Data Smart

Using Data Science to Transform Information into Insight

John W. Foreman

WILEY

Data Smart: Using Data Science to Transform Information into Insight

Published by
John Wiley & Sons, Inc.
10475 Crosspoint Boulevard
Indianapolis, IN 46256
www.wiley.com

Copyright © 2014 by John Wiley & Sons, Inc., Indianapolis, Indiana

Published simultaneously in Canada

ISBN: 978-1-118-66146-8
ISBN: 978-1-118-66148-2 (ebk)
ISBN: 978-1-118-83986-7 (ebk)

Manufactured in the United States of America

10 9 8

For general information on our other products and services please contact our Customer Care Department within the United States at (877) 762-2974, outside the United States at (317) 572-3993 or fax (317) 572-4002.

Wiley publishes in a variety of print and electronic formats and by print-on-demand. Some material included with standard print versions of this book may not be included in e-books or in print-on-demand. If this book refers to media such as a CD or DVD that is not included in the version you purchased, you may download this material at http://booksupport.wiley.com. For more information about Wiley products, visit www.wiley.com.

Library of Congress Control Number: 2013946768

To my wife, Lydia. What you do each day is impossibly rad. If it weren't for you,
I'd have lost my hair (and my mind) eons ago.

Credits

Executive Editor
Carol Long

Senior Project Editor
Kevin Kent

Technical Editors
Greg Jennings
Evan Miller

Production Editor
Christine Mugnolo

Copy Editor
Kezia Endsley

Editorial Manager
Mary Beth Wakefield

Freelancer Editorial Manager
Rosemarie Graham

Associate Director of Marketing
David Mayhew

Marketing Manager
Ashley Zurcher

Business Manager
Amy Knies

Vice President and Executive Group Publisher
Richard Swadley

Associate Publisher
Jim Minatel

Project Coordinator, Cover
Katie Crocker

Proofreader
Nancy Carrasco

Indexer
Johnna van Hoose Dinse

Cover Image
Courtesy of John W. Foreman

Cover Designer
Ryan Sneed

About the Author

John W. Foreman is the Chief Data Scientist for MailChimp.com. He's also a recovering management consultant who's done a lot of analytics work for large businesses (Coca-Cola, Royal Caribbean, Intercontinental Hotels) and the government (DoD, IRS, DHS, FBI). John can often be found speaking about the trials and travails of implementing analytic solutions in business—check John-Foreman .com to see if he's headed to your town.

When he's not playing with data, John spends his time hiking, watching copious amounts of television, eating all sorts of terrible food, and raising three smelly boys.

About the Technical Editors

Greg Jennings is a data scientist, software engineer, and co-founder of ApexVis. After completing a master's degree in materials science from the University of Virginia, he began his career with the Analytics group of Booz Allen Hamilton, where he grew a team providing predictive analytics and data visualization solutions for planning and scheduling problems.

After leaving Booz Allen Hamilton, Greg cofounded his first startup, Decision Forge, where he served as CTO and helped develop a web-based data mining platform for a government client. He also worked with a major media organization to develop an educational product that assists teachers in accessing targeted content for their students, and with a McLean-based startup to help develop audience modeling applications to optimize web advertising campaigns.

After leaving Decision Forge, he cofounded his current business ApexVis, focused on helping enterprises get maximum value from their data through custom data visualization and analytical software solutions. He lives in Alexandria, Virginia, with his wife and two daughters.

Evan Miller received his bachelor's degree in physics from Williams College in 2006 and is currently a PhD student in economics at the University of Chicago. His research interests include specification testing and computational methods in econometrics. Evan is also the author of Wizard, a popular Mac program for performing statistical analysis, and blogs about statistics problems and experiment design at http://www.evanmiller.org.

Acknowledgments

This book started after an improbable number of folks checked out my analytics blog, Analytics Made Skeezy. So I'd like to thank those readers as well as my data science Twitter pals who've been so supportive. And thanks to Aarron Walter, Chris Mills, and Jon Duckett for passing the idea for this book on to Wiley based on my blog's silly premise.

I'd also like to thank the crew at MailChimp for making this happen. Without the supportive and adventurous culture fostered at MailChimp, I'd not have felt confident enough to do something so stupid as to write a technical book while working a job and raising three boys. Specifically, I couldn't have done it without the daily assistance of Neil Bainton and Michelle Riggin-Ransom. Also, I'm indebted to Ron Lewis, Josh Rosenbaum, and Jason Travis for their work on the cover and marketing video for the book.

Thanks to Carol Long at Wiley for taking a chance on me and to all the editors for their expertise and hard work. Big thanks to Greg Jennings for working all the spreadsheets!

Many thanks to my parents for reading my sci-fi novel and not telling me to quit writing.

Contents

Introduction

What Am I Doing Here?

You've probably heard the term *data science* floating around recently in the media, in business books and journals, and at conferences. Data science can call presidential races, reveal more about your buying habits than you'd dare tell your mother, and predict just how many years those chili cheese burritos have been shaving off your life.

Data scientists, the elite practitioners of this art, were even labeled "sexy" in a recent Harvard Business Review article, although there's apparently such a shortage that it's kind of like calling a unicorn sexy. There's just no way to verify the claim, but if you could see me as I type this book with my neck beard and the tired eyes of a parent of three boys, you'd know that sexy is a bit of an overstatement.

I digress. The point is that there's a buzz about data science these days, and that buzz is creating pressure on a lot of businesses. If you're not doing data science, you're gonna lose out to the competition. Someone's going to come along with some new product called the "BlahBlahBlahBigDataGraphThing" and destroy your business.

Take a deep breath.

The truth is most people are going about data science all wrong. They're starting with buying the tools and hiring the consultants. They're spending all their money before they even know what they want, because a purchase order seems to pass for actual progress in many companies these days.

By reading this book, you're gonna have a leg up on those jokers, because you're going to learn exactly what these techniques in data science are and how they're used. When it comes time to do the planning, and the hiring, and the buying, you'll already know how to identify the data science opportunities within your own organization.

The purpose of this book is to introduce you to the practice of data science in a comfortable and conversational way. When you're done, I hope that much of that data science anxiety you're feeling is replaced with excitement and with ideas about how you can use data to take your business to the next level.

A Workable Definition of Data Science

To an extent, *data science* is synonymous with or related to terms like *business analytics*, *operations research, business intelligence, competitive intelligence, data analysis and modeling*, and *knowledge extraction* (also called *knowledge discovery in databases* or *KDD*). It's just a new spin on something that people have been doing for a long time.

There's been a shift in technology since the heyday of those other terms. Advancements in hardware and software have made it easy and inexpensive to collect, store, and analyze large amounts of data whether that be sales and marketing data, HTTP requests from your website, customer support data, and so on. Small businesses and nonprofits can now engage in the kind of analytics that were previously the purview of large enterprises.

Of course, while data science is used as a catch-all buzzword for analytics today, data science is most often associated with data mining techniques such as artificial intelligence, clustering, and outlier detection. Thanks to the cheap technology-enabled proliferation of transactional business data, these computational techniques have gained a foothold in business in recent years where previously they were too cumbersome to use in production settings.

In this book, I'm going to take a broad view of data science. Here's the definition I'll work from:

> *Data science is the transformation of data using mathematics and statistics into valuable insights, decisions, and products.*

This is a *business-centric* definition. It's about a usable and valuable end product derived from data. Why? Because I'm not in this for research purposes or because I think data has aesthetic merit. I do data science to help my organization function better and create value; if you're reading this, I suspect you're after something similar.

With that definition in mind, this book will cover mainstay analytics techniques such as optimization, forecasting, and simulation, as well as more "hot" topics such as artificial intelligence, network graphs, clustering, and outlier detection.

Some of these techniques are as old as World War II. Others were introduced in the last 5 years. And you'll see that age has no bearing on difficulty or usefulness. All these techniques—whether or not they're currently the rage—are equally useful in the right business context.

And that's why you need to understand how they work, how to choose the right technique for the right problem, and how to prototype with them. There are a lot of folks out there who understand one or two of these techniques, but the rest aren't on their radar. If all I had in my toolbox was a hammer, I'd probably try to solve every problem by smacking it real hard. Not unlike my two-year-old.

Better to have a few other tools at your disposal.

But Wait, What about Big Data?

You've heard the term *big data* even more than *data science* most likely. Is this a book on big data?

That depends on how you define big data. If you define big data as computing simple summary statistics on unstructured garbage stored in massive, horizontally scalable, NoSQL databases, then no, this is not a book on big data.

If you define big data as turning transactional business data into decisions and insight using cutting-edge analytics (regardless of where that data is stored), then yes, this is a book about big data.

This is not a book that will be covering database technologies, like MongoDB and HBase. This is not a book that will be covering data science coding packages like Mahout, NumPy, various R libraries, and so on. There are other books out there for that stuff.

But that's a good thing. This book ignores the tools, the storage, and the code. Instead, it focuses as much as possible on the techniques. There are many folks out there who think that data storage and retrieval, with a little bit of cleanup and aggregation mixed in, constitutes all there is to know about big data.

They're wrong. This book will take you beyond the spiel you've been hearing from the big data software sales reps and bloggers to show you what's really possible with your data. And the cool thing is that for many of these techniques, your dataset can be any size, small or large. You don't have to have a petabyte of data and the expenses that come along with it in order to predict the interests of your customer base. If you have a massive dataset, that's great, but there are some businesses that don't have it, need it, and will likely never generate it. Like my local butcher. But that doesn't mean his e-mail marketing couldn't benefit from a little bacon versus sausage cluster detection.

If data science books were workouts, this book would be all calisthenics—no machine weights, no ergs. Once you understand how to implement the techniques with even the most barebones of tools, you'll find yourself free to implement them in a variety of technologies, prototype with them with ease, buy the correct data science products from consultants, delegate the correct approach to your developers, and so on.

Who Am I?

Let me pause a moment to tell you my story. It'll go a long way to explaining why I teach data science the way I do. Many moons ago, I was a management consultant. I worked on analytics problems for organizations such as the FBI, DoD, the Coca-Cola Company, Intercontinental Hotels Group, and Royal Caribbean International. And through all these experiences I walked away having learned one thing—more people than just the scientists need to understand data science.

I worked with managers who bought simulations when they needed an optimization model. I worked with analysts who only understood Gantt charts, so everything needed to be solved with Gantt charts. As a consultant, it wasn't hard to win over a customer with any old white paper and a slick PowerPoint deck, because they couldn't tell AI from BI or BI from BS.

The point of this book is to broaden the audience of who understands and can implement data science techniques. I'm not trying to turn you into a data scientist against your will. I just want you to be able to integrate data science as best as you can into the role you're already good at.

And that brings me to who you are.

Who Are You?

No, I haven't been using data science to spy on you. I have no idea who you are, but thanks for shelling out some money for this book. Or supporting your local library. You can do that, too.

Here are some archetypes (or *personas* for you marketing folks) I had in mind when writing this book. Maybe you are:

- The vice president of marketing who wants to use her transactional business data more strategically to price products and segment customers. But she doesn't understand the approaches her software developers and overpriced consultants are recommending she try.
- The demand forecasting analyst who knows his organization's historical purchase data holds more insight about his customers than just the next quarter's projections. But he doesn't know how to extract that insight.
- The CEO of an online retail start-up who wants to predict when a customer is likely to be interested in buying an item based on their past purchases.

- The business intelligence analyst who sees money going down the tubes from the infrastructure and supply chain costs her organization is accruing, but doesn't know how to systematically make cost-saving decisions.
- The online marketer who wants to do more with his company's free text customer interactions taking place in e-mail, Facebook, and Twitter, but right now they're just being read and saved.

I have in mind that you are a reader who would benefit directly from knowing more about data science but hasn't found a way to get a foothold into all the techniques. The purpose of this book is to strip away all the distractions around data science (the code, the tools, and the hype) and teach the techniques using practical use cases that someone with a semester of linear algebra or calculus in college can understand. Assuming you didn't fail that semester. If you did, just read slower and use Wikipedia liberally.

No Regrets. Spreadsheets Forever

This is not a book about coding. In fact, I'm giving you my "no code" guarantee (until Chapter 10 at least). Why?

Because I don't want to spend a hundred pages at the beginning of this book messing with Git, setting environment variables, and doing the dance of Emacs versus Vi.

If you run Windows and Microsoft Office almost exclusively. If you work for the government, and they don't let you download and install random open source stuff on your box. Even if MATLAB or your TI-83 scared the hell out of you in college, you need not be afraid.

Do you need to know how to write code to put most of these techniques in automated, production settings? Absolutely! Or at least someone you work with needs to be able to handle code and storage technologies.

Do you need to know how to write code in order to understand, distinguish between, and prototype with these techniques? Absolutely not!

This is why I go over every technique in spreadsheet software.

Now, this is all a bit of a lie. The final chapter in this book is actually on moving to the data science-focused programming language, R. It's for those of you that want to use this book as a jumping-off point to deeper things.

But Spreadsheets Are So Démodé!

Spreadsheets are not the sexiest tools around. In fact, they're the Wilford-Brimley-selling-Colonial-Penn of the analytics tool world. Completely unsexy. Sorry, Wilford.

But that's the point. Spreadsheets stay out of the way. They allow you to see the data and to touch (or at least click on) the data. There's a freedom there. In order to learn these techniques, you need something vanilla, something everyone understands, but nonetheless, something that will let you move fast and light as you learn. That's a spreadsheet.

Say it with me: "I am a human. I have dignity. I should not have to write a map-reduce job in order to learn data science."

And spreadsheets are great for prototyping! You're not running a production AI model for your online retail business out of Excel, but that doesn't mean you can't look at purchase data, experiment with features that predict product interest, and prototype a targeting model. In fact, it's the perfect place to do just that.

Use Excel or LibreOffice

All the examples you're going to work through will be visualized in the book in Excel.

On the book's website (www.wiley.com/go/datasmart) are posted companion spreadsheets for each chapter so that you can follow along. If you're really adventurous, you can clear out all but the starting data in the spreadsheet and replicate all the work yourself.

This book is compatible with Excel versions 2007, 2010, 2011 for Mac, and 2013. Chapter 1 will discuss the version differences most in depth.

Most of you have access to Excel, and you probably already use it for reporting or recordkeeping at work. But if for some reason you don't have a copy of Excel, you can either buy it or go for LibreOffice (www.libreoffice.org) instead.

WHAT ABOUT GOOGLE DRIVE?

Now, some of you might be wondering whether you can use Google Drive. It's an appealing option since Google Drive is in the cloud and can run on your mobile devices as well as your beige box. But it just won't work.

Google Drive is great for simple spreadsheets, but for where you're going, Google just can't hang. Adding rows and columns in Drive is a constant annoyance, the implementation of Solver is dreadful, and the charts don't even have trendlines. I wish it were otherwise.

LibreOffice is open source, free, and has nearly all of the same functionality as Excel. I think its native solver is actual preferable to Excel's. So if you want to go that route for this book, feel free.

Conventions

To help you get the most from the text and keep track of what's happening, I've used a number of conventions throughout the book.

SIDEBARS

Sidebars, like the one you just read about Google Drive, touch upon some side issue related to the text in detail.

WARNING

Warnings hold important, not-to-be-forgotten information that is directly relevant to the surrounding text.

NOTE

Notes cover tips, hints, tricks, or asides to the current discussion.

Frequently in this text I'll reference little snippets of Excel code like this:

```
=CONCATENATE("THIS IS A FORMULA", " IN EXCEL!")
```

We *highlight* new terms and important words when we introduce them. We show file names, URLs, and formulas within the text like so:

```
http://www .john-foreman.com.
```

Let's Get Going

In the first chapter, I'm going to fill in a few holes in your Excel knowledge. After that, you'll move right into use cases. By the end of this book, you'll not only know about but actually have experience implementing from scratch the following techniques:

- Optimization using linear and integer programming
- Working with time series data, detecting trends and seasonal patterns, and forecasting with exponential smoothing

- Using Monte Carlo simulation in optimization and forecasting scenarios to quantify and address risk
- Artificial intelligence using the general linear model, logistic link functions, ensemble methods, and naïve Bayes
- Measuring distances between customers using cosine similarity, creating kNN graphs, calculating modularity, and clustering customers
- Detecting outliers in a single dimension with Tukey fences or in multiple dimensions with local outlier factors
- Using R packages to "stand on the shoulders" of other analysts in conducting these tasks

If any of that sounds exciting, read on! If any of that sounds scary, I promise to keep things as clear and enjoyable as possible.

In fact, I prefer clarity well above mathematical correctness, so if you're an academician reading this, there may be times where you should close your eyes and think of England. Without further ado, then, let's get number-crunching.

1

Everything You Ever Needed to Know about Spreadsheets but Were Too Afraid to Ask

This book relies on you having a working knowledge of spreadsheets, and I'm going to assume that you already understand the basics. If you've never used a formula before in your life, then you've got a slight uphill battle here. I'd recommend going through a *For Dummies* book or some other intro-level tutorial for Excel before diving into this.

That said, even if you're a seasoned Excel veteran, there's some functionality that'll keep cropping up in this text that you may not have had to use before. It's not difficult stuff; just things I've noticed not everyone has used in Excel. You'll be covering a wide variety of little features in this chapter, and the example at this stage might feel a bit disjointed. But you can learn what you can here, and then, when you encounter it organically later in the book, you can slip back to this chapter as a reference.

As Samuel L. Jackson says in *Jurassic Park*, "Hold on to your butts!"

EXCEL VERSION DIFFERENCES

As mentioned in the book's introduction, these chapters work with Excel 2007, 2010, 2013, 2011 for Mac, and LibreOffice. Sadly, in each version of Excel, Microsoft has moved stuff around for the heck of it.

For example, things on the Layout tab on 2011 are on the View tab in the other versions. Solver is the same in 2010 and 2013, but the performance is actually better in 2007 and 2011 even though 2007's Solver interface is grotesque.

The screen captures in this text will be from Excel 2011. If you have an older or newer version, sometimes your interactions will look a little different—mostly when it comes to where things are on the menu bar. I will do my best to call out these differences. If you can't find something, Excel's help feature and Google are your friends.

The good news is that whenever we're in the "spreadsheet part of the spreadsheet," everything works exactly the same.

As for LibreOffice, if you've chosen to use open source software for this book, then I'm assuming you're a do-it-yourself kind of person, and I won't be referencing the LibreOffice interface directly. Never you mind, though. It's a dead ringer for Excel.

Some Sample Data

NOTE

The Excel workbook used in this chapter, "Concessions.xlsx," is available for download at the book's website at www.wiley.com/go/datasmart.

Imagine you've been terribly unsuccessful in life, and now you're an adult, still living at home, running the concession stand during the basketball games played at your old high school. (I swear this is only semi-autobiographical.)

You have a spreadsheet full of last night's sales, and it looks like Figure 1-1.

	A	B	C	D
1	Item	Category	Price	Profit
2	Beer	Beverages	$ 4.00	50%
3	Hamburger	Hot Food	$ 3.00	67%
4	Popcorn	Hot Food	$ 5.00	80%
5	Pizza	Hot Food	$ 2.00	25%
6	Bottled Water	Beverages	$ 3.00	83%
7	Hot Dog	Hot Food	$ 1.50	67%
8	Chocolate Dipped Cone	Frozen Treat:	$ 3.00	50%
9	Soda	Beverages	$ 2.50	80%
10	Chocolate Bar	Candy	$ 2.00	75%
11	Hamburger	Hot Food	$ 3.00	67%
12	Beer	Beverages	$ 4.00	50%
13	Hot Dog	Hot Food	$ 1.50	67%
14	Licorice Rope	Candy	$ 2.00	50%
15	Chocolate Dipped Cone	Frozen Treat:	$ 3.00	50%

Figure 1-1: Concession stand sales

Figure 1-1 shows each sale, what the item was, what type of food or drink it was, the price, and the percentage of the sale going toward profit.

Moving Quickly with the Control Button

If you want to peruse the records, you can scroll down the sheet with your scroll wheel, track pad, or down arrow. As you scroll, it's helpful to keep the header row locked at the top of the sheet, so you can remember what each column means. To do that, choose

Freeze Panes or Freeze Top Row from the "View" tab on Windows ("Layout" tab on Mac 2011 as shown in Figure 1-2).

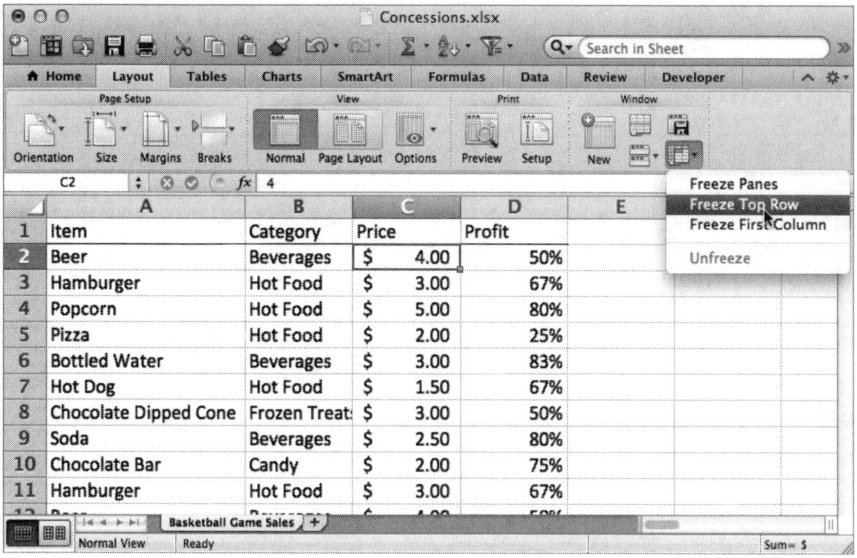

Figure 1-2: Freezing the top row

To move quickly to the bottom of the sheet to look at how many transactions you have, you can select a value in one of the populated columns and press Ctrl+↓ (Command+↓ on a Mac). You'll zip right to the last populated cell in that column. In this sheet, the final row is 200. Also, note that using Ctrl/Command to jump around the sheet from left to right works much the same.

If you want to take an average of the sales prices for the night, below the price column, column C, you can jot the following formula:

```
=AVERAGE(C2:C200)
```

The average is $2.83, so you won't be retiring wealthy anytime soon. Alternatively, you can select the last cell in the column, C200, hold Shift+Ctrl+↑ to highlight the whole column, and then select the Average calculation from the status bar in the bottom right of the spreadsheet to see the simple summary statistic (see Figure 1-3). On Windows, you'll need to right-click the status bar to select the average if it's not there. On Mac, if your status bar is turned off, click the View menu and select "Status Bar" to turn it on.

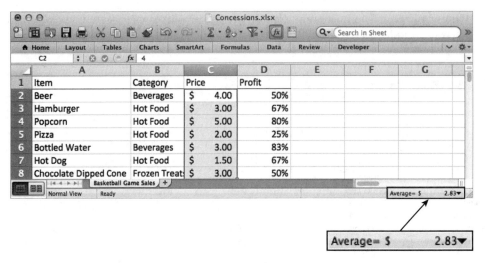

Figure 1-3: Average of the price column in the status bar

Copying Formulas and Data Quickly

Perhaps you'd like to view your profits in actual dollars rather than as percentages. You can add a header to column E called "Actual Profit." In E2, you need only to multiply the price and profit columns together to obtain this:

```
=C2*D2
```

For beer, it's $2. You don't have to rewrite this formula in every cell in the column. Instead, Excel lets you grab the right-bottom corner of the cell and drag the formula where you like. The referenced cells in columns C and D will update relative to where you copy the formula. If, as in the case of the concession data, the column to the left is fully populated, you can double-click the bottom-right corner of the formula to have Excel fill the whole column (see Figure 1-4). Try this double-click action for yourself, because I'll be using it all over the place in this book, and if you get the hang of it now, you'll save yourself a whole lot of heartache.

Now, what if you don't want the cells in the formula to change relative to the target when they're dragged or copied? Whatever you don't want changed, just add a $ in front of it.

For example, if you changed the formula in E2 to:

```
=C$2*D$2
```

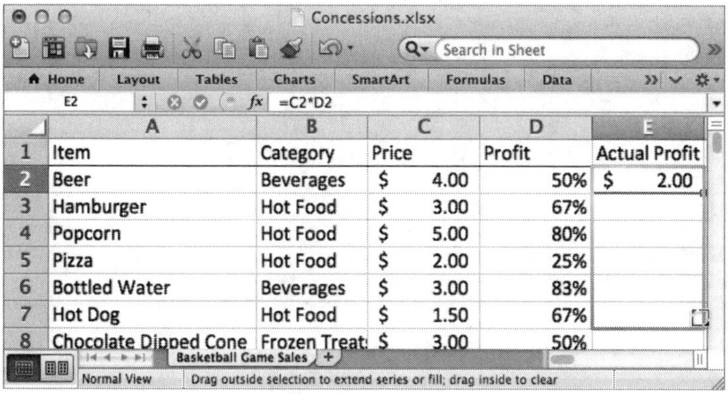

Figure 1-4: Filling in a formula by dragging the corner

Then when you copy the formula down, nothing changes. The formula continues to reference row 2.

If you copy the formula to the right, however, C would become D, D would become E, and so on. If you don't want that behavior, you need to put a $ in front of the column references as well. This is called an *absolute reference* as opposed to a *relative reference*.

Formatting Cells

Excel offers static and dynamic options for formatting values. Take a look at column E, the Actual Profit column you just created. Select column E by clicking on the gray E column label. Then right-click the selection and choose Format Cells.

From within the Format Cells menu, you can tell Excel the type of number to be found in column E. In this case you want it to be Currency. And you can set the number of decimal places. Leave it at two decimals, as shown in Figure 1-5. Also available in Format Cells are options for changing font colors, text alignment, fill colors, borders, and so on.

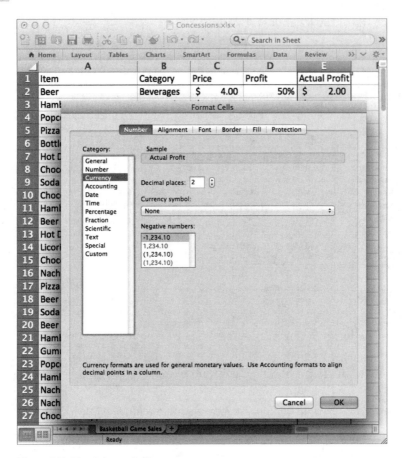

Figure 1-5: The Format Cells menu

But here's a conundrum. What if you want to format only the cells that have a certain value or range of values in them? And what if you want that formatting to change with the values?

That's called *conditional formatting*, and this book makes liberal use of it.

Cancel out of the Format Cells menu and navigate to the Home tab. In the Styles section (Mac calls it Format), you'll find the Conditional Formatting button (see Figure 1-6). Click the button to drop down a menu of options. The conditional formatting most used in this text is Color Scales. Pick a scale for column E and note how each cell in the column is colored based on its high or low value.

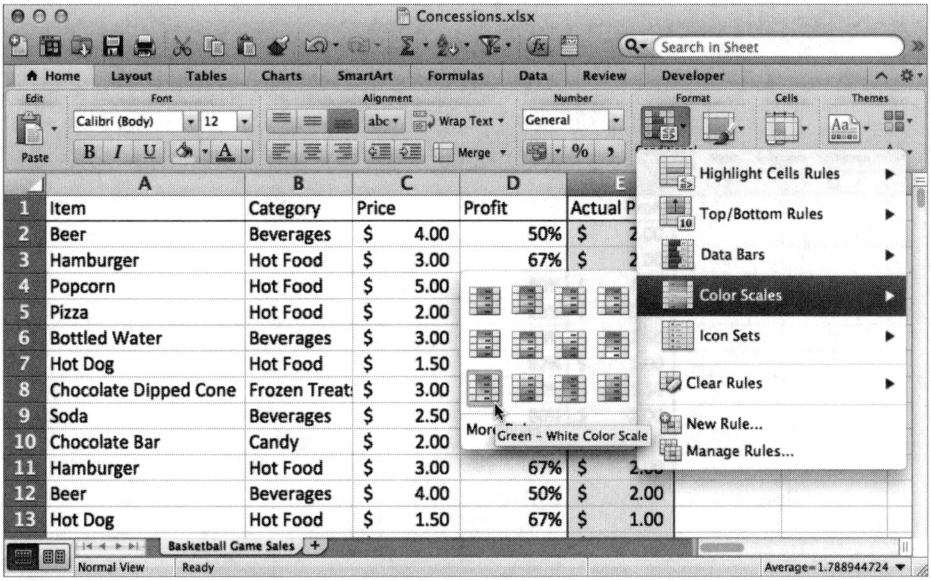

Figure 1-6: Applying conditional formatting to the profit

To remove conditional formatting, use the Clear Rules options under the Conditional Formatting menu.

Paste Special Values

It's often in your best interest not to have a formula lying around like you see in Column E in Figure 1-4. If you were using the RAND() formula to generate a random value, for example, it changes each time the spreadsheet auto-recalculates, which while awesome, can also be extremely annoying. The solution is to copy and paste these cells back to the sheet as flat values.

To convert formulas to values only, simply copy a column filled with formulas (grab column E) and paste it back using the Paste Special option (found on the Home tab under the Paste option on Windows and under the Edit menu on Mac). In the Paste Special window, choose to paste as values (see Figure 1-7). Note also that Paste Special allows you to *transpose* the data from vertical to horizontal and vice versa when pasting. You'll be using that a fair bit in the chapters to come.

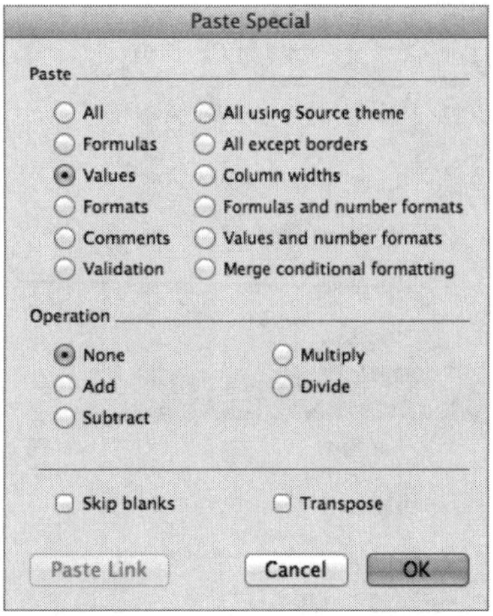

Figure 1-7: The Paste Special window in Excel 2011

Inserting Charts

In the concession stand sales workbook, there's also a tab called Calories with a tiny table that shows the calorie count of each item the concession stand sells. You can chart data like this in Excel easily. On the Insert tab (Charts on a Mac), there is a charts section that provides different visualization options such as bar charts, line graphs, and pie charts.

> **NOTE**
>
> In this book, we're going to use mostly column charts, line graphs, and scatter plots. Never be caught using a pie chart. And especially never use the 3D pie charts Excel offers, or my ghost will personally haunt you when I die. They're ugly, they don't communicate data well, and the 3D effect has less aesthetic value than the seashell paintings hanging on the wall of my dentist's office.

Highlighting columns A:B on the Calories workbook, you can select a Clustered Column chart to visualize the data. Play around with the graph. Sections can be right-clicked to bring up formatting menus. For example, right-clicking the bars, you can select "Format

Data Series…" under which you can change the fill color on the bars from the default Excel blue to any number of pleasing shades—black, for instance.

There's no reason for the default legend, so you should select it and press delete to remove it. You might also want to select various text sections on the graph and increase the size of their font (font size is under the Home tab in Excel). This gives the graph shown in Figure 1-8.

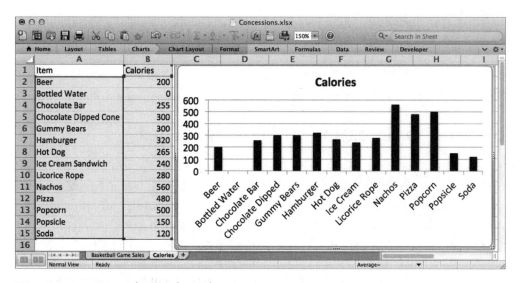

Figure 1-8: Inserting a calories column chart

Locating the Find and Replace Menus

You're going to use find and replace a fair bit in this book. On Windows you can either press Ctrl+F to open up the Find window (Ctrl+H for replace) or navigate to the Home tab and use the Find button in the Editing section. On Mac, there's a search field on the top right of the sheet (press the down arrow for the Replace menu), or you can just press Cmd+F to bring up the Find and Replace menu.

Just to test it out, open up the replace menu on the Calories sheet. You can replace every instance of the word "Calories" with the word "Energy" (see Figure 1-9) by popping the words in the Find and Replace window and pressing Replace All.

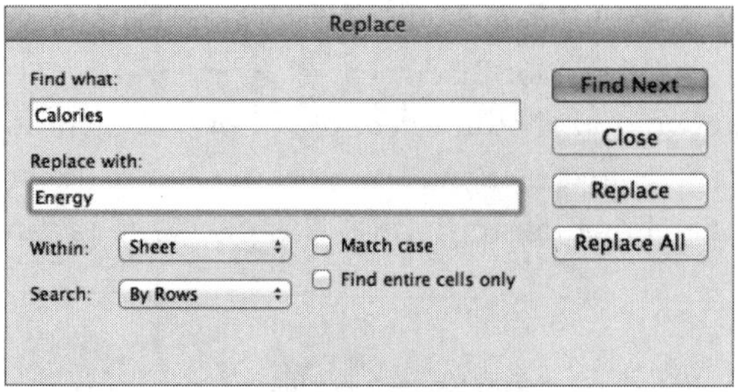

Figure 1-9: Running a Find and Replace

Formulas for Locating and Pulling Values

If I didn't assume you at least knew some formulas in Excel (SUM, MAX, MIN, PERCENTILE, and so on), we'd be here all day. And I want to get started. But there are some formulas used a lot in this book that you've probably not used unless you've dug deep into the wonderful world of spreadsheets. These formulas deal with *finding a value in a range and returning its location* or on the flip side *finding a location in a range and returning its value.*

I want to cover a few of those on the Calories tab.

Sometimes you want to know the place in line of some element in a column or row. Is it first, second, third? The MATCH formula handles that quite nicely. Below your calorie data, label A18 as **Match**. You can implement the formula one cell over in B18 to find where in the item list above the word "Hamburger" appears. To use the formula, you supply it a value to look for, a range to search in, and a 0 to force it to give you back the position of the keyword itself:

```
=MATCH("Hamburger",A2:A15,0)
```

This yields a 6, because "Hamburger" is the sixth item in the list (see Figure 1-10).

Next up is the INDEX formula. Label A19 as **Index**.

This formula takes in a range of values and a row and column number and returns the value in the range at that location. For example, you can feed the INDEX formula our calorie table A1:B15, and to pull back the calorie count for bottled water, feed in 3 rows down and 2 columns over:

```
=INDEX(A1:B15,3,2)
```

This yields a calorie count of 0 as expected (see Figure 1-10).

Another formula you'll see a lot in this text is OFFSET. Go ahead and label A20 as **Offset**, and you can play with the formula in B20.

With this formula, you provide a range that acts like a cursor which is moved around with row and column offsets (similar to INDEX for the single valued case except it's 0-based). For example, you can provide OFFSET with a reference to the top left of the sheet, A1, and then pull back the value 3 cells below by providing a row offset of 3 and a column offset of 0:

```
=OFFSET(A1,3,0)
```

This returns the name of the third item on the list, "Chocolate Bar." See Figure 1-10.

The last formula I want to look at in this section is SMALL (it has a counterpart called LARGE that works the same way). If you have a list of values and you want to return, say, the third smallest, SMALL does that for you. To see this, label A21 as **Small** and in B21 feed in the list of calorie counts and an index of 3:

```
=SMALL(B2:B15,3)
```

This hands back a value of 150 which is the third smallest after 0 (bottled water) and 120 (soda). See Figure 1-10.

Now, there's one more formula used for looking up values that's kind of like MATCH on steroids and that's VLOOKUP (and its horizontal counterpart HLOOKUP). That's got its own section next because it's a beast.

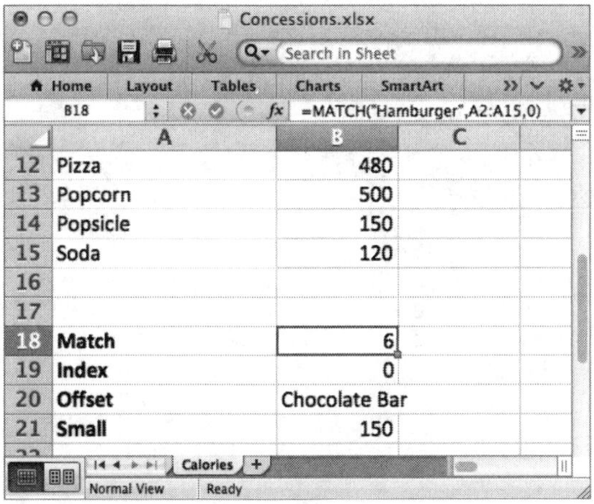

Figure 1-10: Formulas you should learn

Using VLOOKUP to Merge Data

Go ahead and flip back to the Basketball Game Sales tab. You can still reference a cell here from the previous tab, Calories, by simply placing the tab name and "!" in front of a referenced cell. For example, `Calories!B2` is a reference to the calories in beer regardless of what sheet you're working in.

Now, what if you wanted to toss the calorie data into a column back on the sales sheet so that next to each item sold the appropriate calorie count was listed? You'd somehow have to look up the calorie count of each item sold and place it into a column next to the transaction. Well, it turns out there's a formula for that called VLOOKUP.

Go ahead and label Column F in the spreadsheet **Calories** for this purpose. Cell F2 will include the calorie count for the first beer transaction from the Calories table. Using the VLOOKUP formula, you supply the item name from cell A2, a reference to the table `Calories!$A$1:$B$15`, and the relative column offset you want your return value to be read out of, which is to say the second column:

```
=VLOOKUP(A2,Calories!$A$1:$B$15,2,FALSE)
```

The FALSE at the end of the VLOOKUP formula means that you will not accept approximate matches for "Beer." If the formula can't find "Beer" on the calories table, it returns an error.

When you enter the formula, you can see that 200 calories is read in from the table on the Calories tab. Since you've put the $ in front of the table references in the formula, you can copy this formula down the column by double-clicking the bottom-right corner of the cell. *Voila!* As shown in Figure 1-11, you have calorie counts for every transaction.

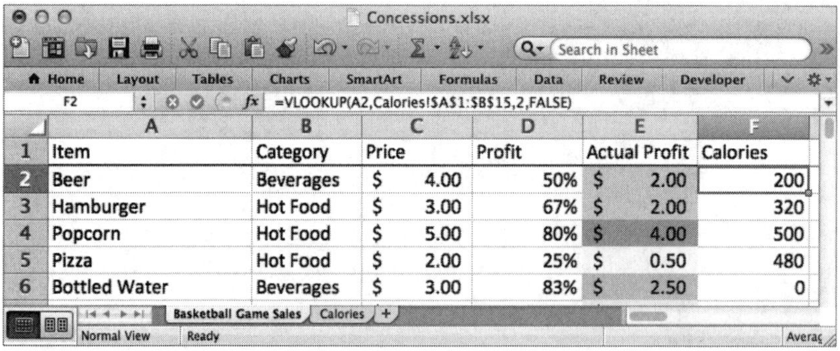

Figure 1-11: Using VLOOKUP to grab calorie counts

Filtering and Sorting

Now that you have calories in there, say you now want to view only those transactions from the Frozen Treats category. What you want to do then is filter the sheet. To do so, first you select the data in range A1:F200. You can put the cursor in A1 and press Shift+Ctrl+↓ then →. An even easier method is to click the top of column A and hold the click as you mouse over to column F to highlight all six columns.

Then to place auto-filtering on these six columns, you press the Filter button in the Data section of the ribbon. It looks like a gray funnel as shown in Figure 1-12.

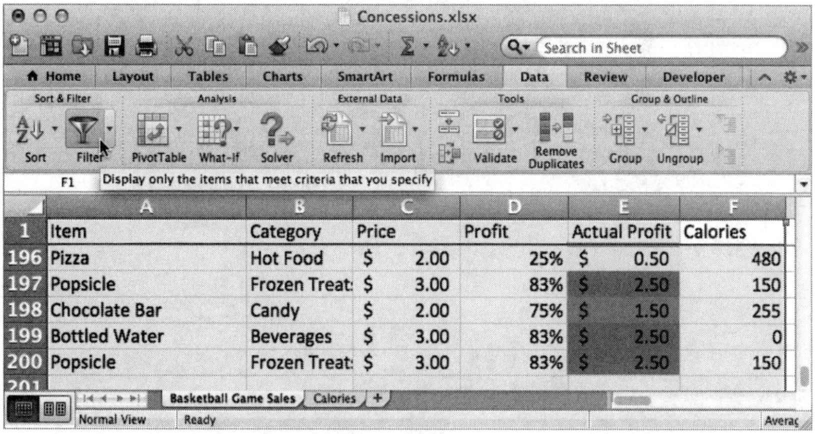

Figure 1-12: Place auto-filter on a selected range

Once auto-filter is activated, you can click the drop-down menu that appears in cell B1 and choose to show only certain categories (in this case, only the Frozen Treats transactions will be displayed). See Figure 1-13.

Once you've filtered, highlighting columns of data allows the summary bar in Excel to give you rolled-up information just on the cells that remain. For example, having filtered just the Frozen Treats, we can highlight the values in column E and use the summary bar to get a quick total of profit just from that category. See Figure 1-14.

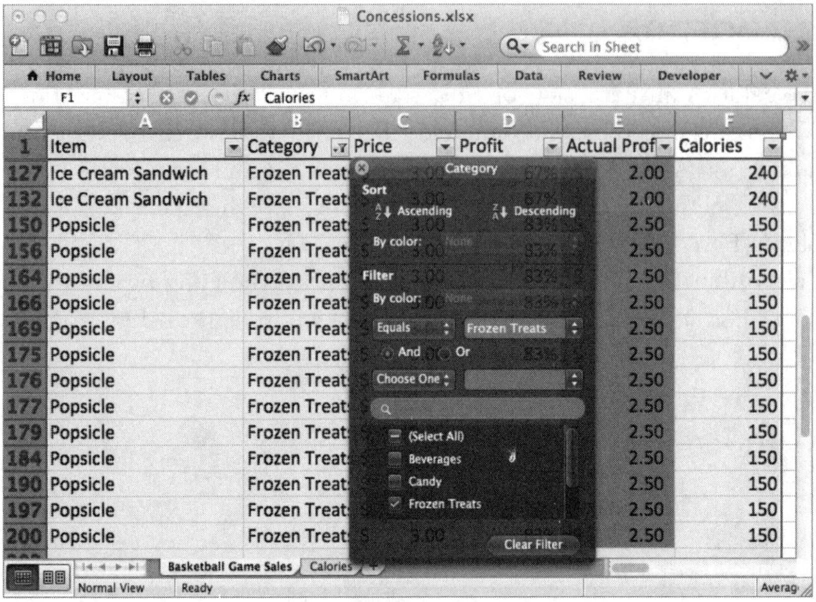

Figure 1-13: Filtering on category

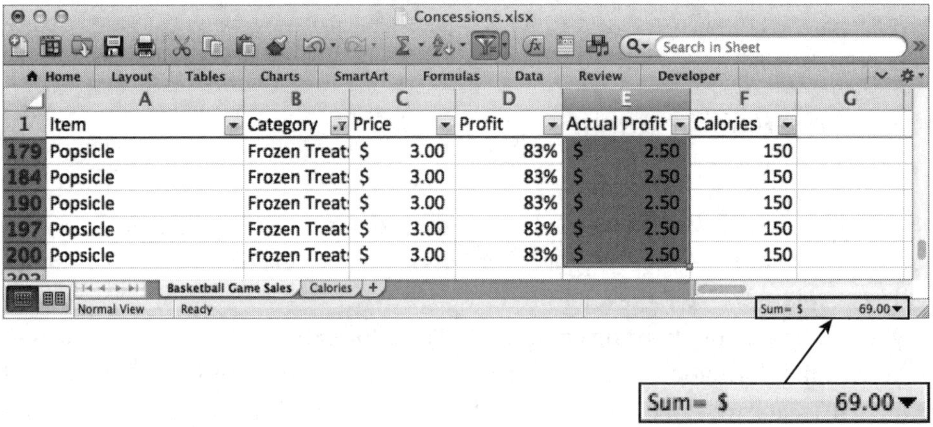

Figure 1-14: Summarizing a filtered column

Auto-filter allows you to sort as well. For example, if you want to sort by profit, just click the auto-filter menu on the Profit cell (D1) and select Sort Ascending (or "Smallest to Largest" in some versions). See Figure 1-15.

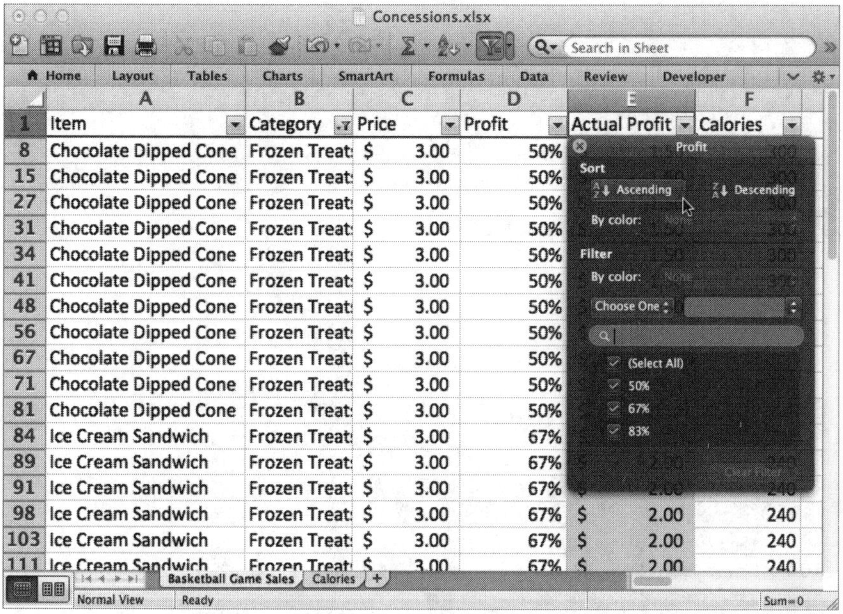

Figure 1-15: Sorting in ascending order by profit

To remove all the filtering you've applied, either you can go back into the Category filter menu and check the other boxes, or you can un-toggle the filter button on the ribbon that you pressed in the first place. You'll see that although you have all of your data back, the Frozen Treats are still in the order you sorted them in.

Excel also offers the Sort interface for doing more complex sorts than might be possible with auto-filter. To use the feature, you highlight the data to be sorted (grab A:F again) and select Sort from the Sort & Filter section of the Data tab in Excel. This will bring up the sort menu. On Mac, to get this window, you must press the down arrow in the sort button and select Custom Sort….

In the sort menu, shown in Figure 1-16, you can note whether your data has column headers or not, and if it does have headers like this example does, then you can select, by name, the columns to be sorted.

Now, the most awesome part of this sorting interface is that under the "Options…" button, you can select to sort left to right instead of column data. That's something you cannot do with auto-filter. In top to bottom of this book you'll need to randomly sort data by both columns and rows in two quick steps, and this interface is going to be your friend. For now, just cancel out of it as the data is already ordered the way you want it.

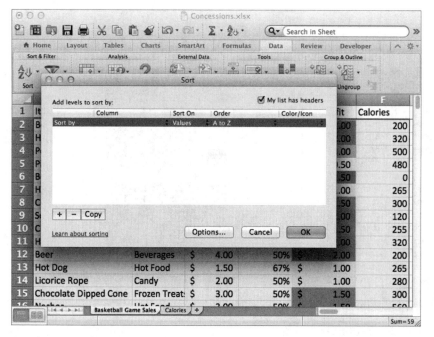

Figure 1-16: Using the Sort menu

Using PivotTables

What if you wanted to know the total counts of each item type you sold? Or you wanted to know revenue totals by item?

These questions are akin to "aggregate" or "group by" queries that you'd run in a traditional SQL database. But this data isn't in a database. It's in a spreadsheet. That's where PivotTables come to the rescue.

Just as when you filtered your data, you start by selecting the data you want to manipulate—in this case, the purchase data in the range A1:F:200. From the Insert tab (Data tab on Mac), you can press the PivotTable button and select for Excel to create a new sheet with a PivotTable. While some versions of Excel allow you to insert a PivotTable into an existing sheet, it's standard practice to select the new sheet option unless you have a really good reason not to.

In this new sheet, the PivotTable Builder will be aligned to the right of the table (it floats on a Mac). The builder allows you to take the columns from the original selected data and use them as report filters, column and row labels for grouping, or values. A report filter is similar in function to a filter from the previous section—it allows you to select only a subset of the data, such as Frozen Treats. The Column Labels and Row Labels fill in the meat of the PivotTable report with distinct values from the selected columns.

On Windows, the initial PivotTable built will be completely empty, while on Mac it is often prepopulated with distinct values from the first selected column down the rows of the table and distinct values from the second column across the columns. If you're on a Mac, go ahead and uncheck all the boxes in the builder, so that you can work along from an empty table.

Now, say you wanted to know total revenue by item. To get at that, you'd drag the Item tile in the PivotTable Builder into the Rows section and the Price tile into the Values section. This means that you'll be operating on revenue grouped by item name.

Initially, however, the PivotTable is set up to merely count the number of price records that are within a group. For example, there are 20 Beer rows. See Figure 1-17.

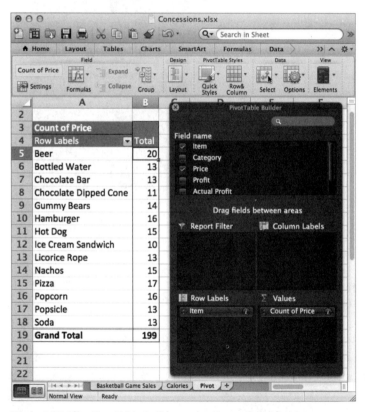

Figure 1-17: The PivotTable builder and a count of sales by item

You need to change the count to a sum in order to examine revenue. To do so, on Windows, drop the menu down on the Price tile in the Values section of the builder and select "Value Field Settings…." On Mac, press the little "*i*" button. From there, "sum" can be selected from the various summary options.

What if you wanted to break out these sums by category? To do so, you drag the Category tile into the Columns section of the builder. This gives the table shown in Figure 1-18. Note that the PivotTable in the figure automatically totals up rows and columns for you.

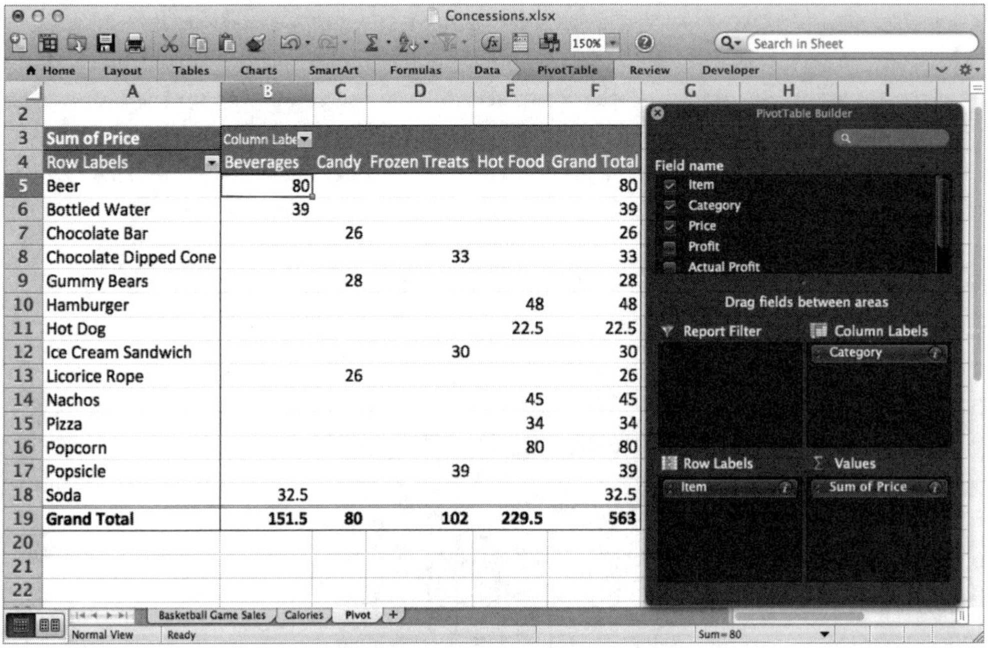

Sum of Price	Column Labels				
Row Labels	Beverages	Candy	Frozen Treats	Hot Food	Grand Total
Beer	80				80
Bottled Water	39				39
Chocolate Bar		26			26
Chocolate Dipped Cone			33		33
Gummy Bears		28			28
Hamburger				48	48
Hot Dog				22.5	22.5
Ice Cream Sandwich			30		30
Licorice Rope		26			26
Nachos				45	45
Pizza				34	34
Popcorn				80	80
Popsicle			39		39
Soda	32.5				32.5
Grand Total	**151.5**	**80**	**102**	**229.5**	**563**

Figure 1-18: Revenue by item and category

And if you want to ever get rid of something from the table, just uncheck it or grab the tile from the section it's in and drag it out of the sheet as if you were tossing it away. Go ahead and drop the Category tile.

Once you get a report you want in a PivotTable, you can always select the values and paste them to another sheet to work on further. In this example, you can copy the table (A5:B18 on Mac) and Paste Special its values into a new tab called Revenue By Item (see Figure 1-19).

Feel free to swap in various row and column labels until you get the hang of what's going on. For instance, try to get a total calorie count sold by category using a PivotTable.

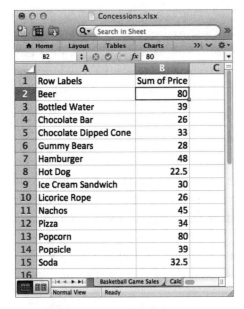

Figure 1-19: Revenue by Item tab created by pasting values from a PivotTable

Using Array Formulas

In the concession transaction workbook, there is a tab called Fee Schedule. As it turns out, Coach O'Shaughnessy would let you run the snack stand only if you kicked some of the profit back to him (perhaps to subsidize his tube sock-buying habit). The Fee Schedule tab shows the percent cut he takes on each item sold.

So how much money do you owe him for last night's game? To answer that question, you need to multiply the total revenue of each item from the PivotTable by the cut for the coach and sum them all up.

There's a great formula for this operation that will do all the multiplication and summation in a single step. Rather creatively named, it's called SUMPRODUCT. In cell E1 on the Revenue By Item sheet, add a label called **Total Cut for Coach**. In C2, determine the SUMPRODUCT of the revenue and the fees by adding this formula:

```
=SUMPRODUCT(B2:B15,'Fee Schedule'!B2:O2)
```

Uh oh. There's an error; the cell just reads #Value. What's going wrong?

Even though you've selected two ranges of equal size and put them in SUMPRODUCT, the formula can't see that the ranges are equal because one range is vertical and one's horizontal.

Fortunately, Excel has a function for flipping arrays in the right direction. It's called TRANSPOSE. You need to write the formula like this:

```
=SUMPRODUCT(B2:B15,TRANSPOSE('Fee Schedule'!B2:O2))
```

Nope! Still getting an error.

The reason you're still getting an error is that every formula in Excel, by default, returns a single value. Even TRANSPOSE returns the first value in the transposed array. If you want the *whole array* returned, you have to turn TRANSPOSE into an "array formula," which means exactly what you might think. Array formulas hand you back arrays, not single values.

You don't have to change the way you type your SUMPRODUCT to make this happen. All you need to do is when you're done typing the formula, instead of pressing Enter, press Ctrl+Shift+Enter. On the Mac, you use Command+Return.

Victory! As shown in Figure 1-20, the calculation now reads $57.60. But I suggest rounding that down to $50, because how many socks does Coach really need?

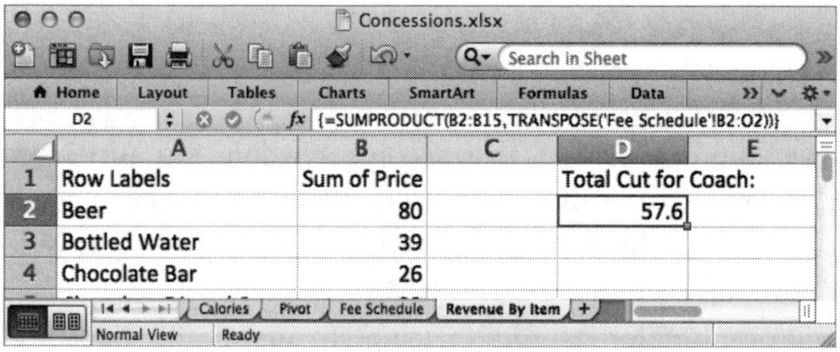

Figure 1-20: Taking a SUMPRODUCT with an array formula

Solving Stuff with Solver

Many of the techniques you'll study in this book can be boiled down to *optimization models*. An optimization problem is one where you have to make the best decision (choose the best investments, minimize your company's costs, find the class schedule with the fewest morning classes, or so on). In optimization models then, the words "minimize" and "maximize" come up a lot when articulating an objective.

In data science, many of the practices, whether that's artificial intelligence, data mining, or forecasting, are actually just some data prep plus a model-fitting step that's actually an optimization model. So it'd make sense to teach optimization first. But learning all there is to know about optimization is tough to do straight off the bat. So you'll do an in-depth optimization study in Chapter 4 *after* you do some more fun machine learning problems in Chapters 2 and 3. To fill in the gaps though, it's best if you get a little practice with optimization now. Just a taste.

In Excel, optimization problems are solved using an Add-In that ships with Excel called Solver.

- On Windows, Solver may be added in by going to File (in Excel 2007 it's the top left Windows button) ⇨ Options ⇨ Add-ins, and under the Manage drop-down choosing Excel Add-ins and pressing the Go button. Check the Solver Add-In box and press OK.
- On Mac, Solver is added by going to Tools then Add-ins and selecting Solver.xlam from the menu.

A Solver button will appear in the Analysis section of the Data tab in every version.

All right! Now that Solver is installed, here's an optimization problem: You are told you need 2,400 calories a day. What's the fewest number of items you can buy from the snack stand to achieve that? Obviously, you could buy 10 ice cream sandwiches at 240 calories a piece, but is there a way to do it for fewer items than that?

Solver can tell you!

To start, make a copy of the Calories sheet, name the sheet **Calories-Solver**, and clear out everything but the calories table on the copy. If you don't know how to make a copy of a sheet in Excel, you simply right-click the tab you'd like to copy and select the Move or Copy menu. This gives you the new sheet shown in Figure 1-21.

To get Solver to work, you need to provide it with a range of cells it can set with decisions. In this case, Solver needs to decide how many of each item to buy. So in Column C next to the calorie counts, label the column **How many?** (or whatever you feel like), and you can allow Solver to store its decisions in this column.

Excel considers blank cells to be 0s so you needn't fill in these cells with anything to start. Solver will do that for you.

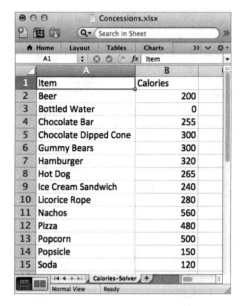

Figure 1-21: The copied Calories-Solver sheet

In cell C16, sum up the number of items to be bought above as:

`=SUM(C2:C15)`

And below that you can sum up the total calorie count of these items (which you'll want eventually to equal 2,400) using the SUMPRODUCT formula:

`=SUMPRODUCT(B2:B15,C2:C15)`

This gives the initial sheet shown in Figure 1-22.

Now you're ready to build the model, so bring up the Solver window by pressing the Solver button on the Data tab.

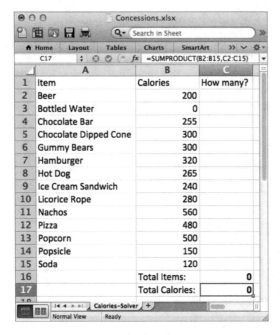

Figure 1-22: Getting calorie and item counts set up

The main elements you plug into Solver to solve a problem, as shown in Figure 1-23, are an objective cell, an optimization direction (minimization or maximization), some decision variables that can be changed by Solver, and some constraints.

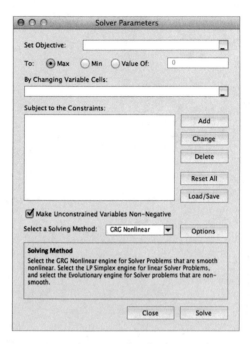

Figure 1-23: The uninitialized Solver window

In your case, the objective is to minimize the total items in cell C16. The cells that can be altered are the item selections in C2:C15. And the constraints are that C17, the total calories, needs to be equal to 2,400. Also, we'll need to add a constraint that our decisions be counting numbers, so we'll need to check the non-negative box (under the options menu in Excel 2007) and add an integer constraint to the decisions. After all, you can't buy 1.7 sodas. These integer constraints will be covered in depth in Chapter 4.

To add in the total calorie constraint, press the Add button and set C17 equal to 2,400 as shown in Figure 1-24.

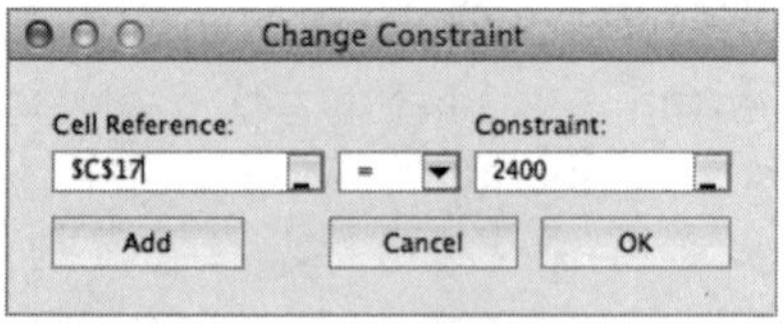

Figure 1-24: Adding the calorie constraint

Similarly, add a constraint setting C2:C15 to be integers as shown in Figure 1-25.

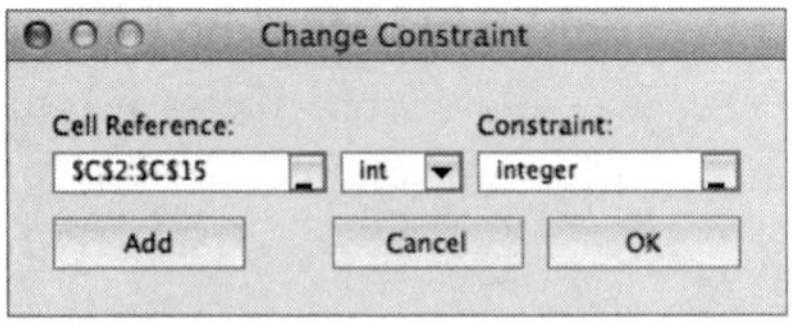

Figure 1-25: Adding an integer constraint

Press OK.

In Excel 2010, 2011, and 2013, make sure the solving method is set to Simplex LP. Simplex LP is appropriate for this problem, because this problem is *linear* (the "L" in LP stands for linear as you'll see in Chapter 4). By linear, I mean that the problem involves nothing but linear combinations of the decisions in C2 through C15 (sums, products with constants such as calorie counts, etc.).

If we had non-linear calculations in the model (perhaps a square root of a decision, a logarithm, or an exponential function), then we could use one of the other algorithms Excel provides in Solver. Chapter 4 covers this in great detail.

In Excel 2007, you would denote the problem as linear by clicking the Assume Linear Model under the Options screen. Your final setup should appear as in Figure 1-26.

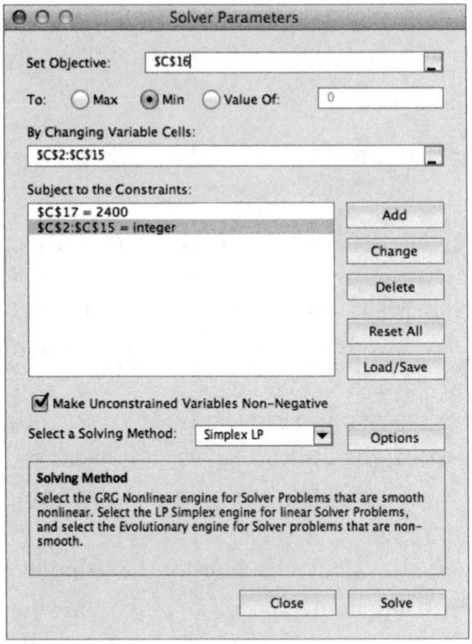

Figure 1-26: Final Solver setup for minimizing items needed for 2,400 calories

All right! Go ahead and press the Solve button. Excel should find a solution almost immediately. And that solution, as shown in Figure 1-27, is 5. Now, your Excel might pick a different 5 items than mine in the screenshot, but the minimum is 5 nonetheless.

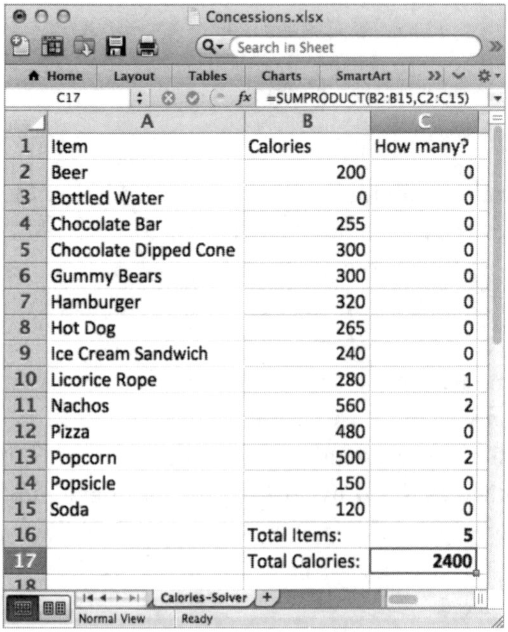

	A	B	C
1	Item	Calories	How many?
2	Beer	200	0
3	Bottled Water	0	0
4	Chocolate Bar	255	0
5	Chocolate Dipped Cone	300	0
6	Gummy Bears	300	0
7	Hamburger	320	0
8	Hot Dog	265	0
9	Ice Cream Sandwich	240	0
10	Licorice Rope	280	1
11	Nachos	560	2
12	Pizza	480	0
13	Popcorn	500	2
14	Popsicle	150	0
15	Soda	120	0
16		Total Items:	5
17		Total Calories:	2400

C17 ▸ *fx* =SUMPRODUCT(B2:B15,C2:C15)

Figure 1-27: The optimized item selection

OpenSolver: I Wish We Didn't Need This, but We Do

This book was originally designed to work completely with Excel's built-in Solver. However, as it turns out, functionality was *removed* from Solver in later versions for mysterious and unadvertised reasons.

What that means is that while this whole book works using vanilla Solver in Excel 2007 and Excel 2011 for Mac, in Excel 2010 and Excel 2013, the built-in Solver will occasionally complain that a linear optimization model is too large (I'll give you a heads-up in this book whenever a model gets that complex).

Luckily, there's an excellent free tool called OpenSolver that's available for the Windows versions of Excel that addresses this deficiency. With OpenSolver, you can still build your model in the regular Solver interface, but OpenSolver provides a button that you press to use its Simplex LP algorithm implementation, which is blazingly fast.

To set up OpenSolver, navigate to `http://OpenSolver.org` and download the zip file. Uncompress the file into a folder, and whenever you want to solve a beefy model, just set it up in a spreadsheet like normal and double-click the OpenSolver.xlam file, which will give you an OpenSolver section on the Data tab in Excel. Press the Solve button to solve an existing model. As shown in Figure 1-28, I've applied OpenSolver in Excel 2013 to the model from the previous section, and it buys five slices of pizza.

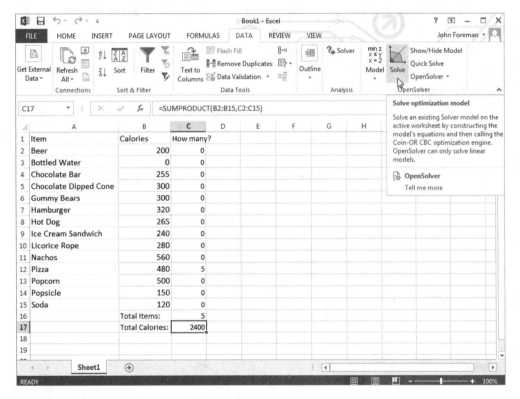

Figure 1-28: OpenSolver buys pizza like a madman

Wrapping Up

All right, you've learned how to navigate and select ranges quickly, how to leverage absolute references, how to paste special values, how to use VLOOKUP and other matching formulas, how to sort and filter data, how to create PivotTables and charts, how to execute array formulas, and how and when to bust out Solver.

Here's either a depressing or fun fact depending on your perspective. I've known management consultants at prominent firms who earn excellent salaries by doing what I call the "consulting two-step":

1. Talk about nonsense with clients (sports, vacation, barbeque ... not that there's anything nonsensical about smoked meats).
2. Summarize data in Excel.

You may not know all there is to know about college football (I certainly don't), but if you internalize this chapter, you'll have point number two knocked out.

But you're not here to become a management consultant. You're here to drive deep into data science, and that starts in the next chapter where we'll get started with a little bit of unsupervised machine learning.

2

Cluster Analysis Part I: Using K-Means to Segment Your Customer Base

I work in the e-mail marketing industry for a website called MailChimp.com. We help customers send e-mail newsletters to their audience, and every time someone uses the term "e-mail blast," a little part of me dies.

Why? Because e-mail addresses are no longer black boxes that you lob "blasts" at like flash grenades. No, in e-mail marketing (as with many other forms of online engagement, including tweets, Facebook posts, and Pinterest campaigns), a business receives feedback on how their audience is engaging *at the individual level* through click tracking, online purchases, social sharing, and so on. This data is not noise. It characterizes your audience. But to the uninitiated, it might as well be Greek. Or Esperanto.

How do you take a bunch of transactional data from your customers (or audience, users, subscribers, citizens, and so on) and use it to understand them? When you're dealing with lots of people, it's hard to understand each customer personally, especially if they all have their own different ways in which they've engaged with you. Even if you could understand everyone at a personal level, that can be tough to act on.

You need to take this customer base and find a happy medium between "blasting" everyone as if they were the same faceless entity and understanding everything about everyone to create personalized marketing for each individual recipient. One way to strike this balance is to use *clustering* to create a *market segmentation* of your customers so that you can market to segments of your base with targeted content, deals, etc.

Cluster analysis is the practice of gathering up a bunch of objects and separating them into groups of similar objects. By exploring these different groups—determining how they're similar and how they're different—you can learn a lot about the previously amorphous pile of data you had. And that insight can help you make better decisions at a level that's more detailed than before.

In this way, clustering is called *exploratory data mining*, because these clustering techniques help tease out relationships in large datasets that are too hard to identify with an eyeball. And revealing relationships in your population is useful across industries whether it's for recommending films based on the habits of folks in a taste cluster, identifying crime hot spots within urban areas, or grouping return-related financial investments to ensure a diversified portfolio spans clusters.

One of my favorite uses for clustering is image clustering—lumping together image files that "look the same" to the computer. For example, in photo sharing services like Flickr, a user will generate a lot of content, and there may end up being too many photos to navigate simply. But using clustering techniques, you can cluster similar images together and allow users to navigate between these clusters before drilling down.

SUPERVISED VERSUS UNSUPERVISED MACHINE LEARNING

By definition, in exploratory data mining, you don't know ahead of time what you're looking for. You're an explorer. Like Dora. You may be able to articulate when two customers look the same and when they look different, but you don't know the best way to segment your customer base. So when you ask a computer to segment your customers for you, that's called *unsupervised machine learning*, because you're not "supervising"—telling the computer how to do its job.

This is in contrast to *supervised machine learning*, which usually crops up when artificial intelligence makes the front page of the paper. If I know I want to divide customers into two groups—say "likely to purchase" and "not likely to purchase"—and I provide the computer with historical examples of such customers and tell it to assign all new leads to one of these two groups, that's supervised.

If instead I say, "here's what I know about my customers and here's how to measure whether they're different or similar. Tell me what's interesting," that's unsupervised.

This chapter looks at the most common type of clustering, called *k-means clustering*, which originated in the 1950s and has since become a go-to clustering technique for knowledge discovery in databases (KDD) across industries and the government.

K-means isn't the most mathematically rigorous of techniques. It's born of the kind of practicality and common sense you might see in soul food. Soul food doesn't have the snooty pedigree of French cuisine, but it hits the spot sometimes. Cluster analysis with k-means, as you'll soon see, is part math, part story-telling. But its intuitive simplicity is part of the attraction.

To see how it works, you'll start with a simple example.

Girls Dance with Girls, Boys Scratch Their Elbows

The goal in k-means clustering is to take some points in space and put them into k groups (where k is any number you want to pick). Those k groups are each defined by a point in the center, kind of like a flag stuck in the moon that says, "Hey, this is the center of my group. Join me if you're closer to this flag than any others." This group center (formally called the *cluster centroid*) is the *mean* from which k-means gets its name.

Take as an example a middle school dance. If you've blocked the horror of middle school dances from your mind, I apologize for resurfacing such painful memories.

Those in attendance at the McAcne Middle School dance, romantically called the "Under the Sea Gala," are scattered about the floor as shown in Figure 2-1. I've even Photoshopped some parquet floor into the figure to help with the illusion.

And here's a sampling of the songs these young leaders of the free world will be dancing awkwardly to if you'd like to listen along in Spotify:

- Styx: Come Sail Away
- Everything But the Girl: Missing
- Ace of Bass: All that She Wants
- Soft Cell: Tainted Love
- Montell Jordan: This is How We Do It
- Eiffel 65: Blue

Figure 2-1: McAcne Middle School students tearing up the dance floor

Now, k-means clustering demands that you specify how many clusters you want to put the attendees in. Let's pick three clusters to start (later in this chapter we'll look at how to choose k). The algorithm is going to plant three flags on the dance floor, starting with some initial feasible solution, such as that pictured in Figure 2-2, where you have three initial means spread on the floor, denoted by black circles.

Figure 2-2: Initial cluster centers placed

In k-means clustering, dancers are assigned to the cluster that's nearest them, so between any two cluster centers on the floor, you can draw a line of demarcation, whereby if a dancer is on one side of the line they're in one group, but if they're on the other side, their group changes (see Figure 2-3).

Using these lines of demarcation, you can assign dancers to their groups and shade them appropriately, as in Figure 2-4. This diagram, one that divides the space into polytopes based on which regions are assigned to which cluster centers by distance, is called a *Voronoi diagram*.

Now, this initial assignment doesn't feel right, does it? You've sliced the space up in a rather odd way, leaving the bottom-left group empty and a lot of folks on the border of the top-right group.

The k-means clustering algorithm slides these three cluster centers around the dance floor until it gets the best fit.

How is "best fit" measured? Well, each attendee is some distance away from their cluster center. Whichever arrangement of cluster centers minimizes the average distance of attendees from their center is best.

Figure 2-3: Lines denote the borders of the clusters.

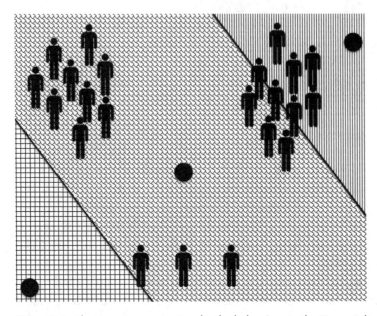

Figure 2-4: Cluster assignments given by shaded regions in the Voronoi diagram

Now, as I mentioned in Chapter 1, the word "minimize" is a tip-off that you'll need optimization modeling to best place the cluster centers. So in this chapter, you'll be busting out Solver to move the cluster centers around. The way Solver is going to get the centers placed just right is by intelligently and iteratively moving them around, keeping track of many of the good placements it has found and combining them (literally mating them like race horses) to get the best placement.

So while the diagram in Figure 2-4 looks pretty bad, Solver might eventually bump the centers to something like Figure 2-5. This gets the average distance between each dancer and their center down a bit.

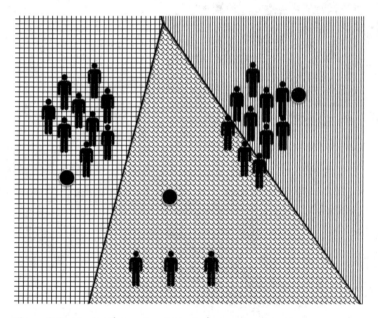

Figure 2-5: Moving the centers just a tad

Eventually though, Solver would figure out that the centers should be placed in the middle of our three groups of dancers as shown in Figure 2-6.

Nice! This is what an ideal clustering looks like. The cluster centroids are at the centers of each group of dancers, minimizing the average distance between dancer and nearest center. And now that you have a clustering, you can move on to the fun part: trying to understand what the clusters *mean*.

If you investigated the dancers' hair colors, political persuasions, or mile run speeds, the clusters may not make much sense. But the moment you were to evaluate the genders and ages of the attendees in each cluster, you'd start to see some common themes. The small group at the bottom is all old people—they must be the dance chaperones. The left group is all young males, and the right group is all young females. Everyone is too afraid to dance with each other.

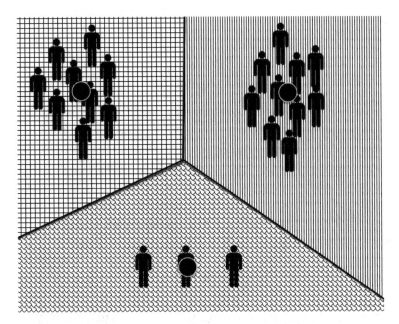

Figure 2-6: Optimal 3-means clustering of the McAcne dance

All right! So k-means has allowed you to segment this dance attendee population and correlate attendee descriptors with cluster membership to understand the *why* behind the assignments.

Now, you're probably saying to yourself, "Yeah, but that's stupid. I already knew the answer to start." You're right. In this example, you did. The reason this is a toy problem, is that you can already solve it by just *looking* at the points. Everything is in two-dimensional space, which is super easy for your eyeballs to cluster.

But what if you ran a store that sold thousands of products? Some customers have bought one or two in the past year. Other customers have bought tens. And the items purchased vary from customer to customer.

How do you cluster them on their "dance floor?" Well, your dance floor isn't in a two-dimensional space or three-dimensional space. It's in a thousand-dimensional product purchase space in which a customer has either purchased or not purchased the product in each single dimension. Very quickly, you see, a clustering problem can exceed the limits of the "Mark I Eyeball," as my military friends like to say.

Getting Real: K-Means Clustering Subscribers in E-mail Marketing

Let's move on to a more substantive use case. I'm an e-mail-marketing guy, so I'm going to use an example from `MailChimp.com` where I work. But this same example would work on retail purchase data, ad conversion data, social media data, and so on. It works with basically any type of data where you're reaching out to customers with marketing material, and they're choosing to engage with you.

Joey Bag O' Donuts Wholesale Wine Emporium

Let's imagine that you live in New Jersey where you run Joey Bag O' Donuts Wholesale Wine Emporium. It's an import-export business focused on bringing bulk wine to the states and selling it to select wine and liquor stores across the country. The way the business works is that Joey Bags travels the globe finding incredible deals on large quantities of wine. Joey ships it back to Jersey, and it's your job to sell this stuff on to stores at a profit.

You reach out to customers in a number of ways—a Facebook page, Twitter, even the occasional direct mailing—but the e-mail newsletter drums up the most business. For the past year, you've sent one newsletter per month. Usually there are two or three wine deals in each e-mail, perhaps one would be on Champagne, another on Malbec. Some deals are amazing, 80 percent or more off of retail. In total, you've offered 32 deals this year, all of which have gone quite well.

But just because things are going well, doesn't mean you can't do better. It'd be nice if you could understand the customers a little more. Sure, you can look at a particular purchase—like how some person with the last name Adams bought some Espumante in July at a 50 percent discount—but you can't tell whether that's because he liked that the minimum purchase requirement was one six-bottle box or the price or that it hadn't passed its peak yet.

It would be nice if you could segment the list into groups based on interest. Then, you could customize the newsletter to each segment and maybe drum up some more business. Whichever deal you thought matched up better with the segment could go in the subject line and would come first in the newsletter. That type of targeting can result in a bump in sales.

But how do you segment the list? Where do you start?

This is an opportunity to let the computer segment the list for you. Using k-means clustering, you can find the best segments and then try to understand *why* they're the best segments.

The Initial Dataset

NOTE

The Excel workbook used in this chapter, "WineKMC.xlsx," is available for download at the book's website at www.wiley.com/go/datasmart. This workbook includes all the initial data if you want to work from it. Or you can just read along using the sheets I've put together in the workbook.

Starting out, you have two interesting sources of data:

- The metadata on each offer is saved in a spreadsheet, including varietal, minimum bottle quantity for purchase, discount off retail, whether the wine is past its peak, and country or state of origin. This data is housed in a tab called OfferInformation, as shown in Figure 2-7
- You also know which customers bought which offers, so you can dump that information out of MailChimp and into the spreadsheet with the offer metadata in a tab called Transactions. This transactional data, as shown in Figure 2-8, is simply represented as the customer who made the purchase and which offer they purchased.

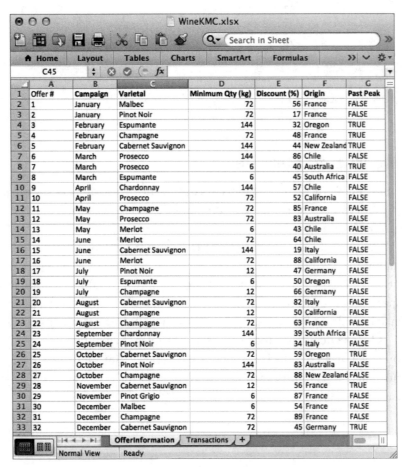

Offer #	Campaign	Varietal	Minimum Qty (kg)	Discount (%)	Origin	Past Peak
1	January	Malbec	72	56	France	FALSE
2	January	Pinot Noir	72	17	France	FALSE
3	February	Espumante	144	32	Oregon	TRUE
4	February	Champagne	72	48	France	TRUE
5	February	Cabernet Sauvignon	144	44	New Zealand	TRUE
6	March	Prosecco	144	86	Chile	FALSE
7	March	Prosecco	6	40	Australia	TRUE
8	March	Espumante	6	45	South Africa	FALSE
9	April	Chardonnay	144	57	Chile	FALSE
10	April	Prosecco	72	52	California	FALSE
11	May	Champagne	72	85	France	FALSE
12	May	Prosecco	72	83	Australia	FALSE
13	May	Merlot	6	43	Chile	FALSE
14	June	Merlot	72	64	Chile	FALSE
15	June	Cabernet Sauvignon	144	19	Italy	FALSE
16	June	Merlot	72	88	California	FALSE
17	July	Pinot Noir	12	47	Germany	FALSE
18	July	Espumante	6	50	Oregon	FALSE
19	July	Champagne	12	66	Germany	FALSE
20	August	Cabernet Sauvignon	72	82	Italy	FALSE
21	August	Champagne	12	50	California	FALSE
22	August	Champagne	72	63	France	FALSE
23	September	Chardonnay	144	39	South Africa	FALSE
24	September	Pinot Noir	6	34	Italy	FALSE
25	October	Cabernet Sauvignon	72	59	Oregon	TRUE
26	October	Pinot Noir	144	83	Australia	FALSE
27	October	Champagne	72	88	New Zealand	FALSE
28	November	Cabernet Sauvignon	12	56	France	TRUE
29	November	Pinot Grigio	6	87	France	FALSE
30	December	Malbec	6	54	France	FALSE
31	December	Champagne	72	89	France	FALSE
32	December	Cabernet Sauvignon	72	45	Germany	TRUE

Figure 2-7: The details of the last 32 offers

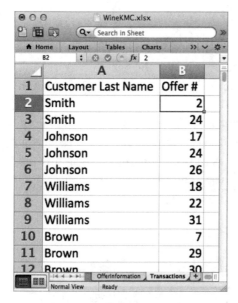

Figure 2-8: A list of offers taken by customer

Determining What to Measure

So here's a conundrum. In the middle school dance problem, measuring distances between dancers and cluster centers was easy, right? Just break out the measuring tape!

But what do you do here?

You know there were 32 deals offered in the last year, and you have a list in the Transactions tab of the 324 purchases, broken out by customer. But in order to measure the distance between each customer and a cluster center, you need to position them in this 32-deal space. In other words, you need to understand the deals *they did not take*, and create a matrix of deals-by-customers, where each customer gets their own 32-deal column full of 1s for the deals they took and 0s for the ones they didn't.

In other words, you need to take this row-oriented Transactions tab and turn it into a matrix with customers in columns and offers in rows. And the best way to create such a matrix is to use a PivotTable.

> **NOTE**
>
> For a primer on PivotTables, see Chapter 1.

So here's what you're going to do. In the Transactions tab, highlight columns A and B and then insert a PivotTable. Using the PivotTable Builder, simply select deals as row labels, customers as column labels, and take a count of deals for the values. This count will be 1 if a customer/deal pair was present in the original data and 0 otherwise (0 ends up as a blank cell in this case). The resulting PivotTable is pictured in Figure 2-9.

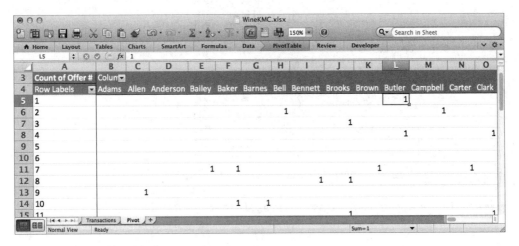

Figure 2-9: PivotTable of deals versus customers

Now that you have your purchases in matrix form, copy the OfferInformation tab and name it **Matrix**. In this new sheet, paste the values from the PivotTable (you don't need to copy and paste the deal number, because it's already in the offer information) into the new tab starting at column H. You end up with a fleshed out version of the matrix that has consolidated the deal descriptions with the purchase data, as pictured in Figure 2-10.

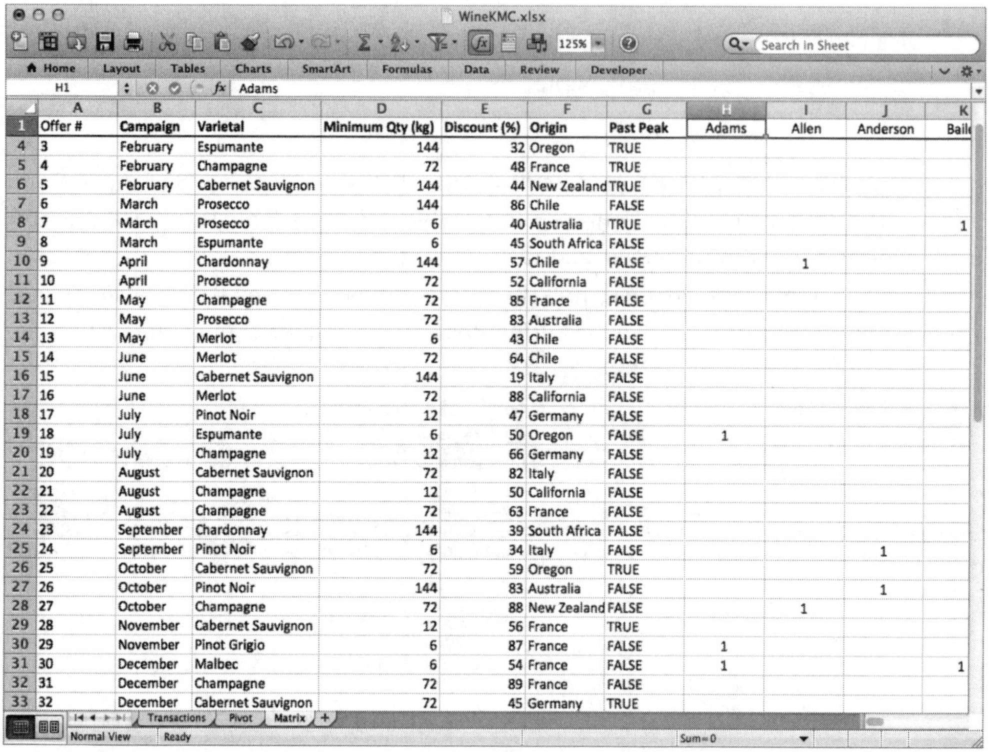

	A	B	C	D	E	F	G	H	I	J	K
1	Offer #	Campaign	Varietal	Minimum Qty (kg)	Discount (%)	Origin	Past Peak	Adams	Allen	Anderson	Bail
4	3	February	Espumante	144	32	Oregon	TRUE				
5	4	February	Champagne	72	48	France	TRUE				
6	5	February	Cabernet Sauvignon	144	44	New Zealand	TRUE				
7	6	March	Prosecco	144	86	Chile	FALSE				
8	7	March	Prosecco	6	40	Australia	TRUE				1
9	8	March	Espumante	6	45	South Africa	FALSE				
10	9	April	Chardonnay	144	57	Chile	FALSE		1		
11	10	April	Prosecco	72	52	California	FALSE				
12	11	May	Champagne	72	85	France	FALSE				
13	12	May	Prosecco	72	83	Australia	FALSE				
14	13	May	Merlot	6	43	Chile	FALSE				
15	14	June	Merlot	72	64	Chile	FALSE				
16	15	June	Cabernet Sauvignon	144	19	Italy	FALSE				
17	16	June	Merlot	72	88	California	FALSE				
18	17	July	Pinot Noir	12	47	Germany	FALSE				
19	18	July	Espumante	6	50	Oregon	FALSE	1			
20	19	July	Champagne	12	66	Germany	FALSE				
21	20	August	Cabernet Sauvignon	72	82	Italy	FALSE				
22	21	August	Champagne	12	50	California	FALSE				
23	22	August	Champagne	72	63	France	FALSE				
24	23	September	Chardonnay	144	39	South Africa	FALSE				
25	24	September	Pinot Noir	6	34	Italy	FALSE			1	
26	25	October	Cabernet Sauvignon	72	59	Oregon	TRUE				
27	26	October	Pinot Noir	144	83	Australia	FALSE			1	
28	27	October	Champagne	72	88	New Zealand	FALSE		1		
29	28	November	Cabernet Sauvignon	12	56	France	TRUE				
30	29	November	Pinot Grigio	6	87	France	FALSE	1			
31	30	December	Malbec	6	54	France	FALSE	1			1
32	31	December	Champagne	72	89	France	FALSE				
33	32	December	Cabernet Sauvignon	72	45	Germany	TRUE				

Figure 2-10: Deal description and purchase data merged into a single matrix

STANDARDIZING YOUR DATA

In this chapter, each dimension of your data is the same type of binary purchase data. But in many clustering problems, this is not the case. Envision a scenario where people are clustered based on height, weight, and salary. These three types of data are all on different scales. Height may range from 60 inches to 80 inches while weight may range from 100 to 300 pounds.

In this context, measuring the distance between customers (like dancers on the dance floor) gets tricky. So it's common to *standardize* each column of data by subtracting out the average and dividing through by a measure of spread we'll encounter in Chapter 4 called the standard deviation. This puts each column on the same scale, centered around 0.

While our data in Chapter 2 does not require standardization, you can see it in action in the outlier detection chapter, Chapter 9.

Start with Four Clusters

All right, so now you have all of your data consolidated into a single, useable format. In order to begin clustering, you need to pick k, which is the number of clusters in the k-means clustering algorithm. Often the approach in k-means is to try a bunch of different values for k (I'll get to how to choose between them later), but for the sake of starting, you need to choose just one.

You'll want to choose a number of clusters to start with that's in the ball park of what you're willing to act on. You're not going to create 50 clusters and send 50 targeted ad campaigns to a couple of folks in each group. That defeats the purpose of the exercise in the first place. You want something small in this case. For this example, then, start with four—in an ideal world, maybe you'd get your list divided into four perfectly understandable groups of 25 customers each (this isn't likely).

All right then, if you were to split the customers into four groups, what are the best four groups for that?

Rather than dirty up the pretty Matrix tab, copy the data into a new tab and call it **4MC**. You can then insert four columns after Past Peak in columns H through K that will be the cluster centers. (To insert a column, right-click Column H and select Insert. A column will be added to the left.) Label these clusters **Cluster 1** through **Cluster 4**. You can also place some conditional formatting on them so that whenever each cluster center is set you can see how they differ.

The 4MC tab will appear as shown in Figure 2-11.

These cluster centers are all 0s at this point. But technically, they can be anything you want, and what you'd like to see is that they, like in the middle school dance case, distribute themselves to minimize the distances between each customer and their closest cluster center.

Obviously then, these centers will have values between 0 and 1 for each deal since all the customer vectors are binary.

But what does it mean to measure the distance between a cluster center and a customer?

Euclidean Distance: Measuring Distances as the Crow Flies

You now have a single column per customer, so how do you measure the dance-floor distance between them? Well, the official term for that is "as-the-crow-flies," measuring tape distance is the *Euclidean distance*.

Let's return to the dance floor problem to understand how to compute it.

I'm going to lay down a horizontal and a vertical axis on the dance floor, and in Figure 2-12, you can see that you have a dancer at (8, 2) and a cluster center at (4, 4). To compute the Euclidean distance between them, you have to remember the Pythagorean theorem you learned back in middle school.

Offer #	Campaign	Varietal	Minimum Qty	Discount (%)	Origin	Past Peak	Cluster 1	Cluster 2	Cluster 3	Cluster 4	Adams	Allen	Anderson	Bailey
1	January	Malbec	72	56	France	FALSE								
2	January	Pinot Noir	72	17	France	FALSE								
3	February	Espumante	144	32	Oregon	TRUE								
4	February	Champagn	72	48	France	TRUE								
5	February	Cabernet S	144	44	New Zealai	TRUE								
6	March	Prosecco	144	86	Chile	FALSE								
7	March	Prosecco	6	40	Australia	TRUE								1
8	March	Espumante	6	45	South Afric	FALSE								
9	April	Chardonna	144	57	Chile	FALSE						1		
10	April	Prosecco	72	52	California	FALSE								
11	May	Champagn	72	85	France	FALSE								
12	May	Prosecco	72	83	Australia	FALSE								
13	May	Merlot	6	43	Chile	FALSE								
14	June	Merlot	72	64	Chile	FALSE								
15	June	Cabernet S	144	19	Italy	FALSE								
16	June	Merlot	72	88	California	FALSE								
17	July	Pinot Noir	12	47	Germany	FALSE								
18	July	Espumante	6	50	Oregon	FALSE					1			
19	July	Champagn	12	66	Germany	FALSE								
20	August	Cabernet S	72	82	Italy	FALSE								
21	August	Champagn	12	50	California	FALSE								
22	August	Champagn	72	63	France	FALSE								
23	September	Chardonna	144	39	South Afric	FALSE								
24	September	Pinot Noir	6	34	Italy	FALSE							1	
25	October	Cabernet S	72	59	Oregon	TRUE								
26	October	Pinot Noir	144	83	Australia	FALSE							1	
27	October	Champagn	72	88	New Zealai	FALSE						1		

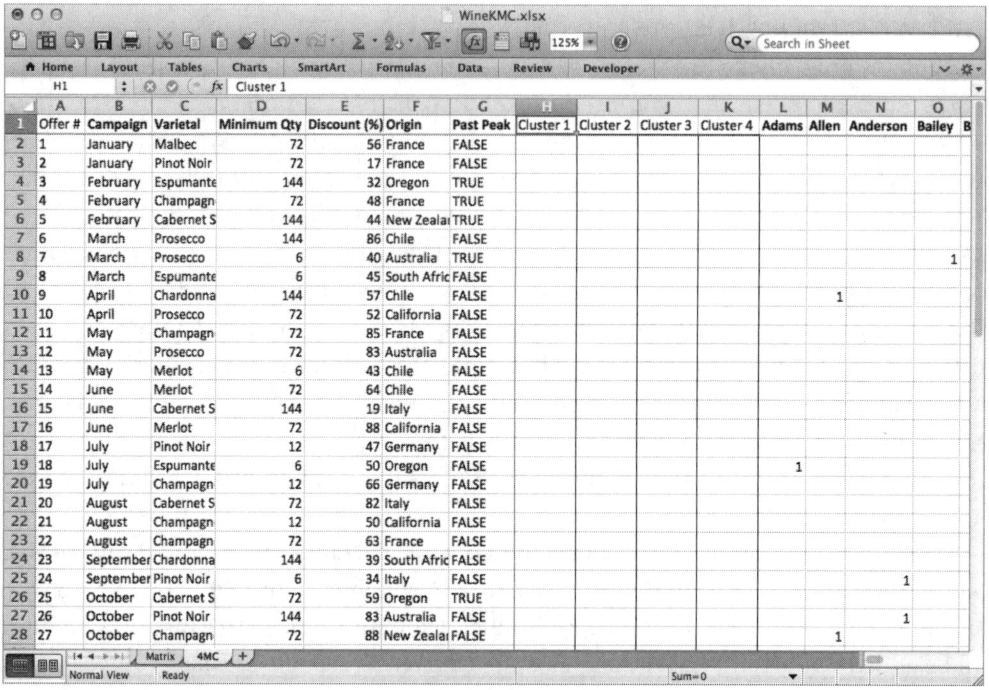

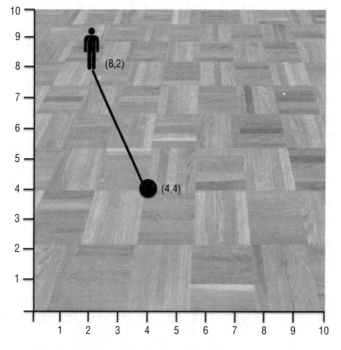

Figure 2-11: Blank cluster centers placed on the 4MC tab

Figure 2-12: A dancer at (8,2) and a cluster center at (4,4)

These two points are 8 – 4 = 4 feet apart in the vertical direction. They're 4 – 2 = 2 feet apart in the horizontal direction. By the Pythagorean theorem then, the squared distance between these two points is 4^2 + 2^2 = 16 + 4 = 20 feet. So the distance between them is the square root of 20, which is approximately 4.47 feet (see Figure 2-13).

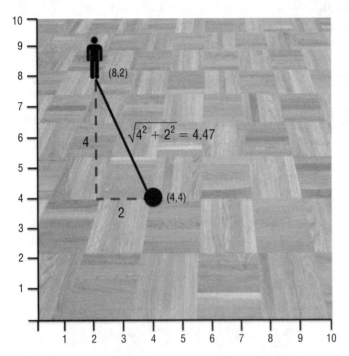

Figure 2-13: Euclidean distance is the square root of the sum of squared distances in each single direction

In the context of the newsletter subscribers, you have more than two dimensions, but the same concept applies. Distance between a customer and a cluster center is calculated by taking the difference between the two points for each deal, squaring them, summing them up, and taking the square root.

So for instance, let's say in the 4MC tab, you wanted to take the Euclidean distance between the Cluster 1 center in column H and the purchases of customer Adams in column L.

In cell L34, below Adams' purchases, you can take the difference of Adams' vector and the cluster center, square it, sum it, and square root the sum, using the following array formula (note the absolute references that allow you to drag this formula to the right or down without the cluster center reference changing):

```
{=SQRT(SUM((L$2:L$33-$H$2:$H$33)^2))}
```

You have to use an array formula (enter the formula and press Ctrl + Shift + Enter or Cmd + Return on Mac as covered in Chapter 1) because the $(L2:L33 - H2:H33)^2$ portion of the formula needs to know to go item by item taking differences and squaring them. The end result, however, is a single number: 1.732 in this case (see Figure 2-14). This makes sense because Adams took three deals, but the initial cluster center is all 0s, and the square root of 3 is 1.732.

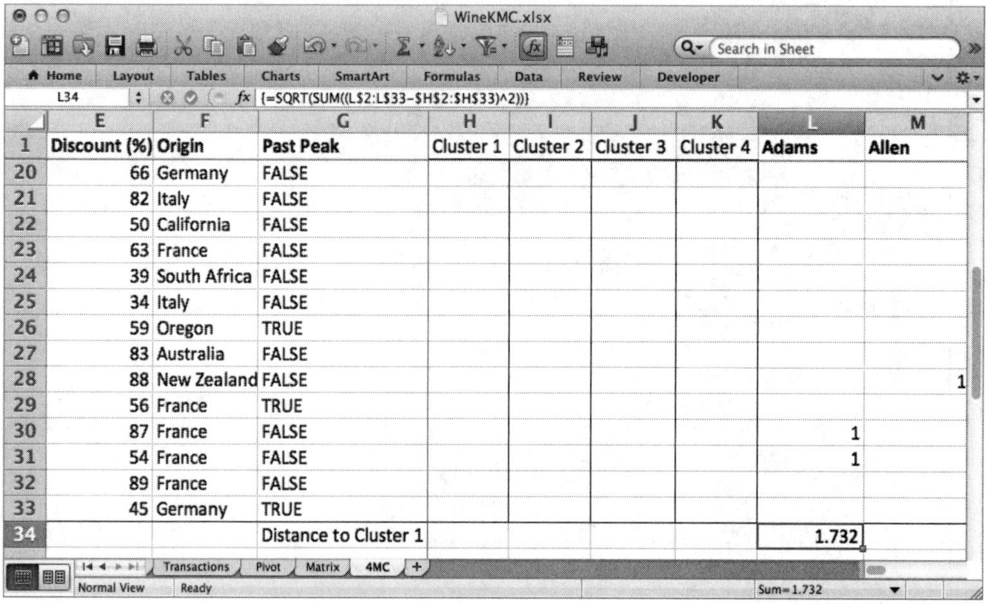

	E	F	G	H	I	J	K	L	M
1	Discount (%)	Origin	Past Peak	Cluster 1	Cluster 2	Cluster 3	Cluster 4	**Adams**	**Allen**
20	66	Germany	FALSE						
21	82	Italy	FALSE						
22	50	California	FALSE						
23	63	France	FALSE						
24	39	South Africa	FALSE						
25	34	Italy	FALSE						
26	59	Oregon	TRUE						
27	83	Australia	FALSE						
28	88	New Zealand	FALSE						1
29	56	France	TRUE						
30	87	France	FALSE					1	
31	54	France	FALSE					1	
32	89	France	FALSE						
33	45	Germany	TRUE						
34			Distance to Cluster 1					1.732	

Cell reference: L34 `{=SQRT(SUM((L$2:L$33-$H$2:$H$33)^2))}`
Sum=1.732

Figure 2-14: The distance between Adams and Cluster 1

In the spreadsheet shown in Figure 2-14, I've frozen panes (see Chapter 1) between columns G and H and labeled row 34 in G34 as Distance to Cluster 1 just to keep track of things when you scroll to the right.

Distances and Cluster Assignments for Everybody!

So now you know how to calculate the distance between a purchase vector and a cluster center.

It's time to add the distance calculations for Adams to the other centers by dragging cell L34 down through L37 and then changing the cluster center reference *manually* from column H to I, J, and K in the descending cells. You end up with the following 4 formulas in L34:L37:

```
{=SQRT(SUM((L$2:L$33-$H$2:$H$33)^2))}
{=SQRT(SUM((L$2:L$33-$I$2:$I$33)^2))}
```

```
{=SQRT(SUM((L$2:L$33-$J$2:$J$33)^2))}
{=SQRT(SUM((L$2:L$33-$K$2:$K$33)^2))}
```

Since you've used absolute references (the $ sign in the formulas; see Chapter 1 for more details) for the cluster centers, you can drag L34:L37 over through DG34:DG37 to calculate distances between each customer and all four cluster centers. Also, in column G, label rows 35 through 37 **Distance to Cluster 2**, and so on. These new distances are pictured in Figure 2-15.

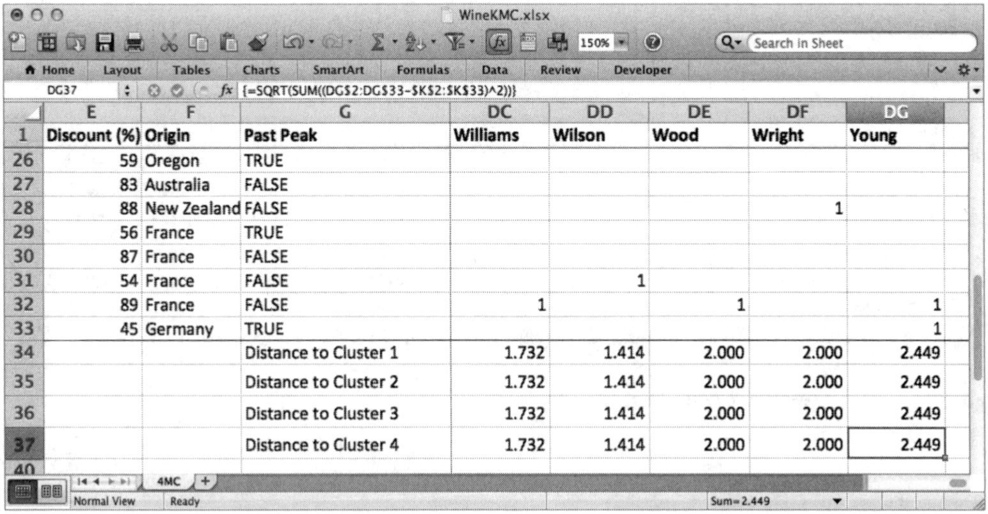

Figure 2-15: Distance calculations from each customer to each cluster

For each customer then, you know their distance to all four cluster centers. Their cluster assignment is to the nearest one, which you can calculate in two steps.

First, going back to customer Adams in column L, let's calculate the minimum distance to a cluster center in cell L38. That's just:

```
=MIN(L34:L37)
```

And then to determine which cluster center matches that minimum distance, you can use the MATCH formula (see Chapter 1 for more details). Placing the following MATCH formula in L39, you can determine which cell index in the range L34 to L37 counting up from 1 matches the minimum distance:

```
=MATCH(L38,L34:L37,0)
```

In this case the minimum distance is a tie between all four clusters, so MATCH picks the first (L34) by returning index 1 (see Figure 2-16).

You can drag these two formulas across the sheet through DG38:DG39 as well. Add Minimum Cluster Distance and Assigned Cluster in Column G as labels for rows 38 and 39 just to keep things organized.

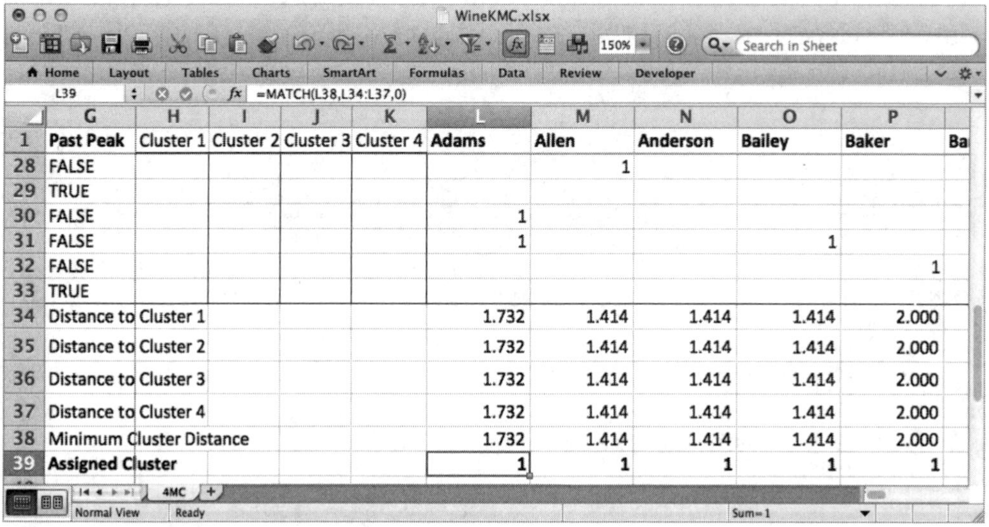

	G	H	I	J	K	L	M	N	O	P	
1	**Past Peak**	**Cluster 1**	**Cluster 2**	**Cluster 3**	**Cluster 4**	**Adams**	**Allen**	**Anderson**	**Bailey**	**Baker**	**Ba**
28	FALSE						1				
29	TRUE										
30	FALSE					1					
31	FALSE					1			1		
32	FALSE									1	
33	TRUE										
34	Distance to Cluster 1					1.732	1.414	1.414	1.414	2.000	
35	Distance to Cluster 2					1.732	1.414	1.414	1.414	2.000	
36	Distance to Cluster 3					1.732	1.414	1.414	1.414	2.000	
37	Distance to Cluster 4					1.732	1.414	1.414	1.414	2.000	
38	Minimum Cluster Distance					1.732	1.414	1.414	1.414	2.000	
39	Assigned Cluster					1	1	1	1	1	

Figure 2-16: Cluster matches added into the sheet

Solving for the Cluster Centers

You now have distance calculations and cluster assignments in the spreadsheet. To set the cluster centers to their best locations, you need to find the values in columns H through K that minimize the total distance between the customers and their assigned clusters denoted on row 39 beneath each customer.

And if you read Chapter 1, you know exactly what to think when you hear the word *minimize*: This is an optimization step, and an optimization step means using Solver.

In order to use Solver, you need an objective cell, so in cell A36, let's sum up all the distances between customers and their cluster assignments:

```
=SUM(L38:DG38)
```

This sum of customers' distances from their closest cluster center is exactly the objective function encountered earlier when clustering on the McAcne Middle School dance floor. But Euclidean distance with its squares and square roots is crazy non-linear (read "wicked non-linear" if you live in Massachusetts), so you need to use the evolutionary solving method instead of the simplex method to set the cluster centers.

In Chapter 1, you used the simplex algorithm. Simplex is faster than other methods when it's allowable, but it's not possible when you're squaring, square rooting, or otherwise, taking non-linear functions of your decisions. Likewise, OpenSolver (introduced in Chapter 1), which uses an implementation of simplex on steroids is of no use here.

In this case, the evolutionary algorithm built into Solver uses a combination of random search and good solution "breeding" to find good solutions similarly to how evolution works in biological contexts.

NOTE

For a full treatment of optimization, see Chapter 4.

Notice that you have everything you need to set up a problem in Solver:

- **Objective:** Minimize the total distances of customers from their cluster centers (A36).
- **Decision variables:** The deal values of each row within the cluster center (H2:K33).
- **Constraints:** Cluster centers should have values somewhere between 0 and 1.

Open Solver and hammer in the requirements. You'll set Solver to minimize A36 by changing H2:K33 with the constraint that H2:K33 be <= 1 just like all the deal vectors. Make sure that the variables are checked as non-negative and that the evolutionary solver is chosen. See Figure 2-17.

Also, setting these clusters isn't a cakewalk for Solver, so you should beef up some of the evolutionary solver's options by pressing the options button within the Solver window and toggling over to the evolutionary tab. It's useful to bump up the Maximum Time Without Improvement parameter somewhere north of 30 seconds, depending on how long you want to wait for the Solver to finish. In Figure 2-18, I've set mine to 600 seconds (10 minutes). That way, I can set the Solver to run and go to dinner. And if you ever want to kill Solver early, just press Escape and then exit with the best solution it's found so far.

If you're curious, the inner workings of the evolutionary solver are covered in greater detail in Chapter 4 and at `http://www.solver.com`.

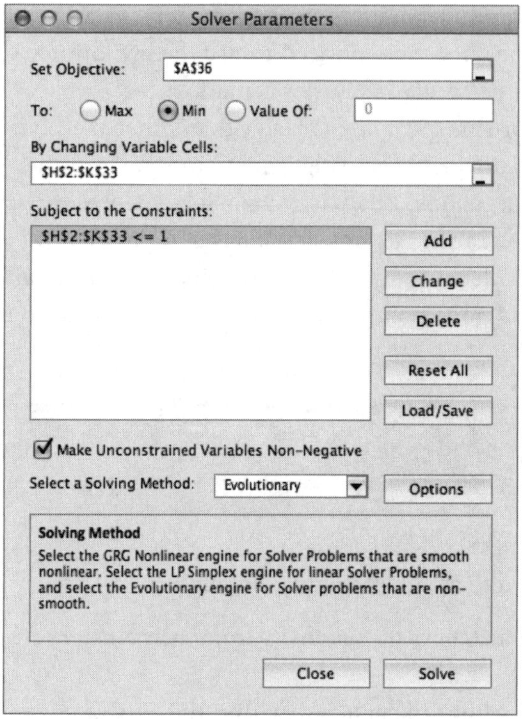

Figure 2-17: The Solver setup for 4-means clustering

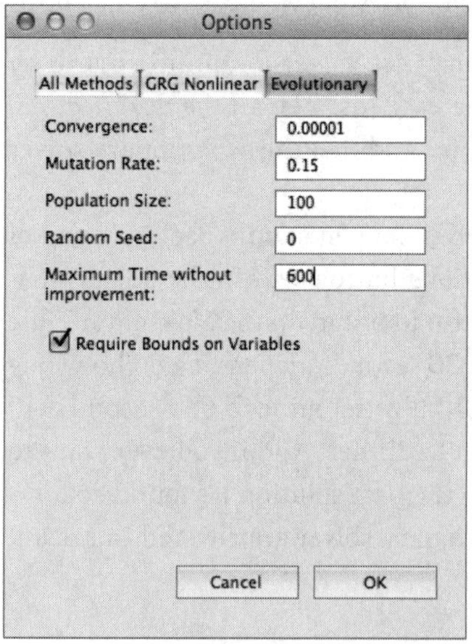

Figure 2-18: The evolutionary solver options tab

Press Solve and watch Excel do its thing until the evolutionary algorithm converges.

Making Sense of the Results

Once Solver gives you the optimal cluster centers, the fun starts. You get to mine the groups for insight! So in Figure 2-19, you can see that Solver calculated an optimal total distance of 140.7, and the four cluster centers, thanks to the conditional formatting, all look very different.

Note that your cluster centers may look different from the spreadsheet provided with the book, because the evolutionary algorithm employs random numbers and does not give the same answer each time. The clusters may be fundamentally different or, more likely, they may be in a different order (for example, my Cluster 1 is very close to your Cluster 4, and so on).

Because you pasted the deal descriptions in columns B through G when you set up the tab, you can read off the details of the deals in Figure 2-19 that seem important to the cluster centers.

	A	B	C	D	E	F	G	H	I	J	K	L	M	N	O
1	Offer #	Campaign	Varietal	Min. Qty	Discount (%)	Origin	Past Peak	Cluster 1	Cluster 2	Cluster 3	Cluster 4	Adams	Allen	Anderson	Bailey
29	28	November	Cabernet	12	56	France	TRUE	0.026	0.017	0.090	0.030				
30	29	November	Pinot Gri	6	87	France	FALSE	0.012	0.619	0.043	0.038	1			
31	30	December	Malbec	6	54	France	FALSE	0.020	0.729	0.079	0.136	1			1
32	31	December	Champag	72	89	France	FALSE	0.023	0.027	0.211	0.259				
33	32	December	Cabernet	72	45	Germany	TRUE	0.093	0.013	0.053	0.125				
34							Distance to Cluster 1					2.166	1.939	0.740	1.924
35	Total Distance						Distance to Cluster 2					1.044	1.886	1.865	1.042
36	140.7						Distance to Cluster 3					1.691	1.339	1.428	1.359
37							Distance to Cluster 4					2.012	1.731	1.781	1.749
38							Minimum Cluster Distance					1.044	1.339	0.740	1.042
39							Assigned Cluster					2	3	1	2

Figure 2-19: The four optimal cluster centers

For Cluster 1 in column H, the conditional formatting calls out deals 24, 26, 17, and to a lesser degree, 2. Reading through the details of those deals, the main thing they have in common: *They're all Pinot Noir.*

If you look at column I, the green cells all have a low minimum quantity in common. These are the buyers who don't want to have to buy in bulk to get a deal.

But I'll be honest; the last two cluster centers are kind of hard to interpret. Well, how about instead of interpreting the cluster center, you investigate the members of the cluster and determine which deals they like? That might be more elucidating.

Getting the Top Deals by Cluster

So instead of looking at which dimensions are closer to 1 for a cluster center, let's check who is assigned to each cluster and which deals they prefer.

To do this, let's start by making a copy of the OfferInformation tab and calling it **4MC – TopDealsByCluster**. On this new tab, label columns H through K as **1, 2, 3,** and **4** (see Figure 2-20).

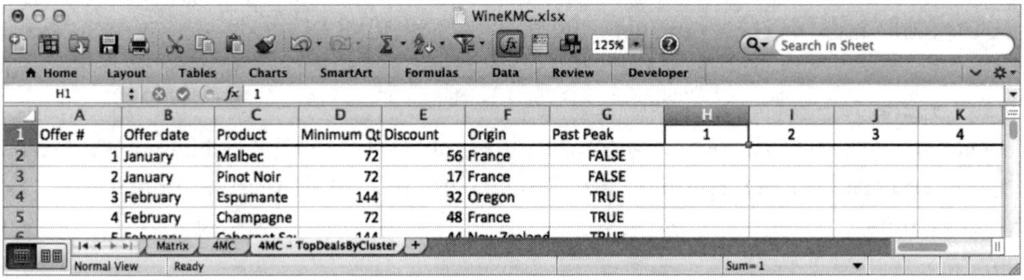

A	B	C	D	E	F	G	H	I	J	K
Offer #	Offer date	Product	Minimum Qt	Discount	Origin	Past Peak	1	2	3	4
1	January	Malbec	72	56	France	FALSE				
2	January	Pinot Noir	72	17	France	FALSE				
3	February	Espumante	144	32	Oregon	TRUE				
4	February	Champagne	72	48	France	TRUE				

Figure 2-20: Setting up a tab to count popular deals by cluster

Back on tab 4MC, you have cluster assignments listed (1-4) on row 39. All you need to do to get deal counts by cluster is check the column title on tab 4MC – TopDealsByCluster in columns H through K, see who on 4MC was assigned to that cluster using row 39, and then sum up their values for each deal row. That'll give you the total customers from a given cluster that took a deal.

Start with cell H2, that is, the count of customers in Cluster 1 who took offer #1, the January Malbec offer. You want to sum across L2:DG2 on the 4MC tab but only for those customers who are in Cluster 1, and that is a classic use case for the SUMIF formula. The formula looks like this:

```
=SUMIF('4MC'!$L$39:$DG$39,'4MC - TopDealsByCluster'!H$1,'4MC'!$L2:$DG2)
```

The way the SUMIF statement works is that you provide it with some values to check in the first section '4MC'!$L$39:$DG$39, which are checked against the 1 in the column header ('4MC - TopDealsByCluster'!H$1), and then for any match, you sum up row 2 by specifying '4MC'!$L2:$DG2 in the third section of the formula.

Note that you've used absolute references (the $ in the formula) in front of everything in the cluster assignment row, in front of the row number for our column headers, and in front of the column letter for our deals taken. By making these references absolute, you can then drag this formula through range H2:K33 to get deal counts for every cluster center and deal combination, as pictured in Figure 2-21. You can place some conditional formatting on these columns to make them more readable.

By selecting columns A through K and auto-filtering (see Chapter 1), you can make this data sortable. Sorting from high to low on column H, you can then see which deals are most popular within Cluster 1 (see Figure 2-22).

Just as noted earlier, the four top deals for this cluster are all Pinot. These folks have watched *Sideways* one too many times. When you sort on Cluster 2, it becomes abundantly clear that these are the low volume buyers (see Figure 2-23).

But when you sort on Cluster 3, things aren't quite as clear. There are more than a handful of top deals; the drop-off between in deals and out deals is not as stark. But the most popular ones seem to have a few things in common—the discounts are quite good, five out of the top six deals are bubbly in nature, and France is in three of the top four deals. But nothing is conclusive (see Figure 2-24).

As for Cluster 4, these folks really loved the August Champaign deal for whatever reason. Also, five out of the top six deals are from France, and nine of the top 10 deals are high volume (see Figure 2-25). Perhaps this is the French-leaning high volume Cluster? The overlap between clusters 3 and 4 is somewhat troubling.

This leads to a question: Is 4 the right number for k in k-means clustering? Perhaps not. But how do you tell?

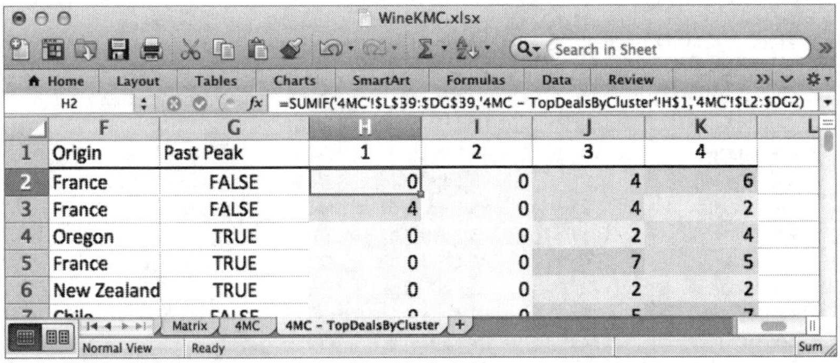

Figure 2-21: Totals of each deal taken broken out by cluster

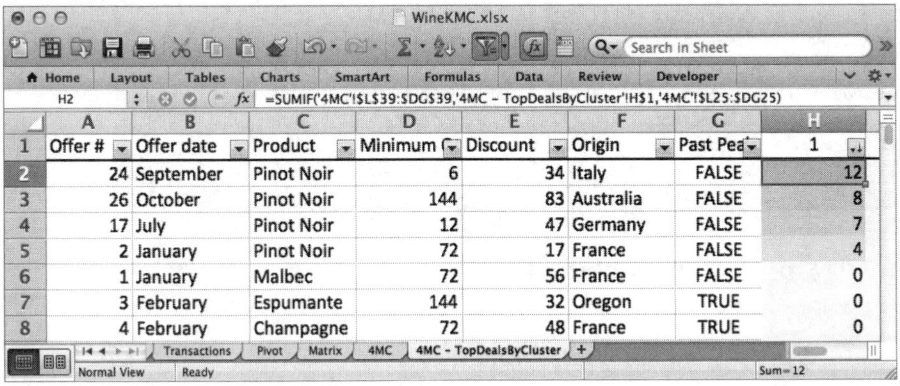

Figure 2-22: Sorting on Cluster 1—Pinot, Pinot, Pinot!

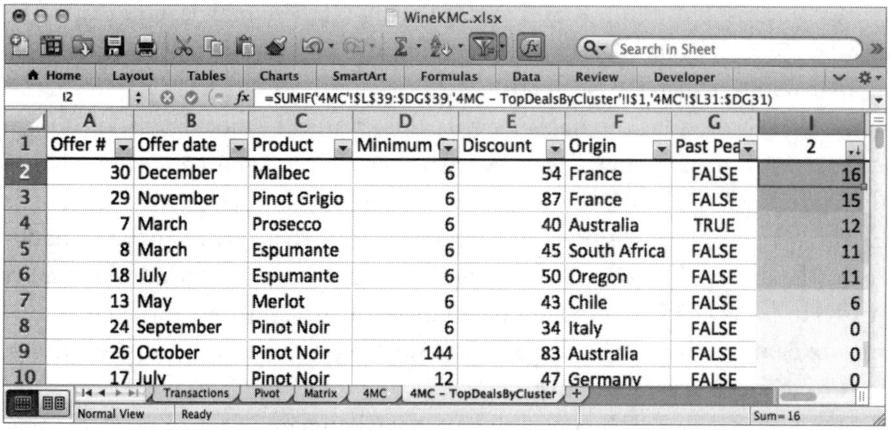

Offer #	Offer date	Product	Minimum Q	Discount	Origin	Past Peak	2
30	December	Malbec	6	54	France	FALSE	16
29	November	Pinot Grigio	6	87	France	FALSE	15
7	March	Prosecco	6	40	Australia	TRUE	12
8	March	Espumante	6	45	South Africa	FALSE	11
18	July	Espumante	6	50	Oregon	FALSE	11
13	May	Merlot	6	43	Chile	FALSE	6
24	September	Pinot Noir	6	34	Italy	FALSE	0
26	October	Pinot Noir	144	83	Australia	FALSE	0
17	July	Pinot Noir	12	47	Germany	FALSE	0

Figure 2-23: Sorting on Cluster 2—small-timers

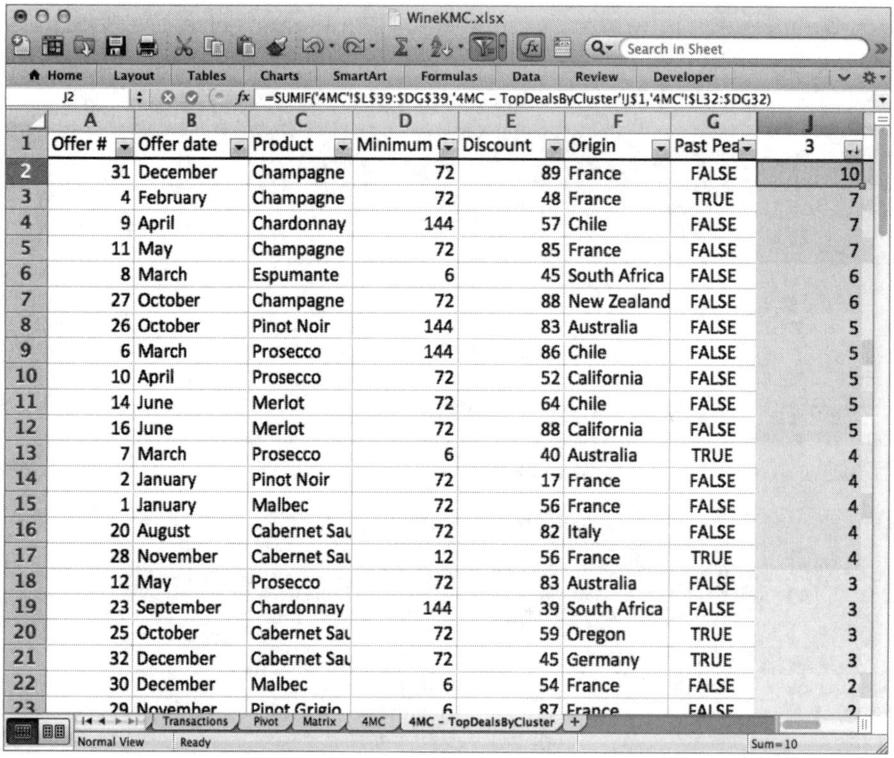

Offer #	Offer date	Product	Minimum Q	Discount	Origin	Past Peak	3
31	December	Champagne	72	89	France	FALSE	10
4	February	Champagne	72	48	France	TRUE	7
9	April	Chardonnay	144	57	Chile	FALSE	7
11	May	Champagne	72	85	France	FALSE	7
8	March	Espumante	6	45	South Africa	FALSE	6
27	October	Champagne	72	88	New Zealand	FALSE	6
26	October	Pinot Noir	144	83	Australia	FALSE	5
6	March	Prosecco	144	86	Chile	FALSE	5
10	April	Prosecco	72	52	California	FALSE	5
14	June	Merlot	72	64	Chile	FALSE	5
16	June	Merlot	72	88	California	FALSE	5
7	March	Prosecco	6	40	Australia	TRUE	4
2	January	Pinot Noir	72	17	France	FALSE	4
1	January	Malbec	72	56	France	FALSE	4
20	August	Cabernet Sau	72	82	Italy	FALSE	4
28	November	Cabernet Sau	12	56	France	TRUE	4
12	May	Prosecco	72	83	Australia	FALSE	3
23	September	Chardonnay	144	39	South Africa	FALSE	3
25	October	Cabernet Sau	72	59	Oregon	TRUE	3
32	December	Cabernet Sau	72	45	Germany	TRUE	3
30	December	Malbec	6	54	France	FALSE	2
29	November	Pinot Grigio	6	87	France	FALSE	2

Figure 2-24: Sorting on Cluster 3 is a bit of a mess

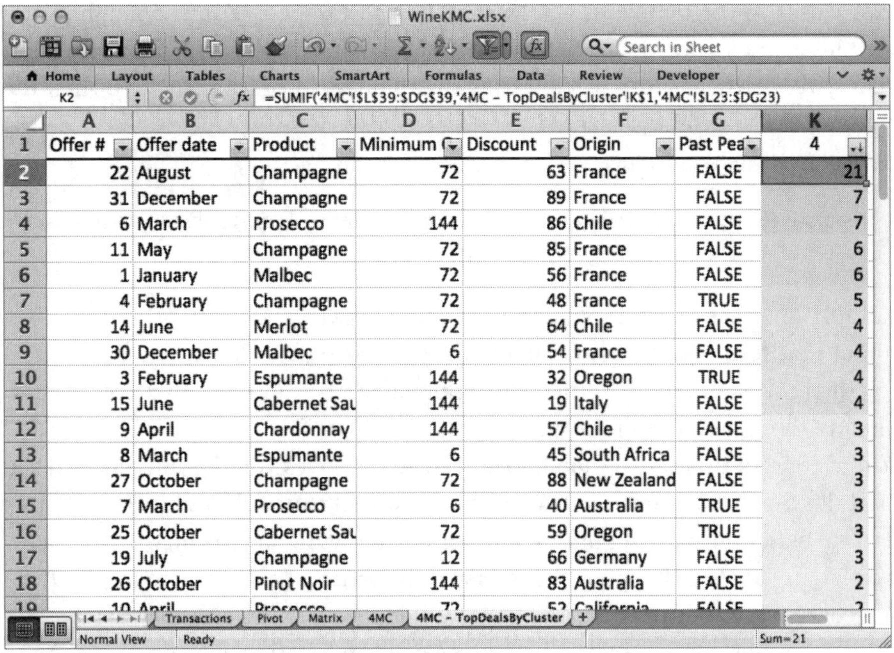

	A	B	C	D	E	F	G	K
1	Offer #	Offer date	Product	Minimum	Discount	Origin	Past Pea	4
2	22	August	Champagne	72	63	France	FALSE	21
3	31	December	Champagne	72	89	France	FALSE	7
4	6	March	Prosecco	144	86	Chile	FALSE	7
5	11	May	Champagne	72	85	France	FALSE	6
6	1	January	Malbec	72	56	France	FALSE	6
7	4	February	Champagne	72	48	France	TRUE	5
8	14	June	Merlot	72	64	Chile	FALSE	4
9	30	December	Malbec	6	54	France	FALSE	4
10	3	February	Espumante	144	32	Oregon	TRUE	4
11	15	June	Cabernet Sau	144	19	Italy	FALSE	4
12	9	April	Chardonnay	144	57	Chile	FALSE	3
13	8	March	Espumante	6	45	South Africa	FALSE	3
14	27	October	Champagne	72	88	New Zealand	FALSE	3
15	7	March	Prosecco	6	40	Australia	TRUE	3
16	25	October	Cabernet Sau	72	59	Oregon	TRUE	3
17	19	July	Champagne	12	66	Germany	FALSE	3
18	26	October	Pinot Noir	144	83	Australia	FALSE	2

Figure 2-25: Sorting on Cluster 4—these folks just like Champagne in August?

The Silhouette: A Good Way to Let Different K Values Duke It Out

There's nothing wrong with just doing k-means clustering for a few values of k until you find something that makes intuitive sense to you. Of course, maybe the reason that a given k doesn't "read well" is not because k is wrong but because the offer information is leaving something out that would help describe the clusters better.

So is there another way (other than just eyeballing the clusters) to give a thumbs-up or -down to a particular value of k?

There is—by computing a score for your clusters called the *silhouette*. The cool thing about the silhouette is that it's relatively agnostic to the value of k, so you can compare different values of k using this single score.

The Silhouette at a High Level: How Far Are Your Neighbors from You?

You can compare the average distance between each customer and their friends in the cluster they've been assigned to with the average distance to the customers in the cluster with the next nearest center.

If I'm a lot closer to the people in my cluster than to the people in the neighboring cluster, these folks are a good group for me, right? But what if the folks from the next nearest cluster are nearly as close to me as my own clustered brethren? Well, then my cluster assignment is a bit shaky, isn't it?

A formal way to write this value is:

(Average distance to those in the nearest neighboring cluster – Average distance to those in my cluster)/The maximum of those two averages

The denominator in the calculation keeps the value between -1 and 1.

Think about that formula. As the residents of the next closet cluster get farther and farther away (more ill-suited to me), the value approaches 1. And if the two average distances are nearly the same? Then the value approaches 0.

Taking the average of this calculation for each customer gives you the silhouette. If the silhouette is 1, it's perfect. If it's 0, the clusters are rather ill suited. If it's less than 0, lots of customers are better off hanging out in another cluster, which is the pits.

And for different values of k, you can compare silhouettes to see if you're improving.

To see this concept more clearly, go back to the middle school dance example. Figure 2-26 shows an illustration of the distance calculations used in forming the silhouette. Note that one of the chaperone's distance from the other two chaperones is being compared to the distances from the next nearest cluster, which is the flock of middle school boys.

Now, the other two chaperones are by far closer than the herd of awkward teenagers, so that would make the distance ratio calculation far greater than 0 for this chaperone.

Figure 2-26: The distances considered for a chaperone's contribution to the silhouette calculation

Creating a Distance Matrix

In order to implement the silhouette, there's one major piece of data you need: the distance between customers. And while cluster centers may move around, the distance between two customers never changes. So you can just create a single Distances tab and use it in all of your silhouette calculations no matter what value of k you use or where those centers end up.

Let's start by creating a blank sheet called **Distances** and pasting in customers across the top and down the rows. A cell in the matrix will hold the distance between the customer on the row and the customer on the column. To paste customers down the rows, copy H1:DC1 from the Matrix tab and use Paste Special to paste the values, making sure to choose the Transpose option in the Paste Special window.

You need to keep track of where customers are on the Matrix tab, so number the customers from 0 to 99 in both directions. Let's put these numbers in column A and row 1, so insert blank rows and columns to the left and above the names you've already pasted by right-clicking column A and row 1 and inserting a new row 1 and a new column A.

> **NOTE**
>
> FYI, there are a lot of ways to put those 0–99 counts into Excel. For instance, you can type the first few in, 0, 1, 2, 3, and then highlight them and drag the bottom corner of the selection through the rest of the customers. Excel will understand and extend the count. The resulting empty matrix is pictured in Figure 2-27.

Consider cell C3, which is the distance between Adams and Adams, in other words between Adams and himself. This should be 0, right? You can't get any closer to you than you!

So how do you calculate that? Well, column H on the Matrix tab shows Adams' deal vector. To calculate the Euclidean distance between Adams and himself, it's just column H minus column H, square the differences, sum them up, and take the square root.

But how do you drag that calculation around to every cell in the matrix? I'd hate to type them in manually. That'd take forever. What you need to use is the OFFSET formula in cell C3 (see Chapter 1 for an explanation of OFFSET).

The OFFSET formula takes in an anchoring range of cells; in this case make it Adams' deal vector Matrix!$H$2:$H$33, and moves the entire range a given number of rows and columns in the direction you specify.

So for instance, OFFSET(Matrix!$H$2:$H$33,0,0) is just Adams' deal vector because you're moving the original range 0 rows down and 0 columns to the right.

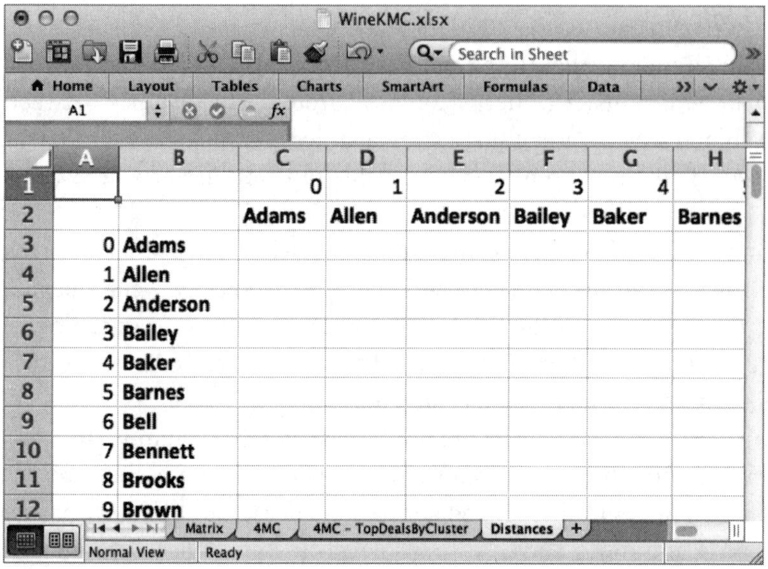

Figure 2-27: The bare bones Distances tab

But `OFFSET(Matrix!$H$2:$H$33,0,1)` is Allen's deal column.

`OFFSET(Matrix!$H$2:$H$33,0,2)` is Anderson, and so on.

And this is where those indices 0 – 99 in row 1 and column A are going to come in handy. For example:

```
{=SQRT(SUM((OFFSET(Matrix!$H$2:$H$33,0,Distances!C$1)-OFFSET(Matrix!$H$2:$
H$33,0,Distances!$A3))^2))}
```

That's the distance between Adams and himself. Note that you're pulling `Distances!C$1` for the column offset in the first deal vector and `Distances!$A3` for the column offset in the second deal vector.

That way, when you drag this calculation across and down in the sheet, everything is anchored to Adams' deal vector, but the `OFFSET` formula shifts the vectors over the appropriate amount using the indices in column A and row 1. This way, it will grab the appropriate two deal vectors for the customers you care about. Figure 2-28 shows the filled out distance matrix.

Also, keep in mind that just like on tab 4MC, these distances are array formulas.

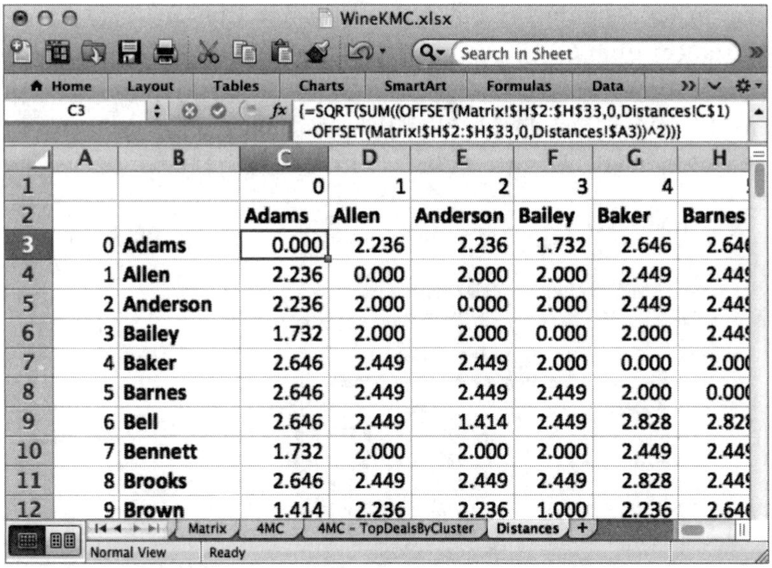

	A	B	C	D	E	F	G	H
1			0	1	2	3	4	
2			Adams	Allen	Anderson	Bailey	Baker	Barnes
3	0	Adams	0.000	2.236	2.236	1.732	2.646	2.64
4	1	Allen	2.236	0.000	2.000	2.000	2.449	2.44
5	2	Anderson	2.236	2.000	0.000	2.000	2.449	2.44
6	3	Bailey	1.732	2.000	2.000	0.000	2.000	2.44
7	4	Baker	2.646	2.449	2.449	2.000	0.000	2.00
8	5	Barnes	2.646	2.449	2.449	2.449	2.000	0.00
9	6	Bell	2.646	2.449	1.414	2.449	2.828	2.82
10	7	Bennett	1.732	2.000	2.000	2.000	2.449	2.44
11	8	Brooks	2.646	2.449	2.449	2.449	2.828	2.44
12	9	Brown	1.414	2.236	2.236	1.000	2.236	2.64

Figure 2-28: The completed distance matrix

Implementing the Silhouette in Excel

All right, now that you have a Distances tab, you can create another tab called **4MC Silhouette** for the final silhouette calculation.

To start, let's copy the customers and their community assignments from the 4MC tab and Paste Special the customer names down column A and the assignments down B (don't forget to check that Transpose box in the Paste Special window).

Next, you can use the Distances tab to calculate the average distance between each customer and those in a particular cluster. So label columns C through F **Distance from People in 1** through **Distance from People in 4**.

In my workbook, Adams has been assigned to Cluster 2, so calculate in cell C2 the distance between him and all the customers in Cluster 1. You need to look up customers and see which ones are in Cluster 1 and then average their distances from Adams on row 3 of the Distances tab.

Sounds like a case for the `AVERAGEIF` formula:

```
=AVERAGEIF('4MC'!$L$39:$DG$39,1,Distances!$C3:$CX3)
```

AVERAGEIF checks the cluster assignments and matches them to Cluster 1 before averaging the appropriate distances from C3:CX3.

For columns D through F, the formulas are the same except Cluster 1 is replaced with 2, 3, and 4 in the formula. You can then double-click these formulas to copy them to all customers, yielding the table shown in Figure 2-29.

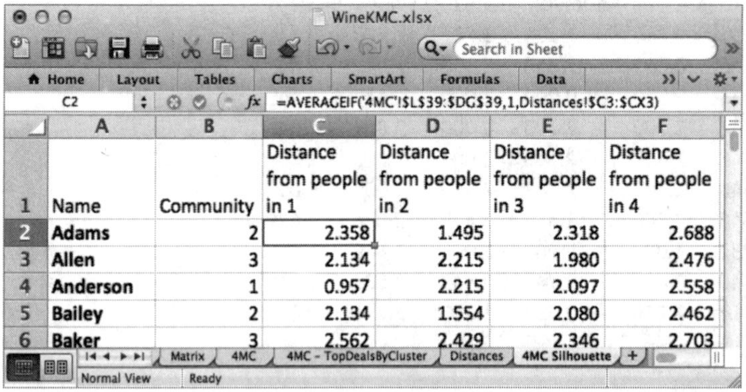

	A	B	C	D	E	F
1	Name	Community	Distance from people in 1	Distance from people in 2	Distance from people in 3	Distance from people in 4
2	Adams	2	2.358	1.495	2.318	2.688
3	Allen	3	2.134	2.215	1.980	2.476
4	Anderson	1	0.957	2.215	2.097	2.558
5	Bailey	2	2.134	1.554	2.080	2.462
6	Baker	3	2.562	2.429	2.346	2.703

C2 : fx =AVERAGEIF('4MC'!$L$39:$DG$39,1,Distances!$C3:$CX3)

Figure 2-29: Average distance between each customer and the customers in every cluster

In column G, you can calculate the closest group of customers using the MIN formula. For instance, for Adams, it's simply:

```
=MIN(C2:F2)
```

And in column H, you can calculate the second closest group of customers using the SMALL formula (the 2 in the formula is for second place):

```
=SMALL(C2:F2,2)
```

Likewise, you can calculate the distance to your own community members (which is probably the same as column G but not always) in column I as:

```
=INDEX(C2:F2,B2)
```

The INDEX formula is used to count over to the appropriate distance column in C through F using the assignment value in B as an index.

And for the silhouette calculation, you also need the distance to the closest group of customers who are *not* in your cluster, which is most likely column H but not always. To get this in column J, you check your own cluster distance in I against the closest cluster in G, and if they match, the value is H. Otherwise, it's G.

```
=IF(I2=G2,H2,G2)
```

Copying all these values down, you'll get the spreadsheet shown in Figure 2-30.

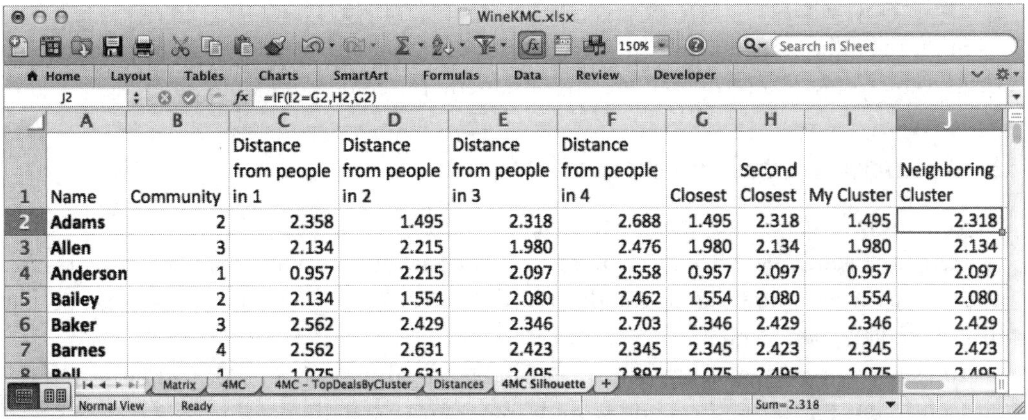

	A	B	C	D	E	F	G	H	I	J
1	Name	Community	Distance from people in 1	Distance from people in 2	Distance from people in 3	Distance from people in 4	Closest	Second Closest	My Cluster	Neighboring Cluster
2	Adams	2	2.358	1.495	2.318	2.688	1.495	2.318	1.495	2.318
3	Allen	3	2.134	2.215	1.980	2.476	1.980	2.134	1.980	2.134
4	Anderson	1	0.957	2.215	2.097	2.558	0.957	2.097	0.957	2.097
5	Bailey	2	2.134	1.554	2.080	2.462	1.554	2.080	1.554	2.080
6	Baker	3	2.562	2.429	2.346	2.703	2.346	2.429	2.346	2.429
7	Barnes	4	2.562	2.631	2.423	2.345	2.345	2.423	2.345	2.423

Figure 2-30: Average distances to the folks in my own cluster and to the closest group whose cluster I'm not in

Once you've placed those values together, adding the silhouette values for a particular customer in column K is simple:

```
=(J2-I2)/MAX(J2,I2)
```

You can just copy that formula down the sheet to get these ratios for each customer.

You'll notice that for some customers, these values are closer to 1. For example, the silhouette value for Anderson in my clustering solution is 0.544 (see Figure 2-31). Not bad! But for other customers, such as Collins, the value is actually less than 0, implying that all things being equal Collins would be better off in his neighboring cluster than in his current one. Poor guy.

Now, you can average these values to get the final silhouette figure. In my case, as shown in Figure 2-31, it's 0.1492, which seems a lot closer to 0 than 1. That's disheartening, but not entirely surprising. After all, two out of four of the clusters were very shaky when you tried to interpret them with the deal descriptions.

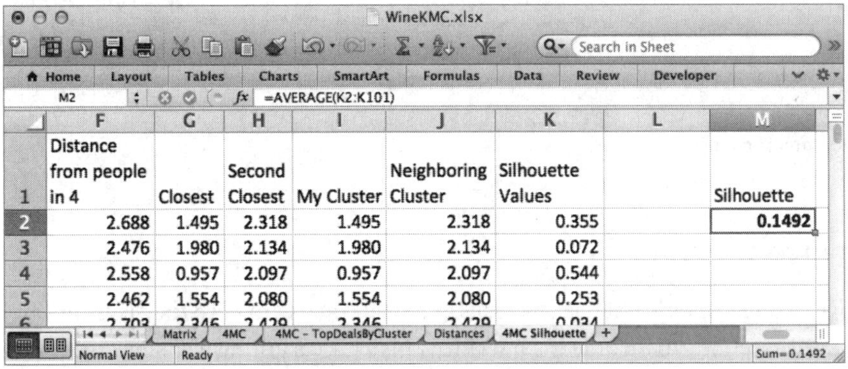

	F	G	H	I	J	K	L	M
1	Distance from people in 4	Closest	Second Closest	My Cluster	Neighboring Cluster	Silhouette Values		Silhouette
2	2.688	1.495	2.318	1.495	2.318	0.355		0.1492
3	2.476	1.980	2.134	1.980	2.134	0.072		
4	2.558	0.957	2.097	0.957	2.097	0.544		
5	2.462	1.554	2.080	1.554	2.080	0.253		

Figure 2-31: The final silhouette for 4-means clustering

Okay. Now what?

Sure, the silhouette is 0.1492. But what does that mean? How do you use it? You try other values of k! Then you can use the silhouette to see if you're doing better.

How about Five Clusters?

Try bumping k up to 5 and see what happens.

Here's the good news: Because you've already done four clusters, you don't have to start the spreadsheets from scratch. You don't have to do anything with the Distances sheet at all. That one's good to go.

You start by creating a copy of the 4MC tab and calling it **5MC**. All you need to do is add a fifth cluster to the sheet and work it into your calculations.

First, let's right-click column L and insert a new column called **Cluster 5**. You also need to insert a Distance to Cluster 5 row by right-clicking row 38 and selecting Insert. You can copy down the Distance to Cluster 4 row into row 38 and change column K to L, to create the Distance to Cluster 5 row. As for the Minimum Cluster Distance and Assigned Cluster rows, references to row 37 should be revised to 38 to include the new cluster distance.

You'll end up with the sheet pictured in Figure 2-32.

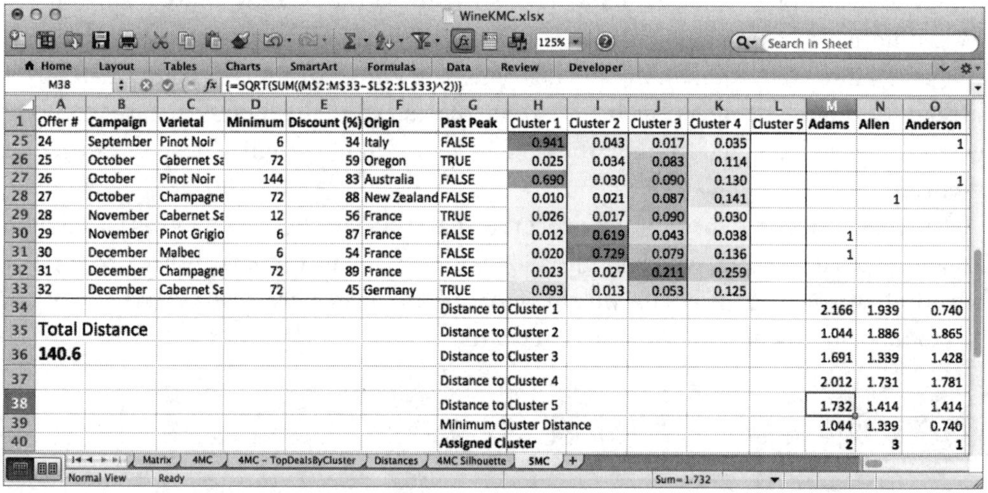

Figure 2-32: The 5-means clustering tab

Solving for Five Clusters

Opening up Solver, you need only change $H$2:$K$33 to $H$2:$L$33 in both the decision variables and constraints sections to include the new fifth cluster. Everything else stays the same.

Press Solve and let this new problem run.

In my run, the Solver terminated with a total distance of 135.1, as shown in Figure 2-33.

	A	B	C	D	E	F	G	H	I	J	K	L
1	Offer #	Campaign	Varietal	Minimum Qty	Discount (%)	Origin	Past Peak	Cluster 1	Cluster 2	Cluster 3	Cluster 4	Cluster 5
2	1	January	Malbec	72	56	France	FALSE	0.006	0.007	0.001	0.216	0.102
3	2	January	Pinot Noir	72	17	France	FALSE	0.266	0.003	0.000	0.080	0.101
4	3	February	Espumante	144	32	Oregon	TRUE	0.007	0.010	0.013	0.191	0.024
5	4	February	Champagne	72	48	France	TRUE	0.011	0.004	0.012	0.159	0.159
6	5	February	Cabernet Sau	144	44	New Zeal:	TRUE	0.011	0.010	0.000	0.033	0.081
7	6	March	Prosecco	144	86	Chile	FALSE	0.008	0.010	0.013	0.255	0.102
8	7	March	Prosecco	6	40	Australia	TRUE	0.011	0.607	0.000	0.113	0.113
9	8	March	Espumante	6	45	South Afr	FALSE	0.011	0.320	1.000	0.127	0.001
10	9	April	Chardonnay	144	57	Chile	FALSE	0.009	0.010	0.000	0.080	0.209
11	10	April	Prosecco	72	52	California	FALSE	0.011	0.005	0.012	0.084	0.085
12	11	May	Champagne	72	85	France	FALSE	0.006	0.009	0.000	0.263	0.166
13	12	May	Prosecco	72	83	Australia	FALSE	0.011	-0.003	0.002	0.110	0.071
14	13	May	Merlot	6	43	Chile	FALSE	0.011	0.205	0.016	0.010	0.005
15	14	June	Merlot	72	64	Chile	FALSE	0.007	0.011	0.000	0.156	0.123
16	15	June	Cabernet Sau	144	19	Italy	FALSE	0.011	0.002	0.005	0.149	0.048
17	16	June	Merlot	72	88	California	FALSE	0.011	0.008	0.001	0.012	0.105
18	17	July	Pinot Noir	12	47	Germany	FALSE	0.611	0.001	0.008	0.004	0.009
19	18	July	Espumante	6	50	Oregon	FALSE	0.010	0.475	0.028	0.057	0.027
20	19	July	Champagne	12	66	Germany	FALSE	0.008	0.008	0.000	0.116	0.052
21	20	August	Cabernet Sau	72	82	Italy	FALSE	0.011	0.008	0.003	0.033	0.100
22	21	August	Champagne	12	50	California	FALSE	0.011	0.010	0.005	0.085	0.048
23	22	August	Champagne	72	63	France	FALSE	0.007	0.009	0.004	1.000	0.004
24	23	September	Chardonnay	144	39	South Afr	FALSE	0.011	0.007	0.008	0.077	0.072
25	24	September	Pinot Noir	6	34	Italy	FALSE	1.000	0.011	0.004	0.005	0.009
26	25	October	Cabernet Sau	72	59	Oregon	TRUE	0.011	0.010	0.008	0.099	0.082
27	26	October	Pinot Noir	144	83	Australia	FALSE	0.719	0.008	0.000	0.033	0.147
28	27	October	Champagne	72	88	New Zeal:	FALSE	0.010	0.011	0.021	0.152	0.112
29	28	November	Cabernet Sau	12	56	France	TRUE	0.010	0.011	0.000	0.068	0.100
30	29	November	Pinot Grigio	6	87	France	FALSE	0.005	0.679	0.044	0.008	0.048
31	30	December	Malbec	6	54	France	FALSE	0.006	0.769	0.021	0.182	0.051
32	31	December	Champagne	72	89	France	FALSE	0.008	0.006	0.013	0.310	0.239
33	32	December	Cabernet Sau	72	45	Germany	TRUE	0.000	0.003	0.004	0.039	0.065
34							Distance to Cluster 1					
35	Total Distance						Distance to Cluster 2					
36	135.1						Distance to Cluster 3					

Figure 2-33: The optimal 5-means clusters

Getting the Top Deals for All Five Clusters

All right. Let's see how you did.

You can create a copy of the 4MC – TopDealsByCluster tab and rename it 5MC – TopDealsByCluster, but you'll need to revise a few of the formulas to get it to work.

First of all, you need to make sure that this worksheet is ordered by Offer # in column A. Then label column L with a 5 and drag the formulas from K over to L. You should also highlight columns A through L and reapply the auto-filtering to make Cluster 5's deal purchases sortable.

Everything on this sheet is currently pointing to tab 4MC, so it's time to break out the ol' Find and Replace. The cluster assignments on tab 5MC are shifted one row down and one column to the right, so the reference to '4MC'!$L$39:$DG$39 in the SUMIF formulas should become '5MC'!$M$40:$DH$40. As shown in Figure 2-34, you can use Find and Replace to change this.

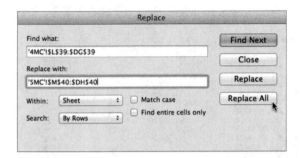

Figure 2-34 Replacing 4-means cluster assignments with 5-means cluster assignments

---

NOTE

Keep in mind that your results will differ from mine due to the evolutionary solver.

Sorting on Cluster 1, you clearly have your Pinot Noir cluster again (see Figure 2-35).

	A	B	C	D	E	F	G	H
	Offer #	Offer date	Product	Minimum	Discount	Origin	Past Peak	1
1								
2	24	September	Pinot Noir	6	34	Italy	FALSE	12
3	26	October	Pinot Noir	144	83	Australia	FALSE	8
4	17	July	Pinot Noir	12	47	Germany	FALSE	7
5	2	January	Pinot Noir	72	17	France	FALSE	4
6	1	January	Malbec	72	56	France	FALSE	0
7	3	February	Espumante	144	32	Oregon	TRUE	0
8	4	February	Champagne	72	48	France	TRUE	0
9	5	February	Cabernet Sau	144	44	New Zealand	TRUE	0
10	6	March	Prosecco	144	86	Chile	FALSE	0
11	7	March	Prosecco	6	40	Australia	TRUE	0

Formula bar: `=SUMIF('5MC'!$M$40:$DH$40,'5MC – TopDealsByCluster'!H$1,'5MC'!$M25:$DH25)`

Figure 2-35: Sorting on Cluster 1—Pinot Noir out the ears

Cluster 2 is the low-volume buyer cluster (see Figure 2-36).

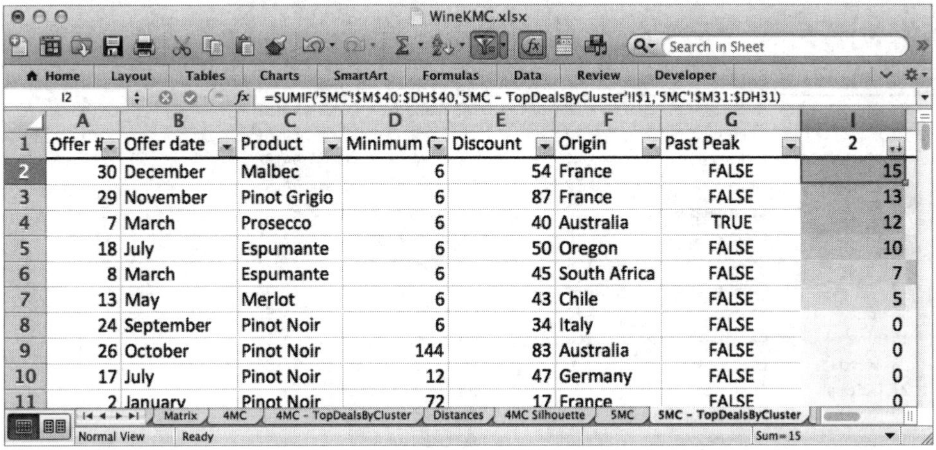

Figure 2-36: Sorting on Cluster 2—small quantities only, please

As for Cluster 3, this one hurts my head. It seems only to be a South African Espumante that's important for some reason (Figure 2-37).

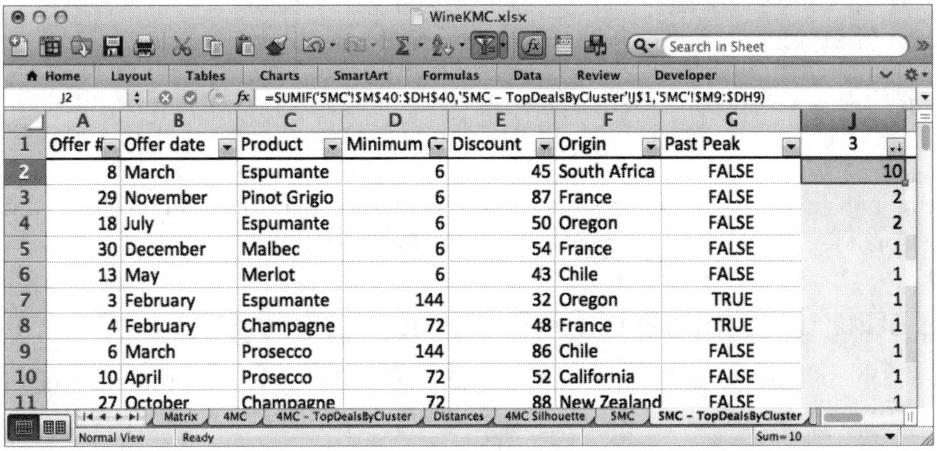

Figure 2-37: Sorting on Cluster 3—is Espumante that important?

The Cluster 4 customers are interested in high volume, primarily French deals with good discounts. There may even be a propensity toward sparkling wines. This cluster is tough to read; there's a lot going on (see Figure 2-38).

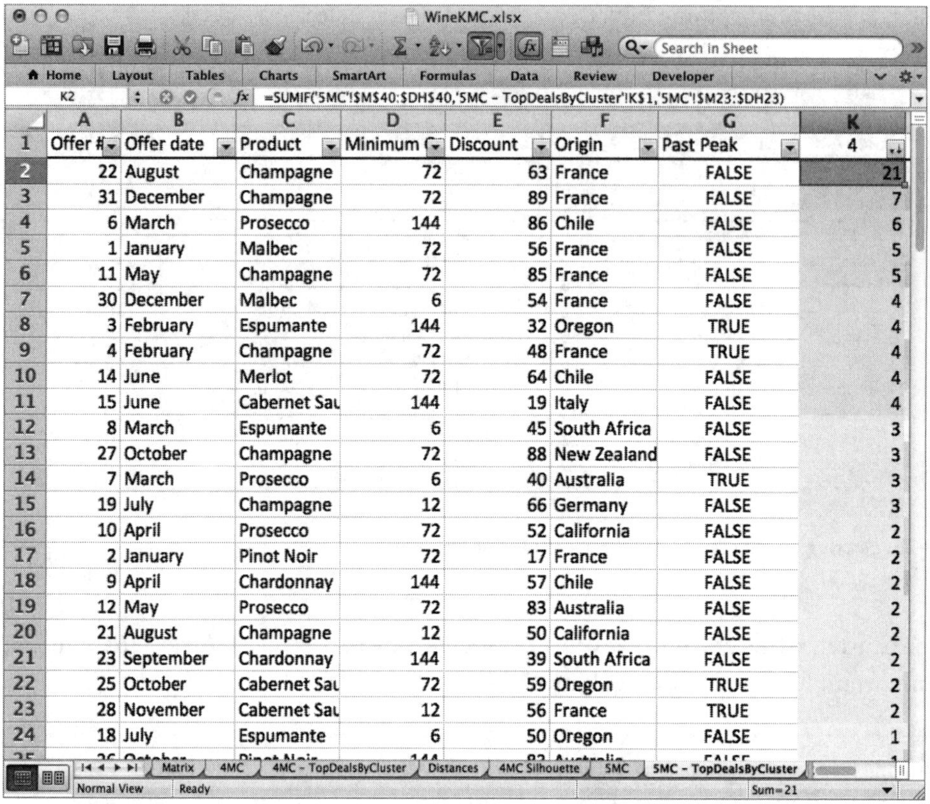

	A	B	C	D	E	F	G	K
1	Offer #	Offer date	Product	Minimum Q	Discount	Origin	Past Peak	4
2	22	August	Champagne	72	63	France	FALSE	21
3	31	December	Champagne	72	89	France	FALSE	7
4	6	March	Prosecco	144	86	Chile	FALSE	6
5	1	January	Malbec	72	56	France	FALSE	5
6	11	May	Champagne	72	85	France	FALSE	5
7	30	December	Malbec	6	54	France	FALSE	4
8	3	February	Espumante	144	32	Oregon	TRUE	4
9	4	February	Champagne	72	48	France	TRUE	4
10	14	June	Merlot	72	64	Chile	FALSE	4
11	15	June	Cabernet Sau	144	19	Italy	FALSE	4
12	8	March	Espumante	6	45	South Africa	FALSE	3
13	27	October	Champagne	72	88	New Zealand	FALSE	3
14	7	March	Prosecco	6	40	Australia	TRUE	3
15	19	July	Champagne	12	66	Germany	FALSE	3
16	10	April	Prosecco	72	52	California	FALSE	2
17	2	January	Pinot Noir	72	17	France	FALSE	2
18	9	April	Chardonnay	144	57	Chile	FALSE	2
19	12	May	Prosecco	72	83	Australia	FALSE	2
20	21	August	Champagne	12	50	California	FALSE	2
21	23	September	Chardonnay	144	39	South Africa	FALSE	2
22	25	October	Cabernet Sau	72	59	Oregon	TRUE	2
23	28	November	Cabernet Sau	12	56	France	TRUE	2
24	18	July	Espumante	6	50	Oregon	FALSE	1

Figure 2-38: Sorting on Cluster 4—all sorts of interests

Sorting on Cluster 5 gives you results similar to Cluster 4, although high volume and high discounts seem to be the primary drivers (see Figure 2-39).

Computing the Silhouette for 5-Means Clustering

You may be wondering whether five clusters did any better than four. From an eyeball perspective, there doesn't seem to be a whole lot of difference. Let's compute the silhouette for five clusters and see what the computer thinks.

Start by making a copy of 4MC Silhouette and renaming it **5MC Silhouette**. Next, right-click column G, insert a new column, and name it **Distance From People in 5**. Drag the formula from F2 over into G2, change the cluster check from 4 to 5, and then double-click the cell to shoot it down the sheet.

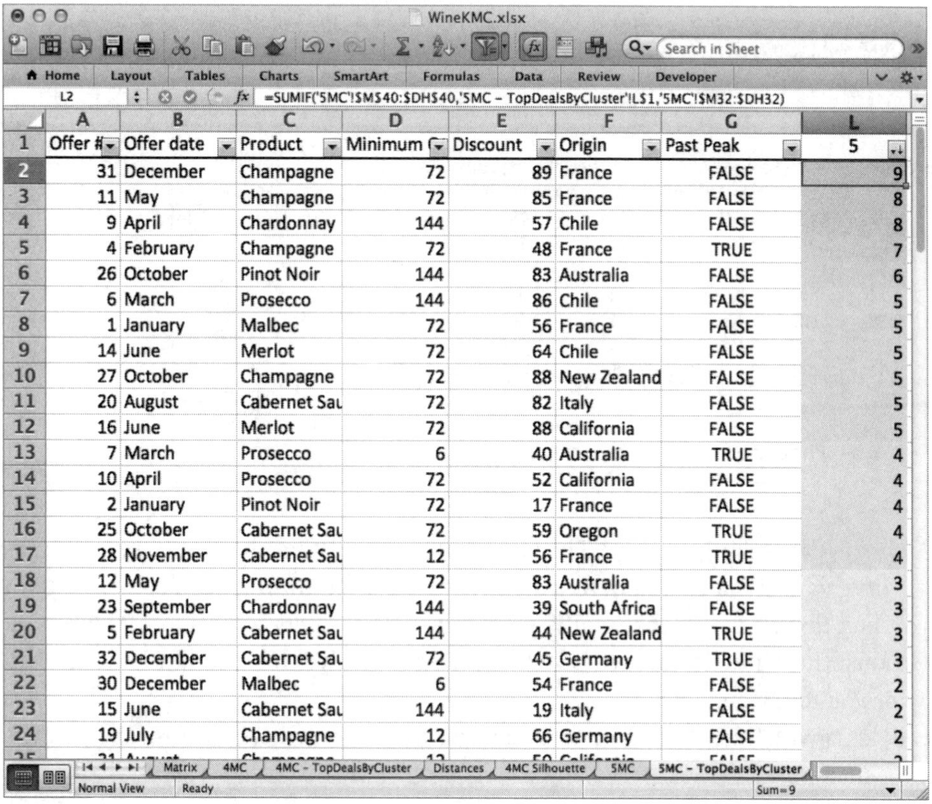

	A	B	C	D	E	F	G	L
1	Offer #	Offer date	Product	Minimum (	Discount	Origin	Past Peak	5
2	31	December	Champagne	72	89	France	FALSE	9
3	11	May	Champagne	72	85	France	FALSE	8
4	9	April	Chardonnay	144	57	Chile	FALSE	8
5	4	February	Champagne	72	48	France	TRUE	7
6	26	October	Pinot Noir	144	83	Australia	FALSE	6
7	6	March	Prosecco	144	86	Chile	FALSE	5
8	1	January	Malbec	72	56	France	FALSE	5
9	14	June	Merlot	72	64	Chile	FALSE	5
10	27	October	Champagne	72	88	New Zealand	FALSE	5
11	20	August	Cabernet Sau	72	82	Italy	FALSE	5
12	16	June	Merlot	72	88	California	FALSE	5
13	7	March	Prosecco	6	40	Australia	TRUE	4
14	10	April	Prosecco	72	52	California	FALSE	4
15	2	January	Pinot Noir	72	17	France	FALSE	4
16	25	October	Cabernet Sau	72	59	Oregon	TRUE	4
17	28	November	Cabernet Sau	12	56	France	TRUE	4
18	12	May	Prosecco	72	83	Australia	FALSE	3
19	23	September	Chardonnay	144	39	South Africa	FALSE	3
20	5	February	Cabernet Sau	144	44	New Zealand	TRUE	3
21	32	December	Cabernet Sau	72	45	Germany	TRUE	3
22	30	December	Malbec	6	54	France	FALSE	2
23	15	June	Cabernet Sau	144	19	Italy	FALSE	2
24	19	July	Champagne	12	66	Germany	FALSE	2

Figure 2-39: Sorting on Cluster 5—high volume

Identical to the previous section, you'll need to Find and Replace `'4MC'!$L$39:$DG$39` with `'5MC'!$M$40:$DH$40`.

In cells H2, I2, and J2, you should include distances to folks in Cluster 5 in your calculations, so any ranges that stop at F2 should be expanded to include G2. You can then highlight H2:J2 and double-click the bottom right to send these updated calculations down the sheet.

Lastly, you need to copy and Paste Special values from the cluster assignments on row 40 of the 5MC tab into column B on the 5MC Silhouette tab. This means you have to check the Transpose button when using Paste Special.

Once you've revised the sheet, you should get something like what's pictured in Figure 2-40.

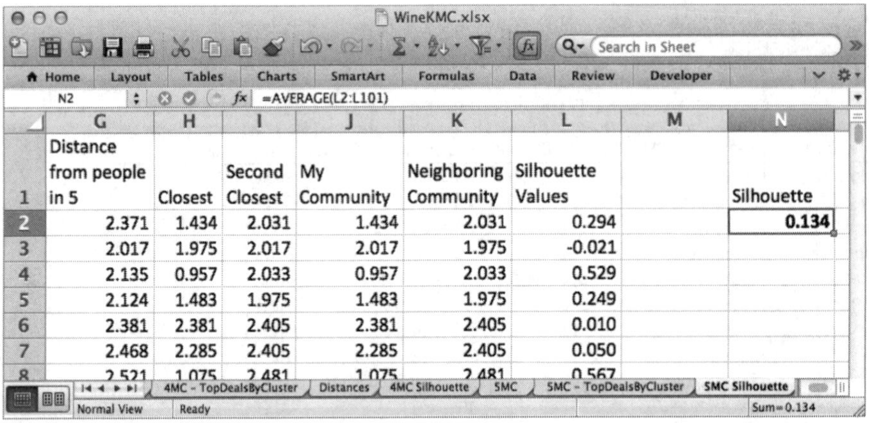

	G: Distance from people in 5	H: Closest	I: Second Closest	J: My Community	K: Neighboring Community	L: Silhouette Values	M	N: Silhouette
2	2.371	1.434	2.031	1.434	2.031	0.294		0.134
3	2.017	1.975	2.017	2.017	1.975	-0.021		
4	2.135	0.957	2.033	0.957	2.033	0.529		
5	2.124	1.483	1.975	1.483	1.975	0.249		
6	2.381	2.381	2.405	2.381	2.405	0.010		
7	2.468	2.285	2.405	2.285	2.405	0.050		
8	2.521	1.075	2.481	1.075	2.481	0.567		

Figure 2-40: The silhouette for 5-means clustering

Well, this is depressing, isn't it? The silhouette isn't all that different. At 0.134, it's actually a little worse! But that's not much of a surprise after mining the clusters. In both cases, you had three clusters that really made sense. The others were noisy. Maybe you should go the other direction and try k=3? If you want to give this a shot, I leave it as an exercise for you to try on your own.

Instead, let's give a little thought to what may be going wrong here to cause these noisy, perplexing clusters.

K-Medians Clustering and Asymmetric Distance Measurements

Usually doing vanilla k-means clustering with Euclidean distance is just fine, but you've run into some problems here that many who do clustering on sparse data (whether that's in retail or text classification or bioinformatics) often encounter.

Using K-Medians Clustering

The first obvious problem is that your cluster centers are decimals even though each customer's deal vector is made of solid 0s and 1s. What does 0.113 of a deal really mean? I want cluster centers that commit to a deal or don't!

If you modify the clustering algorithm to use only values present in the customers' deal vectors, this is called *K-medians* clustering, rather than K-means clustering.

And if you wanted to stick with Euclidean distance, all you'd need to do is add a binary constraint, (bin) in Solver to all of your cluster centers.

But if you make your cluster centers binary, is Euclidean distance what you want?

Getting a More Appropriate Distance Metric

When folks switch from k-means to k-medians, they typically stop using Euclidean distance and start using something called *Manhattan distance*.

Although a crow can fly from point A to B in a straight line, a cab in Manhattan has to stay on the grid of straight streets; it can only go north, south, east, and west. So while in Figure 2-13, you saw that the distance between a middle school dancer and their cluster center was approximately 4.47, their Manhattan distance was 6 feet (that's 4 feet down plus 2 feet across).

In terms of binary data, like the purchase data, the Manhattan distance between a cluster center and a customer's purchase vector is just the count of the mismatches. If the cluster center has a 0 and I have a 0, in that direction there's a distance of 0, and if you have mismatched 0 and 1, you have a distance of 1 in that direction. Summing them up, you get the total distance, which is just the number of mismatches. When working with binary data like this, Manhattan distance is also commonly called *Hamming distance*.

Does Manhattan Distance Solve the Issues?

Before you dive headfirst into doing k-medians clustering using Manhattan distance, stop and think about the purchase data.

What does it mean when customers take a deal? It means they really wanted that product!

What does it mean when customers don't take a deal? Does it mean that they didn't want the product as much as they did want the one they bought? Is a negative signal as strong as a positive one? Perhaps they like Champagne but already have a lot in stock. Maybe they just didn't see your e-mail newsletter that month. There are a lot of reasons why someone doesn't take an action, but there are few reasons why someone does.

In other words, you should care about purchases, not non-purchases.

The fancy way to say this is that there's an "asymmetry" in the data. The 1s are worth more than the 0s. If a customer matches another customer on three 1s, that's more important than matching some other customer on three 0s. What stinks though is that while the 1s are so important, there are very few of them in the data—hence, the term "sparse."

But think about what it means for a customer to be close to a cluster center from a Euclidean perspective. If I have a customer with a 1 for one deal and a 0 for another, both of those are just as important in calculating whether a customer is near a cluster center.

What you need is an *asymmetric distance calculation*. And for binary encoded transactional data, like these wine purchases, there are a bunch of good ones.

Perhaps the most widely used asymmetric distance calculation for 0-1 data is something called *cosine distance*.

Cosine Distance Isn't Scary Despite the Trigonometry

The easiest way to explain cosine distance is to explain its opposite: *cosine similarity.*

Say you had a couple of two-dimensional binary purchase vectors (1,1) and (1,0). In the first vector, both products were purchased, whereas in the second, only the first product was purchased. You can visualize these two purchase vectors in space and see that they have a 45-degree angle between them (see Figure 2-41). Go on, break out the protractor and check it.

You can say that they have a cosine similarity then of cos(45 degrees) = 0.707. But why? It turns out the cosine of an angle between two binary purchase vectors is equal to:

The count of matched purchases in the two vectors divided by the product of the square root of the number of purchases in the first vector times the square root of the number of purchases in the second vector.

In the case of the two vectors (1,1) and (1,0), they have one matched purchase, so the calculation is 1 divided by the square root of 2 (two deals taken), times the square root of one deal taken. And that's 0.707 (see Figure 2-41).

Why is this calculation so cool?

Three reasons:

- The numerator in the calculation counts numbers of matched purchases only, so this is an asymmetric measure, which is what you're looking for.
- By dividing through by the square root of the number of purchases in each vector, you're accounting for the fact that a vector where *everything is purchased*, call it a promiscuous purchase vector, is farther away from another vector than one who matches on the same deals and has not taken as many other deals. You want to match up vectors whose taste matches, not where one vector encompasses the taste of another.
- For binary data, this similarity value ranges between 0 and 1, where two vectors don't get a 1 unless their purchases are identical. This means that *1 – cosine similarity*

can be used as a distance metric called cosine distance, which also ranges between 0 and 1.

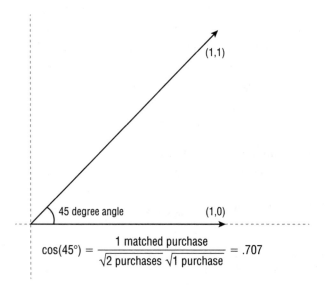

Figure 2-41: An illustration of cosine similarity on two binary purchase vectors

Putting It All in Excel

It's time to give k-medians clustering with cosine distance in Excel a shot.

> **NOTE**
>
> Clustering with cosine distance is also sometimes called *spherical k-means*. In Chapter 10, you'll look at spherical k-means in R.

For consistency's sake, continue using k = 5.

Start by making a copy of the 5MC tab and naming it **5MedC**. Since the cluster centers need to be binary, you might as well delete what Solver left in there.

The only items you need to change (other than adding the binary constraint in Solver for k-medians) are the distance calculations on rows 34 through 38. Start in cell M34, which is the distance between Adams and the center of Cluster 1.

To count the deal matches between Adams and Cluster 1, you need to take a SUMPRODUCT of the two columns. If either or both have 0s, they get nothing for that row, but if both have a 1, that match will get totaled by the SUMPRODUCT (since 1 times 1 is 1 after all).

As for taking the square root of the number of deals taken in a vector, that's just a SQRT laid on a SUM of the vector. Thus, the overall distance equation can be written as:

```
=1-SUMPRODUCT(M$2:M$33,$H$2:$H$33)/
    (SQRT(SUM(M$2:M$33))*SQRT(SUM($H$2:$H$33)))
```

Note the 1- at the beginning of the formula, which changes from cosine similarity to distance. Also, unlike with Euclidean distance, the cosine distance calculation does not require the use of array formulas.

However, when you stick this into cell M34, you should add an error check in case the cluster center is all 0s:

```
=IFERROR(1-SUMPRODUCT(M$2:M$33,$H$2:$H$33)/
    (SQRT(SUM(M$2:M$33))*SQRT(SUM($H$2:$H$33))),1)
```

Adding the IFERROR formula prevents you from having a division by 0 situation. If for some reason Solver picks an all-0s cluster center, then you can consider that center to have a distance of 1 from everything instead (1 being the largest possible distance in this binary setup).

You can then copy M34 down through M38 and change the references from column H to I, J, K, and L respectively. Just like in the Euclidean distance case, you use absolute references ($) in the formula so that you can drag it across without the cluster center columns changing.

This gives you a 5MedC sheet (see Figure 2-42) that's remarkably similar to the earlier 5MC tab.

Now, to find the clusters, you need to open Solver and change the <= 1 constraint for H2:L33 to instead read as a binary or bin constraint.

Press Solve. You can take a load off for a half hour while the computer finds the optimal clusters. Now, you'll notice visually that the cluster centers are all binary, so likewise the conditional formatting goes to two shades, which is much more stark.

The Top Deals for the 5-Medians Clusters

When Solver completes, you end up with five cluster centers, each which have a smattering of 1s, indicating which deals are preferred by that cluster. In my Solver run, I ended up with an optimal objective value of 42.8, although yours may certainly vary (see Figure 2-43).

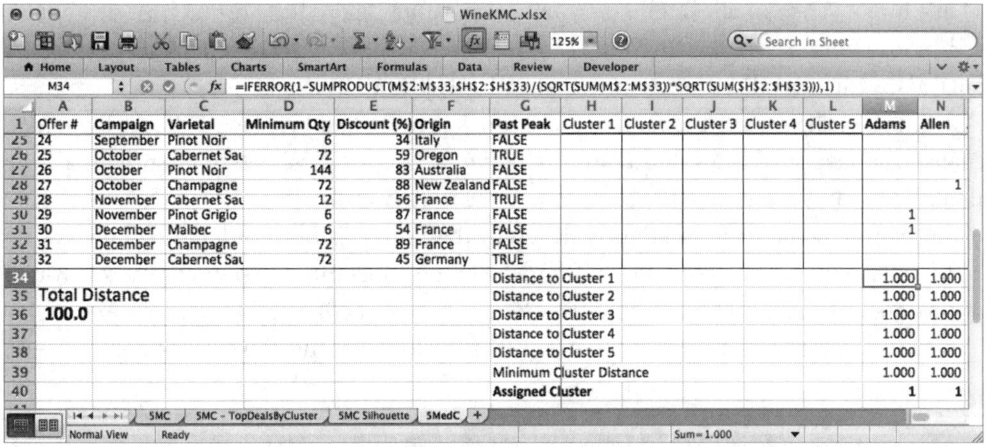

Figure 2-42: The 5MedC tab not yet optimized

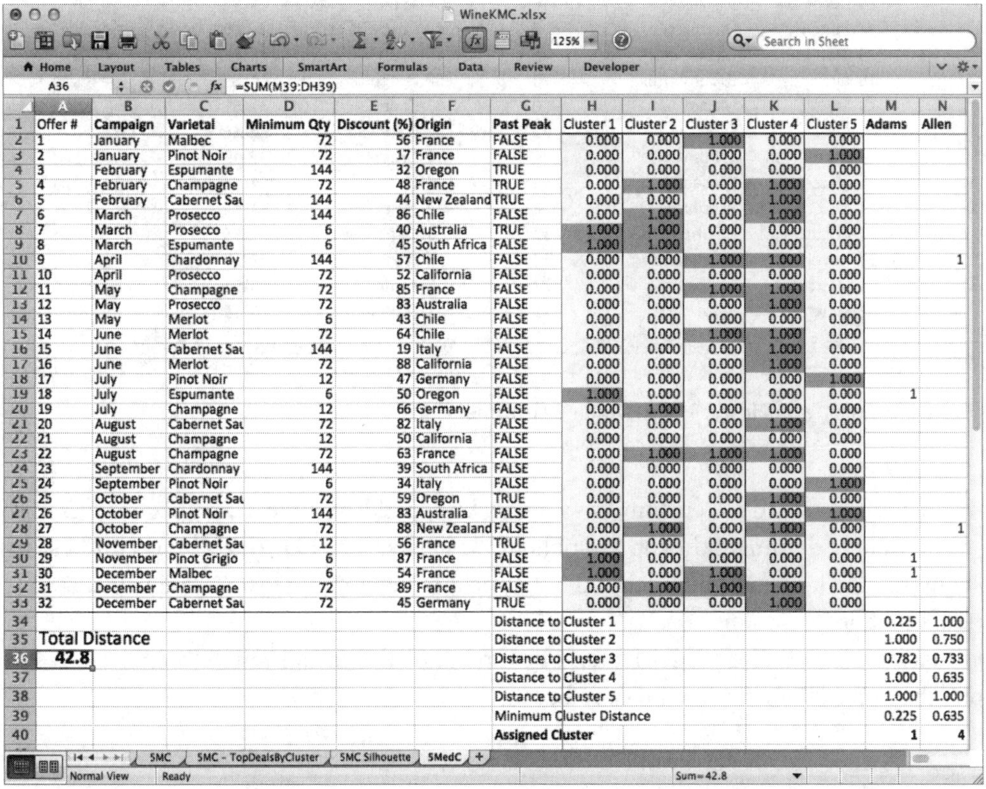

Figure 2-43: The five-cluster medians

Let's make sense of these clusters using the same deal counting techniques you've used in k-means. To do so, the first thing you need to do is make a copy of the 5MC – TopDealsByCluster tab and rename it **5MedC – TopDealsByCluster**.

On this tab, all you need to do to make it work is to find and replace 5MC with **5MedC**. Because the layout of rows and columns between these two sheets is identical, all the calculations carry over once the sheet reference is changed.

Now, your clusters may be slightly different than mine in both order and composition due to the evolutionary algorithm, but hopefully not substantively so. Let's walk through my clusters one at a time to see how the algorithm has partitioned the customers.

Sorting on Cluster 1, it's apparent that this is the low-volume cluster (see Figure 2-44).

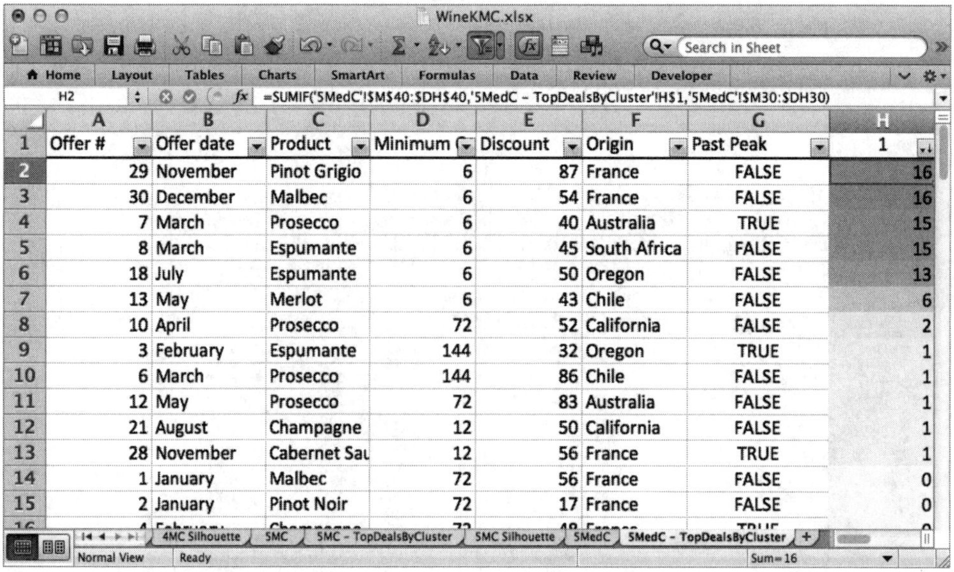

Offer #	Offer date	Product	Minimum	Discount	Origin	Past Peak	1
29	November	Pinot Grigio	6	87	France	FALSE	16
30	December	Malbec	6	54	France	FALSE	16
7	March	Prosecco	6	40	Australia	TRUE	15
8	March	Espumante	6	45	South Africa	FALSE	15
18	July	Espumante	6	50	Oregon	FALSE	13
13	May	Merlot	6	43	Chile	FALSE	6
10	April	Prosecco	72	52	California	FALSE	2
3	February	Espumante	144	32	Oregon	TRUE	1
6	March	Prosecco	144	86	Chile	FALSE	1
12	May	Prosecco	72	83	Australia	FALSE	1
21	August	Champagne	12	50	California	FALSE	1
28	November	Cabernet Sau	12	56	France	TRUE	1
1	January	Malbec	72	56	France	FALSE	0
2	January	Pinot Noir	72	17	France	FALSE	0

Figure 2-44: Sorting on Cluster 1—low-volume customers

Cluster 2 has carved out customers who only buy sparkling wine. Champagne, Prosecco, and Espumante dominate the top 11 spots in the cluster (see Figure 2-45). It's interesting to note that the k-means approach did not so clearly demonstrate the bubbly cluster with k equal to 4 or 5.

Cluster 3 is our Francophile cluster. The top five deals are all French (see Figure 2-46). Don't they know California wines are better?

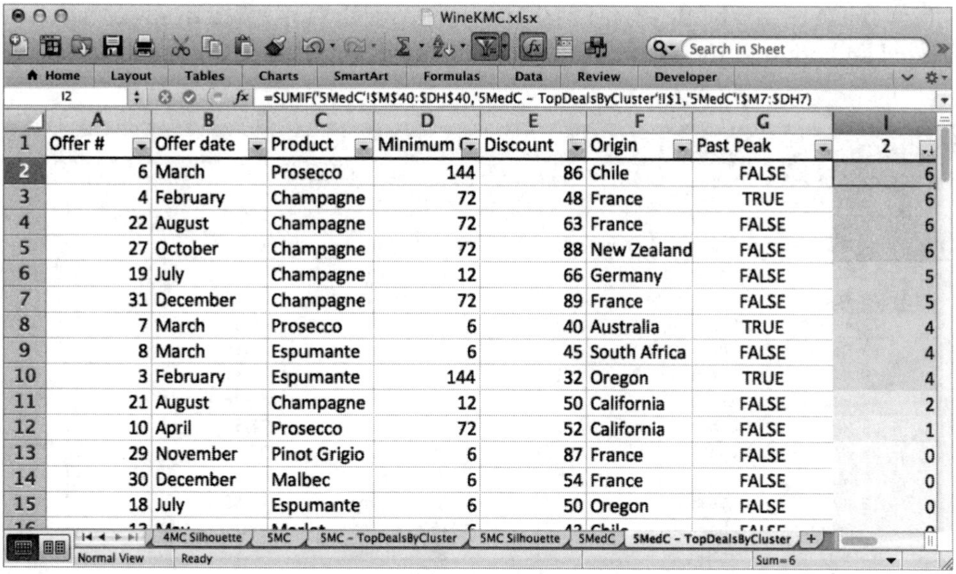

WineKMC.xlsx

I2 =SUMIF('5MedC'!$M$40:$DH$40,'5MedC - TopDealsByCluster'!I$1,'5MedC'!$M7:$DH7)

	Offer #	Offer date	Product	Minimum Q	Discount	Origin	Past Peak	2
2	6	March	Prosecco	144	86	Chile	FALSE	6
3	4	February	Champagne	72	48	France	TRUE	6
4	22	August	Champagne	72	63	France	FALSE	6
5	27	October	Champagne	72	88	New Zealand	FALSE	6
6	19	July	Champagne	12	66	Germany	FALSE	5
7	31	December	Champagne	72	89	France	FALSE	5
8	7	March	Prosecco	6	40	Australia	TRUE	4
9	8	March	Espumante	6	45	South Africa	FALSE	4
10	3	February	Espumante	144	32	Oregon	TRUE	4
11	21	August	Champagne	12	50	California	FALSE	2
12	10	April	Prosecco	72	52	California	FALSE	1
13	29	November	Pinot Grigio	6	87	France	FALSE	0
14	30	December	Malbec	6	54	France	FALSE	0
15	18	July	Espumante	6	50	Oregon	FALSE	0

Figure 2-45: Sorting on Cluster 2—not all who sparkle are vampires

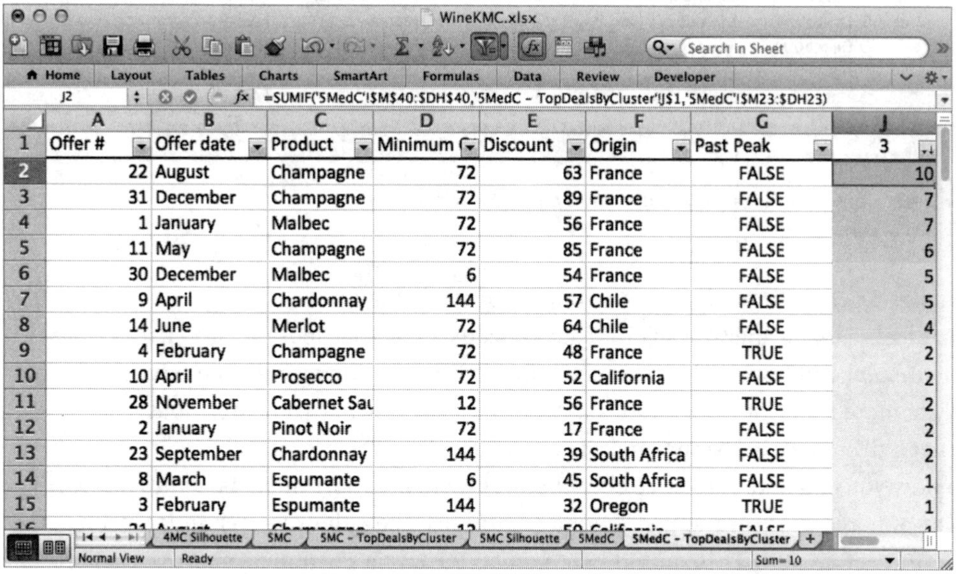

WineKMC.xlsx

J2 =SUMIF('5MedC'!$M$40:$DH$40,'5MedC - TopDealsByCluster'!J$1,'5MedC'!$M23:$DH23)

	Offer #	Offer date	Product	Minimum Q	Discount	Origin	Past Peak	3
2	22	August	Champagne	72	63	France	FALSE	10
3	31	December	Champagne	72	89	France	FALSE	7
4	1	January	Malbec	72	56	France	FALSE	7
5	11	May	Champagne	72	85	France	FALSE	6
6	30	December	Malbec	6	54	France	FALSE	5
7	9	April	Chardonnay	144	57	Chile	FALSE	5
8	14	June	Merlot	72	64	Chile	FALSE	4
9	4	February	Champagne	72	48	France	TRUE	2
10	10	April	Prosecco	72	52	California	FALSE	2
11	28	November	Cabernet Sau	12	56	France	TRUE	2
12	2	January	Pinot Noir	72	17	France	FALSE	2
13	23	September	Chardonnay	144	39	South Africa	FALSE	2
14	8	March	Espumante	6	45	South Africa	FALSE	1
15	3	February	Espumante	144	32	Oregon	TRUE	1

Figure 2-46: Sorting on cluster—Francophiles

As for Cluster 4, all the deals are high volume. And the top rated deals are all well discounted and not past their peak (Figure 2-47).

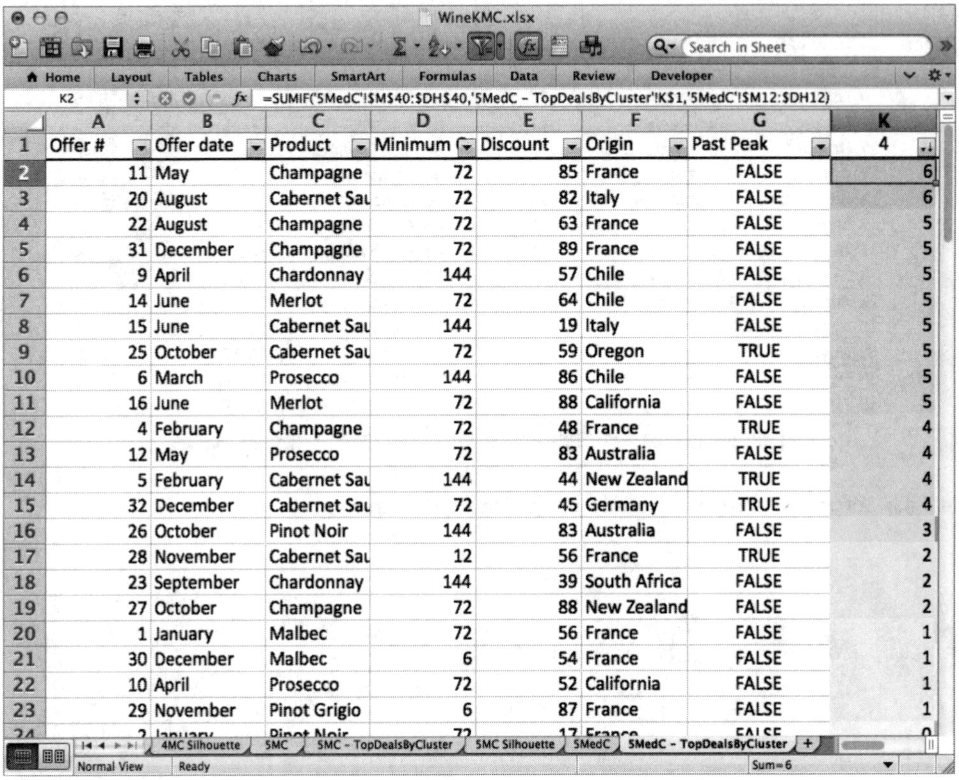

	A	B	C	D	E	F	G	K
1	Offer #	Offer date	Product	Minimum	Discount	Origin	Past Peak	4
2	11	May	Champagne	72	85	France	FALSE	6
3	20	August	Cabernet Sau	72	82	Italy	FALSE	6
4	22	August	Champagne	72	63	France	FALSE	5
5	31	December	Champagne	72	89	France	FALSE	5
6	9	April	Chardonnay	144	57	Chile	FALSE	5
7	14	June	Merlot	72	64	Chile	FALSE	5
8	15	June	Cabernet Sau	144	19	Italy	FALSE	5
9	25	October	Cabernet Sau	72	59	Oregon	TRUE	5
10	6	March	Prosecco	144	86	Chile	FALSE	5
11	16	June	Merlot	72	88	California	FALSE	5
12	4	February	Champagne	72	48	France	TRUE	4
13	12	May	Prosecco	72	83	Australia	FALSE	4
14	5	February	Cabernet Sau	144	44	New Zealand	TRUE	4
15	32	December	Cabernet Sau	72	45	Germany	TRUE	4
16	26	October	Pinot Noir	144	83	Australia	FALSE	3
17	28	November	Cabernet Sau	12	56	France	TRUE	2
18	23	September	Chardonnay	144	39	South Africa	FALSE	2
19	27	October	Champagne	72	88	New Zealand	FALSE	2
20	1	January	Malbec	72	56	France	FALSE	1
21	30	December	Malbec	6	54	France	FALSE	1
22	10	April	Prosecco	72	52	California	FALSE	1
23	29	November	Pinot Grigio	6	87	France	FALSE	1
24	2	January	Pinot Noir	72	17	France	FALSE	0

K2 : =SUMIF('5MedC'!$M$40:$DH$40,'5MedC - TopDealsByCluster'!K$1,'5MedC'!$M12:$DH12)

Figure 2-47: Sorting on Cluster 4—high volume for 19 deals in a row

Cluster 5 is the Pinot Noir cluster once again (see Figure 2-48).

That feels a lot cleaner doesn't it? That's because in the k-medians case, using an asymmetric distance measure like cosine distance, you can cluster customers based on their interests more than their disinterests. And that's really what you care about.

What a difference a distance measure makes!

So now you can take these five cluster assignments, import them back into MailChimp .com as a merge field on the list of e-mails, and use the values to customize your e-mail marketing per cluster. This should help you better target customers and drive sales.

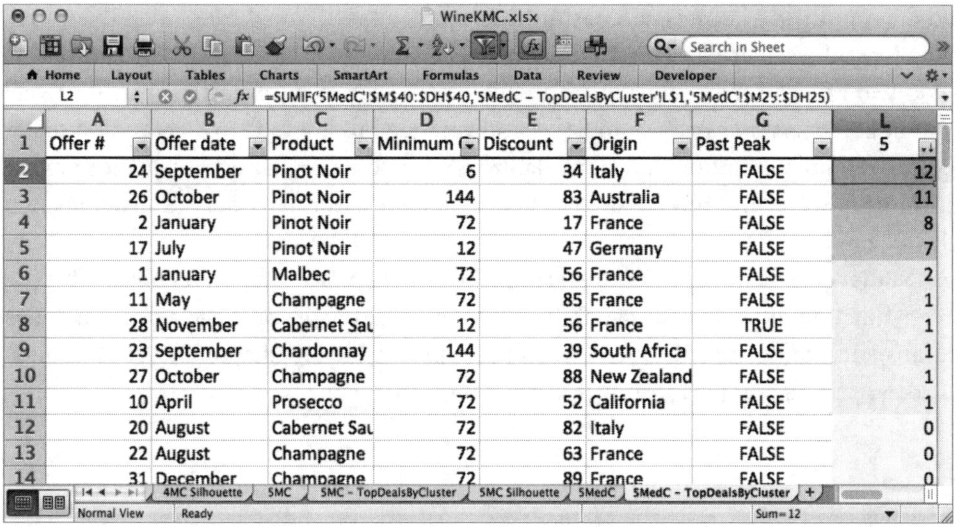

Figure 2-48: Sorting on cluster 5—mainlining Pinot Noir

Wrapping Up

This chapter covered all sorts of good stuff. To summarize, you looked at:

- Euclidean distance
- k-means clustering using Solver to optimize the centers
- How to understand the clusters once you have them
- How to calculate the silhouette of a given k-means run
- K-medians clustering
- Manhattan/Hamming distance
- Cosine similarity and distance

If you made it through the chapter, you should feel confident not only about how to cluster data, but also which questions can be answered in business through clustering, and how to prepare your data to make it ready to cluster.

K-means clustering has been around for decades and is definitely the place to start for anyone looking to segment and pull insights from their customer data. But it's not the most "current" clustering technique. In Chapter 5, you'll explore using network graphs to find communities of customers within this same dataset. You'll even take a field trip outside of Excel, very briefly, to visualize the data.

If you want to go further with k-means clustering, keep in mind that vanilla Excel tops out at 200 decision variables in Solver, so you need to upgrade to a better *non-linear* Solver (for example Premium Solver available at Solver.com or just migrate over to using the non-linear Solver in LibreOffice) to cluster on data with many deal dimensions and a high value of k.

Most statistical software offers clustering capabilities. For example, R comes with the `kmeans()` function; however, the capabilities of the `fastcluster` package, which includes k-medians and a variety of distance functions, is preferable. In Chapter 10, you'll look at the `skmeans` package for performing spherical k-means.

3

Naïve Bayes and the Incredible Lightness of Being an Idiot

In the previous chapter, you hit the ground running with a bit of unsupervised learning. You looked at k-means clustering, which is like the chicken nugget of the data mining world: simple, intuitive, and useful. Delicious too.

In this chapter you're going to move from unsupervised into supervised artificial intelligence models by training up a *naïve Bayes model*, which is, for lack of a better metaphor, also a chicken nugget, albeit a supervised one.

As mentioned in Chapter 2, in supervised artificial intelligence, you "train" a model to make predictions using data that's already been classified. The most common use of naïve Bayes is for *document classification*. Is this e-mail spam or ham? Is this tweet happy or angry? Should this intercepted satellite phone call be classified for further investigation by the spooks? You provide "training data," i.e. classified examples, of these documents to the training algorithm, and then going forward, the model can classify new documents into these categories using its knowledge.

The example you'll work through in this chapter is one that's close to my own heart. Let me explain.

When You Name a Product Mandrill, You're Going to Get Some Signal and Some Noise

Recently the company I work for, MailChimp, started a new product called Mandrill.com. It has the most frightening logo I've seen in a while (see Figure 3-1).

Mandrill is a transactional e-mail product for software developers who want their apps to send one-off e-mails, receipts, password resets, and anything else that's one-to-one. Because it allows you to track opens and clicks of individual transactional e-mails, you can even wire it into your personal e-mail account and track whether your relatives are actually viewing those pictures of your cat you keep sending them. (Take it from a data scientist—they're not.)

Figure 3-1: The trance-inducing Mandrill logo

But ever since Mandrill was released, one thing has perpetually annoyed me. Whereas a "MailChimp" is a something we invented, a mandrill, also a primate, has been kicking it here on earth for a while. And they're quite popular. Heck, Darwin called the mandrill's colorful butt "extraordinary."

That means that if you go onto Twitter and want to look at any tweets mentioning the product Mandrill, you get something like what you see in Figure 3-2. The bottom tweet is about a new module hooking up the Perl programming language to Mandrill. That one is relevant. But the two above it are about Spark Mandrill from the Super Nintendo game Megaman X and a band called Mandrill.

Ryan Seguin @kerish42   1h
I liked a @YouTube video from @smoothmcgroove youtu.be/hyx9-
kWYjDI?a Megaman X - Spark **Mandrill** Acapella
▶ View media

KZKO The Vibe @KzkoTheVibe   1h
Git It All - **Mandrill** rdo.to/KZKO #nowplaying #listenlive
Expand

CPAN New Modules @cpan_new   2h
WebService-**Mandrill** 0.3 by LEV - metacpan.org/release/LEV/We...
▯ View summary

Figure 3-2: Three tweets, only one of which matters

Yuck.

Even if you enjoyed Megaman X when you were a teen, many of these tweets aren't relevant to your search. Indeed, there are more tweets about the band plus the game plus the animal plus other Twitter users with "mandrill" in their handle combined than there are about Mandrill.com. That's a lot of noise.

So is it possible to create a model that can distinguish the signal from the noise? Can an AI model alert you only to the tweets about the e-mail product Mandrill?

This then is a classic document classification problem. If a document, such as a Mandrill tweet, can belong to multiple classes (about Mandrill.com, about other things), which class should it go in?

And the most typical way of attacking this problem is using a *bag of words model* in combination with a naïve Bayes classifier. A bag of words model treats documents as a collection of unordered words. "John ate Little Debbie" is the same as "Debbie ate Little John"; they both are treated as a collection of words {"ate," "Debbie," "John," "Little"}.

A naïve Bayes classifier takes in a training set of these bags of words that are already classified. For instance, you might feed it some bags of about-Mandrill-the-app words and some bags of about-other-mandrills words and train it to distinguish between the two. Then in the future, you can feed it an unknown bag of words, and it'll classify it for you.

So that's what you're going to build in this chapter—a naïve Bayes document classifier that treats the Mandrill tweets as bags of words and gives you back a classification. And it's going to be really fun. Why?

Because naïve Bayes is often called "idiot's Bayes." As you'll see, you get to make lots of sloppy, idiotic assumptions about your data, and it still works! It's like the splatter-paint of AI models, and because it's so simple and easy to implement (it can be done in 50 lines of code), companies use it all the time for simple classification jobs. You can use it to classify company e-mails, customer support transcripts, AP wire articles, the police blotter, medical documents, movie reviews, whatever!

Now, before you get started implementing this thing in Excel (which is really quite easy), you're going to have to learn some probability theory. My apologies. If you get lost in the math, press on to the implementation, and you'll see how simply it all shakes out.

The World's Fastest Intro to Probability Theory

In the next couple sections I'm going to use the notation $p()$ to talk about probability. For instance:

$p(Michael\ Bay's\ next\ film\ will\ be\ terrible) = 1$
$p(John\ Foreman\ will\ ever\ go\ vegan) = 0.0000001$

Sorry, it's extremely unlikely that I'll ever give up Conecuh smoked sausage—the one thing I like that comes out of Alabama.

Totaling Conditional Probabilities

Now, the previous two examples are simple probabilities, but what you're going to be working with a lot in this chapter are *conditional probabilities*. Here's a conditional probability:

$p(John Foreman will go vegan \mid you pay him \$1B) = 1$

Although the odds of me ever going vegan are extremely low, the probability of me going vegan *given* you pay me a billion dollars is 100 percent. That vertical bar | in the statement is used to separate the event from what it's being conditioned on.

How do you reconcile the 0.0000001 overall vegan probability with the virtually assured conditional probability? Well, you can use the *law of total probability*. The way it works is the probability of my going vegan equals the sum of the probabilities of my going vegan *conditioned on* all possible cases times their probability of happening:

$p(vegan) = p(\$1B) * p(vegan \mid \$1B) + p(not \$1B)* p(vegan \mid not \$1B) = .0000001$

The overall probability is the weighted sum of all conditional probabilities multiplied by the probability of that condition. And the probability of the condition that you will pay me one billion dollars is 0 (pretty sure that's a safe assumption). Which means that $p(not \$1B)$ is 1, so you get:

$p(vegan) = 0*p(vegan \mid \$1B) + 1* p(vegan \mid not \$1B) = .0000001$
$p(vegan) = 0*1 + 1*.0000001 = .0000001$

Joint Probability, the Chain Rule, and Independence

Another concept in probability theory is that of the *joint probability*, which is just a fancy way of saying "and." Think back to your SAT days.

Here's the probability that I'll eat Taco Bell for lunch today:

$p(John eats Taco Bell) = .2$

It's a once-a-week thing for me. And here's the probability that I'll listen to some cheesy electronic music today:

$p(John listens to cheese) = .8$

It's highly likely.

So what are the odds that I *do both* today? That's called the joint probability, and it's written as follows:

p(John eats Taco Bell, John listens to cheese)

You just separate the two events with a comma.

Now, in this case these events are *independent*. That means that my listening doesn't affect my eating and vice versa. Given this independence, you can then multiply these two probabilities together to get their joint likelihood:

p(John eats Taco Bell, John listens to cheese) = .2 * .8 = .16

This is sometimes called the *multiplication rule of probability*. Note that the joint probability is less than the probability of either occurring, which makes perfect sense. Winning the lottery on the day you get struck by lightning is far less likely to happen than either event alone.

One way to see this is through the *chain rule of probability*, which goes like this:

p(John eats Taco Bell, John listens to cheese) = p(John eats Taco Bell) * p(John listens to cheese | John eats Taco Bell)

The joint probability is the probability of one event happening times the probability of the other event happening given that the first event happens. But since these two events are independent, the condition doesn't matter. I'm going to listen to cheesy techno the same amount regardless of lunch, so:

p(John listens to cheese | John eats Taco Bell) = p(John listens to cheese)

That reduces the chain rule setup to simply:

p(John eats Taco Bell, John listens to cheese) = p(John eats Taco Bell) * p(John listens to cheese) = .16

What Happens in a Dependent Situation?

I'll introduce another probability, the probability that I listen to Depeche Mode today:

p(John listens to Depeche Mode) = .3

There's a 30 percent chance I'll rock some DM today. Don't judge. I now have two events that have dependencies on each other: listening to Depeche Mode and listening to cheesy electronic music. Why? Because Depeche Mode *is* cheesy techno. That means that:

p(John listens to cheese | John listens to Depeche Mode) = 1

If I listen to Depeche Mode today then there's a 100 percent chance I'm listening to cheesy techno. It's a tautology. Since Depeche Mode is cheesy, the probably that I'm listening to cheesy techno given that I'm listening to Depeche Mode must be 1.

And that means that when I want to calculate their joint probability, I'm not just going to get the product of the two probabilities. Using the chain rule:

*p(John listens to cheese, John listens to DM) = p(John listens to Depeche Mode) * p(John listens to cheese | John listens to Depeche Mode) = .3 * 1 = .3*

Bayes Rule

Since I've defined Depeche Mode as cheesy techno, the probability of my listening to cheesy techno *given* I listen to Depeche Model is 1. But what about the other way around? You don't yet have a probability for this statement:

p(John listens to Depeche Mode | John listens to cheese)

After all, there are other techno groups out there. Kraftwerk anyone? The new Daft Punk album, maybe?

Well, a kindly gentleman named Bayes came up with this rule:

*p(cheese) * p(DM | cheese) = p(DM) * p(cheese | DM)*

This rule allows you to relate the probability of a conditional event to the probability when the event and condition are swapped.

Rearranging the terms then, we can isolate the probability we do not know (the probability that I'm listening to Depeche Mode given that I'm listening to cheesy music):

*p(DM | cheese) = p(DM) * p(cheese | DM) / p(cheese)*

The preceding formula is the way you'll encounter *Bayes Rule* most often. It's merely a way of flipping around conditional probabilities. When you know a conditional probability going only one way, yet you know the total probabilities of the event and the condition, you can flip everything around.

Plugging in values, you'll get:

*p(DM | cheese) = .3 * 1 / .8 = .375*

I typically have a 30 percent chance of listening to Depeche Mode on any day. However, if I know I'm going to listen to some kind of cheesy techno today, the odds of listening to Depeche Mode jump up to 37.5 percent given that knowledge. Cool!

Using Bayes Rule to Create an AI Model

All right, it's time to leave my music taste behind and think on this Mandrill tweet problem. You're going to treat each tweet as a bag of words, meaning you'll break each tweet up into words (often called *tokens*) at spaces and punctuation. There are two classes of tweets—called *app* for the Mandrill.com tweets and *other* for everything else.

You care about these two probabilities:

$$p(app \mid word_1, word_2, word_3, \ldots)$$
$$p(other \mid word_1, word_2, word_3, \ldots)$$

These are the probabilities of a tweet being either about the app or about something else given that we see the words "$word_1$," "$word_2$," "$word_3$," etc.

The standard implementation of a naïve Bayes model classifies a new document based on which of these two classes is most likely given the words. In other words, if:

$$p(app \mid word_1, word_2, word_3, \ldots) > p(other \mid word_1, word_2, word_3, \ldots)$$

then you have a tweet about the Mandrill app.

This decision rule—which picks the class that's most likely given the words—is called the *maximum a posteriori rule (MAP rule)*.

But how do you calculate these two probabilities? The first step is to use the Bayes Rule on them. Using the Bayes Rule, you can rewrite the conditional app probability as follows:

$$p(app \mid word_1, word_2, \ldots) = p(app) \, p(word_1, word_2, \ldots \mid app) \, / \, p(word_1, word_2, \ldots)$$

Similarly, you get:

$$p(other \mid word_1, word_2, \ldots) = p(other) \, p(word_1, word_2, \ldots \mid other) \, / \, p(word_1, word_2, \ldots)$$

But note that both of these calculations have the same denominator:

$p(word1, word2, \ldots)$

This is just the probability of getting these words in a document in general. Because this quantity doesn't change based on the class, you can drop it out of the MAP comparison, meaning you care only about which of these two values is larger:

$$p(app) \, p(word_1, word_2, \ldots \mid app)$$
$$p(other) \, p(word_1, word_2, \ldots \mid other)$$

But how do you calculate the probability of getting a bag of words given that it's an *app* tweet or an *other* tweet?

This is where things get idiotic!

Assume that the probabilities of these words being in the document are independent from one another. Then you get:

$p(app)\ p(word_1, word_2, ...| app) = p(app)\ p(word_1| app)\ p(word_2| app)\ p(word_3| app)...$
$p(other)\ p(word_1, word_2, ...| other) = p(other)\ p(word_1| other)\ p(word_2| other)$
$p(word_3| other)...$

The independence assumption allows you to break that joint conditional probability of the bag of words given the class into probabilities of single words given the class.

And why is this idiotic? Because words are not independent of one another in a document!

If you were classifying spam e-mails and you had two words in the document,— "erectile" and "dysfunction"—this would assume:

$p(erectile, dysfunction \mid spam) = p(erectile \mid spam)\ p(dysfunction \mid spam)$

But this is idiotic, isn't it? It's naïve, because if I told you that I got a spam e-mail with the word "dysfunction" in it and I asked you to guess what the previous word was, you'd almost certainly guess "erectile." There's a dependency there that's being blatantly ignored.

The funny thing is though that for many practical applications, somehow this idiocy doesn't matter. That's because the MAP rule doesn't really care that you calculated your class probabilities correctly; it just cares about which incorrectly calculated probability is larger. And by assuming independence of words, you're injecting all sorts of error into that calculation, but at least this sloppiness is across the board. The comparisons used in the MAP rule tend to come out in the same direction they would have had you applied all sorts of fancier linguistic understanding to the model.

High-Level Class Probabilities Are Often Assumed to Be Equal

So then to recap, in the case of the Mandrill app, you want to classify tweets based on which of these two values is higher:

$p(app)\ p(word_1| app)\ p(word_2| app)\ p(word_3| app)...$
$p(other)\ p(word_1| other)\ p(word_2| other)\ p(word_3| other)...$

So what are $p(app)$ and $p(other)$? You can log on to Twitter and see that $p(app)$ is really about 20 percent. Eighty percent of tweets using the word mandrill are about other stuff.

Although this is true now, it may shift over time, and I'd prefer to get too many tweets classified as app tweets (false positives) rather than filter some relevant ones out (false negatives), so I'm going to assume my odds are 50/50. You'll see this assumption constantly in naïve Bayes classification in the real world, especially in spam filtering where the percentage of e-mail that's spam shifts over time and may be hard to measure globally.

But if you assume both $p(app)$ and $p(other)$ are 50 percent, then when comparing the two values using the MAP decision rule, you might as well just drop them out. Thus, you can classify a tweet as app-related if:

$$p(word_1| app)\ p(word_2| app)\ \ldots\ >=\ p(word_1| other)\ p(word_2| other)\ \ldots$$

But how do you calculate the probability of a word given the class it's in? For example, contemplate the following probability:

$$p(\text{``spark''} | app)$$

To figure this out, you can pull a set of training tweets in for the app, tokenize them into words, count up the words, and figure out what percentage of those words are "spark." It'll probably be 0 percent since most "spark" mandrill tweets are about video games.

Pause a moment and contemplate this point. To build a naïve Bayes classification model, you need only track frequencies of historic app-related and non-app-related words. Well that's not hard!

A Couple More Odds and Ends

Now, before you get started in Excel, you have to address two practical hurdles in implementing naïve Bayes in Excel or in any programming language:

- Rare words
- Floating-point underflow

Dealing with Rare Words

The first is the problem of *rare words*. What if you get a tweet that you're supposed to classify, but there's the word "Tubal-cain" in it? Based on past data in the training set, perhaps one or both classes have never seen this word. A place where this happens a lot on Twitter is with shortened URLs, since each new tweet of a URL might have a different, never-seen-before encoding.

You can assume:

$$p(\text{``Tubal-cain''} | app) = 0$$

But then you'd get:

$$p(\text{``Tubal-cain''} | app)\ p(word_2| other)\ p(word_3| other)\ldots = 0$$

Tubal-cain effectively "zeros out" the entire probability calculation.

Instead, assume that you've seen "Tubal-cain" once before. You can do this for all rare words.

But wait—that's unfair to the words *you actually have seen once*. Okay, so add 1 to them, too.

But that's unfair to the words *you've actually seen twice*. Okay, so add one to every count.

This is called *additive smoothing*, and it's often used to accommodate heretofore-unseen words in bag of words models.

Dealing with Floating-Point Underflow

Now that you've addressed rare words, the second problem you have to face is called floating-point underflow.

A lot of these words are rare, so you end up with very small probabilities. In this data, most of the word probabilities will be less than 0.001. And because of the independence assumption, you'll be multiplying these individual word probabilities together.

What if you have a 15-word tweet with probabilities all under 0.001? You'll end up with a value in the MAP comparison that's tiny, such as 1×10^{-45}. Now, in truth, Excel can handle a number as small as 1x10-45. It craps out somewhere in the hundreds of 0s after the decimal place. So for classifying tweets, you'd probably be all right. But for longer documents (e.g. e-mails, news articles), tiny numbers can wreak havoc on calculations.

Just to be on the safe side, you need to find a way to not make the MAP evaluation directly:

$$p(word_1|\ app)\ p(word_2|\ app)\ \ldots\ >=\ p(word_1|\ other)\ p(word_2|\ other)\ \ldots$$

You can solve this problem using the log function (natural log in Excel is available through the LN formula).

Here's a math fun fact for you. Say you have a product:

$$.2 * .8$$

If you take the log of it, the following is true:

$$ln(.2 * .8) = ln(.2) + ln(.8)$$

And when you take the natural log of any value between 0 and 1, instead of getting a tiny decimal, you get a solid negative number. So you can take the natural log of each of the probabilities and sum them to conduct the maximum a posteriori comparison. This gives a value that the computer won't barf on.

If you're a bit confused, don't worry. This will become very clear in Excel.

Let's Get This Excel Party Started

> **NOTE**
>
> The Excel workbook used in this chapter, "Mandrill.xlsx," is available for download at the book's website at `www.wiley.com/go/datasmart`. This workbook includes all the initial data if you want to work from that. Or you can just read along using the sheets I've already put together in the workbook.

In this chapter's workbook, called Mandrill.xlsx, you have two tabs of input data to start with. One tab, AboutMandrillApp, contains 150 tweets, one per row, pertaining to Mandrill.com. The other tab, AboutOther, contains 150 tweets about other mandrill-related things.

I just want to say before you get started—welcome to the world of *natural language processing* (*NLP*). Natural language processing concerns itself with chewing on human-written text and spitting out knowledge. And that almost always means prepping that human-written content (like tweets) for computer consumption. It's time to get prepping.

Removing Extraneous Punctuation

The primary step in creating a bag of words from a tweet is tokenizing the words wherever there's a space between them. But before you divide the words wherever there's whitespace, you must lowercase everything and replace most of the punctuation with spaces since punctuation in tweets isn't always meaningful. The reason why you lowercase everything is because the words "e-mail" and "E-mail" aren't meaningfully different.

So in cell B2 on the two tweet tabs, add this formula:

```
=LOWER(A2)
```

This will lowercase the first tweet. In C2, strip out any periods. You don't want to mangle the URLs, so strip out any periods with a space after them using the SUBSTITUTE command:

```
=SUBSTITUTE(B2,". "," ")
```

This formula substitutes the string ". " for a single space " ".

You can also point cell D2 at cell C2 and replace any colons with a space after them with a single space:

```
=SUBSTITUTE(C2,": "," ")
```

In cells E2 through H2, you should make similar substitutions with the strings "?", "!", ";", and ",":

```
=SUBSTITUTE(D2,"?"," ")
=SUBSTITUTE(E2,"!"," ")
```

```
=SUBSTITUTE(F2,";"," ")
=SUBSTITUTE(G2,","," ")
```

You don't need to add a space after the punctuation in the previous four formulas because they don't appear in URLs (especially in shortened links) that often.

Highlight cells B2:H2 on both tabs and double-click the formulas to send them down through row 151. This gives you two tabs like the ones shown in Figure 3-3.

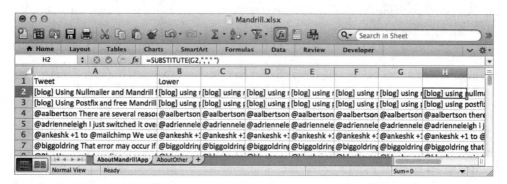

Figure 3-3: Prepped tweet data

Splitting on Spaces

Next, create two new tabs and call them **AppTokens** and **OtherTokens**.

You need to count how many times each word is used across all tweets in a category. That means you need all the tweets' words in a single column. It's safe to assume that each tweet contains no more than 30 words (feel free to expand this to 40 or 50 if you like), so if you're going to extract one token from a tweet per row, that means you need 150 x 30 = 4,500 rows.

To start, in these two tabs label A1 as **Tweet**.

Highlight A2:A4501 and Paste Special the tweet values from column H of the initial two tabs. This will give you a list of the processed tweets, as shown in Figure 3-4. Note that because you're pasting 150 tweets into 4,500 rows, Excel automatically repeats everything for you. Ginchy.

That means that if you extract the first word from the first tweet on row 2, that same tweet is repeated to extract the second word from it on row 152, then the third word on row 302, and so on.

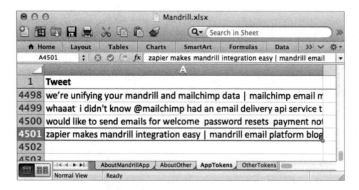

Figure 3-4: The initial AppTokens sheet

In column B, you need to indicate the position of each successive space between words in a tweet. You can label this column something like **Space Position**. Because there is no space at the beginning of each tweet, begin by placing a 0 in A2:A151 to indicate that words begin at the first character of each tweet.

Beginning at B152 when the tweets repeat for the first time, you can calculate the next space as follows:

```
=FIND(" ",A152,B2+1)
```

The FIND formula will search the tweet for the next empty space beginning with the character after the previous space referenced in cell B2, which is 150 cells above. See Figure 3-5.

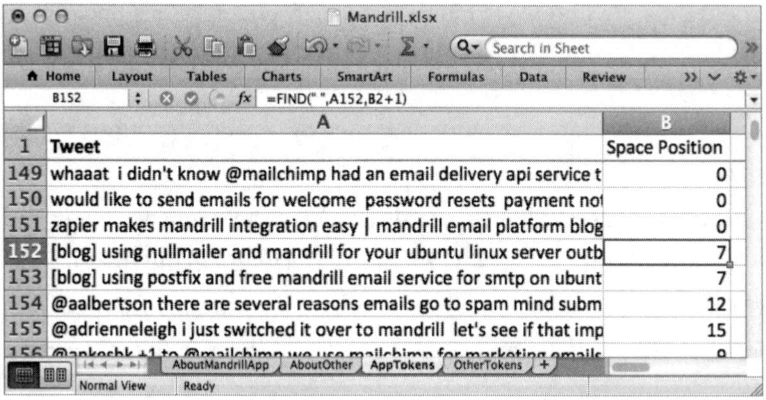

Figure 3-5: The space position of the second word in the tweet on row 152

However, note that this formula will give an error once you run out of spaces if there are fewer words than the 30 you've planned for, so to accommodate this, you need to wrap the formula in an IFERROR statement and just return one plus the tweet length to indicate the position after the last word:

```
=IFERROR(FIND(" ",A152,B2+1),LEN(A152)+1)
```

You can then double-click this formula to send it down the sheet through A4501. This will produce the sheet shown in Figure 3-6.

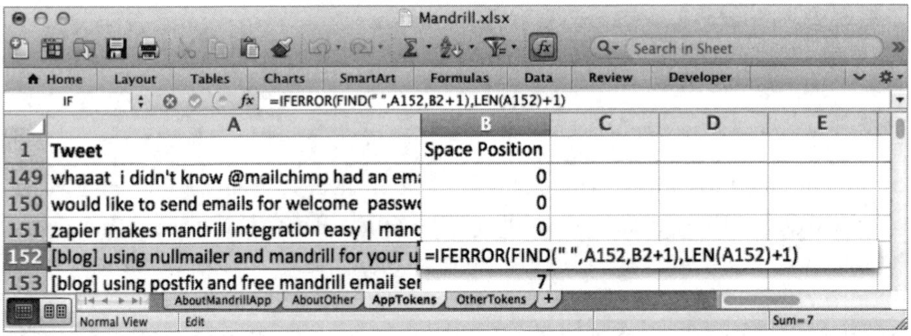

Figure 3-6: Positions of each space in the tweet

Next in column C, you can begin to extract single tokens from the tweets. Label column C as **Token**, and beginning in cell C2, you can pull the appropriate word from the tweet using the MID function. MID takes in a string of text, a start position, and the number of characters to yank. So in C2, your text is in A2, the starting position is one past the last space (B2 + 1), and the length is the difference between the subsequent space position in cell B152 and the current space position in B2 minus 1 (keeping in mind that identical tweets are offset by 150 rows).

This yields the following formula:

```
MID(A2,B2+1,B152-B2-1)
```

Now, once again, you can get into some tight spots at the end of the string when you run out of words. So, if there's an error, turn the token into " . " so it will be easy to ignore later:

```
=IFERROR(MID(A2,B2+1,B152-B2-1),".")
```

You can then double-click this formula and send it down the sheet to tokenize every tweet, as shown in Figure 3-7.

Add a Length column to column D, and in cell D2 take the length of the token in C2 as:

```
=LEN(C2)
```

You can double-click this to send it down the sheet. This value allows you to find and delete any token three characters or less, which tend overall to be meaningless.

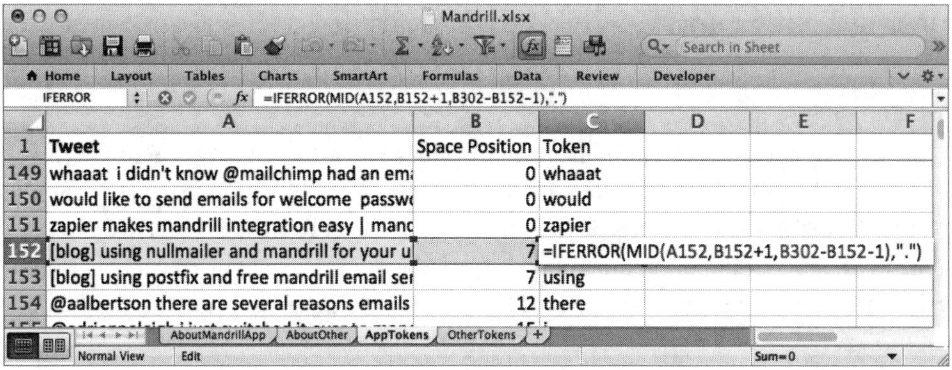

Figure 3-7: Every tweet token

NOTE

Typically in these kind of natural language processing tasks, rather than drop all the short words, a list of *stop words* for the particular language (English in this case) would be removed. Stop words are words which have very little *lexical content*, which is like nutritional content, for bag of words models.

For instance, "because" or "instead" might be stop words, because they're common and they don't really do much to distinguish one type of document from another. The most common stop words in English do happen to be short, such as "a," "and," "the," etc., which is why in this chapter you'll take the easier, yet more Draconian, route of removing short words from tweets only.

If you follow these steps, you'll have the AppTokens sheet shown in Figure 3-8 (the OtherTokens sheet is identical except for the tweets pasted in column A).

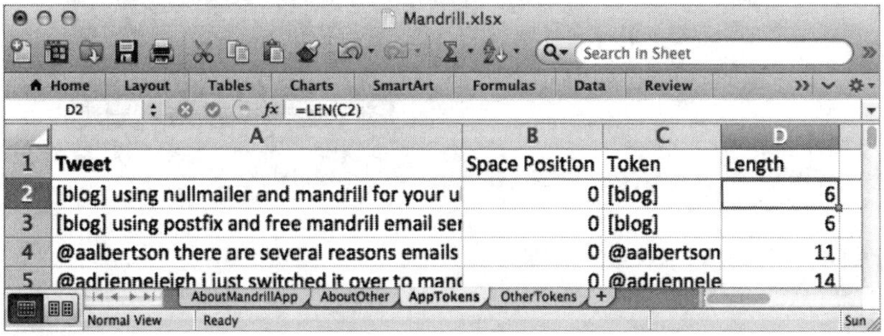

Figure 3-8: App tokens with their respective lengths

Counting Tokens and Calculating Probabilities

Now that you've tokenized your tweets, you're ready to calculate the conditional probability of a token, $p(token \mid class)$.

To do so, you need to determine how many times each token is used. Start with the AppTokens tab by selecting the token and length range C1:D4501 and then inserting the data into a PivotTable. Rename the created pivot table tab **AppTokensProbability**.

In the PivotTable Builder, filter on token length, make the tokens the row labels, and in the values box set the value to be a count of each token. This gives you the Builder setup shown in Figure 3-9.

In the actual pivot, drop down the length filter and uncheck tokens of length 0, 1, 2, or 3 from being used. (On Windows you have to instruct Excel to Select Multiple Items in the drop-down.) This is also pictured in Figure 3-9.

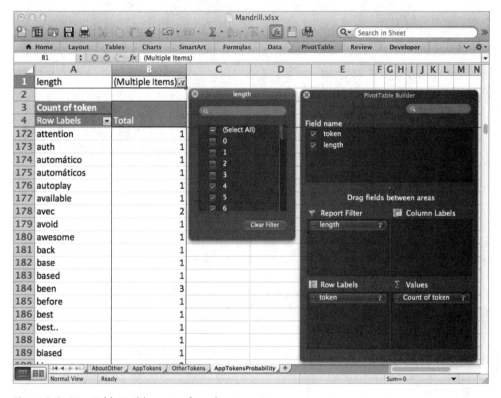

Figure 3-9: PivotTable Builder setup for token counting

You now have only the longer tokens from each tweet, all counted up.

You can now tack on the probabilities to each token, but before you run the numbers, apply the additive smoothing concept discussed earlier in the chapter by adding one to each token.

Label column C **Add One To Everything**, and set C5 = B5+1 (C4 = B4+1 on Windows, where Excel builds pivot tables one row higher just to annoy this book). You can double-click the formula to send it down the page.

Since you've added one to everything, you'll also need a new grand total token count. So at the bottom of the table (row 828 in the AppTokensProbability tab), set the cell to sum the counts above it. Once again, note that if you're on Windows everything is one row higher (C4:C826 for the summation range):

```
=SUM(C5:C827)
```

In column D, you can calculate the probability of each token as its count in column C divided by the total token count. Label column D as **P(Token|App)**. The probability of the first token in D5 (D4 on Windows) is calculated as:

```
=C5/C$828
```

Note the absolute reference to the token total count. This allows you to double-click the formula and send it down column D. Then in column E (call it **LN(P)**), you can take the natural log of the probability in D5 as follows:

```
=LN(D5)
```

Sending this down the sheet, you now have the values you need for the MAP rule. See Figure 3-10.

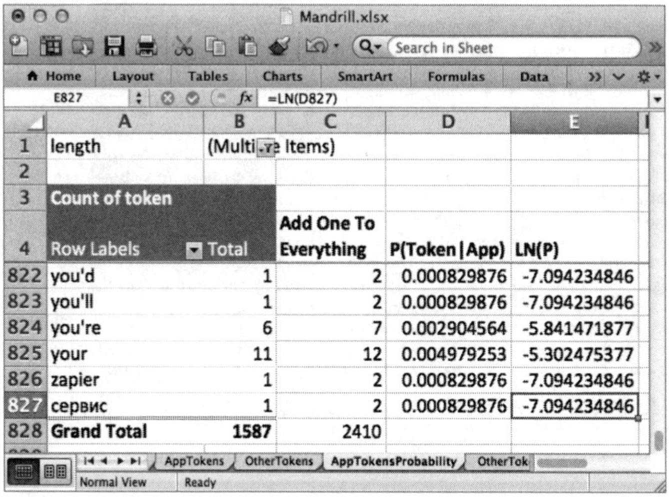

Figure 3-10: The logged probabilities for the app tokens

Also, create an identical tab using the non-app tokens called **OtherTokensProbabilies**.

And We Have a Model! Let's Use It

Unlike with a regression model (which you'll encounter in Chapter 6), there's no optimization step here. No Solver, no model fitting. A naïve Bayes model is nothing more than these two conditional probability tables.

This is one of the reasons why programmers love this model. There's no complicated model-fitting step—they just chunk up some tokens and count them. And you can dump that dictionary of tokens out to disk for later use. It's terribly easy.

Okay, so now that the naïve Bayes model is trained, you can use it. In the TestTweets tab of the workbook, you'll find 20 tweets, 10 about the app and 10 about other mandrills. You're going to prep these tweets, tokenize them (you'll do the tokenizing a bit differently this time for kicks), calculate their logged token probabilities for both classes, and determine which class is most likely.

To begin then, copy cells B2:H21 from AboutMandrillApp and paste them into D2:J21 of the TestTweets tab in order to prep the tweets. This gives you the sheet shown in Figure 3-11.

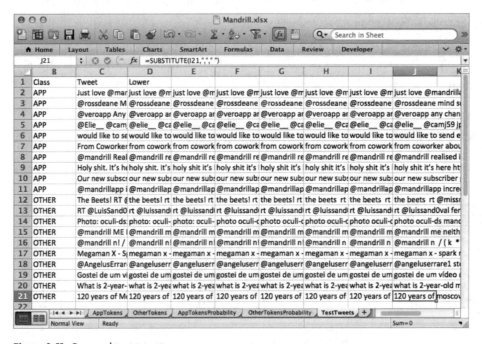

Figure 3-11: Prepped test tweets

Next, create a tab called **TestPredictions**. In the tab, paste the Number and Class columns from TestTweets. Name column C **Prediction**, which you'll fill in with the predicted class values. Then label column D as **Tokens**, and in D2:D21, paste the values from column J on the TestTweets tab. This gives you the sheet shown in Figure 3-12.

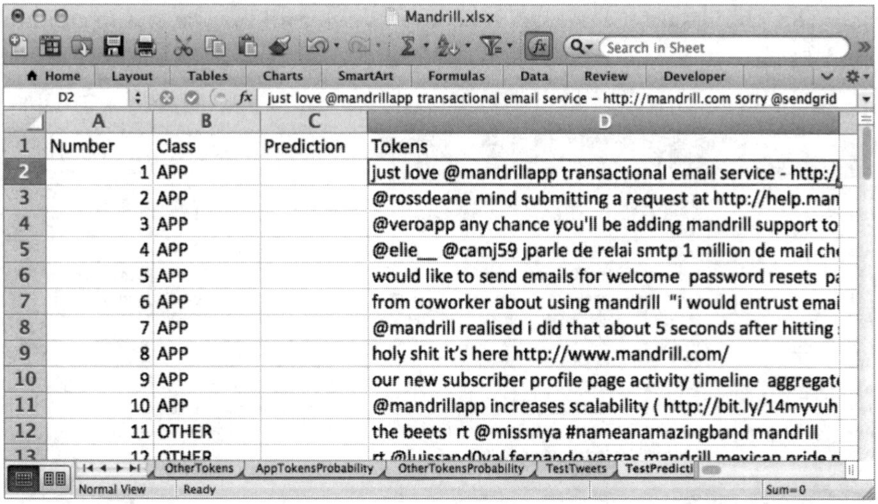

Figure 3-12: The TestPredictions tab

Unlike when you built the probability tables, you don't want to combine these tokens across tweets. You want to evaluate each tweet separately, and this makes tokenizing rather simple.

To start, highlight the tweets in D2:D21 and choose Text to Columns on the Data tab of the Excel ribbon. In the Convert Text to Columns wizard that pops up, select Delimited and press Next.

On the second screen of the wizard, specify Tab and Space as delimiters. You can also choose Treat Consecutive Delimiters As One and make sure that the Text Qualifier is set to {none}. This gives the setup shown in Figure 3-13.

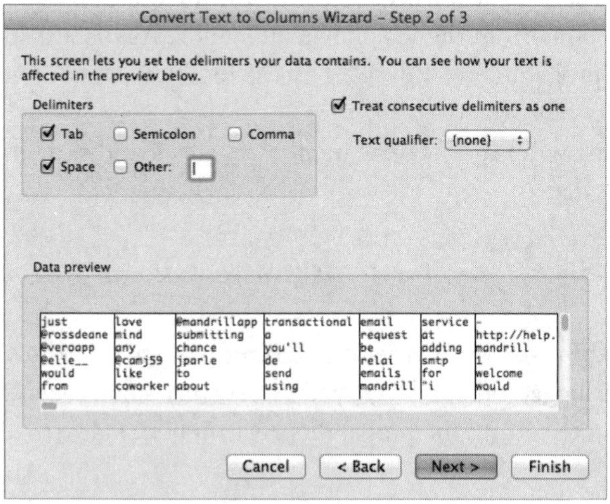

Figure 3-13: The Text to Columns Wizard setup

Press Finish. This chunks up the tweets into columns going all the way out to column AI (see Figure 3-14).

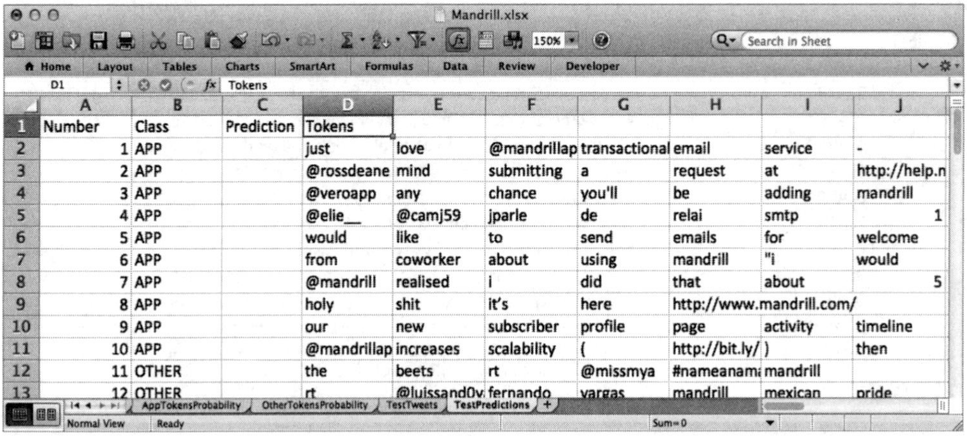

Figure 3-14: The tokens from the test tweets

Below the tokens starting in column D on row 25, you should look up the app probabilities for each token. To do so, you can use the VLOOKUP function (see Chapter 1 for more on VLOOKUP), starting with cell D25:

```
=VLOOKUP(D2,AppTokensProbability!$A$5:$E$827,5,FALSE)
```

The VLOOKUP function takes the corresponding token from D2 and tries to find it in column A on the AppTokensProbability tab. When it finds the token, the lookup grabs the value from column E.

But this isn't sufficient, because you need to deal with the rare words not on the lookup table—these tokens will get an N/A value from the VLOOKUP as it stands. As discussed earlier, these rare words should get a probability of 1 divided by the total token count in cell B828 on the AppTokensProbability tab.

To handle these rare words, you just wrap the VLOOKUP in an ISNA check and slide in the rare word logged probability if needed:

```
IF(ISNA(VLOOKUP(D2,AppTokensProbability!$A$5:$E$827,5,FALSE)),
LN(1/AppTokensProbability!$C$828),VLOOKUP(D2,AppTokensProbability!
$A$5:$E$827,5,FALSE))
```

The one thing this solution hasn't addressed yet are the small tokens you want to throw away. Since you're going to sum these logged probabilities, you can set any small token's logged probability to zero (this is akin to setting the probability to 1 on both sides, that is, throwing it away).

To do this, you just wrap the whole formula in one more IF statement that checks length:

```
=IF(LEN(D2)<=3,0,IF(ISNA(VLOOKUP(D2,AppTokensProbability!
$A$5:$E$827,5,FALSE)),LN(1/AppTokensProbability!$C$828),
VLOOKUP(D2,AppTokensProbability!$A$5:$E$827,5,FALSE)))
```

Note that absolute references are used on the AppTokensProbability tab so that you can drag this formula around.

Since the tweet tokens reach all the way to column AI, you can drag this formula from D25 through AI44 to score each token. This gives the worksheet shown in Figure 3-15.

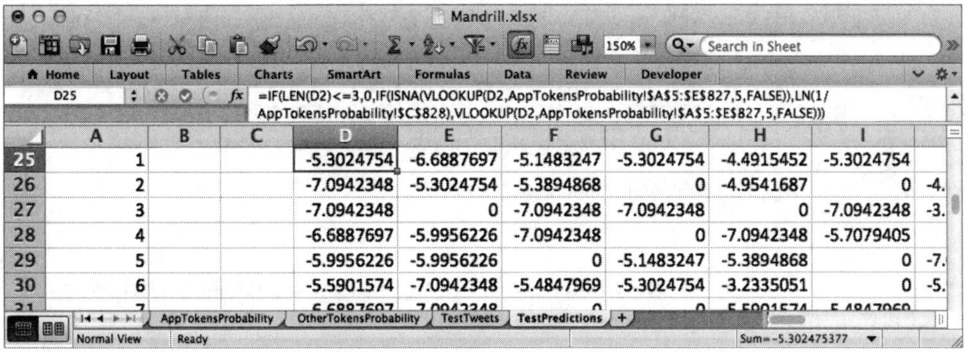

Figure 3-15: App logged probabilities assigned to tokens

Starting at cell D48, you can use the same formula as in D25 except that it should reference the OtherTokensProbability tab, and the range on the probability tab changes to $A$5:$E$810 in the VLOOKUP with the total token count being on $C$811.

This then yields the sheet shown in Figure 3-16.

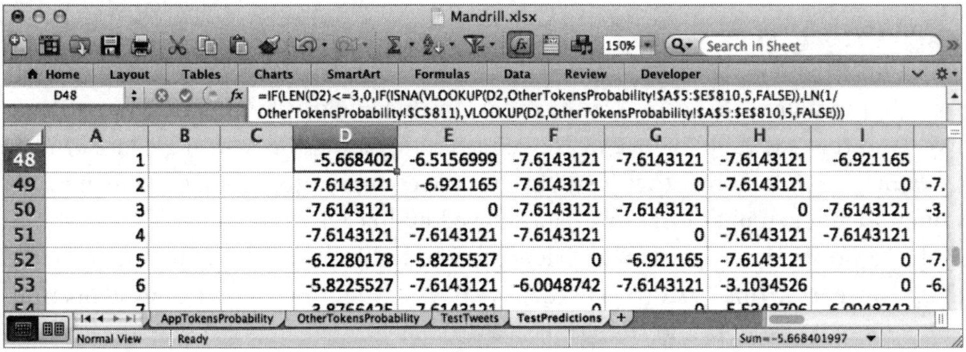

Figure 3-16: Both sets of logged probabilities assigned to the test tweets

In column C, you can sum each row of probabilities, yielding the sheet shown in Figure 3-17. For example, C25 is simply:

```
=SUM(D25:AI25)
```

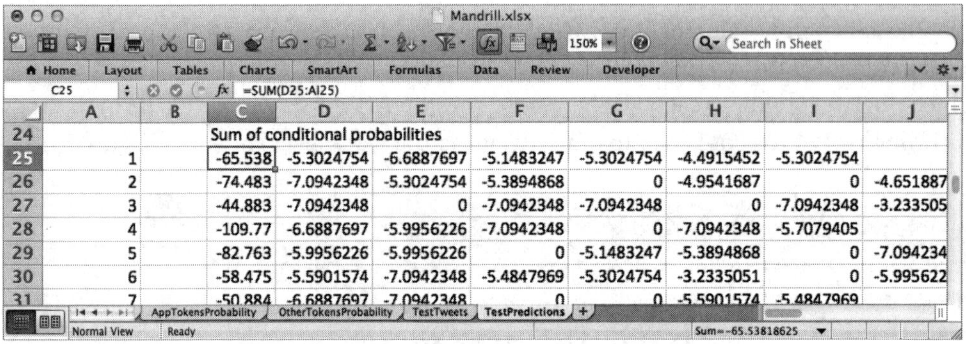

Figure 3-17: Sums of logged conditional token probabilities

In cell C2, you can classify this first tweet by simply comparing its scores below in cells C25 and C48 using the following IF statement:

```
=IF(C25>C48,"APP","OTHER")
```

Copying this formula down through C21, you get all of the classifications, as shown in Figure 3-18.

It gets 19 out of 20 correct! Not bad. If you look at the one tweet that was misclassified, the language is quite vague—the scores are close to tied.

And that's it. Model built, predictions done.

Wrapping Up

This chapter is super short compared to others in this book. Why? Because naïve Bayes is easy! And that's why folks love it. Naïve Bayes appears to be working some kind of complex magic when in reality it just relies on the computer to have a good memory of how often each token in the training data showed up in each class.

There's a proverb that goes, "Experience is the father of wisdom and memory the mother." Nowhere is this truer than with naïve Bayes. Its entire faux-wisdom stems from a combination of past data and storage with a little bit of mathematical duct tape.

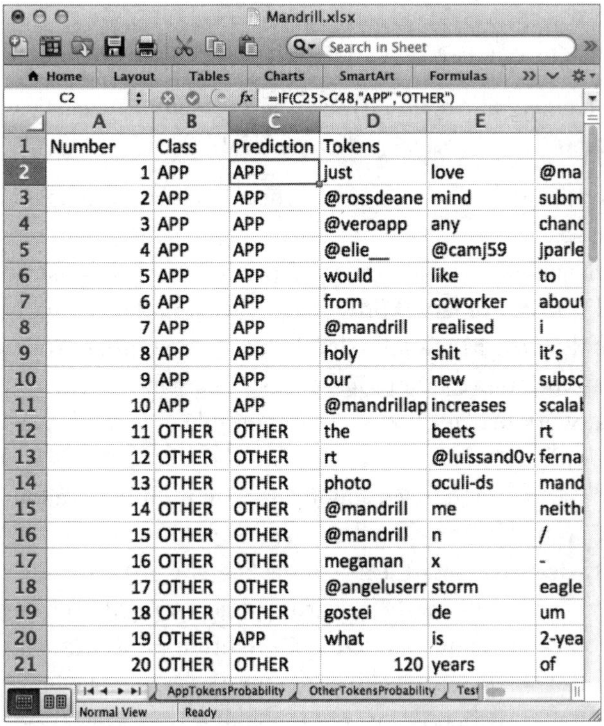

	A	B	C	D	E	
1	Number	Class	Prediction	Tokens		
2	1	APP	APP	just	love	@ma
3	2	APP	APP	@rossdeane	mind	subm
4	3	APP	APP	@veroapp	any	chanc
5	4	APP	APP	@elie__	@camj59	jparle
6	5	APP	APP	would	like	to
7	6	APP	APP	from	coworker	about
8	7	APP	APP	@mandrill	realised	i
9	8	APP	APP	holy	shit	it's
10	9	APP	APP	our	new	subsc
11	10	APP	APP	@mandrillap	increases	scalal
12	11	OTHER	OTHER	the	beets	rt
13	12	OTHER	OTHER	rt	@luissandOv	ferna
14	13	OTHER	OTHER	photo	oculi-ds	mand
15	14	OTHER	OTHER	@mandrill	me	neith
16	15	OTHER	OTHER	@mandrill	n	/
17	16	OTHER	OTHER	megaman	x	-
18	17	OTHER	OTHER	@angeluserr	storm	eagle
19	18	OTHER	OTHER	gostei	de	um
20	19	OTHER	APP	what	is	2-yea
21	20	OTHER	OTHER	120	years	of

Figure 3-18: Test tweets classified

Naïve Bayes lends itself particularly well to simple implementations in code. For example, here's a C# implementation:

```
http://msdn.microsoft.com/en-us/magazine/jj891056.aspx
```

Here's a tiny version someone posted online in Python:

```
http://www.mustapps.com/spamfilter.py
```

Here's one in Ruby:

```
http://blog.saush.com/2009/02/11/naive-bayesian-classifiers-and-ruby/
```

One of the great things about this type of model is that it works well even when there are a boatload of *features* (AI model inputs) you're predicting with (in the case of this data, each word was a feature). But that said, keep in mind that a simple bag of words model does have some drawbacks. Chiefly, the naïve bit of the model can cause problems. I'll give you an example.

Suppose I build a naïve Bayes classifier that tries to classify tweets about movies into "thumbs up" and "thumbs down." When someone says something like:

> *Michael Bay's new movie is a steaming pile of misogynistic garbage, full of explosions and poor acting, signifying nothing. And I, for one, loved the ride!*

Is the model going to get that correct? You have a bunch of thumbs-down tokens followed by a thumbs-up token at the end.

Since a bag of words model throws away the structure of the text and tokens are assumed to be unordered, this could be a problem. Many naïve Bayes models actually take in phrases rather than individual words as tokens. That helps contextualize words a little bit (and makes the naïve assumption even more ludicrous...but who cares!). You need more training data to make that work because the space of possible n-word phrases is larger than the space of possible words.

For something like this movie review you might need a model that actually cares about the position of a word in the review. Which phrase "had the last word?" Incorporating that kind of information immediately does away with this simple bag of words concept.

But, hey, this is nitpicking. Naïve Bayes is a straightforward and versatile AI tool. It's easy to prototype and test with. So you can try out a modeling idea with naïve Bayes, and if it works well enough, you're good. If it shows promise but is poor, you can move on to something beefier, like an ensemble model (which is covered in Chapter 7).

4 Optimization Modeling: Because That "Fresh Squeezed" Orange Juice Ain't Gonna Blend Itself

Business Week recently published an article about how The Coca-Cola Company uses a large analytics model to determine how to blend raw orange juices to create the perfect not-from-concentrate product.

I was discussing this article with some folks, and one of them blurted something like, "But you could never do that with an artificial intelligence model!"

They were right. You can't. Because Coca-Cola doesn't use an *artificial intelligence* model. It uses an *optimization* model. Huh? What's the difference?

An artificial intelligence model predicts the result of a process by analyzing its inputs. That's not what Coca-Cola is doing. Coca-Cola doesn't need to predict the outcome when they combine juice A with juice B. It needs to decide which combination of juice A, B, C, D, and so on to buy and blend together. Coca-Cola is taking some data and some business rules (their inventory, their demand, their specs, and so on) and *deciding* how to blend a product. These decisions enable Coca-Cola to blend juices with complementary strengths and weaknesses (maybe one is too sweet and another not sweet enough) to get exactly the right taste for the minimum cost and the maximum profit.

There's no one outcome that needs predicting. The model gets to change the future. Optimization modeling is analytics' Arminianism to AI's Calvinism. Free will, baby! (Sorry, that's the last historical theological joke in this book.)

Companies across industries use optimization models every day to answer questions such as these:

- How do I schedule my call center employees to accommodate their vacation requests, balance overtime, and eliminate back-to-back graveyard shifts for any one employee?
- Which oil drilling opportunities do I explore to maximize return while keeping risk under control?
- When do I place new orders to China, and how do I get them shipped to minimize cost and meet anticipated demand?

Optimization, you see, is the practice of mathematically formulating a business problem and then solving that mathematical representation for the best solution. And as noted in Chapter 1, this objective is always a minimization or a maximization where the "best solution" gets to mean whatever you like—lowest cost, highest profit, or least likely to land you in jail.

The most widely used and understood form of mathematical optimization, called *linear programming*, was developed in secret by the Soviet Union in the late 1930s and gained traction through its extensive use in World War II for transportation planning and resource allocation to minimize cost and risk and maximize damage to the enemy.

In this chapter, I'll go into detail on the *linear* part of linear programming. The *programming* part is a holdover from wartime terminology and has nothing to do with computer programming. Just ignore it.

This chapter covers linear, integer, and a bit of non-linear optimization. It focuses on how to formulate business problems in a language in which the computer can solve them. The chapter also discusses at a high level how the industry-standard optimization methods built into Excel's Solver tool attack these problems and close in on the best solutions.

Why Should Data Scientists Know Optimization?

If you watch a bunch of James Bond or *Mission Impossible* movies, you'll notice that they often have a big action sequence before the opening credits. Nothing draws viewers in like an explosion.

The previous chapters on data mining and artificial intelligence were just that—our explosions. But now, like in any good action movie, the plot must advance. In Chapter 2 you used a bit of optimization modeling in finding the optimal placement of cluster centroids, but you had only been given enough optimization knowledge in Chapter 1 to make that happen. In this chapter, you're going to dive deep into optimization and get lots of experience with how to formulate models that solve business problems.

Artificial intelligence is making waves these days for its use at tech companies and start-ups. Optimization, on the other hand, seems to be more of a Fortune 500 business practice. Reengineering your supply chain to reduce the fuel costs of your fleet is anything but sexy. But optimization, whether it's trimming the fat or making the most of economies of scale, is *fundamental* to effectively running a business.

And when we talk data science, the truth is that optimization is fundamental there too. As you'll see in this book, not only is optimization a worthwhile analytic practice to understand on its own, but any data science practitioner worth their salt is going to need to use optimization on the way to implementing other data science techniques. In this book alone, optimization makes a cameo in four other chapters:

- Determining optimal cluster centers in k-means clustering as seen in Chapter 2
- Maximizing modularity for community detection (Chapter 5)

- Training coefficients for an AI model (fitting a regression in Chapter 6)
- Optimally setting smoothing parameters in a forecasting model (Chapter 8)

Optimization problems are embedded everywhere in data science, so you need to master solving them before you move on.

Starting with a Simple Trade-Off

This section begins by discussing economists' two favorite resources—guns and butter. The year is 1941, and you've been airdropped behind enemy lines where you've assumed the identity of one Jérémie (or Ameline) Galiendo, a French dairy farmer.

Your day job: milking cows and selling sweet, creamy butter to the local populace.

Your night job: building and selling machine guns to the French resistance.

Your job is complex and fraught with peril. You've been cut off from HQ and are left on your own to run the farm while not getting caught by the Nazis. You only have so much money in the budget to make ends meet while producing guns and butter; you must stay solvent throughout the war. You cannot lose the farm and your cover along with it.

After sitting and thinking about your plight, you've found a way to characterize your situation in terms of three elements:

- **The objective:** You get $195 dollars (or, uh, francs, although honestly my Excel is set to dollars, and I'm not going to change it for the figures here) in revenue from every machine gun you sell to your contact, Pierre. You get $150 for every ton of butter you sell in the market. You need to bring in as much revenue as you can each month to keep the farm going.
- **The decisions:** You need to figure out what mix of guns and tons of butter to produce each month to maximize total profit.
- **The constraints:** It costs $100 to produce a ton of butter and $150 to produce a machine gun. You have a budget of $1,800 a month to devote to producing new product for sale. You also have to store this stuff in your 21 cubic meter cellar. Guns take up 0.5 cubic meters once packaged, and a ton of butter takes up 1.5 cubic meters. You can't store the butter elsewhere or it'll spoil. You can't store the guns elsewhere or you'll get caught by the Nazis.

Representing the Problem as a Polytope

This problem as it's been laid out is called a *linear program*. A linear program is characterized as a set of decisions that need to be made to optimize an objective in light of some constraints, where both the constraints and the objective are *linear*. Linear in this case means that any equation in the problem can only add decisions, subtract decisions, multiply decisions by constants, or some combination of those things.

In linear programming, you can't shove your decisions through any non-linear functions, which might include:

- Multiplying decisions together (guns *times* butter cannot be used anywhere)
- Sending a decision variable through a kind of logic check, such as an `if` statement ("If you only store butter in the cellar, then you can give it a little squish and make the capacity 22 cubic meters.")

As you'll see later in this chapter, restrictions breed creativity.

Now, back to the problem. Start by graphing the "feasible region" for this problem. The feasible region is the set of possible solutions. Can you produce no guns and no butter? Sure, that's feasible. It won't maximize revenue, but it's feasible. Can you produce 100 guns and 1,000 tons of butter? Nope, not in the budget, and not in the cellar. Not feasible.

Okay, so where do you start graphing? Well, you can't produce negative quantities of guns or butter. This isn't theoretical physics. So you're dealing with the first quadrant of the x-y plane.

In terms of the budget, at $150 a pop you can make 12 guns from the $1,800 budget. At $100 a ton, you can make 18 tons of butter.

So if you graph the budget constraint as a line on the x-y plane, it'd pass right through 12 guns and 18 tons of butter. As shown in Figure 4-1, the feasible region is then a triangle of positive values in which you can produce, at most, 12 guns and 18 tons of butter, or some middling linear combination of the two extremes.

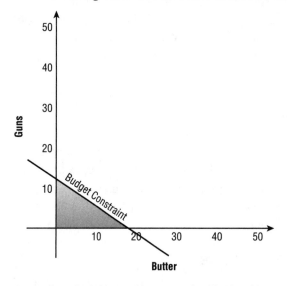

Figure 4-1: The budget constraint makes the feasible region a triangle.

Now, this triangle is more generally called a *polytope*. A polytope is nothing more than a geometric shape with flat sides. You've probably heard the term *polygon*. Well, a polygon is just a polytope in a two-dimensional space. If you've got a big fat rock of an engagement ring on your hand…Bam! The diamond is a polytope.

All linear programs can have their feasible regions expressed as polytopes. Some algorithms, as you'll see momentarily, exploit this fact to arrive quickly at solutions to linear programming problems.

Concerning the problem at hand, it's time to consider the second constraint—the cellar. If you produced only guns, you'd be able to pack 42 of them in the cellar. On the other hand, you could shove 14 tons of butter in the cellar, maximum. So adding this constraint to the polytope, you shave off part of the feasible region, as shown in Figure 4-2.

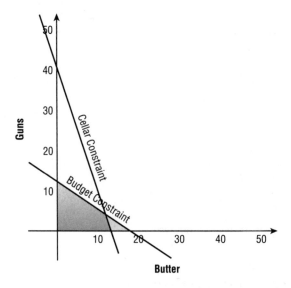

Figure 4-2: The cellar constraint cuts a chunk out of the feasible region.

Solving by Sliding the Level Set

Now that you've determined the feasible region, you can begin to ask the question, "Where in that region is the best guns/butter mix?"

To answer that question, begin by defining something called the *level set*. A level set for your optimization model is a region in the polytope where all the points give the same revenue.

Because your revenue function is $150*Butter + $195*Guns, each level set can be defined by the line $150*Butter + $195*Guns = C, where C is a fixed amount of revenue.

Consider the case where C is $1950. For the level set *$150*Butter + $195*Guns = $1950*, both the points (0,10) and (13,0) exist in the level set as does any combination of guns and butter where *$150*Butter + $195*Guns* comes out to $1950. This level set is pictured in Figure 4-3.

Using this idea of the level set, you could then think of solving the revenue maximization problem by sliding the level set in the direction of increasing revenue (this is perpendicular to the level set itself) until *the last possible moment before you left the feasible region.*

In Figure 4-3, a level set is pictured with a dashed line, while the arrow and dashed line together represent your objective function.

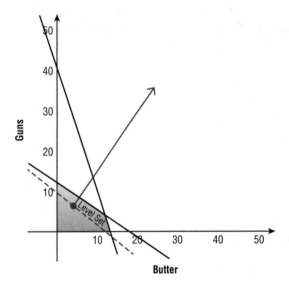

Figure 4-3: The level set and objective function for the revenue optimization

The Simplex Method: Rooting around the Corners

To reiterate, if you want to know which feasible points are optimal, you can just slide that level set along the direction of increasing revenue. Right at the border before the level set leaves the polytope, that's where the best points would be. And here's what's cool about that:

One of these optimal points at the border will always be a corner of the polytope.

Go ahead and confirm this in Figure 4-3. Lay a pencil on the level set and move it up and right in the direction of increasing revenue. See how it leaves the polytope at a corner?

Why is that cool? Well, the polytope in Figure 4-3 has an infinite number of feasible solutions. Searching the entire space would be hell. Even the edges have an infinite number of points! But there are only four corners, and there's an optimal solution in one of them. Much better odds.

It turns out there's an algorithm that's been designed to check corners. And even in problems with hundreds of millions of decisions, it's very effective. The algorithm is called the *simplex method*.

Basically, the simplex method starts at a corner of the polytope and slides along edges of the polytope that benefit the objective. When it hits a corner whose departing edges all are detrimental to the objective, well, then that corner is the best one.

In the case of selling guns and butter, assume that you start out at point (0,0). It's a corner, but it's got $0 in revenue. Surely you can do better.

Well, as seen in Figure 4-3, the bottom edge of the polytope increases revenue as you move right. So sliding along the bottom edge of the polytope in this direction, you hit the corner (14,0)—14 tons of butter and no guns will produce $2,100 dollars (see Figure 4-4).

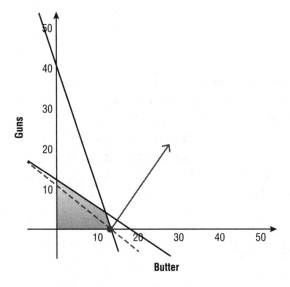

Figure 4-4: Testing out the all-butter corner

From the all-butter corner, you can then slide along the cellar storage edge in the direction of increasing revenue. The next corner you hit is (12.9, 3.4), which gives you revenue just shy of $2,600. All the edges departing the corner lead to worse nodes, so you're done. As pictured in Figure 4-5, this is the optimum!

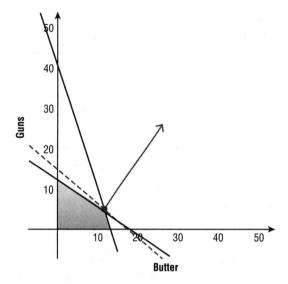

Figure 4-5: Located the optimal corner

Working in Excel

Before you leave this simple problem behind for something a little tougher, I want to build and solve it in Excel. The first thing you're going to do in a blank Excel workbook is create spaces for the objective and decision variables, so you'll label cell B2 as the spot where the total revenue will go and cells B4:C4 as the range where the production decisions will go.

Below the objective and decision sections, add the size and price information for guns and butter, the limits on storage space and budget, and each item's contribution to revenue.

The barebones spreadsheet should look like Figure 4-6.

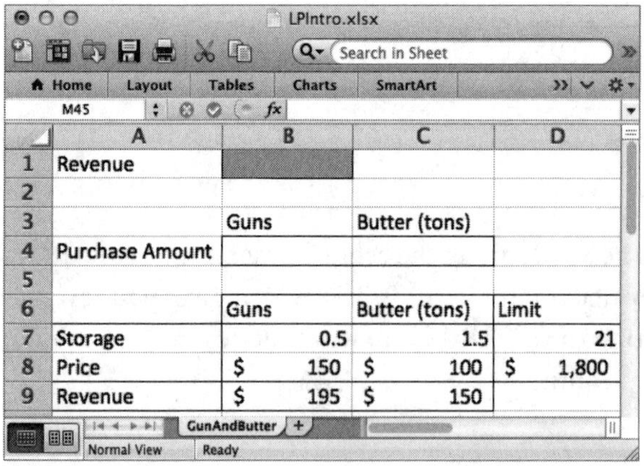

	A	B	C	D
1	Revenue			
2				
3		Guns	Butter (tons)	
4	Purchase Amount			
5				
6		Guns	Butter (tons)	Limit
7	Storage	0.5	1.5	21
8	Price	$ 150	$ 100	$ 1,800
9	Revenue	$ 195	$ 150	

Figure 4-6: Guns and butter data placed, lovingly, in Excel

To this data, you need to add several calculations, namely, the constraint calculations and the revenue calculation. In Column E, next to the Limit cells, you can multiply the amounts of guns and butter produced times their respective sizes and prices, and sum them up in a Used column. For example, in E7 you can place how much space is used in the cellar using the formula:

```
=SUMPRODUCT(B4:C4,B7:C7)
```

Note that this formula is linear because only one range, B4:C4, is a decision range. The other range just houses the storage coefficients. You can do the same calculation to gather the total amount spent on guns and butter.

For the objective function, you need only take a SUMPRODUCT of the purchased quantities on row 4 with their revenue on row 9. Placing a feasible solution, such as 1 gun, 1 ton of butter, into the decision cells now yields a sheet like that pictured in Figure 4-7.

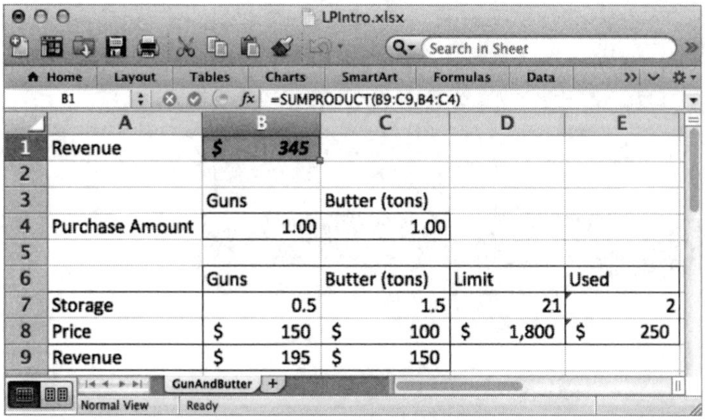

Figure 4-7: Revenue and constraint calculations within the guns and butter problem

All right, so how do you now get Excel to set the decision variables to their optimal values? To do this, you use Solver! Start by popping open an empty Solver window (pictured in Figure 4-8). For more on adding Solver to Excel see Chapter 1.

Just as was mocked up earlier in the chapter, you need to provide Solver with an objective, decisions, and constraints. The objective is the revenue cell created in B1. Also, make sure that you choose the Max radio button since you're maximizing, not minimizing, revenue. If you were working a problem with cost or risk in the objective function, you would use the Min option instead.

The decisions are in B4:C4. After you add them to the "By Changing Variable Cells" section, the Solver window will look like Figure 4-9.

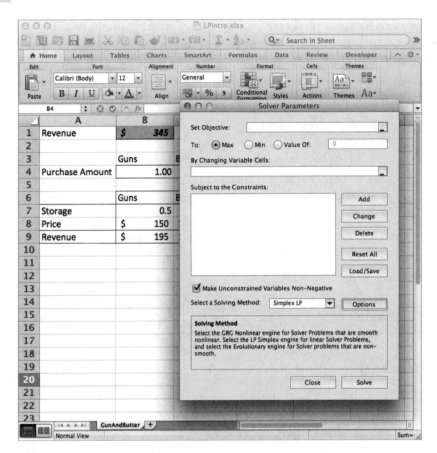

Figure 4-8: The Solver window

As for the constraints, there are two you have to add. Start with the cellar storage constraint. Click on the Add button next to the constraints section. Filling out the small dialog box, you need to indicate that cell E7 must be less than or equal to (≤) cell D7 (see Figure 4-10). The amount of space you're using must be less than the limit.

> **NOTE**
>
> Note that Solver will add absolute references ($) to everything in your formulation. It doesn't matter that Solver does this. Honestly, I don't know why it does because you can't drag formulas in the context of a Solver model. See Chapter 1 for more on absolute references.

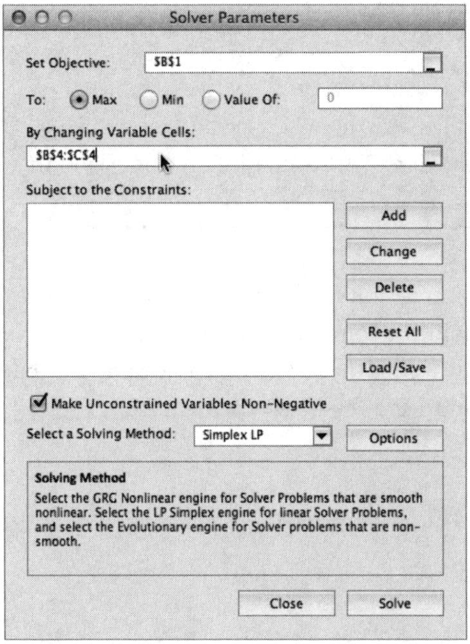

Figure 4-9: Objective and decisions populated in Solver

> **NOTE**
>
> Before pressing OK, look at the other constraint types Solver offers you. Beyond ≤, ≥, and =, there are some funky ones, namely int, bin, and dif. These odd constraints can be placed on cells to make them integers, binary (0 or 1), or "all different." Keep the int constraint in mind. You're going to return to it in a second.

Press OK to add the constraint, and then add the budget constraint the same way (E8 ≤ D8). Confirm also that the Make Unconstrained Variables Non-Negative box is checked to make sure the guns and butter production doesn't become negative for some odd reason. (Alternatively, you can just add a B4:C4 ≥ 0 constraint, but the check box makes it easy.)

Now, from Select a Solving Method, make sure the Simplex LP algorithm is selected. You're ready to go (see Figure 4-11).

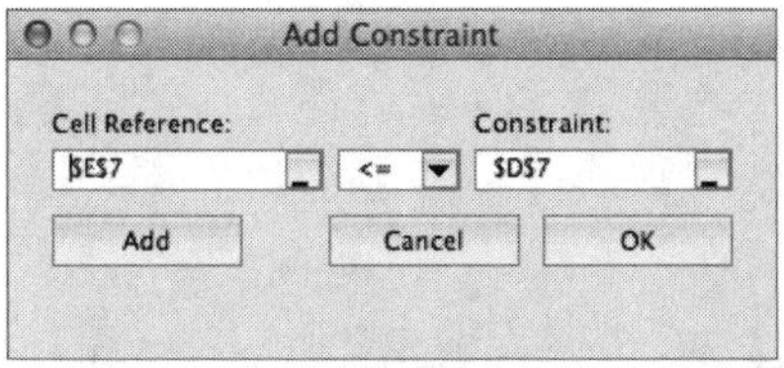

Figure 4-10: The Add Constraint dialog box

USING EXCEL 2007

In Excel 2007, there is no Make Unconstrained Variables Non-Negative checkbox. Instead, go to the Options screen and check off the Assume Non-negative box. Also, there's no Solving Method selection. Instead, check the Assume Linear Model box in order to activate the simplex algorithm.

When you press Solve, Excel quickly finds the solution to the problem and pops up a box letting you know. You can either accept the solution found or restore the values in the decision cells (see Figure 4-12). If you press OK to accept the solution, you would see that it's 3.43 guns and 12.86 tons of butter just like you'd graphed (see Figure 4-13).

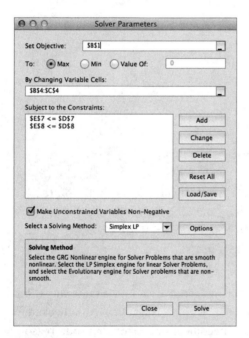

Figure 4-11: Completed Guns and Butter formulation in Solver

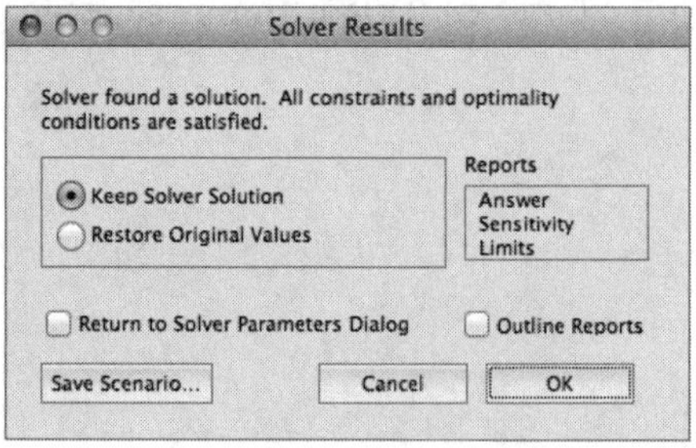

Figure 4-12: Solver lets you know when it's solved the problem.

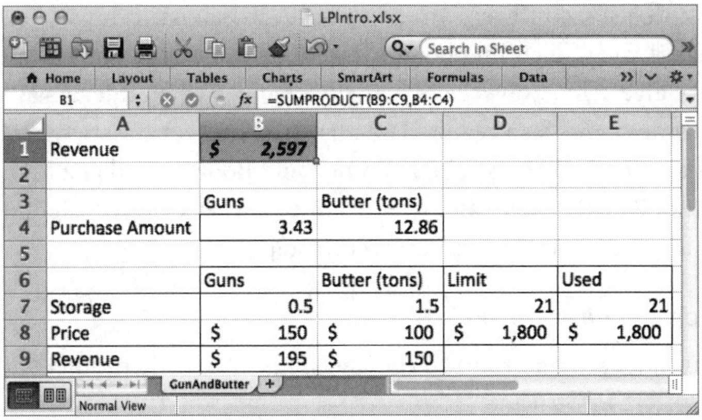

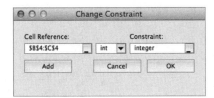

Figure 4-13: Optimized guns and butter workbook

But You Can't Make 3.43 Guns

Now, your French alter ego is most likely shouting, "*Zut alors!*" Why? Because you can't make 43 percent of a gun. And I concede this point.

When working with linear programs, the fractional solutions can sometimes be an annoyance. If you were producing guns and butter in the millions, the decimal could be ignored without too much danger of infeasibility or revenue changes. But for this problem, the numbers are small enough to where you really need Solver to make them integers.

So, hopping back into the Solver window, add a constraint to force the decision cells B4:C4 to be integers (see Figure 4-14). Click OK to return to the Solver Parameters window.

Figure 4-14: Making the guns and butter decisions integers

Under the Options section next to Simplex LP, make sure that the Ignore Integer Constraints box is not checked. Press OK.

Press Solve and a new solution pops up. At $2,580, you've only lost about $17. Not bad! Note that by forcing the decisions to be integers, you can never do better, only worse, because you're tightening up the possible solutions.

Guns have moved up to an even 4 while butter has dropped to 12. And while the budget is completely used up, note that you've got a spare 1 cubic meter of storage left in the cellar.

So why not just make your decisions integers all the time? Well, sometimes you just don't need them. For instance, if you're blending liquids, fractions can be just fine.

Also, behind the scenes the algorithm Solver uses actually changes when integers are introduced, and performance degrades as a result. The algorithm Solver uses when it encounters the integer or binary constraints is called "Branch and Bound," and at a high level, it has to run the simplex algorithm over and over again on pieces of your original problem, rooting around for integer-feasible solutions at each step.

Let's Make the Problem Non-Linear for Kicks

Even though you've added an integer constraint to the decisions, the basic problem at hand is still a linear one.

What if you got a $500 bonus from your contact Pierre if you were able to bring him 5 or more guns each month? Well, you can place an IF statement in the revenue function that checks gun production in cell B4:

```
=SUMPRODUCT(B9:C9,B4:C4) + IF(B4>=5,500,0)
```

Once you tack on that IF statement, the objective function becomes non-linear. By graphing the IF statement in Figure 4-15, you can easily see the large non-linear discontinuity at 5 guns.

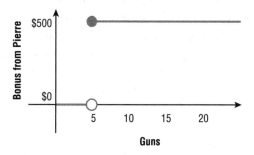

Figure 4-15: A graph of Pierre's $500 bonus

If you were to open Solver and use Simplex LP again to solve this problem, Excel would politely complain that "the linearity conditions required by this LP Solver are not satisfied" (see Figure 4-16).

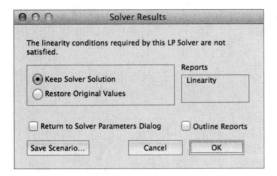

Figure 4-16: Excel won't let you put the decision variables through an IF statement when using Simplex LP.

Luckily, Solver provides two other algorithms for resolving this problem, called the "Evolutionary" and "GRG Nonlinear" algorithms. You'll give the evolutionary approach a shot here, with which you're already familiar if you've worked through Chapter 2. (In Excel 2007, since there is no algorithm selection box, leaving the Assume Linear Model box *unchecked* will activate a non-linear optimization algorithm.)

The way an evolutionary algorithm works is loosely modeled on the way evolution works in biology:

- Generate a pool of initial solutions (kind of like a "gene pool"), some feasible and some infeasible.
- Each solution has some level of fitness for survival.
- Solutions breed through *crossover*, meaning components are selected and combined from two or three existing solutions.
- Solutions *mutate* to create new solutions.
- Some amount of *local search* takes place, wherein new solutions are generated within the close vicinity of the current best solution in the population.
- *Selection* occurs when randomly selected poor performing candidate solutions are dropped from the gene pool.

Note that this approach does not inherently require that the problem structure be linear, quadratic, or otherwise. To an extent, the problem can be treated like a black box.

What that means is that when modeling a linear program in Excel, you're limited to things like the +/- signs, the SUM and AVERAGE formulas, and the SUMPRODUCT formula, where only one range contains decisions. But with the evolutionary solver, your formula choices expand to just about anything your little heart desires, including these useful non-linear functions:

- Logical checks:
  - IF
  - COUNTIF
  - SUMIF
- Statistical functions:
  - MIN
  - MAX
  - MEDIAN
  - LARGE
  - NORMDIST, BINOMDIST, and so on
- Lookup functions:
  - VLOOKUP
  - HLOOKUP
  - OFFSET
  - MATCH
  - INDEX

Now, I know you're getting pumped, so let me deflate the excitement just a little bit. There are a number of problems with the evolutionary solver:

- It gives no guarantees that it can find an optimal solution. All it does is keep track of the best solution in a population until time runs out, until the population hasn't changed enough in a while to merit continuing, or until you kill Solver with the Esc key. You can modify these "stopping criteria" in the evolutionary algorithm options section of Excel Solver.
- The evolutionary solver can be quite slow. With complex feasible regions, it often barfs, unable to find even a good starting place.
- In order to get the evolutionary algorithm to work well in Excel, you should specify hard bounds for each decision variable. If you have a decision that's more or less unbounded, you have to pick a really large number to bound it.

Concerning this last bullet point, for the guns and butter problem, you should add a constraint that both decisions must stay below 25, giving the new setup pictured in Figure 4-17.

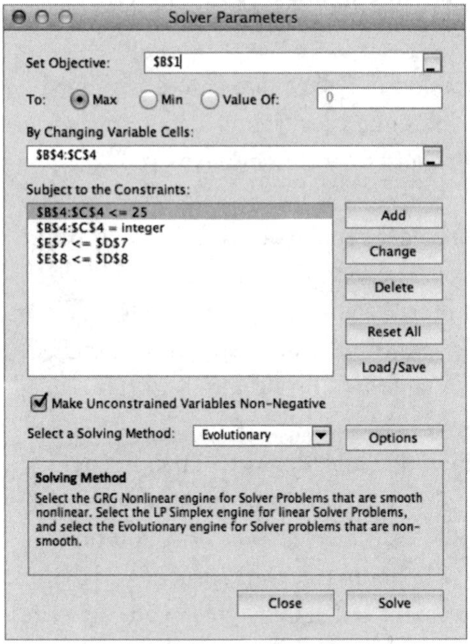

Figure 4-17: Formulation for the evolutionary solver

Press OK then Solve. The algorithm kicks off and should eventually find a solution of 6 guns and 9 tons of butter. So the evolutionary algorithm decided to take Pierre up on his $500 bonus. Nice! But notice that even on such a small problem, this took a while. About 30 seconds on my laptop. Think about what that might mean for a production model.

There's a Monster at the End of This Chapter

Okay, so that's an imaginary problem. In the next section, I'm going to demonstrate the powers of Solver on something a bit meatier. You'll also spend time learning how to model non-linear functions (such as Pierre's $500 gun bonus) in linear ways, so that you can still use the fast Simplex LP algorithm.

If you're chomping at the bit to move on to another topic, you now know most of what you need to know to succeed in the following chapters. Stick around at least through the If-Then and the "Big M" Constraint section of this chapter in order to learn what you need for Chapter 5 on clustering in graphs. Or, better yet, strap in and work through all the remaining problems here! But be warned, the last two business rules modeled in this chapter are monsters.

OTHER TOOLS

Huge models don't fit very well in Excel. The version of Solver that comes packaged with Excel allows only 100 – 200 decision variables and constraints, depending on the version you're running. That's going to limit the size of the problems you can attack in this book.

If you want to go larger in Excel, you can buy a bigger version of Solver from Frontline Systems. Even better, if you're on a Windows box, use OpenSolver just as you'll do in the later sections of this chapter. OpenSolver, introduced in Chapter 1, calls an open source solver called COIN Branch and Cut (`http://www.coin-or.org/`) that is excellent for midsized optimization problems. I've used OpenSolver on hundreds of thousands of variables effectively.

Other beefier linear programming engines include Gurobi and CPLEX. I generally recommend that developers and other people who like their software "in the cloud" check out Gurobi, whereas CPLEX, owned by IBM, is the go-to enterprise solution.

Interfacing with these industrial strength tools happens in all sorts of ways. For instance, CPLEX comes packaged with an environment called OPL where you can write models in a specialized language that's got excellent hooks into spreadsheets. There are plenty of hooks into programming languages for embedding these algorithms and models within production systems.

My favorite tool for plugging into the heavy-duty solvers like CPLEX and Gurobi is called AIMMS (`www.AIMMS.com`). The software lets you build out optimization models and then slap a user interface on them without having to write code. Also, the software can talk to spreadsheets and databases.

For the rest of this book, you're going to stick with Excel and Solver, but just know that there are cutting-edge modeling environments out there for solving bigger problems, should your needs grow beyond what Excel can handle.

Fresh from the Grove to Your Glass...with a Pit Stop through a Blending Model

NOTE

The Excel workbook used in this chapter, "OrangeJuiceBlending.xlsx," is available for download at the book's website at `www.wiley.com/go/datasmart`. This workbook includes all the initial data if you want to work from that. Or you can just read along using the sheets I've already put together in the workbook."

When you were a child, perhaps there came that day when someone explained to you that Santa Claus didn't exist, outside of men with bad rosacea dressed up at the mall.

Well, today I'm going to shatter another belief: your not-from-concentrate premium orange juice was not hand squeezed. In fact, the pulp in it is probably from different oranges than the juice, and the juice has been pulled from different vats and blended according to mathematical models to ensure that each carafe you drink tastes the same as the last.

Consistent taste in OJ year round isn't something that just anyone can pull off. Oranges aren't in season in Florida year round. And at different times of the year, different orange varietals are ripe. Pull fruit too early and it tastes "green." Get fruit from another country that's in season instead, and the juice might be another color. Or sweeter. Consumers demand consistency. That might be easy with Sunny D, but how do you get that out of a bunch of vats of freshly squeezed, very chilled orange juice?

You Use a Blending Model

On the hit TV show *Downton Abbey*, the wealthy Lord Grantham invests all his family's money in a single railroad venture. It's risky. And he loses big. Apparently in the early 1900s, diversification was not a popular concept.

By averaging the risk and return of an investment portfolio across multiple investments, the odds of you striking it rich probably decrease, but so do the odds of your going broke. This same approach applies to orange juice production today.

Juice can be procured from all around the world, from different oranges in different seasons. Each product has different specs—some might be a bit more tart, some a bit more astringent, and others might be sickly sweet. By blending this "portfolio" of juices, a single consistent taste can be maintained.

That's the problem you'll work through in this section. How do you build a blending model that reduces cost while maintaining quality, and what type of wrenches might get thrown into the works that would need to get mathematically formulated along the way?

Let's Start with Some Specs

Let's say you're an analyst working at JuiceLand and your boss, Mr. Juice R. Landingsly III (your company is full of nepotism), has asked you to plan the procurement of juice from your suppliers for January, February, and March of this coming year. Along with this assignment, Mr. Landingsly hands you a sheet of specs from your suppliers containing the country of origin and varietal, the quantity available for purchase over the next three months, and the price and shipping cost per 1,000 gallons.

The specs sheet rates the color of the juice on a scale from one to ten and three flavor components:

- **Brix/Acid ratio:** Brix is a measure of sweetness in the juice, so Brix/Acid ratio is a measure of sweetness to tartness, which in the end, is really what orange juice is all about.
- **Acid (%):** Acid as a percentage of the juice is broken out individually, because at a certain point, it doesn't really matter how sweet the juice is, it's still too acidic.
- **Astringency (1–10 scale):** A measure of the "green" quality of the juice. It's that bitter, unripe, planty flavor that can creep in. This scale is assessed by a panel of tasters at each juicing facility on a scale of 1–10.

All of these specifications are represented in the specifications spreadsheet pictured in Figure 4-18.

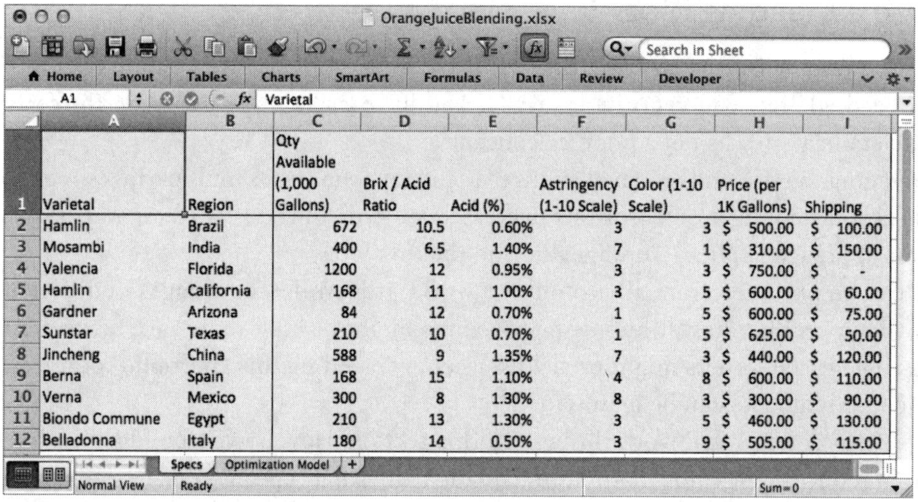

Varietal	Region	Qty Available (1,000 Gallons)	Brix / Acid Ratio	Acid (%)	Astringency (1-10 Scale)	Color (1-10 Scale)	Price (per 1K Gallons)	Shipping
Hamlin	Brazil	672	10.5	0.60%	3	3	$ 500.00	$ 100.00
Mosambi	India	400	6.5	1.40%	7	1	$ 310.00	$ 150.00
Valencia	Florida	1200	12	0.95%	3	3	$ 750.00	$ -
Hamlin	California	168	11	1.00%	3	5	$ 600.00	$ 60.00
Gardner	Arizona	84	12	0.70%	1	5	$ 600.00	$ 75.00
Sunstar	Texas	210	10	0.70%	1	5	$ 625.00	$ 50.00
Jincheng	China	588	9	1.35%	7	3	$ 440.00	$ 120.00
Berna	Spain	168	15	1.10%	4	8	$ 600.00	$ 110.00
Verna	Mexico	300	8	1.30%	8	3	$ 300.00	$ 90.00
Biondo Commune	Egypt	210	13	1.30%	3	5	$ 460.00	$ 130.00
Belladonna	Italy	180	14	0.50%	3	9	$ 505.00	$ 115.00

Figure 4-18: The specs sheet for raw orange juice procurement

Whatever juice you choose to buy will be shipped to your blending facility in large, aseptic chilled tanks, either by cargo ship or rail. That's why there isn't a shipping cost for the Florida Valencia oranges—the blending facility is located in your Florida grove (where, back in the good old days, you grew all the oranges you needed).

Look over the specs pictured in Figure 4-18. What can you say about them? The juice is coming from an international selection of varietals and localities.

Some juice, such as that from Mexico, is cheap but a bit off. In Mexico's case, the astringency is very high. In other cases, such as the Sunstar oranges from Texas, the juice is sweeter and less astringent, but the cost is higher.

Which juice you buy for the next three months depends on some considerations:

- If you're minimizing cost, can you buy whatever you want?
- How much juice do you need?
- What are the flavor and color bounds for each batch?

Coming Back to Consistency

Through taste tests and numerous customer interviews, JuiceLand has determined what their orange juice should taste and look like. Any deviation outside the allowable range of these specs and customers are more likely to label the juice as generic, cheap, or even worse, *from concentrate*. Eek.

Mr. Landingsly III lays out the requirements for you:

- He wants the lowest cost purchase plan for January, February, and March that meets a projected demand of 600,000 gallons of juice in January and February and 700,000 gallons in March.
- JuiceLand has entered an agreement with the state of Florida which provides the company tax incentives so long as the company buys at least 40 percent of its juice each month from Florida Valencia growers. Under no circumstances are you to violate this agreement.
- The Brix/Acid ratio (BAR) must stay between 11.5 and 12.5 in each month's blend.
- The acid level must remain between 0.75 and 1 percent.
- The astringency level must stay at 4 or lower.
- Color must remain between 4.5 and 5.5. Not too watery, not too dark.

Real quickly shove those requirements into an outline of an LP formulation:

- **Objective:** Minimize procurement costs.
- **Decisions:** Amount of each juice to buy each month
- **Constraints:**
    - Demand
    - Supply
    - Florida Valencia requirement
    - Flavor
    - Color

Putting the Data into Excel

To model the problem in Excel, the first thing you need to do is create a new tab to house the formulation. Call it **Optimization Model**.

In cell A2, under the label **Total Cost**, put a placeholder for the objective.

Below that, in cell A5, paste everything from the Specs tab, but insert four columns between the Region and Qty Available columns to make way for the decision variables as well as their totals by row.

The first three columns will be labeled January, February, and March, while the fourth will be their sum, labeled Total Ordered. In the Total Ordered column, you need to sum the three cells to the left, so for example in the case of Brazilian Hamlin oranges, cell F6 contains:

```
=SUM(C6:E6)
```

You can drag cell F6 down through F16. Placing some conditional formatting on the range C6:E16, the resulting spreadsheet looks like the one in Figure 4-19.

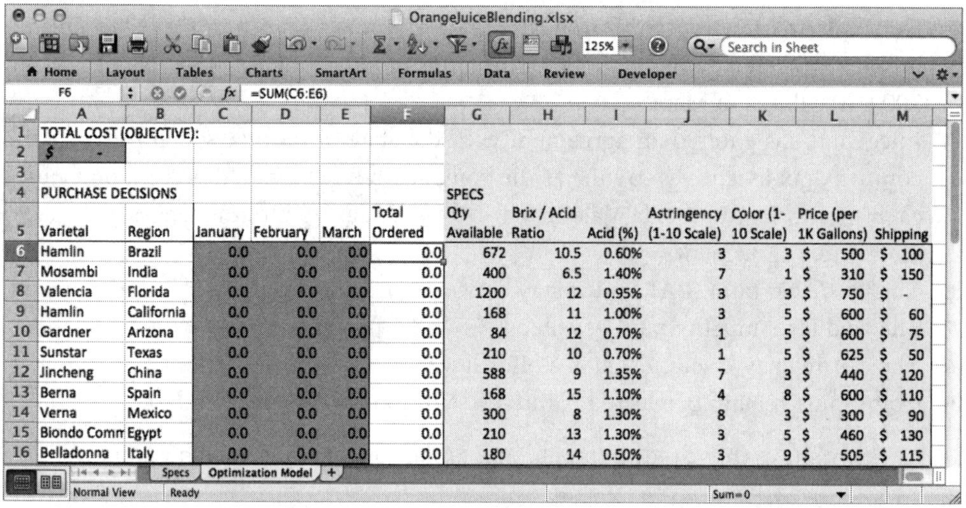

	A	B	C	D	E	F	G	H	I	J	K	L	M
1	TOTAL COST (OBJECTIVE):												
2	$ -												
3													
4	PURCHASE DECISIONS						SPECS						
5	Varietal	Region	January	February	March	Total Ordered	Qty Available	Brix / Acid Ratio	Acid (%)	Astringency (1-10 Scale)	Color (1-10 Scale)	Price (per 1K Gallons)	Shipping
6	Hamlin	Brazil	0.0	0.0	0.0	0.0	672	10.5	0.60%	3	3	$ 500	$ 100
7	Mosambi	India	0.0	0.0	0.0	0.0	400	6.5	1.40%	7	1	$ 310	$ 150
8	Valencia	Florida	0.0	0.0	0.0	0.0	1200	12	0.95%	3	3	$ 750	$ -
9	Hamlin	California	0.0	0.0	0.0	0.0	168	11	1.00%	3	5	$ 600	$ 60
10	Gardner	Arizona	0.0	0.0	0.0	0.0	84	12	0.70%	1	5	$ 600	$ 75
11	Sunstar	Texas	0.0	0.0	0.0	0.0	210	10	0.70%	1	5	$ 625	$ 50
12	Jincheng	China	0.0	0.0	0.0	0.0	588	9	1.35%	7	3	$ 440	$ 120
13	Berna	Spain	0.0	0.0	0.0	0.0	168	15	1.10%	4	8	$ 600	$ 110
14	Verna	Mexico	0.0	0.0	0.0	0.0	300	8	1.30%	8	3	$ 300	$ 90
15	Biondo Comm	Egypt	0.0	0.0	0.0	0.0	210	13	1.30%	3	5	$ 460	$ 130
16	Belladonna	Italy	0.0	0.0	0.0	0.0	180	14	0.50%	3	9	$ 505	$ 115

Figure 4-19: Setting up the blending spreadsheet

Below the monthly purchase fields, add some fields for monthly procurement and shipping costs. For January, place the monthly procurement cost in cell C17 as follows:

```
=SUMPRODUCT(C6:C16,$L6:$L16)
```

Once again, since only the C column is a decision variable, this calculation is linear. Similarly, you need to add the following calculation to C18 to calculate shipping costs for the month:

```
=SUMPRODUCT(C6:C16,$M6:$M16)
```

Dragging these formulas across columns D and E, you'll have all of your procurement and shipping costs calculated. You can then set the objective function in cell A2 as the sum of C17:E18. The resulting spreadsheet is pictured in Figure 4-20.

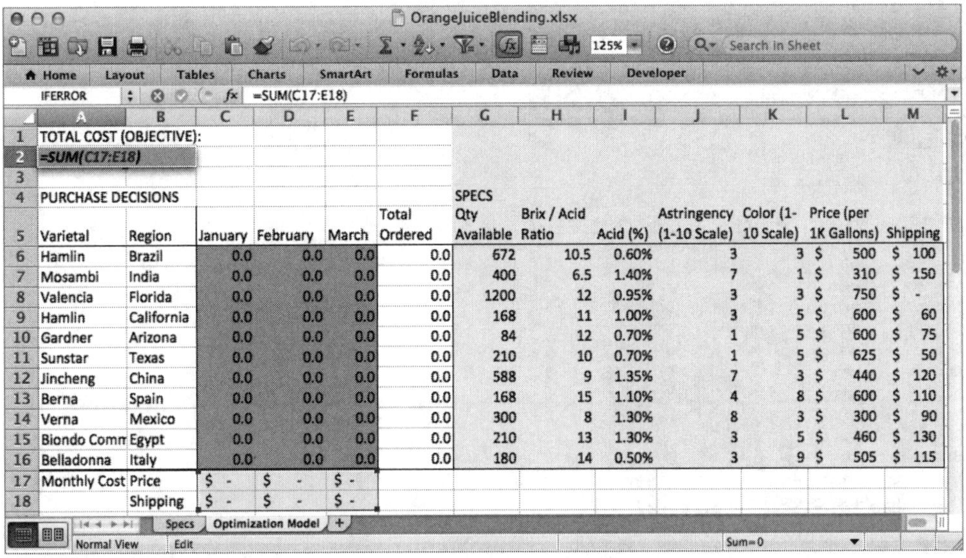

	A	B	C	D	E	F	G	H	I	J	K	L	M
1	TOTAL COST (OBJECTIVE):												
2	=SUM(C17:E18)												
3													
4	PURCHASE DECISIONS						SPECS						
5	Varietal	Region	January	February	March	Total Ordered	Qty Available	Brix / Acid Ratio	Acid (%)	Astringency (1-10 Scale)	Color (1-10 Scale)	Price (per 1K Gallons)	Shipping
6	Hamlin	Brazil	0.0	0.0	0.0	0.0	672	10.5	0.60%	3	3	$ 500	$ 100
7	Mosambi	India	0.0	0.0	0.0	0.0	400	6.5	1.40%	7	1	$ 310	$ 150
8	Valencia	Florida	0.0	0.0	0.0	0.0	1200	12	0.95%	3	3	$ 750	$ -
9	Hamlin	California	0.0	0.0	0.0	0.0	168	11	1.00%	3	5	$ 600	$ 60
10	Gardner	Arizona	0.0	0.0	0.0	0.0	84	12	0.70%	1	5	$ 600	$ 75
11	Sunstar	Texas	0.0	0.0	0.0	0.0	210	10	0.70%	1	5	$ 625	$ 50
12	Jincheng	China	0.0	0.0	0.0	0.0	588	9	1.35%	7	3	$ 440	$ 120
13	Berna	Spain	0.0	0.0	0.0	0.0	168	15	1.10%	4	8	$ 600	$ 110
14	Verna	Mexico	0.0	0.0	0.0	0.0	300	8	1.30%	8	3	$ 300	$ 90
15	Biondo Comm	Egypt	0.0	0.0	0.0	0.0	210	13	1.30%	3	5	$ 460	$ 130
16	Belladonna	Italy	0.0	0.0	0.0	0.0	180	14	0.50%	3	9	$ 505	$ 115
17	Monthly Cost	Price	$ -	$ -	$ -								
18		Shipping	$ -	$ -	$ -								

Figure 4-20: Cost calculations added to the juice blending worksheet

Now add the calculations you need to satisfy the demand and Florida Valencia constraints. On row 20, sum the total quantity of juice procured on that month, and on row 21, place the required levels of 600, 600, and 700, respectively into columns C through E.

As for total Valencia ordered from Florida, map C8:E8 to cells C23:E23 and place the required 40 percent of total demand (240, 240, 280) below the values.

This yields the spreadsheet shown in Figure 4-21.

Now that you've covered the objective function, the decision variables, and the supply, demand, and Valencia calculations, all you have left are the taste and color calculations based on what you order.

Let's tackle Brix/Acid ratio first. In cell B27, put the minimum BAR of the blend, which is 11.5. Then in cell C27, you can use the SUMPRODUCT of the January orders (column C) with their Brix/Acid specs in column H, divided by *total demand*, to get the average Brix/Acid ratio.

WARNING

Do not divide through by total ordered, as that's a function of your decision variables! Decisions divided by decisions are highly non-linear.

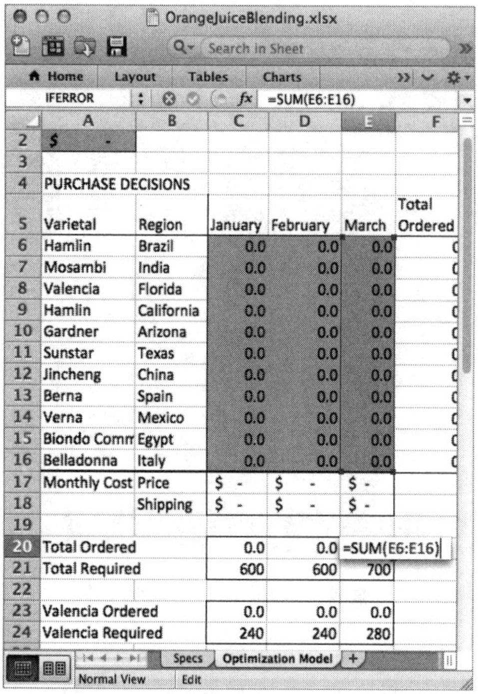

Figure 4-21: Demand and Valencia calculations added

Just remember, you'll be setting the total ordered amount equal to projected demand as a constraint, so there's no reason not to just divide through by demand when getting the average BAR of the blend. Thus, cell C27 looks as follows:

```
=SUMPRODUCT(C$6:C$16,$H$6:$H$16)/C$21
```

You can drag that formula to the right through column E. In column F, you'll finish off the row by typing in the maximum BAR of **12.5**. You can then repeat these steps to set up calculations for acid, astringency, and color in rows 28 through 30. The resulting spreadsheet is pictured in Figure 4-22.

Setting Up the Problem in Solver

All right, so you have all the data and calculations you need to set up the blending problem in Solver. The first thing you need to specify in Solver is the total cost function in A2 that you're minimizing.

The decision variables are the monthly purchase amounts of each varietal housed in the cell range C6:E16. Once again, these decisions can't be negative, so make sure the

Make Unconstrained Variables Non-Negative box is checked (Assume Linear Model is checked in Excel 2007).

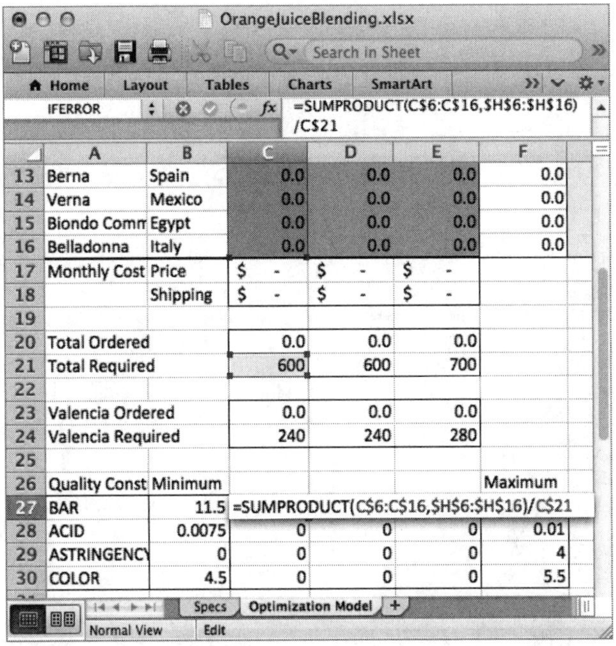

	A	B	C	D	E	F
13	Berna	Spain	0.0	0.0	0.0	0.0
14	Verna	Mexico	0.0	0.0	0.0	0.0
15	Biondo Comm	Egypt	0.0	0.0	0.0	0.0
16	Belladonna	Italy	0.0	0.0	0.0	0.0
17	Monthly Cost	Price	$ -	$ -	$ -	
18		Shipping	$ -	$ -	$ -	
19						
20	Total Ordered		0.0	0.0	0.0	
21	Total Required		600	600	700	
22						
23	Valencia Ordered		0.0	0.0	0.0	
24	Valencia Required		240	240	280	
25						
26	Quality Const	Minimum				Maximum
27	BAR		11.5 =SUMPRODUCT(C$6:C$16,$H$6:$H$16)/C$21			
28	ACID	0.0075	0	0	0	0.01
29	ASTRINGENCY	0	0	0	0	4
30	COLOR	4.5	0	0	0	5.5

Figure 4-22: Adding taste and color constraints to the worksheet

When it comes to adding constraints, this problem really deviates from the guns and butter example. There are a lot of them.

The first constraint is that the orders on row 20 must equal demand on row 21 for each month. Similarly, the Florida Valencia orders on row 23 should be greater than or equal to the required amount on row 24. Also, the total quantity ordered from each geography, calculated in F6:F16, should be less than or equal to what's available in G6:G16.

With supply and demand constraints added, you need to add the taste and color constraints.

Now, Excel won't let you put a constraint on two differently sized ranges, so if you enter C27:E30 ≥ B27:B30, it's not going to understand how to handle that. (I find this terribly irritating.) Instead, you have to add constraints for columns C, D, and E individually. For example, for January orders you have C27:C30 ≥ B27:B30 and C27:C30 ≤ F27:F30. And the same goes for February and March.

After you add all those constraints, make sure that Simplex LP is the chosen solving method. The final formulation should look like Figure 4-23.

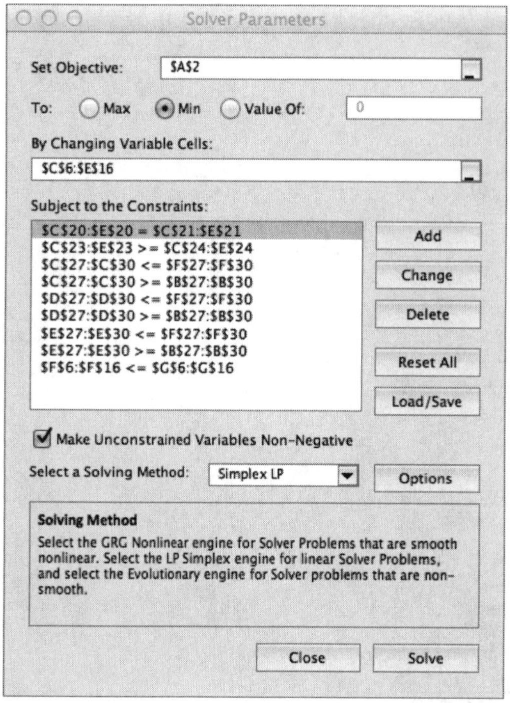

Figure 4-23: The populated Solver dialog for the blending problem

Solving, you get an optimal cost of $1.23 million dollars in procurement costs (see Figure 4-24). Note how Florida Valencia purchases hug their lower bound. Obviously, these oranges aren't the best deal, but the model is being forced to make do for tax purposes. The second most popular orange is the Verna out of Mexico, which is dirt cheap but otherwise pretty awful. The model balances this bitter, acidic juice with mixtures of Belladonna, Biondo Commune, and Gardner, which are all milder, sweeter, and superior in color. Pretty neat!

Lowering Your Standards

Excited, you bring your optimal blend plan to your manager, Mr. Landingsly III. You explain how you arrived at your answer, and he eyes it with suspicion. Even though you claim it's optimal, he wants you to shave an additional 5 percent off the cost. He explains his seemingly nonsensical position using mostly sports analogies about "playing all four quarters" and "giving 110 percent."

There's no use arguing against sports analogies. If $1,170,000 is the sweet spot, then so be it. You explain that there's no way to achieve that within the current quality bounds, and he merely grunts and tells you to "bend reality a bit."

Hmmm...

You return to your spreadsheet flustered.

How do you get the best blend for a cost of $1,170,000?

After the heart to heart with Mr. Landingsly, cost is no longer an objective. It's a constraint! So what's the objective?

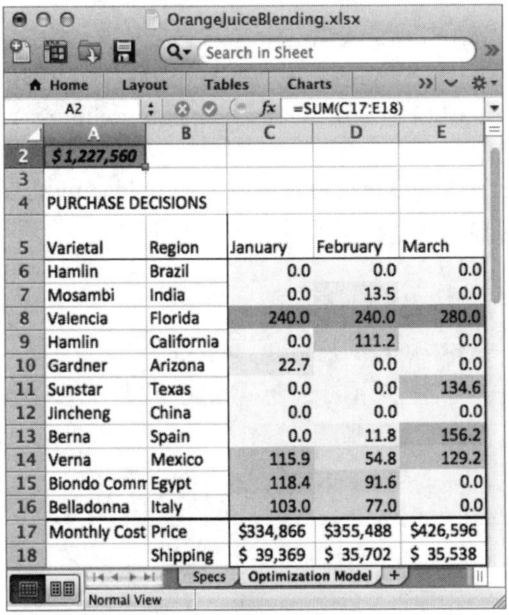

	A	B	C	D	E
2	$1,227,560				
3					
4	PURCHASE DECISIONS				
5	Varietal	Region	January	February	March
6	Hamlin	Brazil	0.0	0.0	0.0
7	Mosambi	India	0.0	13.5	0.0
8	Valencia	Florida	240.0	240.0	280.0
9	Hamlin	California	0.0	111.2	0.0
10	Gardner	Arizona	22.7	0.0	0.0
11	Sunstar	Texas	0.0	0.0	134.6
12	Jincheng	China	0.0	0.0	0.0
13	Berna	Spain	0.0	11.8	156.2
14	Verna	Mexico	115.9	54.8	129.2
15	Biondo Comm	Egypt	118.4	91.6	0.0
16	Belladonna	Italy	103.0	77.0	0.0
17	Monthly Cost	Price	$334,866	$355,488	$426,596
18		Shipping	$ 39,369	$ 35,702	$ 35,538

Figure 4-24: Solution to the orange juice-blending problem

Your new objective based on the bossman's grunts appears to be finding the solution that *degrades quality the least* for 1.17 million dollars. And the way to implement that is to stick a decision variable in the model that loosens up the quality constraints.

Go ahead and copy the Optimization Model tab into a new sheet, called Relaxed Quality. You don't have to change a whole lot to make this work.

Take a moment and think about how you might change things around to accommodate the new relaxed quality objective and cost constraint. Don't peak ahead until your head hurts!

All right.

The first thing you do is pop $1,117,000 as the cost limit in cell B2 right next to the old objective. Also, copy and paste *values* of the old minima and maxima for taste and color into columns H and I, respectively. And in column G on rows 27 through 30, add a new decision variable called % **Relaxed**.

Now consider how you might use the Brix/Acid relaxation decision in cell G27 to relax the lower bound of 11.5. Currently, the allowable band of Brix/Acid is 11.5 to 12.5, which is a width of 1. So a 10 percent broadening at the bottom of the constraint would make the minimum 11.4.

Following this approach, replace the minimum in B27 with this formula:

```
=H27-G27*(I27-H27)
```

This takes the old minimum, now in H27, and subtracts from it the percent relaxation times the distance of the old maximum from the old minimum (I27 minus H27). You can copy this formula down through row 30. Similarly, implement the relaxed maximum in column F.

For the objective, take the average of the relaxation decisions in G27:G30. Placing this calculation in cell D2, the new sheet now looks like Figure 4-25.

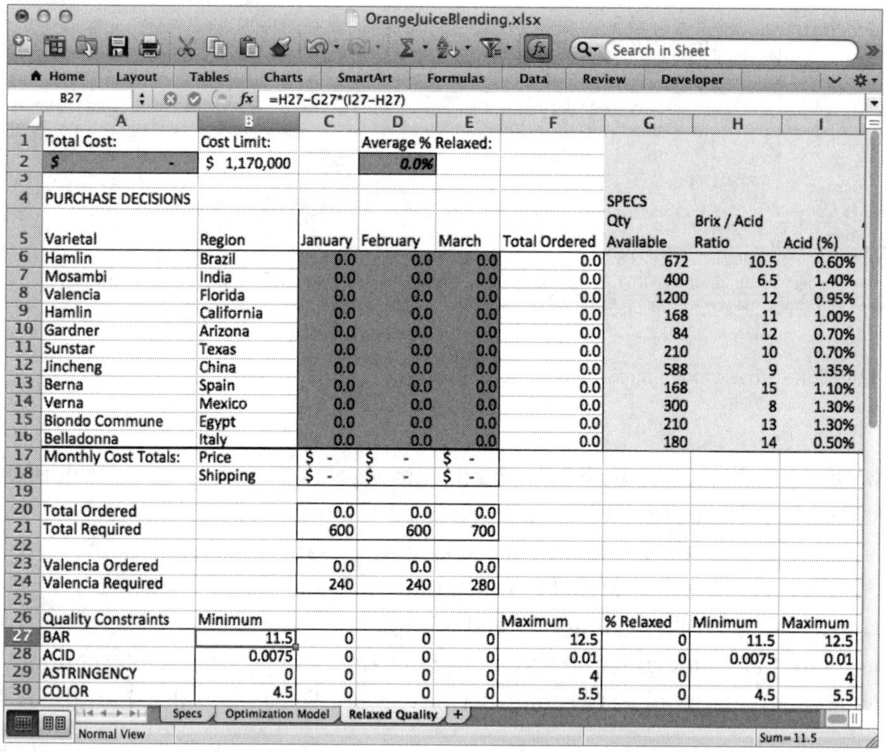

	A	B	C	D	E	F	G	H	I
1	Total Cost:	Cost Limit:		Average % Relaxed:					
2	$ -	$ 1,170,000		0.0%					
3									
4	PURCHASE DECISIONS						SPECS		
5	Varietal	Region	January	February	March	Total Ordered	Qty Available	Brix / Acid Ratio	Acid (%)
6	Hamlin	Brazil	0.0	0.0	0.0	0.0	672	10.5	0.60%
7	Mosambi	India	0.0	0.0	0.0	0.0	400	6.5	1.40%
8	Valencia	Florida	0.0	0.0	0.0	0.0	1200	12	0.95%
9	Hamlin	California	0.0	0.0	0.0	0.0	168	11	1.00%
10	Gardner	Arizona	0.0	0.0	0.0	0.0	84	12	0.70%
11	Sunstar	Texas	0.0	0.0	0.0	0.0	210	10	0.70%
12	Jincheng	China	0.0	0.0	0.0	0.0	588	9	1.35%
13	Berna	Spain	0.0	0.0	0.0	0.0	168	15	1.10%
14	Verna	Mexico	0.0	0.0	0.0	0.0	300	8	1.30%
15	Biondo Commune	Egypt	0.0	0.0	0.0	0.0	210	13	1.30%
16	Belladonna	Italy	0.0	0.0	0.0	0.0	180	14	0.50%
17	Monthly Cost Totals:	Price	$ -	$ -	$ -				
18		Shipping	$ -	$ -	$ -				
19									
20	Total Ordered		0.0	0.0	0.0				
21	Total Required		600	600	700				
22									
23	Valencia Ordered		0.0	0.0	0.0				
24	Valencia Required		240	240	280				
25									
26	Quality Constraints	Minimum				Maximum	% Relaxed	Minimum	Maximum
27	BAR	11.5	0	0	0	12.5	0	11.5	12.5
28	ACID	0.0075	0	0	0	0.01	0	0.0075	0.01
29	ASTRINGENCY	0	0	0	0	4	0	0	4
30	COLOR	4.5	0	0	0	5.5	0	4.5	5.5

Figure 4-25: Relaxed quality model

Open Solver and change the objective to minimize the average relaxation of the quality bounds calculated in cell D2. You also need to add G27:G30 to the list of decision variables and set the cost in A2 as less than or equal to the limit in B2. This new formulation is pictured in Figure 4-26.

To recap then, you've transformed your previous cost objective into a constraint with an upper bound. You've also transformed your hard constraints on quality into soft constraints that can be relaxed by altering G27:G30. Your objective in D2 is to minimize the average amount you must degrade quality across your specs. Press Solve.

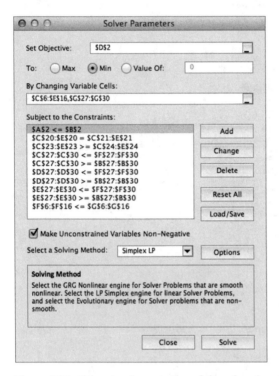

Figure 4-26: Solver implementation of the relaxed quality model

Excel finds that with an average relaxation of 35 percent on each end of the bounds, a solution can be achieved that meets the cost constraint, as shown in Figure 4-27.

Now that you have the model set up, one thing you can do is provide more information to Mr. Landingsly than he asked for. You know that for $1.23 million you get a quality degradation of 0 percent, so why not step down the cost in increments of 20 grand or so and see what quality degradation results? At $1.21 million it's 5 percent, at $1.19 million it's 17 percent, and so forth, including 35 percent, 54 percent, 84 percent, and 170 percent. If you try to dip below $1.1 million the model becomes infeasible.

Creating a new tab called Frontier, you can paste all these solutions and graph them to illustrate the trade-off between cost and quality (see Figure 4-28). To insert a graph like the one pictured in Figure 4-28, simply highlight the two columns of data on the Frontier sheet and insert a Smoothed Line Scatter plot from the Scatter selection in Excel (see Chapter 1 for more on inserting charts).

OrangeJuiceBlending.xlsx — A2 =SUM(C17:E18)

Total Cost:	Cost Limit:		Average % Relaxed:	
$ 1,170,000	$ 1,170,000		34.8%	
PURCHASE DECISIONS				
Varietal	Region	January	February	March
Hamlin	Brazil	79.3	77.6	90.6
Mosambi	India	73.5	48.8	56.9
Valencia	Florida	240.0	240.0	280.0
Hamlin	California	0.0	0.0	0.0
Gardner	Arizona	0.0	0.0	0.0
Sunstar	Texas	0.0	0.0	0.0
Jincheng	China	0.0	0.0	0.0
Berna	Spain	23.4	0.0	0.0
Verna	Mexico	78.0	102.5	119.5
Biondo Commune	Egypt	51.9	73.0	85.2
Belladonna	Italy	54.0	58.2	67.9
Monthly Cost Totals:	Price	$ 330,976	$327,616	$ 382,218
	Shipping	$ 41,494	$ 40,475	$ 47,221

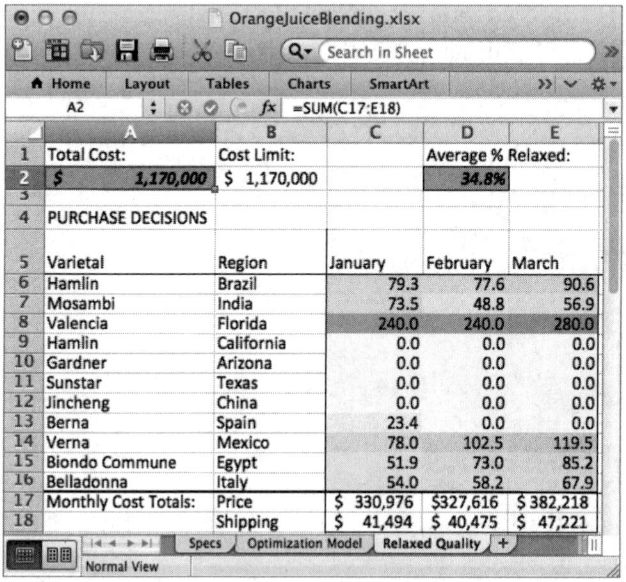

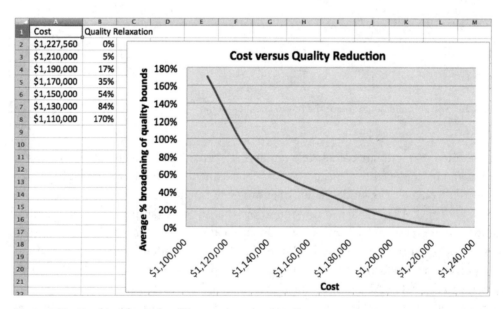

Figure 4-27: Solution to the relaxed quality model

Cost	Quality Relaxation
$1,227,560	0%
$1,210,000	5%
$1,190,000	17%
$1,170,000	35%
$1,150,000	54%
$1,130,000	84%
$1,110,000	170%

Figure 4-28: Graphing the trade-off between cost and quality

Dead Squirrel Removal: The Minimax Formulation

If you look at the relaxed quality solution for a cost bound of $1.17 million, there's a potential problem. Sure, the average relaxation across the taste and color bounds is 35 percent, but for color it's 80 percent and for Brix/Acid ratio it's 51 percent. The average hides this variability.

What you'd rather do in this situation is *minimize the maximum* relaxation across the four quality bounds. This problem is commonly called a "minimax" problem because you're minimizing a maximum, and it's fun to say really fast. Minimax, minimax, minimax.

But how can you do that? If you make your objective function MAX(G27:G30), you'll be non-linear. You could try that with the evolutionary solver, but it'll take forever to solve. It turns out there's a way to model this non-linear problem in a linear way.

First, copy the relaxed model to a new tab called **Minimax Relaxed Quality**.

Now, how many of you have had to pick up and get rid of a dead animal? Last summer I had a squirrel die in my blisteringly hot attic here in Atlanta, and the smell knocked many brave men and women to their knees.

How did I get rid of that squirrel?

I refused to touch it or deal with it directly.

Instead, I scooped it from below with a shovel and pressed down on it from above with a broom handle. It was like picking it up with giant salad tongs or chopsticks. Ultimately, this pincer move had the same effect as grabbing the squirrel with my bare hands, but it was less gross.

You can handle the calculation MAX(G27:G30) in the same way I handled that dead squirrel. Since you're no longer computing the average of G27:G30, you can clear out the objective in D2. That's where you would compute the MAX() function, but you can leave the cell blank. It needs to be lifted up to the max somehow without being touched directly.

Here's how you can do it:

1. Set the objective, D2, to be a decision variable, so that the algorithm can move it as needed. Keep in mind that since you've set the model to be a minimization, Simplex is going to try to send this cell down as far as it can go.

2. Set G27:G30 to be less than or equal to D2 using the Add Constraint window. D2 must go in the right side of the Add Constraint dialogue for Excel to allow an unequal number of cells (4 cells in a range on the left side and 1 upper bound on the right side). Unlike elsewhere in this chapter where you couldn't use two different sized ranges in a constraint, this works because Excel has been designed to understand the case where the right side of the constraint is a single cell.

Okay, so what did you just do?

Well, as the objective function of the model, simplex will try to force D2 down to 0, while the taste and color constraints will force it up to maintain a workable blend. Where will cell D2 land? The lowest it can go will be the maximum of the four relaxation percentages in G27 through G30.

Once the objective strikes that maximum, the only way the Solver can make progress is by forcing that maximum down. Just like with the squirrel, the constraints are the shovel under the squirrel and the minimization objective is the mop handle pressing down. Hence, you get the term "minimax." Pretty cool, ain't it? Or gross...depending on how you feel about dead squirrels.

Now that you've cleared out the formula in D2, the implementation in Solver (making D2 a variable and adding G27:G30 ≤ D2) looks like Figure 4-29.

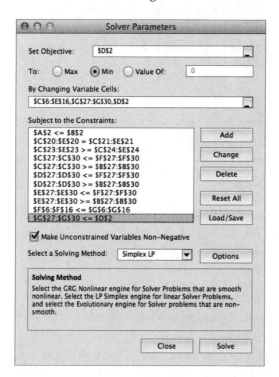

Figure 4-29: Solver setup for minimax quality reduction

Solving this setup yields a quality reduction of 58.7 percent, which, while greater than the average 34.8 percent from the previous model, is a vast improvement over the worst-case color relaxation of 84 percent.

If-Then and the "Big M" Constraint

Now that you have a feel for vanilla linear modeling, you can add some integers. Mr. Landingsly III eventually signs off on your original procurement plan, but when you deliver it to the supply chain team, their eyes start twitching uncontrollably.

They refuse to procure juice in any given month from more than four suppliers. Too much paperwork, apparently.

Okay, so how do you handle this within the model?

Take a minute and think about what model modifications might be required before moving on.

Start by copying the original Optimization Model sheet to a new tab called Optimization Model (Limit 4).

Now, regardless of how much juice you buy from a supplier, whether it's 1,000 gallons or 1,000,000 gallons, that counts as an order from one supplier. In other words, you need to find a way to flick a switch the moment you order a drop of juice from a supplier.

In integer programming, a "switch" is a binary decision variable, which is merely a cell that Solver can set to 0 or 1 only.

So what you want to do is define a range the same size as your order variables only it'll hold 0s and 1s, where a 1 is set when an order gets placed.

You can place these variables in range C34:E44. Now, assuming they're going to be set to 1 when you place an order from the supplier, you can sum up each column in row 45 and make sure the sum is less than the limit of 4, which you can toss in row 46. The resulting spreadsheet is pictured in Figure 4-30.

Here's the tricky part though. You can't use an IF formula that sets the indicator to 1 when the order quantity above is nonzero. That would be non-linear, which would force you to use the much slower evolutionary algorithm. For truly large problems with if-then constraints, the slower non-linear algorithms become useless. So you'll need to "turn on" the indicator using linear constraints instead.

But say you add a constraint to have the Brazilian Hamlin indicator variable turn on when you place an order by using the constraint C34 ≥ C6.

If C34 is supposed to be binary, then that's going to limit C6 to a max of 1 (that is, 1,000 gallons ordered).

Thus, you have to model this if-then statement, "if we order, then turn on the binary variable," using something colloquially called a "Big M" constraint. "Big M" is just a number, a big number, called M. In the case of C34, M should be big enough that you'd never order more Brazilian Hamlin than M. Well, you'll never order more juice than is available, right? For Hamlin, the available quantity is 672 thousand gallons. So make that M.

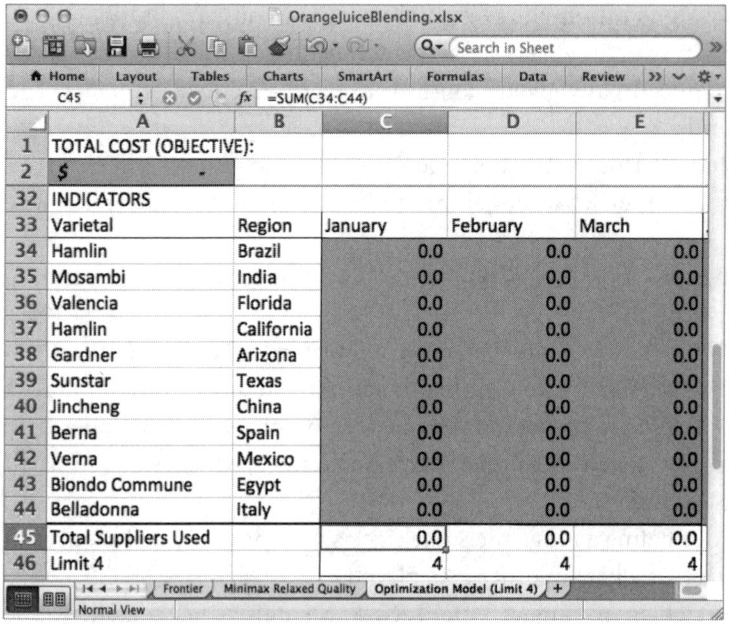

	A	B	C	D	E
1	TOTAL COST (OBJECTIVE):				
2	$ -				
32	INDICATORS				
33	Varietal	Region	January	February	March
34	Hamlin	Brazil	0.0	0.0	0.0
35	Mosambi	India	0.0	0.0	0.0
36	Valencia	Florida	0.0	0.0	0.0
37	Hamlin	California	0.0	0.0	0.0
38	Gardner	Arizona	0.0	0.0	0.0
39	Sunstar	Texas	0.0	0.0	0.0
40	Jincheng	China	0.0	0.0	0.0
41	Berna	Spain	0.0	0.0	0.0
42	Verna	Mexico	0.0	0.0	0.0
43	Biondo Commune	Egypt	0.0	0.0	0.0
44	Belladonna	Italy	0.0	0.0	0.0
45	Total Suppliers Used		0.0	0.0	0.0
46	Limit 4		4	4	4

Figure 4-30: Adding indicator variables to the spreadsheet

Then you can set a constraint where 672*C34 ≥ C6. When C6 is 0, C34 is *allowed* to be zero. And when C6 is greater than zero, C34 is *forced* to flip to 1 in order to raise the upper bound from 0 to 672.

To implement this in the spreadsheet, you set up a new range of cells in F34:H44 where you'll multiply the indicators to the left times their respective available quantities in range G6:G16. The result is pictured in Figure 4-31.

In Solver, you need to add C34:E44 to the range of decision variables. You also need to make them binary, which you accomplish by putting a `bin` constraint on the range.

To put the "Big M" constraint in effect, you set C6:E16 ≤ F34:H44. You can then check the supplier counts and make sure they're under four by setting C45:E45 ≤ C46:E46. The resulting spreadsheet is pictured in Figure 4-32.

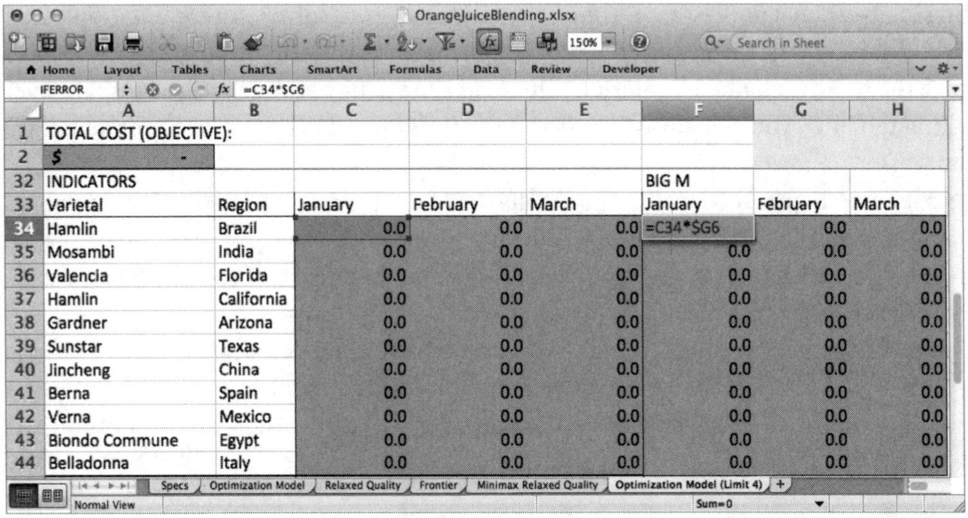

Figure 4-31: Setting up our "Big M" constraint values

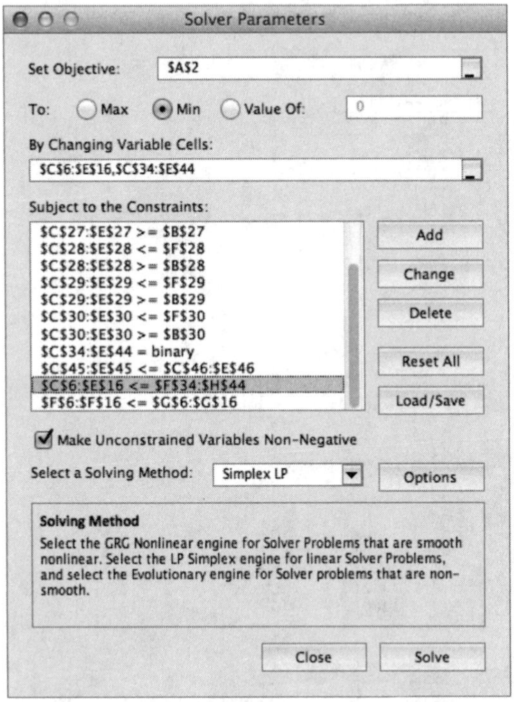

Figure 4-32: Initializing Solver

Press Solve. You'll notice that the problem takes longer to solve with the addition of the binary variables. When using integer and binary variables in your formulation, Solver will display the best "incumbent" solution it finds in the status bar. If for some reason Solver is taking too long, you can always press the Escape key and keep the best incumbent it's found so far.

As shown in Figure 4-33, the optimal solution of the model restricted to four suppliers per month is $1.24 million, about $16,000 more than the original optimum. Armed with this plan, you can return to the supply chain team and ask them if their reduced paperwork is worth an extra $16,000.

Quantifying the introduction of new business rules and constraints in this way is one of the hallmarks of employing optimization modeling in a business. You can place a dollar figure to a business practice and make an informed decision to the question, "Is it worth it?"

			OrangeJuiceBlending.xlsx					
Home	Layout	Tables	Charts	SmartArt	Formulas	Data	Review	
A2		fx	=SUM(C17:E18)					
	A	B	C	D	E	F	G	H
1	TOTAL COST (OBJECTIVE):							
2	$	1,243,658						
4	PURCHASE DECISIONS						SPECS	
							Qty	Brix / Acid
5	Varietal	Region	January	February	March	Total Orde	Available	Ratio
6	Hamlin	Brazil	0.0	0.0	0.0	0.0	672	10.5
7	Mosambi	India	0.0	0.0	0.0	0.0	400	6.5
8	Valencia	Florida	259.7	253.3	280.0	793.1	1200	12
9	Hamlin	California	0.0	0.0	0.0	0.0	168	11
10	Gardner	Arizona	0.0	84.0	0.0	84.0	84	12
11	Sunstar	Texas	75.4	0.0	134.6	210.0	210	10
12	Jincheng	China	0.0	0.0	0.0	0.0	588	9
13	Berna	Spain	0.0	0.0	156.2	156.2	168	15
14	Verna	Mexico	0.0	137.6	129.2	266.8	300	8
15	Biondo Commune	Egypt	210.0	0.0	0.0	210.0	210	13
16	Belladonna	Italy	54.9	125.1	0.0	180.0	180	14
17	Monthly Cost Totals:	Price	$366,233	$344,840	$426,596			
18		Shipping	$ 37,379	$ 33,071	$ 35,538			
31								
32	INDICATORS					BIG M		
33	Varietal	Region	January	February	March	January	February	March
34	Hamlin	Brazil	0.0	0.0	0.0	0.0	0.0	0.0
35	Mosambi	India	0.0	0.0	0.0	0.0	0.0	0.0
36	Valencia	Florida	1.0	1.0	1.0	1200.0	1200.0	1200.0
37	Hamlin	California	0.0	0.0	0.0	0.0	0.0	0.0
38	Gardner	Arizona	0.0	1.0	0.0	0.0	84.0	0.0
39	Sunstar	Texas	1.0	0.0	1.0	210.0	0.0	210.0
40	Jincheng	China	0.0	0.0	0.0	0.0	0.0	0.0
41	Berna	Spain	0.0	0.0	1.0	0.0	0.0	168.0
42	Verna	Mexico	0.0	1.0	1.0	0.0	300.0	300.0
43	Biondo Commune	Egypt	1.0	0.0	0.0	210.0	0.0	0.0
44	Belladonna	Italy	1.0	1.0	0.0	180.0	180.0	0.0
45	Total Suppliers Used		4.0	4.0	4.0			
46	Limit 4		4	4	4			

Frontier / Minimax Relaxed Quality / Optimization Model (Limit 4) / +

Normal View

Figure 4-33: Optimal solution limited to four suppliers per period

That's how "Big M" constraints are set up; you'll encounter them again in the graph clustering problem in Chapter 5.

Multiplying Variables: Cranking Up the Volume to 11

> ### OPENSOLVER NEEDED FOR EXCEL 2010 AND EXCEL 2013
>
> That last bit was tough, but it was child's play compared to this next business rule you're going to model.
>
> For this next problem, please keep the worked spreadsheet available for download with you for reference. This is a tough one but worth learning if your business is confronted with complex optimization problems. Also, nothing in the book is dependent on you learning this section, so if it gets too hard, just skip ahead. That said, I urge you to dig deep and give it a shot.
>
> If you're working in Excel 2010 or Excel 2013, you'll want to have OpenSolver installed and loaded (see Chapter 1 for an explanation). If you don't use OpenSolver to solve the problem in those versions of Excel, you'll get an error saying the optimization model is too large. To use OpenSolver in this chapter, set up the problem normally as shown in this section, but when it comes time to solve, use OpenSolver's Solve button on the ribbon.

Before you implement the limited supplier plan, you're informed that the new "acid-reducers" have been hooked up in the blending facility. Using ion exchange with a bed of calcium citrate, the technology is able to neutralize 20 percent of the acid in the juice that's run through it. This not only reduces acid percent by 20 but also increases the Brix/Acid ratio by 25 percent.

But the power and raw materials needed to run the reducer cost $20 per 1,000 gallons of juice put through it. Not all orders from suppliers need to be put through the de-acidification process; however, if an order is processed through the ion exchanger, the entire order must be pumped through.

Can you create a new optimal plan that tries to use ion exchange to reduce the optimal cost? Think about how you might set this one up. You now have to make a new set of decisions regarding when and when not to reduce the acid. How might those decisions interact with order quantities?

Start by copying the Optimization Model (Limit 4) tab to a new tab. Call it **Optimization Model Integer Acid.**

The problem with this business rule is that the natural way to model it is non-linear, and that would force you to use a slow optimization algorithm. You could have a binary variable that you "turn on" when you want to de-acidify an order, but that means that the cost of that de-acidifcation is:

```
De-acid indicator * Amount purchased * $20
```

You can't multiply two variables together unless you want to switch to using the non-linear solver, but that thing is never gonna figure out the complexities of this model. There has to be a better way to do this. Keep this in mind when doing linear programming: There are very few things that cannot be linearized through the judicious use of new variables manipulated by additional constraints and the objective function like a pair of salad tongs.

The first thing you're going to need is a set of new binary variables that get "turned on" when you choose to de-acidify a batch of juice. You can insert a new chunk of them in a rectangle between the Valencia orders and the quality constraints (cells C26:E36).

Furthermore, you can't use the product of De-acid indicator * Amount purchased, so instead you'll create a new grid of variables below the indicators that you're going to force to equal this amount without expressly touching them (a la dead squirrel). Insert these empty cells in C38:E48.

The spreadsheet now has two empty grids of variables—the indicators and the total amount of juice being fed through acid reduction—as shown in Figure 4-34.

Now, if you want to multiply a de-acidification binary variable times the amount of juice you've ordered, what are the values that product can take on? There are a number of distinct possibilities:

- If both the indicator and the product purchase amount are 0, their product is 0.
- If you order some juice but decide to not reduce the acid, the product is still 0.
- If you choose to reduce, the product is merely the amount of juice ordered.

In every case, the total possible juice that can be de-acidified is limited by the de-acidification indicator variable times the total juice available to purchase. If you don't reduce the acid, this upper bound goes to zero. If you choose to reduce, the upper bound pops up to the max available for purchase. This is a "Big M" constraint just like in the last section.

For Brazilian Hamlin then, this "Big M" constraint could be calculated as the indicator in cell C26 times the amount available for purchase, 672,000 gallons, in cell G6. Adding this calculation next to the indicator variables in cell G26, you can copy it to the remaining months and varietals.

This yields the worksheet shown in Figure 4-35.

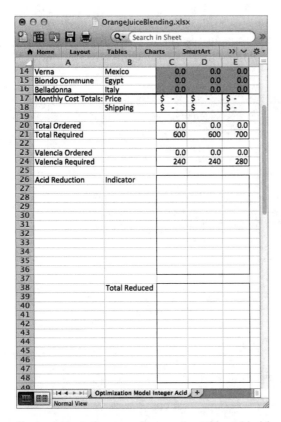

Figure 4-34: Indicator and amount variables added for the de-acidification decision

On the flip side, the total possible juice that can be de-acidified is limited by the amount you decide to purchase, given in C6:E16. So now you have two upper bounds on this product:

- De-acid indicator * Amount available for purchase
- Amount purchased

That's one upper bound per variable in the original non-linear product.

But you can't stop there. If you decide to de-acidify a batch, you need to send the *whole* batch through. That means you have to add a lower bound to the two upper bounds to help "scoop up" the de-acidified amount in C38:E48.

So how about just using the purchase amount as the lower bound? In the case where you decide to de-acidify, that works perfectly. You'll have a lower bound of the purchase amount, an upper bound of the purchase amount, and an upper bound of the total amount available for purchase times a de-acidification indicator set to 1. These upper and lower bounds force the amount going through de-acidification to be the whole shipment, which is what you want.

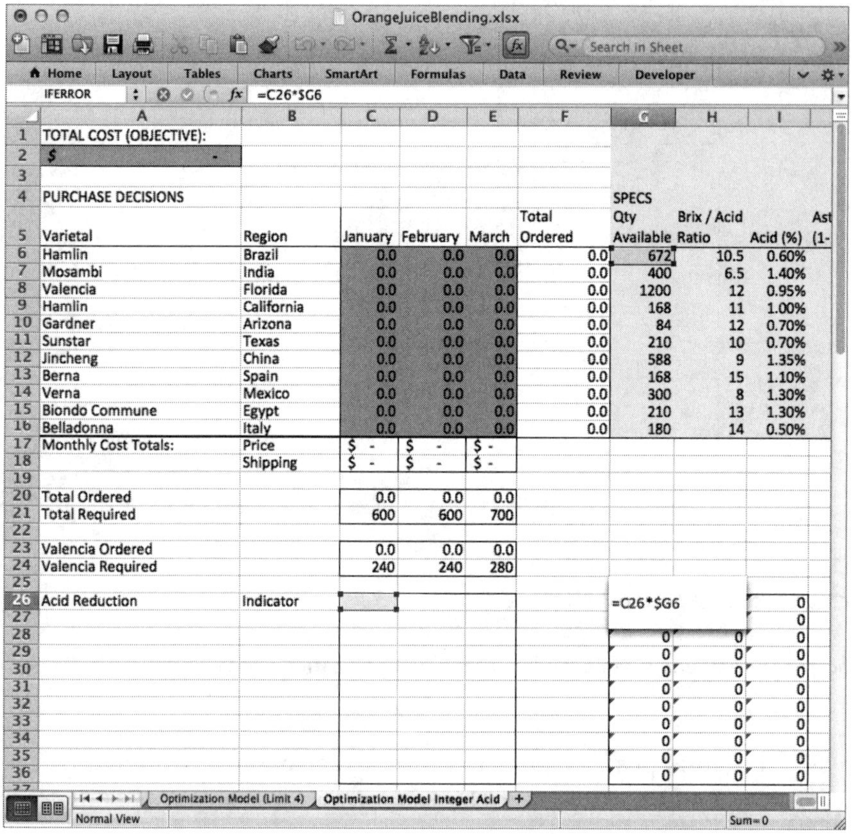

Figure 4-35: Calculation added for upper bound on how much juice can be de-acidified

But what if you choose not to de-acidify a batch? Then one of the upper bounds becomes an indicator of 0 times the amount available to purchase, whereas the lower bound is still the amount purchased. In that case, a non-zero purchase amount that's not de-acidified becomes impossible.

Hmmm.

So you need a way to "turn off" this lower bound in the situation where you choose not to de-acidify the juice.

Instead of making the lower bound the amount you ordered, why not make it the following:

```
Amount purchased - Amount available for purchase * (1 - de-acid
indicator)
```

In the case where you choose to de-acidify, this lower bound bounces up to the amount you purchased. In the case where you don't de-acidify, this value becomes less than or equal to 0. The constraint still exists, but it's for all intents worthless.

It's a bit janky, I know.

Try working it through an example. You buy 40,000 gallons of the Brazilian Hamlin juice. Furthermore, you decide to de-acidify.

The upper bounds on the amount you're de-acidifying are the amount purchased of 40 and the de-acid indicator times the amount available of 672.

The lower bound on the amount you're de-acidifying is 40 – 672 * (1-1) = 40. In other words, you have upper and lower bounds of 40, so you've sandwiched the amount you're de-acidifying right into `De-acid indicator * Amount purchased` without ever calculating this quantity.

If I choose not to de-acidify the Hamlin, the indicator is set to 0. In that case you have upper bounds of 40 and 672*0 = 0. You have a lower bound of 40 – 672 * (1-0) = -632. And since you've checked the box making all the variables be non-negative, that means that the amount of Hamlin you're de-acidifying is sandwiched between 0 and 0.

Perfect!

All right, so let's add this lower bound in a grid to the right of the upper bound calculation. In cell K26 you'd type:

```
=C6-$G6*(1-C26)
```

And you can copy that formula to each varietal and month, giving you the spreadsheet in Figure 4-36.

Next to the Total Reduced section, subtract that value from the total purchases in C6:E16 to get the remaining Not Reduced quantities of juice. For example, in cell G38, you place:

```
=C6 - C38
```

You can drag this across and down to the remaining cells in the grid (see Figure 4-37).

Wrapping up the formulation, you need to alter the cost, Brix/Acid, and Acid % calculations. For cost, you can just add $20 times the sum of the month's Total Reduced values into the Price cell. For example, January's Price calculation would become:

```
=SUMPRODUCT(C6:C16,$L6:$L16)+20*SUM(C38:C48)
```

which you can then drag across to February and March.

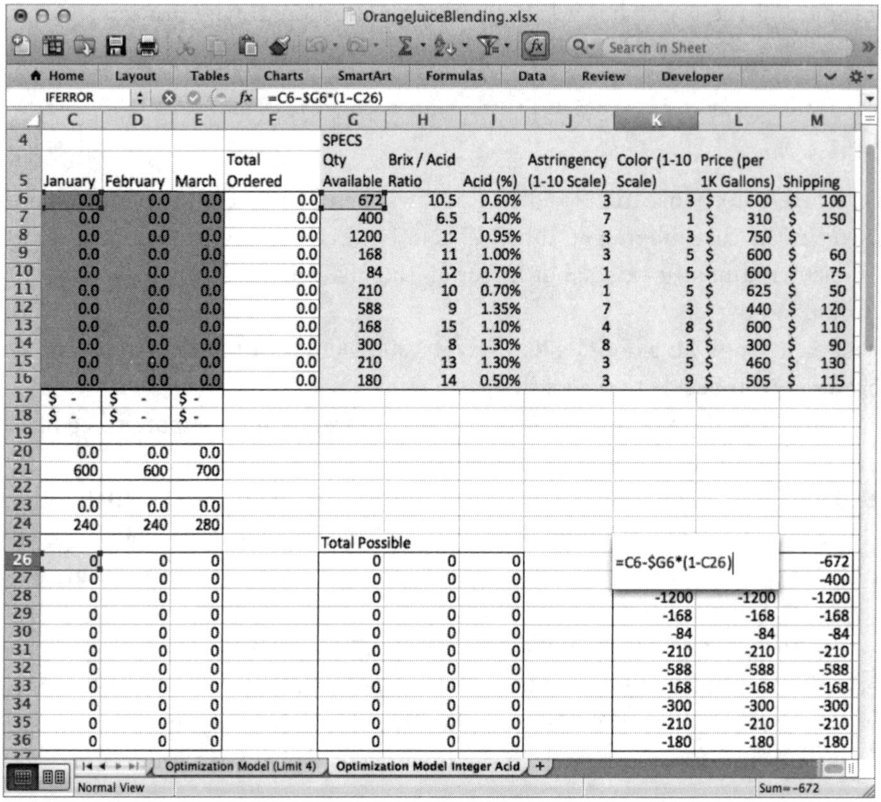

Figure 4-36: Adding in a lower bound on de-acidification

The Brix/Acid and Acid % calculations will now be calculated off of the split quantities in the Total Reduced and Not Reduced sections of the spreadsheet. Not Reduced values will be put through a SUMPRODUCT with their original specs, whereas the same SUMPRODUCT using the reduced acid juice will be scaled by 1.25 and 0.8, respectively, for BAR and Acid and added to the total in the monthly averages.

For example, Brix/Acid for January in C51 can be calculated as:

```
=(SUMPRODUCT(G38:G48,$H6:$H16)+SUMPRODUCT(C38:C48,$H6:$H16)*1.25)/C21
```

Now you need to modify the model in Solver. The objective function remains the same (sum of price and shipping), but the decision variables now include the de-acid indicators and amounts to be reduced located in C26:E36 and C38:E48.

As for the constraints, you need to indicate that C26:E36 is bin. Also, C38:C48 is less than or equal to the two upper bounds in C6:C16 and G26:I36. Also, you need a lower bound constraint where C38:E48 is greater than or equal to K26:M36.

This all yields the new model pictured in Figure 4-38.

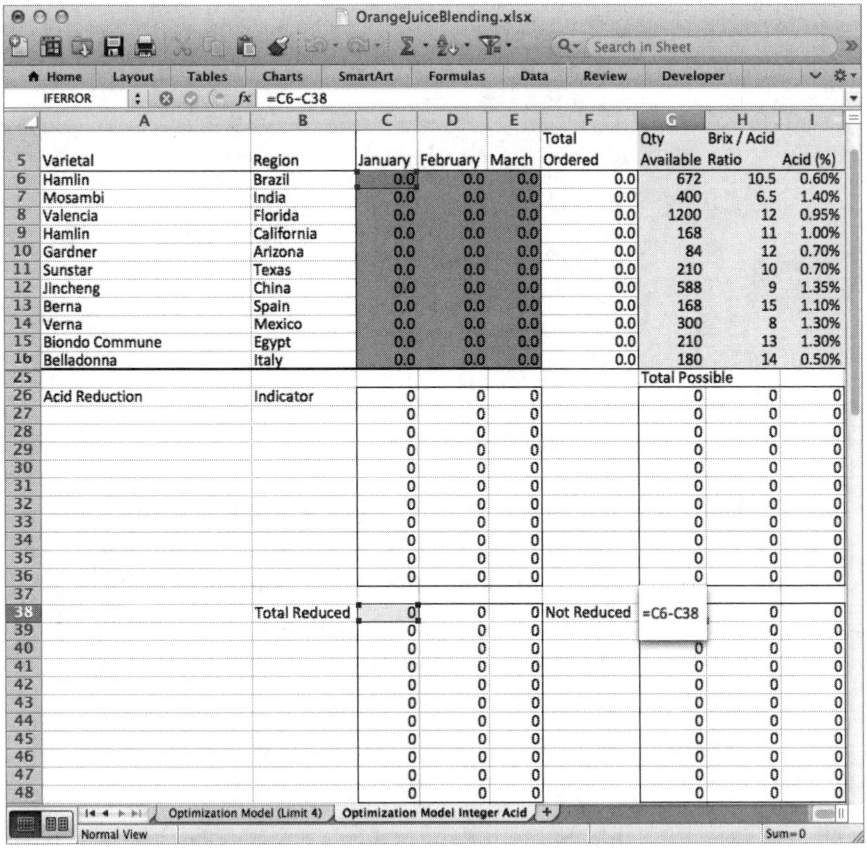

Figure 4-37: Adding a "Not Reduced" calculation

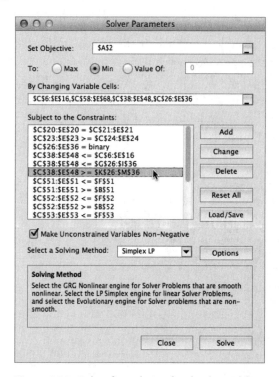

Figure 4-38: Solver formulation for the de-acidification problem

Press Solve and let the Branch and Bound do its thing. You'll end up with an optimal solution that's about $4,000 lower than in the previous formulation. Examining the new decision variables, you find that two batches—one from Arizona and one from Texas—are going through the de-acidification process. The lower and upper bounds for those two batches match precisely to force the product of the variables into place (see Figure 4-39).

Modeling Risk

That last business rule was a toughie, but it illustrates how a modeler can linearize most business problems by adding more constraints and variables. However, no matter how easy or hard the previous problems were, they all had one thing in common—they treat the input data as gospel.

This doesn't always conform to the reality many businesses find themselves in. Parts are not all to spec, shipments don't always arrive on time, demand doesn't match the forecast, and so on. In other words, there's variability and *risk* in the data.

So how do you take that risk and model it within an optimization model?

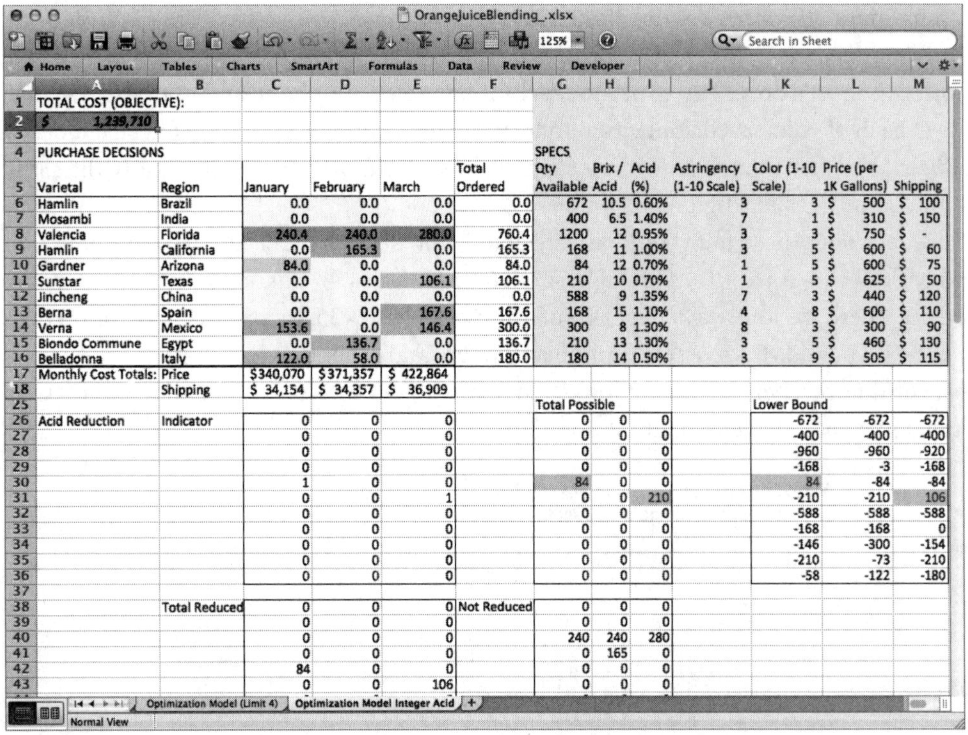

OrangeJuiceBlending_.xlsx

		PURCHASE DECISIONS				SPECS						
TOTAL COST (OBJECTIVE):												
$ 1,239,710												

Varietal	Region	January	February	March	Total Ordered	Qty Available	Brix/Acid	Acid (%)	Astringency (1-10 Scale)	Color (1-10 Scale)	Price (per 1K Gallons)	Shipping
Hamlin	Brazil	0.0	0.0	0.0	0.0	672	10.5	0.60%	3	3	$ 500	$ 100
Mosambi	India	0.0	0.0	0.0	0.0	400	6.5	1.40%	7	1	$ 310	$ 150
Valencia	Florida	240.4	240.0	280.0	760.4	1200	12	0.95%	3	3	$ 750	$ -
Hamlin	California	0.0	165.3	0.0	165.3	168	11	1.00%	3	5	$ 600	$ 60
Gardner	Arizona	84.0	0.0	0.0	84.0	84	12	0.70%	1	5	$ 600	$ 75
Sunstar	Texas	0.0	0.0	106.1	106.1	210	10	0.70%	1	5	$ 625	$ 50
Jincheng	China	0.0	0.0	0.0	0.0	588	9	1.35%	7	3	$ 440	$ 120
Berna	Spain	0.0	0.0	167.6	167.6	168	15	1.10%	4	8	$ 600	$ 110
Verna	Mexico	153.6	0.0	146.4	300.0	300	8	1.30%	8	3	$ 300	$ 90
Biondo Commune	Egypt	0.0	136.7	0.0	136.7	210	13	1.30%	3	5	$ 460	$ 130
Belladonna	Italy	122.0	58.0	0.0	180.0	180	14	0.50%	3	9	$ 505	$ 115
Monthly Cost Totals: Price		$340,070	$371,357	$422,864								
Shipping		$ 34,154	$ 34,357	$ 36,909								

						Total Possible				Lower Bound		
Acid Reduction	Indicator	0	0	0		0	0	0		-672	-672	-672
		0	0	0		0	0	0		-400	-400	-400
		0	0	0		0	0	0		-960	-960	-920
		0	0	0		0	0	0		-168	-3	-168
		1	0	0		84	0	0		84	-84	-84
		0	0	1		0	0	210		-210	-210	106
		0	0	0		0	0	0		-588	-588	-588
		0	0	0		0	0	0		-168	-168	0
		0	0	0		0	0	0		-146	-300	-154
		0	0	0		0	0	0		-210	-73	-210
		0	0	0		0	0	0		-58	-122	-180
Total Reduced		0	0	0	Not Reduced	0	0	0				
		0	0	0		0	0	0				
						240	240	280				
						0	165	0				
		84	0	0		0	0	0				
		0	0	106		0	0	0				

Optimization Model (Limit 4) | Optimization Model Integer Acid | +
Normal View

Figure 4-39: Solved de-acidification model

Normally Distributed Data

In the orange juice problem, you're trying to blend juices to take out variability, so is it reasonable to expect that the product you're getting from your suppliers won't have variable specs?

Chances are that shipment of Biondo Commune orange juice you're getting from Egypt won't have an exact 13 Brix/Acid ratio. That may be the expected number, but there's probably some give around it. And oftentimes, that wiggle room can be characterized using a *probability distribution*.

A probability distribution, loosely speaking, gives a likelihood to each possible outcome of some situation, and all the probabilities add up to 1. Perhaps the most famous and widely used distribution is the normal distribution, otherwise known as the "bell curve." The reason why the bell curve crops up a lot is because when you have a bunch of independent, complex, real-world factors added together that produce randomly distributed data, that data will *often* be distributed in a normal or bell-like way. This is called the *central limit theorem*.

To see this, let's do a little experiment. Pull out your cell phone and grab the last four digits of each of your saved contacts' phone numbers. Digit one will probably be *uniformly distributed* between 0 and 9, meaning each of those digits will show up roughly the same amount. Same goes for digits 2, 3, and 4.

Now, let's take these four "random variables" and sum them. The lowest number you could get is 0 (0 + 0 + 0 + 0). The highest is 36 (9 + 9 + 9 + 9). There's only one way to get 0 and 36. There are four ways to get 1 and four ways to get 35, but there's a ton of ways to get 20. So if you did this to enough phone numbers and graphed a bar chart of the various sums, you'd have a bell curve that looks like Figure 4-40 (I used 1,000 phone numbers to get the figure, because I'm just that popular).

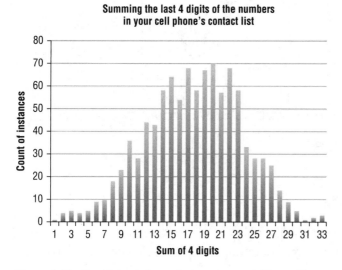

Figure 4-40: Combining independent random variables to illustrate how they gather into a bell curve

The Cumulative Distribution Function

There's another way of drawing this distribution that's going to be super helpful, and it's called the *cumulative distribution function (CDF)*. The cumulative distribution function gives the probability of an outcome that's *less than or equal* to a particular value.

In the case of the cell phone data, only 12 percent of the cases are less than or equal to 10, whereas 100 percent of the cases are less than or equal to 36 (since that's the largest possible value). This cumulative distribution is pictured in Figure 4-41.

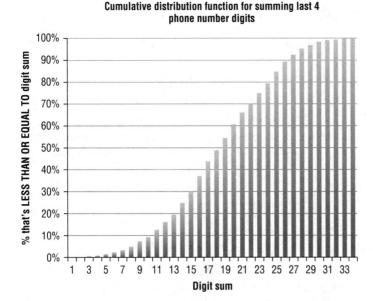

Figure 4-41: The cumulative distribution function for the cell phone contact sums

And here's the cool thing about the cumulative distribution function—*you can read it backward to generate samples from the distribution.*

For example, if you wanted to generate a random value from this contact list four-digit sum distribution, you could generate a random number between 0 and 100 percent. Say you come up with 61 percent as your random value. Looking that up on the vertical axis of the CDF, 61 percent lines up with 19 on the horizontal axis. And you could do this over and over to generate a lot of samples from the distribution.

Now, a normal CDF can be described completely by two numbers: a *mean* and a *standard deviation*. The mean is nothing more than the center of the distribution. The standard deviation measures the variability or spread of the bell curve around the mean.

Say in the case of the juice you order from Egypt, it has a Brix/Acid mean of 13 and a standard deviation of 0.9. That means that 13 is the center of the probability distribution and 68 percent of orders are going to be within +/-0.9 of 13, 95 percent will be within two standard deviations (+/-1.8), and 99.7 percent will be within three standard deviations (+/-2.7). This is sometimes called the "68-95-99.7" rule.

In other words, it's pretty likely you'll receive a 13.5 Brix/Acid batch from Egypt, but it's very unlikely you'll receive a 10 Brix/Acid batch.

CALCULATING THE SAMPLE MEAN AND STANDARD DEVIATION

For those of you who haven't calculated standard deviation before and are interested to know how it's done, it's super easy.

Figure 4-42 shows the past 11 orders of the Biondo Commune orange juice from Egypt and their respective Brix/Acid measurements in column B. The sample mean of those measures is 13, as given in the original specs spreadsheet.

The sample estimate of the standard deviation is just the square root of the mean squared error. By "error," I just mean the deviation of each order from the expected value of 13.

In column C of Figure 4-42, you can see the error calculation, and the squared error calculation is in column D. The mean squared error is AVERAGE(D2:D12), which comes out to 0.77. The square root of the mean squared error is then 0.88. Easy enough!

In practice however, when calculating the sample standard deviation for a small number of orders, you get a better estimate if you sum the squared error and divide through by 1 less than your total orders (in this case 10 instead of 11).

If you make this adjustment, the standard deviation becomes 0.92, as shown in Figure 4-42.

	A	B	C	D	E	F
1	Order	BAR	Error	Squared Error		MEAN
2	1	14	1	1		13
3	2	13	0	0		
4	3	13	0	0		Mean Squared Error
5	4	13.5	0.5	0.25		0.77
6	5	14	1	1		Standard Deviation
7	6	13	0	0		0.88
8	7	12.5	-0.5	0.25		
9	8	11	-2	4		Sum Squared Error / N-1
10	9	13	0	0		0.85
11	10	12	-1	1		Adjusted Standard Deviation
12	11	14	1	1		0.92

Figure 4-42: An example of the sample standard deviation calculation

---

Generating Scenarios from Standard Deviations in the Blending Problem

NOTE

Just as in the previous section, those using Excel 2010 and Excel 2013 will need to employ OpenSolver. Just set the problem up normally and use the OpenSolver Solve button on the ribbon when the time comes. See Chapter 1 for more detail on OpenSolver.

Imagine instead of receiving the Specs tab, you received standard deviations along with your specifications in a tab titled Specs Variability, as shown in Figure 4-43. The goal is to find a blending plan that's less than $1.25 million dollars that best meets the quality expectations in light of supplier variability.

You can create a copy of the original Minimax Relaxed Quality tab called the Robust Optimization Model, where the new standard deviations will go in N6:Q16 adjacent to the old specifications.

Once they're in there, what do you do with them?

You're going to use the mean and standard deviation for the specs to take a *Monte Carlo simulation* approach to solving this problem. The Monte Carlo method means that instead of somehow incorporating the distribution directly into the model, you sample the distribution, creating scenarios or instantiations from each set of samples, and then include those samples in the model.

A scenario is one possible answer to the question, "If these are the distributions for my stats, what would an actual order look like?" To draw a scenario, you read the normal CDF—characterized by the mean and standard deviation—backward, as discussed previously with Figure 4-41.

		SPECS								Standard Deviations			
		Qty Available	Brix / Acid	Acid	Astringency	Color (1-10	Price (per			Brix / Acid		Astringency	Color (1-10
Varietal	Region	(1,000 Gallons)	Ratio	(%)	(1-10 Scale)	Scale)	1K Gallons)	Shipping		Ratio	Acid (%)	(1-10 Scale)	Scale)
Hamlin	Brazil	672	10.5	0.60%	3	3	$ 500.00	$100.00		2	0.12%	0.7	1
Mosambi	India	400	6.5	1.40%	7	1	$ 310.00	$150.00		1.1	0.09%	0.05	1.3
Valencia	Florida	1200	12	0.95%	3	3	$ 750.00	$ -		0.2	0.19%	0.7	1.4
Hamlin	California	168	11	1.00%	3	5	$ 600.00	$ 60.00		1	0.18%	0.9	0.9
Gardner	Arizona	84	12	0.70%	1	5	$ 600.00	$ 75.00		1.3	0.13%	0.6	0.3
Sunstar	Texas	210	10	0.70%	1	5	$ 625.00	$ 50.00		1.4	0.09%	0.4	1
Jincheng	China	588	9	1.35%	7	3	$ 440.00	$120.00		0.3	0.19%	0.2	0.3
Berna	Spain	168	15	1.10%	4	8	$ 600.00	$110.00		0.8	0.12%	0.4	0.9
Verna	Mexico	300	8	1.30%	8	3	$ 300.00	$ 90.00		1	0.17%	0.5	0.2
Biondo Com	Egypt	210	13	1.30%	3	5	$ 460.00	$130.00		0.9	0.17%	0.7	0.1
Belladonna	Italy	180	14	0.50%	3	9	$ 505.00	$115.00		0.6	0.07%	0.9	0.1

Figure 4-43: Specifications with standard deviation added

The formula in Excel for reading the normal CDF backward (or "inverted" if you like) is NORMINV.

So generate a scenario in column B, starting at row 33 below everything that's in the worksheet already. You can call this Scenario 1.

In B34:B44 you'll generate an actual scenario of Brix/Acid values for all the suppliers. In B34 generate a random value for Brazilian Hamlin where its mean Brix/Acid is 10.5 (H6) and its standard deviation is 2 (N6) using the NORMINV formula:

```
=NORMINV(RAND(),$H6,$N6)
```

You're feeding a random number between 0 and 100 percent into NORMINV along with the mean and standard deviation, and out pops a random Brix/Acid value. Let's drag that formula down to B44.

Starting at B45, you can do the same thing for Acid, then Astringency, then Color. The range B34:B77 now contains a single scenario, randomly drawn from the distributions. Dragging this scenario across the columns all the way to CW (note the absolute references that allow for this), you can generate 100 such random spec scenarios. Solver can't understand them if they remain non-linear formulas, so go ahead and copy and paste the scenarios on top of themselves *as values only*. Now the scenarios are fixed data.

This mound of scenario data in B34:CW77 is pictured in Figure 4-44.

	A	B	C	D	E	F	G	H	I	J	K
33	SCENARIO	1	2	3	4	5	6	7	8	9	10
34	BAR	7.7	11.8	6.5	13.7	12.2	8.0	8.8	11.9	11.9	12.7
35		6.8	6.6	6.8	6.2	4.2	7.8	8.0	5.3	6.4	4.6
36		12.1	12.3	11.5	12.1	12.1	11.8	11.8	12.0	12.1	12.0
37		8.8	12.5	11.7	10.4	9.6	10.8	10.4	11.0	9.0	10.5
38		12.1	12.7	13.2	12.2	10.2	13.1	11.2	11.9	12.5	10.6
39		9.2	9.9	8.6	10.5	9.1	7.3	9.7	9.4	8.5	8.4
40		8.9	9.0	8.8	9.1	8.9	9.3	8.6	9.4	9.1	9.2
41		16.2	16.3	15.6	16.1	16.0	16.3	15.2	13.2	14.6	15.5
42		7.8	8.2	6.9	7.2	7.3	6.8	7.9	8.3	8.8	8.3
43		13.7	13.4	13.7	14.6	12.3	13.4	11.2	14.2	12.3	12.9
44		13.1	13.2	13.7	13.6	13.9	13.6	14.1	13.9	14.1	14.3
45	Acid	0.56%	0.64%	0.68%	0.71%	0.46%	0.33%	0.49%	0.65%	0.43%	0.62%
46		1.38%	1.44%	1.33%	1.40%	1.33%	1.46%	1.37%	1.34%	1.44%	1.33%
47		0.93%	0.78%	1.07%	1.15%	0.89%	0.89%	0.60%	1.12%	0.75%	0.71%
48		1.23%	1.14%	0.77%	0.82%	0.88%	1.31%	0.93%	1.28%	1.11%	0.66%
49		0.76%	0.67%	0.79%	0.61%	0.74%	0.84%	0.69%	0.64%	0.57%	0.66%
50		0.60%	0.83%	0.76%	0.71%	0.71%	0.73%	0.82%	0.72%	0.71%	0.64%
51		1.58%	1.27%	1.46%	1.55%	1.45%	1.56%	1.42%	1.47%	1.44%	1.52%
52		1.23%	1.04%	1.20%	1.05%	1.23%	1.22%	1.14%	0.97%	1.10%	1.21%
53		1.24%	1.34%	1.21%	1.34%	1.19%	1.66%	1.38%	1.14%	1.35%	1.53%
54		1.50%	1.31%	1.41%	1.04%	1.57%	1.66%	1.20%	1.19%	1.60%	1.37%
55		0.55%	0.51%	0.52%	0.50%	0.48%	0.53%	0.49%	0.60%	0.57%	0.55%
56	Astringency	3.5	2.0	2.9	4.3	2.8	3.3	3.1	2.1	3.3	3.1
57		7.0	6.8	7.0	6.9	6.9	7.0	7.1	6.9	7.0	7.0
58		2.8	3.5	2.6	2.9	1.7	3.8	3.9	3.1	2.9	3.0
59		2.5	2.6	0.5	2.2	1.8	1.2	1.8	3.9	3.5	2.2
60		0.7	0.9	1.2	1.4	1.3	1.1	2.1	0.0	1.3	1.2
61		0.8	1.1	0.7	0.6	0.8	1.1	0.7	1.3	0.9	0.4
62		7.0	6.9	7.2	6.9	7.0	7.1	6.9	6.8	7.2	6.5
63		3.5	3.4	3.7	4.2	3.9	4.6	4.0	4.5	4.3	4.5
64		7.7	7.7	8.2	8.4	7.7	8.4	7.7	7.4	7.9	8.7
65		2.6	3.3	3.0	3.1	2.9	2.0	2.8	3.3	3.2	2.6
66		2.7	2.8	3.1	3.2	2.7	3.4	3.3	4.1	2.5	2.6
67	Color	1.7	2.2	3.5	3.4	3.2	3.9	3.0	1.9	5.0	3.5
68		1.0	1.1	-0.7	-2.0	0.1	1.2	-1.7	0.0	0.5	1.5

Cell B34: =NORMINV(RAND(),$H6,$N6)

Sheet tabs: Specs Variability / Robust Optimization Model / +

Figure 4-44: 100 generated juice spec scenarios

Setting Up the Scenario Constraints

Okay, so what you want to do is find a solution that relaxes the quality bounds *the least* in order to meet them in each and every scenario you've generated. Just find a solution that protects the product.

So under the first scenario in cell B79 calculate the BAR for January as:

```
=SUMPRODUCT($C$6:$C$16,B34:B44)/$C$21
```

You can do the same for February and March on rows 80 and 81 and then drag the entire calculation right through column CW to get a Brix/Acid for each scenario.

Doing the same for the other specs, you end up with calculations on each scenario, as shown in Figure 4-45.

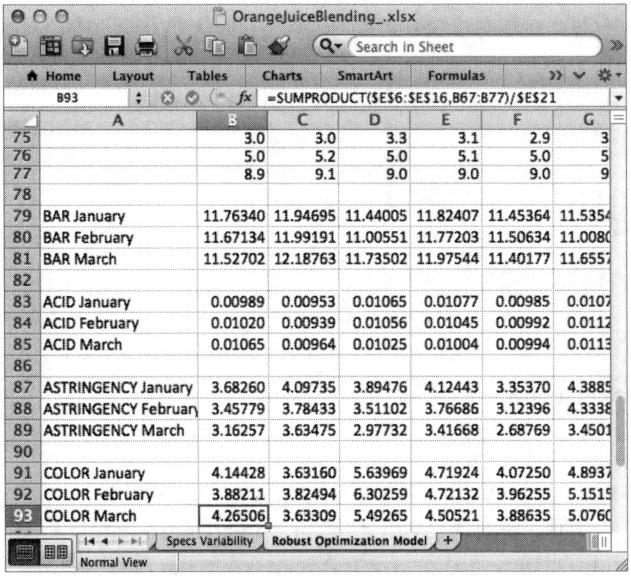

	A	B	C	D	E	F	G
75		3.0	3.0	3.3	3.1	2.9	3
76		5.0	5.2	5.0	5.1	5.0	5
77		8.9	9.1	9.0	9.0	9.0	9
78							
79	BAR January	11.76340	11.94695	11.44005	11.82407	11.45364	11.535
80	BAR February	11.67134	11.99191	11.00551	11.77203	11.50634	11.008
81	BAR March	11.52702	12.18763	11.73502	11.97544	11.40177	11.655
82							
83	ACID January	0.00989	0.00953	0.01065	0.01077	0.00985	0.010
84	ACID February	0.01020	0.00939	0.01056	0.01045	0.00992	0.011
85	ACID March	0.01065	0.00964	0.01025	0.01004	0.00994	0.011
86							
87	ASTRINGENCY January	3.68260	4.09735	3.89476	4.12443	3.35370	4.388
88	ASTRINGENCY Februar	3.45779	3.78433	3.51102	3.76686	3.12396	4.333
89	ASTRINGENCY March	3.16257	3.63475	2.97732	3.41668	2.68769	3.450
90							
91	COLOR January	4.14428	3.63160	5.63969	4.71924	4.07250	4.893
92	COLOR February	3.88211	3.82494	6.30259	4.72132	3.96255	5.151
93	COLOR March	4.26506	3.63309	5.49265	4.50521	3.88635	5.076

Figure 4-45: Spec calculations for each scenario

Setting up the model isn't all that difficult. You put a cost upper bound of $1.25 million in B2. You're still minimizing D2, the quality relaxation, in a minimax setup. All you need to do is place the quality bounds around all of the scenarios rather than just the expected quality values.

Thus, for BAR, you add that B79:CW81 ≥ B27 and ≤ F27 and similarly for Acid, Astringency, and Color, yielding the formulation shown in Figure 4-46.

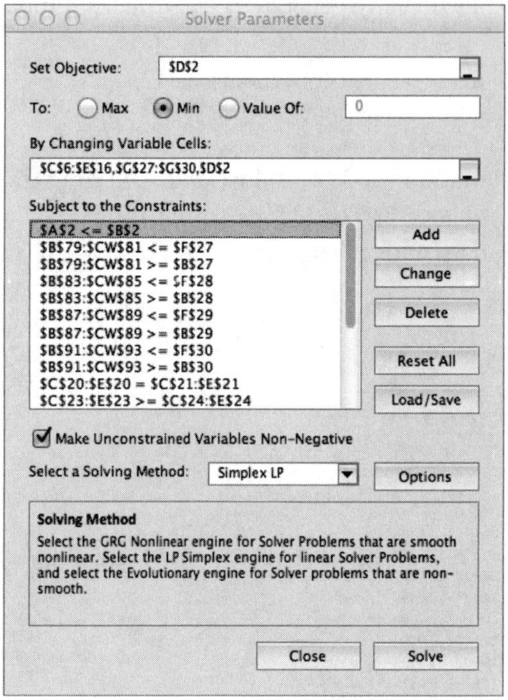

Figure 4-46: Solver setup for robust optimization

Press Solve. You'll get a solution rather quickly. Now, if you generated the random scenarios yourself rather than keeping the ones provided in the spreadsheet available for download, the solution you get will be different. For my 100 scenarios, the best quality I could get is a 133 percent relaxation while keeping cost under $1.25 million.

For giggles, you can up the cost upper bound to $1.5 million and solve again. You get a 114 percent relaxation without the cost even going to the upper bound but rather staying at about $1.3 million. It seems that upping the cost higher than that doesn't give you any more leeway to improve quality (see the solution in Figure 4-47).

And that's it! You now have a balance of cost and quality that meets constraints even in random, real-world situations.

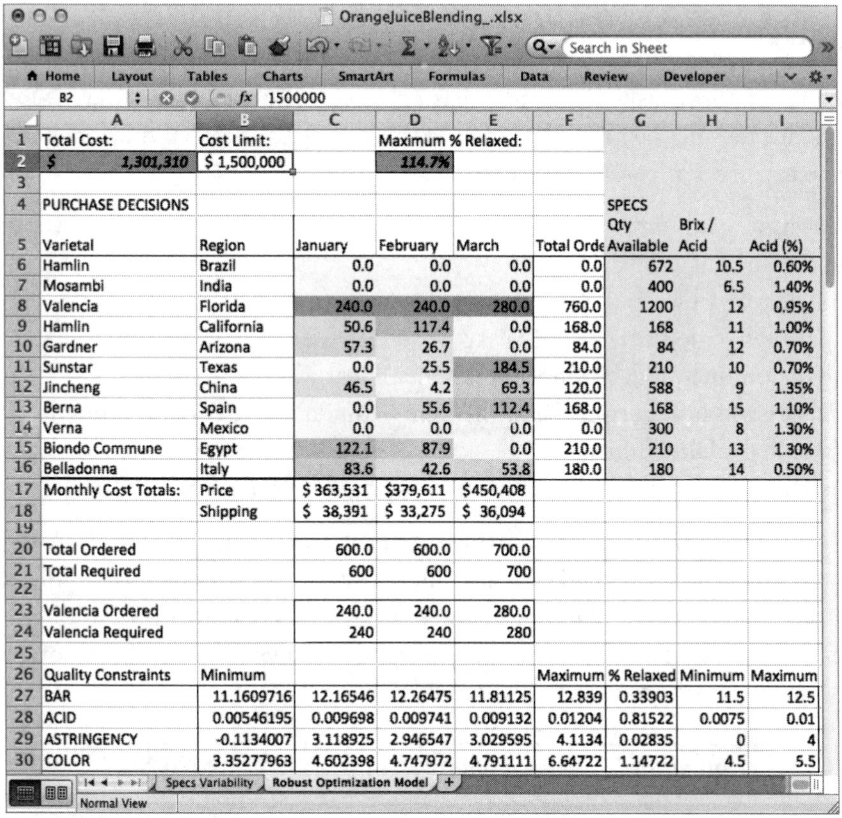

Figure 4-47: Solution to the robust optimization model

The spreadsheet shown in the figure contains:

Toolbar: OrangeJuiceBlending_.xlsx — Home, Layout, Tables, Charts, SmartArt, Formulas, Data, Review, Developer

Cell B2: fx 1500000

	A	B	C	D	E	F	G	H	I
1	Total Cost:	Cost Limit:			Maximum % Relaxed:				
2	$ 1,301,310	$ 1,500,000			114.7%				
3									
4	PURCHASE DECISIONS						SPECS		
5	Varietal	Region	January	February	March	Total Orde	Qty Available	Brix / Acid	Acid (%)
6	Hamlin	Brazil	0.0	0.0	0.0	0.0	672	10.5	0.60%
7	Mosambi	India	0.0	0.0	0.0	0.0	400	6.5	1.40%
8	Valencia	Florida	240.0	240.0	280.0	760.0	1200	12	0.95%
9	Hamlin	California	50.6	117.4	0.0	168.0	168	11	1.00%
10	Gardner	Arizona	57.3	26.7	0.0	84.0	84	12	0.70%
11	Sunstar	Texas	0.0	25.5	184.5	210.0	210	10	0.70%
12	Jincheng	China	46.5	4.2	69.3	120.0	588	9	1.35%
13	Berna	Spain	0.0	55.6	112.4	168.0	168	15	1.10%
14	Verna	Mexico	0.0	0.0	0.0	0.0	300	8	1.30%
15	Biondo Commune	Egypt	122.1	87.9	0.0	210.0	210	13	1.30%
16	Belladonna	Italy	83.6	42.6	53.8	180.0	180	14	0.50%
17	Monthly Cost Totals:	Price	$ 363,531	$379,611	$450,408				
18		Shipping	$ 38,391	$ 33,275	$ 36,094				
19									
20	Total Ordered		600.0	600.0	700.0				
21	Total Required		600	600	700				
22									
23	Valencia Ordered		240.0	240.0	280.0				
24	Valencia Required		240	240	280				
25									
26	Quality Constraints	Minimum				Maximum	% Relaxed	Minimum	Maximum
27	BAR	11.1609716	12.16546	12.26475	11.81125	12.839	0.33903	11.5	12.5
28	ACID	0.00546195	0.009698	0.009741	0.009132	0.01204	0.81522	0.0075	0.01
29	ASTRINGENCY	-0.1134007	3.118925	2.946547	3.029595	4.1134	0.02835	0	4
30	COLOR	3.35277963	4.602398	4.747972	4.791111	6.64722	1.14722	4.5	5.5

Sheet tabs: Specs Variability | Robust Optimization Model | +
Normal View

AN EXERCISE FOR THE READER

If you're a glutton for pain, I'd like to offer one more formulation to work through. In the previous problem, you minimized the percent you had to lower and raise the quality bounds such that every constraint was satisfied. But what if you cared only that 95 percent of the scenarios were satisfied?

You would still minimize the quality relaxation percentage, but you'd need to stick an indicator variable on each scenario and use constraints to set it to 1 when the scenario's quality constraints were violated. The sum of these indicators could then be set ≤5 as a constraint.

Give it a shot. See if you can work it.

Wrapping Up

If you stuck with me on those last couple of models, then *bravo*. Those suckers weren't toy problems. In fact, this may be the hardest chapter in this book. It's all downhill from here!

Here's a little recap of what you just learned:

- Simple linear programming
- The minimax formulation
- Adding integer variables and constraints
- Modeling if-then logic using a "Big M" constraint
- Modeling the product of decision variables in a linear way
- The normal distribution, central limit theorem, cumulative distribution functions, and the Monte Carlo method
- Using the Monte Carlo method to model risk within a linear program

Your head is probably spinning with all sorts of applications of this stuff to your business right now. Or you've just downed a stiff drink and never want to deal with linear programming again. I hope it's the former, because the truth is, you can get arbitrarily creative and complex with linear programming. In many business contexts you'll often find models with tens of millions of decision variables.

PRACTICE, PRACTICE, PRACTICE! AND READ SOME MORE

Modeling linear programs, especially when you have to execute funky "squirrel removal" tricks, can be rather non-intuitive. The best way to get good at it is to find some opportunities in your own line of work that could use modeling and have at it. You can't memorize this stuff; you have to get a feel for how to address certain modeling peculiarities. And that comes with practice.

If you want some additional linear programming literature to supplement your practice, here are some free online resources that I highly recommend:

- The AIMMS optimization modeling book available at `http://www.aimms.com/downloads/manuals/optimization-modeling` is an incredible resource. Don't skip their two Tips and Tricks chapters; those things are awesome.
- "Formulating Integer Linear Programs: A Rogue's Gallery" from Brown and Dell of the Naval Postgraduate School: `http://faculty.nps.edu/gbrown/docs/Brown_Dell_INFORMS_Transactions_on_Education_January2007.pdf`.

5

Cluster Analysis
Part II: Network Graphs
and Community
Detection

This chapter continues the discussion on cluster identification and analysis using the wholesale wine dataset from Chapter 2. Although it's perfectly fine to jump around in this book, in this case I recommend at least skimming Chapter 2 before reading this chapter, because I don't repeat the data preparation steps, and you're going to be using cosine similarity, which was discussed at the end of Chapter 2.

Also, the techniques used here rely on the "Big M" constraint optimization techniques introduced in Chapter 4, so some familiarity with that will be helpful.

This chapter continues addressing the problem of detecting interesting groups of customers based on their purchases, but it approaches the problem from a fundamentally different direction.

Rather than thinking about customers huddling around flags planted on the dance floor to assign them to groups, as you did with k-means clustering (Chapter 2), you're going to look at your customers in a more relational way. Customers buy similar things, and in that way, they're related to each other. Some are more "friendly" than others, in that they're interested in the same stuff. So by thinking about how related or not related each customer is to the others, you can identify communities of customers without needing to plant a set number of flags in the data that get moved around until people feel at home.

The key concept that allows you to approach customer clustering in this relational way is called a *network graph*. A network graph, as you'll see in the next section, is a simple way to store and visualize entities (such as customers) that are connected (by purchase data for instance).

These days, network visualization and analysis are all the rage, and the techniques used to mine insights from network graphs often work better than traditional techniques (such as k-means clustering in Chapter 2), so it's important that a modern analyst understand and be able to leverage network graphs in their work.

When doing cluster analysis on a network, people often use the term *community detection* instead, which makes sense because many network graphs are social in nature and their clusters do indeed make up communities. This chapter focuses on a particular community detection algorithm called *modularity maximization*.

At a high level, modularity maximization rewards you every time you place two good friends in a cluster together and penalizes you every time you shove some strangers together. By grabbing all the rewards you can and avoiding as many penalties as possible, the technique leads to a natural clustering of customers. And here's the cool part, which you'll see later—unlike the k-means clustering approach, you don't need to choose k. The algorithm does it for you! In this way, the clustering technique used here takes *unsupervised* machine learning to a whole new level of knowledge discovery.

Also, from a mathematical-sex-appeal perspective, k-means clustering, while rad, has been around for over half a century. The techniques you'll use in this chapter were developed in just the past several years. This is cutting edge stuff.

What Is a Network Graph?

A network graph is a collection of things called *nodes* that are connected by relationships called *edges*. Social networks like Facebook provide a lot of network-graphable data, such as friends who are connected to you and possibly to each other. Hence, the term "the social graph" has come up a lot in recent years.

The nodes in a network graph don't have to be people of course, and the edges that represent relationships don't have to be interpersonal relationships. For instance, you could have nodes that are Facebook users and other nodes that are product pages they like. Those "likes" comprise the edges of the graph. Similarly, you could create a network graph of all the stops on your city's transportation system. Or all the destinations and routes on Delta's flight map (in fact, if you look at the route map on any airline's website, you'll see it's a canonical network graph).

Or you could get all spy-like and graph anyone who has called anyone on a GPS sat phone within al-Qaeda in the Islamic Magreb. With the release of material on the NSA's spying efforts by Edward Snowden, this last type of network graph has been getting a lot of attention in the media. One example is the congressional discussion around NSA's ability to perform a "three-hop" query—that is go into their network graph of phone call data and find people three hops from a known terrorist (nodes connected to a terrorist by a three edge path in the graph).

Whatever your business is, I guarantee you have a graph hiding in your data. One of my favorite network graphing projects is called DocGraph (`http://notonlydev.com/docgraph/`). Some intrepid folks have used a Freedom of Information Act request to create a graph of all kinds of Medicare referral data. Doctors get connected to other doctors via referrals, and the graph can be used to identify communities, influential providers (the doctor everyone goes to for the final opinion on a tricky diagnosis), and even cases of fraud and abuse.

Network graphs are a rare contradiction in the analytics world. They are aesthetically beautiful and yet extremely utilitarian in the way they store and enable certain analyses. These graphs allow analysts to discover all sorts of insights both visually and algorithmically, such as clusters, outliers, local influencers, and bridges between different groups.

In the next section, you'll visualize some network data to get a feel for how these things work.

Visualizing a Simple Graph

The TV show *Friends* was one of the most popular sitcoms of the 1990s and early 2000s. The show centered around six friends: Ross, Rachel, Joey, Chandler, Monica, and Phoebe. If you've never heard of the show or these characters, you're either super young or trapped in a cave.

These six characters become involved in a lot of romances with each other of various types: real romances, fantasy romances that never amount to anything, play romances based on some dare or competition, and so on.

Think of these characters as six nodes or vertices on the graph. The relationships between them are edges. Off the top of my head, I can think of these edges:

- Ross and Rachel, obviously
- Monica and Chandler end up married.
- Joey and Rachel have a little romance going but ultimately decide it's too weird.
- Chandler and Rachel meet each other in a flashback episode over a pool table mishap, and Rachel imagines what it'd be like to be with Chandler.
- Chandler and Phoebe play at a relationship and end up having to kiss, because Chandler refuses to admit he's with Monica.

These six characters and their five edges can be visualized as shown in Figure 5-1.

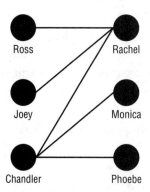

Figure 5-1: Diagram of ro(faux)mances on *Friends*

Pretty simple, right? Nodes and edges. That's all a network graph is. And note how network graphs have nothing whatsoever to do with the graphs you may be familiar with, such as dot plots, line charts, and bar charts. No, these graphs are a different animal entirely.

Figure 5-1 is what's called an *undirected* network graph, because the relationships are mutual by definition. Something like Twitter data on the other hand is *directed*, that is, I can follow you, but you don't have to follow me. When visualizing a directed graph, the edges are usually directional arrows.

Now, one of the drawbacks about using Excel to work on network graphs is that, unlike other graphing and charting capabilities, Excel does not provide tools for visualizing network graphs.

NODEXL

If you're in Excel 2007 or 2010, the Social Media Research Foundation has released a template that allows network visualization in Excel called NodeXL. It's not covered in this book because it's still early days for the software, and LibreOffice and Excel 2011 for Mac users wouldn't be able to follow along. If you're interested, you can check out NodeXL for yourself at `http://www.smrfoundation.org/nodexl/`.

So for this chapter, I'm going to break my own ground rules for this book and use an external tool called Gephi for some visualization and computation, which is discussed more in the next section. That said, *you can ignore all the Gephi aspects of this chapter if you want to*. All the actual data mining on network data can be done without visualizing the network in Gephi; you're just doing that part for fun.

But visualization aside, if you want to work on this type of graph, you need a numerical representation of the data. One intuitive representation is called an *adjacency matrix*. An adjacency matrix is just a node-by-node grid of 0s and 1s, where a 1 in a particular cell means "put an edge here" and a 0 means "these nodes are unconnected."

You can create an adjacency matrix out of the *Friends* data, as shown in Figure 5-2 (the matrix looks a bit like a Galaga-style lobster to me). The friends' names line the columns and rows, and relationships between them are shown with 1s. Notice how the graph is *symmetric* along the diagonal, because the graph is undirected. If Joey has an edge with Rachel, then the converse is true, and the adjacency matrix shows this. If relationships were one-sided, you could have a matrix without this symmetry.

Although the edges here are represented with 1s, they don't have to be. You can add weights to the edges, such as capacities—think of different planes with different capacities flying routes or varying bandwidths available on different links of an IT network. A weighted adjacency matrix is also called an *affinity matrix*.

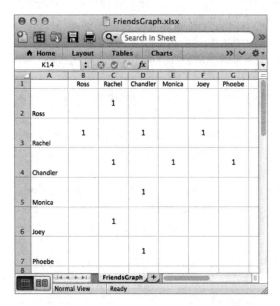

Figure 5-2: An adjacency matrix for the *Friends* data

Brief Introduction to Gephi

Let's go ahead and get Gephi running so you can import and visualize the *Friends* dataset. Then you'll know your way around later when things get real all up in here.

Gephi is an open source network visualization tool written in Java, and it's the main culprit behind many of the network visualization graphics you see in the media today. It's easy to produce striking pictures, and people seem to have taken to it for graphing tweets like bunnies to carrots.

The reason why I've waived my usual hesitancy to stay in Excel is that Gephi fills in the network visualization gap in Excel, it's free, and it works on Windows, Mac OS, and Linux, so no matter what computer you're using, you can follow along.

You don't have to do these visualization steps. If you just want to follow along in the figures feel free, but I recommend getting your hands dirty. It's fun. Keep in mind, though, that this book is not about Gephi. If you want to get really crazy with this tool, check out the resources at wiki.gephi.org for deeper instruction.

Gephi Installation and File Preparation

To download Gephi, navigate to gephi.org in your browser, and then download and install the package following the instructions for your OS at http://gephi.org/users/install/.

If you want a general tutorial on Gephi, check out the quick start guide at https://gephi.org/users/quick-start/. Also, inside the application, Gephi has a Help selection in the menu bar if you need it.

Once Gephi is installed, you need to prep the adjacency matrix for importing into the visualization tool.

Now, I find that importing an adjacency matrix into Gephi takes one step more than it should. Why? Because Gephi doesn't accept comma-separated adjacency matrices. Each value has to be separated by a semicolon.

Although Kurt Vonnegut said in *A Man Without A Country*, "Do not use semicolons. They are transvestite hermaphrodites representing absolutely nothing. All they do is show you've been to college," Gephi has ignored his sound advice. My apologies. So follow along, and I'll take you through the import process.

I've made the FriendsGraph.xlsx spreadsheet available with the book (download at the book's website at www.wiley.com/go/datasmart), or if you like, you can just hand-jam in the small dataset from the adjacency matrix pictured in Figure 5-2.

The first thing you're going to do to import this graph into Gephi is save it as a CSV, which is a plain-text, comma-separated file format. To do so, go to Save As in Excel and choose CSV from the format list. The filename will end up as FriendsGraph.csv, and when you save it, Excel may bark some warnings at you, which I give you permission to ignore.

Once you've exported the file, you need to replace all the commas in it with semicolons. To do this, open the file in a text editor (such as Notepad on Windows or TextEdit on Mac OS) and find and replace the commas with semicolons. Save the file. Figure 5-3 shows this process in Mac OS TextEdit.

Figure 5-3: Replacing commas with semicolons in the *Friends* graph CSV

Once that's completed, open your freshly installed copy of Gephi, and using the Open Graph File option on the Welcome screen (see Figure 5-4), select the FriendsGraph.csv file you just edited.

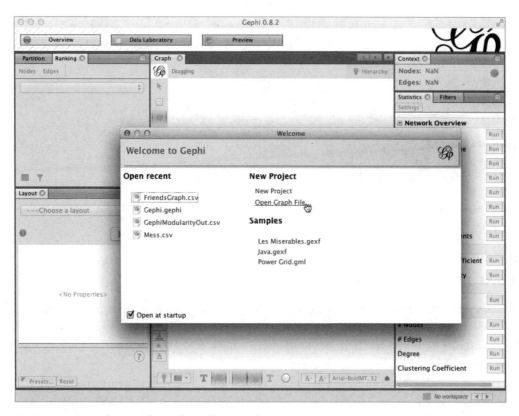

Figure 5-4: Open the FriendsGraph.csv file in Gephi.

When you attempt to open the file, an Import Report window will pop up. Note that six nodes and ten edges have been detected. The reason why ten edges are listed is because the adjacency matrix is symmetric, so each relationship is duplicated. To resolve this duplication, change the Graph Type from directed to undirected in the import window (see Figure 5-5). Press OK.

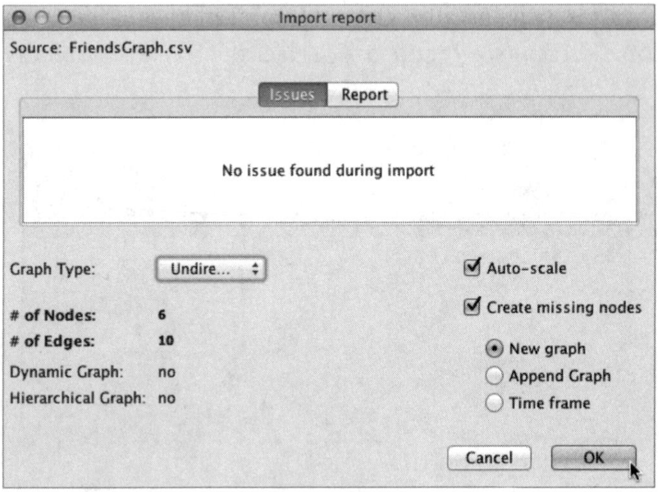

Figure 5-5: Importing the *Friends* graph

Laying Out the Graph

Make sure the Overview tab is selected in the top left of the Gephi window. If it is selected, your Gephi window should look something like Figure 5-6. The nodes and edges are laid out haphazardly in space. The zoom is all out of whack so the graph is barely visible. Your initial layout will likely appear different.

Let's make this graph a little prettier. A couple of navigational items you should be aware of—you can zoom in with the scroll wheel on your mouse, and you can move the canvas around by right-clicking in the space and dragging the graph until it's centered.

By clicking the T button at the foot of the overview window, you can add labels to the graph nodes so you know which character is which node. After zooming in, adjusting, and adding labels, the graph now looks as shown in Figure 5-7.

You need to lay this graph out in a nicer fashion. And luckily, Gephi has a bunch of algorithms for automating this process. Many of them use forces such as gravity between connected nodes and repulsion between unconnected nodes to settle things into place. The layout section of Gephi is in the bottom-left window of the overview panel. Feel free to select things haphazardly from the menu to try them out.

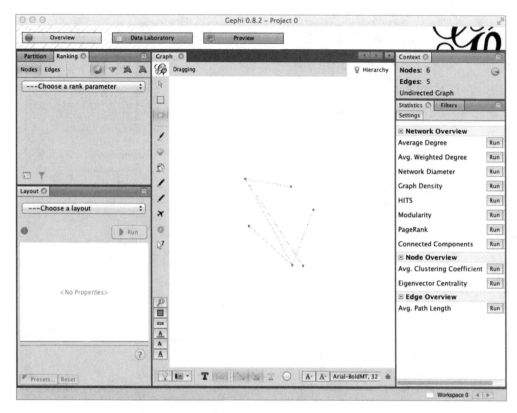

Figure 5-6: Initial layout of the *Friends* graph

NOTE

Be warned that some of the layout algorithms are going to shrink or expand the graph such that you'll have to zoom in or out to see the graph again. Also, the sizes of your labels are going to get out of whack, but there's a Label Adjust selection under the Layout drop-down menu to fix that.

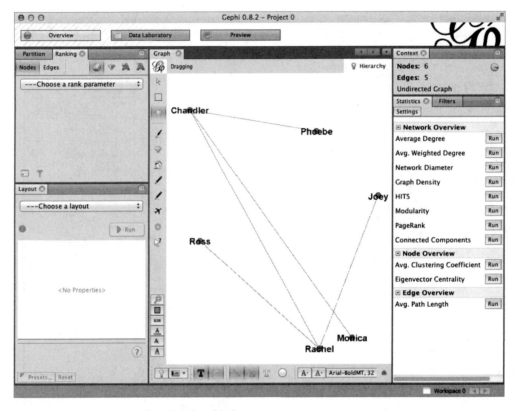

Figure 5-7: The *Friends* graph is decipherable but messy.

To get my preferred layout, the first thing I'm going to do is select ForceAtlas 2 from the layout menu and press the Run button. This is going to move my nodes around to better positions. But the labels are now huge (see Figure 5-8).

Select Label Adjust from the menu and press Run. You'll get something that looks much better. I can see that Rachel and Chandler are really the most well-connected in the graph. Obviously, Monica and Ross are distant because they're brother and sister, and so on.

Node Degree

One concept in network graphing that's going to be important in this chapter is that of *degree*. The degree of a node is simply the count of edges connected to it. So Chandler has a degree of 3, whereas Phoebe has a degree of 1. You can use these degrees in Gephi to resize nodes.

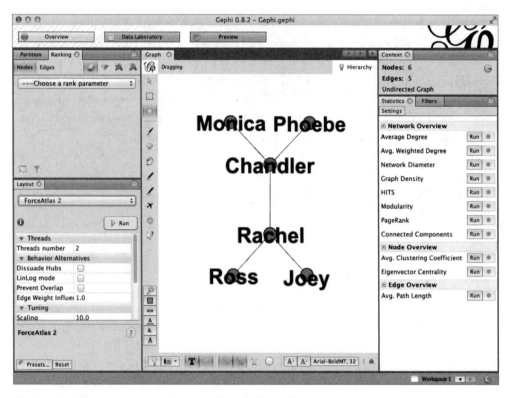

Figure 5-8: After running ForceAtlas 2 on the *Friends* graph

---

INDEGREE, OUTDEGREE, IMPORTANCE, AND BAD BEHAVIOR

In a directed graph, the count of edges going into a node is called the *indegree*. The count of outbound edges is the *outdegree*. Indegree in a social network is a simple way to gauge the prestige of a node. This is often the first value people look at on Facebook or Twitter to gauge importance. "Oh, they have a lot of followers…they must be a big deal."

Now, this metric can certainly be gamed. Who exactly are these followers whose edges flow into your node? Maybe they're all fake users you signed up for to heighten your own prestige.

Google uses indegree (in search engine speak this is a *backlink* count) in their PageRank algorithm. When someone fakes inbound links to their website to heighten its prestige and move up the search results, that's called *link spam*. In contexts such as an Internet search where rankings mean big business, more complex measures of prestige, influence, and centrality have evolved to account for such bad behavior.

As you'll see in Chapter 9, these network graph concepts are useful in *outlier detection*. Rather than finding who is central in a graph, you can use indegree to find who's on the periphery.

To get a sense of the average degree of the graph and who has what degree, press the Average Degree button on the right side of Gephi in the Statistics section. This will pop up a window like the one shown in Figure 5-9, where the average degree of the graph is 1.6667 with four nodes of degree 1 and two nodes of degree 3 (Rachel and Chandler).

Close this window and navigate to the Ranking section of the Overview window in the top left box. Select the Nodes section and the red gemstone label that indicates node resizing. Select Degree from the drop-down and toggle the minimum and maximum sizes for nodes. When you press Apply, Gephi will resize the nodes using degree as a proxy for importance. I've called out this section of the Overview window in Figure 5-10.

Pretty Printing

Although these pictures look okay, you're not going to hang them on your wall. To prepare the graph for printing an image, click the Preview pane at the top of Gephi.

Under the Preview Settings tab, select the Black Background preset from the Presets drop-down (because you have hacker delusions), and click the Refresh button at the bottom left of the window.

Gephi will paint the graph with stunning, curvy beauty (see Figure 5-11). Note how the labels are resized with the nodes, which is awesome. I find the edges of this graph a little on the thin side, so I bumped the edge thickness up from 1 to 3 on the left settings pane.

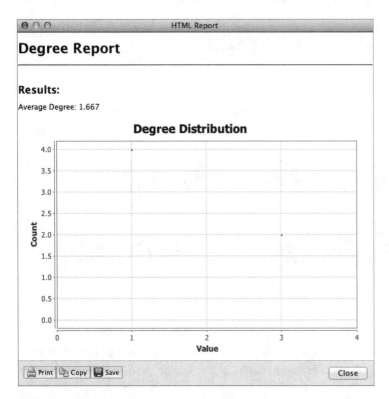

Figure 5-9: Calculating the average degree of a graph

Figure 5-10: Resizing the graph according to node degree

If you want to export this image to a graphics file (for example, a .png file), press the Export button in the bottom left of the preview settings section. You can then distribute the graph on a website, in a PowerPoint presentation, or even in a book on data science.

Touching the Graph Data

Before you move back to Excel to confront the wholesale wine problem from Chapter 2, I want to take you through the Data Laboratory section of Gephi. Click Data Laboratory at the top of Gephi to see the underlying data that you've imported into the graph.

Note that there are two sections of data: Nodes and Edges. In the Nodes section, you see the six characters. And because you went through the Average Degree calculation earlier, a column for Degree has been added to the node dataset. If you want to, you can export this column back to Excel by pressing the Export Table button on the menu bar. See Figure 5-12.

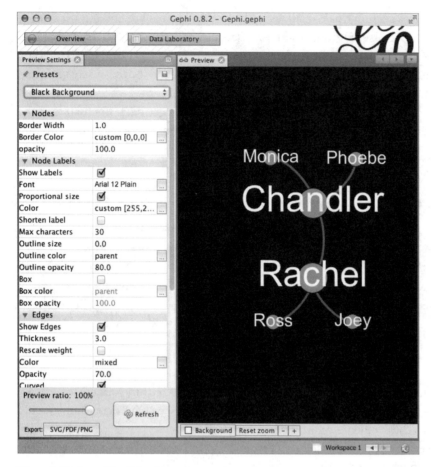

Figure 5-11: A prettier *Friends* graph

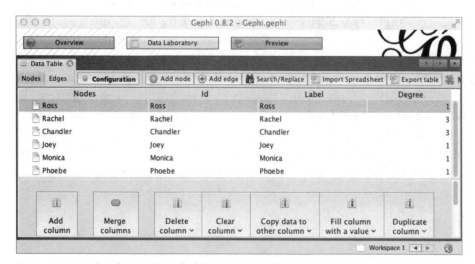

Figure 5-12: Node information with degree count in the Data Laboratory

Clicking the edges section, the five edges with their endpoints are laid out. Each edge was a weight of 1, because you imported an adjacency matrix with all 1s. If you had changed some of those values to be higher in the case of, say, an actual marriage then those higher weights would be reflected in this column (they also would have affected the ForceAtlas 2 layout).

All right! So there's your 30,000-foot tour of Gephi. Let's get back to clustering the wholesale wine data, and you'll return to Gephi later to do some more visualizations and computations.

Building a Graph from the Wholesale Wine Data

NOTE

The Excel workbook used in this chapter, "WineNetwork.xlsx," is available for download at the book's website at www.wiley.com/go/datasmart. This workbook includes all the initial data if you want to work from that. Or you can just read along using the sheets I've already put together in the workbook.

In this chapter, I want to demonstrate how to detect clusters within your customer purchase data by representing that data as a graph. Some businesses have data that's already graphable, such as the Medicare referral data discussed earlier.

But in this case, the wine purchase matrix from Chapter 2 does not represent customer-to-customer relationships out of the box.

To start, you should figure out how to graph the wholesale wine dataset as a network. And that means constructing an adjacency matrix similar to the *Friends* adjacency matrix shown in Figure 5-2. From there you'll be able to visualize and compute whatever you want on the graph.

I'll pick up the analysis using the Matrix tab in the WineNetwork.xlsx workbook (available for download with this book). If you remember, this is the same Matrix tab you created at the beginning of Chapter 2 from the wine sale transactional data and the wholesale deal metadata.

Pictured in Figure 5-13, the rows of the Matrix tab give details of the 32 wine deals offered by Joey Bag O' Donuts Wine Emporium last year. In the columns of the sheet are customer names, and each (deal, customer) cell has a value of 1 if that customer purchased that deal.

	B	C	D	E	F	G	H	I	J	K	L	
1	Campaign	Varietal	Minimum Qty (kg)	Discount (%)	Origin	Past Peak	Adams	Allen	Anderson	Bailey	Baker	Bar
2	January	Malbec	72	56	France	FALSE						
3	January	Pinot Noir	72	17	France	FALSE						
4	February	Espumante	144	32	Oregon	TRUE						
5	February	Champagne	72	48	France	TRUE						
6	February	Cabernet Sauvignon	144	44	New Zealand	TRUE						
7	March	Prosecco	144	86	Chile	FALSE						
8	March	Prosecco	6	40	Australia	TRUE				1	1	
9	March	Espumante	6	45	South Africa	FALSE						
10	April	Chardonnay	144	57	Chile	FALSE			1			
11	April	Prosecco	72	52	California	FALSE					1	
12	May	Champagne	72	85	France	FALSE						
13	May	Prosecco	72	83	Australia	FALSE						
14	May	Merlot	6	43	Chile	FALSE						
15	June	Merlot	72	64	Chile	FALSE						
16	June	Cabernet Sauvignon	144	19	Italy	FALSE						
17	June	Merlot	72	88	California	FALSE						
18	July	Pinot Noir	12	47	Germany	FALSE						
19	July	Espumante	6	50	Oregon	FALSE	1					
20	July	Champagne	12	66	Germany	FALSE					1	
21	August	Cabernet Sauvignon	72	82	Italy	FALSE						
22	August	Champagne	12	50	California	FALSE						
23	August	Champagne	72	63	France	FALSE						
24	September	Chardonnay	144	39	South Africa	FALSE						
25	September	Pinot Noir	6	34	Italy	FALSE			1			
26	October	Cabernet Sauvignon	72	59	Oregon	TRUE						
27	October	Pinot Noir	144	83	Australia	FALSE			1			
28	October	Champagne	72	88	New Zealand	FALSE		1				
29	November	Cabernet Sauvignon	12	56	France	TRUE						
30	November	Pinot Grigio	6	87	France	FALSE	1					
31	December	Malbec	6	54	France	FALSE	1			1		
32	December	Champagne	72	89	France	FALSE					1	
33	December	Cabernet Sauvignon	72	45	Germany	TRUE						

Matrix +

Normal View   Ready   Sum=0

Figure 5-13: The Matrix tab showing who bought what

So you need to turn this data from Chapter 2 into something similar to the *Friends* adjacency matrix, but how do you go about doing that?

If you created the Distances matrix for the k-means silhouette in Chapter 2, you've already seen something similar. For that calculation, you created a matrix of distances between each customer based on the deals they took (shown in Figure 5-14).

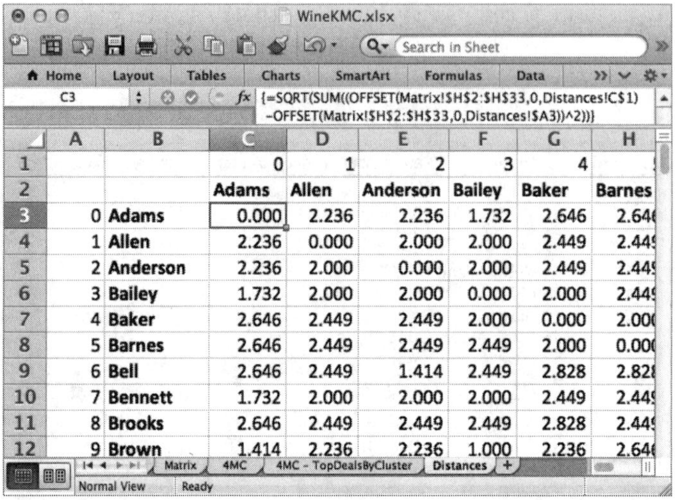

	A	B	C	D	E	F	G	H
1			0	1	2	3	4	
2			Adams	Allen	Anderson	Bailey	Baker	Barnes
3		0 Adams	0.000	2.236	2.236	1.732	2.646	2.64
4		1 Allen	2.236	0.000	2.000	2.000	2.449	2.44
5		2 Anderson	2.236	2.000	0.000	2.000	2.449	2.44
6		3 Bailey	1.732	2.000	2.000	0.000	2.000	2.44
7		4 Baker	2.646	2.449	2.449	2.000	0.000	2.00
8		5 Barnes	2.646	2.449	2.449	2.449	2.000	0.00
9		6 Bell	2.646	2.449	1.414	2.449	2.828	2.82
10		7 Bennett	1.732	2.000	2.000	2.000	2.449	2.44
11		8 Brooks	2.646	2.449	2.449	2.449	2.828	2.44
12		9 Brown	1.414	2.236	2.236	1.000	2.236	2.64

Figure 5-14: The customer distances tab from Chapter 2

This dataset was oriented in a customer-to-customer fashion just like the *Friends* dataset. Connections between customers were characterized by how their purchases aligned.

But there are a couple of problems with this customer-to-customer distance matrix created in Chapter 2:

- At the end of Chapter 2 you discovered that asymmetric similarity and distance measures between customers work much better than Euclidean distance in the case of purchase data. You care about purchases, not "non-purchases."
- If you want to draw edges between two customers, you want to do so because the two customers are similar not because they are distant, so this calculation needs to be reversed. This closeness of purchases is captured via cosine *similarity*, so you need to create a similarity matrix in contrast to Chapter 2's distance matrix.

Creating a Cosine Similarity Matrix

In this section, you'll take the Matrix tab in your notebook and construct from it a customer-to-customer graph using cosine similarity. The process for doing this in Excel, using numbered rows and columns together with the `OFFSET` formula, is identical to that used in Chapter 2 for the Euclidean distances sheet. For more on `OFFSET`, see Chapter 1.

You'll start by creating a tab called **Similarity** in which you will paste a customer-by-customer grid, whereby each customer is numbered in each direction. Remember that copying and pasting customers from the Matrix tab down the rows requires using the Paste Special feature in Excel with the Transpose box checked.

This empty grid is shown in Figure 5-15.

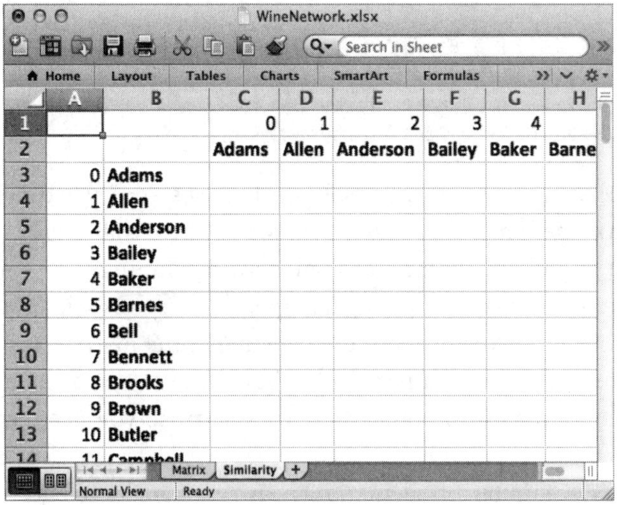

	A	B	C	D	E	F	G	H
1			0	1	2	3	4	
2			Adams	Allen	Anderson	Bailey	Baker	Barne
3	0	Adams						
4	1	Allen						
5	2	Anderson						
6	3	Bailey						
7	4	Baker						
8	5	Barnes						
9	6	Bell						
10	7	Bennett						
11	8	Brooks						
12	9	Brown						
13	10	Butler						

Figure 5-15: The empty grid for the cosine similarity matrix

Start by computing the cosine similarity between Adams and himself (which should be 1). As a refresher, recall the definition of cosine similarity between two customers' binary purchase vectors that you read in Chapter 2:

The count of matched purchases in the two vectors divided by the product of the square root of the number of purchases in the first vector times the square root of the number of purchases in the second vector.

Adams' purchase vector is `Matrix!$H$2:$H$33`; so in order to compute the cosine similarity of Adams to himself, you use the following formula in cell C3:

```
=SUMPRODUCT(Matrix!$H$2:$H$33,Matrix!$H$2:$H$33)/
  (SQRT(SUM(Matrix!$H$2:$H$33))*SQRT(SUM(Matrix!$H$2:$H$33)))
```

In the top of the formula you take the `SUMPRODUCT` of the purchase vectors you care about to count matched purchases. In the denominator, you take the square roots of the number of purchases for each customer and multiply them.

Now, this computation works for Adams, but you want to drag it around the sheet so you don't have to type each formula individually. And to make that happen, you use the `OFFSET` formula. By replacing `Matrix!$H$2:$H$33` with `OFFSET(Matrix!$H$2:$H$33,0,Similarity!C$1)` for the columns and, similarly using

OFFSET(Matrix!$H$2:$H$33,0,Similarity!$A3) for the rows, you get a formula that uses the customer numbers in column A and row 1 to shift the purchase vectors being used in the similarity calculation.

This leads to a slightly more ugly (sorry!) formula for cell C3:

```
=SUMPRODUCT(OFFSET(Matrix!$H$2:$H$33,0,Similarity!C$1),
    OFFSET(Matrix!$H$2:$H$33,0,Similarity!$A3))/
    (SQRT(SUM(OFFSET(Matrix!$H$2:$H$33,0,Similarity!C$1)))
    *SQRT(SUM(OFFSET(Matrix!$H$2:$H$33,0,Similarity!$A3))))
```

This formula locks down Matrix!$H$2:$H$33 by the absolute references, so as you drag the formula around the sheet, it stays the same. Similarity!C$1 will change columns but will stay on row 1 where you want it, and Similarity!$A3 will stay in column A.

But you're not quite done. You're interested in creating a graph of customers who are similar to each other, but honestly, you don't care about the diagonal of the matrix. Yes, Adams is identical to himself and has a cosine similarity of 1, but you're not interested in drawing a graph with edges that loop back to point where they start, so you need to make all those entries 0 instead.

This just means wrapping the cosine similarity calculation in an IF statement to check whether the customer on the row equals the one in the column. Thus, you get the final formula of:

```
IF(C$1=$A3,0,SUMPRODUCT(OFFSET(Matrix!$H$2:$H$33,0,Similarity!C$1),
    OFFSET(Matrix!$H$2:$H$33,0,Similarity!$A3))/
    (SQRT(SUM(OFFSET(Matrix!$H$2:$H$33,0,Similarity!C$1)))
    *SQRT(SUM(OFFSET(Matrix!$H$2:$H$33,0,Similarity!$A3))))))
```

Now that you have a formula that you can drag around, grab the bottom-right corner of C3, drag it across the sheet to CX3, and drag it down to CX102.

You now have a cosine similarity matrix that shows which customers match each other. Placing some conditional formatting on the grid, you get what's pictured in Figure 5-16.

Producing an r-Neighborhood Graph

The Similarity tab is a weighted graph. Each pair of customers either has a 0 between them or some non-zero cosine similarity value that shows how strong their edge should be. As it is, this similarity matrix is an affinity matrix.

So why not just dump this affinity matrix out and peek at it in Gephi? Maybe you're all set to do the analysis on the graph as is.

Sure, exporting the CSV and importing it into Gephi is possible at this step. But let me save you the heartache and just throw up an image (Figure 5-17) of the graph after it's been laid out in Gephi. It's a huge mess of edges going every which way. Too many connections prevent the layout algorithms from properly moving nodes away from each other, so in the end you have an oblong chunk of noise.

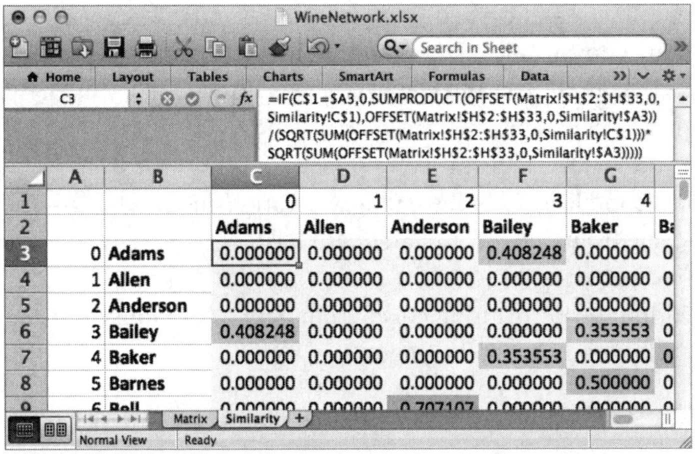

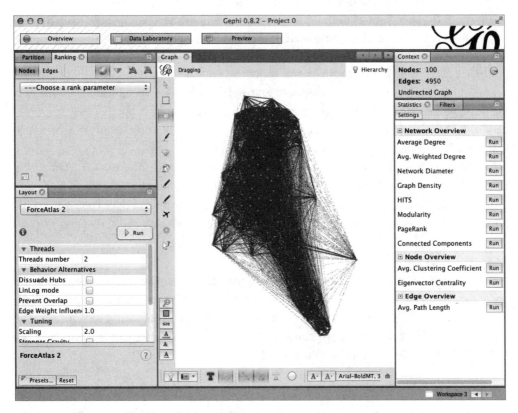

Figure 5-16: The completed customer cosine similarity matrix

Figure 5-17: The mess of a cosine similarity customer-to-customer graph

You've taken about 300 purchases and turned them into thousands of edges in the graph. Some of these edges you can probably chalk up to randomness. Yeah, maybe you and I lined up on 1 of our 10 wine purchases, and you have a teeny tiny cosine similarity, but is that edge worth drawing on the graph?

In order to make sense of the data, it's best if you *prune* edges from the graph that really don't matter all that much, and keep only the strongest relationships on there—the relationships that don't just come from one lucky shared purchase.

Okay, so which edges should you drop?

There are two popular techniques for pruning edges from network graphs. You can take the affinity matrix and build one of the following:

- **An r-neighborhood graph:** In an r-neighborhood graph, you keep only the edges that are of a certain strength. For instance, in the affinity matrix, edge weights range from 0 to 1. Maybe you should drop all edges below 0.5. That'd be an example of an r-neighborhood graph where *r* is 0.5.
- **A k nearest neighbors (kNN) graph:** In a kNN graph, you keep a set number of edges (k) going out of each node. For instance, if you set k to 5, you'd keep the five edges coming out of each node that have the highest affinities.

Neither graph is superior to the other. It depends on the situation.

This chapter focuses on the first option, an r-neighborhood graph. I leave it as an exercise for you to go back and work the problem with a kNN graph. It's pretty easy to implement in Excel using the LARGE formula (see Chapter 1 for more on LARGE). In Chapter 9, we'll use a kNN graph for outlier detection.

All right. So how do you take the Similarity tab and turn it into an r-neighborhood adjacency matrix? Well, first you need to settle on what *r* should be.

In the white space below the similarity matrix, count how many edges (non-zero similarity values) you have in the affinity matrix using the formula in cell C104:

```
=COUNTIF(C3:CX102,">0")
```

This returns 2,950 edges made from the original 324 sales. What if you kept only the top 20 percent of them? What would the value of *r* have to be to make that happen? Well, because you have 2,950 edges, the 80th percentile similarity value would be whatever the 590th edge has. So below the edge count in C105, you can use the LARGE formula to get the 590th largest edge weight (see Figure 5-18):

```
=LARGE(C3:CX102,590)
```

This returns a value of 0.5. So you can keep the top 20 percent of edges by throwing away everything with a cosine similarity of less than 0.5.

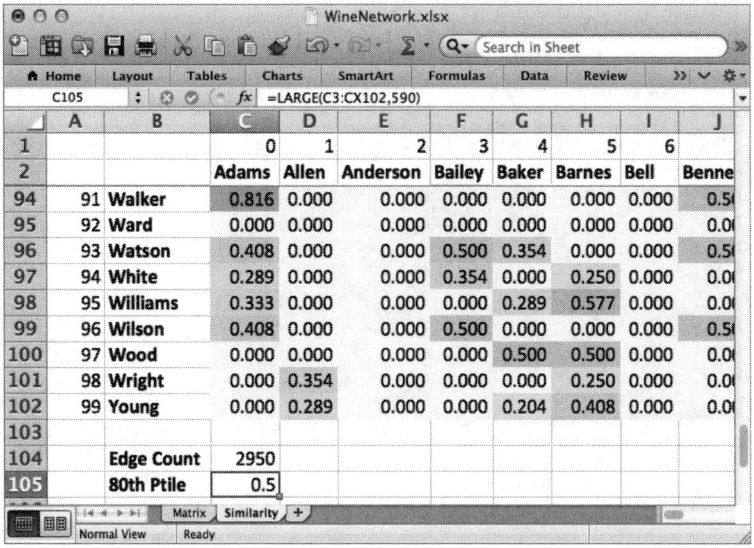

	A	B	C	D	E	F	G	H	I	J
1			0	1	2	3	4	5	6	
2			Adams	Allen	Anderson	Bailey	Baker	Barnes	Bell	Benne
94	91	Walker	0.816	0.000	0.000	0.000	0.000	0.000	0.000	0.5
95	92	Ward	0.000	0.000	0.000	0.000	0.000	0.000	0.000	0.0
96	93	Watson	0.408	0.000	0.000	0.500	0.354	0.000	0.000	0.5
97	94	White	0.289	0.000	0.000	0.354	0.000	0.250	0.000	0.0
98	95	Williams	0.333	0.000	0.000	0.000	0.289	0.577	0.000	0.0
99	96	Wilson	0.408	0.000	0.000	0.500	0.000	0.000	0.000	0.5
100	97	Wood	0.000	0.000	0.000	0.000	0.500	0.500	0.000	0.0
101	98	Wright	0.000	0.354	0.000	0.000	0.000	0.250	0.000	0.0
102	99	Young	0.000	0.289	0.000	0.000	0.204	0.408	0.000	0.0
103										
104		Edge Count	2950							
105		80th Ptile	0.5							

Figure 5-18: Calculating the 80th percentile of edge weights

Now that you have the cutoff for the r-neighborhood graph, construction of the adjacency matrix is super easy. First create a new tab in the workbook called **r-NeighborhoodAdj**, and paste the customer names in column A and row 1 to create a grid.

In any cell in the grid, you put a 1 if the similarity value on the previous Similarity tab is greater than 0.5. So, for example, in cell B2, you can use the following formula:

```
=IF(Similarity!C3>=Similarity!$C$105,1,0)
```

The `IF` formula simply checks the appropriate similarity value against the cutoff in `Similarity$C$105` (0.5) and assigns a 1 if it's large enough. Because `Similarity$C$105` is locked down with absolute references, you can drag this formula across the columns and down the rows to fill in the whole adjacency matrix, as shown in Figure 5-19 (I've used some conditional formatting for the benefit of the figure).

You now have the r-neighborhood graph of the customer purchase data. You've transformed the purchase data into customer relationships and then whittled those down to a set of meaningful ones.

If you were to now export the r-neighborhood adjacency matrix to Gephi and lay it out, you would get something much improved over Figure 5-17. Export the graph yourself, do the semicolon two-step, and take a peek along with me.

As shown in Figure 5-20, there are at least two tightly knit communities in the graph that kinda look like tumors. One of them is well-separated from the rest of the herd, which is awesome, because it means their interests separate them from other customers.

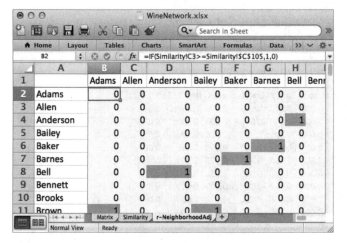

Figure 5-19: The 0.5-neighborhood adjacency matrix

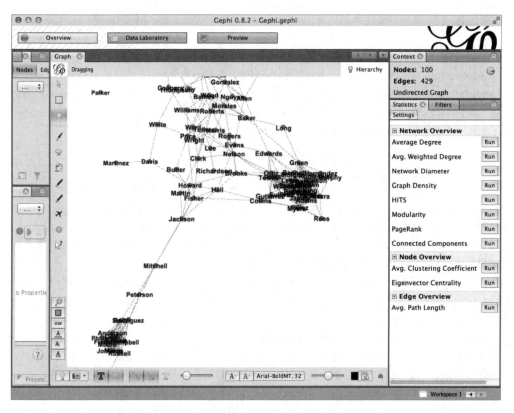

Figure 5-20: Gephi visualization of the r-neighborhood graph

And then there's poor old Parker, the one customer who didn't end up with any edges greater than or equal to 0.5 cosine similarity. So he's by himself, crying in his tea. I honestly feel bad for the guy, because the layout algorithms are going to try to toss him as far as possible from the connected part of the graph.

All right! So now you have a graph that you can eyeball. And in fact, just laying a graph out and eyeballing it—separating it into communities by inspection—isn't half bad. You've taken high-dimensional data and distilled it into something flat like the middle school dance floor from Chapter 2. But if you had thousands of customers instead of a hundred, your eyeballs wouldn't be terribly helpful. Indeed, even now, there's a mesh of customers in the graph who are hard to group together. Are they in one community or several?

This is where modularity maximization comes into play. The algorithm uses these relationships in the graph to make community assignment decisions even when your eyeballs might have trouble.

How Much Is an Edge Worth? Points and Penalties in Graph Modularity

Pretend that I'm a customer hanging out in my graph, and I want to know who belongs in a community with me.

How about that lady who's connected to me by an edge? Maybe. Probably. We are connected after all.

How about the guy on the other side of the graph who shares no edge with me? Hmmm, it's much less likely.

Graph modularity quantifies this gut feeling that *communities are defined by connections*. The technique assigns scores to each pair of nodes. If two nodes aren't connected, I need to be penalized for putting them in a community. If two nodes are connected, I need to be rewarded. Whatever community assignment I make, the modularity of the graph is driven by the sum of those scores for each pair of nodes that ends up in a community together.

Using an optimization algorithm (you knew Solver was coming!), you can "try out" different community assignments on the graph and see which one rakes in the most points with the fewest penalties. This will get you a winning modularity score.

What's a Point and What's a Penalty?

In modularity maximization you give yourself one point every time you cluster two nodes that share an edge in the adjacency matrix. You get zero points every time you cluster those who don't.

Easy.

What about penalties?

This is where the modularity maximization algorithm really gets creative. Consider again the *Friends* graph, originally pictured in Figure 5-1.

Modularity maximization bases its penalties for putting two nodes together on one question:

If you had this graph and you erased the middle of each edge and "rewired" it a bunch of times at random, what is the expected number of edges you'd get between two nodes?

That expected number of edges is the penalty.

Why is the expected number of edges between two nodes the penalty? Well, you don't want to reward the model as much for clustering people based on a relationship that was likely to happen anyway because both parties are extremely social.

I want to know how much of that graph is *intentional* relationship and connection, and how much of it is just because, "Yeah, well, Chandler's connected to a lot of people, so odds are Phoebe would be one of them." This means that edges between two highly selective individuals are "less random" and worth more than edges between two socialites.

To understand this more clearly, look at a version of the *Friends* graph in which I've erased the middle of each edge. These half-edges are called *stubs*. See Figure 5-21.

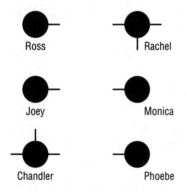

Figure 5-21: Stubby *Friends* graph

Now, think about wiring the graph up randomly. In Figure 5-22, I've drawn an ugly random rewiring. And yes, in a random rewiring it's totally possible to connect someone to him or herself if they have multiple stubs coming out of them. Trippy.

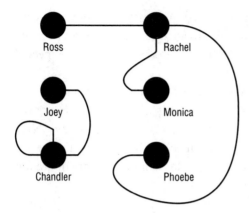

Figure 5-22: A rewiring of the *Friends* graph

Figure 5-22 is just one way to wire it up, right? There are tons of possibilities even with a graph with just five edges. Notice that Ross and Rachel were chosen. What were the odds of that happening? Based on that probability, what is the expected number of edges between the two if you rewired the graph randomly over and over and over again?

Well, when drawing a random edge, you need to select two stubs at random. So what's the probability that a node's stubs will be selected?

In the case of Rachel, she has three stubs out of a total of ten (two times the number of edges) on the graph. Ross has one stub. So the probability that you'd select Rachel for any edge is 30 percent, and the probability that you'd select Ross's stub for any edge is 10 percent. The node selection probabilities are shown in Figure 5-23.

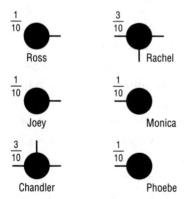

Figure 5-23: Node selection probabilities on the *Friends* graph

So if you were randomly selecting nodes to link up, you could select Ross and then Rachel or Rachel and then Ross. That's roughly 10 percent *times* 30 percent or 30 percent *times* 10 percent, which is 2 times 0.3 times 0.1. That comes out to 6 percent.

But you're not drawing just one edge, are you? You need to draw a random graph with five edges, so you get five tries to pick that combo. The expected number of edges between Ross and Rachel then is roughly 6 percent times 5, or 0.3 edges. Yes, that's right, expected edges can be fractional.

Did I just blow your mind *Inception*-style? Think of it like this. If I flip a Sacagawea dollar coin, which you get to keep if it lands on heads but not tails, then fifty percent of the time you're going to get a dollar and fifty percent of the time you get nothing. Your *expected* payoff is 0.5 * $1 = $0.50, even though you'll never actually win fifty cents in a game.

Similarly here, you'll only ever encounter graphs where Ross and Rachel are or are not connected, but their expected edge value is nevertheless 0.3.

Figure 5-24 shows these calculations in detail.

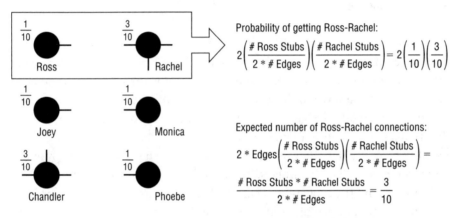

Figure 5-24: The expected number of edges between Ross and Rachel

Bringing the points and penalties together, things should now become clear.

If you put Ross and Rachel in a community together, you don't get a full 1 point. This is because you get penalized 0.3 points since that's the expected number of edges a random graph would have anyway. That leaves you with a score of 0.7.

If you didn't cluster Ross and Rachel, then you would receive 0 rather than 0.7 points.

On the other hand, Rachel and Phoebe *aren't* connected. They have the same expected edge value of 0.3 though. That means that if you put them in a community together, you'd still get the penalty but you'd receive no points, so the score would be adjusted by –0.3.

Why? Because the fact that there's no edge between Rachel and Phoebe means something! The expected number of edges was 0.3 and yet this graph doesn't have one, so the score should account for that possibly intentional separation.

If you didn't put Rachel and Phoebe in a community together, then they'd receive no score at all, so all things being equal, you're best separating them into different clusters.

To sum it all up then, the points and penalties capture the amount that the graph's structure deviates from the *expected* graph structure. You need to assign communities that account for these deviations.

The modularity of a community assignment is just the sum of these points and penalties for pairs of nodes placed in community together, divided by the *total number of stubs* in the graph. You divide by the number of stubs so that whatever the size of the graph, the maximum modularity score is 1, which facilitates comparisons across graphs.

Setting Up the Score Sheet

Enough talk! Let's actually calculate these scores for each pair of customers in the graph.

To start, let's count how many stubs are coming out of each customer and how many total stubs there are in the graph. Note that the stub count of a customer is just the degree of the node.

So on the r- NeighborhoodAdj tab you can count the degree of a node simply by summing down a column or across a row. If there's a 1, that's an edge, hence a stub, hence it's counted. So, for example, how many stubs does Adams have? In cell B102, you can just place the following formula to count them:

```
=SUM(B2:B101)
```

You get 14. Similarly, you could sum across row 2 by placing in cx2 the formula:

```
=SUM(B2:CW2)
```

You get 14 in that case as well, which is what you'd expect since the graph is undirected.

Copying these formulas across and down respectively, you can count the stubs for each node. And by simply summing column CX in row 102, you get the total number of stubs for the graph. As shown in Figure 5-25, the graph has a total of 858 stubs.

Now that you have the stub counts, you can create a Scores tab in your workbook where you place the customers' names across row 1 and down column A, just as in the r-NeighborhoodAdj tab.

Consider cell B2, which is the score for Adams connecting with himself. Does this get one point or none? Well, you can read in the value from the adjacency matrix, `'r-NeighborhoodAdj'!B2`, and you're done. If the adjacency matrix is a 1, it's copied in. Simple.

As for the expected edge calculation that you need to tack on as a penalty, you can calculate it the same way that was shown in Figure 5-24:

*# stubs customer A * # stubs customer B / Total stubs*

By bringing these points and penalties together in cell B2, you end up with this formula:

```
='r-NeighborhoodAdj'!B2 -
(('r-NeighborhoodAdj'!$CX2*'r-NeighborhoodAdj'!B$102)/
'r-NeighborhoodAdj'!$CX$102)
```

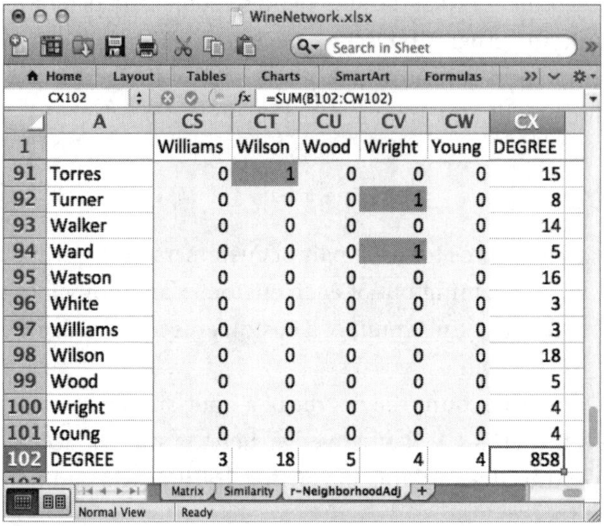

Figure 5-25: Counting edge stubs on the r-Neighborhood graph

You have the 0/1 adjacency score minus the expected count.

Note that the formula uses absolute cell references on the stub values so that when you drag the formula, everything changes appropriately. Thus, dragging the formula across and down the Scores tab, you end up with the values shown in Figure 5-26.

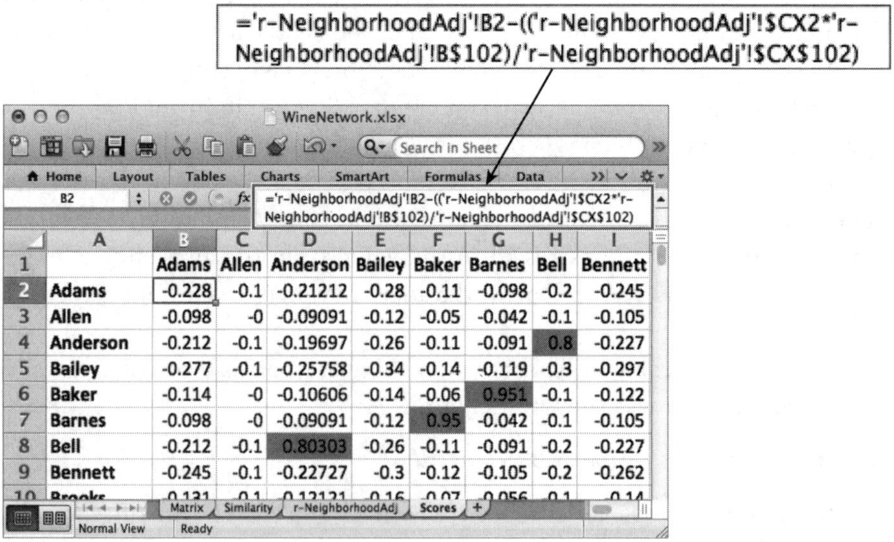

```
='r-NeighborhoodAdj'!B2-(('r-NeighborhoodAdj'!$CX2*'r-
NeighborhoodAdj'!B$102)/'r-NeighborhoodAdj'!$CX$102)
```

Figure 5-26: The Scores tab

To drive this score home, check out cell K2. This is the score for an Adams/Brown clustering. It's 0.755.

Adams and Brown share an edge on the adjacency matrix so you get 1 point for clustering them (`'r-NeighborhoodAdj'!K2` in the formula), but Adams has a stub count of 14 and Brown is a 15, so their expected edge count is 14 * 15 / 858. That second part of the formula looks like this:

```
(('r-NeighborhoodAdj'!$CX2*'r-NeighborhoodAdj'!K$102)/
'r-NeighborhoodAdj'!$CX$102)
```

which comes out to 0.245. Bringing it all together, you get 1 - 0.245 = 0.755 for the score.

Let's Get Clustering!

You now have the scores you need. All you need to do now is set up an optimization model to find optimal community assignments.

Now, I'm going to be honest with you up front. Finding optimal communities using graph modularity is a more intense optimization setup than what you encountered in Chapter 2. This problem is often solved with complex heuristics such as the popular "Louvain" method (see `http://perso.uclouvain.be/vincent.blondel/research/louvain.html` for more info), but this is a code-free zone, so you're going to make do with Solver.

To make this possible, you're going to attack the problem using an approach called *divisive clustering* or *hierarchical partitioning*. All that means is that you're going to set up the problem to find the best way to split the graph into two communities. Then you're going to split those two into four, and on and on until Solver decides that the best way to maximize modularity is to stop dividing the communities.

> **NOTE**
>
> Divisive clustering is the opposite of another often-used approach called *agglomerative clustering*. In agglomerative clustering, each customer starts in their own cluster, and you recursively glom together the two closest clusters until you reach a stopping point.

Split Number 1

All right. So you start this divisive clustering process by dividing the graph into two communities so the modularity score is maximized.

First create a new sheet called **Split1** and paste customers down column A. Each customer's community assignment will go in column B, which you should label **Community**. Since you're splitting the graph in half, have the Community column be a binary decision variable in Solver, where the 0/1 value will denote whether you're in community 0 or community 1. Neither community is better than the other. There's no shame in being a 0.

Scoring Each Customer's Community Assignment

In column C, you're going to calculate the scores you get by placing each customer in their respective community. By that, I mean if you place Adams in community 1, you'll calculate his piece of the total modularity score by summing all the values from his row in the Scores tab whose customer columns also landed in community 1.

Consider how you'd add these scores in a formula. If Adams is in community 1, you need to sum all values from the Scores tab on row 2 where the corresponding customer in the optimization model is also assigned a 1. Because assignment values are 0/1, you can use SUMPRODUCT to multiply the community vector by the score vector and then sum the result.

Although the score values go across the Scores tab, in the optimization model, the assignments go top to bottom, so you need to TRANSPOSE the score values in order to make this work (and using TRANSPOSE means making this an array formula):

```
{=SUMPRODUCT(B$2:B$101,TRANSPOSE(Scores!B2:CW2))}
```

The formula simply multiplies the Scores values for Adams times the community assignments. Only scores matching community assignment 1 stay, whereas the others get set to 0. The SUMPRODUCT just sums everything.

But what if Adams were assigned to community 0? You need only flip the community assignments by subtracting them from 1 in order to make the sum of scores work.

```
{=SUMPRODUCT(1-(B$2:B$101),TRANSPOSE(Scores!B2:CW2))}
```

In an ideal world, you could put these two together with an IF formula that checks Adams' community assignment and then uses one of these two formulas to sum up the correct neighbors' scores. But in order to use an IF formula, you need to use the non-linear solver (see Chapter 4 for details), and in this particular case, maximizing modularity is too hard for the non-linear solver to handle efficiently. You need to make the problem linear.

Making the Score Calculation into a Linear Model

If you read Chapter 4, you'll recall a method for modeling the IF formula using linear constraints, called a "Big M" constraint. You're going to use this tool here.

Both of the previous two formulas are linear; so what if you just set a score variable for Adams to be less than both of them? You're trying to maximize the total modularity scores, so Adams' score will want to rise until it bumps up against the lowest of these two constraining formulas.

But how do you know which score calculation corresponding to Adams' actual community assignment is the lowest? You don't.

To fix that, you need to *deactivate* whichever of those two formulas isn't in play. If Adams is assigned a 1, the first formula becomes an upper bound and the second formula is *turned off*. If Adams is a zero, you have the opposite.

How do you turn off one of the two upper bounds? Add a "Big M" to it— just big enough that its bound is meaningless, because the legit bound is lower.

Consider this modification to the first formula:

```
{=SUMPRODUCT(B$2:B$101,TRANSPOSE(Scores!B2:CW2))+
(1-B2)*SUM(ABS(Scores!B2:CW2))}
```

If Adams is assigned to community 1, the addition you made at the end of the formula turns to 0 (because you're multiplying by 1-B2). In this way, the formula becomes identical to the first one you examined. But if Adams gets assigned to community 0, this formula no longer applies and needs to be turned off. So the `(1-B2)*SUM(ABS(Scores!B2:CW2)` piece of the formula adds one times the sum of all the absolute values of the scores Adams could possibly get, which guarantees the formula is higher than its flipped version that's now in play:

```
{=SUMPRODUCT(1-(B$2:B$101),TRANSPOSE(Scores!B2:CW2))+
B2*SUM(ABS(Scores!B2:CW2))}
```

All you're doing is setting Adams' score to be less than or equal to the correct calculation and removing the other formula from consideration by making it larger. It's a ghetto-hacked `IF` statement.

Thus, in column C you can create a score column that will be a decision variable, whereas in columns D and E in the spreadsheet you can place these two formulas as upper bounds on the score (see Figure 5-27).

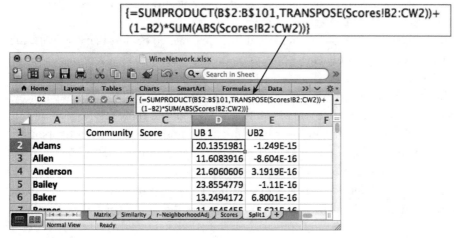

Figure 5-27: Adding two upper bounds to each customer's score variable

Note that in the formula absolute references are used on the community assignment range, so that as you drag the formulas down, nothing shifts.

Summing the scores in cell G2 for each eventual community assignment in column C, you get the total score, which you can normalize by the total stub count in `'r-NeighborhoodAdj'!CX102` in order to get the modularity calculation:

```
=SUM(C2:C101)/'r-NeighborhoodAdj'!CX102
```

This gives the sheet shown in Figure 5-28.

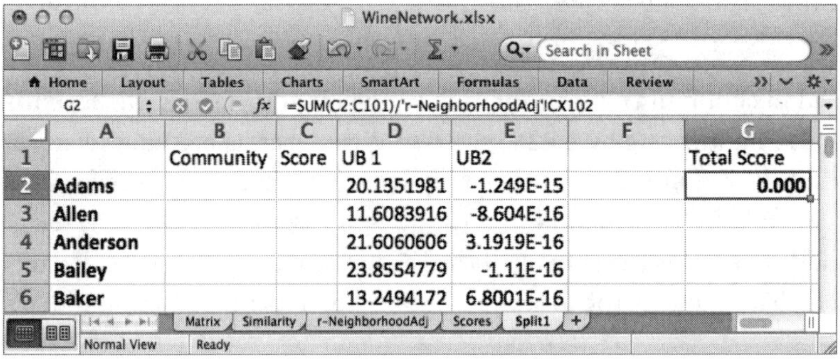

Figure 5-28: Filled out Split1 tab, ready for optimization

Setting Up the Linear Program

Now everything is set up for optimizing. Open the Solver window and specify that you're maximizing the graph modularity score in cell G2. The decision variables are the community assignments in B2:B101 and their modularity scores are in C2:C101.

You need to add a constraint forcing the community assignments in B2:B101 to be binary. Also, you need to make the customer score variables in column C less than both the upper bounds in columns D and E.

As shown in Figure 5-29, you can then set all the variables to be non-negative with the checkbox and select Simplex LP as the optimization algorithm.

But wait. There's more!

One of the problems with using a "Big M" constraint is that Solver often has trouble confirming it's actually found the optimal solution. So it'll just sit there and spin its wheels even though it's got a great solution in its back pocket. To prevent that from happening, press the Options button in Solver and set the Max Subproblems value to 15,000. That ensures that Solver quits after about 20 minutes on my laptop.

Go ahead and press Solve—regardless of whether you're using Solver or OpenSolver (see the nearby sidebar) when the algorithm terminates due to a user-defined limit, it may tell you that while it found a feasible solution, it didn't solve to optimality. This just means that the algorithm didn't prove optimality (similar to how non-linear solvers are unable to prove optimality), but in this case, your solution should be strong nonetheless.

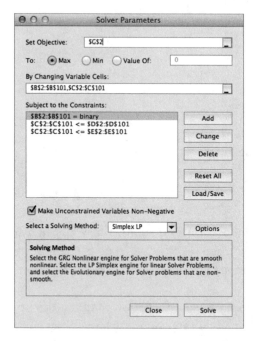

Figure 5-29: The LP formulation for the first split

Once you have a solution, the Split1 tab should appear as in Figure 5-30.

EXCEL 2010 AND 2013 MUST USE OPENSOLVER

If you're in Excel 2010 or 2013 on Windows, this problem is too hard for the Solver provided you, and you'll need to use OpenSolver, as discussed in Chapters 1 and 4.

If you use OpenSolver, set up the problem with regular Solver, but before solving, open the OpenSolver plugin to beef up your system. OpenSolver has the same difficulty with "Big M" constraints, so before running the model, click the OpenSolver options button and set the time limit to 300 seconds. If you don't do this, the default run time on OpenSolver is really high, and it may just spin its wheels, forcing you to kill Excel.

If you're in Excel 2007 or Excel 2011 for Mac, you're good to go with vanilla Solver, although if you'd like to use OpenSolver with Excel 2007, you can. If you're in LibreOffice, you should be just fine.

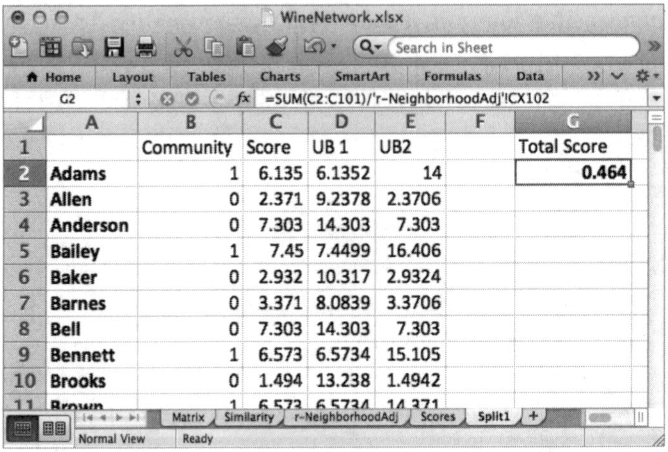

	A	B	C	D	E	F	G
1		Community	Score	UB 1	UB2		Total Score
2	Adams	1	6.135	6.1352	14		0.464
3	Allen	0	2.371	9.2378	2.3706		
4	Anderson	0	7.303	14.303	7.303		
5	Bailey	1	7.45	7.4499	16.406		
6	Baker	0	2.932	10.317	2.9324		
7	Barnes	0	3.371	8.0839	3.3706		
8	Bell	0	7.303	14.303	7.303		
9	Bennett	1	6.573	6.5734	15.105		
10	Brooks	0	1.494	13.238	1.4942		
11	Brown	1	6.573	6.5734	14.371		

Figure 5-30: Optimal solution for the first split

My Solver run came up with 0.464 for the modularity; your solution may be better if you use OpenSolver. Running down column B, you can see who ended up in community 0 and who's in community 1. The question then is, are you done? Are there only two communities or are there more?

In order to answer that question, you need to try to split these two communities up. If you're done, Solver won't have any of it. But if making three or four communities from these two improves modularity, well, then Solver is going to do it.

Split 2: Electric Boogaloo

All right. Split these communities up like you're doing cell division. You start by making a copy of the Split1 tab and calling it **Split2.**

The first thing you need to do is insert a new column after the community values in column B. Label this new column C **Last Run** and copy the values over from B into C. This gives the sheet pictured in Figure 5-31.

In this model, the decisions are the same—customers are given a 1 or a 0. But you need to keep in mind that if two customers are given 1s this time around they're not necessarily in the same community. If one of them was in community 0 on the first run and the other was in community 1, they're in two different communities.

In other words, the only scores Adams might get for being in, say, community 1-0 are from those customers who were also placed in community 0 on the first split and in community 1 on the second. Thus, you need to change the upper bounds on the score calculation. The score calculation for column E (here you show E2) then requires a check against the previous run in column C:

```
{=SUMPRODUCT(B$2:B$101,IF(C$2:C$101=C2,1,0),TRANSPOSE(Scores!B2:CW2))}
```

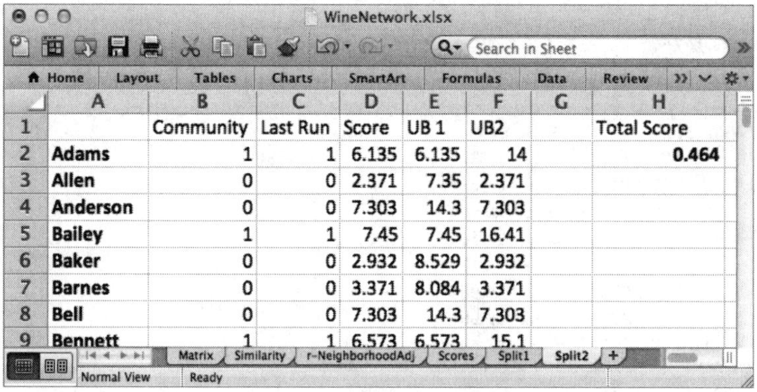

Figure 5-31: The Split2 tab with previous run values

The IF statement IF(C$2:C$101=C2,1,0) prevents Adams from getting points unless his neighbors are with him on the first split.

You can use an IF statement here, because column C isn't a decision variable this time around. That split was fixed on the last run, so there's nothing non-linear about this. You can add the same IF statement into the "Big M" part of the formula to make the final calculation in column E:

```
=SUMPRODUCT(B$2:B$101,IF(C$2:C$101=C2,1,0),TRANSPOSE(Scores!B2:CW2))+
(1-B2)*SUMPRODUCT(IF(C$2:C$101=C2,1,0),TRANSPOSE(ABS(Scores!B2:CW2)))
```

Similarly, you can add the same IF statements into the second upper bound in column F:

```
=SUMPRODUCT(1-(B$2:B$101),IF(C$2:C$101=C2,1,0),TRANSPOSE(Scores!B2:CW2))
+B2*SUMPRODUCT(IF(C$2:C$101=C2,1,0),TRANSPOSE(ABS(Scores!B2:CW2)))
```

All you've done is silo-ed the problem—those who were split into community 0 the first time around have their own little world of scores to play with and the same goes for those who ended up in 1 the first time.

And here's the cool part—you don't have to change the Solver formulation at all! Same formulation, same options! If you're using OpenSolver, it may not have saved your maximum time limit options from the previous tab. Reset the option to three hundred seconds. Solve again.

In my run on Split2, I ended up with a final modularity of 0.546 (see Figure 5-32), which is a substantial improvement over 0.464. That means that splitting was a good idea. (Your solution may end up different and possibly better.)

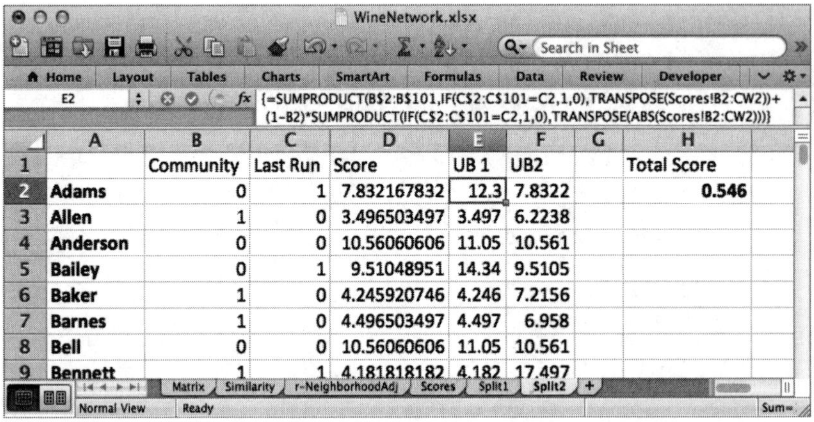

	A	B	C	D	E	F	G	H
1		Community	Last Run	Score	UB 1	UB2		Total Score
2	Adams	0	1	7.832167832	12.3	7.8322		0.546
3	Allen	1	0	3.496503497	3.497	6.2238		
4	Anderson	0	0	10.56060606	11.05	10.561		
5	Bailey	0	1	9.51048951	14.34	9.5105		
6	Baker	1	0	4.245920746	4.246	7.2156		
7	Barnes	1	0	4.496503497	4.497	6.958		
8	Bell	0	0	10.56060606	11.05	10.561		
9	Bennett	1	1	4.181818182	4.182	17.497		

Figure 5-32: The optimal solution for Split2

And...Split 3: Split with a Vengeance

Okay, so should you stop here or should you keep going? The way to tell is to split again, and if Solver can't do better than 0.546, you're through.

Start by creating a Split3 tab, renaming Last Run to **Last Run 2**, and then inserting a new Last Run in column C. Then copy the values from column B into C.

Add more `IF` statements to the upper bounds to check for community assignments in the previous run. For example, F2 becomes:

```
=SUMPRODUCT(B$2:B$101,
IF(D$2:D$101=D2,1,0),IF(C$2:C$101=C2,1,0),
TRANSPOSE(Scores!B2:CW2))+
(1-B2)*SUMPRODUCT(
IF(C$2:C$101=C2,1,0),IF(D$2:D$101=D2,1,0),
TRANSPOSE(ABS(Scores!B2:CW2)))
```

Once again, the Solver formulation doesn't change. Reset your maximum solving time if need be, press Solve, and let the model run its course. In the case of my model, I saw no improvement in modularity (see Figure 5-33).

Splitting again added nothing, so this means that modularity was effectively maximized on Split2. Let's take the cluster assignments from that tab and investigate.

Encoding and Analyzing the Communities

In order to investigate these community assignments, the first thing you should do is take this *binary tree* that's been created by the successive splits and turn those columns into single cluster labels.

Create a tab called **Communities** and paste the customer name, community, and last run values from the Split2 tab. You can rename the two binary columns **Split2** and **Split1**. To turn their binary values into single numbers, Excel provides a nifty binary-to-decimal formula called BIN2DEC. So in column D, starting at D2, you can add:

```
=BIN2DEC(CONCATENATE(B2,C2))
```

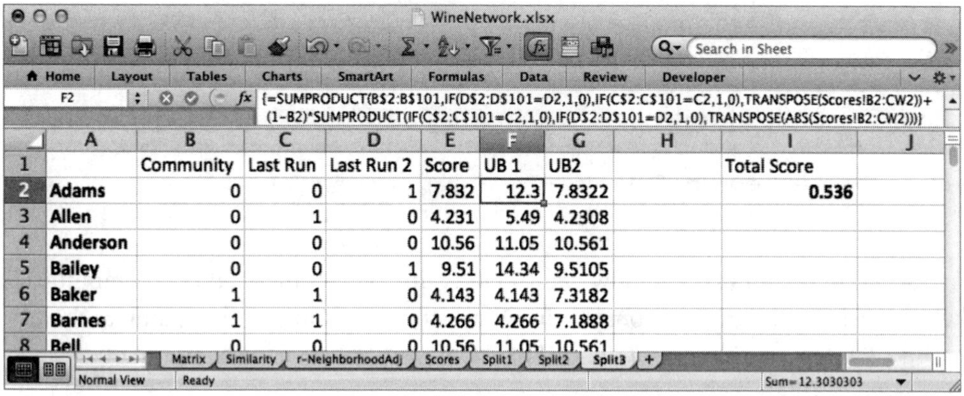

Figure 5-33: No modularity improvement in Split 3

Copying that formula down, you get the community assignments shown in Figure 5-34 (your assignments may vary depending on Solver).

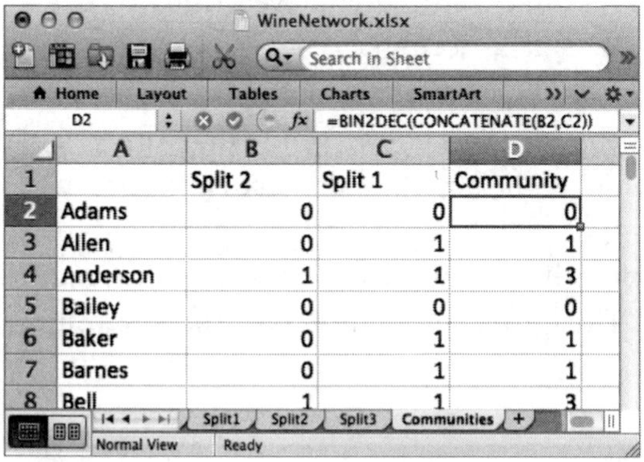

Figure 5-34: Final community labels for modularity maximization

You get four clusters with labels 0 to 3 out of the decimal encoding. So what are these four optimal clusters? Well, you can find out in the same way you delved into clusters in Chapter 2—by investigating the most popular purchases of their members.

To begin, just as in Chapter 2, create a tab called **TopDealsByCluster** and paste the deal information from columns A through G on the Matrix tab. Next to the matrix, place the cluster labels 0, 1, 2, and 3 in columns H through K. This gives you the sheet pictured in Figure 5-35.

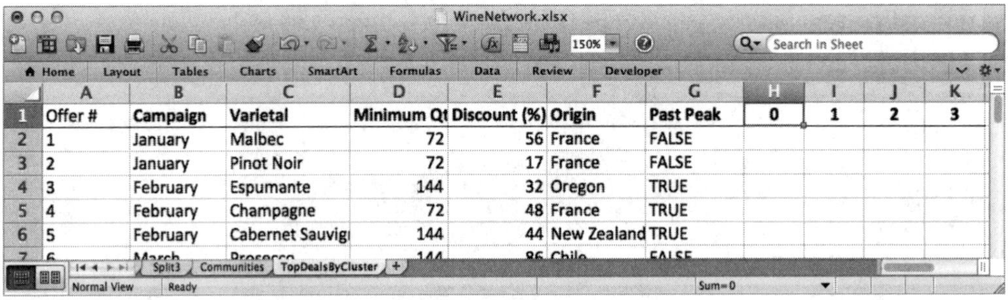

	A	B	C	D	E	F	G	H	I	J	K
1	Offer #	Campaign	Varietal	Minimum Qt	Discount (%)	Origin	Past Peak	0	1	2	3
2	1	January	Malbec	72	56	France	FALSE				
3	2	January	Pinot Noir	72	17	France	FALSE				
4	3	February	Espumante	144	32	Oregon	TRUE				
5	4	February	Champagne	72	48	France	TRUE				
6	5	February	Cabernet Sauvig	144	44	New Zealand	TRUE				
7	6	March	Prosecco	144	86	Chile	FALSE				

Figure 5-35: The initial TopDealsByCluster tab

For label 0 in column H, you now want to look up all customers on the Communities tab who have been assigned to community 0 and sum how many of them took each deal. Just as in Chapter 2 and in the previous Split tabs, you use SUMPRODUCT with an IF statement to achieve this:

```
{=SUMPRODUCT(IF(Communities!$D$2:$D$101=TopDealsByCluster!H$1,1,0),
    TRANSPOSE(Matrix!$H2:$DC2))}
```

In this formula you check which customers match the 0 in the column label at H1, and when they do match, you sum whether or not they took the first deal by checking H2:DC2 on the Matrix tab. Note that you use TRANSPOSE in order to orient everything vertically. This means you have to make the calculation an array formula.

Note that you've used absolute references on the customer community assignments, the header rows, and the purchase matrix columns. This allows you to drag the formula to the right and down, giving you a full picture of the popular purchases for each cluster (see Figure 5-36).

Just as in Chapter 2, you need to apply filtering to the sheet and sort by descending deal count on community 0 in column H. This gives you Figure 5-37, the low-volume customer community (your clusters may vary in their order and composition depending on the solution Solver terminated with at each step).

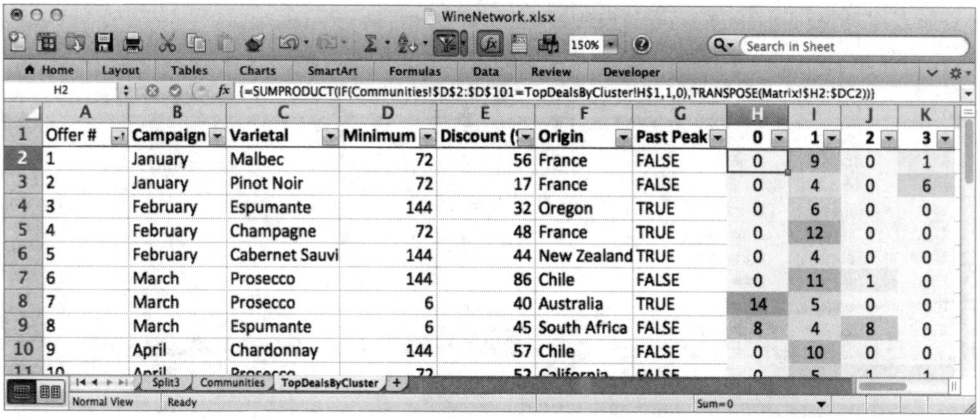

Offer #	Campaign	Varietal	Minimum	Discount (%	Origin	Past Peak	0	1	2	3
1	January	Malbec	72	56	France	FALSE	0	9	0	1
2	January	Pinot Noir	72	17	France	FALSE	0	4	0	6
3	February	Espumante	144	32	Oregon	TRUE	0	6	0	0
4	February	Champagne	72	48	France	TRUE	0	12	0	0
5	February	Cabernet Sauvi	144	44	New Zealand	TRUE	0	4	0	0
6	March	Prosecco	144	86	Chile	FALSE	0	11	1	0
7	March	Prosecco	6	40	Australia	TRUE	14	5	0	0
8	March	Espumante	6	45	South Africa	FALSE	8	4	8	0
9	April	Chardonnay	144	57	Chile	FALSE	0	10	0	0

Figure 5-36: TopDealsByCluster with completed purchase counts

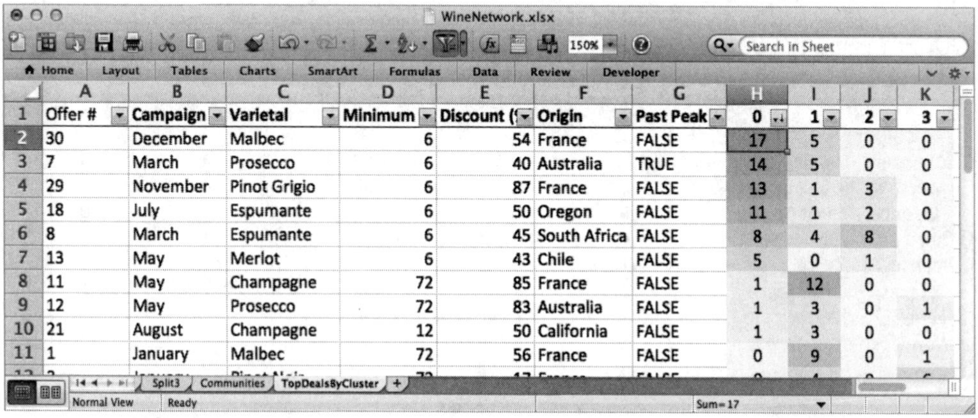

Offer #	Campaign	Varietal	Minimum	Discount (%	Origin	Past Peak	0	1	2	3
30	December	Malbec	6	54	France	FALSE	17	5	0	0
7	March	Prosecco	6	40	Australia	TRUE	14	5	0	0
29	November	Pinot Grigio	6	87	France	FALSE	13	1	3	0
18	July	Espumante	6	50	Oregon	FALSE	11	1	2	0
8	March	Espumante	6	45	South Africa	FALSE	8	4	8	0
13	May	Merlot	6	43	Chile	FALSE	5	0	1	0
11	May	Champagne	72	85	France	FALSE	1	12	0	0
12	May	Prosecco	72	83	Australia	FALSE	1	3	0	1
21	August	Champagne	12	50	California	FALSE	1	3	0	0
1	January	Malbec	72	56	France	FALSE	0	9	0	1

Figure 5-37: Top deals for community 0

Sorting by community 1, you get what appears to be the high-volume French Champagne cluster (see Figure 5-38). Fascinating.

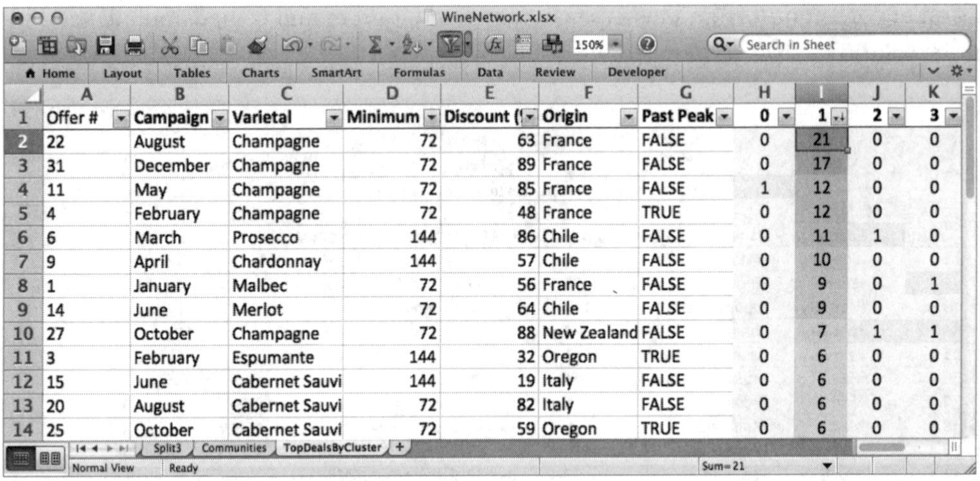

	Offer #	Campaign	Varietal	Minimum	Discount (%	Origin	Past Peak	0	1	2	3
2	22	August	Champagne	72	63	France	FALSE	0	21	0	0
3	31	December	Champagne	72	89	France	FALSE	0	17	0	0
4	11	May	Champagne	72	85	France	FALSE	1	12	0	0
5	4	February	Champagne	72	48	France	TRUE	0	12	0	0
6	6	March	Prosecco	144	86	Chile	FALSE	0	11	1	0
7	9	April	Chardonnay	144	57	Chile	FALSE	0	10	0	0
8	1	January	Malbec	72	56	France	FALSE	0	9	0	1
9	14	June	Merlot	72	64	Chile	FALSE	0	9	0	0
10	27	October	Champagne	72	88	New Zealand	FALSE	0	7	1	1
11	3	February	Espumante	144	32	Oregon	TRUE	0	6	0	0
12	15	June	Cabernet Sauvi	144	19	Italy	FALSE	0	6	0	0
13	20	August	Cabernet Sauvi	72	82	Italy	FALSE	0	6	0	0
14	25	October	Cabernet Sauvi	72	59	Oregon	TRUE	0	6	0	0

Figure 5-38: Poppin' bottles in community 1

As for community 2, it looks similar to community 0, except that the March Espumante deal is the main driver (see Figure 5-39).

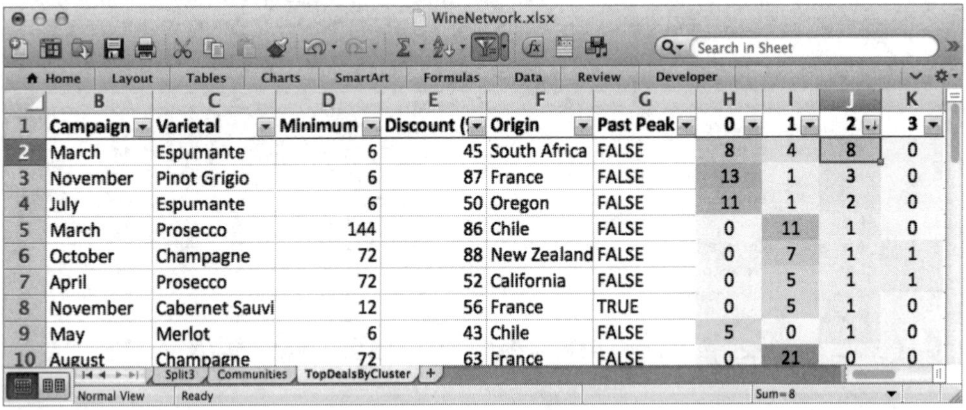

	Campaign	Varietal	Minimum	Discount (%	Origin	Past Peak	0	1	2	3
2	March	Espumante	6	45	South Africa	FALSE	8	4	8	0
3	November	Pinot Grigio	6	87	France	FALSE	13	1	3	0
4	July	Espumante	6	50	Oregon	FALSE	11	1	2	0
5	March	Prosecco	144	86	Chile	FALSE	0	11	1	0
6	October	Champagne	72	88	New Zealand	FALSE	0	7	1	1
7	April	Prosecco	72	52	California	FALSE	0	5	1	1
8	November	Cabernet Sauvi	12	56	France	TRUE	0	5	1	0
9	May	Merlot	6	43	Chile	FALSE	5	0	1	0
10	August	Champagne	72	63	France	FALSE	0	21	0	0

Figure 5-39: People who liked the March Espumante deal

And for community 3, it's the Pinot Noir folks. Haven't you ever heard of Cabernet Sauvignon, people!? Admittedly, I have a terrible palate for wine. See Figure 5-40.

That's it! You have four clusters, and honestly, three of them make perfect sense, although I suppose it's possible that you have a group of people who really just love Espumante in March. And you may get that in your work—some indecipherable outlier clusters.

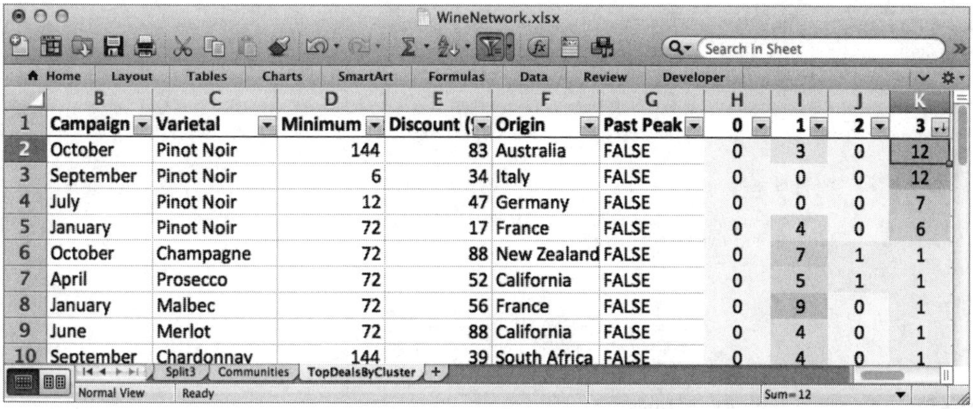

	B	C	D	E	F	G	H	I	J	K
1	Campaign	Varietal	Minimum	Discount (%	Origin	Past Peak	0	1	2	3
2	October	Pinot Noir	144	83	Australia	FALSE	0	3	0	12
3	September	Pinot Noir	6	34	Italy	FALSE	0	0	0	12
4	July	Pinot Noir	12	47	Germany	FALSE	0	0	0	7
5	January	Pinot Noir	72	17	France	FALSE	0	4	0	6
6	October	Champagne	72	88	New Zealand	FALSE	0	7	1	1
7	April	Prosecco	72	52	California	FALSE	0	5	1	1
8	January	Malbec	72	56	France	FALSE	0	9	0	1
9	June	Merlot	72	88	California	FALSE	0	4	0	1
10	September	Chardonnay	144	39	South Africa	FALSE	0	4	0	1

Figure 5-40: Pinot peeps

Note how similar this solution is to the clusters found in Chapter 2, however. In Chapter 2, you used a whole different methodology by keeping each customer's deal vector in the mix and using it to measure their distances from a cluster center. Here, there's no concept of a center and even which deals a customer has purchased have been obfuscated. What's important is the distance to other customers.

There and Back Again: A Gephi Tale

Now that you've gone through the entire clustering process, I'd like to show you that same process in Gephi. In Figure 5-20, you examined a laid out export of the r-Neighborhood graph into Gephi, which I return to in this section.

This next step is going to make you envious, but here it goes. In Excel you had to solve for the optimal graph modularity using divisive clustering. In Gephi, there's a Modularity button. You'll find it on the right side of the window in the Network Overview section of the Statistics tab.

When you press the Modularity button, a settings window opens. You needn't use edge weights since you exported an adjacency matrix (see Figure 5-41 for the Gephi modularity settings window).

Press OK. The modularity optimization will run using an approximation algorithm that's blindingly fast. A report is then displayed with a total modularity score of 0.549 as well as the size of each detected cluster (see Figure 5-42). Note that if you run this in Gephi, the solution may come out different since the calculation is randomized.

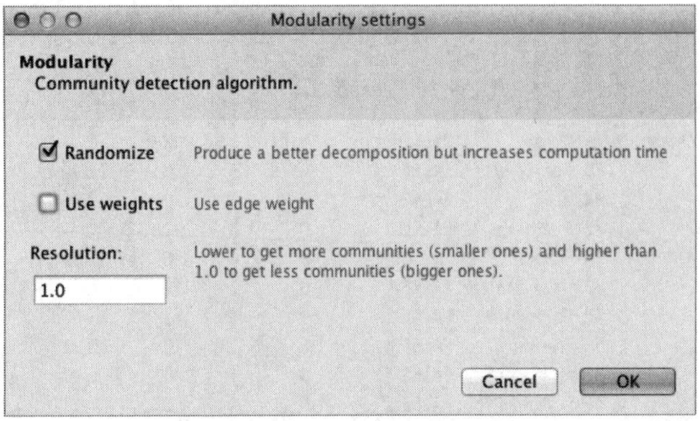

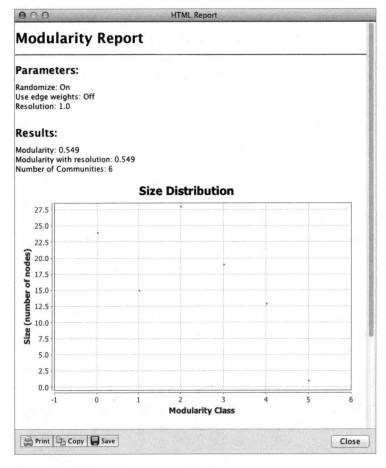

Figure 5-41: Gephi modularity settings

Figure 5-42: Modularity score from Gephi

Once you have your clusters from Gephi, you can do a few things with them.

First, you can recolor the graph using the modularity. Just as you resized the *Friends* graph using node degree, you can navigate to the Ranking window in the upper left of window in Gephi and go into the Nodes section. From there, you can select Modularity Class from the drop-down menu, pick any color scheme you want, and press Apply to recolor the graph (see Figure 5-43).

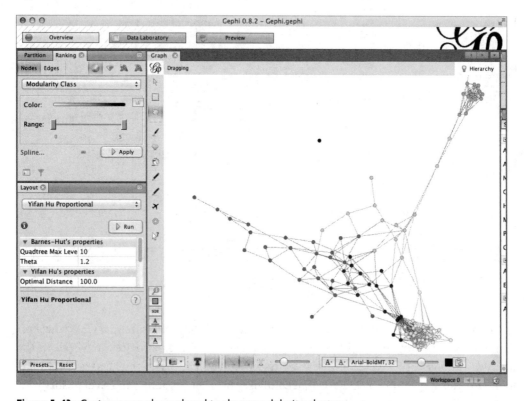

Figure 5-43: Customer graph recolored to show modularity clusters

Cool! You can now see that the two "tumor-esque" parts of the graph are indeed communities. The spread-out middle section of the graph was divided into three clusters. And poor Parker was placed in his own cluster, unconnected to anyone. How lonely and sad.

The second thing you can do with the modularity information is export it back into Excel to examine it, just as you did with your own clusters. To accomplish this, go into the Data Laboratory tab you visited earlier in Gephi. You'll notice that the modularity classes have already been populated as a column in the Nodes data table. Pressing the Export Table button, you can select the label and modularity class columns to dump to a CSV file (see Figure 5-44).

Figure 5-44: Exporting modularity classes back to Excel

Press OK on the export window to export your modularity classes to a CSV wherever you like and then open that file in Excel. From there, you can create a new tab in the main workbook called **CommunitiesGephi**, where you can paste the classes Gephi has found for you (see Figure 5-45). You'll need to use the filter capability in Excel to sort your customers by name just as they are in the rest of the workbook.

Just for kicks, let's confirm that this clustering really does beat the original score in column C. You're not bound by linear modeling constraints anymore, so you can total each customer's modularity scores using the following formula (shown here using our favorite customer, Adams, in cell C2):

```
{=SUMPRODUCT(IF($B$2:$B$101=B2,1,0),TRANSPOSE(Scores!B2:CW2))}
```

The formula merely checks for customers in the same cluster using an IF statement, gives those customers 1s and all else 0s, and then uses a SUMPRODUCT to sum their modularity scores.

You can double-click this formula to send it down column C. Summing the column in cell E2 and dividing through by the total stub count from 'r-NeighborhoodAdj'!CX102, you do indeed get a modularity score of 0.549 (see Figure 5-46). So Gephi's heuristic has beat out the divisive clustering heuristic by 0.003. Oh well! Pretty close. (If you used OpenSolver, you may actually be able to beat Gephi.)

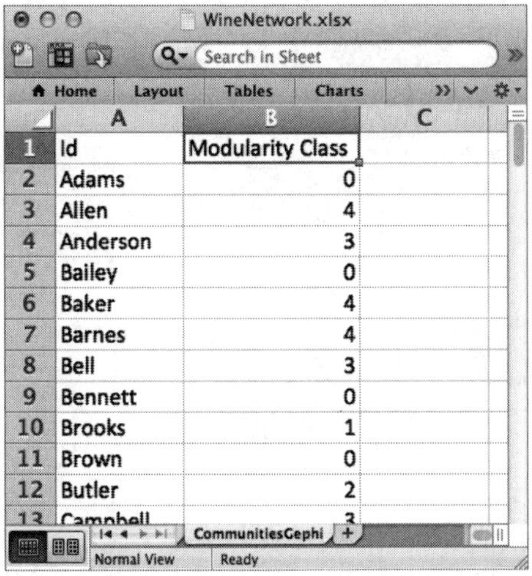

Figure 5-45: Gephi modularity classes back in Excel

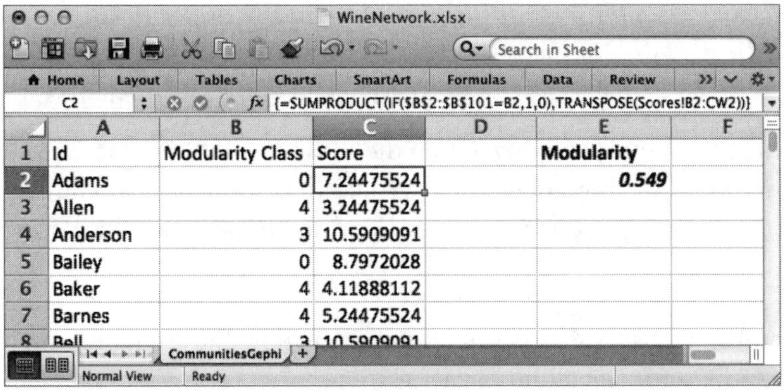

Figure 5-46: Reproducing the modularity score for the communities detected by Gephi

Let's see which clusters Gephi actually came up with. To start, let's make a copy of the TopDealsByCluster tab, which you should rename **TopDealsByClusterGephi**. Once you've made a copy, sort the deals back in order by column A and drop the filtering placed on the table. Now, in Gephi's clustering, you have six clusters with labels 0 through 5 (your results may be different since Gephi uses a randomized algorithm), so let's add 4 and 5 to the mix in columns L and M.

The formula in cell H2 need only be modified to reference column B on the CommunitiesGephi tab instead of column D on the Communities tab. You can then drag this formula to the rest of the sheet, yielding Figure 5-47.

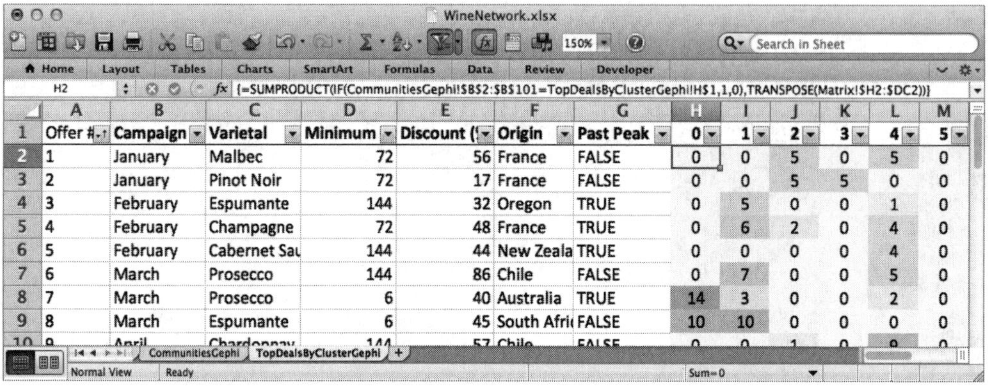

Offer #	Campaign	Varietal	Minimum	Discount (%)	Origin	Past Peak	0	1	2	3	4	5
1	January	Malbec	72	56	France	FALSE	0	0	5	0	5	0
2	January	Pinot Noir	72	17	France	FALSE	0	0	5	5	0	0
3	February	Espumante	144	32	Oregon	TRUE	0	5	0	0	1	0
4	February	Champagne	72	48	France	TRUE	0	6	2	0	4	0
5	February	Cabernet Sau	144	44	New Zeala	TRUE	0	0	0	0	4	0
6	March	Prosecco	144	86	Chile	FALSE	0	7	0	0	5	0
7	March	Prosecco	6	40	Australia	TRUE	14	3	0	0	2	0
8	March	Espumante	6	45	South Afri	FALSE	10	10	0	0	0	0

Figure 5-47: Top purchases per cluster from Gephi

If you sort once again by column, you see the all too familiar clusters—low volume, sparkling wine, Francophiles, Pinot people, high volume, and last but not least, Parker by himself.

Wrapping Up

In Chapter 2, you looked at k-means clustering. Using the same data in this chapter, you tackled network graphs and clustering via modularity maximization. You should feel pretty good about your data mining chops by now. In more detail, here are some items you learned:

- How network graphs are visually represented as well as how they're represented numerically using adjacency and affinity matrices
- How to load a network graph into Gephi to augment Excel's visualization deficiencies
- How to prune edges from network graphs via the r-neighborhood graph. You also learned the concept of a kNN graph, which I recommend you go back and tinker with.
- The definitions of node degree and graph modularity and how to calculate modularity scores for grouping two nodes together

- How to maximize graph modularity using a linear optimization model and divisive clustering
- How to maximize graph modularity in Gephi and export the results

Now, you may be wondering, "John, why in the world did you take me through that graph modularity maximization process when Gephi does it for me?"

Remember, the point of this book is not to press buttons blindly, without understanding what they do. Now you know how to construct and prep graph data for cluster detection. And you know how community detection on graph data works. You've done it. So next time you do this, even if you're just pushing a button, you'll know what's going on behind the scenes, and that level of understanding and confidence in the process is invaluable.

Although Gephi is one of the best places to do this analysis, if you're looking for a place to code with graph data, the igraph library, which has hooks in R and Python, is excellent for working with network graphs.

Also worth mentioning are the Neo4J and Titan graph databases. These databases are designed to store graph data for querying later, whether that query is something as simple as "get John's friends' favorite films" or as complex as "find the shortest path on Facebook between John and Kevin Bacon."

So that's it. Go forth, graph, and find communities!

6

The Granddaddy of Supervised Artificial Intelligence— Regression

Wait, What? You're Pregnant?

In a recent *Forbes* article, it was reported that Target had created an artificial intelligence (AI) model that could predict when a customer was pregnant and use that information to start targeting them with pregnancy-related marketing and offers. New parents blow a lot of money on the accouterments of child rearing, and what better time to turn them into loyal customers than before the baby even shows up? They'll be buying the store brand diapers for years!

This story about Target is just one of many that have peppered the press recently. Watson won *Jeopardy!*. Netflix offered a million dollar prize to improve its recommendation system. The Obama re-election campaign used artificial intelligence to help direct ground, online, and on the air media and fundraising operations. And then there's Kaggle.com, where competitions are popping up to predict everything from whether a driver is getting sleepy to how much a grocery shopper will spend on groceries.

But those are only the headline-catching applications. AI is useful across nearly any industry you can think of. Your credit card company uses it to identify odd transactions on your account. The enemy in your shoot-em-up Xbox game runs on AI. There's e-mail spam filtering, tax fraud detection, spelling auto-correction, and friend recommendation on social networks.

Quite simply, a good AI model can help a business make better decisions, market better, increase revenue, and decrease costs. An AI model can help your sales and support staff prioritize leads and support calls. AI can help predict what offers will bring a customer back to your brick and mortar store. AI can identify applicants who lie on their online dating profile or are going to have a coronary in the next year. You name it; if there's good historical data, a trained AI model can help.

Don't Kid Yourself

Folks who don't know how AI models work often experience some combination of awe and creepiness when hearing about how these models can predict the future. But to paraphrase the great 1992 film *Sneakers*, "Don't kid yourself. It's not that [intelligent]."

Why? Because AI models are no smarter than the sum of their parts. At a simplistic level, you feed a *supervised* AI algorithm some historical data, purchases at Target for example, and you tell the algorithm, "Hey, these purchases were from pregnant people, and these other purchases were from not-so-pregnant people." The algorithm munches on the data and out pops a model. In the future, you feed the model a customer's purchases and ask, "Is this person pregnant?" and the model answers, "No, that's a 26-year-old dude living in his mom's basement."

That's extremely helpful, but the model isn't a magician. It just cleverly turns past data into a formula or set of rules that it uses to predict a future case. As we saw in the case of naïve Bayes in Chapter 3, it's the AI model's ability to recall this data and associated decision rules, probabilities, or coefficients that make it so effective.

We do this all the time in our own non-artificially intelligent lives. For example, using personal historical data, my brain knows that when I eat a sub sandwich with brown-looking alfalfa sprouts on it, there's a good chance I may be ill in a few hours. I've taken past data (I got sick) and *trained* my brain on it, so now I have a rule, formula, model, whatever you'd like to call it: brown sprouts = gastrointestinal nightmare.

In this chapter, we're going to implement two different *regression models* just to see how straightforward AI can be. Regression is the granddaddy of supervised predictive modeling with research being done on it as early as the turn of the 19th century. It's an oldie, but its pedigree contributes to its power—regression has had time to build up all sorts of rigor around it in ways that some newer AI techniques have not. In contrast to the MacGyver feel of naïve Bayes in Chapter 3, you'll feel the weight of the statistical rigor of regression in this chapter, particularly when we investigate significance testing.

Similarly to how we used the naïve Bayes model in Chapter 3, we'll use these models for classification. However as you'll see, the problem at hand is very different from the bag-of-words document classification problem we encountered earlier.

Predicting Pregnant Customers at RetailMart Using Linear Regression

Pretend you're a marketing manager at RetailMart's corporate headquarters in charge of infant merchandise. Your job is to help sell more diapers, formula, onesies, cribs, strollers, pacifiers, etc. to new parents, but you have a problem.

You know from focus groups that new parents get into habits with baby products. They find diaper brands they like early on and stores that have the best prices on their brands. They find the pacifier that works with their baby, and they know where to go to get the cheap two-pack. You want RetailMart to be the first store these new parents buy diapers at. You want to maximize RetailMart's chances of being a parent's go-to for baby purchases.

But to do that, you need to market to these parents before they buy their first package of diapers somewhere else. You need to market to the parents before the baby shows up. That way, when the baby arrives, the parents have already received and possibly already used that coupon they got in the mail for diapers and ointment.

Quite simply, you need a predictive model to help identify potential pregnant customers for targeted direct marking.

The Feature Set

You have a secret weapon at your disposal for building this model: customer account data. You don't have this data for every customer; no, you're up the creek for the guy who lives in the woods and only pays cash. But for those who use a store credit card or have an online account tied to their major credit card, you can tie purchases not necessarily to an individual but at least to a household.

However, you can't just feed an entire purchase history, unstructured, into an AI model and expect things to happen. You have to be smart about pulling relevant predictors out of the dataset. So the question you should ask yourself is which past purchases are predictive for or against a household being pregnant?

The first purchase that comes to mind is a pregnancy test. If a customer buys a pregnancy test, they're more likely to be pregnant than the average customer. These predictors are often called model *features* or *independent variables*, while the thing we're trying to predict "Pregnant (yes/no)?" would be the *dependent variable* in the sense that its value is dependent on the independent variable data we're pushing into the model.

Pause a moment, and jot down your thoughts on possible features for the AI model. What purchase history should RetailMart consider?

Here's a list of example features that could be generated from a customer's purchase records and associated account information:

- Account holder is Male/Female/Unknown by matching surname to census data.
- Account holder address is a home, apartment, or PO box.
- Recently purchased a pregnancy test
- Recently purchased birth control
- Recently purchased feminine hygiene products
- Recently purchased folic acid supplements
- Recently purchased prenatal vitamins
- Recently purchased prenatal yoga DVD
- Recently purchased body pillow
- Recently purchased ginger ale
- Recently purchased Sea-Bands
- Bought cigarettes regularly until recently, then stopped
- Recently purchased cigarettes
- Recently purchased smoking cessation products (gum, patch, etc.)
- Bought wine regularly until recently, then stopped
- Recently purchased wine
- Recently purchased maternity clothing

None of these predictors are perfect. Customers don't buy everything at RetailMart; a customer might choose to buy their pregnancy test at the local drug store instead of RetailMart or their prenatal supplements might be prescription. Even if the customer did buy everything at RetailMart, pregnant *households* can still have a smoker or a drinker. Maternity clothing is often worn by non-pregnant folks, especially when the Empire waist is in style—thank goodness RetailMart doesn't exist in a Jane Austen novel. Ginger ale may help nausea, but it's also great with bourbon. You get the picture.

None of these predictors are going to cut it, but the hope is that with their powers combined Captain-Planet-style, the model will be able to classify customers reasonably well.

Assembling the Training Data

Six percent of RetailMart's customer households are pregnant at any given time according to surveys the company has conducted. You need to grab some examples of this group from the RetailMart database and assemble your modeling features on their purchase history before they gave birth. Likewise, you need to assemble these features for a sample of customers who aren't pregnant.

Once you assemble these features for a bunch of pregnant and non-pregnant households, you can use these known examples to train an AI model.

But how should you go about identifying past pregnant households in the data? Surveying customers to build a training set is always an option. You're just building a prototype, so perhaps approximating households who just had a baby by looking at buying habits is good enough. For customers who suddenly began buying newborn diapers and continued to buy diapers of increasing size on and off for at least a year, you can reasonably assume the customer's household has a new baby.

So by looking at the purchase history for the customer before the diaper-buying event, you can assemble the features listed previously for a pregnant household. Imagine you pull 500 examples of pregnant households and assemble their feature data from the RetailMart database.

As for non-pregnant customers, you can assemble purchase history from a random selection of customers in RetailMart's database that don't meet the "ongoing diaper purchasing" criteria. Sure, one or two pregnant people might slip into the not-pregnant category, but because pregnant households only make up a small percentage of the RetailMart population (and that's before excluding diaper-buyers), this random sample should be clean enough. Imagine you grab another 500 examples of these non-pregnant customers.

If you plopped the 1,000 rows (500 preggers, 500 not) into a spreadsheet it'd look like Figure 6-1.

Gender	Implied Home/ Apt/ PO Box	Pregnancy Test	Birth Control	Feminine Hygiene	Folic Acid	Prenatal Vitamins	Prenatal Yoga	Body Pillow	Ginger Ale	Sea Bands	Stopped buying ciggies	Cigar ettes	Smoking Cessation	Stopped buying wine	Wine	Maternity Clothes	PREGNANT
M	A	1	0	0	0	1	0	0	0	0	0	0	0	0	0	0	1
M	H	1	0	0	0	1	0	0	0	0	0	0	0	0	0	0	1
M	H	1	0	0	0	0	0	0	1	0	0	0	0	0	0	0	1
U	H	0	0	0	0	0	0	1	0	0	0	0	0	0	0	0	1
F	A	0	0	0	0	1	0	0	0	0	0	0	1	0	0	0	1
F	H	0	0	0	1	0	0	0	0	1	0	0	0	0	0	0	1
M	H	0	1	0	1	1	0	0	0	0	0	0	0	0	0	0	1
F	H	0	0	0	0	0	0	0	0	0	0	0	0	0	1	0	1
F	H	0	0	0	0	0	0	1	0	0	0	0	0	0	0	0	1
F	H	0	0	0	1	0	0	0	0	0	0	0	0	0	1		1

Figure 6-1: Raw training data

RESOLVING CLASS IMBALANCE

Now, you know that only 6 percent of our customer population in the wild is pregnant at any given time, but the training set you've assembled is 50/50. This is called *over*-sampling. Pregnancy would be the "minority" or rare class in the data, and by balancing the sample, the classifier you're going to train won't become overwhelmed by non-pregnant customers. After all, if you left the sample at a natural 6/94 split, then just labeling everyone as not pregnant leads to a 94 percent accuracy rate. That's dangerous since pregnancy, while in the minority, is actually the class you care about marketing to.

This rebalancing of the training data will introduce a bias to the model—it'll think pregnancy is more common than it really is. But that's fine, because you don't need to get actual probabilities of being pregnant out of the model. As you'll see later in this chapter, you just need to find the sweet spot for pregnancy scores coming out of the model that balances the *true positives* and *false positives*.

In the first two columns of the training dataset, you have categorical data for gender and address type. The rest of the features are binary where a 1 means TRUE. So for example, if you look at the first row in the spreadsheet, you can see that this customer was confirmed pregnant (column S). That's the column you're going to train the model to predict. And if you look at this customer's past purchasing history, you can see that they purchased a pregnancy test and some prenatal vitamins. Also, they have *not* purchased cigarettes or wine recently.

If you scroll through the data, you'll see all types of customers, some with lots of indicators and some with little. Just as expected, pregnant households will occasionally buy cigarettes and wine, while non-pregnant households will buy products associated with pregnancy.

Creating Dummy Variables

You can think of an AI model as nothing more than a formula that takes numbers in, chews on them a bit, and spits out a prediction that should look something like the 1s (pregnant) and 0s (not) in column S of the spreadsheet.

But the problem with this data is that the first two columns aren't numbers, now are they? They're letters standing for categories, like male and female.

This issue, handling *categorical data*, that is, data that's grouped by a finite number of labels without inherent numeric equivalents, is one that constantly nips at data miners' heels. If you send out a survey to your customers and they have to report back what line of work they're in, their marital status, the country they live in, the breed of dog they own, or their favorite episode of *Gilmore Girls*, then you're going to be stuck dealing with categorical data.

This is in contrast to *quantitative data*, which is already numeric and ready to be devoured by data mining techniques.

So what do you do to handle categorical data? Well, in short you need to make it quantitative.

Sometimes, your categorical data may have a natural ordering that you can use to assign each category a value. For instance, if you had a variable in your dataset where folks reported whether they drove a Scion, a Toyota, or a Lexus, maybe you could just make those responses 1, 2, and 3. *Voila*, numbers.

But more frequently, there is no ordering, such as with gender. For example, male, female, and unknown are distinct labels without a notion of ordering. In this case, it's common to use a technique called *dummy coding* to convert your categorical data to quantitative data.

Dummy coding works by taking a single categorical column (consider the Implied Gender column) and turning it into multiple binary columns. You could take the Implied Gender column and instead have one column for male, another for female, and another for unknown gender. If a value in the original column were "M," that instead could be coded as a 1 in the male column, a 0 in the female column, and a 0 in the unknown gender column.

This is actually overkill, because if the male and female columns were both 0, then the unknown gender is already implied. You don't need a third column.

In this way, when dummy coding a categorical variable, you always need one less column than you have category values—the last category is always implied by the other values. In stats-speak, you'd say that the gender categorical variable has only two *degrees of freedom*, because the degrees of freedom are always one less than the possible values the variable can take.

In this particular example, start by creating a copy of the Training Data sheet called **Training Data w Dummy Vars**. You're going to split the first two predictors into *two columns each*, so go ahead and clear out column A and B and insert another two blank columns to the left of column A.

Label these four empty columns **Male**, **Female**, **Home**, and **Apt** (unknown gender and PO box become implied). As shown in Figure 6-2, you should now have four empty columns to house the dummy coding of your two categorical variables.

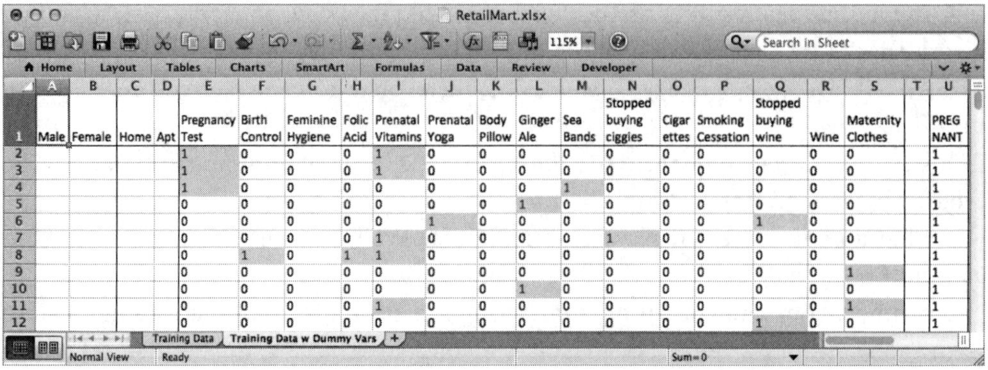

	A	B	C	D	E	F	G	H	I	J	K	L	M	N	O	P	Q	R	S	T	U
1	Male	Female	Home	Apt	Pregnancy Test	Birth Control	Feminine Hygiene	Folic Acid	Prenatal Vitamins	Prenatal Yoga	Body Pillow	Ginger Ale	Sea Bands	Stopped buying ciggies	Cigarettes	Smoking Cessation	Stopped buying wine	Wine	Maternity Clothes		PREGNANT
2					1	0	0	0	1	0	0	0	0	0	0	0	0	0	0		1
3					1	0	0	0	1	0	0	0	0	0	0	0	0	0	0		1
4					1	0	0	0	0	0	0	0	1	0	0	0	0	0	0		1
5					0	0	0	0	0	0	0	1	0	0	0	0	0	0	0		1
6					0	0	0	0	0	1	0	0	0	0	0	0	1	0	0		1
7					0	0	0	0	1	0	0	0	0	1	0	0	0	0	0		1
8					0	1	0	1	1	0	0	0	0	0	0	0	0	0	0		1
9					0	0	0	0	0	0	0	0	0	0	0	0	0	0	1		1
10					0	0	0	0	0	0	0	1	0	0	0	0	0	0	0		1
11					0	0	0	0	1	0	0	0	0	0	0	0	0	0	1		1
12					0	0	0	0	0	0	0	0	0	0	0	0	1	0	0		1

Figure 6-2: Training Data w Dummy Vars tab with new columns for the dummy variables

Consider the first row of training data. To turn the "M" in the gender column into dummy encoded data, you place a 1 in the Male column and a 0 in the Female column. (The 1 in the Male column naturally implies that the gender is not Unknown.)

In cell A2 on the Training Data w Dummy Vars tab, check the old category on the Training Data tab and set a 1 if the category was set to "M":

```
=IF('Training Data'!A2="M",1,0)
```

Same goes for values "F" in the Female column, "H" in the Home column, and "A" in the Apt column. To copy these four formulas down through all the rows of the training data, you can either drag them, or better yet, as explained in Chapter 1, highlight all four formulas and then double-click the bottom right corner of D2. That'll fill in the sheet with the converted values through D1001. Once you've converted these two categorical columns into four binary dummy variables (see Figure 6-3), you're ready to get modeling.

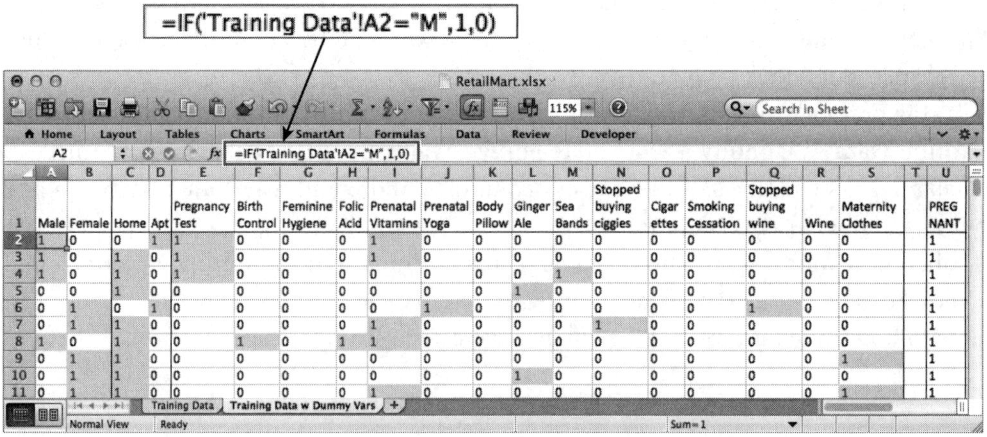

	A	B	C	D	E	F	G	H	I	J	K	L	M	N	O	P	Q	R	S	T	U
1	Male	Female	Home	Apt	Pregnancy Test	Birth Control	Feminine Hygiene	Folic Acid	Prenatal Vitamins	Prenatal Yoga	Body Pillow	Ginger Ale	Sea Bands	Stopped buying ciggies	Cigarettes	Smoking Cessation	Stopped buying wine	Wine	Maternity Clothes		PREGNANT
2	1	0	0	1	1	0	0	0	1	0	0	0	0	0	0	0	0	0	0		1
3	1	0	1	0	1	0	0	0	1	0	0	0	0	0	0	0	0	0	0		1
4	1	0	1	0	1	0	0	0	0	0	0	0	1	0	0	0	0	0	0		1
5	0	0	1	0	0	0	0	0	0	0	0	1	0	0	0	0	0	0	0		1
6	0	1	0	1	0	0	0	0	0	1	0	0	0	0	0	0	1	0	0		1
7	0	1	1	0	0	0	0	0	1	0	0	0	0	1	0	0	0	0	0		1
8	1	0	1	0	0	1	0	1	1	0	0	0	0	0	0	0	0	0	0		1
9	0	1	1	0	0	0	0	0	0	0	0	0	0	0	0	0	0	0	1		1
10	0	1	1	0	0	0	0	0	0	0	0	1	0	0	0	0	0	0	0		1
11	0	1	1	0	0	0	0	0	1	0	0	0	0	0	0	0	0	0	1		1

Figure 6-3: Training data with dummy variables populated

Let's Bake Our Own Linear Regression

Every time I say this, a statistician loses its wings, but I'm going to say it anyway—If you're ever shoved a trendline through a cloud of points on a scatter plot, then you've built an AI model.

You're probably thinking, "But there's no way! I would've known had I created a robot that could travel back in time to stop John Conner!"

The Simplest of Linear Models

Let me explain by showing some simple data in Figure 6-4.

	A	B
1	Number of cats owned	Likelihood I'll sneeze in your home
2	0	3%
3	1	20%
4	2	36%
5	3	45%
6	4	67%
7	5	80%

Figure 6-4: Cat ownership versus me sneezing

In the pictured table, you have the number of cats in a house in the first column and the likelihood that I'll sneeze inside that house in the second column. No cats? Three percent of the time I sneeze any way just because I know a Platonic cat exists somewhere. Five cats? Well, then my sneezing is just about guaranteed. Now, we can scatter plot this data in Excel and look at it as shown in Figure 6-5 (For more on inserting plots and charts see Chapter 1).

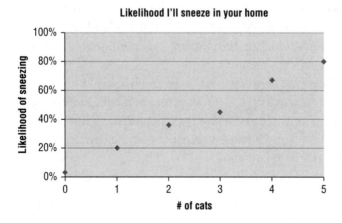

Figure 6-5: Scatter plot of cats versus sneezing

By right-clicking on the data points in the graph (you have to right-click an actual data point, not just the graph itself) and selecting Add Trendline from the menu, you can select a linear regression model to add to the graph. Under the "Options" section of the "Format Trendline" window, you can select to "Display equation on chart." Pressing OK, you can now see the trendline and formula for the line (Figure 6-6).

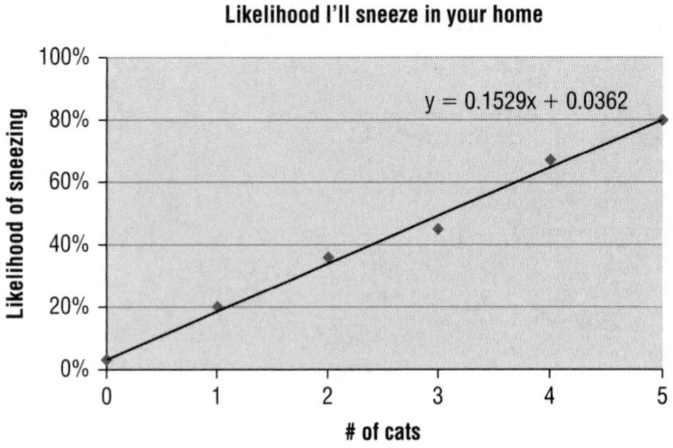

Figure 6-6: Linear model displayed on the graph

The trendline in the graph rightly shows the relationship between cats and sneezing with a formula of:

```
Y = 0.1529x + 0.0362
```

In other words, when x is 0, the linear model thinks I've got about a 3-4 percent chance of sneezing, and the model gives me an extra 15 percent chance per cat.

That baseline of 3-4 percent is called the *intercept* of the model, and the 15 percent per cat is called a *coefficient* for the cats variable. Making a prediction with a linear model like this requires nothing more than taking my future data and combining it with the coefficients and the intercept of the model.

In fact, you can copy the formula =0.1529x+0.0362 out of the graph if you like and paste it in a cell to make predictions by replacing the x with an actual number., For example, if in the future I went into a home with three and a half cats (poor Timmy lost his hind paws in a boating accident), then I'd take a "linear combination" of the coefficients and my data, add in the intercept, and get my prediction:

```
0.1529*3.5 cats + 0.0362 = 0.57
```

A 57 percent chance of sneezing! This is an AI model in the sense that we've taken an independent variable (cats) and a dependent variable (sneezing) and asked the computer to describe their relationship as a formula that best fits our historical data.

Now, you might wonder how the computer figured this trendline out from the data. It looks good, but how'd it know where to put it? Basically, the computer looked for a trendline that *best fit* the data, where by *best fit* I mean the trendline that minimizes the *sum of squared error* with the training data.

To get a handle on what the sum of squared error means, if you evaluate the trendline for one cat you get:

```
0.1529*1 cat + 0.0362 = 0.1891
```

But the training data gives a likelihood of 20 percent, not 18.91 percent. So then your error at this point on the trendline is 1.09 percent. This error value is squared to make sure it a positive value, regardless of whether the trendline is above or below the data point. 1.09 percent squared is 0.012 percent. Now if you summed each of these squared error values for the points in our training data, you'd get the sum of the squared error (often just called the *sum of squares*). And that's what Excel minimized when fitting the trendline to the sneeze graph.

Although your RetailMart data has way too many dimensions to toss into a scatter plot, in these next sections, you'll fit the exact same type of line to the data from scratch.

Back to the RetailMart Data

OK, so it's time to build a linear model like the Kitty Sneeze model on the RetailMart dataset. First, create a new tab called **Linear Model**, and paste the values from the Training Data w Dummy Vars tab, except when you paste it, start in column B to save room for some row labels in column A and on row 7 to leave space at the top of the sheet for the linear model's coefficients and other evaluative data you'll be tracking.

Paste the header row for your dependent variables again on row 1 to stay organized. And in column U, add the label **Intercept** because your linear model will need a baseline just like in the previous example. Furthermore, to incorporate the intercept into the model easier, fill in your intercept column (U8:U1007) with 1s. This will allow you to evaluate the model by taking a SUMPRODUCT of the coefficient row with a data row that will incorporate the intercept value.

All the coefficients for this model are going to go on row 2 of the spreadsheet, so label row 2 as **Model Coefficients** and place a starting value of 1 in each cell. You can also lay on some conditional formatting on the coefficient row so you can see differences in them once they're set.

Your dataset now looks like Figure 6-7.

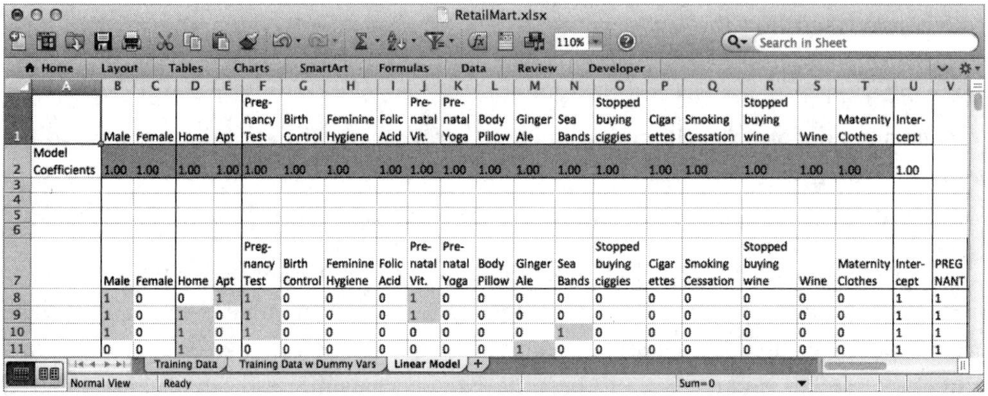

Figure 6-7: Linear modeling setup

Once the coefficients in row 2 are set, you can take a linear combination (formula SUMPRODUCT) of the coefficients with a row of customer data and get a pregnancy prediction.

You have too many columns here, to build a linear model by graphing it the way I did with the cats, so instead you're going to train the model yourself. The first step is to add a column to the spreadsheet with a prediction on one of the rows of data.

In column W, next to the customer data, add the column label **Linear Combination (Prediction)** to row 7 and below it take a linear combination of coefficients and customer data (intercept column included). The formula you plug into row 8 to do this for your first customer is:

```
=SUMPRODUCT(B$2:U$2,B8:U8)
```

The absolute reference should be placed on row 2, so that you can drag this formula down to all the other customers without the coefficient row changing.

> **TIP**
>
> Also, you may want to highlight column W, right-click, select "Format Cells…," and format the values as a number with two decimal places just to keep your eyes from bleeding at the sight of so many decimals.

Once you've added this column, your data will look like Figure 6-8.

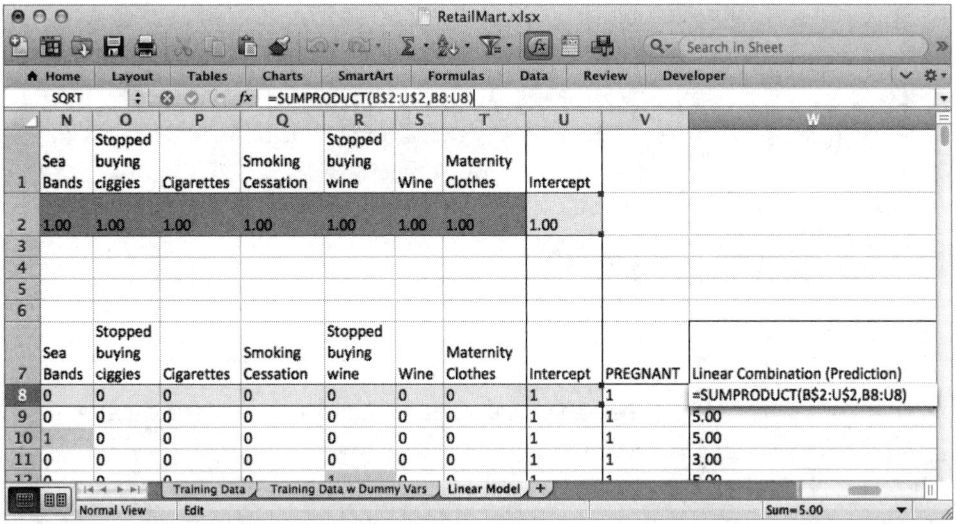

Figure 6-8: The prediction column for a linear model

Ideally, the prediction column (column W) would look identical to what we know to be the truth (column V), but using coefficients of 1 for every variable, it's easy to see you're way off. The first customer gets a prediction of 5 even though pregnancy is indicated with a 1 and non-pregnancy with a 0. What's a 5? Really, really pregnant?

Adding in an Error Calculation

You need to get the computer to set these model coefficients for you, but in order for it to know how to do that, you need to let the machine know when a prediction is right and when it's wrong.

To that end, add an error calculation in column X. Use squared error, which is just the square of the distance of the value of PREGNANT (column V) from the predicted value (column W).

Squaring the error allows each error calculation to be positive, so that you can sum them together to get a sense of overall error of the model. You don't want positive and negative errors canceling each other out. So for the first customer in the sheet, you'd have the following formula:

```
=(V8-W8)^2
```

You can drag that cell down the rest of the column to give each prediction its own error calculation.

Now, add a cell above the predictions in cell X1 (labeled in W1 as **Sum Squared Error**) where you'll sum the squared error column using the formula:

```
=SUM(X8:X1007)
```

Your spreadsheet looks like Figure 6-9:

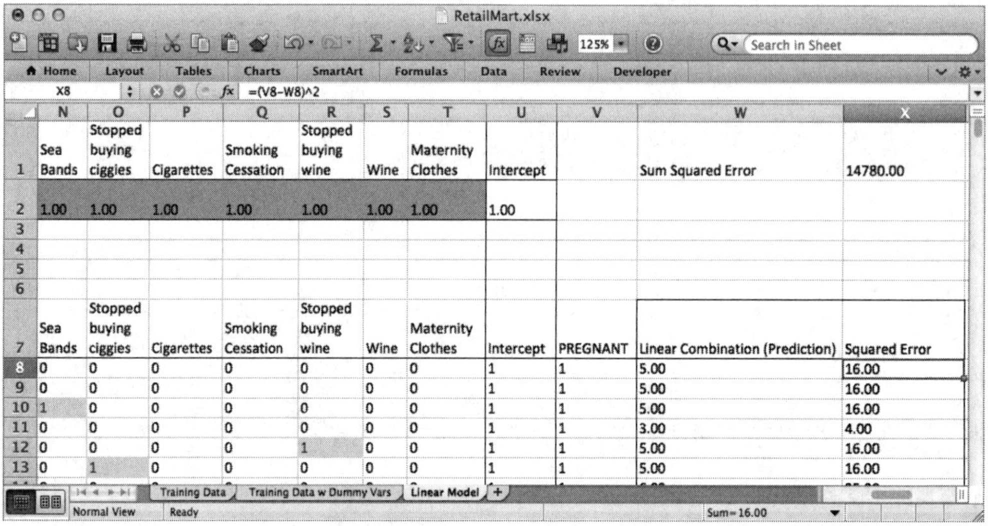

	N	O	P	Q	R	S	T	U	V	W	X
1	Sea Bands	Stopped buying ciggies	Cigarettes	Smoking Cessation	Stopped buying wine	Wine	Maternity Clothes	Intercept		Sum Squared Error	14780.00
2	1.00	1.00	1.00	1.00	1.00	1.00	1.00	1.00			
3											
4											
5											
6											
7	Sea Bands	Stopped buying ciggies	Cigarettes	Smoking Cessation	Stopped buying wine	Wine	Maternity Clothes	Intercept	PREGNANT	Linear Combination (Prediction)	Squared Error
8	0	0	0	0	0	0	0	1	1	5.00	16.00
9	0	0	0	0	0	0	0	1	1	5.00	16.00
10	1	0	0	0	0	0	0	1	1	5.00	16.00
11	0	0	0	0	0	0	0	1	1	3.00	4.00
12	0	0	0	0	1	0	0	1	1	5.00	16.00
13	0	1	0	0	0	0	0	1	1	5.00	16.00

Figure 6-9: Predictions and sum of squared error

Training with Solver

Now you're ready to train your linear model. You want to set the coefficients for each variable such that the sum of squared error is as low as it can be. If this sounds like a job for Solver to you, you're right. Just as you did in Chapters 2, 4, and 5, you're going to open up Solver and get the computer to find the best coefficients for you.

The objective function will be the Sum Squared Error value from cell X1, which you'll want to minimize "by changing variable cells" B2 through U2, which are your model coefficients.

Now, squared error is a quadratic function of your decision variables, the coefficients, so you can't use Simplex-LP as the solving method like you used extensively in Chapter 4. Simplex is super-fast and guarantees finding the best answer, but it requires that the model only consider linear combinations of the decisions. You'll need to use the evolutionary algorithm in Solver.

REFERENCE

For more on non-linear optimization models and the inner workings of the evolutionary optimization algorithm, see Chapter 4. If you like, you can also play with the other non-linear optimization algorithm Excel offers called GRG.

Basically, Solver is going to sniff around for coefficient values that make the sum of squares fall until it feels like it's found a really good solution. But in order to use the evolutionary algorithm effectively, you need to set upper and lower bounds on each of the coefficients you're trying to set.

I urge you to play around with these upper and lower bounds. The tighter they are (without getting too tight!), the better the algorithm works. For this model, I've set them to be between -1 and 1.

Once you've completed these items, your Solver setup should look like Figure 6-10.

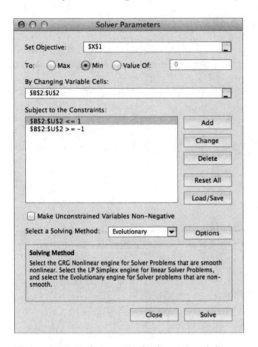

Figure 6-10: Solver setup for linear model

Press the Solve button and wait! As the Evolutionary Solver tries out various coefficients for the model, you'll see the values change. The conditional formatting on the cells will give you a sense of magnitude. Furthermore, the sum of the squared error should bounce around but generally decrease over time. Once Solver finishes, it will tell you the problem is optimized. Click OK, and you'll have your model back.

In Figure 6-11, you'll see that the Solver run finished with a 135.52 sum of squared error. If you're following along and would like to run Solver yourself, be aware that two runs of the evolutionary algorithm don't have to end up in the same place—your sum of squares might end up being higher or lower than the book's, with slightly different final model coefficients. The optimized linear model is pictured in Figure 6-11.

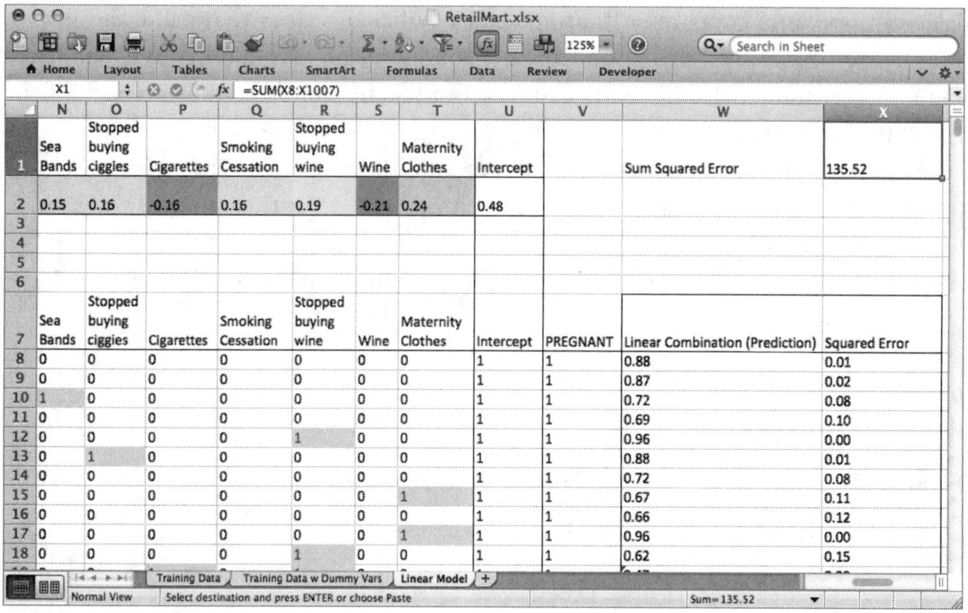

	N	O	P	Q	R	S	T	U	V	W	X
1	Sea Bands	Stopped buying ciggies	Cigarettes	Smoking Cessation	Stopped buying wine	Wine	Maternity Clothes	Intercept		Sum Squared Error	135.52
2	0.15	0.16	-0.16	0.16	0.19	-0.21	0.24	0.48			
3											
4											
5											
6											
7	Sea Bands	Stopped buying ciggies	Cigarettes	Smoking Cessation	Stopped buying wine	Wine	Maternity Clothes	Intercept	PREGNANT	Linear Combination (Prediction)	Squared Error
8	0	0	0	0	0	0	0	1	1	0.88	0.01
9	0	0	0	0	0	0	0	1	1	0.87	0.02
10	1	0	0	0	0	0	0	1	1	0.72	0.08
11	0	0	0	0	0	0	0	1	1	0.69	0.10
12	0	0	0	0	1	0	0	1	1	0.96	0.00
13	0	1	0	0	0	0	0	1	1	0.88	0.01
14	0	0	0	0	0	0	0	1	1	0.72	0.08
15	0	0	0	0	0	0	1	1	1	0.67	0.11
16	0	0	0	0	0	0	0	1	1	0.66	0.12
17	0	0	0	0	0	0	1	1	1	0.96	0.00
18	0	0	0	0	1	0	0	1	1	0.62	0.15

Figure 6-11: Optimized linear model

USING THE LINEST() FORMULA FOR LINEAR REGRESSION

Some readers may be aware that Excel has its own linear regression formula called LINEST(). In one stroke, this formula can, indeed, do what you just did by hand. It craps out at 64 features, however, so for truly large regressions, you'll need to roll your own anyway.

Feel free to try it out on this dataset. But beware! Read the Excel help documentation on the formula. In order to get all your coefficients out of it, you'll need to use it as an array formula (see Chapter 1). Also, it spits the coefficients out in reverse order (Male will be the final coefficient before the intercept), which is truly annoying.

Where LINEST() comes in super handy is that it automatically computes many of the values needed for performing statistical testing on your linear model, such as the dreaded coefficient standard error calculation that you'll see in the next section.

But in this chapter, you're going to do everything by hand so that you'll know a great deal about what LINEST() (and other software packages' linear modeling functions) is doing and will feel comfortable leaning on it in the future. Also, doing things by hand will aid the transition into logistic regression, which Excel *does not* support.

USING MEDIAN REGRESSION TO BETTER HANDLE OUTLIERS

In *median regression*, you minimize the sum of the *absolute values of the errors* instead of the sum of the squared errors. That's the only change from linear regression.

What does it get you?

In linear regression, *outliers* (values that are markedly distant from the rest of the data) in your training set have more pull and can throw off the model fitting process. When an outlier's error values are large, the linear regression will chase them more, striking a different balance between a large error and a bunch of other normal points' smaller errors than the balance that is struck in median regression. In median regression, the line that's fit to the data will stay close to the typical, inlying data points rather than chase the outliers so much.

While I won't work through median regression in this chapter, it's not hard to try out on your own. Just swap the squared error term for the absolute value (Excel has the ABS function) and you're off and running.

That said, if you're on Windows and have OpenSolver installed (see Chapter 1), then here's a huge bonus problem!

Since in median regression, you're minimizing error, and since an absolute value can also be thought of as a max function (the max of a value and -1 times that value), try to linearize the median regression as a *minimax*-esque optimization model (see Chapter 4 for more on minimax optimization models). Hint: You'll need to create one variable per row of training data, which is why you need OpenSolver—regular Solver can't handle a thousand decisions and two thousand constraints.

Good luck!

Linear Regression Statistics: R-Squared, F Tests, t Tests

NOTE

This next section is the heaviest statistical section in the whole book. Indeed, this section arguably houses the most complex calculation in this entire book—the calculation of model coefficient standard error. I've tried to describe everything as intuitively as possible, but some of the calculations defy explanation at a level appropriate for the text. And I don't want to get sidetracked teaching a linear algebra course here.

Try to understand these concepts as best you can. Practice them. And if you want to know more, grab an intro level stats textbook (for example, *Statistics in Plain English* by Timothy C. Urdan [Routledge, 2010]).

If you get bogged down, know that this section is self-contained. Skip it and come back if you need to.

You have a linear model now that you fit by minimizing the sum of squares. Glancing at the predictions in Column Y, they look all right to the eye. For example, the pregnant customer on row 27 who bought a pregnancy test, prenatal vitamins, and maternity clothes gets a score of 1.07 while the customer on row 996 who's only ever bought wine gets a score of 0.15. That said, questions remain:

- How well does the regression *actually fit the data* from a quantitative, non-eyeball perspective?
- Is this overall fit by chance or is it statistically significant?
- How useful are each of the features to the model?

To answer these questions for a linear regression, you can compute the *R-squared*, an overall *F test*, and *t tests* for each of your coefficients.

R-Squared—Assessing Goodness of Fit

If you knew nothing about a customer in the training set (columns B through T were missing) but you were forced to make a prediction on pregnancy anyway, the best way to minimize the sum of squared error in that case would be to just put the average of column V in the sheet for each prediction. In this case the average is 0.5 given the 500/500 split in the training data. And since each actual value is either a 0 or 1, each error would be 0.5, making each squared error 0.25. At 1000 predictions then, this strategy of predicting the average, would give a sum of squares of 250.

This value is called the *total sum of squares*. It's the sum of squared deviations of each value in column V from the average of column V. And Excel offers a nifty formula for calculating it in one step, DEVSQ.

In X2, you can calculate the total sum of squares as:

```
=DEVSQ(V8:V1007)
```

But while putting the mean for every prediction would yield a sum of squared error of 250, the sum of the squared error given by the linear model you fit earlier is far less than that. Only 135.52.

That means 135.52 out of the total 250 sum of squares remains *unexplained* after you fit your regression (in this context, the sum of squared error is often called the *residual sum of squares*).

Flipping this value around, the *explained sum of squares* (which is exactly what it says— the amount you explained with your model) is 250 – 135.52. Put this in X3 as:

```
=X2-X1
```

This gives 114.48 for the explained sum of squares (if you didn't obtain a sum of squared error of 135.52 when you fit your regression, then your results might vary slightly).

So how good of a fit is this?

Generally, this is answered by looking at the ratio of the explained sum of squares to the total sum of squares. This value is called the *R-squared*. We can calculate the ratio in X4:

```
=X3/X2
```

As shown in Figure 6-12, this gives an R-squared of 0.46. If the model fit perfectly, you'd have 0 squared error, the explained sum of squares would equal the total, and the R-squared would be a perfect 1. If the model didn't fit at all, the R-squared would be closer to 0. So then in the case of this model, given the training data's inputs, the model can do an okay-but-not-perfect job of replicating the training data's independent variable (the Pregnancy column).

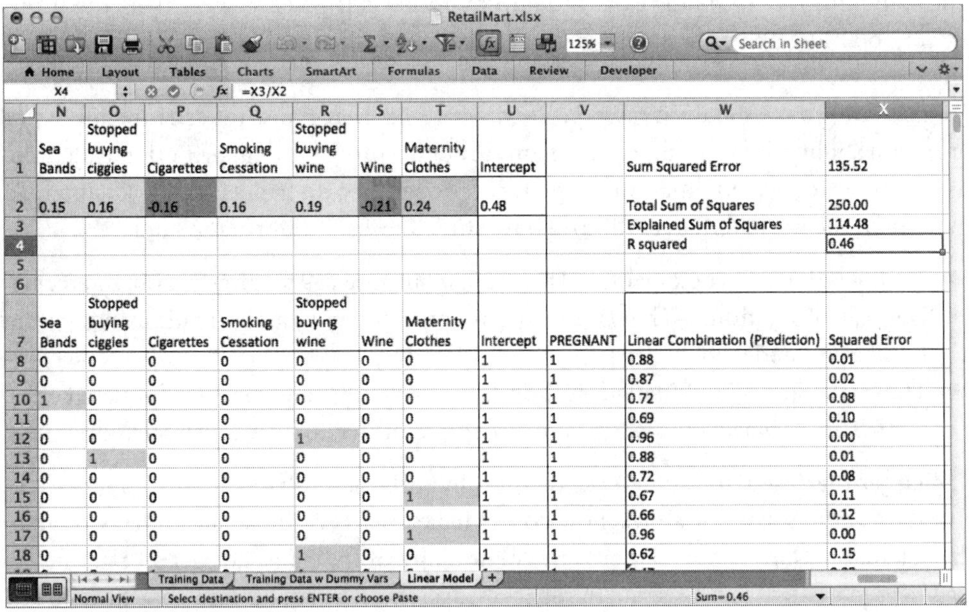

Figure 6-12: R-squared of 0.46 for the linear regression

Now, keep in mind that the R-squared calculation only works in finding linear relationships between data. If you have a funky, non-linear relationship (maybe a V or U shape) between a dependent and independent variable in a model, the R-squared value could not capture that relationship.

The F Test—Is the Fit Statistically Significant?

Oftentimes, people stop at R-squared when analyzing the fit of a regression.

"Hey, the fit looks good! I'm done."

Don't do that.

The R-squared only tells you how well the model fits the data. What it doesn't tell you is whether this fit is *statistically significant*.

It is easy, especially with sparse datasets (only a few observations), to get a model that fits quite well but whose fit is *statistically insignificant*, meaning that the relationship between the features and the independent variable may not actually be real.

Is your model's fit due to chance? Some stroke of luck? For a model to be statistically significant, you must reject this fit-by-fluke *hypothesis*. So *assume* for a moment, that your model's fit is a complete fluke. That the entire fit is due to luck of the draw on the random 1,000 observations you pulled from the RetailMart database. This devil's advocate assumption is called the *null hypothesis*.

The standard practice is to reject the null hypothesis if given it were true, the probability of obtaining a fit at least this good is less than 5 percent. This probability is often called a *p value*.

To calculate that probability, we perform an F test. An *F test* takes three pieces of information about our model and runs them through a probability distribution called the F distribution (for an explanation of the term probability distribution, see Chapter 4's discussion of the normal distribution). Those three pieces of information are:

- **Number of model coefficients**—This is 20 in our case (19 features plus an intercept).
- **Degrees of freedom**—This is the number of training data observations minus the number of model coefficients.
- **The F statistic**—The F statistic is the ratio of explained to unexplained squared error (X3/X1 in the sheet) *times* the ratio of degrees of freedom to dependent variables.

The larger the F statistic, the lower the null hypothesis probability is. And given the explanation of the F statistic above, how do you make it larger? Make one of the two ratios in the calculation larger. You can either explain more of the data (i.e., get a better fit) or you can get more data for the same number of variables (i.e., make sure your fit holds in a larger sample).

Returning then to the sheet, we need to count up the number of observations and the number of model coefficients we have.

Label Y1 as **Observation Count** and in Z1 count up all the pregnancy values in column V:

```
=COUNT(V8:V1007)
```

You should, as you'd expect, get 1,000 observations.

In Z2, get the Model Coefficient Count by counting them on row 2:

```
=COUNT(B2:U2)
```

You should get 20 counting the intercept. You can then calculate the Degrees of Freedom in Z3 by subtracting the model coefficient count from the observation count:

```
=Z1-Z2
```

You'll get a value of 980 degrees of freedom.

Now for the F statistic in Z4. As noted above, this is just the ratio of explained to unexplained squared error (X3/X1) times the ratio of degrees of freedom to dependent variables (Z3/(Z2-1)):

```
=(X3/X1)*(Z3/(Z2-1))
```

We can then plug these values into the F distribution in Z5 using the Excel function FDIST. Label the cell **F Test P Value**. FDIST takes the F statistic, the number of dependent variables in the model, and the degrees of freedom:

```
=FDIST(Z4,Z2-1,Z3)
```

As shown in Figure 6-13, the probability of getting a fit like this given the null hypothesis is effectively 0. Thus, you may reject the null hypothesis and conclude that the fit is statistically significant.

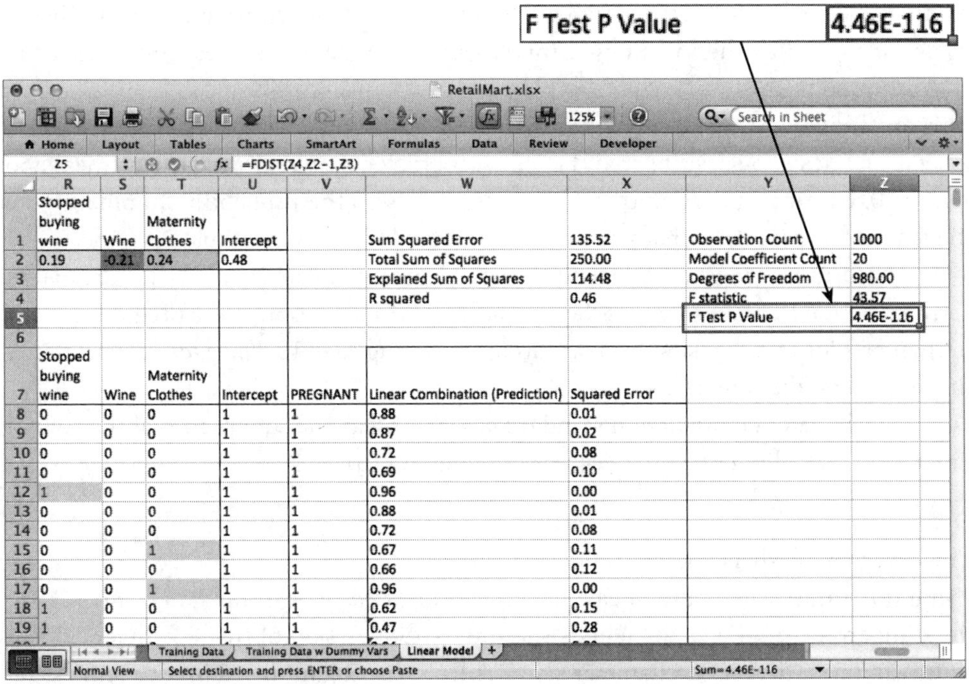

Figure 6-13: The result of the F test

Coefficient t Tests—Which Variables Are Significant?

WARNING: MATRIX MATH AHEAD!

While the previous two statistics weren't hard to compute, performing a t test on a multiple linear regression requires matrix multiplication and inversion. If you don't remember how these operations work from high school or intro college math, check out a linear algebra or calculus book. Or just read up on Wikipedia. And use the workbook that's available for download with this chapter to make sure your math is correct.

In Excel, matrix multiplication uses the MMULT function while inversion uses the MINVERSE function. Since a matrix is nothing more than a rectangular array of numbers, these formulas are array formulas (see Chapter 1 for using array formulas in Excel).

While the F test verified that the entire regression was significant, you can also check the significance of individual variables. By testing the significance of single features, you can gain insight into what's driving your model's results. Statistically insignificant variables might be able to be eliminated, or if you're sure in your gut that the insignificant variable *should matter*, then you might investigate if there are data cleanliness issues in your training set.

This test for model coefficient significance is called a *t test*. When performing a t test, much like an F test, you assume that the model coefficient you're testing is worthless and should be 0. Given that assumption, the t test calculates the probability of obtaining a coefficient as far from 0 as what you actually obtained from your sample.

When performing a t test on a dependent variable, the first value you should calculate is the *prediction standard error*. This is the sample standard deviation of the prediction error (see Chapter 4 for more on standard deviation), meaning that it's a measure of variability in the model's prediction errors.

You can calculate the prediction standard error in X5 as the square root of the sum of squared error (X1) divided by the degrees of freedom (Z3):

```
=SQRT(X1/Z3)
```

This gives us the sheet shown in Figure 6-14.

Using this value, you can then calculate the model's *coefficient standard errors*. Think of the standard error of a coefficient as the standard deviation of that coefficient if you kept drawing new thousand-customer samples from the RetailMart database and fitting new linear regressions to those training sets. You wouldn't get the same coefficients each time; they'd vary a bit. And the coefficient standard error quantifies the variability you'd expect to see.

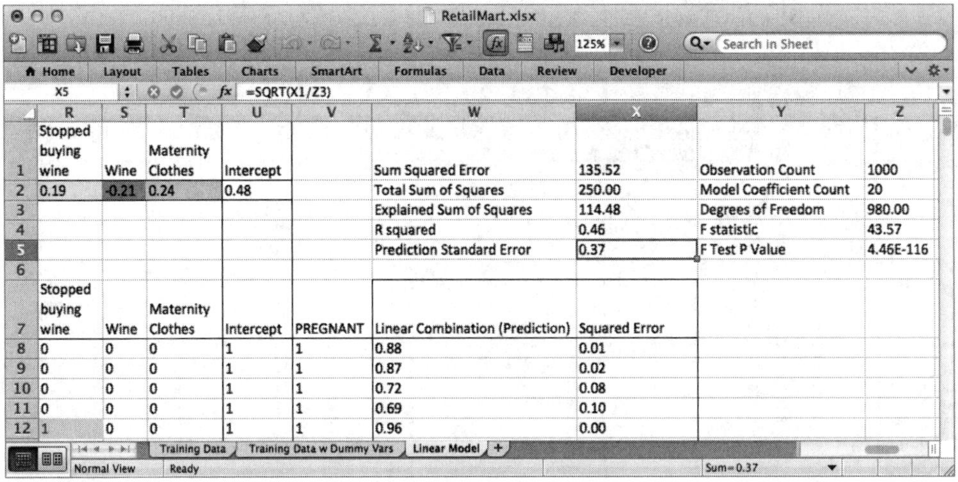

Figure 6-14: The prediction standard error for the linear regression

To start this calculation, create a new tab in the workbook called **ModelCoefficientStandardError**. Now, the thing that makes computing the standard error so difficult is that we need to understand both how the training data for a coefficient varies by itself and *in concert* with the other variables. The first step in nailing that down is multiplying the training set as one gigantic matrix (often called the *design matrix* in linear regression) by itself.

This product of the design matrix (B8:U1007) with itself forms what's called a *sum of squares and cross products* (SSCP) matrix. To see what this looks like, first paste the row headers for the training data in the ModelCoefficientStdError tab in B1:U1 and transposed down the rows in A2:A21. This includes the Intercept header.

To multiply the design matrix times itself, you feed it into the Excel's MMULT function, first transposed, then right-side up:

```
{=MMULT(TRANSPOSE('Linear Model'!B8:U1007),'Linear Model'!B8:U1007)}
```

Since this function returns a variables-by-variables sized matrix, you actually have to highlight the entire range of B2:U21 on the ModelCoefficientStdError tab and execute the function as an array formula (see Chapter 1 for more on array formulas).

This yields the tab shown in Figure 6-15.

Note the values in the SSCP matrix. Along the diagonal, you're counting matches of each variable with itself—the same as just summing up the 1s in each column of the design matrix. The intercept gets 1000, for example, in cell U21, because in the original training data, that column is made up of 1000 ones.

In the off-diagonal cells, you end up with counts of the matches between different predictors. While Male and Female obviously never match by design, Pregnancy Test and Birth Control appear together in six customer rows in the training data.

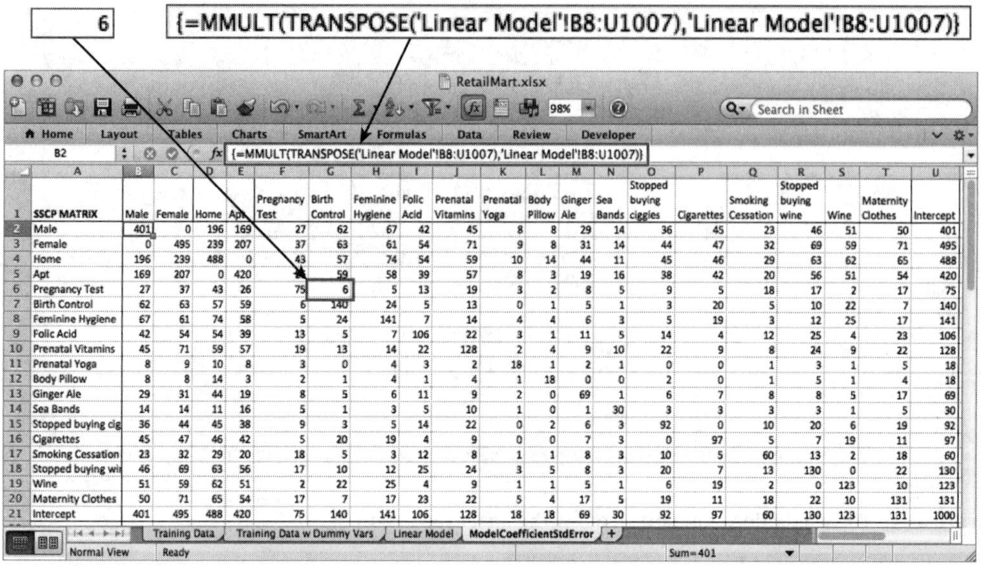

| 6 | {=MMULT(TRANSPOSE('Linear Model'!B8:U1007),'Linear Model'!B8:U1007)} |

RetailMart.xlsx

Home | Layout | Tables | Charts | SmartArt | Formulas | Data | Review | Developer

B2   fx {=MMULT(TRANSPOSE('Linear Model'!B8:U1007),'Linear Model'!B8:U1007)}

SSCP MATRIX	Male	Female	Home	Apt	Pregnancy Test	Birth Control	Feminine Hygiene	Folic Acid	Prenatal Vitamins	Prenatal Yoga	Body Pillow	Ginger Ale	Sea Bands	Stopped buying ciggies	Cigarettes	Smoking Cessation	Stopped buying wine	Wine	Maternity Clothes	Intercept
Male	401	0	196	169	27	62	67	42	45	8	8	29	14	36	45	23	46	51	50	401
Female	0	495	239	207	37	63	61	54	71	9	8	31	14	44	47	32	69	59	71	495
Home	196	239	488	0	43	57	74	54	59	10	14	44	11	45	46	29	63	62	65	488
Apt	169	207	0	420	26	59	58	39	57	8	3	19	16	38	42	20	51	54	54	420
Pregnancy Test	27	37	43	26	75	6	5	13	19	3	2	8	5	9	5	18	17	2	17	75
Birth Control	62	63	57	59	6	140	24	5	13	0	1	5	1	3	20	5	10	22	7	140
Feminine Hygiene	67	61	74	58	5	24	141	7	14	4	4	6	3	5	19	3	12	25	17	141
Folic Acid	42	54	54	39	13	5	7	106	22	3	1	11	5	14	4	12	25	4	23	106
Prenatal Vitamins	45	71	59	57	19	13	14	22	128	2	4	9	10	22	9	8	24	9	22	128
Prenatal Yoga	8	9	10	8	3	0	4	3	2	18	1	2	1	0	0	1	3	1	5	18
Body Pillow	8	8	14	3	2	1	4	1	4	1	18	0	0	2	0	1	5	1	4	18
Ginger Ale	29	31	44	19	8	5	6	11	9	2	0	69	1	6	7	8	8	5	17	69
Sea Bands	14	14	11	16	5	1	3	5	10	1	0	1	30	3	3	3	3	1	5	30
Stopped buying ciggies	36	44	45	38	9	3	5	14	22	0	2	6	3	92	0	10	20	6	19	92
Cigarettes	45	47	46	42	5	20	19	4	9	0	0	7	3	0	97	5	7	19	11	97
Smoking Cessation	23	32	29	20	18	5	3	12	8	1	1	8	3	10	5	60	13	2	18	60
Stopped buying wine	46	69	63	51	17	10	12	25	24	3	5	8	3	20	7	13	130	0	22	130
Wine	51	59	62	54	2	22	25	4	9	1	1	5	1	6	19	2	0	123	10	123
Maternity Clothes	50	71	65	54	17	7	17	23	22	5	4	17	5	19	11	18	22	10	131	131
Intercept	401	495	488	420	75	140	141	106	128	18	18	69	30	92	97	60	130	123	131	1000

Training Data | Training Data w Dummy Vars | Linear Model | ModelCoefficientStdError | +

Normal View   Ready   Sum=401

Figure 6-15: The SSCP matrix

The SSCP matrix then gives you a glimpse into the magnitudes of each variable and how much they overlap and move with each other.

The coefficient standard error calculation uses the inverse of the SSCP matrix. To obtain the inverse, paste the variable headers again below the SSCP matrix in B24:U24 and in A25:A44. The inverse of the SSCP matrix in B2:U21 is then calculated by highlighting B25:U44 and employing the MINVERSE function as an array formula:

{=MINVERSE(B2:U21)}

This yields the sheet shown in Figure 6-16.

The values required in the coefficient standard error calculation are those on the diagonal of the SSCP inverse matrix. Each coefficient standard error is calculated as the prediction standard error for the entire model (calculated as 0.37 on the Linear Model tab earlier in cell X5) scaled by the square root of the appropriate value from the SSCP inverse diagonal.

For example, the coefficient standard error for Male would be the square root of its Male-to-Male entry in the inverse SSCP matrix (square root of 0.0122) times the prediction standard error.

To calculate this for all variables, number each variable starting with 1 in B46 through 20 in U46. The appropriate diagonal value can then be read for each predictor using the INDEX formula. For example, INDEX(ModelCoefficientStdError!B25:B44,ModelCoefficientStdError!B46) returns the Male-to-Male diagonal entry (see more on the INDEX formula in Chapter 1).

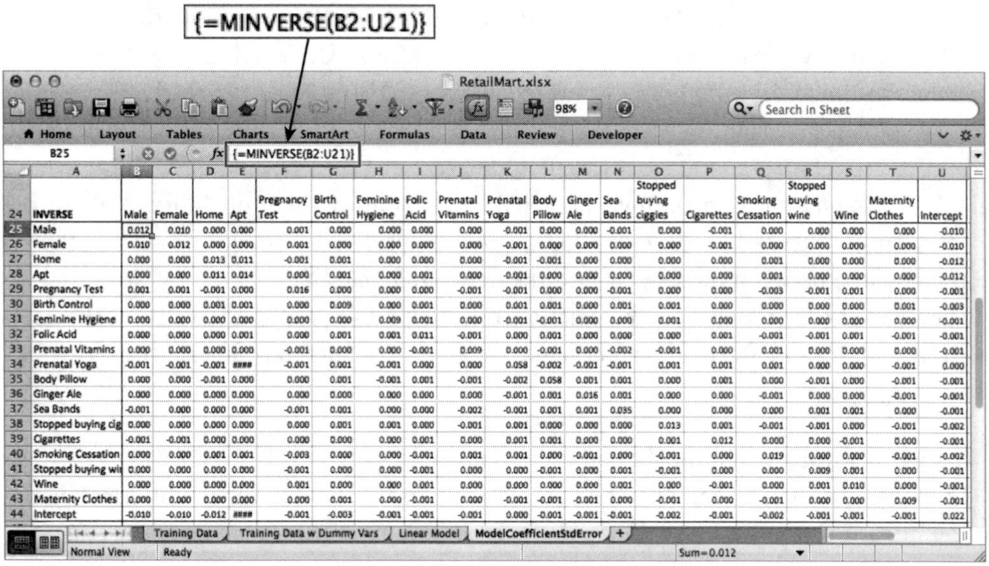

$$\{=MINVERSE(B2:U21)\}$$

Figure 6-16: The inverse of the SSCP matrix

Taking the square root of this value and multiplying it times the prediction standard error, the Male coefficient standard error is calculated in cell B47 as:

```
='Linear Model'!$X5*SQRT(INDEX(ModelCoefficientStdError!B25:B44,
ModelCoefficientStdError!B46))
```

This comes out to 0.04 for the model fit in the book.

Drag this formula through column U to obtain all the coefficient standard error values as shown in Figure 6-17.

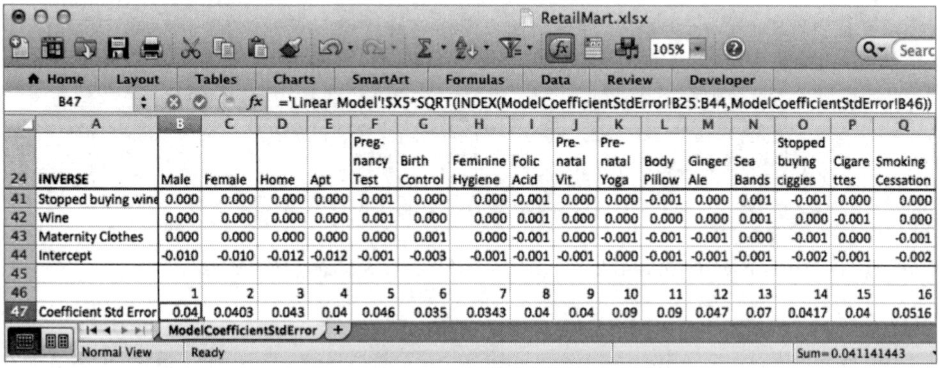

Figure 6-17: The standard error of each model coefficient

On the Linear Model tab, label A3 as **Coefficient Standard Error**. Copy the coefficient standard errors, and paste their values back on the Linear Model tab in row 3 (B3:U3).

Phew! It's downhill from here. No more matrix math for the rest of the book. I swear.

Now you have everything you need to calculate each coefficient's *t statistic* (similar to the entire model's F statistic from the previous section). You will be performing what's called a two-tailed t test, meaning that you'll be calculating the probability of obtaining a coefficient at least as large in *either the positive or negative direction* if, in reality, there's no relationship between the feature and the dependent variable.

The t statistic for the test can be calculated in row 4 as the absolute value of the coefficient normalized by the coefficient's standard error. For the Male feature this is:

```
=ABS(B2/B3)
```

Copy this through column U to all the variables.

The t test can then be called by evaluating the *t distribution* (another statistical distribution like the normal distribution introduced in Chapter 4) at the value of the t statistic for your particular degrees of freedom value. Label row 5 then as t Test p Value, and in B5 use the formula TDIST to calculate the probability of a coefficient at least this large given the null hypothesis:

```
=TDIST(B4,$Z3,2)
```

The two in the formula indicates you're performing the two-tailed t test. Copying this formula across to all variables and applying conditional formatting to cells over 0.05 (5percent probability), you can see which features are not statistically significant. While your results may vary based on the fit of your model, in the workbook shown in Figure 6-18, the Female, Home, and Apt columns are shown to be insignificant.

	A	B	C	D	E	F	G	H	I	J	K	L	M
1		Male	Female	Home	Apt	Pregnancy Test	Birth Control	Feminine Hygiene	Folic Acid	Prenatal Vitamins	Prenatal Yoga	Body Pillow	Ginger Ale
2	Model Coefficients	-0.10	-0.03	-0.03	-0.01	0.22	-0.27	-0.24	0.35	0.29	0.33	0.19	0.23
3	Coefficient Standard Error	0.041	0.040	0.043	0.043	0.046	0.035	0.034	0.039	0.036	0.089	0.089	0.047
4	t Statistic	2.39	0.6651	0.6516	0.307	4.654338	7.8738	6.939359	8.83	8.16017	3.645	2.166	4.882
5	t Test p Value	0.02	0.51	0.51	0.76	0.00	0.00	0.00	0.00	0.00	0.00	0.03	0.00

Figure 6-18: Female, Home, and Apt are insignificant predictors according to the test

You could remove these columns from your model in future training runs.

Now that you've learned how to evaluate the model using statistical tests, let's change gears and look at measuring the model's performance by making actual predictions on a test set.

Making Predictions on Some New Data and Measuring Performance

That last section was all statistics. Lab work you could say. It's not the most fun you've ever had, but validating goodness of fit and significance are important skills to have. But now it's time to take this model to the racetrack and have some fun!

How do you know your linear model actually will predict well in the real world? After all, your training set does not encapsulate every possible customer record, and your coefficients have been purpose built to fit the training set (although if you've done your job right, the training set, very nearly, resembles the world at large).

To get a better sense of how the model will perform in the real world, you should run some customers through the model that were not used in the training process. You'll see this separate set of examples used for testing a model often called a *validation set, test set, or holdout set*.

To assemble your test set, you can just return to the customer database and select another set of data from random customers (paying special attention to not pull the same customers used in training). Now, as noted earlier, 6 percent of RetailMart's customers are pregnant, so if you randomly selected a thousand customers from the database, roughly 60 of them would be pregnant.

While you oversampled the pregnant class in training the model, for testing you'll leave the ratio of pregnant households at 6 percent so that our measurements of the precision of the model are accurate for how the model would perform in a live setting.

In the RetailMart spreadsheet available for download that accompanies this chapter, you'll find a tab called Test Set, which is populated with a thousand rows of data identical to the training data. The first 60 customers are pregnant, while the other 940 are not (see Figure 6-19).

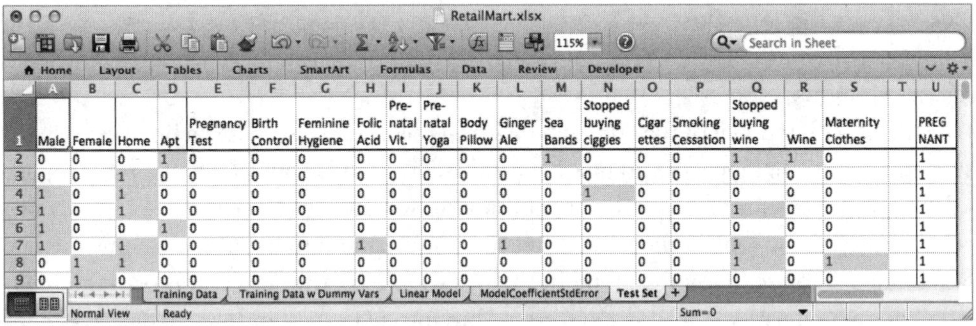

Figure 6-19: Test set data

Just as you did on the Linear Model tab, run this new data through the model by taking a linear combination of customer data and coefficients and adding in the intercept.

Placing this prediction in column V, you have the following formula for the first customer on row 2 (since the test set doesn't have an Intercept column, you add it in separately):

```
=SUMPRODUCT('Linear Model'!B$2:T$2,'Test Set'!A2:S2)+'Linear Model'!U$2
```

Copy this calculation down to all the customers. The resulting spreadsheet looks as shown in Figure 6-20.

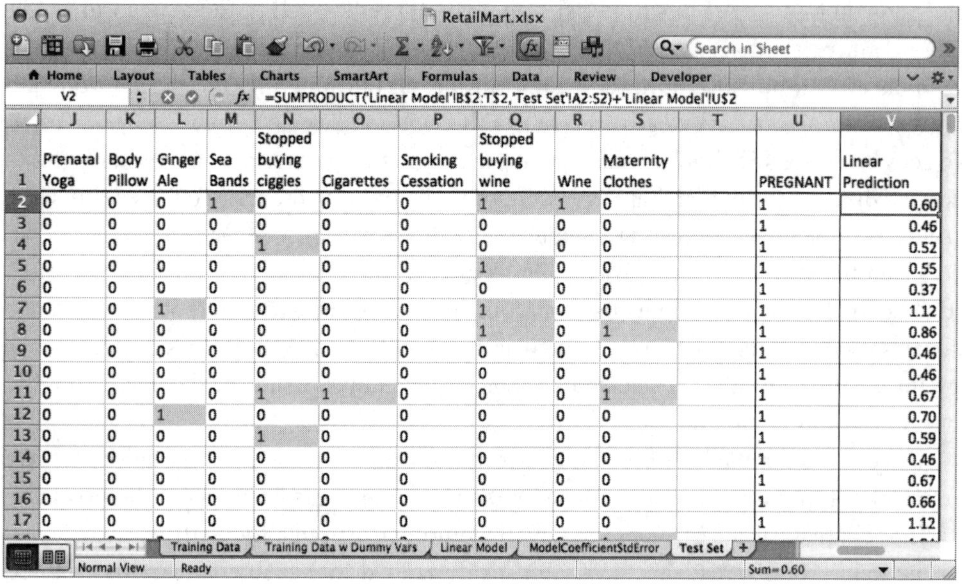

	Prenatal Yoga	Body Pillow	Ginger Ale	Sea Bands	Stopped buying ciggies	Cigarettes	Smoking Cessation	Stopped buying wine	Wine	Maternity Clothes		PREGNANT	Linear Prediction
2	0	0	0	1	0	0	0	1	1	0		1	0.60
3	0	0	0	0	0	0	0	0	0	0		1	0.46
4	0	0	0	0	1	0	0	0	0	0		1	0.52
5	0	0	0	0	0	0	0	1	0	0		1	0.55
6	0	0	0	0	0	0	0	0	0	0		1	0.37
7	0	0	1	0	0	0	0	1	0	0		1	1.12
8	0	0	0	0	0	0	0	1	0	1		1	0.86
9	0	0	0	0	0	0	0	0	0	0		1	0.46
10	0	0	0	0	0	0	0	0	0	0		1	0.46
11	0	0	0	0	1	1	0	0	0	1		1	0.67
12	0	0	1	0	0	0	0	0	0	0		1	0.70
13	0	0	0	0	1	0	0	0	0	0		1	0.59
14	0	0	0	0	0	0	0	0	0	0		1	0.46
15	0	0	0	0	0	0	0	0	0	0		1	0.67
16	0	0	0	0	0	0	0	0	0	0		1	0.66
17	0	0	0	0	0	0	0	0	0	0		1	1.12

Figure 6-20: Predictions on the test set

You can see in Figure 6-20 that the model has identified many of the pregnant households with predictions closer to 1 than they are to 0. The highest prediction values are for households that bought a product clearly related to pregnancy, such as folic acid or prenatal vitamins.

On the other hand, out of the 60 pregnant households, there are some who never bought anything to indicate they were pregnant. Of course, they *didn't* buy alcohol or tobacco, but as their low pregnancy scores indicate, not buying something doesn't mean a whole lot.

Conversely, if you look at the predictions for non-pregnant folks there are some misses. For instance if you're following along in the workbook, on row 154 a non-pregnant customer bought maternity clothing and stopped buying cigarettes, and the model gave them a score of 0.76.

It's clear then that if you are going to use these predictions in real marketing efforts, you need to set a score threshold for when you can assume someone is pregnant and reach out to that person with marketing materials. Perhaps you only send someone marketing materials if they're scored at 0.8 or above. Perhaps that cutoff should be 0.95, so that you're extra sure.

In order to set this classification threshold, you need to look at trade-offs in model performance metrics. Most predictive model performance metrics are based on counts and ratios of four values that come from the predictions on our test set:

- **True positives**—Labeling a pregnant customer as pregnant
- **True negatives**—Labeling a not pregnant customer as not pregnant
- **False positives (also called *type I error*)**—Calling a not-so-pregnant customer pregnant. In my experience, this specific false positive is very insulting face-to-face. Do not try this at home.
- **False negatives (also called *type II error*)**—Failing to identify a pregnant customer as such. This is not nearly as insulting in my experience.

As you'll see, while there are lots of different performance metrics for a predictive model, they all feel a bit like Tex Mex food—they're all basically combinations of the same four ingredients listed above.

Setting Up Cutoff Values

Create a new sheet called **Performance**. The lowest value that could practically be used as a cutoff between pregnant and not pregnant is the lowest prediction value from the test set. Label A1 as **Min Prediction** and in A2, you can calculate this as:

```
=MIN('Test Set'!V2:V1001)
```

Similarly, the highest cutoff value would be the max prediction from the test set. Label A4 as **Max Prediction**, and in A5, you can calculate this as:

```
=MAX('Test Set'!V2:V1001)
```

The values given back are -0.35 and 1.25 respectively. Keep in mind that your linear regression can make predictions below 0 and above 1 because it's not actually returning class probabilities (we'll address this with another model later).

In column B, then, add the header Probability Cutoff for Pregnant Classification and below that specify a range of cutoff values starting with -0.35. In the sheet shown in Figure 6-21, the cutoff values have been chosen to increase in increments of 0.05 all the way to the max of 1.25 (just enter the first three by hand, highlight them, and drag down to fill in the rest).

Alternatively, you could specify every single prediction value from the test set as a cutoff if you wanted to be thorough. No more than that would be needed.

Precision (Positive Predictive Value)

Let's now fill in some model performance metrics for each of these cutoff values using the Test Set data predictions starting with *precision*, also known as *positive predictive value*.

Precision is the measure of how many pregnant households we correctly identify out of all the households the model says are pregnant. In business-speak, precision is the percent of fish in your net that are tuna and not dolphins.

Label column C as **Precision**. Consider the cutoff score in B2 of -0.35. What's the precision of our model if we consider anyone scoring at least a -0.35 to be pregnant?

To calculate that, we can go to the "Test Set" tab and count the number of cases where a *pregnant* household scored greater than or equal to -0.35 divided by the number of total rows with a score over -0.35. Using the COUNTIFS formula to check actuals and predictions, the formula in cell C2 would look as follows:

```
=COUNTIFS('Test Set'!$V$2:$V$1001,">=" & B2,
'Test Set'!$U$2:$U$1001,"=1")/COUNTIF('Test Set'!$V$2:$V$1001,">=" & B2)
```

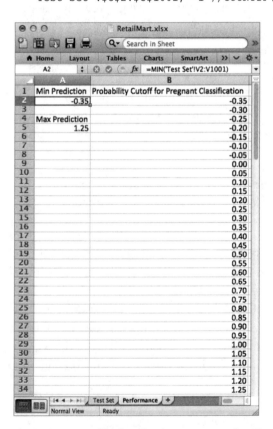

Figure 6-21: Cutoff values for the pregnancy classification

The first COUNTIFS statement in the formula matches both on actual pregnancy and model prediction, while the COUNTIF in the denominator just cares about only those who scored higher that -0.35 regardless of pregnancy. You can copy this formula to all the thresholds you're evaluating.

As seen in Figure 6-22, the precision of the model increases with the cutoff value, and at a cutoff value of 1, the model becomes completely precise. A completely precise model identifies only pregnant customers as pregnant.

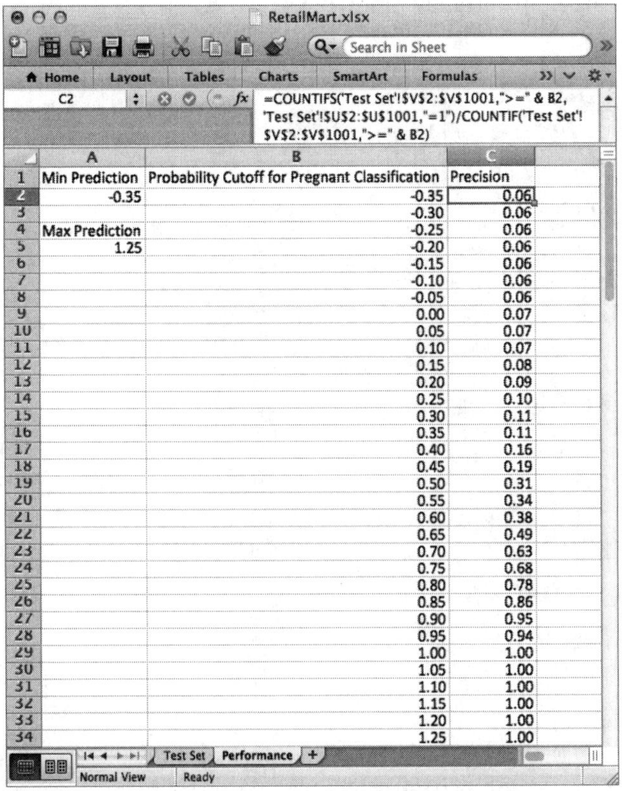

Figure 6-22: Precision calculations on the test set

Specificity (True Negative Rate)

Another performance metric that increases with the cutoff value is called *Specificity*. Specificity, also called the *True Negative Rate* is a count of how many not pregnant customers are correctly predicted as such (true negatives) divided by the total number of not pregnant cases.

Labeling column D as **Specificity/True Negative Rate**, you can calculate it in D2 by using COUNTIFS in the numerator to count true negatives, and COUNTIF in the denominator to count total customers who aren't pregnant:

```
=COUNTIFS('Test Set'!$V$2:$V$1001,"<" & B2,
'Test Set'!$U$2:$U$1001,"=0")/COUNTIF('Test Set'!$U$2:$U$1001,"=0")
```

Copying this calculation down through the other cutoff values, you should see it increase (see Figure 6-23). Once a cutoff value of 0.85 is reached, 100 percent of not pregnant customers in the test set are appropriately predicted.

	A	B	C	D
1	Min Prediction	Probability Cutoff for Pregnant Classification	Precision	Specificity / True Negative Rate
2	-0.35	-0.35	0.06	0.00
3		-0.30	0.06	0.00
4	Max Prediction	-0.25	0.06	0.01
5	1.25	-0.20	0.06	0.02
6		-0.15	0.06	0.03
7		-0.10	0.06	0.05
8		-0.05	0.06	0.08
9		0.00	0.07	0.11
10		0.05	0.07	0.13
11		0.10	0.07	0.18
12		0.15	0.08	0.23
13		0.20	0.09	0.34
14		0.25	0.10	0.44
15		0.30	0.11	0.50
16		0.35	0.11	0.53
17		0.40	0.16	0.69
18		0.45	0.19	0.76
19		0.50	0.31	0.89
20		0.55	0.34	0.91
21		0.60	0.38	0.93
22		0.65	0.49	0.96
23		0.70	0.63	0.98
24		0.75	0.68	0.98
25		0.80	0.78	0.99
26		0.85	0.86	1.00
27		0.90	0.95	1.00
28		0.95	0.94	1.00
29		1.00	1.00	1.00
30		1.05	1.00	1.00
31		1.10	1.00	1.00
32		1.15	1.00	1.00
33		1.20	1.00	1.00
34		1.25	1.00	1.00

Figure 6-23: Specificity calculations on the test set

False Positive Rate

The *false positive rate* is a common metric looked at to understand model performance. And since you already have the true negative rate, this can quickly be calculated as one minus the true negative rate. Label column E as **False Positive Rate/(1 – Specificity)** and fill in the cells as one minus the value in the adjacent cell in D. For E2, that's written as:

```
=1-D2
```

Copying this formula down, you can see that as the cutoff value increases, you get less false positives. In other words, you're committing fewer type I errors (calling customers pregnant who aren't).

True Positive Rate/Recall/Sensitivity

The final metric you can calculate on your model's performance is call *true positive rate*. And *recall*. And *sensitivity*. Geez. They should just pick one name and stick with it.

The true positive rate is the ratio of correctly identified pregnant women divided by the total of actual pregnant women in the test set. Label column F as **True Positive Rate/Recall/Sensitivity**. In F2 then you can calculate the true positive rate of a cutoff value of -0.35 as:

```
=COUNTIFS('Test Set'!$V$2:$V$1001,">=" & B2,
'Test Set'!$U$2:$U$1001,"=1")/COUNTIF('Test Set'!$U$2:$U$1001,"=1")
```

Looking back at the true negative rate column, this calculation is exactly the same except "<" becomes ">=" and 0s become 1s.

Copying this metric down, you can see that as the cutoff increases, some of the pregnant women cease to be identified as such (these are type II errors) and the true positive rate falls. Figure 6-24 shows the false and true positive rates in columns E and F.

	Probability Cutoff for		Specificity / True	False Positive Rate	True Positive Rate /
1	Min Prediction	Pregnant Classification	Precision	Negative Rate	(1 - Specificity)	Recall / Sensitivity
2	-0.35	-0.35	0.06	0.00	1.00	1.00
3		-0.30	0.06	0.00	1.00	1.00
4	Max Prediction	-0.25	0.06	0.01	0.99	1.00
5	1.25	-0.20	0.06	0.02	0.98	1.00
6		-0.15	0.06	0.03	0.97	1.00
7		-0.10	0.06	0.05	0.95	1.00
8		-0.05	0.06	0.08	0.92	1.00
9		0.00	0.07	0.11	0.89	1.00
10		0.05	0.07	0.13	0.87	0.98
11		0.10	0.07	0.18	0.82	0.98
12		0.15	0.08	0.23	0.77	0.98
13		0.20	0.09	0.34	0.66	0.97
14		0.25	0.10	0.44	0.56	0.95
15		0.30	0.11	0.50	0.50	0.95
16		0.35	0.11	0.53	0.47	0.95
17		0.40	0.16	0.69	0.31	0.90
18		0.45	0.19	0.76	0.24	0.87
19		0.50	0.31	0.89	0.11	0.78
20		0.55	0.34	0.91	0.09	0.75
21		0.60	0.38	0.93	0.07	0.72
22		0.65	0.49	0.96	0.04	0.65
23		0.70	0.63	0.98	0.02	0.58
24		0.75	0.68	0.98	0.02	0.53
25		0.80	0.78	0.99	0.01	0.47
26		0.85	0.86	1.00	0.00	0.40
27		0.90	0.95	1.00	0.00	0.33
28		0.95	0.94	1.00	0.00	0.28
29		1.00	1.00	1.00	0.00	0.23
30		1.05	1.00	1.00	0.00	0.18
31		1.10	1.00	1.00	0.00	0.15
32		1.15	1.00	1.00	0.00	0.03
33		1.20	1.00	1.00	0.00	0.03
34		1.25	1.00	1.00	0.00	0.02

Figure 6-24: The false positive rate and the true positive rate

Evaluating Metric Trade-Offs and the Receiver Operating Characteristic Curve

When choosing a threshold value for a binary classifier, it's important to select the best balance of these performance metrics. The higher the cutoff, the more precise the model but the lower the recall, for example. One of the most common visualizations used to assess these performance trade-offs is the receiver operating characteristic (ROC) curve. The ROC curve is just a plot of the False Positive Rate versus the True Positive Rate (columns E and F in the Performance sheet).

WHY IS IT CALLED THE RECEIVER OPERATING CHARACTERISTIC?

The reason why such a simple graph has such a complex name is that it was developed during World War II by radar engineers rather than by marketers predicting when customers are pregnant.

These folks were using signals to detect enemies and their equipment in the battlefield, and they wanted to better visualize the trade-off between correctly and incorrectly identifying something as a foe.

To insert this graph, simply highlight the data in columns E and F and select the *straight lined scatter plot* in Excel (see Chapter 1 for more on inserting charts and graphs). With a little formatting (setting the axes between 0 and 1, bumping up the font), the ROC curve looks as shown in Figure 6-25.

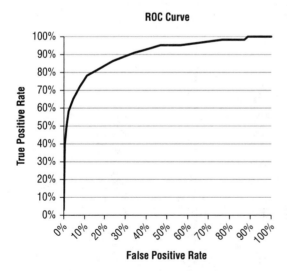

Figure 6-25: The ROC curve for the linear regression

This curve allows you to quickly assess the false positive rate that's associated with a true positive rate in order to understand your options. For example, in Figure 6-25, you can see that the model is capable of identifying 40 percent of pregnant customers using a cutoff of 0.85 without a single false positive. Nice!

And if you were okay with occasionally sending a not pregnant household some pregnancy-related coupons, the model could achieve a 75 percent true positive rate with only a 9 percent false positive rate.

Where you decide to set the threshold for acting on someone's pregnancy score *is a business decision*, not purely an analytic one. If there were little downside to predicting someone was pregnant, then a low precision might be a fine trade-off for a high true positive rate. But if you're predicting likelihood of default for loan applications, you're going to want specificity and precision to be a *bit higher*, right? On the extreme end, if a model like this were being used to validate the legitimacy of overseas threats based on a body of intelligence, then you'd hope that the operator of the model would want a very high level of precision before calling in a drone strike.

So whether we're talking sending coupons in the mail, approving loans, or dropping bombs, the balance you strike between these performance metrics is a strategic decision.

COMPARING ONE MODEL TO ANOTHER

As we'll see a bit later, the ROC curve is also good for choosing one predictive model over another. Ideally, the ROC curve would jump straight up to 1 on the y-axis as fast as possible and stay there all the way across the graph. So the model that looks most like that (also said to have the highest *area under the curve* or *AUC*) is often considered superior.

All right! So now you've run the model on some test data, made some predictions, computed its performance on the test set for different cutoff values, and visualized that performance with the ROC curve.

But in order to compare model performance, you need another model to race against.

Predicting Pregnant Customers at RetailMart Using Logistic Regression

If you look at the predicted values coming out your linear regression, it's clear that while the model is useful for classification, the prediction values themselves are certainly in no way class probabilities. You can't be pregnant with 125 percent probability or -35 percent probability.

So is there a model whose predictions are actually class probabilities? Once such model that we can build is called a *logistic regression*.

First You Need a Link Function

Think about the predictions currently coming out of your linear model. Is there a formula you can shove these numbers through that will make them stay between 0 and 1? It turns out, this kind of function is called a *link function*, and there's a great one for doing just that:

```
exp(x)/(1 + exp(x))
```

In this formula, x is our linear combination from column W on the Linear Model tab, and exp is the exponential function. The exponential function exp(x) is just the mathematical constant e (2.71828…it's like pi, but a little lower) raised to the power of x.

Look at a graph of the function pictured in Figure 6-26.

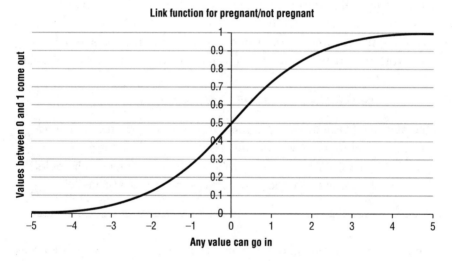

Figure 6-26: The link function

This link function looks like a really wide S. It takes in any values given from multiplying the model coefficients times a row of customer data, and it outputs a number between 0 and 1. But why does this odd function look like this?

Well, just round e to 2.7 real quick and think about the case where the input to this function is pretty big, say 10. Then the link function is:

```
exp(x)/(1 + exp(x)) = 2.7^10 / (1+ 2.7^10) = 20589/20590
```

Well, that's basically 1, so we can see that as x gets larger, that 1 in the denominator just doesn't matter much. But as x goes negative? Look at -10:

```
exp(x)/(1 + exp(x)) = 2.7^-10 / (1+ 2.7^-10) = 0.00005/1.00005
```

Well, that's just 0 for the most part. In this case the 1 in the denominator means everything and the teeny numbers are more or less 0s.

Isn't that handy? In fact, this link function has been so useful that someone gave it a name along the way. It's called the "logistic" function.

Hooking Up the Logistic Function and Reoptimizing

Now create a copy of the Linear Model tab in the spreadsheet and call it **Logistic Link Model**. Delete all of the statistical testing data from the sheet since that was primarily applicable to linear regression. Specifically, highlight and delete rows 3 through 5, and clear out all the values at the top of columns W through Z except for the Sum Squared Error placeholder. Also, clear out the squared error column and rename it **Prediction (after Link Function)**. See Figure 6-27 to see what the sheet should look like.

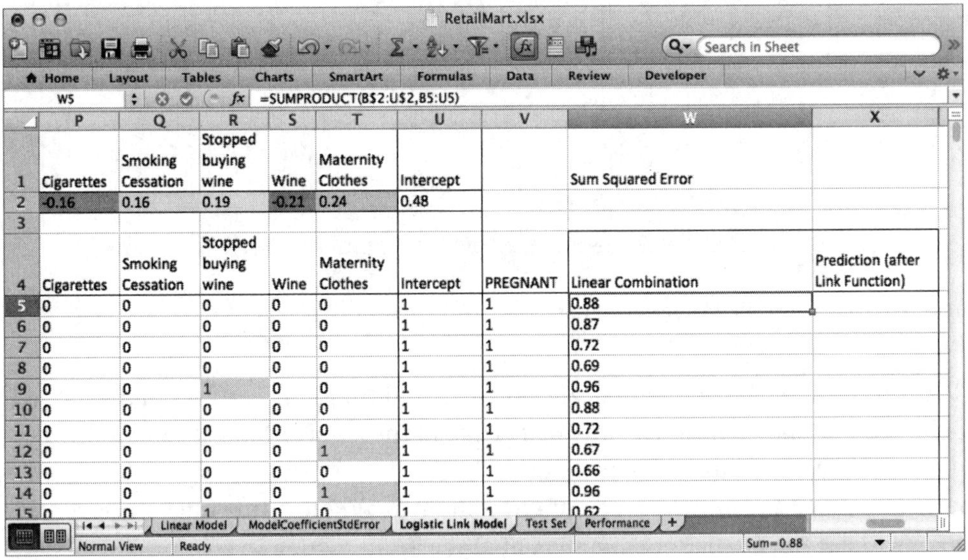

Figure 6-27: The initial logistic model sheet

You're going use column X to suck in the linear combination of coefficients and data from column W and put it through your logistic function. For example, the first row of modeled customer data would be sent through the logistic function by putting this formula in cell X5:

```
=EXP(W5)/(1+EXP(W5))
```

If you copy this formula down the column, you can see that the new values are all between 0 and 1 (see Figure 6-28).

NOTE

Your sheet might have slightly different values in columns W and X to start since the model coefficients are coming from the evolutionary algorithm run on the previous tab.

	P	Q	R	S	T	U	V	W	X
1	Cigarettes	Smoking Cessation	Stopped buying wine	Wine	Maternity Clothes	Intercept		Sum Squared Error	
2	-0.16	0.16	0.19	-0.21	0.24	0.48			
3									
4	Cigarettes	Smoking Cessation	Stopped buying wine	Wine	Maternity Clothes	Intercept	PREGNANT	Linear Combination	Prediction (after Link Function)
5	0	0	0	0	0	1	1	0.88	0.71
6	0	0	0	0	0	1	1	0.87	0.70
7	0	0	0	0	0	1	1	0.72	0.67
8	0	0	0	0	0	1	1	0.69	0.67
9	0	0	1	0	0	1	1	0.96	0.72
10	0	0	0	0	0	1	1	0.88	0.71
11	0	0	0	0	0	1	1	0.72	0.67
12	0	0	0	0	1	1	1	0.67	0.66
13	0	0	0	0	0	1	1	0.66	0.66
14	0	0	0	0	1	1	1	0.96	0.72
15	0	0	1	0	0	1	1	0.62	0.65

Figure 6-28: Values through the logistic function

However, most of the predictions appear to be middling, between 0.4 and 0.7. Well, that's because we didn't optimize our coefficients in the "Linear Model" tab for this new kind of model. We need to optimize again.

So add back in a squared error column to column Y, although this time, the error calculation will use the predictions coming out of the link function in column X:

```
=(V5-X5)^2
```

Which you'll again sum up just as in the linear model in cell X1 as:

```
=SUM(Y5:Y1004)
```

You can then minimize the sum of squares in this new model using the exact same Solver setup (see Figure 6-29) as in the linear model, except if you experiment with the variable bounds, you'll find it's best to broaden them a bit for a logistic model. In Figure 6-29, the bounds have been set to keep each coefficient between -5 and 5.

Once you've reoptimized for the new link function, you can see that your predictions on the training data now all fall between 0 and 1 with many predictions confidently being committed to either a 0 or a 1. As you can see in Figure 6-30, from an aesthetic perspective, these predictions feel nicer than those from the linear regression.

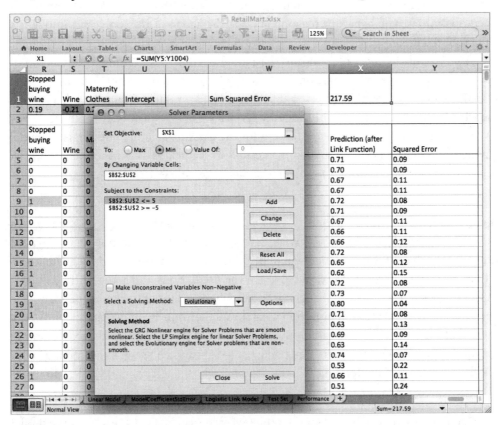

Figure 6-29: Identical Solver setup for logistic model

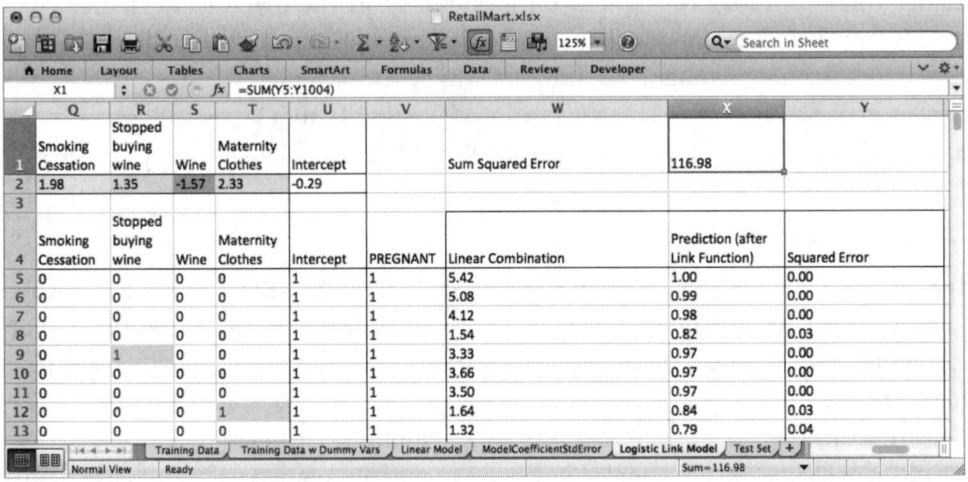

Figure 6-30: Fitted logistic model

Baking an Actual Logistic Regression

The truth is that in order to do an actual logistic regression that gives accurate, unbiased class probabilities, you can't, for reasons outside the scope of this book, minimize the sum of squared error.

Instead, you fit the model by finding the model coefficients that maximize the joint probability (see Chapter 3 for more on joint probability) of you having pulled this training set from the RetailMart database given that the model accurately explains reality.

So what is the likelihood of a training row given a set of logistic model parameters? For a given row in the training set, let p stand in for the class probability your logistic model is giving in column X. Let y stand for the actual pregnancy value housed in column V. The likelihood of that training row, given the model parameters is:

$$p^y(1-p)^{(1-y)}$$

For a pregnant customer (column V is 1) with a prediction of 1 (column X has a 1 in it), this likelihood calculation is, likewise, 1. But if the prediction were 0 for a pregnant customer, then the above calculation would be 0 (plug in the numbers and check it). Thus, the likelihood of each row is maximized when the predictions and actuals all line up.

Assuming each row of data is independent (see Chapter 3 for more on independence) as is the case in any good random pull from a database, then you can calculate the log of the joint probability of the data by taking the log of each of these likelihoods and summing them up. The log of the above equation, using the same rules you saw in the floating-point underflow section in Chapter 3, is:

$$y*\ln(p)+(1-y)*\ln(1-p)$$

The log likelihood is near 0 when the previous formula is near 1 (i.e., when the model fits well).

Rather than minimize the sum of the squared error then, you can calculate this *log-likelihood* value on each prediction and sum them up instead. The model coefficients that *maximize* the joint likelihood of the data will be the best ones.

To start, make a copy of the Logistic Link Model tab and call it **Logistic Regression**. In column Y, change the squared error column to read Log Likelihood. In cell Y5, the first log likelihood can be calculated as:

```
=IFERROR(V5*LN(X5)+(1-V5)*LN(1-X5),0)
```

The entire log likelihood calculation is wrapped in an IFERROR formula, because when the model coefficients generate a prediction very, very near the actual 0/1 class value, you can get numerical instability. In that case, it's fair just to set the log-likelihood to a perfect match score of 0.

Copy this formula down column Y, and in X1, sum the log likelihoods. Optimizing, you get a set of coefficients that look similar to the sum of squares coefficients with some small shifts here and there. See Figure 6-31.

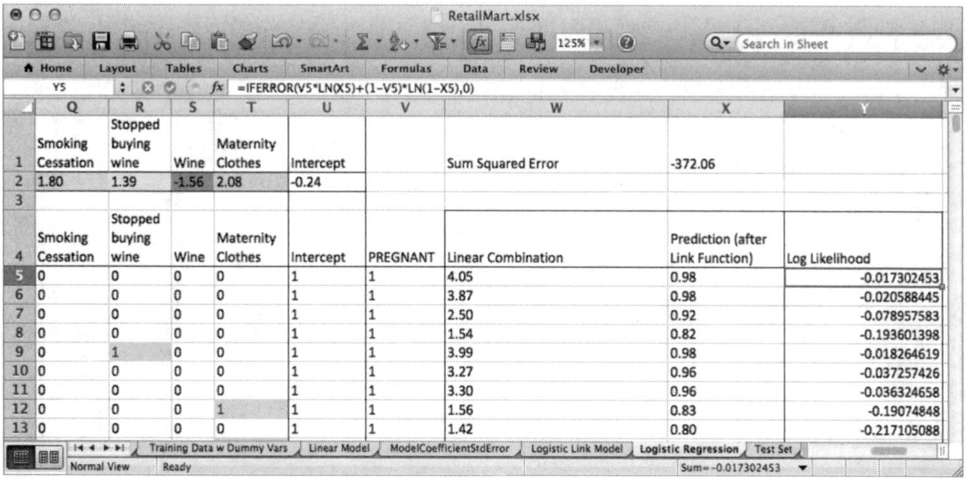

	Q	R	S	T	U	V	W	X	Y
	Smoking Cessation	Stopped buying wine	Wine	Maternity Clothes	Intercept		Sum Squared Error		
1									
2	1.80	1.39	-1.56	2.08	-0.24			-372.06	
3									
4	Smoking Cessation	Stopped buying wine	Wine	Maternity Clothes	Intercept	PREGNANT	Linear Combination	Prediction (after Link Function)	Log Likelihood
5	0	0	0	0	1	1	4.05	0.98	-0.017302453
6	0	0	0	0	1	1	3.87	0.98	-0.020588445
7	0	0	0	0	1	1	2.50	0.92	-0.078957583
8	0	0	0	0	1	1	1.54	0.82	-0.193601398
9	0	1	0	0	1	1	3.99	0.98	-0.018264619
10	0	0	0	0	1	1	3.27	0.96	-0.037257426
11	0	0	0	0	1	1	3.30	0.96	-0.036324658
12	0	0	0	1	1	1	1.56	0.83	-0.19074848
13	0	0	0	0	1	1	1.42	0.80	-0.217105088

Cell reference: Y5 = IFERROR(V5*LN(X5)+(1-V5)*LN(1-X5),0)

Sheet tabs: Training Data w Dummy Vars / Linear Model / ModelCoefficientStdError / Logistic Link Model / Logistic Regression / Test Set

Figure 6-31: The Logistic Regression sheet

If you check the sum of squared error associated with your actual logistic regression, it's nearly optimal for that metric anyway.

STATISTICAL TESTS ON A LOGISTIC REGRESSION

Analogous statistical concepts to the R-squared, F test, and t test are available in logistic regression. Computations such as pseudo R-squared, model deviance, and the Wald statistic lend logistic regression much of the same rigor as linear regression. For more information, see *Applied Logistic Regression* by David W. Hosmer, Jr., Stanley Lemeshow, and Rodney X. Sturdivant (John Wiley & Sons, 2013).

Model Selection—Comparing the Performance of the Linear and Logistic Regressions

Now that you have a second model, you can run it on the test set and compare its performance to that of your linear regression. Predictions using the logistic regression are made in exactly the same way they were modeled in the Logistic Regression tab in columns W and X.

In cell W2 on the Test Set tab, take the linear combination of model coefficients and test data as:

```
=SUMPRODUCT('Logistic Regression'!B$2:T$2,'Test Set'!A2:S2)+
'Logistic Regression'!U$2
```

In X2, run this through the link function to get your class probability:

```
=EXP(W2)/(1+EXP(W2))
```

Copy these cells down through the test set to obtain the sheet shown in Figure 6-32.

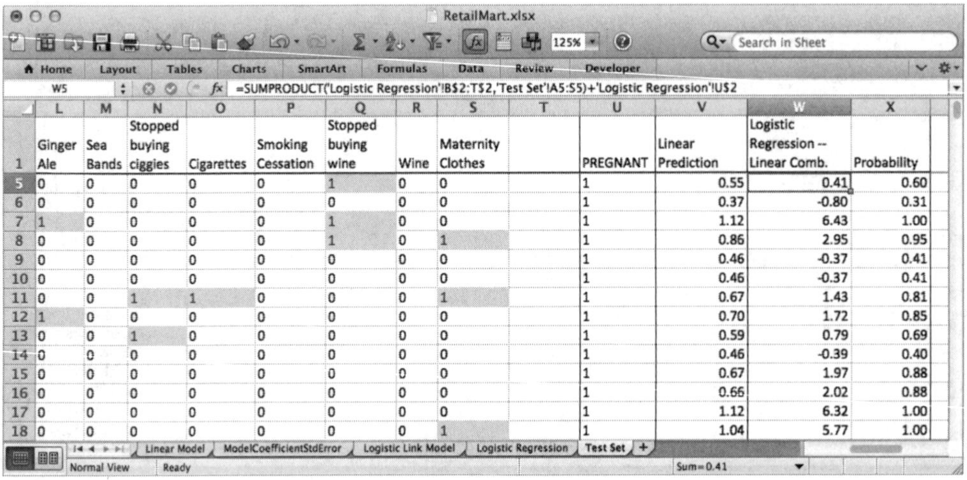

	L	M	N	O	P	Q	R	S	T	U	V	W	X
1	Ginger Ale	Sea Bands	Stopped buying ciggies	Cigarettes	Smoking Cessation	Stopped buying wine	Wine	Maternity Clothes		PREGNANT	Linear Prediction	Logistic Regression -- Linear Comb.	Probability
5	0	0	0	0	0	1	0	0		1	0.55	0.41	0.60
6	0	0	0	0	0	0	0	0		1	0.37	-0.80	0.31
7	1	0	0	0	0	1	0	0		1	1.12	6.43	1.00
8	0	0	0	0	0	1	0	1		1	0.86	2.95	0.95
9	0	0	0	0	0	0	0	0		1	0.46	-0.37	0.41
10	0	0	0	0	0	0	0	0		1	0.46	-0.37	0.41
11	0	0	1	1	0	0	0	1		1	0.67	1.43	0.81
12	1	0	0	0	0	0	0	0		1	0.70	1.72	0.85
13	0	0	1	0	0	0	0	0		1	0.59	0.79	0.69
14	0	0	0	0	0	0	0	0		1	0.46	-0.39	0.40
15	0	0	0	0	0	0	0	0		1	0.67	1.97	0.88
16	0	0	0	0	0	0	0	0		1	0.66	2.02	0.88
17	0	0	0	0	0	0	0	0		1	1.12	6.32	1.00
18	0	0	0	0	0	0	0	1		1	1.04	5.77	1.00

Figure 6-32: Logistic regression predictions on the test set

To see how the predictions stack up, make a copy of the Performance tab and call it **Performance Logistic**. Changing the minimum and maximum prediction formulas to point to column X from the Test Set tab, the values come back as 0 and 1, just as you'd expect now that your model is giving actual class probabilities unlike the linear regression.

NOTE

While the logistic regression returns class probabilities (actual predictions between 0 and 1), these probabilities are based on the 50/50 split of pregnant and not pregnant customers in the rebalanced training set.

This is fine if all you care about is binary classification at some cutoff value rather than using the actual probabilities.

Choose cutoff values from 0 to 1 in 0.05 increments (actually, you may need to make 1 a 0.999 or so to keep the precision formula from dividing by 0). Everything below row 22 can be cleared, and the performance metrics need only be changed to check column X on the Test Set tab instead of V. This yields the sheet shown in Figure 6-33.

You can set the ROC curve up in exactly the same way as before, however, in order to compare the logistic regression to the linear regression, add in a data series for each model's performance metrics (right-click the chart and choose Select Data to add another series). In Figure 6-34, it's apparent that the ROC curves for the two models are almost exactly on top of each other.

	Probability Cutoff for Pregnant Classification	Precision	Specificity / True Negative Rate	False Positive Rate (1 - Specificity)	True Positive Rate / Recall / Sensitivity
Min Prediction	0.00	0.06	0.00	1.00	1.00
	0.05	0.07	0.21	0.79	0.98
Max Prediction	0.10	0.09	0.41	0.59	0.97
1.00	0.15	0.11	0.49	0.51	0.95
	0.20	0.11	0.51	0.49	0.95
	0.25	0.11	0.54	0.46	0.93
	0.30	0.13	0.61	0.39	0.93
	0.35	0.16	0.69	0.31	0.90
	0.40	0.18	0.74	0.26	0.88
	0.45	0.30	0.88	0.12	0.80
	0.50	0.30	0.88	0.12	0.78
	0.55	0.32	0.89	0.11	0.78
	0.60	0.33	0.90	0.10	0.77
	0.65	0.36	0.92	0.08	0.75
	0.70	0.37	0.92	0.08	0.72
	0.75	0.43	0.94	0.06	0.67
	0.80	0.51	0.96	0.04	0.67
	0.85	0.62	0.98	0.02	0.60
	0.90	0.71	0.99	0.01	0.53
	0.95	0.76	0.99	0.01	0.42
	1.00	1.00	1.00	0.00	0.02

Figure 6-33: The Performance Logistic tab

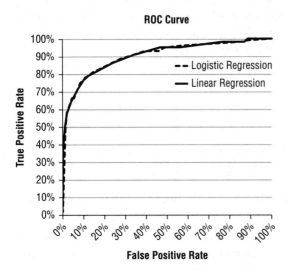

Figure 6-34: The linear and logistic regression ROC curves graphed together

Given that the models' performances are nearly identical, you might consider using the logistic regression if for no other reason than the practicality of getting actual class probabilities bounded between 0 and 1 from the model. It's prettier if nothing else.

A WORD OF CAUTION

You may hear a lot about model selection out there in the real world. Folks may ask, "Why didn't you use support vector machines or neural nets or random forests or boosted trees?" There are numerous types of AI models, all with their strengths and weaknesses. And I would encourage you to read about them, and if in your work you happen to use an AI model, then you should try some of these models head-to-head.
But.

Trying different AI models is not the most important part of an AI modeling project. It's the last step, the icing on the cake. This is where sites like Kaggle.com (an AI modeling competition website) have it all wrong.

You get more bang for your buck spending your time on selecting good data and features than models. For example, in the problem I outlined in this chapter, you'd be better served testing out possible new features like "customer ceased to buy lunch meat for fear of listeriosis" and making sure your training data was perfect than you would be testing out a neural net on your old training data.

Why? Because the phrase "garbage in, garbage out" has never been more applicable to any field than AI. No AI model is a miracle worker; it can't take terrible data and magically know how to use that data. So do your AI model a favor and give it the best and most creative features you can find.

For More Information

If you just love supervised AI, and this chapter wasn't enough for you, then let me make some reading suggestions:

- *Data Mining with R* by Luis Torgo (Chapman & Hall/CRC, 2010) is a great next step. The book covers machine learning in the programming language, R. R is a programming language beloved by statisticians everywhere, and it's not hard to pick up for AI modeling purposes. In fact, if you were going to productionalize something like the model in this chapter, R would be a great place to train up and run that production model.
- *The Elements of Statistical Learning* by Trevor Hastie, Robert Tibshirani, and Jerome Friedman (Springer, 2009) takes an academic look at various AI models. At times

a slog, the book can really up your intellectual game. A free copy can be found on Hastie's Stanford website.

For discussion with other practitioners, I usually head to the CrossValidated forum at StackExchange (`stats.stackexchange.com`). Oftentimes, someone has already asked your question for you, so this forum makes for an excellent knowledge base.

Wrapping Up

Congratulations! You just built a classification model in a spreadsheet. Two of them actually. Maybe even two and a half. And if you took me up on my median regression challenge, then you're a beast.

Let's recap some of the things we covered:

- Feature selection and assembling training data, including creating dummy variables out of categorical predictors
- Training a linear regression model by minimizing the sum of squared error
- Calculating R-squared, showing a model is statistically significant using an F test, and showing model coefficients are individually significant using a t test
- Evaluating model performance on a holdout set at various classification cutoff values by calculating precision, specificity, false positive rate, and recall
- Graphing a ROC curve
- Adding a logistic link function to a general linear model and reoptimizing
- Maximizing likelihood in a logistic regression
- Comparing models with the ROC curve

And while I'll be the first to admit that the data in this chapter is fabricated from whole cloth, let me assure you that the power of such a logistic model is not to be scoffed at. You could use something like it in a production decision support or automated marketing system for your business.

If you'd like to keep going with AI, in the next chapter, I'm going to introduce a different approach to AI called the ensemble model.

7 Ensemble Models: A Whole Lot of Bad Pizza

On the American version of the popular TV show *The Office*, the boss, Michael Scott, buys pizza for his employees. Everyone groans when they learn that he has unfortunately bought pizza from Pizza by Alfredo instead of Alfredo's Pizza. Although it's cheaper, apparently pizza from Pizza by Alfredo is awful.

In response to their protests, Michael asks his employees a question: is it better to have a small amount of really good pizza or a lot of really bad pizza?

For many practical artificial intelligence implementations, the answer is arguably the latter. In the previous chapter, you built a single, good model for predicting pregnant households shopping at RetailMart. What if instead, you got democratic? What if you built a bunch of admittedly crappy models and let them vote on whether a customer was pregnant? The vote tally would then be used as a single prediction.

This type of approach is called *ensemble modeling*, and as you'll see, it turns simple observations into gold.

You'll be going over a type of ensemble model called *bagged decision stumps*, which is very close to an approach used constantly in industry called the *random forest* model. In fact, it's very nearly the approach I use daily in my own life here at MailChimp.com to predict when a user is about to send some spam.

After bagging, you'll investigate another awesome technique called *boosting*. Both of these techniques find creative ways to use the training data over and over and over again to train up an entire ensemble of classifiers. There's an intuitive feel to these approaches that's reminiscent of naïve Bayes—a stupidity that, in aggregate, is smart.

Using the Data from Chapter 6

This chapter's gonna move quickly, because you'll use the RetailMart data from Chapter 6. Using the same data will give you a sense of the differences in these two models' implementations from the regression models in the previous chapter. The modeling techniques demonstrated in this chapter were invented more recently. They're somewhat more intuitive, and yet, are some of the most powerful off the shelf AI technologies we have today.

Also, we'll be building ROC curves identical to those from Chapter 6, so I won't be spending much time explaining performance metric calculations. See Chapter 6 if you really want to understand concepts like precision and recall.

Starting off, the workbook available for download has a sheet called TD which includes the training data from Chapter 6 with the dummy variables already set up properly (for more on this see Chapter 6). Also, the features have been numbered 0 to 18 in row 2. This will come in handy with recordkeeping later (see Figure 7-1).

The workbook also includes the Test Set tab from Chapter 6.

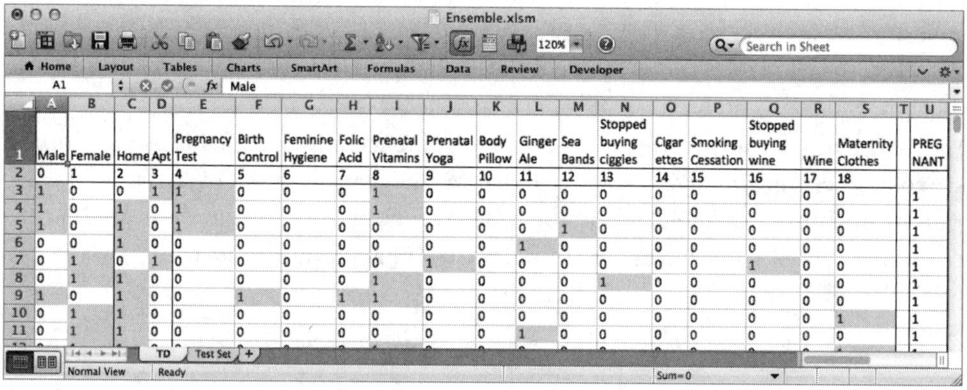

Figure 7-1: The TD tab houses the data from Chapter 6.

You will try to do exactly what you did in Chapter 6 with this data—predict the values in the PREGNANT column using the data to the left of it. Then you'll verify the accuracy on the holdout set.

MISSING VALUE IMPUTATION

In the RetailMart example introduced in Chapter 6 and continued here, you're working with a dataset that doesn't have holes in it. For many models built off of transactional business data, this is often the case. But there will be situations in which elements are missing from some of the rows in a dataset.

For example, if you were building a recommendation AI model for a dating site and you asked users in their profile questionnaire if they listened to the symphonic heavy metal band Evanescence, you might expect that question to be left blank on occasion.

So how do you train a model if some of the folks in your training set leave the Evanescence question blank?

There are all sorts of ways around this issue, but really quickly I'll list some places to start:

- Just drop the rows with missing values. If the missing values are more or less random, losing some rows of training data isn't going to kill you. In the dating site example, these blanks are more likely intentional than random, so dropping the rows could cause the training data to get a skewed view of reality.

- If the column is numeric, fill in the missing value with the median of those records that have values. Filling in missing values is often called *imputation*. If the column is categorical, use the most common category value. Once again, in the case of ashamed Evanescence fans, the most common value is probably No, so filling in with the most common value can be the wrong way to go when people are censoring themselves.

- On top of the previous option, you can add another indicator column that has a 0 in it unless you had a missing value in your original column and a 1 otherwise. That way, you've filled in the missing value as best you could, but you've told the model not to quite trust it.

- Instead of just using the median, you can train a model like the general linear model presented in Chapter 6 to predict the missing value using the data from the other columns. This is a fair bit of work, but it's worth it if you have a small dataset and can't afford to lose accuracy or throw away rows.

continues

(continued)

- Unfortunately, this last approach (like all others mentioned in this note) feels a bit overly confident. It treats the imputed data point as if it's a first-class citizen once it's predicted from the regression line. To get around this, statisticians will often use statistical models to generate multiple regression lines. The empty data will be filled in multiple times using these regression models, each creating a new imputed dataset. Any analysis will be run on each of the imputed datasets and any results will be combined at the end of the analysis. This is called *multiple imputation*.

- Another approach worth trying is called *k nearest neighbors* imputation. Using distance (see Chapter 2) or affinity matrices (Chapter 5), calculate the k nearest neighbors to an entry with missing data. Take a weighted average by distance (or the most common value if you prefer) of the neighbors' values to impute the missing data.

Bagging: Randomize, Train, Repeat

Bagging is a technique used to train multiple classifiers (an ensemble if you will) without them all being trained on the exact same set of training data. Because if you trained the classifiers on the same data, they'd look identical; you want a variety of models, not a bunch of copies of the same model. Bagging lets you introduce some variety in a set of classifiers where there otherwise wouldn't be.

Decision Stump Is an Unsexy Term for a Stupid Predictor

In the bagging model you'll be building, the individual classifiers will be *decision stumps*. A decision stump is nothing more than a single question you ask about the data. Depending on the answer, you say that the household is either pregnant or not. A simple classifier such as this is often called a *weak learner*.

For example, in the training data, if you count the number of times a pregnant household purchased folic acid by highlighting H3:H502 and summing with the summary bar, you'd find that 104 pregnant households made the purchase before giving birth. On the other hand, only two not-pregnant customers bought folic acid.

So there's a relationship between buying folic acid supplements and being pregnant. You can use that simple relationship to construct the following weak learner:

Did the household buy folic acid? If yes, then assume they're pregnant. If no, then assume they're not pregnant.

This predictor is visualized in Figure 7-2.

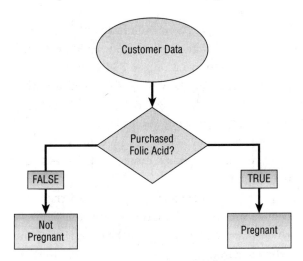

Figure 7-2: The folic acid decision stump

Doesn't Seem So Stupid to Me!

The stump in Figure 7-2 divides the set of training records into two subsets. Now, you might be thinking that that decision stump makes perfect sense, and you're right, it does. But it ain't perfect. After all, there are nearly 400 pregnant households in the training data that didn't buy folic acid but who would be classified incorrectly by the stump.

It's still better than not having a model at all, right?

Undoubtedly. But the question is *how much better* is the stump than not having a model. One way to evaluate that is through a measurement called *node impurity*.

Node impurity measures how often a chosen customer record would be incorrectly labeled as pregnant or not-pregnant if it were assigned a label randomly, according to the distribution of customers in its decision stump subset.

For instance, you could start by shoving all 1,000 training records into the same subset, which is to say, start without a model.

The probability that you'll pull a pregnant person from the heap is 50 percent. And if you label them randomly according to the 50/50 distribution, you have a 50 percent chance of guessing the label correctly.

Thus, you have a 50%*50% = 25 percent chance of pulling a pregnant customer and appropriately guessing they're pregnant. Similarly, you have a 25 percent chance of pulling a not-pregnant customer and guessing they're not pregnant. Everything that's not those two cases is just some version of an incorrect guess.

That means I have a 100% − 25% − 25% = 50 percent chance of incorrectly labeling a customer. So you would say that the impurity of my single starting node is 50 percent.

The folic acid stump splits this set of 1,000 cases into two groups—894 folks who didn't buy folic acid and 106 folks who did. Each of those subsets will have its own impurity, so if you average the impurities of those two subsets (adjusting for their size difference), you can tell how much the decision stump has improved your situation.

For those 894 customers placed into the not-pregnant bucket, 44 percent of them are pregnant and 56 percent are not. This gives an impurity calculation of $100\% − 44\%^2 − 56\%^2 = 49$ percent. Not a whole lot of improvement.

But for the 106 customers placed in the pregnant category, 98 percent of them are pregnant and 2 percent are not. This gives an impurity calculation of $100\% − 98\%^2 − 2\%^2 = 4$ percent. Very nice. Averaging those together, you find that the impurity for the entire stump is 44 percent. That's better than a coin flip!

Figure 7-3 shows the impurity calculation.

SPLITTING A FEATURE WITH MORE THAN TWO VALUES

In the RetailMart example, all the independent variables are binary. You never have to decide how to split the training data when you create a decision tree—the 1s go one way and the 0s go the other. But what if you have a feature that has all kinds of values?

For example, at MailChimp one of the things we predict is whether an e-mail address is alive and can receive mail. One of the metrics we use to do this is how many days have elapsed since someone sent an e-mail to that address. (We send about 7 billion e-mails a month, so we pretty much have data on everyone ...)

This feature isn't anywhere close to being binary! So when we train a decision tree that uses this feature, how do we determine what value to split it on so that some of the training data can go one direction and the rest the other direction?

It's actually really easy.

There's only a finite number of values you can split on. At max, it's one unique value per record in your training set. And there's probably some addresses in your training set that have the exact same number of days since you last sent to them.

You need to consider only these values. If you have four unique values to split on from your training records (say 10 days, 20 days, 30 days, and 40 days), splitting on 35 is no different than splitting on 30. So you just check the impurity scores you get if you chose each value to split on, and you pick the one that gives you the least impurity. Done!

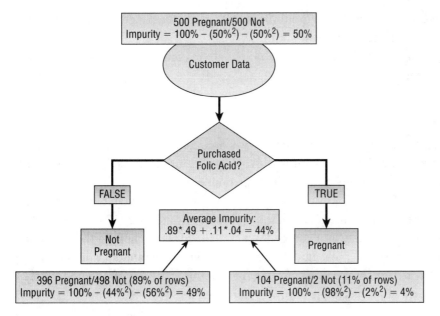

Figure 7-3: Node impurity for the folic acid stump

You Need More Power!

A single decision stump isn't enough. What if you had scads of them, each trained on different pieces of data and each with an impurity slightly lower than 50 percent? Then you could allow them to vote. Based on the percentage of stumps that vote pregnant, you could decide to call a customer pregnant.

But you need more stumps.

Well, you've trained one on the Folic Acid column. Why not just do the same thing on every other feature?

You have only 19 features, and frankly, some of those features, like whether the customer's address is an apartment, are pretty terrible. So you'd be stuck with 19 stumps of dubious quality.

It turns out that through bagging, you can make as many decision stumps as you like. Bagging will go something like this:

1. First, bite a chunk out of the dataset. Common practice is to take roughly the square root of the feature count (four random columns in our case) and a random two thirds of the rows.

2. Build a decision stump for each of those four features you chose using only the random two thirds of the data you picked.

3. Out of those four stumps, single out the purest stump. Keep it. Toss everything back into the big pot and train a new stump.

4. Once you have a load of stumps, grab them all, make them vote, and call them a single model.

Let's Train It

You need to be able to select a random set of rows and columns from the training data. And the easiest way to do that is to shuffle the rows and columns like a deck of cards and then select what you need from the top left of the table.

To start, copy A2:U1002 from the TD tab into the top of a new tab called **TD_BAG** (you won't need the feature names, just their index values from row 2). The easiest way to shuffle TD_BAG will be to add an extra column and an extra row next to the data filled with random numbers (using the RAND() formula). Sorting by the random values from top to bottom and left to right and then skimming the amount you want off the upper left of the table gives you a random sample of rows and features.

Getting the Random Sample

Insert a row above the feature indexes and add the RAND() formula to row 1 (A1:S1) and to column V (V3:V1002). The resulting spreadsheet then looks like Figure 7-4. Note that I've titled column V as **RANDOM.**

	A	B	C	D	E	F	G	H	I	J	K	L	M	N	O	P	Q	R	S	T	U	V
1	0.98	0.83	0.76	0.49	0.08	0.37	0.07	0.96	0.26	0.05	0.02	0.16	0.77	0.88	0.11	0.26	0.62	0.31	0.96			
2	0	1	2	3	4	5	6	7	8	9	10	11	12	13	14	15	16	17	18		PREGNANT	RANDOM
3	1	0	0	1	1	0	0	0	1	0	0	0	0	0	0	0	0	0	0		1	0.69
4	1	0	1	0	1	0	0	0	1	0	0	0	0	0	0	0	0	0	0		1	0.45
5	1	0	1	0	1	0	0	0	0	0	0	0	1	0	0	0	0	0	0		1	0.62
6	0	0	1	0	0	0	0	0	0	0	0	1	0	0	0	0	0	0	0		1	0.02
7	0	1	0	1	0	0	0	0	1	0	0	0	0	0	0	1	0	0		1	0.17
8	0	1	1	0	0	0	0	0	1	0	0	0	0	1	0	0	0	0	0		1	0.83
9	0	1	0	1	0	0	1	0	1	1	0	0	0	0	0	0	0	0	0		1	0.33
10	0	1	1	0	0	0	0	0	0	0	0	0	0	0	0	0	0	1		1	0.26
11	0	1	1	0	0	0	0	0	0	0	1	0	0	0	0	0	0	0		1	0.78
12	0	1	1	0	0	0	0	0	1	0	0	0	0	0	0	0	0	1		1	0.26

Figure 7-4: Adding random numbers to the top and side of the data

Sort the columns and rows randomly. Start with the columns, because side-to-side sorting is kind of funky. To shuffle the columns, highlight columns A through S. Don't highlight the PREGNANT column, because that's not a feature; it's the dependent variable.

Open the custom sort window (see Chapter 1 for a discussion on custom sorting). From the Sort window (Figure 7-5), press the Options button and select to sort left to right in order to sort the columns. Make sure Row 1, which is the row with the random numbers, is selected as the row to sort by. Also, confirm that the My List Has Headers box is unchecked since you have no headers in the horizontal direction.

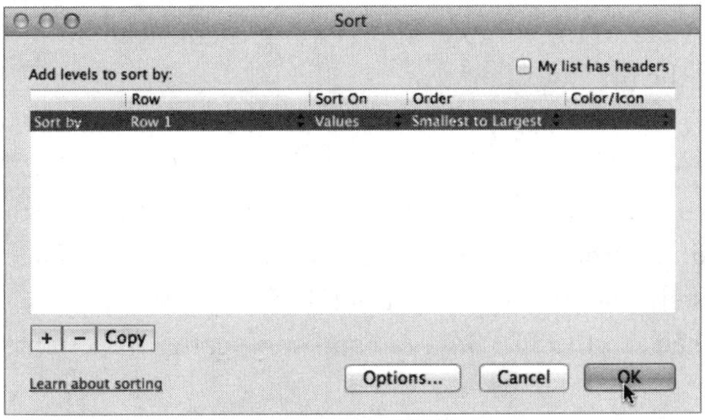

Figure 7-5: Sorting from left to right

Press OK. You'll see the columns on the sheet reorder themselves.

Now you need to do the same thing to the rows. This time around, select the range A2:V1002, including the PREGNANT column so that it remains tied to its data while excluding the random numbers at the top of the sheet.

Access the Custom Sort window again, and under the Options section, select to *sort from top to bottom* this time.

Make sure the My List Has Headers box is checked this time around, and then select the RANDOM column from the drop-down. The Sort window should look like Figure 7-6.

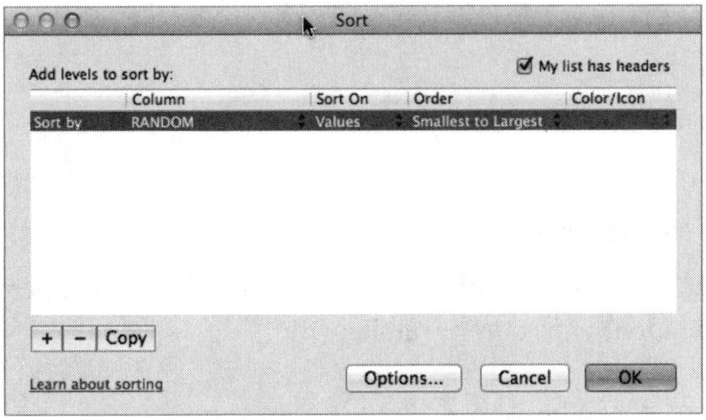

Figure 7-6: Sorting from top to bottom

Now that you've sorted your training data randomly, the first four columns and the first 666 rows form a rectangular random sample that you can grab. Create a new tab called **RandomSelection**. To pull out the random sample, you point the cell in A1 to the following:

```
=TD_BAG!A2
```

And then copy that formula through D667.

You can get the PREGNANT values next to the sample, by mapping them straight into column E. E1 points to cell U2 from the previous tab:

```
=TD_BAG!U2
```

Just double-click that formula to send it down the sheet. Once you complete this, you're left with nothing but the random sample from the data (see Figure 7-7). Note that since the data is sorted randomly, you'll likely end up with four different feature columns.

And what's cool is that if you go back to the TD_BAG tab and sort again, this sample will automatically update!

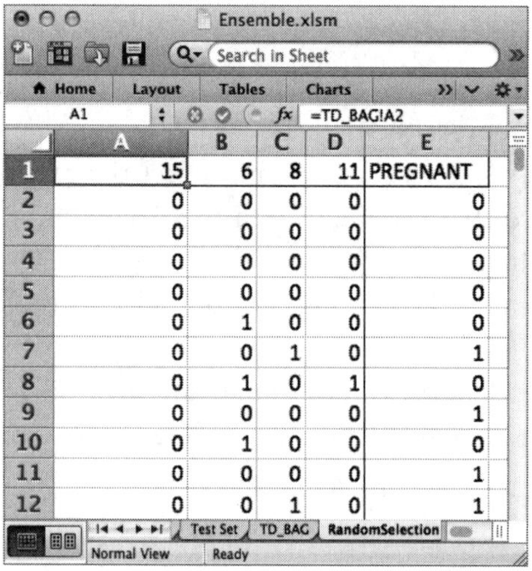

	A	B	C	D	E
1	15	6	8	11	PREGNANT
2	0	0	0	0	0
3	0	0	0	0	0
4	0	0	0	0	0
5	0	0	0	0	0
6	0	1	0	0	0
7	0	0	1	0	1
8	0	1	0	1	0
9	0	0	0	0	1
10	0	1	0	0	0
11	0	0	0	0	1
12	0	0	1	0	1

Figure 7-7: Four random columns and a random two-thirds of the rows

Getting a Decision Stump Out of the Sample

When looking at any one of these four features, there are only four things that can happen between a single feature and the dependent PREGNANT variable:

- The feature can be 0 and PREGNANT can be 1.
- The feature can be 0 and PREGNANT can be 0.

- The feature can be 1 and PREGNANT can be 1.
- The feature can be 1 and PREGNANT can be 0.

You need to get a count of the number of training rows that fall into each of these cases in order to build a stump on the feature similar to that pictured in Figure 7-2. To do this, enumerate the four combinations of 0s and 1s in G2:H5. Set I1:L1 to equal the column indexes from A1:D1.

The spreadsheet then looks like Figure 7-8.

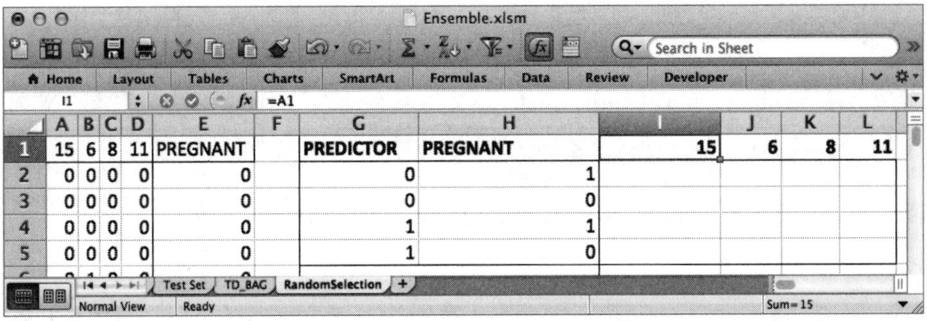

	A	B	C	D	E	F	G	H		I	J	K	L
1	15	6	8	11	PREGNANT		PREDICTOR	PREGNANT		15	6	8	11
2	0	0	0	0	0		0	1					
3	0	0	0	0	0		0	0					
4	0	0	0	0	0		1	1					
5	0	0	0	0	0		1	0					

Figure 7-8: Four possibilities for the training data

Once you've set up this small table, you need to fill it in by getting counts of the training rows whose values match the combination of predictor and pregnant values specified to the left. For the upper-left corner of the table (the first feature in my random sample ended up being number 15), you can count the number of training rows where feature 15 is a 0 and the PREGNANT column is a 1 using the following formula:

```
=COUNTIFS(A$2:A$667,$G2,$E$2:$E$667,$H2)
```

The COUNTIFS() formula allows you to count rows that match *multiple* criteria, hence the s at the end of IFS. The first criterion looks at the feature number 15 range (A2:A667) and checks for rows that are identical to the value in G2 (0), whereas the second criterion looks at the PREGNANT range (E2:E667) and checks for rows that are identical to the value in H2 (1).

Copy this formula into the rest of the cells in the table to get counts for each case (see Figure 7-9).

If you were going to treat each of these features as a decision stump, which value for the feature would indicate pregnancy? It'd be the value with the highest concentration of pregnant customers in the sample.

So in row 6 below the count values you can compare these two ratios. In I6 place the formula:

```
=IF(I2/(I2+I3)>I4/(I4+I5),0,1)
```

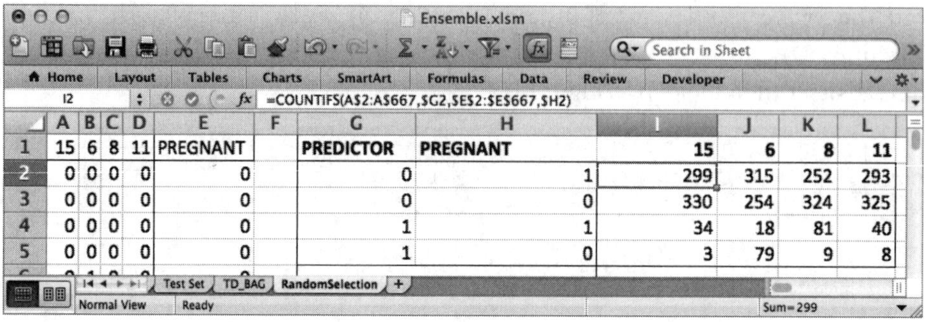

Figure 7-9: Feature/response pairings for each of the features in the random sample

If the ratio of pregnant customers associated with the 0 value for the feature ($I2/(I2+I3)$) is larger than that associated with 1 ($I4/(I4+I5)$), then 0 is predictive of pregnancy in this stump. Otherwise, 1 is. Copy this formula across through column L. This gives the sheet shown in Figure 7-10.

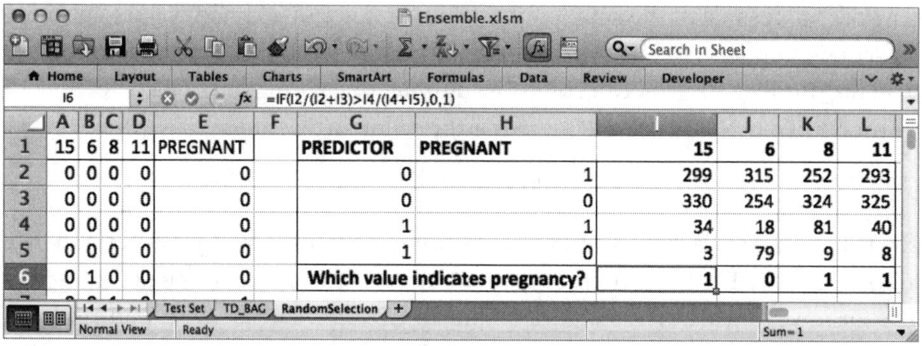

Figure 7-10: Calculating which feature value is associated with pregnancy

Using the counts in rows 2 through 5, you can calculate the impurity values for the nodes of each decision stump should you choose to split on that feature.

Let's insert the impurity calculations on row 8 below the case counts. Just as in Figure 7-3, you need to calculate an impurity value for the training cases that had a feature value of 0 and average it with those that had a value of 1.

If you use the first feature (number 15 for me), 299 pregnant folks and 330 not-pregnant folks ended up in the 0 node, so the impurity is 100% − (299/629)^2 − (330/629)^2, which can be entered in the sheet in cell I8 as follows:

```
=1-(I2/(I2+I3))^2-(I3/(I2+I3))^2
```

Likewise, the impurity for the 1 node can be written as follows:

```
=1-(I4/(I4+I5))^2-(I5/(I4+I5))^2
```

They are combined in a weighted average by multiplying each impurity times the number of training cases in its node, summing them, and dividing by the total number of training cases, 666:

```
=(I8*(I2+I3)+I9*(I4+I5))/666
```

You can then drag these impurity calculations across all four features yielding combined impurity values for each of the possible decision stumps, as shown in Figure 7-11.

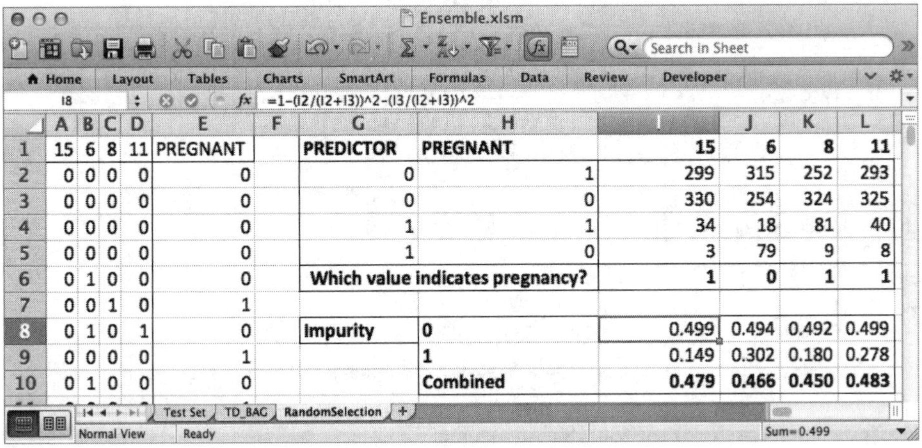

Figure 7-11: Combined impurity values for four decision stumps

Looking over the impurity values, for my workbook (yours will likely be different due to the random sort), the winning feature is number 8 (looking back at the TD sheet, this is Prenatal Vitamins) with an impurity of 0.450.

Recording the Winner

All right, so prenatals won on this sample for me. You probably got a different winner, which you should record somewhere.

Label cells N1 and N2 as **Winner** and **Pregnant Is**. You'll save the winning stump in column O. Start with saving the winning column number in cell O1. This would be the value in I1:L1 that has the lowest impurity (in my case that's 8). You can combine the MATCH and INDEX formulas to do this lookup (see Chapter 1 for more on these formulas):

```
=INDEX(I1:L1,0,MATCH(MIN(I10:L10),I10:L10,0))
```

MATCH(MIN(I10:L10),I10:L10,0) finds which column has the minimum impurity on row 10 and hands it to INDEX. INDEX locates the appropriate winning feature label.

Similarly, in O2 you can put whether 0 or 1 is associated with pregnancy by finding the value on row 6 from the column with the minimum impurity:

```
=INDEX(I6:L6,0,MATCH(MIN(I10:L10),I10:L10,0))
```

The winning decision stump and its pregnancy-associated node are then called out, as pictured in Figure 7-12.

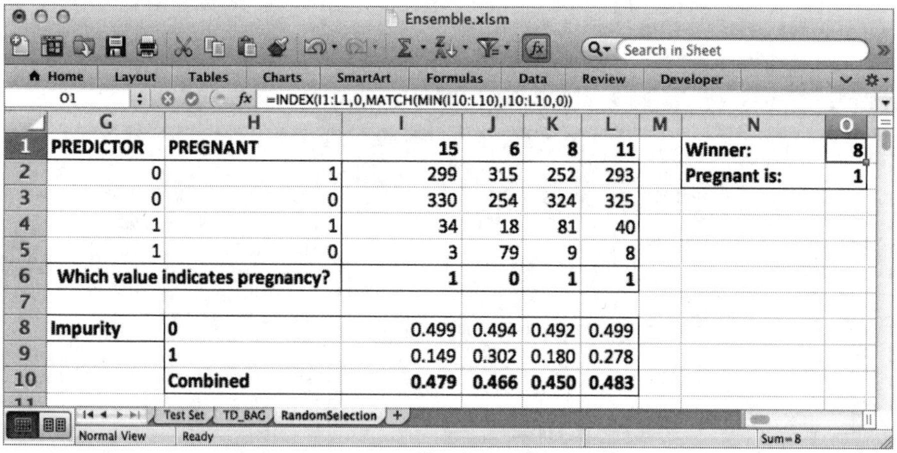

	G	H	I	J	K	L	M	N	O
1	PREDICTOR	PREGNANT	15	6	8	11		Winner:	8
2	0	1	299	315	252	293		Pregnant is:	1
3	0	0	330	254	324	325			
4	1	1	34	18	81	40			
5	1	0	3	79	9	8			
6	Which value indicates pregnancy?		1	0	1	1			
7									
8	Impurity	0	0.499	0.494	0.492	0.499			
9		1	0.149	0.302	0.180	0.278			
10		Combined	0.479	0.466	0.450	0.483			

Figure 7-12: The winner's circle for the four decision stumps

Shake Me Up, Judy!

Phew! I know that was a lot of little steps to create one stump. But now that all the formulas are in place, creating the next couple hundred will be a lot easier.

You can create a second one real quick. But before you do, save the stump you just made. To do that, just copy and paste the values in O1:O2 over to the right into P1:P2.

Then to create a new stump, flip back to the TD_BAG tab and shuffle the rows and columns again.

Click back on the RandomSelection tab. *Voila!* The winner has changed. In my case, it's folic acid, and the value associated with pregnancy is 1 (see Figure 7-13). The previous stump is saved over to the right.

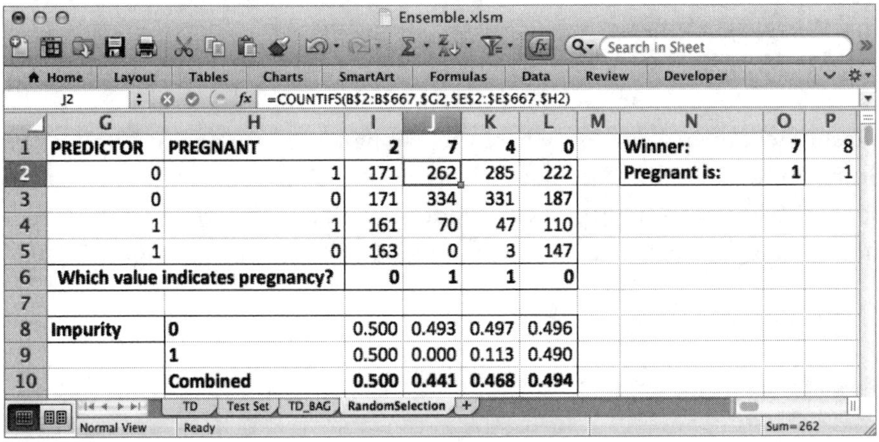

Figure 7-13: Reshuffling the data yields a new stump.

To save this second stump, right-click column P and select Insert to shift the first stump to the right. Then paste the new stump's values in column P. The ensemble now looks like Figure 7-14.

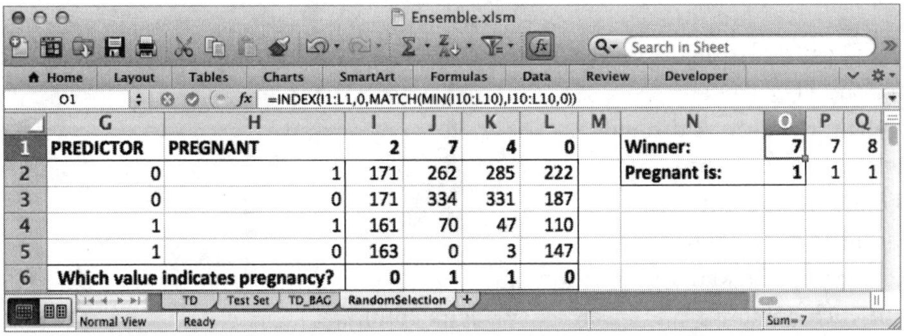

Figure 7-14: And then there were two.

Well, that second one sure took less time than the first. So here's the thing ...

Let's say you want to shoot for 200 stumps in the ensemble model. All you have to do is repeat these steps another 198 times. Not impossible, but annoying.

Why don't you just record a macro of yourself doing it and then play the macro back? As it turns out, this shuffling operation is perfect for a macro.

For those of you who have never recorded a macro, it's nothing more than recording a series of repetitive button presses so you can play them back later instead of giving yourself carpal tunnel syndrome.

So hop on up to View ➪ Macros (Tools ➪ Macro in Mac OS) and select Record New Macro.

Pressing Record will open a window where you can name your macro something like **GetBaggedStump**. And for convenience sake, let's associate a shortcut key with the macro. I'm on a Mac so my shortcut keys begin with Option+Cmd, and I'm going to throw in a z into the shortcut box, because that's the kind of mood I'm in today (see Figure 7-15).

Figure 7-15: Getting ready to record a macro

Press OK to get recording. Here are the steps that'll record a full decision stump:
1. Click the TD_BAG tab.
2. Highlight columns A through S.
3. Custom-sort the columns.
4. Highlight rows 2 through 1002.
5. Custom-sort the rows.
6. Click over to the RandomSelection tab.
7. Right-click column P and insert a new blank column.
8. Select and copy the winning stump in O1:O2.
9. Paste Special the values into P1:P2.

Go to View ➪ Macro ➪ Stop Recording (Tools ➪ Macro ➪ Stop Recording in Excel 2011 for Mac) to end the recording.

You should now be able to generate a new decision stump with a single shortcut key press to activate the macro. Hold on while I go click this thing about 198 hundred times . . .

Evaluating the Bagged Model

That's bagging! All you do is shuffle the data, grab a subset, train a simple classifier, and go again. And once you have a bunch of classifiers in your ensemble, you're ready to make predictions.

Once you've run the decision stump macro a couple hundred times, the RandomSelection sheet should look like Figure 7-16 (your stumps will likely differ).

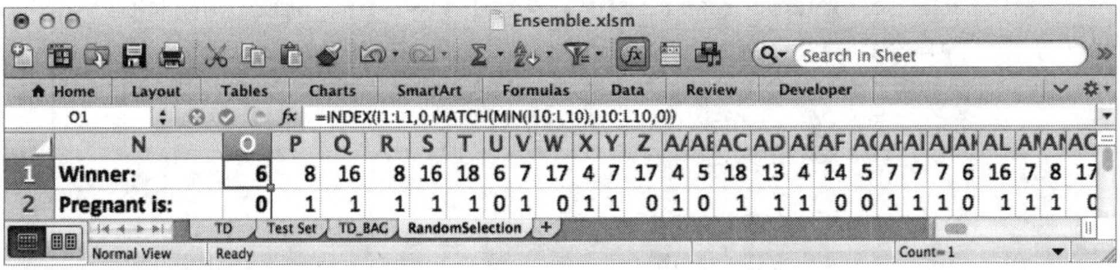

Figure 7-16: The 200 decision stumps

Predictions on the Test Set

Now that you have your stumps, it's time to send your test set data through the model. Create a copy of the Test Set tab and name it **TestBag**.

Moving over to the TestBag tab, insert two blank rows at the top of the sheet to make room for your stumps.

Paste the stump values from the RandomSelection tab (P1:HG2 if you've got 200 of them) onto the TestBag tab starting in column W. This gives the sheet shown in Figure 7-17.

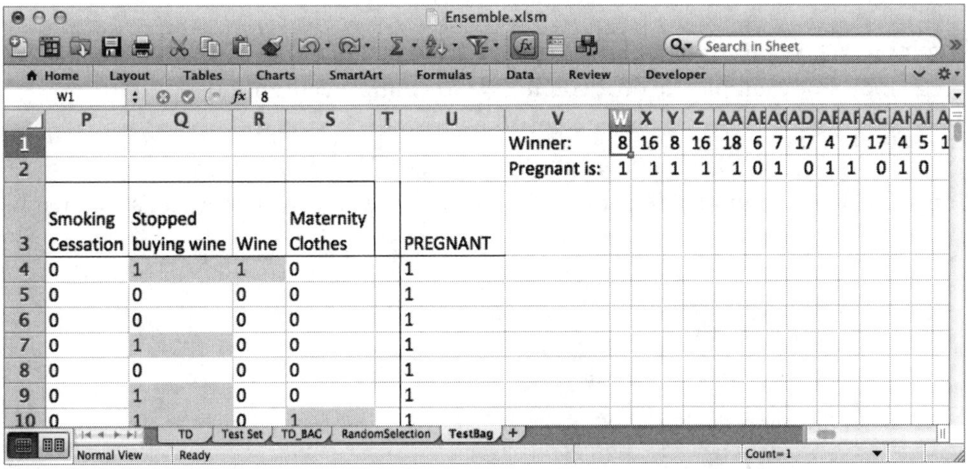

Figure 7-17: Stumps added to the TestBag tab

You can run each row in the Test Set through each stump. Start by running the first row of data (row 4) through the first stump in column W. You can use the OFFSET formula to look up the value from the stump column listed in W1, and if that value equals the one in W2, then the stump predicts a pregnant customer. Otherwise, the stump predicts non-pregnancy. The formula looks like this:

```
=IF(OFFSET($A4,0,W$1)=W$2,1,0)
```

This formula can be copied across all stumps and down the sheet (note the absolute references). This gives the sheet shown in Figure 7-18.

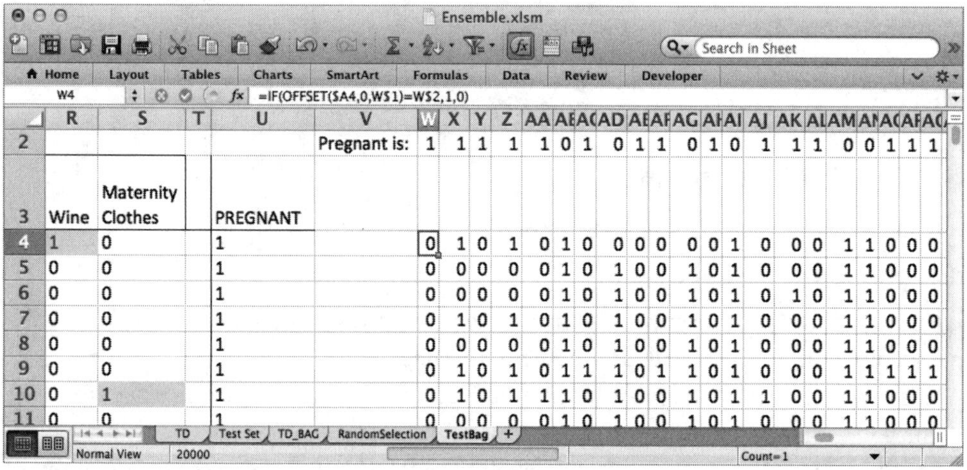

Figure 7-18: Stumps evaluated on the TestBag set

In column V, take the average of the rows to the left in order to obtain a class probability for pregnancy. For example, in V4 if you have 200 stumps, you'd use:

```
=AVERAGE(W4:HN4)
```

Copy this down column V to get predictions for each row in the test set as shown in Figure 7-19.

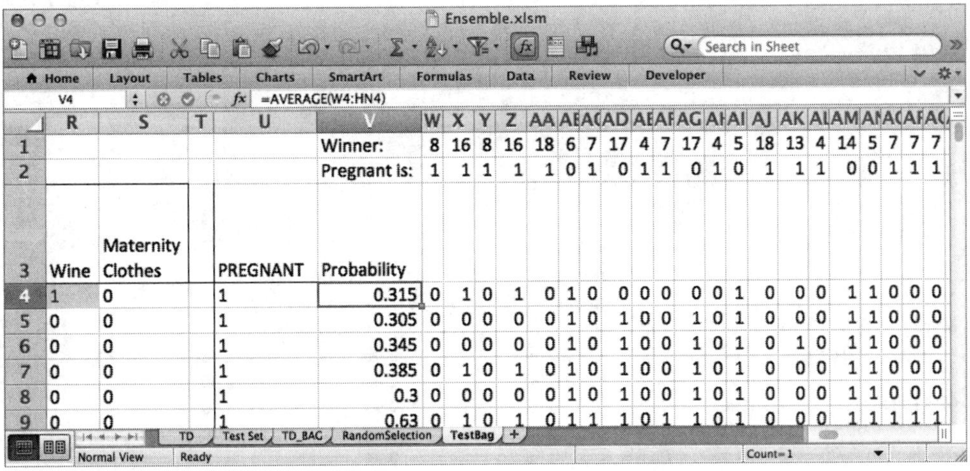

Figure 7-19: Predictions for each row

Performance

You can evaluate these predictions using the same performance measures used in Chapter 6. I won't dwell on these calculations since the technique is exactly the same as that in Chapter 6. First, create a new tab called **PerformanceBag**. In the first column, just as in Chapter 6, calculate the maximum and minimum predictions. For my 200 stumps, that range comes out to 0.02 to 0.75.

In column B, place a range of cutoff values from the minimum to the maximum (in my case, I incremented by 0.02). Precision, specificity, false positive rate, and recall can all then be calculated in the same way as Chapter 6 (flip back to Chapter 6 for the precise details).

This gives the sheet shown in Figure 7-20.

Note that for a prediction cutoff of 0.5, that is, with half of the stumps voting pregnant, you can identify 33 percent of pregnant customers with only a 1 percent false positive rate (your mileage may vary due to the random nature of the algorithm). Pretty sweet for some simple stumps!

You can also insert a ROC curve using the false positive rate and true positive rate (columns E and F) just as you did in Chapter 6. For my 200 stumps, I got Figure 7-21.

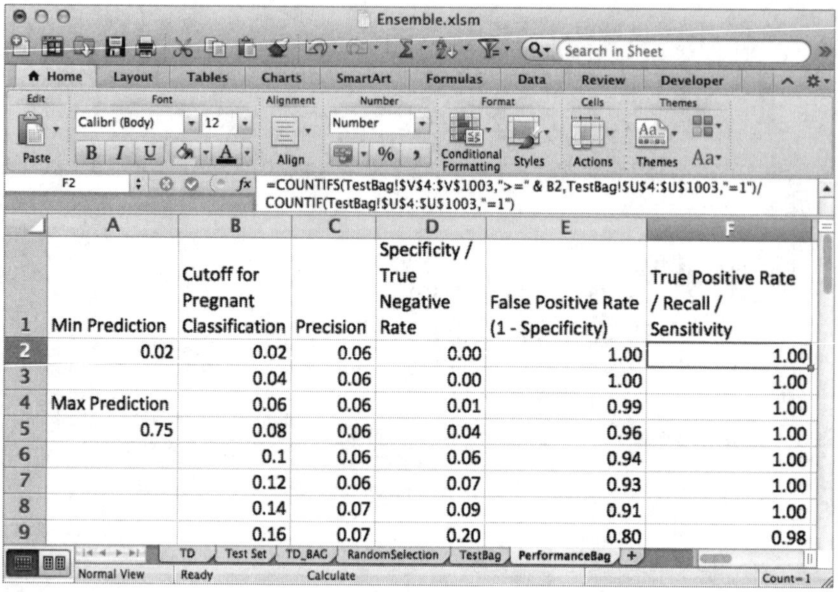

Ensemble.xlsm

| Home | Layout | Tables | Charts | SmartArt | Formulas | Data | Review | Developer |

F2   fx   =COUNTIFS(TestBag!$V$4:$V$1003,">=" & B2,TestBag!$U$4:$U$1003,"=1")/COUNTIF(TestBag!$U$4:$U$1003,"=1")

	A	B	C	D	E	F
1	Min Prediction	Cutoff for Pregnant Classification	Precision	Specificity / True Negative Rate	False Positive Rate (1 - Specificity)	True Positive Rate / Recall / Sensitivity
2	0.02	0.02	0.06	0.00	1.00	1.00
3		0.04	0.06	0.00	1.00	1.00
4	Max Prediction	0.06	0.06	0.01	0.99	1.00
5	0.75	0.08	0.06	0.04	0.96	1.00
6		0.1	0.06	0.06	0.94	1.00
7		0.12	0.06	0.07	0.93	1.00
8		0.14	0.07	0.09	0.91	1.00
9		0.16	0.07	0.20	0.80	0.98

TD / Test Set / TD_BAG / RandomSelection / TestBag / PerformanceBag / +

Normal View   Ready   Calculate   Count=1

Figure 7-20: Performance metrics for bagging

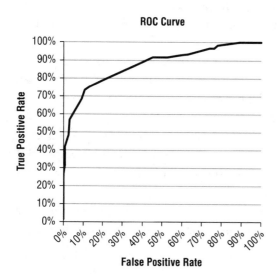

Figure 7-21: The ROC Curve for Bagged Stumps

Beyond Performance

While this bagged stumps model is supported by industry standard packages like R's `randomForest` package, it's important to call out two differences between this and typical random forest modeling settings:

- Vanilla random forests usually sample *with replacement*, meaning that the same row from the training data can be pulled into the random sample more than once. When you sample with replacement, you can sample the same number of records as the actual training set rather than limiting it to two thirds. In practice, while sampling with replacement has nicer statistical properties, if you're working with a large enough dataset, there's virtually no difference between the two sampling methods.
- Random forests by default grow full classification trees rather than stumps. A full tree is one where once you've split the data into two nodes, you pick some new features to split those nodes apart, and on and on until you hit some stopping criteria. Full classification trees are better than stumps when there are interactions between the features that can be modeled.

Moving the conversation beyond model accuracy, here are some advantages to the bagging approach:

- Bagging is resistant to outliers and tends not to *overfit* the data. Overfitting occurs when the model fits more than just the signal in your data and actually fits the noise as well.
- The training process can be parallelized since training an individual weak learner is not dependent on the training of a previous weak learner.
- This type of model can handle tons of decision variables.

The models we use at MailChimp for predicting spam and abuse are random forest models, which we train in parallel using around 10 billion rows of raw data. That's not going to fit in Excel, and I sure as heck wouldn't use a macro to do it!

No, I use the R programming language with the `randomForest` package, which I would highly recommend learning about as a next step if you want to take one of these models into production at your organization. Indeed, the model in this chapter can be achieved by the `randomForest` package merely by turning off sampling with replacement and setting the maximum nodes in the decision trees to 2 (see Chapter 10).

Boosting: If You Get It Wrong, Just Boost and Try Again

What was the reason behind doing bagging, again?

If you trained up a bunch of decision stumps on the whole dataset over and over again, they'd be identical. By taking random selections of the dataset, you introduce some variety to your stumps and end up capturing nuances in the training data that a single stump never could.

Well, what bagging does with random selections, *boosting* does with weights. Boosting doesn't take random portions of the dataset. It uses the whole dataset on each training iteration. Instead, with each iteration, boosting focuses on training a decision stump that resolves some of the sins committed by the previous decision stumps. It works like this:

- At first, each row of training data counts exactly the same. They all have the same weight. In your case, you have 1000 rows of training data, so they all start with a weight of 0.001. This means the weights sum up to 1.
- Evaluate each feature on the entire dataset to pick the best decision stump. Except when it comes to boosting instead of bagging, the winning stump will be the one that has the lowest *weighted error*. Each wrong prediction for a possible stump is given a penalty equal to that row's weight. The sum of those penalties is the weighted error. Choose the decision stump that gives the lowest weighted error.
- The weights are adjusted. If the chosen decision stump accurately predicts a row, then that row's weight decreases. If the chosen decision stump messes up on a row, then that row's weight increases.
- A new stump is trained using these new weights. In this way, as the algorithm rolls on, it concentrates more on the rows in the training data that previous stumps haven't gotten right. Stumps are trained until the weighted error exceeds a threshold.

Some of this may seem a bit vague, but the process will become abundantly clear in a spreadsheet. Off to the data!

Training the Model—Every Feature Gets a Shot

In boosting, each feature is a possible stump on every iteration. You won't be selecting from four features this time.

To start, create a tab called **BoostStumps**. And on it, paste the possible feature/response value combinations from G1:H5 of the RandomSelection tab.

Next to those values, paste the feature index values (0–18) in row 1. This gives the sheet shown in Figure 7-22.

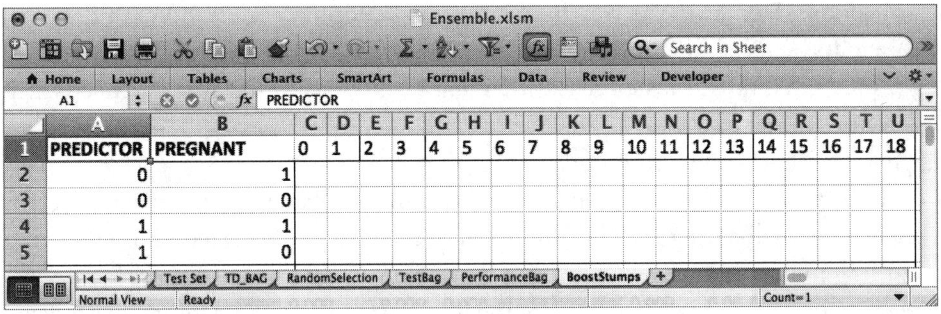

	A	B	C	D	E	F	G	H	I	J	K	L	M	N	O	P	Q	R	S	T	U
1	PREDICTOR	PREGNANT	0	1	2	3	4	5	6	7	8	9	10	11	12	13	14	15	16	17	18
2	0	1																			
3	0	0																			
4	1	1																			
5	1	0																			

Figure 7-22: The initial portions of the BoostStumps tab

Below each index, just as in the bagging process, you must sum up the number of training set rows that fall into each of the four combinations of feature value and independent variable value listed in columns A and B.

Start in cell C2 (feature index 0) by summing the number of training rows that have a 0 for the feature value and also are pregnant. This can be counted using the COUNTIFS formula:

```
=COUNTIFS(TD!A$3:A$1002,$A2,TD!$U$3:$U$1002,$B2)
```

The use of absolute references allows you to copy this formula through U5. This gives the sheet shown in Figure 7-23.

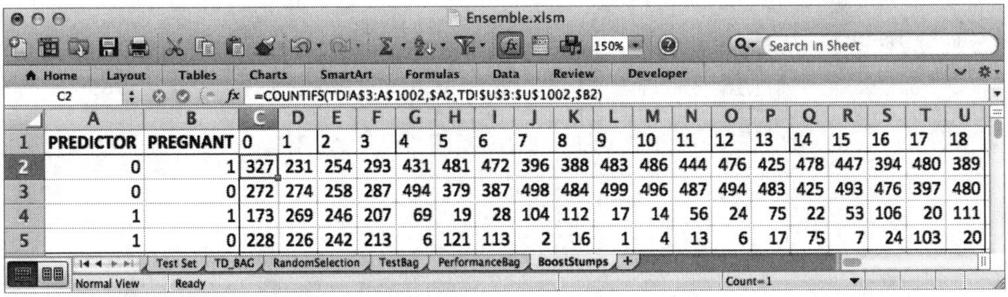

	A	B	C	D	E	F	G	H	I	J	K	L	M	N	O	P	Q	R	S	T	U
1	PREDICTOR	PREGNANT	0	1	2	3	4	5	6	7	8	9	10	11	12	13	14	15	16	17	18
2	0	1	327	231	254	293	431	481	472	396	388	483	486	444	476	425	478	447	394	480	389
3	0	0	272	274	258	287	494	379	387	498	484	499	496	487	494	483	425	493	476	397	480
4	1	1	173	269	246	207	69	19	28	104	112	17	14	56	24	75	22	53	106	20	111
5	1	0	228	226	242	213	6	121	113	2	16	1	4	13	6	17	75	7	24	103	20

Figure 7-23: Counting up how each feature splits the training data

And just as in the case of bagging, in C6 you can find the value associated with pregnancy for feature index 0 by looking at the pregnancy ratios associated with a feature value of 0 and a feature value of 1:

```
=IF(C2/(C2+C3)>C4/(C4+C5),0,1)
```

This too may be copied through column U.

Now, in column B enter in the weights for each data point. Begin in B9 with the label Current Weights, and below that through B1009 put in a 0.001 for each of the thousand training rows. Across row 9, paste the feature names from the TD sheet, just to keep track of each feature.

This gives the sheet shown in Figure 7-24.

For each of these possible decision stumps, you need to calculate its weighted error rate. This is done by locating the training rows that are miscategorized and penalizing each according to its weight.

For instance in C10, you can look back at the first training row's data for feature index 0 (A3 on the TD tab), and if it matches the pregnancy indicator in C6, then you get a penalty (the weight in cell B10) if the row *is not pregnant*. If the feature value does not match C6, then you get a penalty if the row *is pregnant*. This gives the following two IF statements:

```
=IF(AND(TD!A3=C$6,TD!$U3=0),$B10,0)+IF(AND(TD!A3<>C$6,TD!$U3=1),$B10,0)
```

The absolute references allow you to copy this formula through U1009. The weighted error for each possible decision stump may then be calculated in row 7. For cell C7 the calculation of the weighted error is:

```
=SUM(C10:C1009)
```

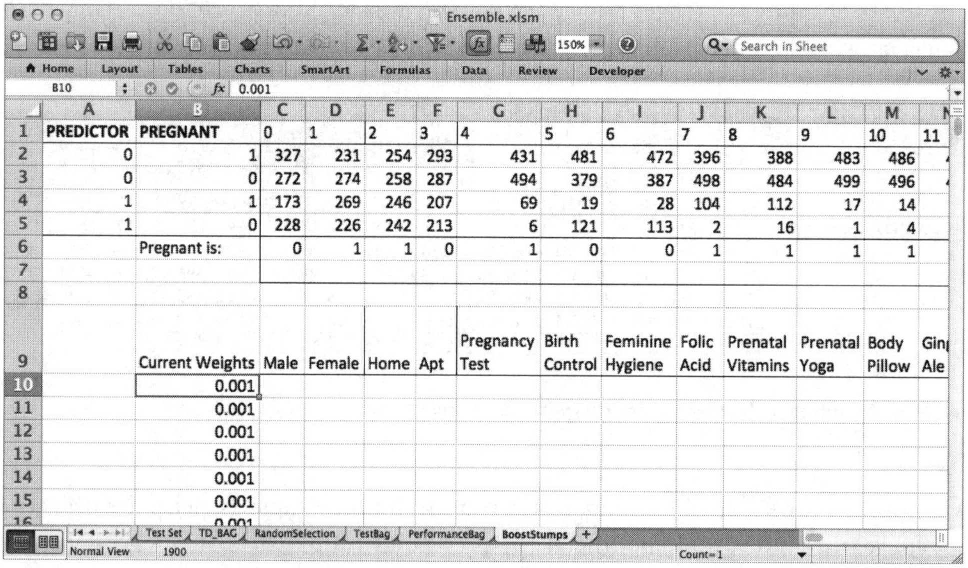

Figure 7-24: Weights for each training data row

Copy this across row 7 to get the weighted error of each decision stump (see Figure 7-25).

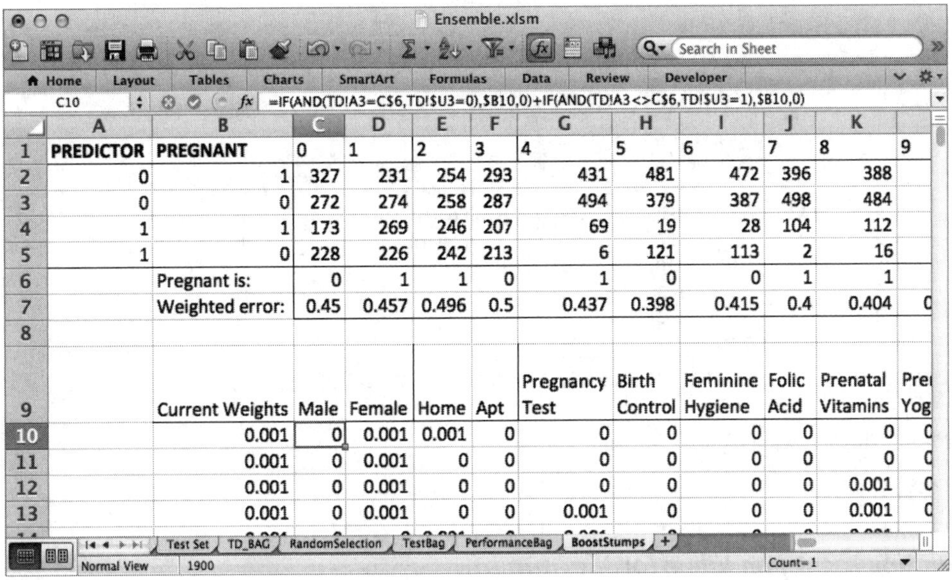

	A	B	C	D	E	F	G	H	I	J	K	
			0	1	2	3	4	5	6	7	8	9
1	PREDICTOR	PREGNANT										
2	0	1	327	231	254	293	431	481	472	396	388	
3	0	0	272	274	258	287	494	379	387	498	484	
4	1	1	173	269	246	207	69	19	28	104	112	
5	1	0	228	226	242	213	6	121	113	2	16	
6		Pregnant is:	0	1	1	0	1	0	0	1	1	
7		Weighted error:	0.45	0.457	0.496	0.5	0.437	0.398	0.415	0.4	0.404	0
8												
9		Current Weights	Male	Female	Home	Apt	Pregnancy Test	Birth Control	Feminine Hygiene	Folic Acid	Prenatal Vitamins	Pre Yog
10		0.001	0	0.001	0.001	0	0	0	0	0	0	0
11		0.001	0	0.001	0	0	0	0	0	0	0	0
12		0.001	0	0.001	0	0	0	0	0	0	0.001	0
13		0.001	0	0.001	0	0	0.001	0	0	0	0.001	0

Cell C10 formula: `=IF(AND(TD!A3=C$6,TD!$U3=0),$B10,0)+IF(AND(TD!A3<>C$6,TD!$U3=1),$B10,0)`

Figure 7-25: The weighted error calculation for each stump

Tallying Up the Winner

Label cell W1 as the **Winning Error**, and in X1, find the minimum of the weighted error values:

```
=MIN(C7:U7)
```

Just as in the bagging section, in X2 combine the INDEX and MATCH formulas to grab the feature index of the winning stump:

```
=INDEX(C1:U1,0,MATCH(X1,C7:U7,0))
```

And in X3, you can likewise grab the value associated with pregnancy for the stump using INDEX and MATCH:

```
=INDEX(C6:U6,0,MATCH(X1,C7:U7,0))
```

This gives the sheet shown in Figure 7-26. Starting with equal weights for each data point, feature index 5 with a value of 0 indicating pregnancy is chosen as the top stump. Flipping back to the TD tab, you can see that this is the Birth Control feature.

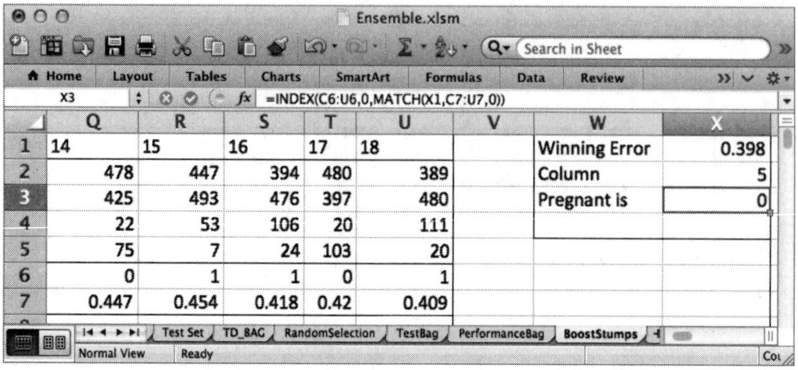

	Q	R	S	T	U	V	W	X
1	14	15	16	17	18		Winning Error	0.398
2	478	447	394	480	389		Column	5
3	425	493	476	397	480		Pregnant is	0
4	22	53	106	20	111			
5	75	7	24	103	20			
6	0	1	1	0	1			
7	0.447	0.454	0.418	0.42	0.409			

Figure 7-26: The first winning boosted stump

Calculating the Alpha Value for the Stump

Boosting works by giving weight to training rows that were misclassified by previous stumps. Stumps at the beginning of the boosting process are then more generally effective, while the stumps at the end of the training process are more specialized—the weights have been altered to concentrate on a few annoying points in the training data.

These stumps with specialized weights help fit the model to the strange points in the dataset. However in doing so, their weighted error will be larger than that of the initial stumps in the boosting process. As their weighted error rises, the overall improvement they contribute to the model falls. In boosting, this relationship is quantified with a value called *alpha*:

*alpha = 0.5 * ln((1 – total weighted error for the stump)/total weighted error for the stump)*

As the total weighted error of a stump climbs, the fraction inside the natural log function grows smaller and closer to 1. Since the natural log of 1 is 0, the alpha value gets tinier and tinier. Take a look at it in the context of the sheet.

Label cell W4 as **Alpha** and in X4 send the weighted error from call X1 through the alpha calculation:

```
=0.5*LN((1-X1)/X1)
```

For this first stump, you end up with an alpha value of 0.207 (see Figure 7-27).

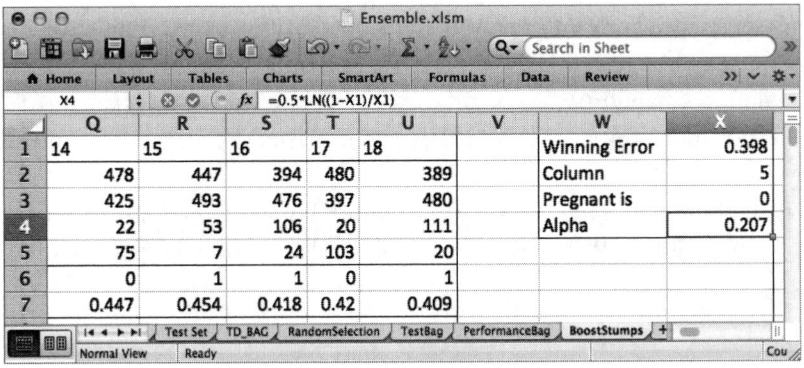
Ensemble.xlsm
Search in Sheet
Home
Layout
Tables
Charts
SmartArt
Formulas
Data
Review
X4
=0.5*LN((1-X1)/X1)
Q R S T U V W X
1 14 15 16 17 18 Winning Error 0.398
2 478 447 394 480 389 Column 5
3 425 493 476 397 480 Pregnant is 0
4 22 53 106 20 111 Alpha 0.207
5 75 7 24 103 20
6 0 1 1 0 1
7 0.447 0.454 0.418 0.42 0.409
Test Set
TD_BAG
RandomSelection
TestBag
PerformanceBag
BoostStumps
Normal View
Ready

Figure 7-27: Alpha value for the first boosting iteration

How exactly are these alpha values used? In bagging, each stump gave a 0/1 vote when predicting. When it comes time to predict with your boosted stumps, each classifier will instead give *alpha* if it thinks the row is pregnant and –*alpha* if not. So for this first stump, when used on the test set, it would give 0.207 points to any customer who had not bought birth control and -0.207 points to any customer who had. The final prediction of the ensemble model is the sum of all these positive and negative alpha values.

As you'll see later on, to determine the overall pregnancy prediction coming from the model, a cutoff is set for the sum of the individual stump scores. Since each stump returns either a positive or negative alpha value for its contribution to the prediction, it is customary to use 0 as the classification threshold for pregnancy, however this can be tuned to suit your precision needs.

Reweighting

Now that you've completed one stump, it's time to reweight the training data. And to do that, you need to know which rows of data this stump gets right and which rows it gets wrong.

So in column V label V9 as **Wrong**. In V10, you can use the OFFSET formula in combination with the winning stump's column index (cell X2) to look up the weighted error for the training row. If the error is nonzero, then the stump is incorrect for that row, and Wrong is set to 1:

```
=IF(OFFSET($C10,0,$X$2)>0,1,0)
```

This formula can be copied down to all training rows (note the absolute references).

Now, the original weights for this stump are in column B. To adjust the weights according to which rows are set to 1 in the Wrong column, boosting multiplies the original weight times *exp(alpha * Wrong)* (where *exp* is the exponential function you encountered when doing logistic regression in Chapter 6).

If the value in the Wrong column is 0, then *exp(alpha * Wrong)* becomes 1, and the weight stays put.

If Wrong is set to 1, then *exp(alpha * Wrong)* is a value larger than 1, so the entire weight is scaled up. Label column W as **Scale by Alpha**, and in W10, you can calculate this new weight as:

```
=$B10*EXP($V10*$X$4)
```

Copy this down through the dataset.

Unfortunately, these new weights don't sum up to one like your old weights. They need to be *normalized* (adjusted so that they sum to one). So label X9 as **Normalize** and in X10, divide the new, scaled weight by the sum of all the new weights:

```
=W10/SUM(W$10:W$1009)
```

This ensures that your new weights sum to one. Copy the formula down. This gives the sheet shown in Figure 7-28.

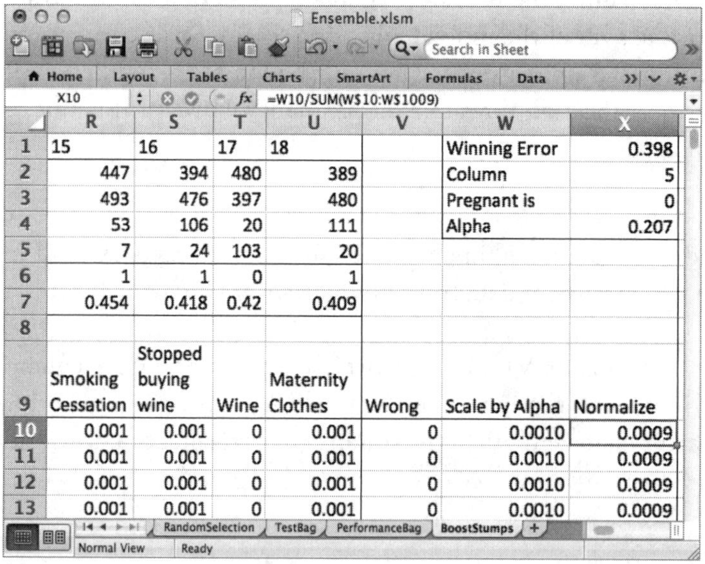

Figure 7-28: The new weight calculation

Do That Again... and Again...

Now you're ready to build a second stump. First, copy the winning stump data from the previous iteration over from X1:X4 to Y1:Y4.

Next, copy the new weight *values* from column X over to column B. The entire sheet will update to select the stump that's best for the new set of weights. As shown in Figure 7-29, the second winning stump is index 7 (Folic Acid) where a 1 indicates pregnancy.

You can train 200 of these stumps in much the same way as you did in the bagging process. Simply record a macro that inserts a new column Y, copies the values from X1:X4 into Y1:Y4, and pastes the weights over from column X to column B.

After 200 iterations, your weighted error rate will have climbed very near to 0.5 while your alpha value will have fallen to 0.005 (see Figure 7-30). Consider that your first stump had an alpha value of 0.2. That means that these final stumps are 40 times less powerful in the voting process than your first stump.

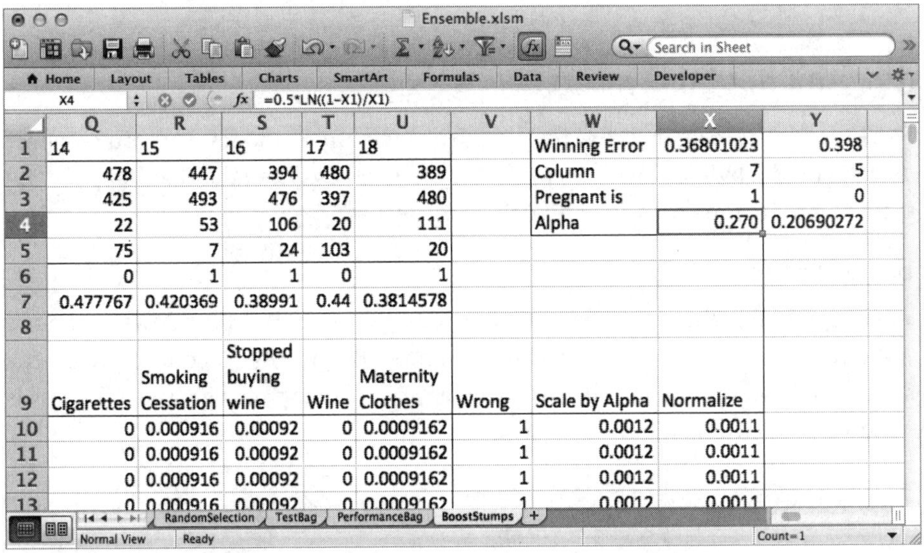

	Q	R	S	T	U	V	W	X	Y
1	14	15	16	17	18		Winning Error	0.36801023	0.398
2		478	447	394	480	389	Column	7	5
3		425	493	476	397	480	Pregnant is	1	0
4		22	53	106	20	111	Alpha	0.270	0.20690272
5		75	7	24	103	20			
6		0	1	1	0	1			
7		0.477767	0.420369	0.38991	0.44	0.3814578			
8									
9	Cigarettes	Smoking Cessation	Stopped buying wine	Wine	Maternity Clothes	Wrong	Scale by Alpha	Normalize	
10		0	0.000916	0.00092	0	0.0009162	1	0.0012	0.0011
11		0	0.000916	0.00092	0	0.0009162	1	0.0012	0.0011
12		0	0.000916	0.00092	0	0.0009162	1	0.0012	0.0011
13		0	0.000916	0.00092	0	0.0009162	1	0.0012	0.0011

Cell X4 formula: =0.5*LN((1−X1)/X1)

Figure 7-29: The second stump

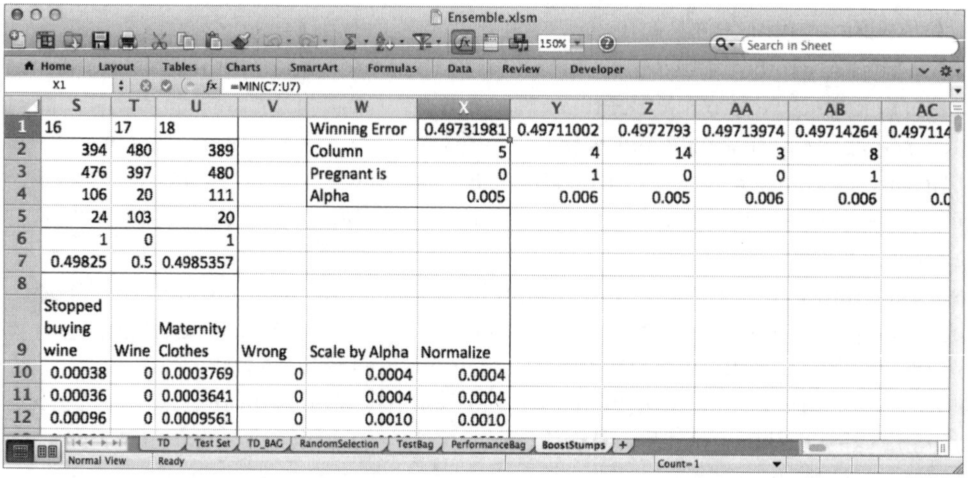

Figure 7-30: The 200th stump

Evaluating the Boosted Model

That's it! You've now trained an entire boosted decision stumps model. You can compare it to the bagged model by looking at its performance metrics. To make that happen, you must first make predictions using the model on the test set data.

Predictions on the Test Set

First make a copy of the Test Set called **TestBoost** and insert four blank rows at the top of it to make room for your winning decision stumps. Beginning in column W on the TestBoost tab, paste your stumps (all 200 in my case) at the top of the sheet. This gives the sheet shown in Figure 7-31.

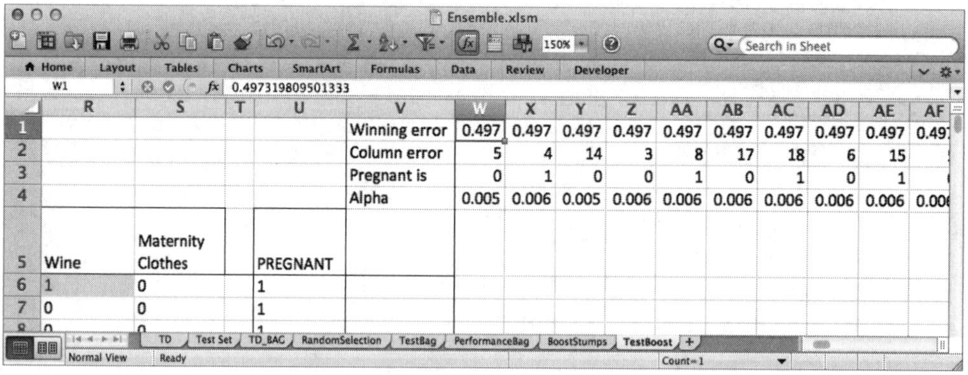

Figure 7-31: Decision stumps pasted to TestBoost

In W6, you can then evaluate the first stump on the first row of test data using OFFSET just as you did with the bagged model. Except this time, a pregnancy prediction returns the stump's alpha value (cell W4) and a non-pregnancy prediction returns –alpha:

```
=IF(OFFSET($A6,0,W$2)=W$3,W$4,-W$4)
```

Copy this formula across to all the stumps and down through all the test rows (see Figure 7-32). To make a prediction for a row, you sum these values across all its individual stump predictions.

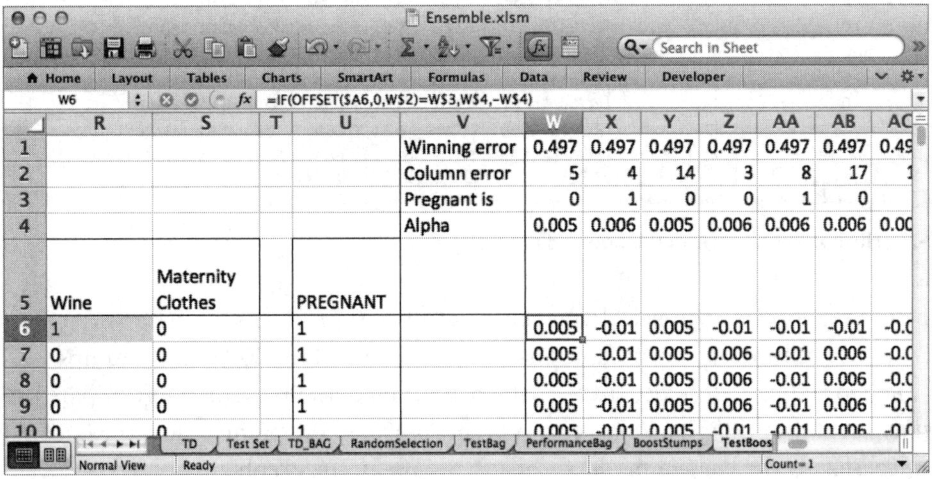

Figure 7-32: Predictions on each row of test data from each stump

Label V5 as **Score**. The score then for V6 is just the sum of the predictions to the right:

```
=SUM(W6:HN6)
```

Copy this sum down. You get the sheet shown in Figure 7-33. A score in column V above 0 means that more alpha-weighted predictions went in the pregnant direction than in the not pregnant direction (see Figure 7-33).

Calculating Performance

To measure the performance of the boosted model on the test set, simply create a copy of the PerformanceBag tab called **PerformanceBoost**, point the formulas at column V on the TestBoost tab, and set the cutoff values to range from the minimum score to the maximum score produced by the boosted model. In my case, I incremented the cutoff values by 0.25 between a minimum prediction score of -8 and a maximum of 4.5. This gives the performance tab shown in Figure 7-34.

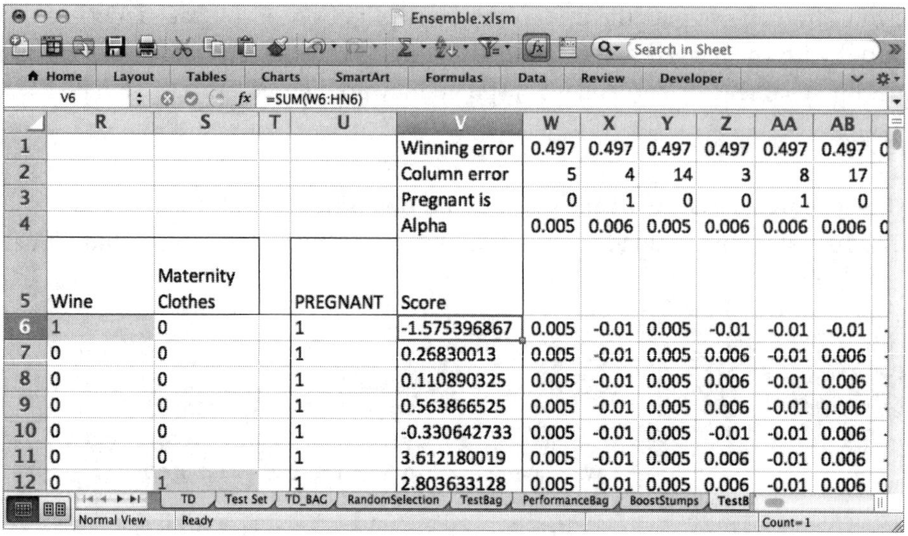

	R	S	T	U	V	W	X	Y	Z	AA	AB
1					Winning error	0.497	0.497	0.497	0.497	0.497	0.497
2					Column error	5	4	14	3	8	17
3					Pregnant is	0	1	0	0	1	0
4					Alpha	0.005	0.006	0.005	0.006	0.006	0.006
5	Wine	Maternity Clothes		PREGNANT	Score						
6	1	0		1	-1.575396867	0.005	-0.01	0.005	-0.01	-0.01	-0.01
7	0	0		1	0.26830013	0.005	-0.01	0.005	0.006	-0.01	0.006
8	0	0		1	0.110890325	0.005	-0.01	0.005	0.006	-0.01	0.006
9	0	0		1	0.563866525	0.005	-0.01	0.005	0.006	-0.01	0.006
10	0	0		1	-0.330642733	0.005	-0.01	0.005	-0.01	-0.01	0.006
11	0	0		1	3.612180019	0.005	-0.01	0.005	0.006	-0.01	0.006
12	0	1		1	2.803633128	0.005	-0.01	0.005	0.006	-0.01	0.006

Figure 7-33: Final predictions from the boosted model

With this model, you can see that a score cutoff of 0 produces a true positive rate 85 percent with only a 27 percent false positive rate. Not bad for 200 stupid stumps.

Add the boosted model's ROC curve to the bagged model's ROC curve to compare the two just as you did in Chapter 6. As seen in Figure 7-35, at 200 stumps each, the boosted model outperforms the bagged model for many points on the graph.

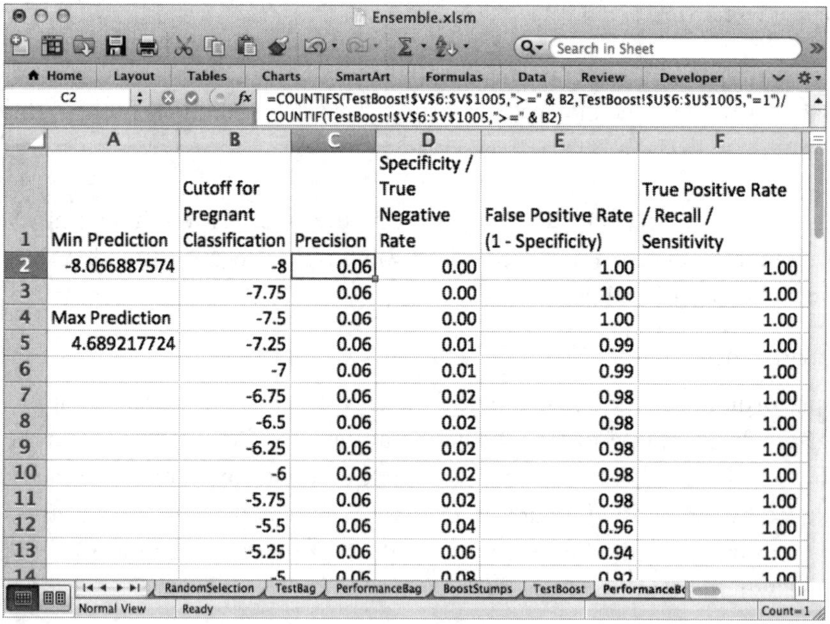

	A	B	C	D	E	F
1	Min Prediction	Cutoff for Pregnant Classification	Precision	Specificity / True Negative Rate	False Positive Rate (1 - Specificity)	True Positive Rate / Recall / Sensitivity
2	-8.066887574	-8	0.06	0.00	1.00	1.00
3		-7.75	0.06	0.00	1.00	1.00
4	Max Prediction	-7.5	0.06	0.00	1.00	1.00
5	4.689217724	-7.25	0.06	0.01	0.99	1.00
6		-7	0.06	0.01	0.99	1.00
7		-6.75	0.06	0.02	0.98	1.00
8		-6.5	0.06	0.02	0.98	1.00
9		-6.25	0.06	0.02	0.98	1.00
10		-6	0.06	0.02	0.98	1.00
11		-5.75	0.06	0.02	0.98	1.00
12		-5.5	0.06	0.04	0.96	1.00
13		-5.25	0.06	0.06	0.94	1.00
14		-5	0.06	0.08	0.92	1.00

Figure 7-34: The performance metrics for boosted stumps

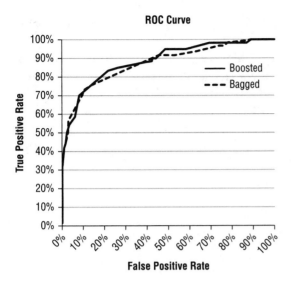

Figure 7-35: The ROC curves for the boosted and bagged models

Beyond Performance

In general, boosting requires fewer trees than bagging to produce a good model. It's not as popular in practice as bagging, because there is a slightly higher risk of overfitting the data. Since each reweighting of the training data is based on the misclassified points in the previous iteration, you can end up in a situation where you're training classifiers to be overly-sensitive to a few noisy points in the data.

Also, the iterative reweighting of the data means that boosting, unlike bagging, cannot be parallelized across multiple computers or CPU cores.

That said, in a neck and neck contest between a well fit boosted model and a well fit bagged model, it's hard for the bagged model to win.

Wrapping Up

You've just seen how a bunch of simple models can be combined via bagging or boosting to form an *ensemble* model. These approaches were unheard of until about the mid-1990s, but today, they stand as two of the most popular modeling techniques used in business.

And you can boost or bag any model that you want to use as a weak learner. These models don't have to be decision stumps or trees. For example, there's been a lot of talk recently about boosting naïve Bayes models like the one you encountered in Chapter 3.

In Chapter 10, you'll implement some of what you've encountered in this chapter using the R programming language.

If you'd like to learn more about these algorithms, I'd recommend reading about them in *The Elements of Statistical Learning* by Trevor Hastie, Robert Tibshirani, and Jerome Friedman (Springer, 2009).

8

Forecasting: Breathe Easy; You Can't Win

As you saw in Chapters 3, 6 and 7, supervised machine learning is about predicting a value or classifying an observation using a model trained on past data. Forecasting is similar. Sure, you can forecast without data (astrology, anyone?). But in quantitative forecasting, past data is used to predict a future outcome. Indeed, some of the same techniques, such as multiple regression (introduced in Chapter 6), are used in both disciplines.

But where forecasting and supervised machine learning differ greatly is in their canonical problem spaces. Typical forecasting problems are about taking some data point over time (sales, demand, supply, GDP, carbon emissions, or population, for example) and projecting that data into the future. And in the presence of trends, cycles, and the occasional act of God, the future data can be wildly outside the bounds of the observed past.

And that's the problem with forecasting: unlike in Chapters 6 and 7 where pregnant women more or less keep buying the same stuff, forecasting is used in contexts where the future often looks nothing like the past.

Just when you think you have a good projection for housing demand, the housing bubble bursts and your forecast is in the toilet. Just when you think you have a good demand forecast, a flood disrupts your supply chain, limiting your supply, forcing you to raise prices, and throwing your sales completely out of whack. Future time series data can and will look different than the data you've observed before.

The only guarantee with forecasting is that your forecast is wrong. You hear that a lot in the world of forecasting. But that doesn't mean you don't try. When it comes to planning your business, you often need some projection. At MailChimp, we might continue to grow like gangbusters, or a hole might open up under Atlanta and swallow us. But we make an effort to forecast growth as best we can so that we can plan our infrastructure and HR pipelines. You don't always want to be playing catch-up.

And as you'll see in this chapter, you can try forecasting the future, but you can also quantify the uncertainty around the forecast. And quantifying the forecast uncertainty by creating *prediction intervals* is invaluable and often ignored in the forecasting world.

As one wise forecaster said, "A good forecaster is not smarter than everyone else; they merely have their ignorance better organized."

So without further ado, let's go organize some ignorance.

The Sword Trade Is Hopping

Imagine with me that you're a rabid *Lord of the Rings* fan. Years ago when the first of the feature films came out, you strapped on some prosthetic hobbit feet and waited in line for hours to see the first midnight showing. Soon you were attending conventions and arguing on message boards about whether Frodo could have just ridden an eagle to Mount Doom.

One day, you decided to give something back. You took a course at the local community college on metalwork and began handcrafting your own swords. Your favorite sword from the book was Anduril, the Flame of the West. You became an expert at hammering out those beefy broadswords in your homemade forge, and you started selling them on Amazon, eBay, and Etsy. These days, your replicas are the go-to swords for the discerning nerd; business is booming.

In the past, you've found yourself scrambling to meet demand with the materials on hand. And so you've decided to forecast your future demand. So you dump your past sales data in a spreadsheet. But how do you take that past data and project it out?

This chapter looks at a set of forecasting techniques called *exponential smoothing* methods. They're some of the simplest and most widely used techniques in business today. Indeed, I know a few Fortune 500s just off the top of my head that forecast with these techniques, because they've proven the most accurate for their data.

This accuracy stems in part from the techniques' simplicity—they resist over-fitting the often-sparse historical data used in forecasting. Furthermore, with these techniques, it's relatively easy to compute prediction intervals *around* exponential smoothing forecasts, so you're going to do a bit of that too.

Getting Acquainted with Time Series Data

NOTE

The Excel workbook used in this chapter, "SwordForecasting.xlsm," is available for download at the book's website at www.wiley.com/go/datasmart. This workbook includes all the initial data if you want to work from that. Or you can just read along using the sheets I've already put together in the workbook.

The workbook for this chapter includes the last 36 months of sword demand starting from January three years ago. The data is shown in the Timeseries tab in Figure 8-1. As mentioned earlier in this chapter, data like this—observations over regular time intervals—is called *time series data*. The time interval can be whatever is appropriate for the problem at hand, whether that's yearly population figures or daily gas prices.

t	Demand
1	165
2	171
3	147
4	143
5	164
6	160
7	152
8	150
9	159
10	169
11	173
12	203
13	169
14	166
15	162
16	147
17	188
18	161
19	162
20	169
21	185
22	188
23	200
24	229
25	189
26	218
27	185
28	199
29	210
30	193
31	211
32	208
33	216
34	218
35	264
36	304

Figure 8-1: Time series data

In this case, you have monthly sword demand data, and the first thing you should do with it is plot it, as shown in Figure 8-2. To insert a plot like this, just highlight columns A and B in Excel and pick Scatter from the charts section of the Excel ribbon (Charts tab on Mac, Insert Tab on Windows). You can adjust the range of your axes by right-clicking them and selecting the Format option.

So what do you see in Figure 8-2? The data ranges from the 140s three years ago to 304 last month. That's a doubling of demand in three years—so maybe there's an upward trend? You'll come back to this thought in a bit.

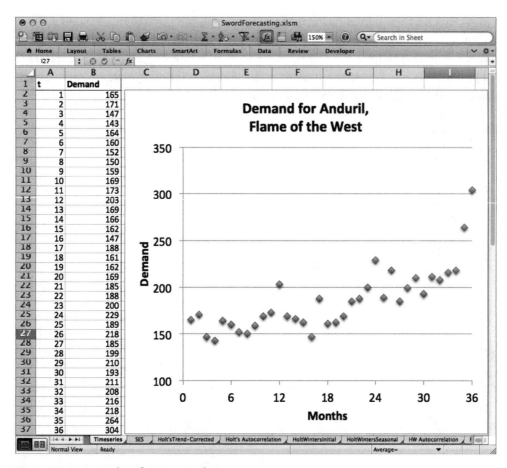

Figure 8-2: Scatter plot of time series data

There are a few ups and downs that may be indicative of some seasonal pattern. For instance, months 12, 24, and 36, which are all Decembers, are the highest demand months for each of their years. But that could just be chance or due to the trend. Let's find out.

Starting Slow with Simple Exponential Smoothing

Exponential smoothing techniques base a future forecast off of past data where the most recent observations are weighted more than older observations. This weighting is done through *smoothing constants*. The first exponential smoothing method you're going to tackle is called *simple exponential smoothing* (SES), and it uses only one smoothing constant, as you'll see.

Simple exponential smoothing assumes that your time series data is made up of two components: a *level* (or mean) and some error around that level. There's no trend, no seasonality, just a level around which the demand hovers with little error jitters here and there. By preferring recent observations, SES can account for shifts in this level. In formula-speak then, you have:

Demand at time t = level + random error around the level at time t

And the most current estimate of the level serves as a forecast for future time periods. If you're at month 36, what's a good estimate of demand at time period 38? The most recent level estimate. And time 40? The level. Simple—hence the name simple exponential smoothing.

So how do you get an estimate of the level?

If you assume that all your historical values are of equal importance, you just take a straight average.

This mean would give you a level, and you'd forecast the future by just saying, "Demand in the future is the average of the past demand." And there are companies that do this. I've seen monthly forecasts at companies where future months were equal to the average of those same months over the past few years. Plus a "fudge factor" for kicks. Yes, forecasting is often done so hand-wavily that even at huge, public companies words like "fudge factor" are still used. Eek.

But when the level shifts over time, you don't want to give equal weight to each historical point in the way that an average does. Should 2008 through 2013 all carry the same weight when forecasting 2014? Maybe, but for most businesses, probably not. So you want a level estimate that gives more weight to your recent demand observations.

So let's think about calculating the level, instead, by rolling over the data points in order, updating the level calculation as you go. To start, say the initial estimate of the level is the average of some of the earliest data points. In this case, pick the first year's worth of data. Call this initial estimate of the level, $level_0$:

$$level_0 = average\ of\ the\ first\ year's\ demand\ (months\ 1-12)$$

That's 163 for the sword demand.

Now, the way exponential smoothing works is that even though you know demand for months 1 through 36, you're going to take your most recent forecast components and use them to forecast one month ahead through the entire series.

So you use $level_0$ (163) as the forecast for demand in month 1.

Now that you've forecasted period 1, you take a step forward in time from period 0 to period 1. The actual demand was 165, so you were off by two swords. You should update the estimate of the level then to account for this error. Simple exponential smoothing uses this equation:

$$level_1 = level_0 + some\ percentage * (demand_1 - level_0)$$

Note that $(demand_1 - level_0)$ is the error you get when you forecast period one with the initial level estimate. Rolling forward:

$$level_2 = level_1 + some\ percentage * (demand_2 - level_1)$$

And again:

$$level_3 = level_2 + some\ percentage * (demand_3 - level_2)$$

Now, the percentage of the error you want to fold back into the level is the *smoothing constant*, and for the level, it's historically been called *alpha*. It can be any value between 0 and 100 percent (0 and 1).

If you set *alpha* to 1, you're accounting for all the error, which just means the level of the current period is the demand of the current period.

If you set *alpha* to 0, you conduct absolutely no error correction on that first level estimate.

You'll likely want something in between those two extremes, but you'll learn how to pick the best *alpha* value later.

So you can roll this calculation forward through time:

$$level_{current\ period} = level_{previous\ period} + alpha * (demand_{current\ period} - level_{previous\ period})$$

Eventually you end up with a final level estimate, $level_{36}$, where the last demand observations count for more because their error adjustments haven't been multiplied by *alpha* a zillion times:

$$level_{36} = level_{35} + alpha * (demand_{36} - level_{35})$$

This final estimate of the level is what you'll use as the forecast of future months. The demand for month 37? Well, that's just $level_{36}$. And the demand for month 40? $level_{36}$. Month 45? $level_{36}$. You get the picture. The final level estimate is the best one you have for the future, so that's what you use.

Let's take a look at it in a spreadsheet.

Setting Up the Simple Exponential Smoothing Forecast

The first thing you'll do is create a new worksheet in the workbook called **SES**. Paste the time series data in columns A and B starting at row 4 to leave some room at the top of the sheet for an *alpha* value. You can put the number of months you have in your data (36) in cell A2, and an initial swag at the *alpha* value in C2. I'm going with 0.5, because it's in between 0 and 1, and that's just how I roll.

Now, in column C, you place the level calculations. You'll need to insert a new row 5 into the time series data at the top for the initial level estimate at time 0. In C5, use the following calculation:

```
=AVERAGE(B6:B17)
```

This averages the first year's worth of data to give the initial level. The spreadsheet then looks as shown in Figure 8-3.

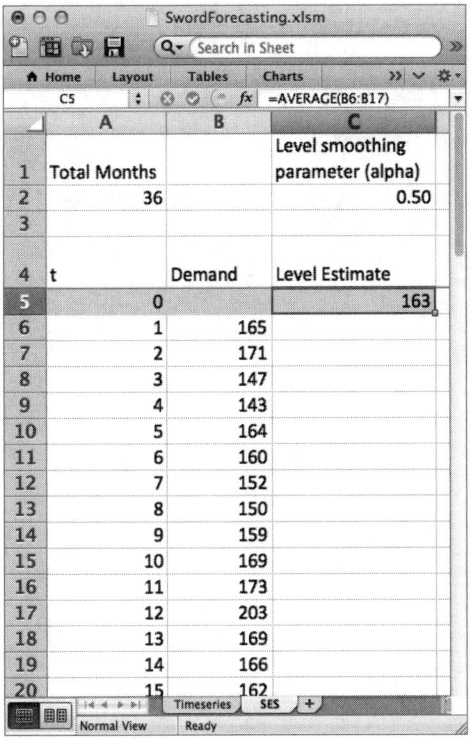

	A	B	C
1	Total Months		Level smoothing parameter (alpha)
2	36		0.50
3			
4	t	Demand	Level Estimate
5	0		163
6	1	165	
7	2	171	
8	3	147	
9	4	143	
10	5	164	
11	6	160	
12	7	152	
13	8	150	
14	9	159	
15	10	169	
16	11	173	
17	12	203	
18	13	169	
19	14	166	
20	15	162	

Figure 8-3: Initial level estimate for simple exponential smoothing

Adding in the One-Step Forecast and Error

Now that you've added the first level value into the sheet, you can roll forward in time using the SES formula laid out in the previous section. To do this, you'll need to add two columns: a one-step forecast column (D) and a forecast error column (E). The one-step forecast for time period 1 is just $level_0$ (cell C5), and the error calculation is then the actual demand minus the forecast:

```
=B6-D6
```

The level estimate then for period 1 is the previous level adjusted by *alpha* times the error, which is:

```
=C5+C$2*E6
```

Note that I've placed a \$ in front of the *alpha* value so that when you drag the formula down the sheet, the absolute row reference leaves *alpha* be. This yields the sheet shown in Figure 8-4.

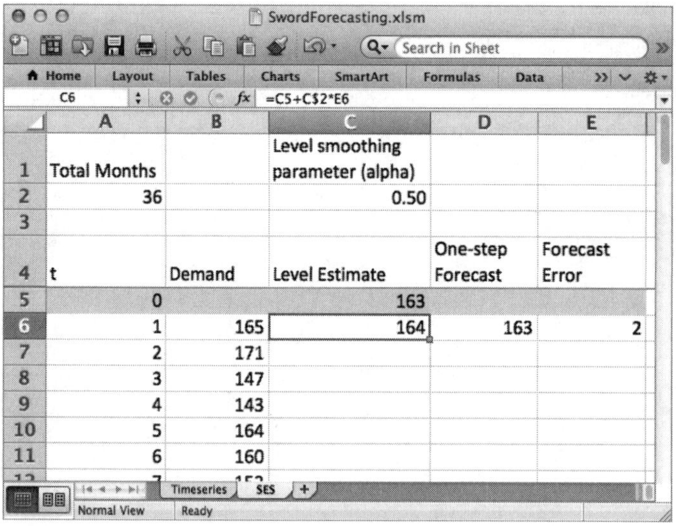

	A	B	C	D	E
1	Total Months		Level smoothing parameter (alpha)		
2	36		0.50		
3					
4	t	Demand	Level Estimate	One-step Forecast	Forecast Error
5	0		163		
6	1	165	164	163	2
7	2	171			
8	3	147			
9	4	143			
10	5	164			
11	6	160			

Figure 8-4: Generating the one-step forecast, error, and level calculation for period 1

Drag That Stuff Down!

Humorously enough, you're pretty much done here. Just drag C6:E6 down through all 36 months, and *voila*, you have $level_{36}$.

Let's add months 37–48 to column A. The forecast for these next 12 months is just $level_{36}$. So in B42, you can just add:

```
=C$41
```

as the forecast and drag it down for the next year.

This gives you a forecast of 272, as shown in Figure 8-5.

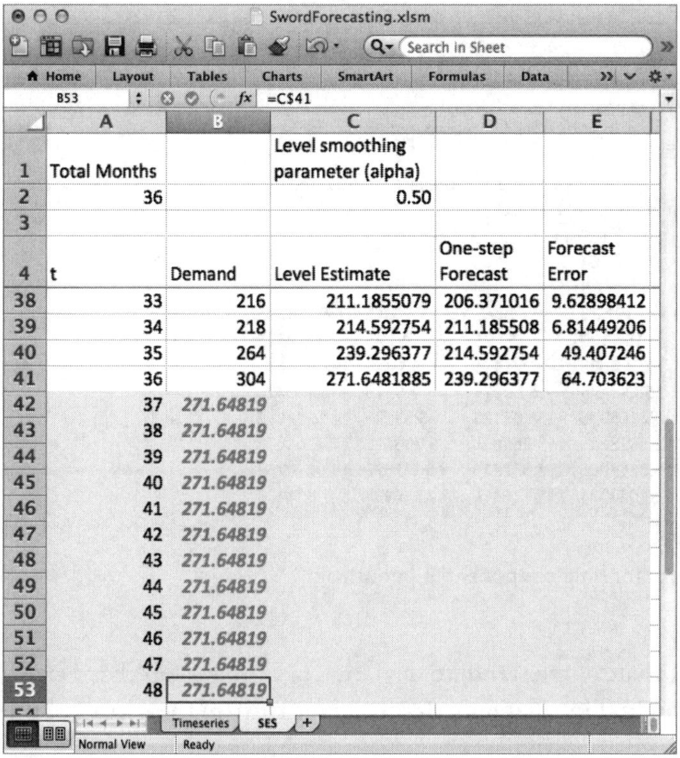

	A	B	C	D	E
1	Total Months		Level smoothing parameter (alpha)		
2	36		0.50		
3					
4	t	Demand	Level Estimate	One-step Forecast	Forecast Error
38	33	216	211.1855079	206.371016	9.62898412
39	34	218	214.592754	211.185508	6.81449206
40	35	264	239.296377	214.592754	49.407246
41	36	304	271.6481885	239.296377	64.703623
42	37	271.64819			
43	38	271.64819			
44	39	271.64819			
45	40	271.64819			
46	41	271.64819			
47	42	271.64819			
48	43	271.64819			
49	44	271.64819			
50	45	271.64819			
51	46	271.64819			
52	47	271.64819			
53	48	271.64819			

Figure 8-5: Simple exponential smoothing forecast with *alpha* of 0.5

But is that the best you can do? Well, the way you optimize this forecast is by setting *alpha*—the larger *alpha* is, the less you care about the old demand points.

Optimizing for One-Step Error

Similar to how you minimized the sum of squared error when fitting the regression in Chapter 6, you can find the best smoothing constant for the forecast by minimizing the sum of the squared error for the one-step ahead forecasts.

Let's add a squared error calculation into column F that's just the value from column E squared, drag that calculation through all 36 months, and sum it in cell E2 as the sum of squared error (SSE). This yields the sheet shown in Figure 8-6.

Also, you're going to add the *standard error* to the spreadsheet in cell F2. The standard error is just the square root of the SSE divided by 35 (36 months minus the number of smoothing parameters in the model, which for simple exponential smoothing is 1).

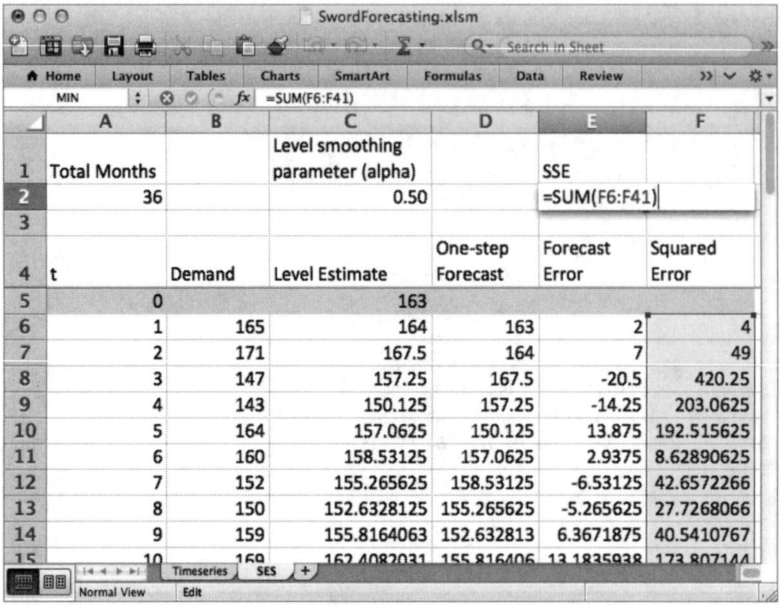

Figure 8-6: The sum of squared error for simple exponential smoothing

The standard error is an estimate of the standard deviation of the one-step ahead error. You saw the standard deviation first in Chapter 4. It's just a measure of the spread of the error.

If you have a nicely fitting forecast model, its error will have a mean of 0. This is to say the forecast is *unbiased*. It over-estimates demand as often as it underestimates. The standard error quantifies the spread around 0 when the forecast is unbiased.

So in cell F2, you can calculate the standard error as:

```
=SQRT(E2/(36-1))
```

For an *alpha* value of 0.5, it comes out to 20.94 (see Figure 8-7). And if you'll recall the 68-95-99.7 rule from the normal distribution discussed in Chapter 4, this is saying that 68 percent of the one-step forecast errors should be less than 20.94 and greater than -20.94.

Now, what you want to do is shrink that spread down as low as you can by finding the appropriate *alpha* value. You could just try a bunch of different values of *alpha*. But you're going to use Solver for the umpteenth time in this book.

The Solver setup for this is super easy. Just open Solver, set the objective to the standard error in F2, set the decision variable to *alpha* in C2, add a constraint that C2 be less than 1, and check the box that the decision be non-negative. The recursive level calculations that go into making each forecast error are highly non-linear, so you'll need to use the evolutionary algorithm to optimize *alpha*.

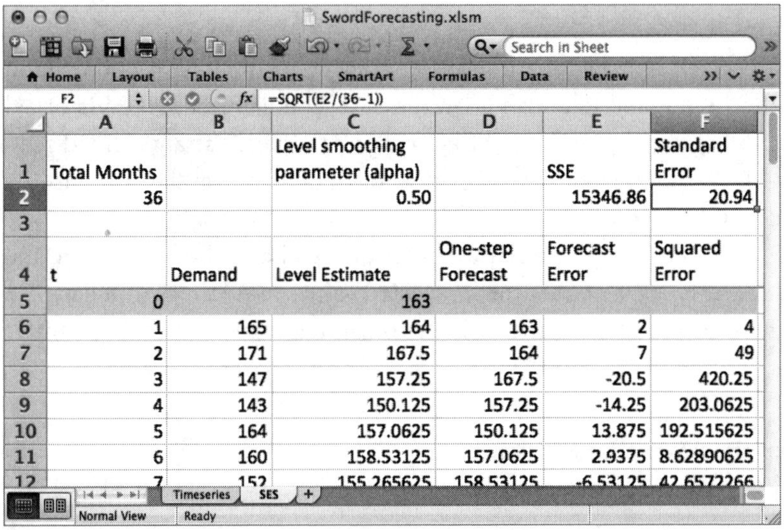

Figure 8-7: The standard error calculation

The Solver formulation should look like what's shown in Figure 8-8. Pressing Solve, you get an *alpha* value of 0.73, which gives a new standard error of 20.39. Not a ton of improvement.

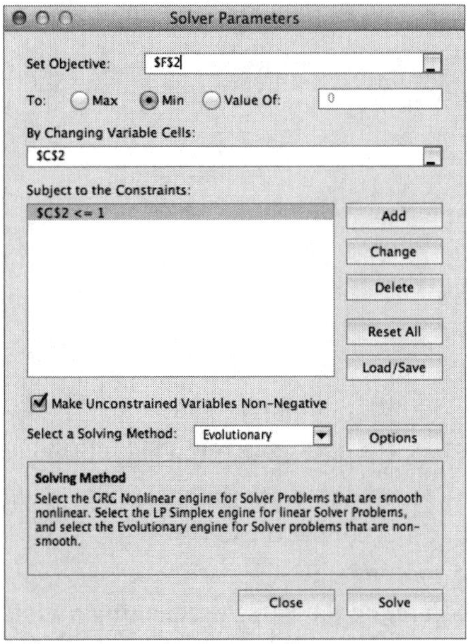

Figure 8-8: Solver formulation for optimizing *alpha*

Let's Graph It

The best way to "gut check" a forecast is to graph it alongside your historical demand and see how the predicted demand takes off from the past. You can select the historical demand data and the forecast and plot them. I like the look of Excel's straight-lined scatter. To start, select A6:B41, which is just the historical data, and choose the straight-line scatter plot from Excel's chart section.

Once you've added that chart, right-click the center of the chart, choose Select Data, and add a new series to the chart with just the forecasted values of A42:B53. You can also add some labels to the axes if you like, after which you should have something similar to Figure 8-9.

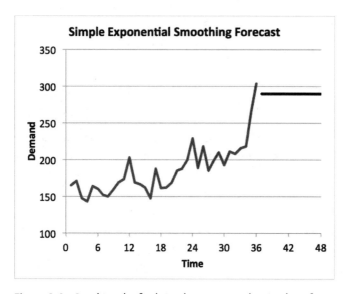

Figure 8-9: Graphing the final simple exponential smoothing forecast

You Might Have a Trend

Just looking at that graph, a few things stand out. First, simple exponential smoothing is just a flat line—the level. But when you look at the demand data from the past 36 months, it's on the rise. There appears to be a trend upward, especially at the end.

Not to denigrate the human eyeball, but how do you prove it?

You prove it by fitting a linear regression to the demand data and performing a *t test* on the slope of that trendline, just as you did in Chapter 6.

If the slope of the line is nonzero and statistically significant (has a p value less than 0.05 in the t test), you can be confident that the data has a trend. If that last sentence makes absolutely no sense to you, check out the statistical testing section in Chapter 6.

Flip back to the Timeseries tab in the workbook to perform the trend test.

Now, in Chapter 6 you proved your mettle by performing both an F test and a t test *by hand*. No one wants to subject you to that again.

In this chapter, you'll use Excel's built-in LINEST function to fit a linear regression, pull the slope, standard error of the slope coefficient, and degrees of freedom (see Chapter 6 to understand these terms). Then you can calculate your t statistic and run it through the TDIST function just as in Chapter 6.

If you've never used LINEST before, Excel's help documentation on the function is very good. You provide LINEST with the dependent variable data (demand in column B) and the independent variable data (you only have one independent variable and it's time in column A).

You also have to provide a flag of TRUE to let the function know to fit an intercept as part of the regression line, and you have to provide a second flag of TRUE to get back detailed stats like standard error and R-squared. For the Timeseries tab data then, a linear regression can be run as:

```
=LINEST(B2:B37,A2:A37,TRUE,TRUE)
```

This call will only return the slope of the regression line however, because LINEST is an array formula. LINEST returns back all the regression stats in an array, so you can either run LINEST as an array formula to dump everything out into a selected range in a sheet, or you can run LINEST through the INDEX formula and pull off just the values you care about one by one.

For instance, the first components of a regression line that LINEST gives are the regression coefficients, so you can pull the slope for the regression in cell B39 on the Timeseries tab by feeding LINEST through INDEX:

```
=INDEX(LINEST(B2:B37,A2:A37,TRUE,TRUE),1,1)
```

You get back a slope of 2.54, meaning the regression line is showing an upward trend of 2.54 additional demanded swords per month. So there is a slope. But is it statistically significant?

To run a t test on the slope, you need to pull the standard error for the slope and the degrees of freedom for the regression. LINEST parks the standard error value in row 2, column 1 of its array of results. So in B40, you can pull it as:

```
=INDEX(LINEST(B2:B37,A2:A37,TRUE,TRUE),2,1)
```

The only change from pulling the slope is that in the INDEX formula you pull row 2, column 1 for the standard error instead of row 1 column 1 for the slope.

The standard error of the slope is given as 0.34. This gives the sheet shown in Figure 8-10.

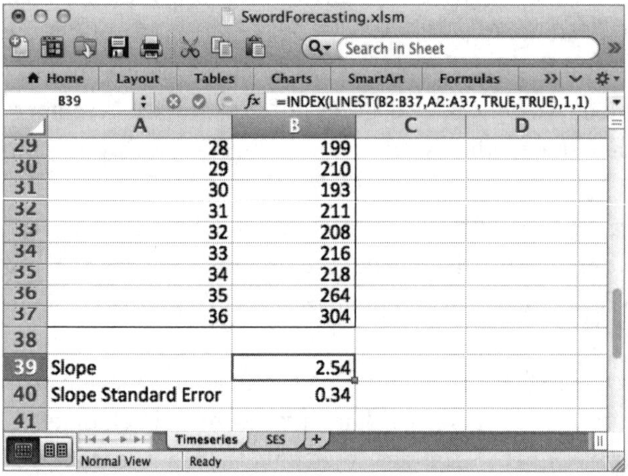

Figure 8-10: The slope and standard error for a regression line fitted to the historical demand

Similarly, Excel's LINEST documentation notes that degrees of freedom for the regression are returned at the fourth row and second column value in the result array. So in B41 you can pull it as follows:

```
=INDEX(LINEST(B2:B37,A2:A37,TRUE,TRUE),4,2)
```

You should get 34 for the degrees of freedom (as noted in Chapter 6, this is calculated as 36 data points minus 2 coefficients from the linear regression).

You now have the three values you need to perform a t test on the statistical significance of your fitted trend. Just as in Chapter 6, you can calculate the test statistic as the absolute value of the slope divided by the standard error for the slope. You can pull the p value for this statistic from the t distribution with 34 degrees of freedom using the TDIST function in B42:

```
=TDIST(ABS(B39/B40),B41,2)
```

This returns a p value near 0 implying that if the trend were nonexistent in reality (slope of 0), there's no chance we would have gotten a slope so extreme from our regression. This is shown in Figure 8-11.

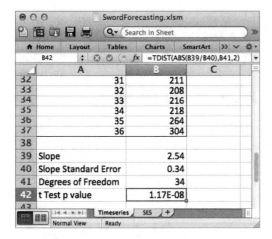

Figure 8-11: Your trend is legit

All right! So you have a trend. Now you just need to incorporate it into your forecast.

Holt's Trend-Corrected Exponential Smoothing

Holt's Trend-Corrected Exponential Smoothing expands simple exponential smoothing to create a forecast from data that has a linear trend. It's often called *double exponential smoothing*, because unlike SES, which has one smoothing parameter *alpha* and one non-error component, double exponential smoothing has two.

If the time series has a linear trend, you can write it as:

Demand at time t = level + t*trend + random error around the level at time t

The most current estimates of the level and trend (times the number of periods out) serve as a forecast for future time periods. If you're at month 36, what's a good estimate of demand at time period 38? The most recent level estimate *plus* two months of the trend. And time 40? The level *plus* four months of the trend. Not as simple as SES but pretty close.

Now, just as in simple exponential smoothing, you need to get some initial estimates of the level and trend values, called $level_0$ and $trend_0$. One common way to get them is just to plot the first half of your demand data and send a trendline through it (just like you did in Chapter 6 in the cat allergy example). The slope of the line is $trend_0$ and the y-intercept is $level_0$.

Holt's Trend-Corrected Smoothing has two update equations, one for the level as you roll through time and one for the trend. The level equation still uses a smoothing parameter called *alpha*, whereas the trend equation uses a parameter often called *gamma*. They're exactly the same—just values between 0 and 1 that regulate how much one-step forecasting error is incorporated back into the estimates.

So, here's the new level update equation:

$$level_1 = level_0 + trend_0 + alpha * (demand_1 - (level_0 + trend_0))$$

Note that $(level_0 + trend_0)$ is just the one-step ahead forecast from the initial values to month 1, so $(demand_1 - (level_0 + trend_0))$ is the one-step ahead error. This equation looks identical to the level equation from SES except you account for one time period's worth of trend whenever you count forward a slot. Thus, the general equation for the level estimate is:

$$level_{current\ period} = level_{previous\ period} + trend_{previous\ period} + alpha * (demand_{current\ period} - (level_{previous\ period} + trend_{previous\ period}))$$

Under this new smoothing technique, you also need a trend update equation. For the first time slot it's:

$$trend_1 = trend_0 + gamma * alpha * (demand_1 - (level_0 + trend_0))$$

So the trend equation is similar to the level update equation. You take the previous trend estimate and adjust it by *gamma* times the amount of error incorporated into the accompanying level update (which makes intuitive sense because only some of the error you're using to adjust the level would be attributable to poor or shifting trend estimation).

Thus, the general equation for the trend estimate is:

$$trend_{current\ period} = trend_{previous\ period} + gamma * alpha * (demand_{current\ period} - (level_{previous\ period} + trend_{previous\ period}))$$

Setting Up Holt's Trend-Corrected Smoothing in a Spreadsheet

To start, create a new tab called **Holt'sTrend-Corrected**. On this tab, just as with the simple exponential smoothing tab, paste the time series data on row 4 and insert an empty row 5 for the initial estimates.

Column C will once again contain the level estimates, and you'll put the trend estimates in column D. So at the top of those two columns you'll put the *alpha* and *gamma* values. You're going to be optimizing them with Solver in a second, but for now, just toss in some 0.5s. This gives the sheet shown in Figure 8-12.

For the initial values of level and trend that go in C5 and D5, let's scatter plot the first 18 months of data and add a trendline to it with the equation (if you don't know how to add a trendline to a scatterplot, see Chapter 6 for an example). This gives an initial trend of 0.8369 and an initial level (intercept of the trendline) of 155.88.

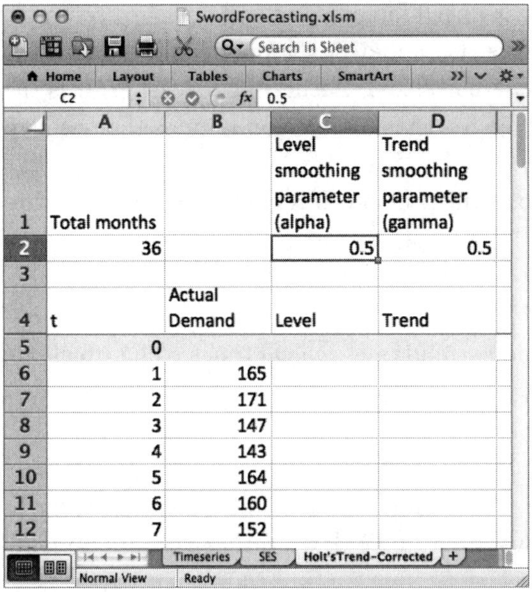

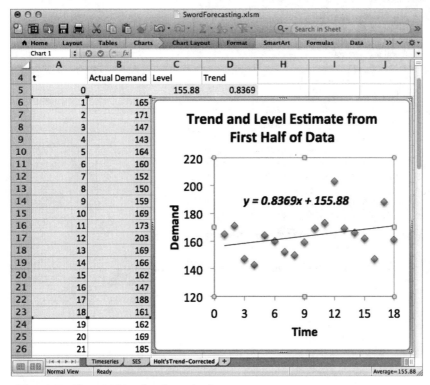

Figure 8-12: Starting with smoothing parameters set to 0.5

Adding these to D5 and C5 respectively, you get the sheet shown in Figure 8-13.

Figure 8-13: The initial level and trend values

Now in Columns E and F, add the one-step ahead forecast and forecast error columns. If you look at row 6, the one-step ahead forecast is merely the previous level plus one month's trend using the previous estimate—that's C5+D5. And the forecast error is the same as in simple exponential smoothing; F6 is just actual demand minus the one-step forecast—B6-E6.

You can then update the level in cell C6 as the previous level plus the previous trend plus *alpha* times the error:

```
=C5+D5+C$2*F6
```

The trend in D6 is updated as the previous trend plus *gamma* times *alpha* times the error:

```
=D5+D$2*C$2*F6
```

Note that you need to use absolute references on both *alpha* and *gamma* in order to drag the formulas down. You'll do that now—drag C6:F6 down through month 36. This is shown in Figure 8-14.

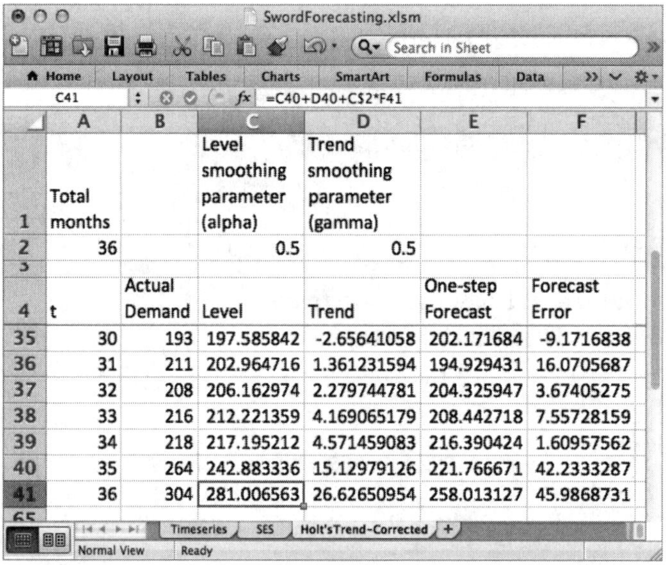

	A	B	C	D	E	F
1	Total months		Level smoothing parameter (alpha)	Trend smoothing parameter (gamma)		
2	36		0.5	0.5		
3						
4	t	Actual Demand	Level	Trend	One-step Forecast	Forecast Error
35	30	193	197.585842	-2.65641058	202.171684	-9.1716838
36	31	211	202.964716	1.361231594	194.929431	16.0705687
37	32	208	206.162974	2.279744781	204.325947	3.67405275
38	33	216	212.221359	4.169065179	208.442718	7.55728159
39	34	218	217.195212	4.571459083	216.390424	1.60957562
40	35	264	242.883336	15.12979126	221.766671	42.2333287
41	36	304	281.006563	26.62650954	258.013127	45.9868731

Figure 8-14: Dragging down the level, trend, forecast, and error calculations

Forecasting Future Periods

To forecast out from month 36, you add the final level (which for an *alpha* and *gamma* of 0.5 is 281) to the number of months out you're forecasting *times* the final trend estimate. You can calculate the number of months between month 36 and the month you care about by subtracting one month in column A from the other.

For example, forecasting month 37 in cell B42, you'd use:

```
=C$41+(A42-A$41)*D$41
```

By using absolute references for month 36, the final trend, and the final level, you can drag the forecast down through month 48, giving the sheet shown in Figure 8-15.

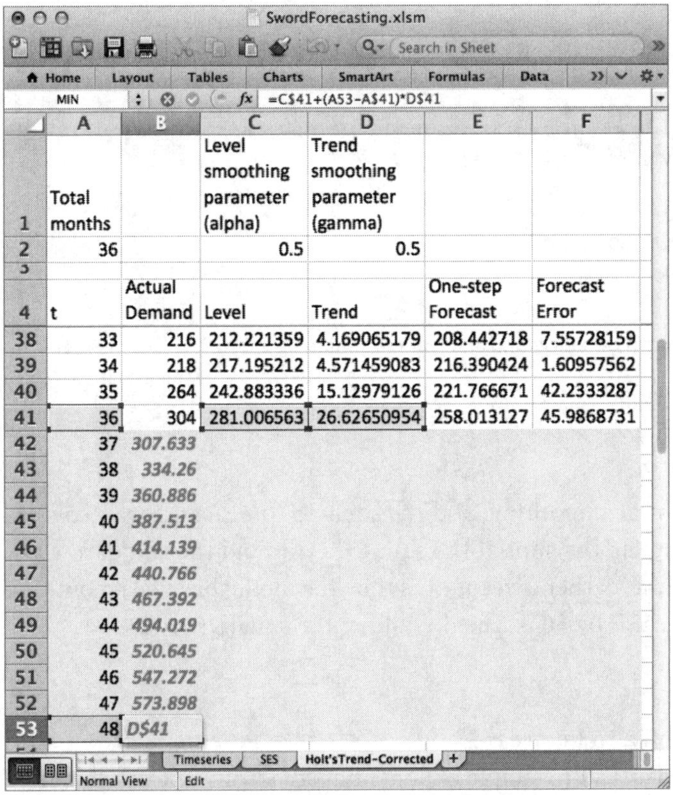

Figure 8-15: Forecasting future months with Holt's Trend-Corrected Exponential Smoothing

Just as on the simple exponential smoothing tab, you can graph the historical demand and the forecast as two series on a straight-line scatter plot, as shown in Figure 8-16.

With an *alpha* and *gamma* of 0.5, that forecast sure looks a bit nutty, doesn't it? It's taking off where the final month ends and increasing at a rather rapid rate from there. Perhaps you should optimize the smoothing parameters.

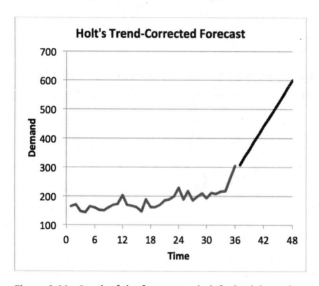

Figure 8-16: Graph of the forecast with default *alpha* and *gamma* values

Optimizing for One-Step Error

As you did for simple exponential smoothing, add the squared forecast error in column G. In F2 and G2, you can calculate the sum of the squared error and the standard error for the one-step forecast exactly as earlier. Except, this time the model has two smoothing parameters so you'll divide the SSE by 36 – 2 before taking the square root:

```
=SQRT(F2/(36-2))
```

This gives you the sheet shown in Figure 8-17.

The optimization setup is identical to simple exponential smoothing except this time around you're optimizing both *alpha* and *gamma* together, as shown in Figure 8-18.

When you solve, you get an optimal *alpha* value of 0.66 and an optimal *gamma* value of 0.05. The optimal forecast is shown in the straight-line scatter in Figure 8-19.

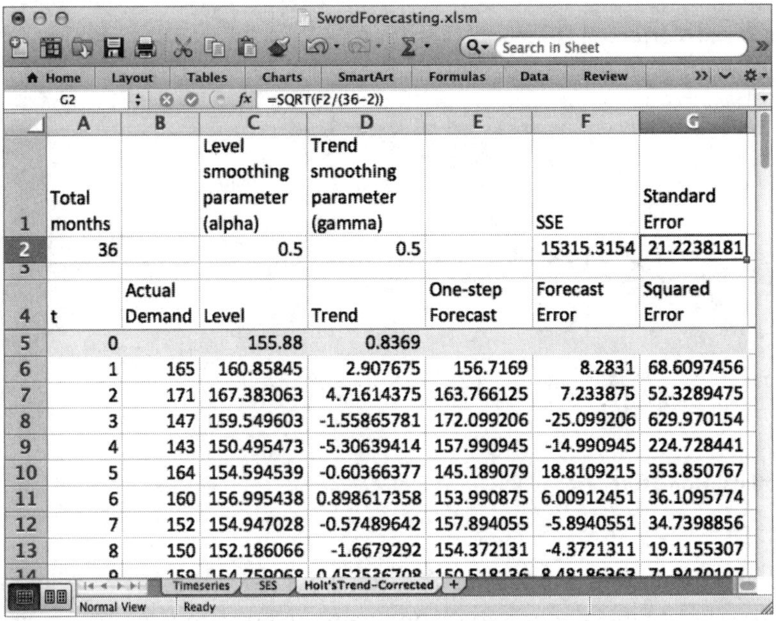

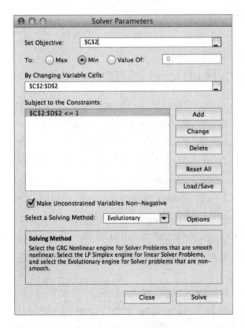

Figure 8-17 shows the spreadsheet interface:

	A	B	C	D	E	F	G
1	Total months		Level smoothing parameter (alpha)	Trend smoothing parameter (gamma)		SSE	Standard Error
2	36		0.5	0.5		15315.3154	21.2238181
3							
4	t	Actual Demand	Level	Trend	One-step Forecast	Forecast Error	Squared Error
5	0		155.88	0.8369			
6	1	165	160.85845	2.907675	156.7169	8.2831	68.6097456
7	2	171	167.383063	4.71614375	163.766125	7.233875	52.3289475
8	3	147	159.549603	-1.55865781	172.099206	-25.099206	629.970154
9	4	143	150.495473	-5.30639414	157.990945	-14.990945	224.728441
10	5	164	154.594539	-0.60366377	145.189079	18.8109215	353.850767
11	6	160	156.995438	0.898617358	153.990875	6.00912451	36.1095774
12	7	152	154.947028	-0.57489642	157.894055	-5.8940551	34.7398856
13	8	150	152.186066	-1.6679292	154.372131	-4.3721311	19.1155307
14	9	159	154.759068	0.452536708	150.518136	8.49186363	71.9420107

Cell G2 formula: `=SQRT(F2/(36-2))`

Figure 8-17: Calculating the SSE and standard error

Figure 8-18: Optimization setup for Holt's Trend-Corrected Exponential Smoothing

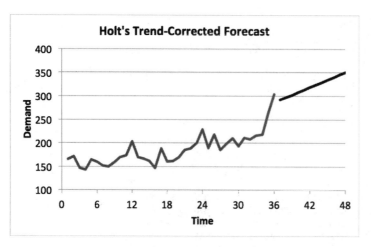

Figure 8-19: Graph of optimal Holt's forecast

The trend you're using from the forecast is an additional five swords sold per month. The reason why this trend is double the one you found using the trendline on the previous tab is because trend-corrected smoothing favors recent points more, and in this case, the most recent demand points have been very "trendy."

Note how this forecast starts very near the SES forecast for month 37 – 290 versus 292. But pretty quickly the trend-corrected forecast begins to grow just like you'd expect with a trend.

So Are You Done? Looking at Autocorrelations

All right. Is this the best you can do? Have you accounted for everything?

Well, one way to check if you have a good model for the forecast is to check the one-step ahead errors. If those errors are random, you've done your job. But if there's a pattern hidden in the error—some kind of repeated behavior at a regular interval—there may be something seasonal in the demand data that is unaccounted for.

And by a "pattern in the error," I mean that if you took the error and lined it up with itself shifted by a month or two months or twelve months, would it move in sync? This concept of the error being correlated with the time-shifted version of itself is called *autocorrelation* (auto means "self" in Greek. It's also a good prefix for ditching vowels in Scrabble).

So to start, create a new tab called **Holt's Autocorrelation**. And in that tab, paste months 1 through 36 along with their one-step errors from the Holt's forecast into columns A and B.

Underneath the errors in B38, calculate the average error. This gives the sheet shown in Figure 8-20.

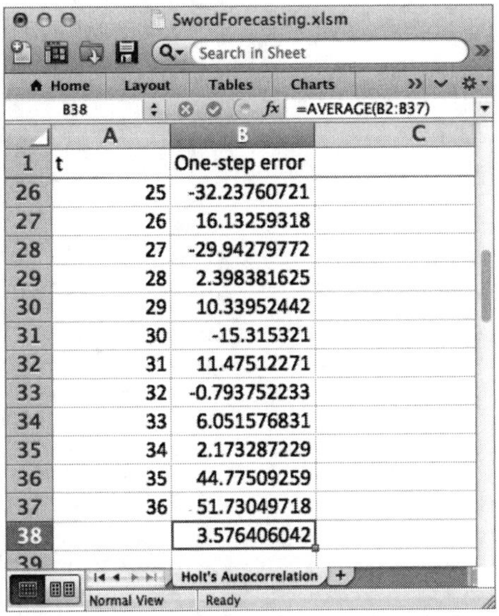

	A	B	C
1	t	One-step error	
26	25	-32.23760721	
27	26	16.13259318	
28	27	-29.94279772	
29	28	2.398381625	
30	29	10.33952442	
31	30	-15.315321	
32	31	11.47512271	
33	32	-0.793752233	
34	33	6.051576831	
35	34	2.173287229	
36	35	44.77509259	
37	36	51.73049718	
38		3.576406042	

Figure 8-20: Months and associated one-step forecast errors

In column C, calculate the deviations of each error in column B from the average in B38. These deviations in the one-step error from the average are where patterns are going to rear their ugly head. For instance, maybe every December the forecast error is substantially above average—that type of seasonal pattern would show up in these numbers.

In cell C2, then, the deviation of the error in B2 from the mean would be:

```
=B2-B$38
```

You can then drag this formula down to give all the mean deviations. In cell C38, calculate the sum of squared deviations as:

```
=SUMPRODUCT($C2:$C37,C2:C37)
```

This gives you the sheet shown in Figure 8-21.

Now, in column D "lag" the error deviations by one month. Label column D with a **1**. You can leave cell D2 blank and set cell D3 to:

```
=C2
```

And then just drag the formula down until D37 equals C36. This gives you Figure 8-22.

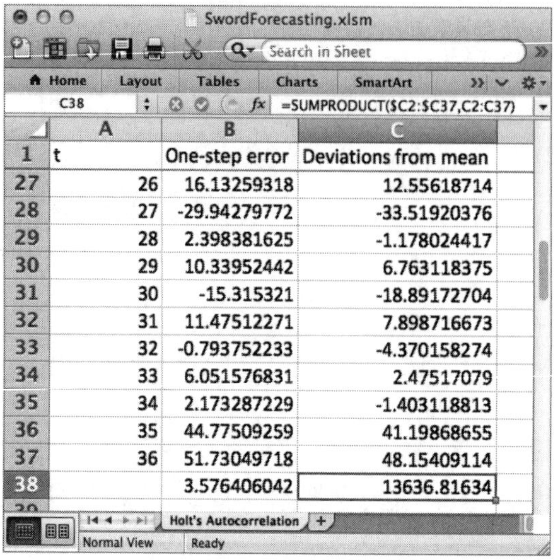

Figure 8-21: Sum of squared mean deviations of Holt's forecast errors

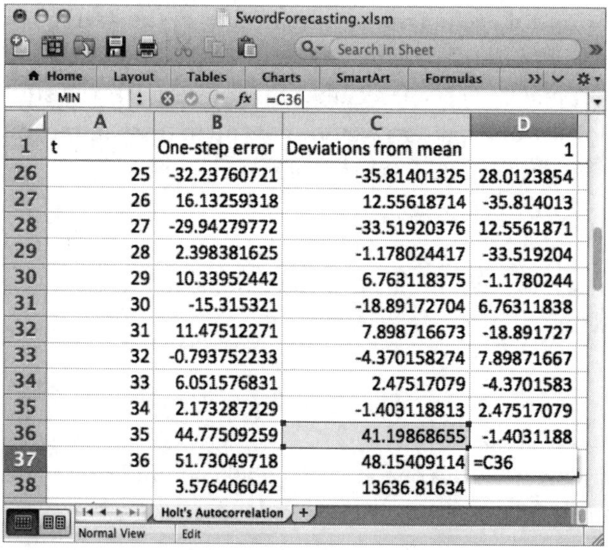

Figure 8-22: One month lagged error deviations

To lag by two months, just select D1:D37 and drag it into column E. Similarly, to lag up to 12 months, just drag the selection through column O. Easy! This gives you a cascading matrix of lagged error deviations, as shown in Figure 8-23.

SwordForecasting.xlsm

O37 — =N36

C	D	E	F	G	H	I	J	K	L	M	N	O
Deviations from mean	1	2	3	4	5	6	7	8	9	10	11	12
4.71												
4.12	4.71	0.00	0.00	0.00	0.00	0.00	0.00	0.00	0.00	0.00	0.00	0.00
-26.35	4.12	4.71	0.00	0.00	0.00	0.00	0.00	0.00	0.00	0.00	0.00	0.00
-15.94	-26.35	4.12	4.71	0.00	0.00	0.00	0.00	0.00	0.00	0.00	0.00	0.00
13.04	-15.94	-26.35	4.12	4.71	0.00	0.00	0.00	0.00	0.00	0.00	0.00	0.00
-2.66	13.04	-15.94	-26.35	4.12	4.71	0.00	0.00	0.00	0.00	0.00	0.00	0.00
-12.04	-2.66	13.04	-15.94	-26.35	4.12	4.71	0.00	0.00	0.00	0.00	0.00	0.00
-8.95	-12.04	-2.66	13.04	-15.94	-26.35	4.12	4.71	0.00	0.00	0.00	0.00	0.00
3.30	-8.95	-12.04	-2.66	13.04	-15.94	-26.35	4.12	4.71	0.00	0.00	0.00	0.00
8.23	3.30	-8.95	-12.04	-2.66	13.04	-15.94	-26.35	4.12	4.71	0.00	0.00	0.00
3.50	8.23	3.30	-8.95	-12.04	-2.66	13.04	-15.94	-26.35	4.12	4.71	0.00	0.00
27.64	3.50	8.23	3.30	-8.95	-12.04	-2.66	13.04	-15.94	-26.35	4.12	4.71	0.00
-29.23	27.64	3.50	8.23	3.30	-8.95	-12.04	-2.66	13.04	-15.94	-26.35	4.12	4.71
-16.71	-29.23	27.64	3.50	8.23	3.30	-8.95	-12.04	-2.66	13.04	-15.94	-26.35	4.12
-12.99	-16.71	-29.23	27.64	3.50	8.23	3.30	-8.95	-12.04	-2.66	13.04	-15.94	-26.35
-22.39	-12.99	-16.71	-29.23	27.64	3.50	8.23	3.30	-8.95	-12.04	-2.66	13.04	-15.94
31.07	-22.39	-12.99	-16.71	-29.23	27.64	3.50	8.23	3.30	-8.95	-12.04	-2.66	13.04
-19.92	31.07	-22.39	-12.99	-16.71	-29.23	27.64	3.50	8.23	3.30	-8.95	-12.04	-2.66
-8.73	-19.92	31.07	-22.39	-12.99	-16.71	-29.23	27.64	3.50	8.23	3.30	-8.95	-12.04
1.26	-8.73	-19.92	31.07	-22.39	-12.99	-16.71	-29.23	27.64	3.50	8.23	3.30	-8.95
13.50	1.26	-8.73	-19.92	31.07	-22.39	-12.99	-16.71	-29.23	27.64	3.50	8.23	3.30
4.07	13.50	1.26	-8.73	-19.92	31.07	-22.39	-12.99	-16.71	-29.23	27.64	3.50	8.23
9.59	4.07	13.50	1.26	-8.73	-19.92	31.07	-22.39	-12.99	-16.71	-29.23	27.64	3.50
28.01	9.59	4.07	13.50	1.26	-8.73	-19.92	31.07	-22.39	-12.99	-16.71	-29.23	27.64
-35.81	28.01	9.59	4.07	13.50	1.26	-8.73	-19.92	31.07	-22.39	-12.99	-16.71	-29.23
12.56	-35.81	28.01	9.59	4.07	13.50	1.26	-8.73	-19.92	31.07	-22.39	-12.99	-16.71
-33.52	12.56	-35.81	28.01	9.59	4.07	13.50	1.26	-8.73	-19.92	31.07	-22.39	-12.99
-1.18	-33.52	12.56	-35.81	28.01	9.59	4.07	13.50	1.26	-8.73	-19.92	31.07	-22.39
6.76	-1.18	-33.52	12.56	-35.81	28.01	9.59	4.07	13.50	1.26	-8.73	-19.92	31.07
-18.89	6.76	-1.18	-33.52	12.56	-35.81	28.01	9.59	4.07	13.50	1.26	-8.73	-19.92
7.90	-18.89	6.76	-1.18	-33.52	12.56	-35.81	28.01	9.59	4.07	13.50	1.26	-8.73
-4.37	7.90	-18.89	6.76	-1.18	-33.52	12.56	-35.81	28.01	9.59	4.07	13.50	1.26
2.48	-4.37	7.90	-18.89	6.76	-1.18	-33.52	12.56	-35.81	28.01	9.59	4.07	13.50
-1.40	2.48	-4.37	7.90	-18.89	6.76	-1.18	-33.52	12.56	-35.81	28.01	9.59	4.07
41.20	-1.40	2.48	-4.37	7.90	-18.89	6.76	-1.18	-33.52	12.56	-35.81	28.01	9.59
48.15	41.20	-1.40	2.48	-4.37	7.90	-18.89	6.76	-1.18	-33.52	12.56	-35.81	28.01
13636.81634												

Holt's Autocorrelation +

Figure 8-23: A beautiful cascading matrix of lagged error deviations fit for a king

Now that you have these lags, think about what it means for one of these columns to "move in sync" with column C. For instance, take the one-month lag in column D. If these two columns were in sync then when one goes negative, the other should. And when one is positive, the other should be positive. That means that the product of the two columns would result in a lot of positive numbers (a negative times a negative or a positive times a positive results in a positive number).

You can sum these products, and the closer this SUMPRODUCT of the lagged column with the original deviations gets to the sum of squared deviations in C38, the more in sync, the more correlated, the lagged errors are with the originals.

You can also get negative autocorrelation where the lagged deviations go negative whenever the originals are positive and vice versa. The SUMPRODUCT in this case will be a larger negative number.

To start, drag the SUMPRODUCT ($C2:$C37,C2:C37) in cell C38 across through column O. Note how the absolute reference to column C will keep the column in place, so you get the SUMPRODUCT of each lag column with the original, as shown in Figure 8-24.

	C	D	E	F	G	H	I	J	K	L	M	N	O
1	Deviations from mean	1	2	3	4	5	6	7	8	9	10	11	12
19	-19.92	31.07	-22.39	-12.99	-16.71	-29.23	27.64	3.50	8.23	3.30	-8.95	-12.04	-2.66
20	-8.73	-19.92	31.07	-22.39	-12.99	-16.71	-29.23	27.64	3.50	8.23	3.30	-8.95	-12.04
21	1.26	-8.73	-19.92	31.07	-22.39	-12.99	-16.71	-29.23	27.64	3.50	8.23	3.30	-8.95
22	13.50	1.26	-8.73	-19.92	31.07	-22.39	-12.99	-16.71	-29.23	27.64	3.50	8.23	3.30
23	4.07	13.50	1.26	-8.73	-19.92	31.07	-22.39	-12.99	-16.71	-29.23	27.64	3.50	8.23
24	9.59	4.07	13.50	1.26	-8.73	-19.92	31.07	-22.39	-12.99	-16.71	-29.23	27.64	3.50
25	28.01	9.59	4.07	13.50	1.26	-8.73	-19.92	31.07	-22.39	-12.99	-16.71	-29.23	27.64
26	-35.81	28.01	9.59	4.07	13.50	1.26	-8.73	-19.92	31.07	-22.39	-12.99	-16.71	-29.23
27	12.56	-35.81	28.01	9.59	4.07	13.50	1.26	-8.73	-19.92	31.07	-22.39	-12.99	-16.71
28	-33.52	12.56	-35.81	28.01	9.59	4.07	13.50	1.26	-8.73	-19.92	31.07	-22.39	-12.99
29	-1.18	-33.52	12.56	-35.81	28.01	9.59	4.07	13.50	1.26	-8.73	-19.92	31.07	-22.39
30	6.76	-1.18	-33.52	12.56	-35.81	28.01	9.59	4.07	13.50	1.26	-8.73	-19.92	31.07
31	-18.89	6.76	-1.18	-33.52	12.56	-35.81	28.01	9.59	4.07	13.50	1.26	-8.73	-19.92
32	7.90	-18.89	6.76	-1.18	-33.52	12.56	-35.81	28.01	9.59	4.07	13.50	1.26	-8.73
33	-4.37	7.90	-18.89	6.76	-1.18	-33.52	12.56	-35.81	28.01	9.59	4.07	13.50	1.26
34	2.48	-4.37	7.90	-18.89	6.76	-1.18	-33.52	12.56	-35.81	28.01	9.59	4.07	13.50
35	-1.40	2.48	-4.37	7.90	-18.89	6.76	-1.18	-33.52	12.56	-35.81	28.01	9.59	4.07
36	41.20	-1.40	2.48	-4.37	7.90	-18.89	6.76	-1.18	-33.52	12.56	-35.81	28.01	9.59
37	48.15	41.20	-1.40	2.48	-4.37	7.90	-18.89	6.76	-1.18	-33.52	12.56	-35.81	28.01
38	13636.81634	-474.069	753.363	-229.306	-2223.642	1544.284	-2442.531	1790.525	-4382.609	-167.700	-1460.419	733.062	O2:O37)

Figure 8-24: SUMPRODUCT of lagged deviations with originals

You calculate the autocorrelation for a given month lag as the SUMPRODUCT of lagged deviations times original deviations divided by the sum of squared deviations in C38. For example, you can calculate the autocorrelation of a one-month lag in cell D40 as:

=D38/$C38

And dragging this across, you can get the autocorrelations for each lag.

Highlighting D40:O40, you can insert a bar chart into the sheet as shown in Figure 8-25 (Right-click and format the series' fill to be slightly transparent if you want to read the month labels under the negative values). This bar chart is called a *correlogram*, and it shows the autocorrelations for each month lag up to a year. (As a personal note, I think the word *correlogram* is really cool.)

All right. So which autocorrelations matter? Well, the convention is that you only worry about the autocorrelations larger than 2/sqrt(number of data points), which in this case is 2/sqrt(36) = 0.333. You should also care about ones with a negative autocorrelation less than -0.333.

You can just eyeball your chart for autocorrelations that are above or below these *critical values*. But it's typical in forecasting to plot some dashed lines at these critical values on the correlogram. For the sake of a pretty picture, I'll show you how to do that here.

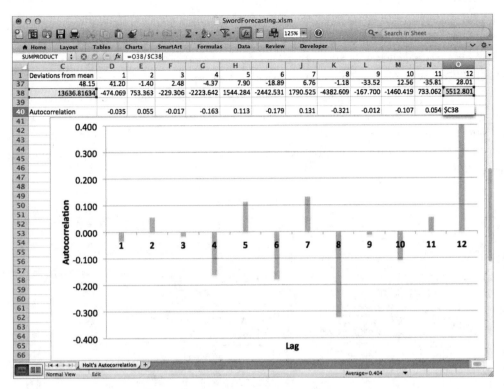

Figure 8-25: This is my correlogram; there are many like it but this is mine.

In D42, add =2/SQRT(36) and drag it across through O. Do the same in D43 only with the negative value =-2/SQRT(36) and drag that across through O. This gives you the critical points for the autocorrelations, as shown in Figure 8-26.

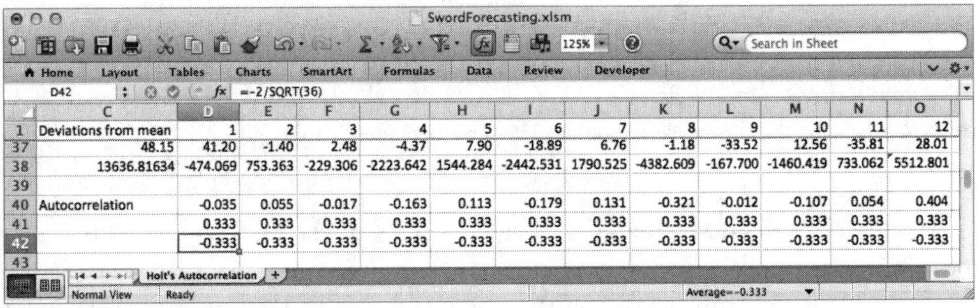

		C	D	E	F	G	H	I	J	K	L	M	N	O
			1	2	3	4	5	6	7	8	9	10	11	12
1		Deviations from mean												
37			48.15	41.20	-1.40	2.48	-4.37	7.90	-18.89	6.76	-1.18	-33.52	12.56	-35.81	28.01
38		13636.81634	-474.069	753.363	-229.306	-2223.642	1544.284	-2442.531	1790.525	-4382.609	-167.700	-1460.419	733.062	5512.801
39														
40		Autocorrelation	-0.035	0.055	-0.017	-0.163	0.113	-0.179	0.131	-0.321	-0.012	-0.107	0.054	0.404
41			0.333	0.333	0.333	0.333	0.333	0.333	0.333	0.333	0.333	0.333	0.333	0.333
42			-0.333	-0.333	-0.333	-0.333	-0.333	-0.333	-0.333	-0.333	-0.333	-0.333	-0.333	-0.333
43														

Average=-0.333

Figure 8-26: Critical points for the autocorrelations

Right-click the correlation bar chart and choose Select Data. From the window that appears, press the Add button to create a new series.

For one series select the range D42:O42 as the y-values. Add a third series using D43:O43. This will add two more sets of bars to the graph.

Right-clicking each of these new bar series, you can select Change Series Chart Type and select the Line chart to turn it into a solid line instead of bars. Right-click these lines and select Format Data Series. Then navigate to the Line (Line Style in some Excel versions) option in the window. In this section, you can set the line to dashed, as shown in Figure 8-27.

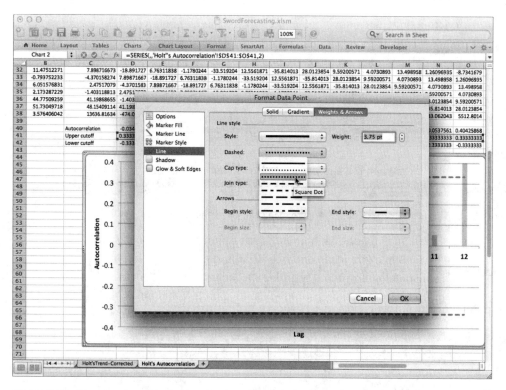

Figure 8-27: Changing the critical values for bars into a dashed line

This yields a correlogram with plotted critical values, as shown in Figure 8-28.

And what do you see?

There's exactly one autocorrelation that's above the critical value, and that's at 12 months.

The error shifted by a year is correlated with itself. That indicates a *12-month seasonal cycle.* This shouldn't be too surprising. If you look at the plot of the demand on the Timeseries tab, it's apparent that there are spikes each Christmas and dips around April/May.

You need a forecasting technique that can account for seasonality. And wouldn't you know it—there's an exponential smoothing technique for that.

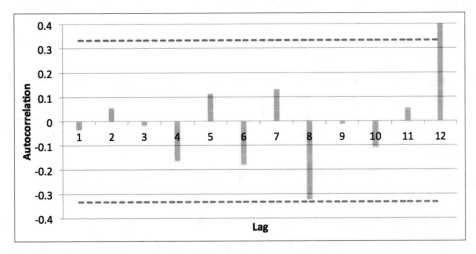

Figure 8-28: Correlogram with critical values

Multiplicative Holt-Winters Exponential Smoothing

Multiplicative Holt-Winters Smoothing is the logical extension of Holt's Trend-Corrected Smoothing. It accounts for a level, a trend, and the need to adjust the demand up or down on a regular basis due to seasonal fluctuations. Note that the seasonal fluctuation needn't be every 12 months like in this example. In the case of MailChimp, we have periodic demand fluctuations every Thursday (people seem to think Thursday is a good day to send marketing e-mail). Using Holt-Winters, we could account for this 7-day cycle.

Now, in most situations you can't just add or subtract a fixed amount of seasonal demand to adjust the forecast. If your business grows from selling 200 to 2,000 swords each month, you wouldn't adjust the Christmas demand in both those contexts by adding 20 swords. No, seasonal adjustments usually need to be multipliers. Instead of adding 20 swords maybe it's *multiplying* the forecast by 120 percent. That's why it's called *Multiplicative Holt-Winters*. Here's how this forecast conceives of demand:

> *Demand at time t = (level +t*trend) * seasonal adjustment for time t * whatever irregular adjustments are left we can't account for*

So you still have the identical level and trend structure you had in Holt's Trend-Corrected Smoothing, but the demand is adjusted for seasonality. And since you can't account for irregular variations in the demand, such as acts of God, you're not going to.

Holt-Winters is also called *triple exponential smoothing*, because, you guessed it, there are three smoothing parameters this time around. There are still *alpha* and *gamma* parameters, but this time you have a seasonal adjustment factor with an update equation and a factor called *delta*.

Now, the three error adjustment equations are slightly more complex than what you've seen so far, but you'll recognize bits.

Before you get started, I want to make one thing clear—so far you've used levels and trends from the previous period to forecast the next and adjust. But with seasonal adjustments, you don't look at the previous period. Instead, you look at the previous estimate of the adjustment factor for that point in the cycle. In this case, that's 12 periods prior rather than one.

That means that if you're at month 36 and you're forecasting three months forward to 39, that forecast is going to look like:

$$Forecast\ for\ month\ 39 = (level_{36}+3*trend_{36})*seasonality_{27}$$

Yep, you're seeing that $seasonality_{27}$ correctly. It's the most recent estimate for the March seasonal adjustment. You can't use $seasonality_{36}$, because that's for December.

All right, so that's how the future forecast works. Let's dig into the update equations, starting with the level. You need only an initial $level_0$ and $trend_0$, but you actually need *twelve* initial seasonality factors, $seasonality_{-11}$ through $seasonality_0$.

For example, the update equation for $level_1$ relies on an initial estimate of the January seasonality adjustment:

$$level_1 = level_0 + trend_0 + alpha * (demand_1 - (level_0 + trend_0)*seasonality_{-11})/seasonality_{-11}$$

You have lots of familiar components here in this level calculation. The current level is the previous level plus the previous trend (just as in double exponential smoothing) plus *alpha* times the one-step ahead forecast error ($demand_1 - (level_0 + trend_0)*seasonality_{-11}$), where the error gets a seasonal adjustment by being divided by $seasonality_{-11}$.

And so as you walk forward in time, the next month would be:

$$level_2 = level_1 + trend_1 + alpha * (demand_2 - (level_1 + trend_1)*seasonality_{-10})/seasonality_{-10}$$

So in general then the level is calculated as:

$$level_{current\ period} = level_{previous\ period} + trend_{previous\ period} + alpha * (demand_{current\ period} - (level_{previous\ period} + trend_{previous\ period})*seasonality_{last\ relevant\ period})/seasonality_{last\ relevant\ period}$$

The trend is updated in relation to the level in exactly the same way as in double exponential smoothing:

$$trend_{current\ period} = trend_{previous\ period} + gamma * alpha * (demand_{current\ period} - (level_{previous\ period} + trend_{previous\ period}) * seasonality_{last\ relevant\ period}) / seasonality_{last\ relevant\ period}$$

Just as in double exponential smoothing, the current trend is the previous trend plus *gamma* times the amount of error incorporated into the level update equation.

And now for the seasonal factor update equation. It's a lot like the trend update equation, except that it adjusts the last relevant seasonal factor using *delta* times the error that the level and trend updates *ignored*:

$$seasonality_{current\ period} = seasonality_{last\ relevant\ period} + delta * (1-alpha) * (demand_{current\ period} - (level_{previous\ period} + trend_{previous\ period}) * seasonality_{last\ relevant\ period}) / (level_{previous\ period} + trend_{previous\ period})$$

In this case you're updating the seasonality adjustment with the corresponding factor from 12 months prior, but you're folding in *delta* times whatever error was left on the cutting room floor from the level update. *Except*, note that rather than seasonally adjusting the error here, you're dividing through by the previous level and trend values. By "level and trend adjusting" the one-step ahead error, you're putting the error on the same multiplier scale as the seasonal factors.

Setting the Initial Values for Level, Trend, and Seasonality

Setting the initial values for SES and double exponential smoothing was a piece of cake. But now you have to tease out what's trend and what's seasonality from the time series. And that means that setting the initial values for this forecast (one level, one trend, and 12 seasonal adjustment factors) is a little tough. There are simple (and wrong!) ways of doing this. I'm going to show you a good way to initialize Holt-Winters, assuming you have at least two seasonal cycles' worth of historical data. In this case, you have three cycles' worth.

Here's what you're going to do:

1. Smooth out the historical data using what's called a 2×12 moving average.
2. Compare a smoothed version of the time series to the original to estimate seasonality.
3. Using the initial seasonal estimates, deseasonalize the historical data.
4. Estimate the level and trend using a trendline on the deseasonalized data.

To start, create a new tab called **HoltWintersInitial** and paste the time series data into its first two columns. Now you need to smooth out some of the time series data using a moving average. Because the seasonality is in 12-month cycles, it makes sense to use a 12-month moving average on the data.

What do I mean by a 12-month moving average?

For a moving average, you take the demand for a particular month as well as the demand around that month in both directions and average them. This tamps down any weird spikes in the series.

But there's a problem with a 12-month moving average. Twelve is an even number. If you're smoothing out the demand for month 7, should you average it as the demand of months 1 through 12 or the demand of months 2 through 13? Either way, month 7 isn't quite in the middle. There is no middle!

To accommodate this, you're going to smooth out the demand with a "2 × 12 moving average," which is the average of both those possibilities—months *1 through 12* and *2 through 13*. (The same goes for any other even number of time periods in a cycle. If your cycle has an odd number of periods, the "2x" part of the moving average is unnecessary and you can just do a simple moving average.)

Now note for the first six months of data and the last six months of data, this isn't even possible. They don't have six months of data on either side of them. You can only smooth the middle months of the dataset (in this case it's months 7–30). This is why you need at least two years' worth of data, so that you get one year of smoothed data.

So starting with month 7, use the following formula:

```
=(AVERAGE(B3:B14)+AVERAGE(B2:B13))/2
```

This is the average of month 7 with the 12 months around it, except that months 1 and 13 count for half of what the other months count for, which makes sense; since months 1 and 13 are in the same month if they were each counted twice then you'd have January over-represented in the moving average.

Dragging this formula down through month 30 and graphing both the original and smoothed data in a straight-line scatter plot, you get the sheet shown in Figure 8-29. In my chart I've labeled the two series smoothed and unsmoothed. It's apparent looking at the smoothed line that any seasonal variation present in the data has, more or less, been smoothed out.

Now, in column D, you can divide the original value by the smoothed value to get an estimate of the seasonal adjustment factor. Starting at month 7, you have for cell D8:

```
B8/C8
```

And you can drag this down through month 30. Note how in both months 12 and 24 (December) you get spikes around 20 percent of normal, whereas you get dips in the spring.

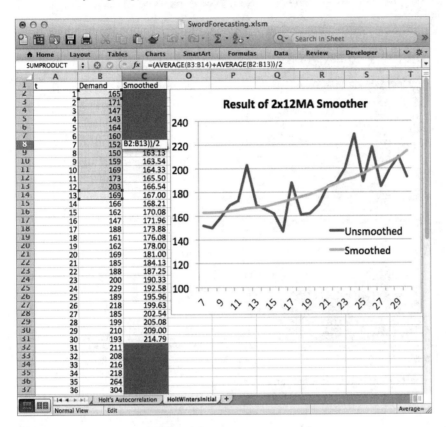

Figure 8-29: The smoothed demand data

This smoothing technique has given you two point estimates for each seasonality factor. In column E, let's average these two points together into a single value that will be the initial seasonal factor used in Holt-Winters.

For example, in E2, which is January, you average the two January points in column D, which are D14 and D26. Since the smoothed data starts in the middle of the year in column D, you can't drag this average down. In E8, which is July, you have to take the average of D8 and D20 for instance.

Once you have these 12 adjustment factors in column E, you can subtract 1 from each of them in column F and format the cells as percentages (highlight the range and right-click Format Cells) to see how these factors move the demand up or down each month. You can even insert a bar chart of these skews into the sheet, as shown in Figure 8-30.

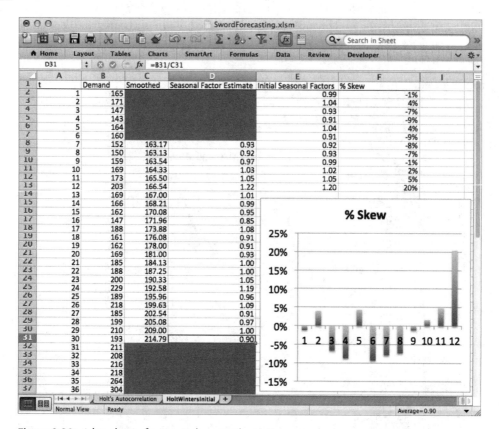

Figure 8-30: A bar chart of estimated seasonal variations

Now that you have these initial seasonal adjustments, you can use them to *deseasonalize* the time series data. Once the entire series is deseasonalized, you can toss a trendline through it and use the slope and intercept as the initial level and trend.

To start, paste the appropriate seasonal adjustment values for each month in G2 through G37. Essentially, you're just pasting E2:E13 three times in a row down column G (make sure to paste values only). In column H you can then divide the original series in column B by the seasonal factors in G to remove the estimated seasonality present in the data. This sheet is shown in Figure 8-31.

Next, as you've done on previous tabs, insert a scatter plot of column H and toss a trendline through it. Displaying the trendline equation on the graph, you get an initial trend estimate of 2.29 additional sword sales per month and an initial level estimate of 144.42 (see Figure 8-32).

t	Demand	Smoothed	Seasonal Factor Estimate	Initial Seasonal	% Skew	Initial Seasonal Factors x3	Deseasonalized Data
1	165			0.99	-1%	0.99	=B2/G2
2	171			1.04	4%	1.04	164.51
3	147			0.93	-7%	0.93	157.57
4	143			0.91	-9%	0.91	156.70
5	164			1.04	4%	1.04	157.24
6	160			0.91	-9%	0.91	176.51
7	152	163.17	0.93	0.92	-8%	0.92	165.07
8	150	163.13	0.92	0.93	-7%	0.93	161.88
9	159	163.54	0.97	0.99	-1%	0.99	160.85
10	169	164.33	1.03	1.02	2%	1.02	166.31
11	173	165.50	1.05	1.05	5%	1.05	165.07
12	203	166.54	1.22	1.20	20%	1.20	168.60
13	169	167.00	1.01			0.99	171.01
14	166	168.21	0.99			1.04	159.70
15	162	170.08	0.95			0.93	173.65
16	147	171.96	0.85			0.91	161.08
17	188	173.88	1.08			1.04	180.25
18	161	176.08	0.91			0.91	177.62
19	162	178.00	0.91			0.92	175.93
20	169	181.00	0.93			0.93	182.38
21	185	184.13	1.00			0.99	187.15
22	188	187.25	1.00			1.02	185.00
23	200	190.33	1.05			1.05	190.83
24	229	192.58	1.19			1.20	190.20
25	189	195.96	0.96			0.99	191.25
26	218	199.63	1.09			1.04	209.72
27	185	202.54	0.91			0.93	198.30
28	199	205.08	0.97			0.91	218.06
29	210	209.00	1.00			1.04	201.34
30	193	214.79	0.90			0.91	212.92
31	211					0.92	229.14
32	208					0.93	224.47
33	216					0.99	218.51
34	218					1.02	214.52
35	264					1.05	251.90
36	304					1.20	252.49

Figure 8-31: The deseasonalized time series

Getting Rolling on the Forecast

Now that you have the initial values for all the parameters, create a new tab called **HoltWintersSeasonal**, where you'll start by pasting the time series data on row 4 just as you did for the previous two forecasting techniques.

In columns C, D, and E next to the time series you're going to put the level, trend, and seasonal values, respectively. And in order to start, unlike on previous tabs where you only needed to insert one new blank row 5, this time around you need to insert blank rows 5 through 16 and label them as time slots -11 through 0 in column A. You can then paste the initial values from the previous tab in their respective spots, as shown in Figure 8-33.

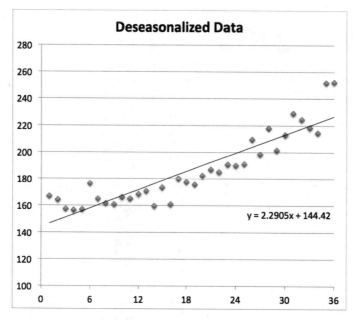

Figure 8-32: Initial level and trend estimates via a trendline on the deseasonalized series

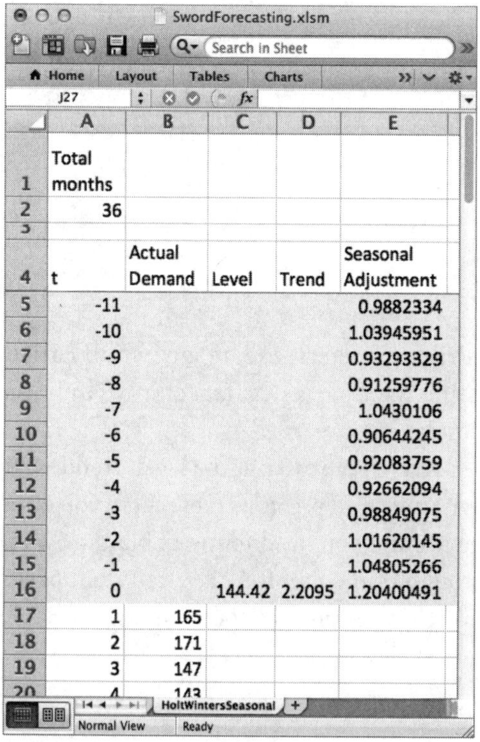

t	Actual Demand	Level	Trend	Seasonal Adjustment
-11				0.9882334
-10				1.03945951
-9				0.93293329
-8				0.91259776
-7				1.0430106
-6				0.90644245
-5				0.92083759
-4				0.92662094
-3				0.98849075
-2				1.01620145
-1				1.04805266
0		144.42	2.2095	1.20400491
1	165			
2	171			
3	147			
4	143			

Figure 8-33: All of the initial Holt-Winters values in one place

In column F you'll do a one-step ahead forecast. So for time period 1, it's the previous level in C16 plus the previous trend in D16. But both of those are adjusted by the appropriate January seasonality estimate 12 rows up in E5. Thus, F17 is written as:

```
=(C16+D16)*E5
```

The forecast error in G17 may then be calculated as:

```
=B17-F17
```

Now you're ready to get started with calculating the level, trend, and seasonality rolling forward. So in cells C2:E2, put the *alpha*, *gamma*, and *delta* values (as always I'm going to start with 0.5). Figure 8-34 shows the worksheet.

	A	B	C	D	E	F	G
1	Total months		Level smoothing parameter (alpha)	Trend smoothing parameter (gamma)	Seasonal smoothing parameter (delta)		
2	36		0.5	0.5	0.5		
3							
4	t	Actual Demand	Level	Trend	Seasonal Adjustment	One-step Forecast	Forecast Error
5	-11				0.9882334		
6	-10				1.03945951		
7	-9				0.93293329		
8	-8				0.91259776		
9	-7				1.0430106		
10	-6				0.90644245		
11	-5				0.92083759		
12	-4				0.92662094		
13	-3				0.98849075		
14	-2				1.01620145		
15	-1				1.04805266		
16	0		144.42	2.2095	1.20400491		
17	1	165				144.9042	20.0958
18	2	171					
19	3	147					
20	4	143					

Figure 8-34: Worksheet with smoothing parameters and first one-step forecast and error

The first item you'll calculate as you roll through the time periods is a new level estimate for period 1 in cell C17:

```
=C16+D16+C$2*G17/E5
```

Just as you saw in the previous section, the new level equals the previous level plus the previous trend plus *alpha* times the deseasonalized forecast error. And the updated trend in D17 is quite similar:

```
=D16+D$2*C$2*G17/E5
```

You have the previous trend plus *gamma* times the amount of deseasonalized error incorporated into the level update.

And for the January seasonal factor update you have:

```
=E5+E$2*(1-C$2)*G17/(C16+D16)
```

That's the previous January factor adjusted by *delta* times the error ignored by the level correction scaled like the seasonal factors by dividing through by the previous level and trend.

Note that in all three of these formulas *alpha*, *gamma*, and *delta* are referenced via absolute references, so that as you drag the calculations down they don't move. Dragging C17:G17 down through month 36, you get the sheet shown in Figure 8-35.

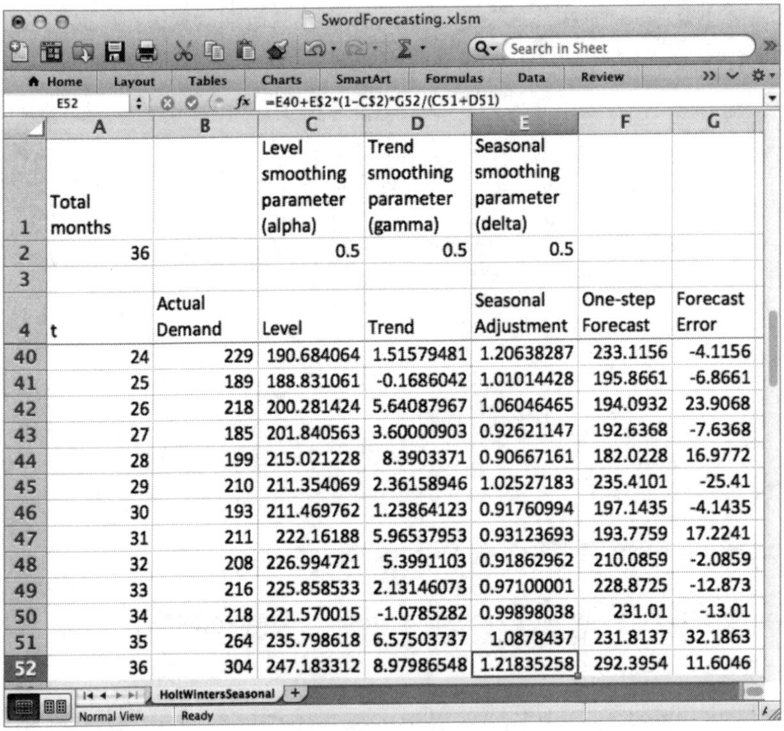

t	Actual Demand	Level	Trend	Seasonal Adjustment	One-step Forecast	Forecast Error
24	229	190.684064	1.51579481	1.20638287	233.1156	-4.1156
25	189	188.831061	-0.1686042	1.01014428	195.8661	-6.8661
26	218	200.281424	5.64087967	1.06046465	194.0932	23.9068
27	185	201.840563	3.60000903	0.92621147	192.6368	-7.6368
28	199	215.021228	8.3903371	0.90667161	182.0228	16.9772
29	210	211.354069	2.36158946	1.02527183	235.4101	-25.41
30	193	211.469762	1.23864123	0.91760994	197.1435	-4.1435
31	211	222.16188	5.96537953	0.93123693	193.7759	17.2241
32	208	226.994721	5.3991103	0.91862962	210.0859	-2.0859
33	216	225.858533	2.13146073	0.97100001	228.8725	-12.873
34	218	221.570015	-1.0785282	0.99898038	231.01	-13.01
35	264	235.798618	6.57503737	1.0878437	231.8137	32.1863
36	304	247.183312	8.97986548	1.21835258	292.3954	11.6046

Figure 8-35: Taking the update equations through month 36

And now that you have your final level, trend, and seasonal estimates, you can forecast the next year's worth of demand. Starting in month 37 in cell B53 you have:

```
=(C$52+(A53-A$52)*D$52)*E41
```

Just as in Holt's Trend-Corrected Smoothing, you're taking the last level estimate and adding to it the trend *times* the number of elapsed months since the most recent trend estimate. The only difference is you're scaling the whole forecast by the most up-to-date seasonal multiplier for January, which is in cell E41. And while the level in C$52 and the trend in D$52 use absolute references so that they won't shift as you drag the forecast down, the seasonal reference in E41 must move down as you drag the forecast through the next 11 months. And so, dragging the calculation down, you get the forecast shown in Figure 8-36.

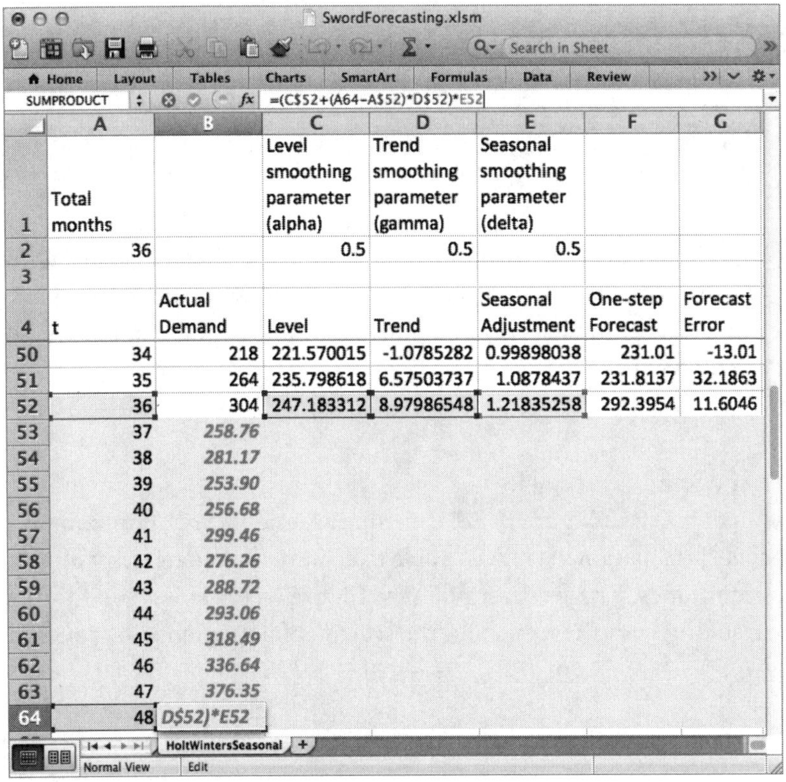

Figure 8-36: Getting the Holt-Winters forecast for future months

You can graph this forecast using Excel's straight-line scatter plot just as in the previous two techniques (see Figure 8-37).

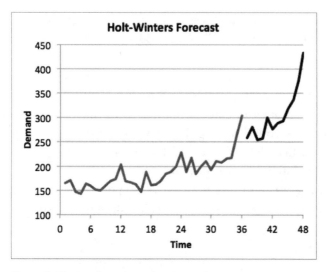

Figure 8-37: Graphing the Holt-Winters forecast

And...Optimize!

You thought you were done, but no. Time to set those smoothing parameters. So just as in the previous two techniques, toss the SSE in cell G2, and place the standard error in H2.

The only difference this time around is that you have three smoothing parameters, so the standard error is calculated as:

```
=SQRT(G2/(36-3))
```

This gives the sheet shown in Figure 8-38.

As for the Solver setup (shown in Figure 8-39), this time around you're optimizing H2 by varying the three smoothing parameters. You're able to achieve a standard error almost half that of previous techniques. The forecast plot (see Figure 8-40) looks good to the eye, doesn't it? You're tracking with the trend and the seasonal fluctuations. Very nice.

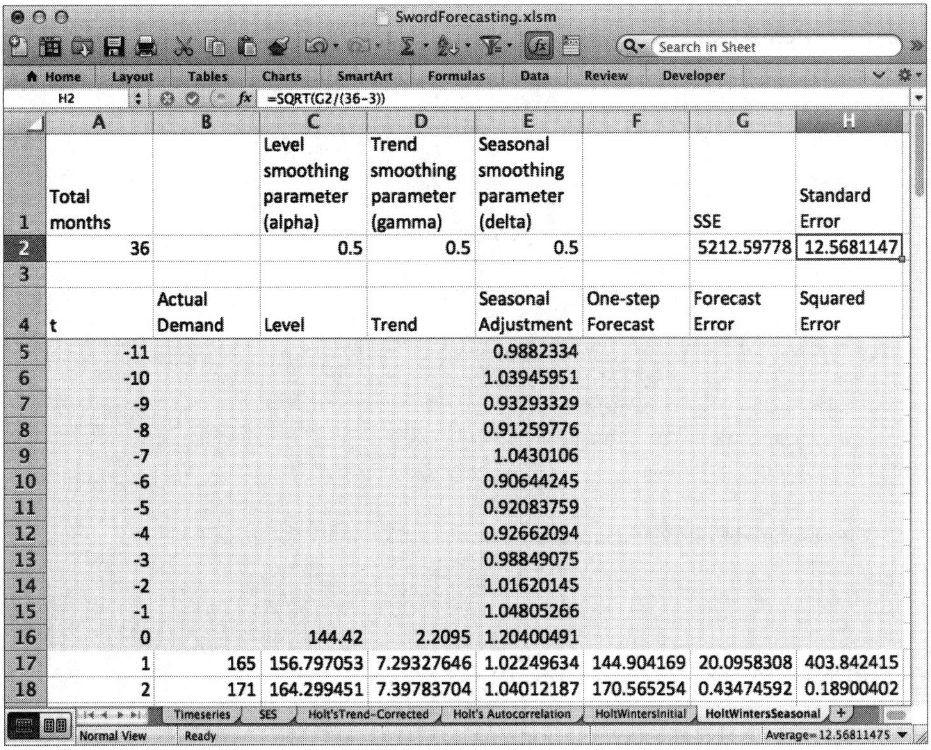

	A	B	C	D	E	F	G	H
1	Total months		Level smoothing parameter (alpha)	Trend smoothing parameter (gamma)	Seasonal smoothing parameter (delta)		SSE	Standard Error
2	36		0.5	0.5	0.5		5212.59778	12.5681147
3								
4	t	Actual Demand	Level	Trend	Seasonal Adjustment	One-step Forecast	Forecast Error	Squared Error
5	-11				0.9882334			
6	-10				1.03945951			
7	-9				0.93293329			
8	-8				0.91259776			
9	-7				1.0430106			
10	-6				0.90644245			
11	-5				0.92083759			
12	-4				0.92662094			
13	-3				0.98849075			
14	-2				1.01620145			
15	-1				1.04805266			
16	0		144.42	2.2095	1.20400491			
17	1	165	156.797053	7.29327646	1.02249634	144.904169	20.0958308	403.842415
18	2	171	164.299451	7.39783704	1.04012187	170.565254	0.43474592	0.18900402

Figure 8-38: Adding SSE and standard error

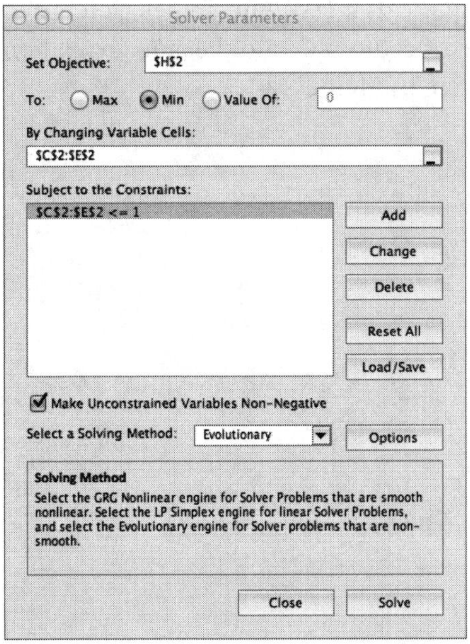

Figure 8-39: The Solver setup for Holt-Winters

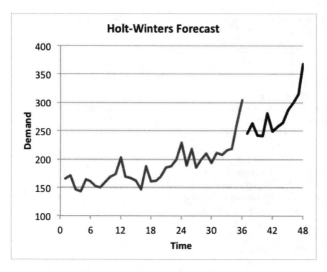

Figure 8-40: The optimized Holt-Winters forecast

Please Tell Me We're Done Now!!!

You now need to check the autocorrelations on this forecast. Since you've already set up the autocorrelation sheet, this time around you just need to make a copy of it and paste in the new error values.

Make a copy of the Holt's Autocorrelation tab and call it **HW Autocorrelation**. Then you need only paste special the values from the error column G into the autocorrelation sheet in column B. This gives the correlogram shown in Figure 8-41.

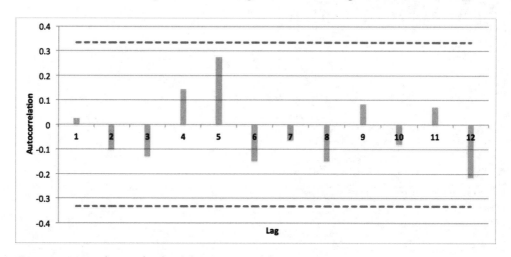

Figure 8-41: Correlogram for the Holt-Winters model

Bam! Since there are no autocorrelations above the critical value of 0.33, you know that the model is doing a nice job at capturing the structure in the demand values.

Putting a Prediction Interval around the Forecast

All right, so you have a forecast that fits well. How do you put some lower and upper bounds around it that you can use to set realistic expectations with the boss?

You're going to do this through Monte Carlo simulation, which you've already seen in Chapter 4. Essentially, you're going to generate future scenarios of what the demand might look like and determine the band that 95 percent of those scenarios fall into. The question is how do you even begin to simulate future demand? It's actually quite easy.

Start by making a copy of the HoltWintersSeasonal tab and calling it **PredictionIntervals**. Delete all the graphs in the tab. They're unnecessary. Furthermore, clear out the forecast in cells B53:B64. You'll be putting "actual" (but simulated) demand in those spots.

Now, like I said at the beginning of this chapter, the forecast is always wrong. There will always be error. But you know how this error will be distributed. You have a well-fitting forecast that you can assume has mean 0 one-step error (unbiased) with a standard deviation of 10.37, as calculated on the previous tab.

Just as in Chapter 4, you can generate a simulated error using the NORMINV function. In future months, you can just feed the NORMINV function the mean (0), the standard deviation (10.37 in cell H$2), and a random number between 0 and 1, and it'll pull an error from the bell curve. (See the discussion on cumulative distribution functions in Chapter 4 for more on how this works.)

Okay, so toss a simulated one-step error into cell G53:

```
=NORMINV(RAND(),0,H$2)
```

Drag it down through G64 to get 12 months of simulated errors in the one-step forecast. This gives you the sheet shown in Figure 8-42 (yours will have different simulated values from these).

But now that you have the forecast error, you have everything you need to update the level, trend, and seasonality estimates going forward as well as the one-step forecast. So grab cells C52:F52 and drag them down through row 64.

Here's where things get analytically badass. You now have a simulated forecast error and a one-step ahead forecast. So if you add the error in G to the forecast in F, you can actually back out a simulated demand for that time period.

Thus, B53 would simply be:

```
=F53+G53
```

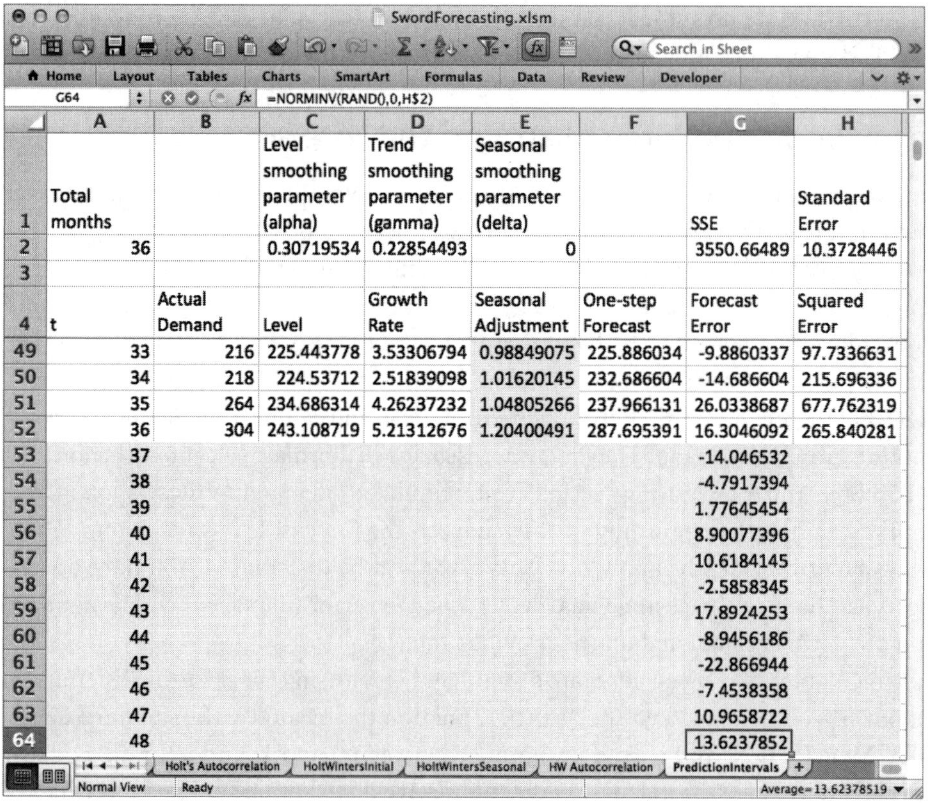

Figure 8-42: Simulated one-step errors

And you can drag that down through B64 to get all 12 months' demand values (see Figure 8-43).

Once you have that one scenario, by simply refreshing the sheet, the demand values change. So you can generate multiple future demand scenarios merely by copy-pasting one of the scenarios elsewhere and watching the sheet refresh itself.

To start then, label cell A69 as **Simulated Demand** and label A70:L70 as months 37 through 48. You can do this by copying A53:A64 and doing a paste special with transposed values into A70:L70.

Similarly, paste special the transposed values of the first demand scenario into A71:L71. To insert a second scenario, simply right-click row 71 and select Insert to insert a new blank row 71. Then paste special some more simulated demand values (they should have updated when you pasted the last set).

You can just keep doing this operation to generate as many future demand scenarios as you want. That's tedious though. Instead, you can record a quick macro.

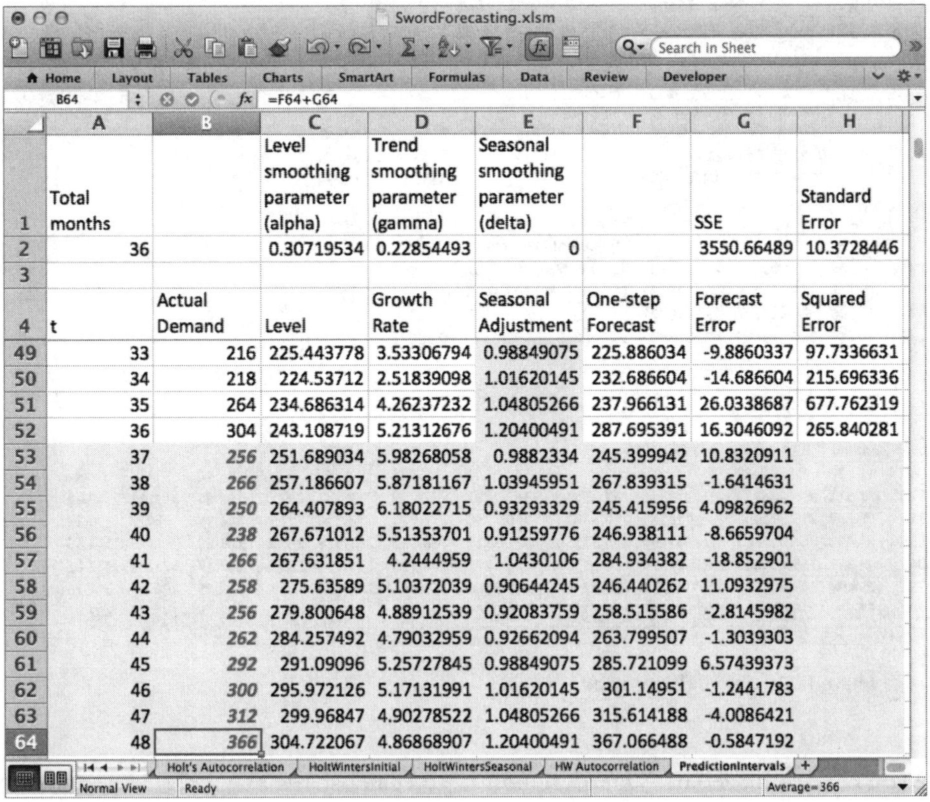

	A	B	C	D	E	F	G	H
1	Total months		Level smoothing parameter (alpha)	Trend smoothing parameter (gamma)	Seasonal smoothing parameter (delta)		SSE	Standard Error
2	36		0.30719534	0.22854493	0		3550.66489	10.3728446
3								
4	t	Actual Demand	Level	Growth Rate	Seasonal Adjustment	One-step Forecast	Forecast Error	Squared Error
49	33	216	225.443778	3.53306794	0.98849075	225.886034	-9.8860337	97.7336631
50	34	218	224.53712	2.51839098	1.01620145	232.686604	-14.686604	215.696336
51	35	264	234.686314	4.26237232	1.04805266	237.966131	26.0338687	677.762319
52	36	304	243.108719	5.21312676	1.20400491	287.695391	16.3046092	265.840281
53	37	256	251.689034	5.98268058	0.9882334	245.399942	10.8320911	
54	38	266	257.186607	5.87181167	1.03945951	267.839315	-1.6414631	
55	39	250	264.407893	6.18022715	0.93293329	245.415956	4.09826962	
56	40	238	267.671012	5.51353701	0.91259776	246.938111	-8.6659704	
57	41	266	267.631851	4.2444959	1.0430106	284.934382	-18.852901	
58	42	258	275.63589	5.10372039	0.90644245	246.440262	11.0932975	
59	43	256	279.800648	4.88912539	0.92083759	258.515586	-2.8145982	
60	44	262	284.257492	4.79032959	0.92662094	263.799507	-1.3039303	
61	45	292	291.09096	5.25727845	0.98849075	285.721099	6.57439373	
62	46	300	295.972126	5.17131991	1.01620145	301.14951	-1.2441783	
63	47	312	299.96847	4.90278522	1.04805266	315.614188	-4.0086421	
64	48	366	304.722067	4.86868907	1.20400491	367.066488	-0.5847192	

Figure 8-43: Simulated future demand

Just as in Chapter 7, record the following steps into a macro:

1. Insert a blank row 71.
2. Copy B53:B64.
3. Paste special transposed values into row 71.
4. Press the Stop recording button.

Once you've recorded those keystrokes, you can hammer on whatever macro shortcut key you selected (see Chapter 7) over and over until you get a ton of scenarios. You can even hold the shortcut key down—1,000 scenarios should do it. (If the idea of holding a button down is abhorrent to you, you can read up on how to put a loop around your macro code using Visual Basic for Applications. Just Google for it.)

When it's all said and done, your sheet should look like Figure 8-44.

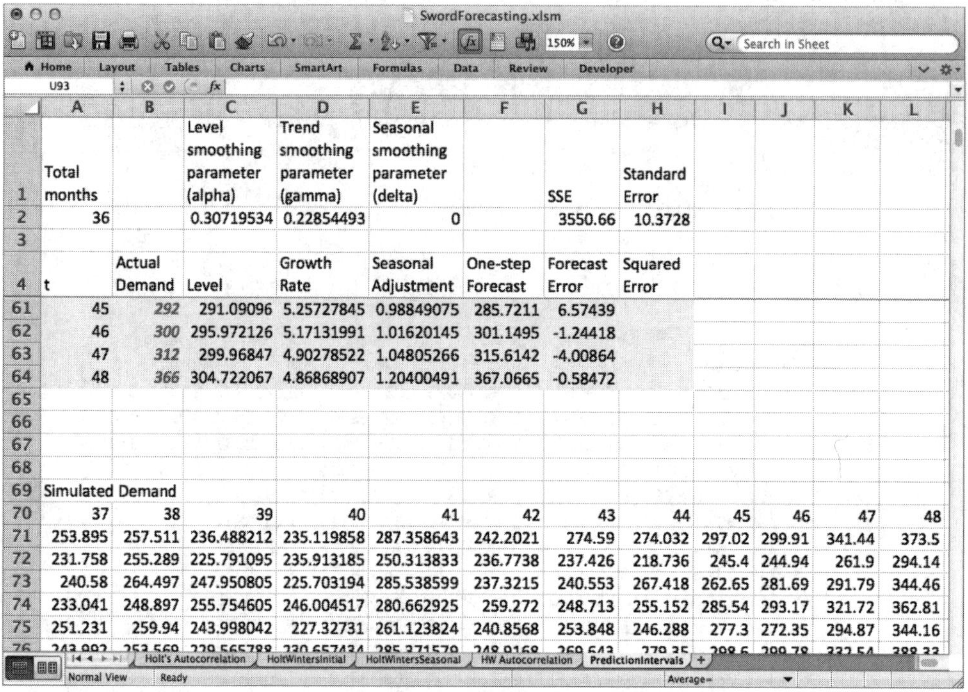

Figure 8-44: I have 1,000 demand scenarios

Once you have your scenarios for each month, you can use the PERCENTILE function to get the upper and lower bounds on the middle 95 percent of scenarios to create a prediction interval.

For instance, above month 37 in A66 you can place the formula:

```
=PERCENTILE(A71:A1070,0.975)
```

This gives you the 97.5th percentile of demand for this month. In my sheet it comes out to about 264. And in A67 you can get the 2.5th percentile as:

```
=PERCENTILE(A71:A1070,0.025)
```

Note that I'm using A71:A1070 because I have 1,000 simulated demand scenarios. You may have more or less depending on the dexterity of your index finger. For me, this lower bound comes out to around 224.

That means that although the forecast for month 37 is 245, the 95 percent prediction interval is 224 to 264.

You can drag these percentile equations across through month 48 in column L to get the entire interval (see Figure 8-45). So now you can provide your superiors with a conservative range plus a forecast if you like! And feel free to swap out the 0.025 and 0.975 with 0.05 and 0.95 for a 90 percent interval or with 0.1 and 0.9 for an 80 percent interval, and so on.

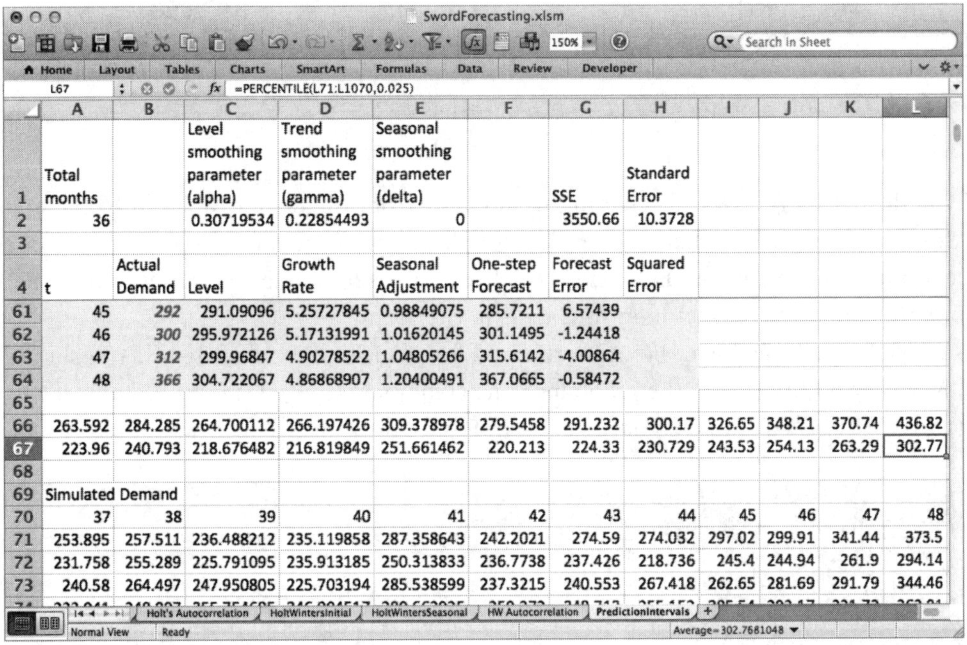
SwordForecasting.xlsm
L67
=PERCENTILE(L71:L1070,0.025)

	A	B	C	D	E	F	G	H	I	J	K	L
1	Total months		Level smoothing parameter (alpha)	Trend smoothing parameter (gamma)	Seasonal smoothing parameter (delta)		SSE	Standard Error				
2	36		0.30719534	0.22854493	0		3550.66	10.3728				
3												
4	t	Actual Demand	Level	Growth Rate	Seasonal Adjustment	One-step Forecast	Forecast Error	Squared Error				
61	45	292	291.09096	5.25727845	0.98849075	285.7211	6.57439					
62	46	300	295.972126	5.17131991	1.01620145	301.1495	-1.24418					
63	47	312	299.96847	4.90278522	1.04805266	315.6142	-4.00864					
64	48	366	304.722067	4.86868907	1.20400491	367.0665	-0.58472					
65												
66	263.592	284.285	264.700112	266.197426	309.378978	279.5458	291.232	300.17	326.65	348.21	370.74	436.82
67	223.96	240.793	218.676482	216.819849	251.661462	220.213	224.33	230.729	243.53	254.13	263.29	302.77
68												
69	Simulated Demand											
70	37	38	39	40	41	42	43	44	45	46	47	48
71	253.895	257.511	236.488212	235.119858	287.358643	242.2021	274.59	274.032	297.02	299.91	341.44	373.5
72	231.758	255.289	225.791095	235.913185	250.313833	236.7738	237.426	218.736	245.4	244.94	261.9	294.14
73	240.58	264.497	247.950805	225.703194	285.538599	237.3215	240.553	267.418	262.65	281.69	291.79	344.46

Holt's Autocorrelation
HoltWintersInitial
HoltWintersSeasonal
HW Autocorrelation
PredictionIntervals
Normal View
Ready
Average=302.7681048

Figure 8-45: The forecast interval for Holt-Winters

Creating a Fan Chart for Effect

Now, this last step isn't necessary, but forecasts with prediction intervals are often shown in something called a *fan chart*. You can create such a chart in Excel.

To start, create a new tab called **Fan Chart** and in that tab, paste months 37 through 48 on row 1 and then paste the values of the upper bound of the prediction interval from row 66 of the PredictionIntervals tab on row 2. On row 3, paste special the transposed values for the actual forecast from the HoltWintersSeasonal tab. And on row 4, paste the values of the lower bound of the prediction interval from row 67 of the intervals sheet.

So you have the months, the upper bound of the interval, the forecast, and the lower bound all right in a row (see Figure 8-46).

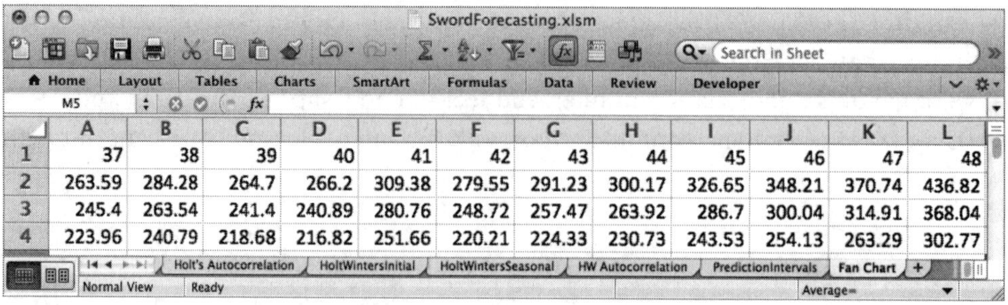

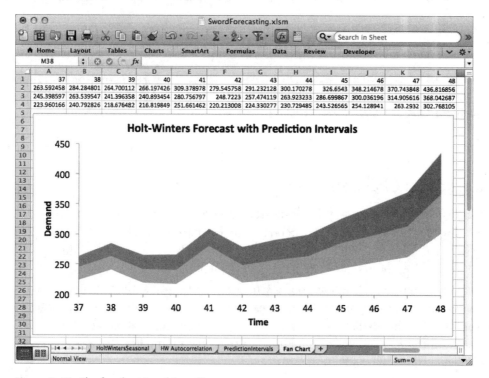

	A	B	C	D	E	F	G	H	I	J	K	L
1	37	38	39	40	41	42	43	44	45	46	47	48
2	263.59	284.28	264.7	266.2	309.38	279.55	291.23	300.17	326.65	348.21	370.74	436.82
3	245.4	263.54	241.4	240.89	280.76	248.72	257.47	263.92	286.7	300.04	314.91	368.04
4	223.96	240.79	218.68	216.82	251.66	220.21	224.33	230.73	243.53	254.13	263.29	302.77

Figure 8-46: The forecast sandwiched by the prediction interval

By highlighting A2:L4 and selecting Area Chart from the charts menu in Excel, you get three solid area charts laid over each other. Right-click one of the series and choose Select Data. You can change the Category (X) axis labels for one of the series to be A1:L1 in order to add in the correct monthly labels to the graph.

Now, right-click the lower bound series and format it to have a white fill. You should also remove grid lines from the graph for consistency's sake. Feel free to add axis labels and a title. This yields the fan chart shown in Figure 8-47.

	A	B	C	D	E	F	G	H	I	J	K	L
1	37	38	39	40	41	42	43	44	45	46	47	48
2	263.592458	284.284801	264.700112	266.197426	309.378978	279.545758	291.232128	300.170278	326.6543	348.214678	370.743848	436.816856
3	245.398597	263.539547	241.396358	240.893454	280.756797	248.7223	257.474119	263.923233	286.699867	300.036196	314.905616	368.042687
4	223.960166	240.792826	218.676482	216.819849	251.661462	220.213008	224.330277	230.729485	243.526565	254.128941	263.2932	302.768105

Figure 8-47: The fan chart is a thing of beauty

The cool thing about this fan chart is that it conveys both the forecast and the intervals in one simple picture. Heck, you could actually layer on an 80 percent interval too if you wanted more shades of gray. There are two interesting items that stand out in the chart:

- The error gets wider as time goes on. This makes sense. The uncertainty from month to month gets compounded.
- Similarly, there is more error in absolute terms during periods of high seasonal demand. When demand dips in a trough, the error bounds tighten up.

Wrapping Up

This chapter covered a ton of content:

- Simple exponential smoothing (SES)
- Performing a t test on a linear regression to verify a linear trend in the time series
- Holt's Trend-Corrected Exponential Smoothing
- Calculating autocorrelations and graphing a correlogram with critical values
- Initializing Holt-Winters Multiplicative Exponential Smoothing using a 2 x 12 moving average
- Forecasting with Holt-Winters
- Creating prediction intervals around the forecast using Monte Carlo simulation
- Graphing the prediction intervals as a fan chart

If you made it through the entire chapter, bravo. Seriously, that's a lot of forecasting for one chapter.

Now if you want to go further with forecasting, there are some excellent textbooks out there. I really like *Forecasting, Time Series, and Regression* by Bowerman et al. (Cengage Learning, 2004). Hyndman has a free forecasting textbook online at `http://otexts.com/fpp/`, and his blog (awesomely called "Hyndsight") is an excellent resource. For questions, `http://stats.stackexchange.com/` is the community to go to.

When it comes to forecasting in a production setting, there are countless products out there. For light jobs, feel free to stay in Excel. If you have tons of products or SKUs, using some code would be helpful.

SAS and R both have excellent packages for forecasting. The ones in R were written by Hyndman himself (see Chapter 10), who came up with the statistical underpinnings for how to do prediction intervals on the exponential smoothing techniques.

And that's it! I hope you now feel empowered to go forth and "organize your ignorance!"

9 Outlier Detection: Just Because They're Odd Doesn't Mean They're Unimportant

Outliers are the odd points in a dataset—the ones that don't fit somehow. Historically, that's meant *extreme* values, meaning quantities that were either too large or small to have come naturally from the same process as the other observations in the dataset.

The only reason people used to care about outliers was because they wanted to get rid of them. Statisticians a hundred years ago had a lot in common with the Borg: a data point needed to assimilate or die. However, this was done with good reason (in the case of the statistician)—outliers can move averages and mess with spread measurements in the data. A good example of outlier removal is in gymnastics, where the highest and lowest judges' scores are always trimmed from the data before taking the average score.

Outliers have a knack for messing up machine learning models. For example, in Chapters 6 and 7 you looked at predicting pregnant customers based on their purchase data. What if a store miscoded some items on the shelves of the pharmacy and were registering multi-vitamin purchases as folic acid purchases? The customers with those faulty purchase vectors are outliers that shift the relationship of pregnancy-to-folic-acid-purchasing in a way that harms the AI model's understanding.

Once upon a time when I consulted for the government, my company found a water storage facility that the United States had in Dubai that had been valued at billions and billions of dollars. The property value was an outlier that was throwing off the results of our analysis—turns out someone had typed it into the database with too many zeroes.

So that's one reason to care about outliers: *to facilitate cleaner data analysis and modeling.* But there's another reason to care about outliers. They're interesting for their own sake!

Outliers Are (Bad?) People, Too

Consider when your credit card company calls you after you make a transaction that is potentially fraudulent. What's your credit card company doing? They're detecting that transaction as being an outlier based on your past behavior. Rather than ignoring the transaction because it's an outlier, they're purposefully flagging the potential fraud and acting on it.

At MailChimp when we predict spammers before they send, we're predicting outliers. These spammers are a small group of people whose behavior lies outside of what we as a company consider normal. We use supervised models similar to those in Chapters 6 and 7 to predict based on past occurrences when a new user is going to send spam.

So in the case of MailChimp, then, an outlier is no more than a small but understood class of data in the population that can be predicted using training data. But what about the cases when you don't know what you're looking for? Like those mislabeled folic acid shoppers? Fraudsters often change their behavior so that the only thing you can expect from them is something unexpected. If that error has never happened before, how do you find those odd points for the first time?

This type of outlier detection is an example of *unsupervised learning* and data mining. It's the intuitive flip side of the analysis performed in Chapters 2 and 5 of this book where you detected clusters of points. In cluster analysis, you look for a data point's group of friends and analyze that group. In outlier detection, you care about data points that differ from the groups. They're odd or exceptional in some way.

This chapter starts with a simple, standard way of calculating outliers in normal-like one-dimensional data. Then it moves on to using k nearest neighbor (kNN) graphs to detect outliers in multidimensional data, similar to how you used r-neighborhood graphs to create clusters in Chapter 5.

The Fascinating Case of Hadlum v. Hadlum

> **NOTE**
>
> The Excel workbook used in this section, "Pregnancy Duration.xlsx," is available for download at the book's website at www.wiley.com/go/datasmart. Later in this chapter, you'll be diving into a larger spreadsheet, "SupportCenter.xlsx," also available on the same website.

Back in the 1940s, a British guy named Mr. Hadlum went off to war. Some days later, 349 of them in fact, his wife Mrs. Hadlum gave birth. Now, the average pregnancy lasts about 266 days. That places Mrs. Hadlum almost 12 weeks *past* her due date. I can't think of a single woman who'd stand for that added discomfort these days, but back then, inducing pregnancy wasn't as common.

Now, Mrs. Hadlum claimed she had nothing more than an exceptionally long pregnancy. Fair enough.

But Mr. Hadlum concluded her pregnancy must have been the result of another man while he'd been away—that a 349-day pregnancy was an anomaly that couldn't be justified given the distribution of typical birth durations.

So, if you had some pregnancy data, what's a quick-and-dirty way to decide whether Mrs. Hadlum's pregnancy should be considered an outlier?

Well, studies have found that gestation length is more or less a normally distributed random variable with a mean of 266 days after conception, with a standard deviation of about 9. So you can evaluate the normal cumulative distribution function (CDF) introduced in Chapter 4 to get the probability of a value less than 349 occurring. In Excel, this is evaluated using the NORMDIST function:

```
=NORMDIST(349,266,9,TRUE)
```

The NORMDIST function is supplied with the value whose cumulative probability you want, the mean, the standard deviation, and a flag set to TRUE, which sets the function to provide the cumulative value.

This formula returns a value of 1.000 all the way out as far as Excel tracks decimals. This means that nearly all babies born from here to eternity are going to be born at or under 349 days. Subtracting this value from 1:

```
=1-NORMDIST(349,266,9,TRUE)
```

You get 0.0000000 as far as the eye can see. In other words, it's nearly impossible for a human baby to gestate this long.

We'll never know for sure, but I'd bet good money Mrs. Hadlum had a little something else going on. Funny thing is, the court ruled in her favor, stating that such a long pregnancy, although highly unlikely, was still possible.

Tukey Fences

This concept of outliers being unlikely points when sampled from the bell curve has led to a rule of thumb for outlier detection called *Tukey fences*. Tukey fences are easy to check and easy to code. They are used by statistical packages the world over for identifying and removing spurious data points from any set of data that fits in a normal bell curve.

Here's the Tukey fences technique in its entirety:

- Calculate the 25th and 75th percentiles in any dataset you'd like to find outliers in. These values are also called the *first quartile* and the *third quartile*. Excel calculates values these using the PERCENTILE function.
- Subtract the first quartile from the third quartile to get a measure of the spread of the data, which is called the *Interquartile Range (IQR)*. The IQR is cool because it's

relatively robust against extreme values as a measure of spread, unlike the typical standard deviation calculation you've used to measure spread in previous chapters of this book.

- Subtract 1.5*IQR from the first quartile to get the *lower inner fence*. Add 1.5*IQR to the third quartile to get the *upper inner fence*.
- Likewise, subtract 3*IQR from the first quartile to get the *lower outer fence*. Add 3*IQR to the third quartile to get the *upper outer fence*.
- Any value less than a lower fence or greater than an upper fence is extreme. In normally distributed data, you'd see about 1 in every 100 points outside the inner fence, but only 1 in every 500,000 points outside the outer fence.

Applying Tukey Fences in a Spreadsheet

I've included a sheet called PregnancyDuration.xlsx for download off the book's website so that you can apply this technique to some actual data. If you open it, you'll see a tab called Pregnancies, with a sample of 1,000 durations in column A.

Mrs. Hadlum's gestation period of 349 days is in cell A2. In column D, place all of the summary statistics and fences. Start with the median (the middle value), which is a more robust statistic of centrality than the average value (averages can be skewed by outliers).

Label C1 as **Median** and in D1, calculate the median as follows:

```
=PERCENTILE(A2:A1001,0.5)
```

That would be the 50th percentile. Below the median, you can calculate the first and third quartiles as:

```
=PERCENTILE(A2:A1001,0.25)
=PERCENTILE(A2:A1001,0.75)
```

And the interquartile range is the difference between them:

```
=D3-D2
```

Tacking on 1.5 and 3 times the IQR to the first and third quartile respectively, you can then calculate all the fences:

```
=D2-1.5*D4
=D3+1.5*D4
=D2-3*D4
=D3+3*D4
```

If you label all these values, you'll get the sheet shown in Figure 9-1.

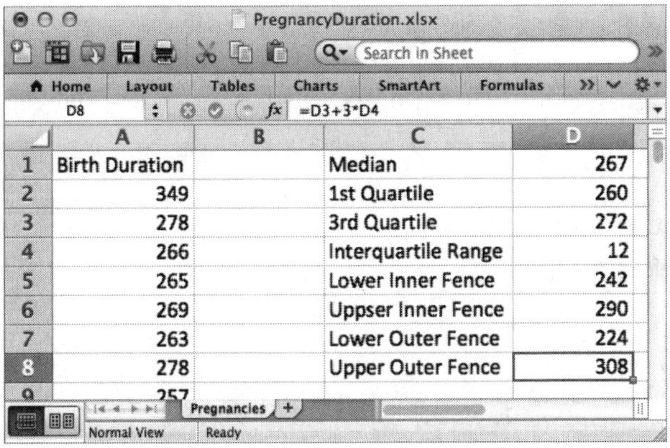

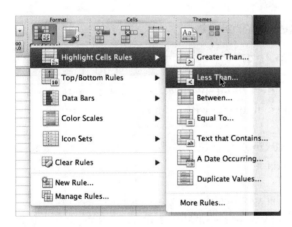

Figure 9-1: Tukey fences for some pregnancy durations

Now you can apply some conditional formatting to the sheet and see who falls outside these fences. Start with the inner fence. To highlight the extreme values, select Conditional Formatting from the Home tab, choose Highlight Cells Rules, and select Less Than, as shown in Figure 9-2.

Figure 9-2: Adding conditional formatting for outliers

Specifying the lower inner fence, feel free to choose a highlight color that tickles your fancy (I'm going to choose a yellow fill for inner fences and a red for outer, because I like traffic lights). Similarly, add formatting for the other three fences (if you're using Excel 2011 for the Mac you can use the Not Between rule to add the formatting with two rules rather than four).

As shown in Figure 9-3, Mrs. Hadlum turns red, meaning her pregnancy was radically extreme. Scrolling down, you'll find no other red pregnancies, but there are nine yellows. This matches up closely with the roughly 1 out of 100 points you'd expect to be flagged in normal data by the rule.

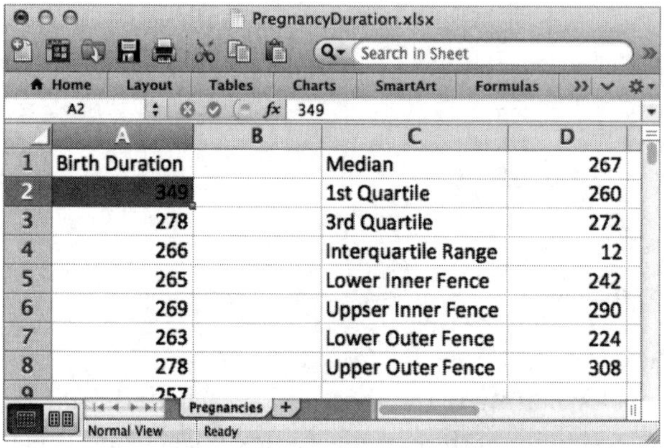

	A	B	C	D
1	Birth Duration		Median	267
2	349		1st Quartile	260
3	278		3rd Quartile	272
4	266		Interquartile Range	12
5	265		Lower Inner Fence	242
6	269		Uppser Inner Fence	290
7	263		Lower Outer Fence	224
8	278		Upper Outer Fence	308
9	257			

Figure 9-3: Uh oh, Mrs. Hadlum. What say you to this conditional formatting?

The Limitations of This Simple Approach

Tukey fences work only when three things are true:

- The data is vaguely normally distributed. It doesn't have to be perfect, but it should be Bell-curve shaped and hopefully symmetric without some long tail jutting out one side of it.
- The definition of an outlier is an extreme value on the perimeter of a distribution.
- You're looking at one-dimensional data.

Let's look at an example of an outlier that violates the first two of these assumptions.

In *The Fellowship of the Ring*, when the adventurers finally form a single company (the fellowship for which the book is named), they all stand in a little group as the leader of the elves, Elrond, pronounces who they are and what their mission is.

This group contains four tall people: Gandalf, Aragorn, Legolas, and Boromir. There are also four short people. The hobbits themselves: Frodo, Merry, Pippin, and Sam.

And in between them, there's a single dwarf: Gimli. Gimli is shorter than the men by a couple heads and taller than the hobbits by about the same (see Figure 9-4).

In the movie, when we see this group presented to us for the first time, Gimli is the clear outlier by height. He belongs to neither group.

Figure 9-4: Gimli, son of Gloin, Dwarven outlier

But how is he the outlier? His height is neither the least nor the greatest. In fact, his height is the closest to the average of the group's.

You see, this height distribution isn't anywhere near normal. If anything, you could call it "multi-modal" (a distribution with multiple peaks). And Gimli is an outlier not because his height is extreme, but because it's between these two peaks. And these types of data points can be even harder to spot when you're looking over several dimensions.

This kind of outlier crops up in fraud pretty frequently. Someone who's *too ordinary* to actually *be ordinary*. Bernie Madoff is a great example of this. Although most Ponzi schemes offer outlier rates of return of 20-plus percent, Madoff offered reliably modest returns that blended into the noise each year—he wasn't jumping any Tukey fences. But across years, his multiyear returns in their reliability became a multi-dimensional outlier.

So how do you find outliers in the case of multi-model, multi-dimensional data (you just as easily could call it "real-world data")?

One awesome way to approach this is to treat the data like a graph, just as you did in Chapter 5 to find clusters in the data. Think about it. What defines Gimli as an outlier is his relationship to the other data points; his distance from them in relation to their distance from each other.

All of those distances, each point from every other point, defines edges on a graph. Using this graph, you can tease out the isolated points. To do that, you start by creating a k nearest neighbor (kNN) graph and going from there.

Terrible at Nothing, Bad at Everything

For this next section, imagine that you manage a large customer support call center. Each call, e-mail, or chat from a customer creates a ticket, and each member of the support team is required to handle at least 140 tickets daily. At the end of each interaction, a customer is given the opportunity to rate the support employee on a five-star scale. Support staff are required to keep an average rating above 2, or they are fired.

High standards, I know.

The company keeps track of plenty of other metrics on each employee as well. How many times they've been tardy over the past year. How many graveyard and weekend shifts they've taken for the team. How many sick days they've taken, and out of those, how many have been on Friday. The company even tracks how many hours the employee uses to take internal training courses (they get up to 40 hours paid) and how many times they've put in a request for a shift swap or been a good Samaritan and fulfilled another employee's request.

You have all this data for all 400 call center employees in a spreadsheet. And the question is which employees are outliers, and what do they teach you about being a call center employee? Are there some baddies slipping through who don't get culled by the ticket requirements and minimum customer ratings? Perhaps the outliers will teach you how to write better rules.

If you open the spreadsheet for this section of the chapter (SupportCenter.xlsx available for download on the book's website at `www.wiley.com/go/datasmart`), you'll find all this tracked performance data on the SupportPersonnel sheet (see Figure 9-5).

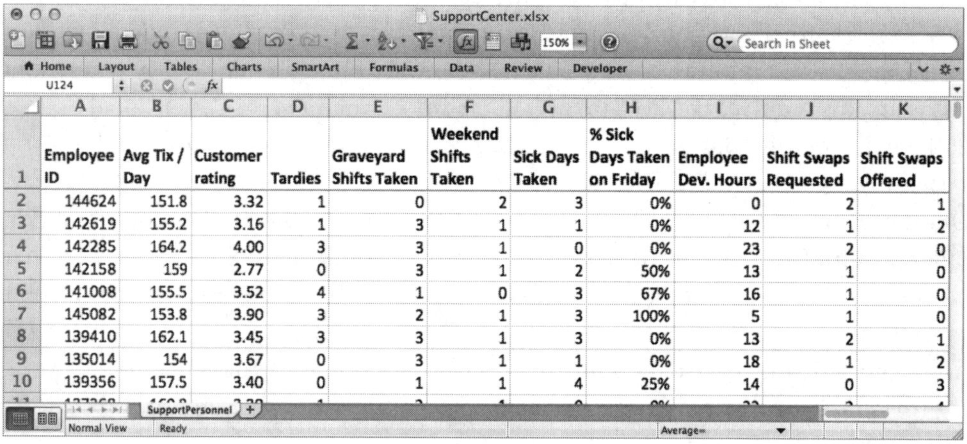

Employee ID	Avg Tix / Day	Customer rating	Tardies	Graveyard Shifts Taken	Weekend Shifts Taken	Sick Days Taken	% Sick Days Taken on Friday	Employee Dev. Hours	Shift Swaps Requested	Shift Swaps Offered
144624	151.8	3.32	1	0	2	3	0%	0	2	1
142619	155.2	3.16	1	3	1	1	0%	12	1	2
142285	164.2	4.00	3	3	1	0	0%	23	2	0
142158	159	2.77	0	3	1	2	50%	13	1	0
141008	155.5	3.52	4	1	0	3	67%	16	1	0
145082	153.8	3.90	3	2	1	3	100%	5	1	0
139410	162.1	3.45	3	3	1	3	0%	13	2	1
135014	154	3.67	0	3	1	1	0%	18	1	2
139356	157.5	3.40	0	1	1	4	25%	14	0	3

Figure 9-5: Multi-dimensional employee performance data

Preparing Data for Graphing

There's a problem with this performance data. You can't measure the distance between employees in order to figure out who's "on the outside" when each column is scaled so differently. What does it mean to have a difference of 5 between two employees on their average tickets versus a difference of 0.2 in customer rating? You need to *standardize* each column so that the values are closer to the same center and spread.

The way that columns of data are usually standardized is:

1. Subtract the mean of a column from each observation.
2. Divide each observation by the standard deviation of the column.

For normally distributed data, this centers the data at 0 (gives it a mean of 0) and gives it a standard deviation of 1. Indeed, a normal distribution with mean 0 and standard deviation 1 is called the *standard normal distribution.*

STANDARDIZING USING ROBUST MEASURES OF CENTRALITY AND SCALE

Not all data you'll want to scale is normally distributed to begin with. Subtracting out the mean and dividing through by the standard deviation tends to work well anyway. But outliers can screw up mean and standard deviation calculations, so sometimes folks like to standardize by subtracting more robust statistics of centrality (the "middle" of the data) and dividing through by more robust measures of scale/statistical dispersion (the spread of the data).

Here are some centrality calculations that work better against one-dimensional outliers than the mean:

- Median—Yep, just the 50th percentile
- Midhinge—The average of the 25th and 75th percentiles
- Trimean—The average of the median and the midhinge. I like this one, because it sounds intelligent.
- Trimmed/truncated mean—The mean, but you throw away the top and bottom N points or top and bottom percentage of points. You see this one in sports a lot (think gymnastics where they throw out the top and bottom scores). If you throw away the top and bottom 25 percent and average the middle 50 percent of the data, that has its own name: the interquartile mean (IQM).
- Winsorized mean—Like the trimmed mean, but instead of throwing away points that are too large or too small, you replace them with a limit.

As for robust measures of scale, here are some others worth using instead of the standard deviation:

- Interquartile range—You saw this one earlier in the chapter. It's just the 75th percentile minus the 25th percentile in the data. You can use other *n*-tiles too. For example, if you use the 90th and 10th percentiles, you get the interdecile range.
- Median absolute deviation (MAD)—Take the median of the data. Then take the absolute value of the difference of each point from the median. The median of these deviations is the MAD. It's kinda like the median's answer to the standard deviation.

To start then, calculate the mean and standard deviation of each column at the bottom of the SupportPersonnel sheet. The first value you'll want in B402 is the mean of the tickets taken per day, which you can write as:

```
=AVERAGE(B2:B401)
```

And below that you take the standard deviation of the column as:

```
=STDEV(B2:B401)
```

Copying those two formulas through column K, you get the sheet shown in Figure 9-6.

Employee ID	Avg Tix / Day	Customer rating	Tardies	Graveyard Shifts Taken	Weekend Shifts Taken	Sick Days Taken	% Sick Days Taken on Friday	Employee Dev. Hours	Shift Swaps Requested	Shift Swaps Offered
141343	159.1	3.60	4	1	0	0	0%	17	0	2
143981	160.3	3.70	1	2	1	0	0%	1	2	4
139820	162.6	3.37	2	3	1	1	100%	6	1	3
144780	159.6	3.50	1	2	1	2	0%	15	1	1
138420	155.4	4.29	3	3	1	2	50%	18	1	3
131547	150.7	3.99	1	2	1	4	25%	30	2	3
137942	160.6	3.87	1	1	1	2	100%	16	1	0
Mean	156.086	3.50	1.465	1.985	0.9525	1.875	35%	11.97	1.4475	1.76
Std. Dev.	4.41664	0.46	0.9727	0.79457749	0.548631	1.673732	39%	7.4708523	0.99987155	1.8126263

Figure 9-6: Mean and standard deviation for each column

Create a new tab called **Standardized** and copy the column labels from row 1 as well as the employee IDs from column A. You can start standardizing the values in cell B2 using Excel's STANDARDIZE formula. This formula just takes the original value, a center, and a spread measure and returns the value with the center subtracted out divided by the spread. So in B2 you would have:

```
=STANDARDIZE(SupportPersonnel!B2,
         SupportPersonnel!B$402,SupportPersonnel!B$403)
```

Note that you're using absolute references on the rows only for the mean and standard deviation, so that they stay put when you copy the formula down. However, when you copy the formula across, the column will change.

Copy and paste B2 across through K2, highlight the range, and then double-click it to send the calculations down through K401. This yields the standardized set of data shown in Figure 9-7.

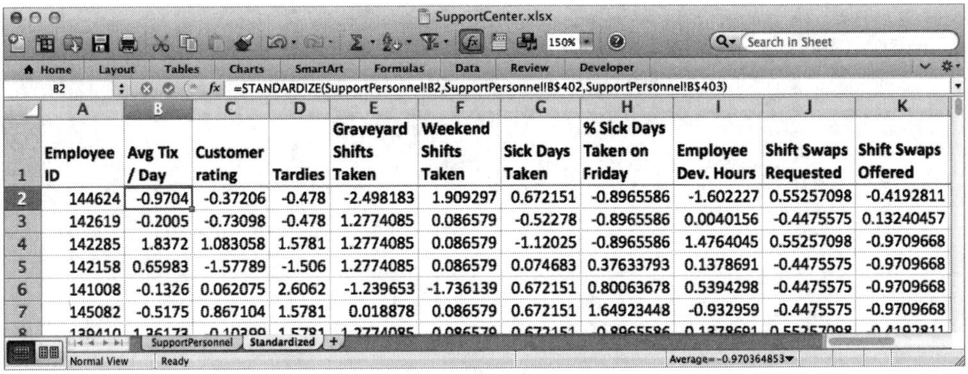

	A	B	C	D	E	F	G	H	I	J	K
1	Employee ID	Avg Tix / Day	Customer rating	Tardies	Graveyard Shifts Taken	Weekend Shifts Taken	Sick Days Taken	% Sick Days Taken on Friday	Employee Dev. Hours	Shift Swaps Requested	Shift Swaps Offered
2	144624	-0.9704	-0.37206	-0.478	-2.498183	1.909297	0.672151	-0.8965586	-1.602227	0.55257098	-0.4192811
3	142619	-0.2005	-0.73098	-0.478	1.2774085	0.086579	-0.52278	-0.8965586	0.0040156	-0.4475575	0.13240457
4	142285	1.8372	1.083058	1.5781	1.2774085	0.086579	-1.12025	-0.8965586	1.4764045	0.55257098	-0.9709668
5	142158	0.65983	-1.57789	-1.506	1.2774085	0.086579	0.074683	0.37633793	0.1378691	-0.4475575	-0.9709668
6	141008	-0.1326	0.062075	2.6062	-1.239653	-1.736139	0.672151	0.80063678	0.5394298	-0.4475575	-0.9709668
7	145082	-0.5175	0.867104	1.5781	0.018878	0.086579	0.672151	1.64923448	-0.932959	-0.4475575	-0.9709668

Figure 9-7: The standardized set of employee performance data

Creating a Graph

A graph is nothing more than some nodes and edges. In this case, each employee is a node, and to start, you can just draw edges between everybody. The length of the edge is the Euclidean distance between the two employees using their standardized performance data.

As you saw in Chapter 2, the Euclidean (as-the-crow-flies) distance between two points is the square root of the sum of the squared differences of each column value for the two.

In a new sheet called **Distances**, create an employee-by-employee distance matrix in the exact same way as in Chapter 2, by using the `OFFSET` formula.

To start, number the employees 0 through 399 starting at A3 going down and at C1 going across. (Tip: Type **0**, **1**, and **2** in the first three cells and then highlight those cells and drag down or across. Excel will fill in the rest for you, because it's smart like that.) Next to these offset values, paste the employee IDs (Paste Special values transposed for the columns). This creates the empty matrix shown in Figure 9-8.

To fill in this matrix, let's start in the first distance cell C3. This is the distance between employee 144624 and themselves.

Now, for all these distance calculations, you're going to use the `OFFSET` formula anchored on the first row of standardized employee data:

```
OFFSET(Standardized!$B$2:$K$2,Some number of rows, 0 columns)
```

In the case of cell C3, `Standardized!$B$2:$K$2` is the actual row you want for employee 144624, so you can take the differences between this employee and themselves using the offset formula as:

```
OFFSET(Standardized!$B$2:$K$2,Distances!$A3,0)-
OFFSET(Standardized!$B$2:$K$2,Distances!C$1,0)
```

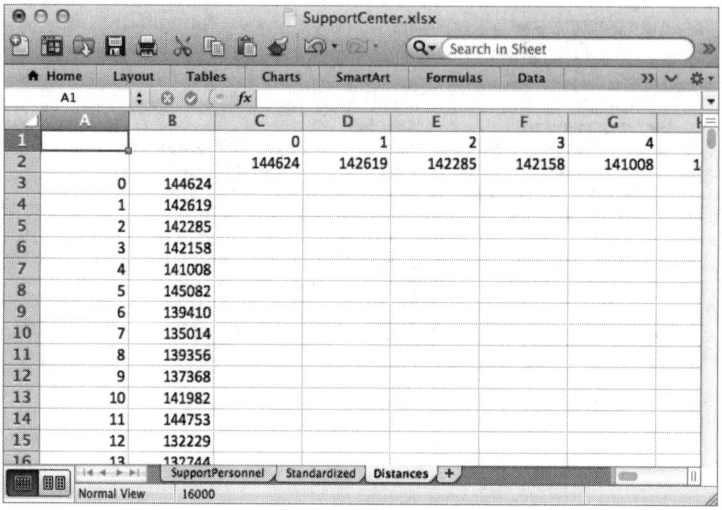

Figure 9-8: Empty employee distance matrix

In the first offset formula, you're moving rows using the value in $A3, while in the second offset formula you use the value in C$1 to move the OFFSET formula to another employee. Absolute references are used on these values in the appropriate places so that as you copy the formula around the sheet, you're still reading row offsets from column A and row 1.

This difference calculation needs to be squared, summed, and then square rooted to get the full Euclidean distance:

```
{=SQRT(SUM((OFFSET(Standardized!$B$2:$K$2,Distances!$A3,0)
  -OFFSET(Standardized!$B$2:$K$2,Distances!C$1,0))^2))}
```

Note that this calculation is an array formula due to the difference of entire rows from each other. So you have to press Ctrl+Shift+Enter (Command+Return on a Mac) to make it work.

The Euclidean distance of employee 144624 from his/herself is, naturally, 0. This formula can be copy and pasted through OL2. Then highlight this range and double-click the bottom corner to send the calculation down through cell OL402. This gives you the sheet shown in Figure 9-9.

And that's it! Now you have an employee-by-employee graph. You could export it to Gephi like you did in Chapter 5 and take a peak at it, but since it has 16,000 edges and only 400 nodes, it would be a mess.

Similarly to how in Chapter 5 you constructed an r-neighborhood graph out of the distance matrix, in this chapter you're going to focus on only the nearest k neighbors of each employee in order to find the outliers.

The first step is ranking the distance of each employee in relation to each other employee. This ranking will yield the first and most basic method for highlighting outliers on the graph.

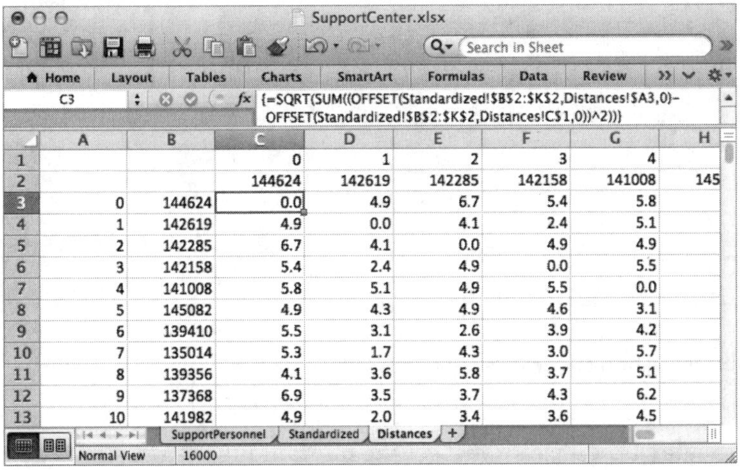

	A	B	C	D	E	F	G	H
1			0	1	2	3	4	
2			144624	142619	142285	142158	141008	145
3	0	144624	0.0	4.9	6.7	5.4	5.8	
4	1	142619	4.9	0.0	4.1	2.4	5.1	
5	2	142285	6.7	4.1	0.0	4.9	4.9	
6	3	142158	5.4	2.4	4.9	0.0	5.5	
7	4	141008	5.8	5.1	4.9	5.5	0.0	
8	5	145082	4.9	4.3	4.9	4.6	3.1	
9	6	139410	5.5	3.1	2.6	3.9	4.2	
10	7	135014	5.3	1.7	4.3	3.0	5.7	
11	8	139356	4.1	3.6	5.8	3.7	5.1	
12	9	137368	6.9	3.5	3.7	4.3	6.2	
13	10	141982	4.9	2.0	3.4	3.6	4.5	

Figure 9-9: The employee distance matrix

Getting the k Nearest Neighbors

Create a new tab called **Rank**. Paste the employee IDs starting down at A2 and across at B1 to form a grid, as on the previous tab.

Now you need to rank each employee going across the top according to his or her distance to each employee in column A. Start the rankings at 0, just so that rank 1 will go to an actual *other* employee, and all the 0s will stay on the diagonal of the graph (due to self-distances always being the smallest).

Starting in B2, the ranking of employee 144624 in relation to him/herself is written using the RANK formula:

```
=RANK(Distances!C3,Distances!$C$3:$OL3,1)-1
```

This -1 at the end of the formula gives this self-distance a rank of 0 instead of 1. Note that you lock down columns C through OL on the Distances tab with absolute references, which allows you to copy this formula to the right.

Copying this formula one to the right, C2, you are now ranking employee 142619 in relationship to their distance from employee 144624:

```
=RANK(Distances!D3,Distances!$C$3:$OL3,1)-1
```

This returns a rank of 194 out of 400, so these two folks aren't exactly buds (see Figure 9-10).

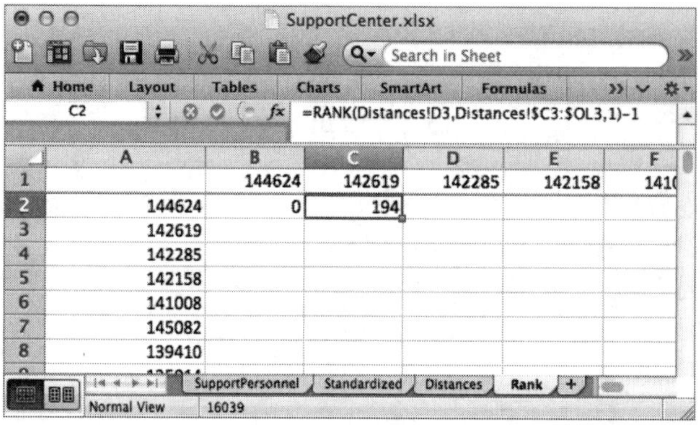

	A	B	C	D	E	F
1		144624	142619	142285	142158	141(
2	144624	0	194			
3	142619					
4	142285					
5	142158					
6	141008					
7	145082					
8	139410					

Figure 9-10: Employee 142619 ranked by distance in relation to 144624

Copy this formula throughout the sheet. You'll get the full ranking matrix pictured in Figure 9-11.

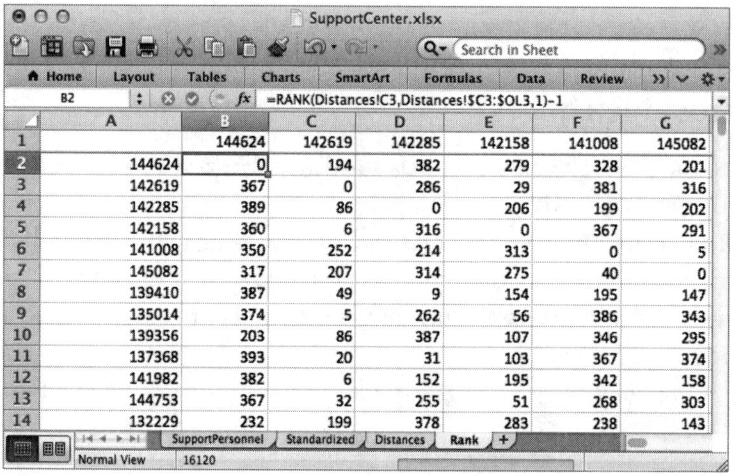

	A	B	C	D	E	F	G
1		144624	142619	142285	142158	141008	145082
2	144624	0	194	382	279	328	201
3	142619	367	0	286	29	381	316
4	142285	389	86	0	206	199	202
5	142158	360	6	316	0	367	291
6	141008	350	252	214	313	0	5
7	145082	317	207	314	275	40	0
8	139410	387	49	9	154	195	147
9	135014	374	5	262	56	386	343
10	139356	203	86	387	107	346	295
11	137368	393	20	31	103	367	374
12	141982	382	6	152	195	342	158
13	144753	367	32	255	51	268	303
14	132229	232	199	378	283	238	143

Figure 9-11: Each employee on the column ranked in relation to each row

Graph Outlier Detection Method 1: Just Use the Indegree

If you wanted to assemble a k nearest neighbors (kNN) graph using the Distances and Rank sheets, all you'd need to do is delete any edge in the Distances sheet (set its cell to blank) whose rank was greater than k. For k = 5, you'd drop all the distances with a rank on the Rank sheet that was 6 or over.

What would it mean to be an outlier in this context? Well, an outlier wouldn't get picked all that often as a "nearest neighbor," now would it?

Say you created a 5NN graph, so you kept only those edges with a rank of 5 or less. If you scroll down a column, such as column B for employee 144624, how many times does this employee end up in the top-five ranks for all the other employees? That is, how many employees choose 144624 as one of their top five neighbors? Not many. I'm eyeballing none, in fact, except for its self-distance on the diagonal with a rank of 0, which you can ignore.

How about if you made a 10NN? Well, in that case employee 139071 on row 23 happens to consider 144624 its ninth nearest neighbor. This means that in the 5NN graph employee 144624 has an *indegree* of 0, whereas in the 10NN graph employee 144624 has an indegree of 1.

The indegree is the count of the number of edges going into any node on a graph. The lower the indegree, the more of an outlier you are, because no one wants to be your neighbor.

At the bottom of column B on the Rank sheet, count up the indegree for employee 144624 for the cases of 5, 10, and 20 nearest neighbor graphs. You can do this using a simple COUNTIF formula (subtracting out 1 for the self-distance on the diagonal which you're ignoring). So, for example, to count up the indegree for employee 144624 in a 5NN graph, you'd use the following formula in cell B402:

```
=COUNTIF(B2:B401,"<=5")-1
```

Similarly below it, you could calculate the employee's indegree if you made a 10NN graph:

```
=COUNTIF(B2:B401,"<=10")-1
```

And below that for a 20NN:

```
=COUNTIF(B2:B401,"<=20")-1
```

Indeed, you could pick any k you wanted between 1 and the number of employees you have. But you can stick with 5, 10, and 20 for now. Using the conditional formatting menu, you can highlight cells whose counts are 0 (which means there are no inbound edges to the node for a graph of that size). This calculation on employee 144624 yields the tab shown in Figure 9-12.

Highlighting B402:B404, you can drag the calculations to the right through column OK. Scrolling through the results, you can see that some employees may be considered outliers at the 5NN mark but not necessarily at the 10NN mark (if you define an outlier as an employee with a 0 indegree—you could use another number if you liked).

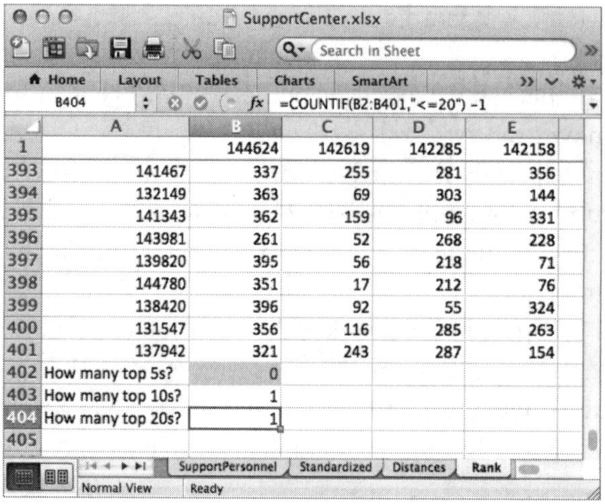

	A	B	C	D	E
1		144624	142619	142285	142158
393	141467	337	255	281	356
394	132149	363	69	303	144
395	141343	362	159	96	331
396	143981	261	52	268	228
397	139820	395	56	218	71
398	144780	351	17	212	76
399	138420	396	92	55	324
400	131547	356	116	285	263
401	137942	321	243	287	154
402	How many top 5s?	0			
403	How many top 10s?	1			
404	How many top 20s?	1			
405					

Figure 9-12: The indegree counts for three different nearest neighbor graphs

There are only two employees who even at the 20NN graph level still have no inbound edges. No one considers them even in the top 20 closest of neighbors. That's pretty distant!

Those two employee IDs are 137155 and 143406. Flipping back to the SupportPersonnel tab, you can investigate. Employee 137155 is on row 300 (see Figure 9-13). They have a high ticket average, high customer rating, and they appear to be a good Samaritan. They've taken lots of weekend shifts, graveyard shifts, and they've offered on seven occasions to swap shifts with an employee who needed it. Nice! This is someone who across multiple dimensions is exceptional enough that they're not even in the top 20 distances to any other employee. That's pretty amazing. Maybe this employee deserves a pizza party or something.

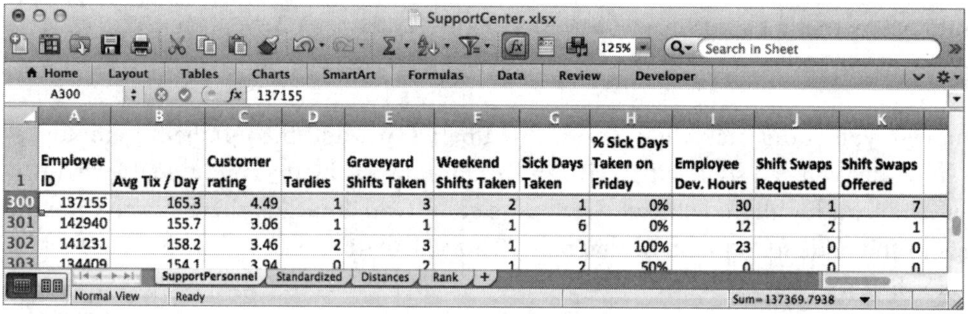

	Employee ID	Avg Tix / Day	Customer rating	Tardies	Graveyard Shifts Taken	Weekend Shifts Taken	Sick Days Taken	% Sick Days Taken on Friday	Employee Dev. Hours	Shift Swaps Requested	Shift Swaps Offered
300	137155	165.3	4.49	1	3	2	1	0%	30	1	7
301	142940	155.7	3.06	1	1	1	6	0%	12	2	1
302	141231	158.2	3.46	2	3	1	1	100%	23	0	0
303	134409	154.1	3.94	0	2	1	2	50%	0	0	0

Figure 9-13: The performance data for employee 137155

What about the other employee—143406? They're on row 375, and they're an interesting contrast to the previous employee (see Figure 9-14). No metric by itself is enough to fire them, but that said, their ticket number is two standard deviations below the average, their customer rating is likewise a couple of standard deviations down the distribution. Their tardies are above average, and they've taken five out of six sick days on a Friday. Hmmm.

This employee has taken plenty of employee development, which is a plus. But maybe that's because they just enjoy getting out of taking tickets. Perhaps employee dev should start being graded. And they've requested four shift swaps without offering to swap with someone else.

This employee feels like they're working the system. While meeting the minimum requirements for employment (note they're not jumping any Tukey fences here), they seem to be skating by at the bad end of every distribution.

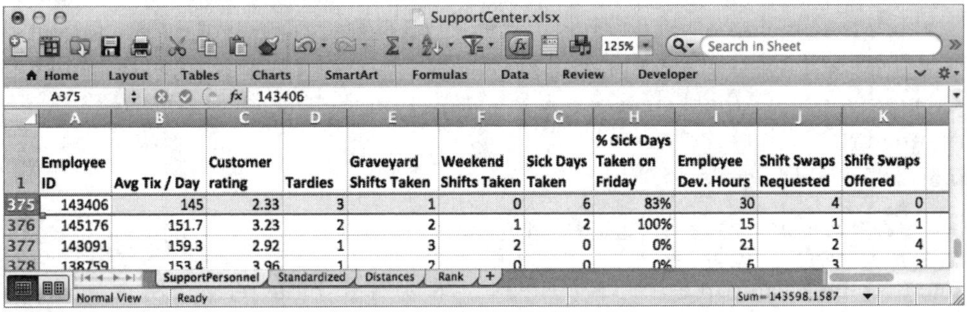

	Employee ID	Avg Tix / Day	Customer rating	Tardies	Graveyard Shifts Taken	Weekend Shifts Taken	Sick Days Taken	% Sick Days Taken on Friday	Employee Dev. Hours	Shift Swaps Requested	Shift Swaps Offered
375	143406	145	2.33	3	1	0	6	83%	30	4	0
376	145176	151.7	3.23	2	2	1	2	100%	15	1	1
377	143091	159.3	2.92	1	3	2	0	0%	21	2	4
378	138759	153.4	3.96	1	2	0	0	0%	6	3	3

Figure 9-14: The performance data for employee 143406

Graph Outlier Detection Method 2: Getting Nuanced with k-Distance

One of the drawbacks of the previous method is that for a given kNN graph you either get an inbound edge from someone or you don't. And that means that you get large shifts in who's an outlier and who's not one, depending on the value of k you pick. This example ended up trying 5, 10, and 20 before you were left with just two employees. And of those two employees, which one was the biggest outlier? Beats me! They both had an indegree of 0 on the 20NN, so they were kinda tied, right?

What would be nice is to have a calculation that assigned an employee a continuous degree of outlying-ness. The next two methods you'll look at attempt to do just that. First, you'll look at ranking outliers using a quantity called the *k-distance*.

The k-distance is the distance from an employee to their kth neighbor.

Nice and simple, but since it's giving back a distance rather than a count, you can get a nice ranking out of the value. Create a new tab in the workbook called **K-Distance** to take a look.

For k, use 5, which means you'll grab everyone's distance to their fifth closest neighbor. One way to think of this is that if the neighborhood where I live has five neighbors and myself, how much land does that neighborhood sit on? If I have to walk 30 minutes to make it to my fifth neighbor's house, then maybe I live in the boonies.

So label A1 as **How many employees are in my neighborhood?** and put a **5** in B1. This is your k value.

Starting in A3, label the column **Employee ID** and paste the employee IDs down. Then you'll start calculating the k-distance with that of employee 144624 in cell B4.

Now, how do you calculate the distance between 144624 and his fifth closest neighbor? The fifth closest employee will be ranked 5 on row 2 (144624's row) of the Rank tab. So you can just use an IF statement to set that value to 1 in a vector of all 0s, and then multiply that vector times the distances row for 144624 on the Distances tab. Finally, sum everything up.

Thus, in B4 you'd have:

```
{=SUM(IF(Rank!B2:OK2=$B$1,1,0)*Distances!C3:OL3)}
```

Note that the k value in cell B1 is locked down with absolute references, so you can copy the formula down. Also, this is an array formula since the IF statement is checking an entire array of values.

Double-click the formula to send it down the sheet and apply some conditional formatting to highlight the large distances. Once again, the two outliers from the previous section rise to the top (see Figure 9-15).

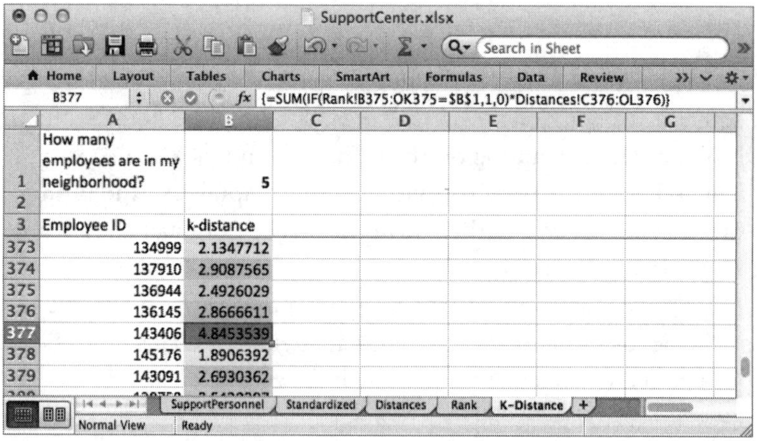

Figure 9-15: Employee 143406 has a high 5-distance

This time around, you get a little more nuance. You can see in this single list that the bad employee, 143406, is substantially more distant than 137155, and both of those values are substantially larger than the next largest value of 3.53.

But there's a drawback to this approach, which is visualized in Figure 9-16. Merely using k-distance gives you a sense of global outlying-ness, that is, you can highlight points that are farther away from their neighbors than any other points. But when you look at Figure 9-16, the triangular point is clearly the outlier, and yet, its k-distance is going to be less than that of some of the diamond shape points.

Are those diamonds really weirder than that triangle? Not to my eyes!

The issue here is that the triangle is not a *global outlier*, so much as it is a *local outlier*. The reason why your eyeballs pick it up as the odd point out is that it's nearest to the tight cluster of circles. If the triangle were among the spaced-out diamonds, it'd be fine. But it's not. Instead, it looks nothing like its circular neighbors.

This leads to a cutting-edge technique called *local outlier factors* (*LOF*).

Figure 9-16: k-distance fails on local outliers

Graph Outlier Detection Method 3: Local Outlier Factors Are Where It's At

Just like using k-distance, local outlier factors provide a single score for each point. The larger the score, the more of an outlier they are. But LOF gives you something a little cooler than that: The closer the score is to 1, the more ordinary the point is locally. As the score increases, the point should be considered less typical and more like an outlier. And unlike k-distance, this "1 is typical" fact doesn't change no matter the size or scale of your graph, which is really cool.

At a high level here's how it works: *You are an outlier if your k nearest neighbors consider you farther away than their neighbors consider them.* The algorithm cares about a point's friends and friends-of-friends. That's how it defines "local."

Looking back at Figure 9-16 this is exactly what makes the triangle an outlier, isn't it? It may not have the highest k-distance, but the ratio of the triangle's distance to its nearest neighbors over their distance to each other is quite high (see Figure 9-17).

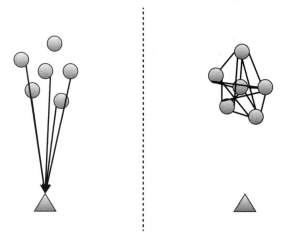

Figure 9-17: The triangle is not nearly as reachable by its neighbors as the neighbors are by each other

Starting with Reach Distance

Before you can put together your local outlier factors for each employee, you need to calculate one more set of numbers, called *reachability distances*.

The reachability distance of employee A with respect to employee B is just their ordinary distance, unless A is within B's k-distance neighborhood, in which case the reachability distance is just B's k-distance.

In other words, if A is inside B's neighborhood, you round up A's distance to B to the size of B's neighborhood; otherwise, you leave it alone.

Using reachability distance rather than ordinary distance for LOF helps stabilize the calculation a bit.

Create a new tab called **Reach-dist** and replace the distances from the Distances tab with the new reach distances.

First thing you'll want to do is Paste Special the transposed values from the K-Distance tab across the top of the tab, and then paste the employee-by-employee grid, like on the Distances tab starting in row 3. This gives you the empty sheet shown in Figure 9-18.

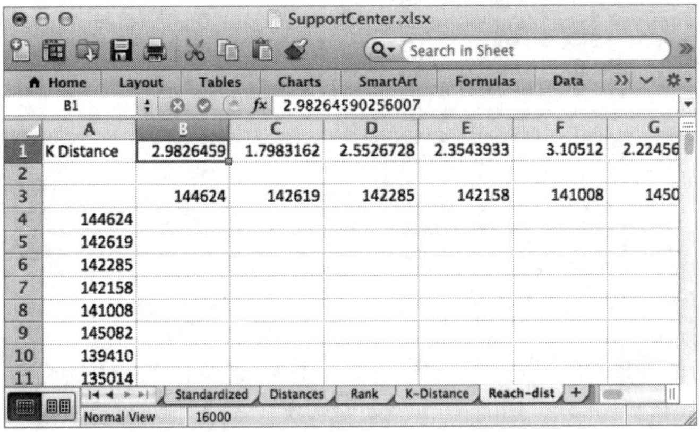

	A	B	C	D	E	F	G
1	K Distance	2.9826459	1.7983162	2.5526728	2.3543933	3.10512	2.22456
2							
3		144624	142619	142285	142158	141008	1450
4	144624						
5	142619						
6	142285						
7	142158						
8	141008						
9	145082						
10	139410						
11	135014						

Figure 9-18: The skeleton of the reach distance tab

Starting in cell B4, you're going to slide in the distance of 144624 to itself from the Distances tab (Distances!C3) unless it's less than the k-distance above in B1. It's a simple MAX formula:

```
=MAX(B$1,Distances!C3)
```

The absolute reference on the k-distance allows you to copy the formula around the sheet. Copying the formula through OK4, you can then highlight the calculations on row 4 and double-click them to send them through row 403. This fills in all the reach distances, as shown in Figure 9-19.

Putting Together the Local Outlier Factors

Now you're ready to calculate each employee's local outlier factor. To start, create a new tab called **LOF** and paste the employee IDs down column A.

As stated earlier, local outlier factors gauge how a point is viewed by its neighbors versus how those neighbors are viewed by their neighbors. If I'm 30 miles outside of town, my closest neighbors may view me as a redneck, whereas they are viewed by their neighbors as members of the community. That means that locally I'm viewed more as an outlier than my neighbors are. You want to capture that phenomenon.

These values hinge on the average reachability of each employee with respect to his k nearest neighbors.

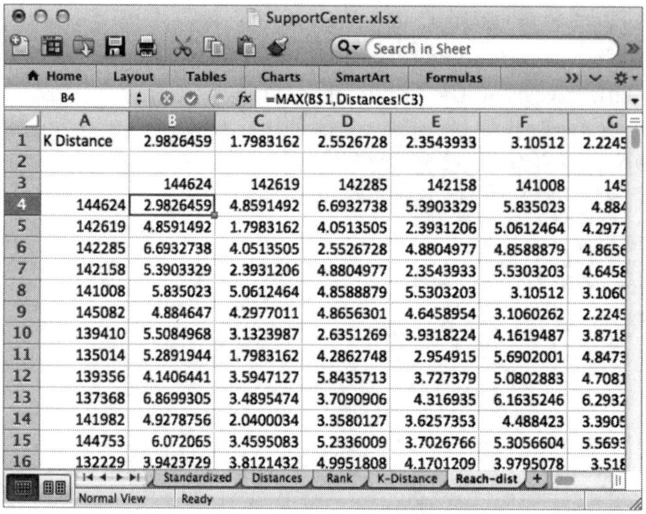

	A	B	C	D	E	F	G
1	K Distance	2.9826459	1.7983162	2.5526728	2.3543933	3.10512	2.2245
2							
3		144624	142619	142285	142158	141008	145
4	144624	2.9826459	4.8591492	6.6932738	5.3903329	5.835023	4.884
5	142619	4.8591492	1.7983162	4.0513505	2.3931206	5.0612464	4.2977
6	142285	6.6932738	4.0513505	2.5526728	4.8804977	4.8588879	4.8656
7	142158	5.3903329	2.3931206	4.8804977	2.3543933	5.5303203	4.6458
8	141008	5.835023	5.0612464	4.8588879	5.5303203	3.10512	3.1060
9	145082	4.884647	4.2977011	4.8656301	4.6458954	3.1060262	2.2245
10	139410	5.5084968	3.1323987	2.6351269	3.9318224	4.1619487	3.8718
11	135014	5.2891944	1.7983162	4.2862748	2.954915	5.6902001	4.8473
12	139356	4.1406441	3.5947127	5.8435713	3.727379	5.0802883	4.7081
13	137368	6.8699305	3.4895474	3.7090906	4.316935	6.1635246	6.2932
14	141982	4.9278756	2.0400034	3.3580127	3.6257353	4.488423	3.3905
15	144753	6.072065	3.4595083	5.2336009	3.7026766	5.3056604	5.5693
16	132229	3.9423729	3.8121432	4.9951808	4.1701209	3.9795078	3.518

Figure 9-19: All reach distances

Consider employee 144624 on row 2. You've already set k to 5, so the question is, what is the average reachability distance of 144624 *with respect to* that employee's five nearest neighbors?

To calculate this, pull a vector of 1s from the Rank tab for the five employees closest to 144624 and 0s for everyone else (similar to what you did on the K-Distance tab). Such a vector can be created using `IF` formulas to grab the top-ranked neighbors while excluding the actual employee:

```
IF(Rank!B2:OK2<='K-Distance'!B$1,1,0)*IF(Rank!B2:OK2>0,1,0)
```

Multiply this indicator vector times 144624's reach distances, sum up the product, and divide them by k=5. In cell B2, then, you have:

```
=SUM(IF(Rank!B2:OK2<='K-Distance'!B$1,1,0)*
IF(Rank!B2:OK2>0,1,0)*
'Reach-dist'!B4:OK4)/'K-Distance'!B$1}
```

Just as when you calculated k-distance, this is an array formula. You can send this formula down the sheet by double-clicking it (see Figure 9-20).

So this column indicates how the five nearest neighbors of each employee view them. *The local outlier factor then for an employee is the average of the ratios of the employee's average reachability distance divided by the average reachability distances of each of their k neighbors.*

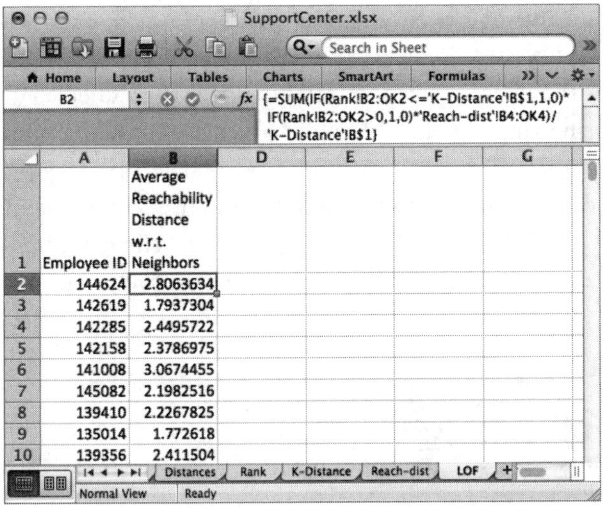

Figure 9-20: Average reachability for each employee with respect to his neighbors

You will tackle the LOF calculation for employee 144624 in cell C2 first. Just as in previous calculations, the following IF statements give you a vector of 1s for 144624's top five nearest neighbors:

```
IF(Rank!B2:OK2<='K-Distance'!B$1,1,0)*IF(Rank!B2:OK2>0,1,0)
```

You then multiply the ratio of 144624's average reachability divided by each neighbor's average reachability as:

```
IF(Rank!B2:OK2<='K-Distance'!B$1,1,0)
  *IF(Rank!B2:OK2>0,1,0)*B2/TRANSPOSE(B$2:B$401)
```

Note that the neighbors' reachability distances referenced in range B2:B401 on the bottom of the ratio are transposed so that the column is turned into a row, just like the vectors coming out of the IF statements in the equation.

You can average these ratios by summing them and dividing by k:

```
{=SUM(IF(Rank!B2:OK2<=
  'K-Distance'!B$1,1,0)
  *IF(Rank!B2:OK2>0,1,0)
  *B2/TRANSPOSE(B$2:B$401))/'K-Distance'!B$1}
```

Note the curly braces since this is an array formula. Press Control+Shift+Enter (Command+Return on Mac) to get back the LOF factor for 144624.

It's 1.34, which is somewhat over a value of 1, meaning that this employee is a bit of a local outlier.

You can send this formula down the sheet by double-clicking and then check out the other employees. Conditional formatting is helpful to highlight the most significant outliers.

Lo and behold, when you scroll down you find that employee 143406, the resident slacker, is the most outlying point with an LOF of 1.97 (see Figure 9-21). His neighbors view him as twice as distant as they are viewed by their neighbors. That's pretty far outside the community.

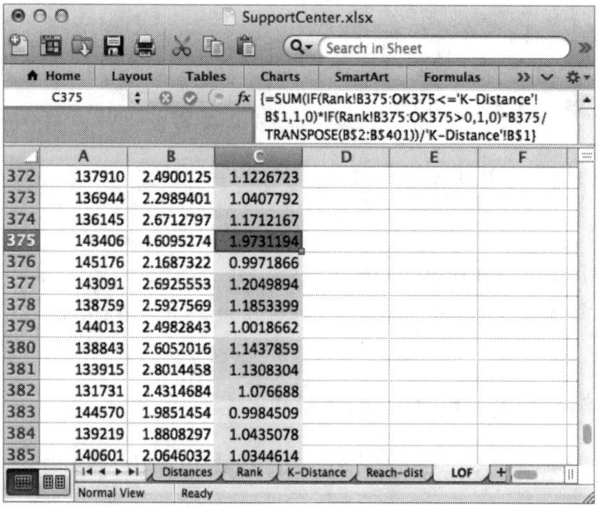

Figure 9-21: LOFs for the employees. Somebody is knocking on the door of 2.

And that's it! You now have a single value assigned to each employee that ranks them as a local outlier and is scaled the same no matter the size of the graph. Pretty flippin' awesome.

Wrapping Up

Between the graph modularity chapter and this chapter on outlier detection, you've been exposed to the power of analyzing a dataset by "graphing" your data, that is, assigning distances and edges between your observations.

Although in the clustering chapters, you mined groups of related points for insights, here you mined the data for points outside of communities. You saw the power of something as simple as indegree to demonstrate who's influential and who's isolated.

For more on outlier detection, check out the 2010 survey put together by Kriegel, Kroger, and Zimek at `http://www.siam.org/meetings/sdm10/tutorial3.pdf` for the 2010 SIAM conference. All the techniques in this chapter show up there along with a number of others.

Note that these techniques don't require any kind of arbitrarily long-running process the way optimization models might. There are a finite number of steps to get LOFs, so this kind of thing can be coded in production on top of a database quite easily.

If you're looking for a good programming language to do this stuff in, R is the way to go. The bplot function in R provides box plots of data with Tukey fences built in. The ability to plot Tukey fences graphically is something so painful in Excel that I didn't even bother putting it in this book, so the bplot function is a huge plus for R.

Also in R, the DMwR package (which accompanies the excellent *Data Mining with R* book by Torgo [Chapman and Hall, 2010]) includes an implementation of LOF in a function called *lofactor*. To construct and analyze the degree of nodes in a graph, the igraph package in Python and R is the way to go.

10

Moving from Spreadsheets into R

After spending the previous nine chapters injecting Excel directly into your veins, I'm now going to tell you to drop it. Well, not for everything, but let's be honest, Excel is not ideal for all analytics tasks.

Excel is awesome for learning analytics, because you can touch and see your data in every state as an algorithm changes it from input into output. But you came, you saw, you learned. Do you really need to go through all those steps manually every time? For example, do you really need to bake up your own optimization formulation to fit your own logistic regressions? Do you need to input the definitions of cosine similarity all yourself?

Now that you've learned it, you're allowed to cheat and have someone else do that for you! Think of yourself as Wolfgang Puck. Does he cook everything at all his restaurants? I sure hope not; otherwise, his skills vary wildly from airport to real world. Now that you've learned this stuff, you too should feel comfortable using other folks' implementations of these algorithms.

And that, among many other things (for example, referencing a whole table of data using one word) is why moving from Excel into the analytics-focused programming language called *R* is worth doing.

This chapter runs some of the previous chapters' analyses in R rather than Excel—same data, same algorithms, different environment. You'll see how easy this stuff can be!

Now, just as a warning, this chapter *is not* an intro tutorial of R. I'm going to be moving at a thousand miles an hour to hit a few algorithms in a single chapter. If you want a more comprehensive introduction, check out the books I recommend at the end of this chapter.

And if you haven't read the previous chapters to this point, this isn't going to make a lick of sense, because I'm going to assume that you are already familiar with the data, problems, and techniques from earlier chapters. This ain't a "choose your own adventure" novel. Read everything else and come back!

Getting Up and Running with R

You can download R from the R website at www.r-project.org. Just click the download link, pick a mirror nearest you, and download the installer for your OS.

Run through the installer (on Windows it's nice to install the software as the administrator) and then open the application. On Windows and Mac, the R console is going to load. It looks something like Figure 10-1.

Figure 10-1: The R console on Mac OS

Inside the R console, you type commands into the > prompt and press Return to get the system to do anything. Here's a couple for you:

```
> print("No regrets. Texas forever.")
[1] "No regrets. Texas forever."
> 355/113
[1] 3.141593
```

You can call the `print` function to get the system to print out text. You can also type in arithmetic directly to make calculations. Now, my standard workflow for using R is:

1. Bring data into an R.
2. Do data-sciency things with data.
3. Dump results out of R where some other person or process can use them.

When it comes to the first step, bringing data in R, there are all sorts of options, but in order to understand variables and datatypes, you'll start simply by entering data manually.

Some Simple Hand-Jamming

The simplest way to get data in R is the same way you get it into Excel. By typing it with your fingers and storing those keystrokes somewhere. You can start by storing a single value in a variable:

```
> almostpi <- 355/113
> almostpi
[1] 3.141593
> sqrt(almostpi)
[1] 1.772454
```

In this little bit of code, you are storing 355/113 in a variable called `almostpi`. Then by typing the variable back into the console and pressing Return, you can print its contents. You can then act on that variable with a variety of functions (this example calls the square root).

For a quick reference of many of the built-in functions R has (functions available without loading packages … something you're building toward), check out the R reference card at `http://cran.r-project.org/doc/contrib/Short-refcard.pdf`.

To understand what a function does, just type a question mark before it when you put it into the console:

```
> ?sqrt
```

This will pop open a Help window on the function (see Figure 10-2 for the Help window on `sqrt`).

You can also type two question marks in front of functions to do a search for information, like the following:

```
> ??log
```

The `log` search yields the results shown in Figure 10-3.

NOTE

There are all sorts of great resources for finding out what functions and packages are available to you in R besides the whole `??` rigmarole. For example, `rseek.org` is a great search engine for R-related content. And you can post specific questions to `stackoverflow.com` (see `http://stackoverflow.com/questions/tagged/r`) and the R mailing list (see `http://www.r-project.org/mail.html`).

Figure 10-2: The Help window for the square root function

Vector Math and Factoring

You can insert a vector of numbers using the `c()` function (the c stands for "combine"). Toss some primes into a variable:

```
> someprimes <- c(1,2,3,5,7,11)
> someprimes
[1]  1  2  3  5  7 11
```

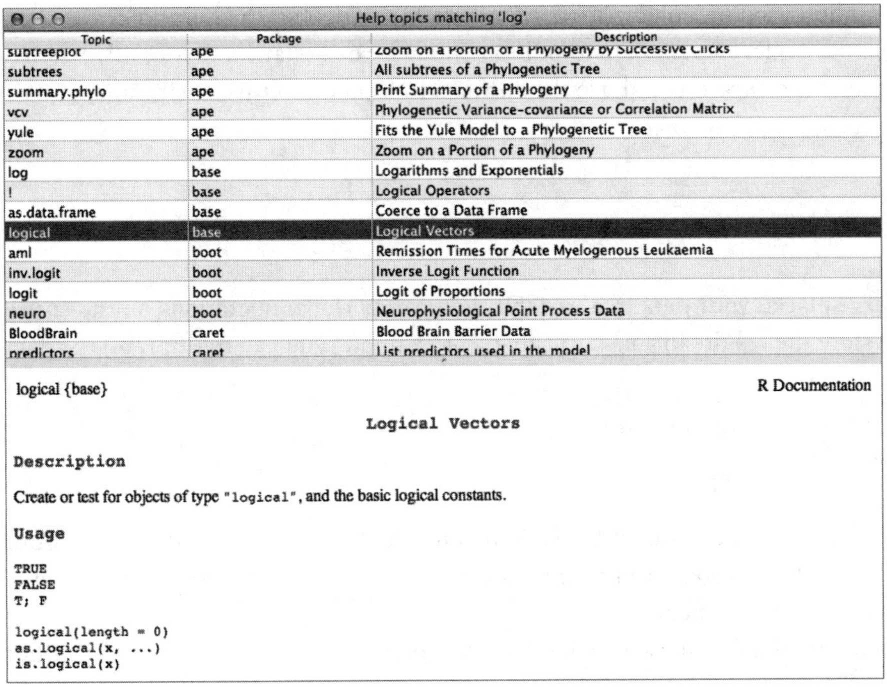

Figure 10-3: Search results for the word log

Using the `Length()` function, you can count the number of elements you have in your vector:

```
> length(someprimes)
[1] 6
```

You can also reference single values in the vector using bracket notation:

```
> someprimes[4]
[1] 5
```

This gives back the fourth value in the vector, which happens to be 5. You can provide vectors of indices using the `c()` function or a `:` character to specify a range:

```
> someprimes[c(4,5,6)]
[1]  5  7 11
> someprimes[4:6]
[1]  5  7 11
```

In both of these cases, you're grabbing the fourth through sixth values of the vector. You can also use logical statements to pull out values. For instance, if you only wanted primes less than seven, you could use the `which()` function to return their indices:

```
> which(someprimes<7)
[1] 1 2 3 4

> someprimes[which(someprimes<7)]
[1] 1 2 3 5
```

Once you've placed your data in a variable, you can perform operations on the entire dataset and store the results in a new variable. For example, you can multiply all the data by two:

```
> primestimes2 <- someprimes*2
> primestimes2
[1]  2  4  6 10 14 22
```

Think about how you do this in Excel. You enter the formula in the adjacent column and copy it down. R lets you name that column or row of data and operate on that variable as a single entity, which is neat.

One useful function for checking your data for wonky entries is the `summary` function:

```
> summary(someprimes)
   Min. 1st Qu.  Median    Mean 3rd Qu.    Max.
  1.000   2.250   4.000   4.833   6.500  11.000
```

And you can work with text data too:

```
> somecolors <- c("blue","red","green","blue",
"green","yellow","red","red")
> somecolors
[1] "blue"   "red"    "green"  "blue"   "green"  "yellow" "red"    "red"
```

If you summarize `somecolors`, all you get is a little bit of descriptive data:

```
> summary(somecolors)
   Length     Class      Mode
        8 character character
```

But you can treat these colors as categories and make this vector into categorical data by "factoring" it:

```
> somecolors <- factor(somecolors)
> somecolors
[1] blue   red    green  blue   green  yellow red    red
Levels: blue green red yellow
```

Now when you summarize the data, you get back counts for each "level" (a level is essentially a category):

```
> summary(somecolors)
  blue   green    red yellow
     2       2      3      1
```

Two-Dimensional Matrices

The vectors you've been playing with so far are one-dimensional. Something more akin to a spreadsheet in R might be a matrix, which is a two-dimensional array of numbers. You can construct one with the matrix function:

```
> amatrix <- matrix(data=c(someprimes,primestimes2),nrow=2,ncol=6)
> amatrix
     [,1] [,2] [,3] [,4] [,5] [,6]
[1,]    1    3    7    2    6   14
[2,]    2    5   11    4   10   22
```

You can count columns and rows:

```
> nrow(amatrix)
[1] 2
> ncol(amatrix)
[1] 6
```

If you want to transpose the data (just as you did throughout the book using Excel's Paste Special transpose functionality), you use the t() function:

```
> t(amatrix)
     [,1] [,2]
[1,]    1    2
[2,]    3    5
[3,]    7   11
[4,]    2    4
[5,]    6   10
[6,]   14   22
```

To grab individual records or ranges, you use the same bracket notation, except you separate column and row references with a comma:

```
> amatrix[1:2,3]
[1]  7 11
```

This gives back rows 1 through 2 for column 3. But you need not reference row 1 and 2 since that's all the rows you have—you can instead leave that portion of the bracket blank and all the rows will be printed:

```
> amatrix[,3]
[1]  7 11
```

Using the `rbind()` and `cbind()` functions, you can smush new rows and columns of data into the matrix:

```
> primestimes3 <- someprimes*3
> amatrix <- rbind(amatrix,primestimes3)
> amatrix
              [,1] [,2] [,3] [,4] [,5] [,6]
                1    3    7    2    6   14
                2    5   11    4   10   22
primestimes3    3    6    9   15   21   33
```

Here you've created a new row of data (`primestimes3`) and used `rbind()` on the `amatrix` variable to tack `primestimes3` onto it and assign the result back into `amatrix`.

The Best Datatype of Them All: The Dataframe

A *dataframe* is the ideal way to work with real world, database table-style data in R. A dataframe in R is a specific version of the "list" datatype. So what's a list? A *list* is a collection of objects in R that can be of different types. For instance, here's a list with some info about yours truly:

```
> John <- list(gender="male", age="ancient", height = 72,
               spawn = 3, spawn_ages = c(.5,2,5))
> John
$gender
[1] "male"

$age
[1] "ancient"

$height
[1] 72

$spawn
[1] 3

$spawn_ages
[1] 0.5 2.0 5.0
```

A dataframe is a type of list that looks eerily similar to an Excel sheet. Essentially, it's a two-dimensional column-oriented sheet of data where columns can be treated as numeric or categorical vectors. You can create a dataframe by calling the `data.frame()` function on arrays of imported or jammed-in data. The following example uses data from James Bond films to illustrate. First, create some vectors:

```
> bondnames <- c("connery","lazenby","moore","dalton","brosnan","craig")
> firstyear <- c(1962,1969,1973,1987,1995,2006)
> eyecolor <- c("brown","brown","blue", "green", "blue", "blue")
> womenkissed <- c(17,3,20,4,12,4)
> countofbondjamesbonds <- c(3,2,10,2,5,1)
```

So at this point you have five vectors—some text, some numeric—and all are the same length. You can combine them into a single dataframe called bonddata like so:

```
> bonddata <- data.frame(bondnames,firstyear,eyecolor,womenkissed,
countofbondjamesbonds)
> bonddata
  bondnames firstyear eyecolor womenkissed countofbondjamesbonds
1   connery      1962    brown          17                     3
2   lazenby      1969    brown           3                     2
3     moore      1973     blue          20                    10
4    dalton      1987    green           4                     2
5   brosnan      1995     blue          12                     5
6     craig      2006     blue           4                     1
```

The data.frame function is going to take care of recognizing which of these columns are factors and which are numeric. You can see this difference by calling the str() and summary() functions (the str stands for "structure"):

```
> str(bonddata)
'data.frame': 6 obs. of  5 variables:
 $ bondnames            : Factor w/ 6 levels "brosnan","connery",..:
2 5 6 4 1 3
 $ firstyear            : num  1962 1969 1973 1987 1995 ...
 $ eyecolor             : Factor w/ 3 levels "blue","brown",..:
2 2 1 3 1 1
 $ womenkissed          : num  17 3 20 4 12 4
 $ countofbondjamesbonds: num  3 2 10 2 5 1
> summary(bonddata)
 bondnames   firstyear     eyecolor  womenkissed    countofbondjamesbonds
 brosnan:1  Min.   :1962  blue :3  Min.   : 3.00  Min.   : 1.000
 connery:1  1st Qu.:1970  brown:2  1st Qu.: 4.00  1st Qu.: 2.000
 craig  :1  Median :1980  green:1  Median : 8.00  Median : 2.500
 dalton :1  Mean   :1982           Mean   :10.00  Mean   : 3.833
 lazenby:1  3rd Qu.:1993           3rd Qu.:15.75  3rd Qu.: 4.500
 moore  :1  Max.   :2006           Max.   :20.00  Max.   :10.000
```

Note that the year is being treated as a number. You could factorize this column using the factor() function if you wanted it treated categorically instead.

And one of the awesome things about dataframes is that you can reference each column using a $ character plus the column name, as shown:

```
> bonddata$firstyear <- factor(bonddata$firstyear)
> summary(bonddata)
  bondnames  firstyear  eyecolor  womenkissed    countofbondjamesbonds
 brosnan:1  1962:1    blue :3  Min.   : 3.00  Min.   : 1.000
 connery:1  1969:1    brown:2  1st Qu.: 4.00  1st Qu.: 2.000
 craig  :1  1973:1    green:1  Median : 8.00  Median : 2.500
 dalton :1  1987:1             Mean   :10.00  Mean   : 3.833
 lazenby:1  1995:1             3rd Qu.:15.75  3rd Qu.: 4.500
 moore  :1  2006:1             Max.   :20.00  Max.   :10.000
```

Thus, when you run the `summary` function, the years are rolled up by category counts instead of by distribution data. Also, keep in mind that whenever you transpose a dataframe, the result is a good old two-dimensional matrix rather than another dataframe. This makes sense since the transposed version of the Bond data would not have consistent datatypes in each column.

Reading Data into R

Okay, so you've learned how to shove data into various datatypes by hand, but how do you read data in from files? The first thing you need to understand is the *working directory*. The working directory is the folder in which you can put data so that the R console can find it and read it in. The `getwd()` function displays the current working directory:

```
> getwd()
[1] "/Users/johnforeman/RHOME"
```

If you don't like the present working directory, you can change it with the `setwd()` command. Keep in mind, even on Windows machines R expects directory paths to be specified with forward slashes. For example:

```
> setwd("/Users/johnforeman/datasmartfiles")
```

Use this command to set your working directory to a place where you're happy to toss some data. You'll start by placing the downloaded WineKMC.csv file in that directory. This comma-delimited file has the data from the Matrix tab in the k-means clustering workbook from Chapter 2. Read it in and take a look.

To read in data, you use the `read.csv()` function:

```
> winedata <- read.csv("WineKMC.csv")
```

This data should look exactly like the Matrix tab from Chapter 2, so when you print the first few columns (I've chosen nine to fit on this page) you see descriptive data about each of the 32 offers followed by some customers' click vectors in columns:

```
> winedata[,1:9]
   Offer Mth   Varietal MinQty Disc  Origin PastPeak Adams Allen
1      1 Jan     Malbec     72   56  France    FALSE    NA    NA
2      2 Jan Pinot Noir     72   17  France    FALSE    NA    NA
```

3	3	Feb	Espumante	144	32	Oregon	TRUE	NA	NA
4	4	Feb	Champagne	72	48	France	TRUE	NA	NA
5	5	Feb	Cab. Sauv.	144	44	NZ	TRUE	NA	NA
6	6	Mar	Prosecco	144	86	Chile	FALSE	NA	NA
7	7	Mar	Prosecco	6	40	Australia	TRUE	NA	NA
8	8	Mar	Espumante	6	45	S. Africa	FALSE	NA	NA
9	9	Apr	Chardonnay	144	57	Chile	FALSE	NA	1
10	10	Apr	Prosecco	72	52	CA	FALSE	NA	NA
11	11	May	Champagne	72	85	France	FALSE	NA	NA
12	12	May	Prosecco	72	83	Australia	FALSE	NA	NA
13	13	May	Merlot	6	43	Chile	FALSE	NA	NA
14	14	Jun	Merlot	72	64	Chile	FALSE	NA	NA
15	15	Jun	Cab. Sauv.	144	19	Italy	FALSE	NA	NA
16	16	Jun	Merlot	72	88	CA	FALSE	NA	NA
17	17	Jul	Pinot Noir	12	47	Germany	FALSE	NA	NA
18	18	Jul	Espumante	6	50	Oregon	FALSE	1	NA
19	19	Jul	Champagne	12	66	Germany	FALSE	NA	NA
20	20	Aug	Cab. Sauv.	72	82	Italy	FALSE	NA	NA
21	21	Aug	Champagne	12	50	CA	FALSE	NA	NA
22	22	Aug	Champagne	72	63	France	FALSE	NA	NA
23	23	Sept	Chardonnay	144	39	S. Africa	FALSE	NA	NA
24	24	Sept	Pinot Noir	6	34	Italy	FALSE	NA	NA
25	25	Oct	Cab. Sauv.	72	59	Oregon	TRUE	NA	NA
26	26	Oct	Pinot Noir	144	83	Australia	FALSE	NA	NA
27	27	Oct	Champagne	72	88	NZ	FALSE	NA	1
28	28	Nov	Cab. Sauv.	12	56	France	TRUE	NA	NA
29	29	Nov	P. Grigio	6	87	France	FALSE	1	NA
30	30	Dec	Malbec	6	54	France	FALSE	1	NA
31	31	Dec	Champagne	72	89	France	FALSE	NA	NA
32	32	Dec	Cab. Sauv.	72	45	Germany	TRUE	NA	NA

It's all in! But you'll notice that the blank spaces in purchase vectors (which Excel treats as zeroes) have become NA values. You need to make those NA values 0, which you can do using the is.na() function inside of brackets:

```
> winedata[is.na(winedata)] <- 0
> winedata[1:10,8:17]
   Adams Allen Anders Bailey Baker Barnes Bell Bennett Brooks Brown
1      0     0      0      0     0      0    0       0      0     0
2      0     0      0      0     0      0    1       0      0     0
3      0     0      0      0     0      0    0       0      1     0
4      0     0      0      0     0      0    0       0      0     0
5      0     0      0      0     0      0    0       0      0     0
6      0     0      0      0     0      0    0       0      0     0
7      0     0      0      1     1      0    0       0      0     1
8      0     0      0      0     0      0    0       1      1     0
9      0     1      0      0     0      0    0       0      0     0
10     0     0      0      0     1      1    0       0      0     0
```

Bam! NA becomes 0.

Doing Some Actual Data Science

At this point you've learned how to work with variables and datatypes, hand-jam data, and read it in from a CSV. But how do you actually use the algorithms you learned earlier in this book? Since you already have the wine data loaded up, you'll start with a little k-means clustering.

Spherical K-Means on Wine Data in Just a Few Lines

In this section, you'll cluster based on cosine similarity (also called *spherical k-means*). And in R, there's a spherical k-means package you can load, called `skmeans`. But `skmeans` doesn't come baked into R; it's written by a third party as a package that you can load into R and use. Essentially, these geniuses have done all the work for you, and you just have to stand on their shoulders.

Like most R packages, you can read up on it and install it from the Comprehensive R Archive Network (CRAN). CRAN is a repository of many of the useful packages that can be loaded into R to extend its functionality. A list of all the packages you can download from CRAN is available here: `http://cran.r-project.org/web/packages/`.

Just search for "spherical k means" in `rseek.org` and a PDF explaining the package comes up as the first result. There's a function called `skmeans()` that you want.

R is initially set up to download packages from CRAN, so to get the `skmeans` package you need only use the `install.packages()` function (R may ask to set up a personal library the first time you do this):

```
> install.packages("skmeans",dependencies = TRUE)
trying URL 'http://mirrors.nics.utk.edu/cran/bin/macosx/leopard/
                    contrib/2.15/skmeans_0.2-3.tgz'
Content type 'application/x-gzip' length 224708 bytes (219 Kb)
opened URL
==================================================
downloaded 219 Kb


The downloaded binary packages are in
    /var/.../downloaded_packages
```

You can see in the code that I set `dependencies = TRUE` in the installation call. This ensures that if the `skmeans` package is dependent on any other packages, R downloads those packages as well. The call downloads the appropriate package for my R installation (version 2.15 on Mac) from a mirror and puts it where it needs to go.

You can then load the package using the `library()` function:

```
> library(skmeans)
```

You can look up how to use the `skmeans()` function using the `?` call. The documentation specifies that `skmeans()` accepts a matrix where each row corresponds to an object to cluster.

Your data on the other hand is column-oriented with a bunch of deal descriptors at the beginning that the algorithm isn't gonna want to see. So you need to transpose it (note that the transpose function coerces a matrix out of the dataframe).

Using the `ncol()` function, you can see that the customer columns go out to column 107, so you can isolate just the purchase vectors as rows for each customer by transposing the data from column 8 to 107 and shoving it in a new variable called `winedata.transposed`:

```
> ncol(winedata)
[1] 107
> winedata.transposed <- t(winedata[,8:107])
> winedata.transposed[1:10,1:10]
        [,1] [,2] [,3] [,4] [,5] [,6] [,7] [,8] [,9] [,10]
Adams     0    0    0    0    0    0    0    0    0    0
Allen     0    0    0    0    0    0    0    0    1    0
Anders    0    0    0    0    0    0    0    0    0    0
Bailey    0    0    0    0    0    0    1    0    0    0
Baker     0    0    0    0    0    0    1    0    0    1
Barnes    0    0    0    0    0    0    0    0    0    1
Bell      0    1    0    0    0    0    0    0    0    0
Bennett   0    0    0    0    0    0    0    1    0    0
Brooks    0    0    1    0    0    0    0    1    0    0
Brown     0    0    0    0    0    0    1    0    0    0
```

Then you can call `skmeans` on the dataset, specifying five means and the use of a genetic algorithm (much like the algorithm you used in Excel). You'll assign the results back to an object called `winedata.clusters`:

```
> winedata.clusters <- skmeans(winedata.transposed, 5, method="genetic")
```

Typing the object back into the console, you can get a summary of its contents (your results may vary due to the optimization algorithm):

```
> winedata.clusters
A hard spherical k-means partition of 100 objects into 5 classes.
Class sizes: 16, 17, 15, 29, 23
Call: skmeans(x = winedata.transposed, k = 5, method = "genetic")
```

Calling `str()` on the clusters object shows you that the actual cluster assignments are stored within the "cluster" list of the object:

```
> str(winedata.clusters)
List of 7
 $ prototypes: num [1:5, 1:32] 0.09 0.153 0 0.141 0 ...
  ..- attr(*, "dimnames")=List of 2
  .. ..$ : chr [1:5] "1" "2" "3" "4" ...
```

```
   .. ..$ : NULL
 $ membership: NULL
 $ cluster   : int [1:100]  5 4 1 5 2 2 1 3 3 5 ...
 $ family    :List of 7
  ..$ description: chr "spherical k-means"
  ..$ D           :function (x, prototypes)
  ..$ C           :function (x, weights, control)
  ..$ init        :function (x, k)
  ..$ e           : num 1
  ..$ .modify     : NULL
  ..$ .subset     : NULL
  ..- attr(*, "class")= chr "pclust_family"
 $ m          : num 1
 $ value      : num 38
 $ call       : language skmeans(x = winedata.transposed,
                            k = 5, method = "genetic")
  - attr(*, "class")= chr [1:2] "skmeans" "pclust"
```

So for instance, if you wanted to pull back the cluster assignment for row 4, you'd just use the matrix notation on the cluster vector:

```
> winedata.clusters$cluster[4]
[1] 5
```

Now, each row is labeled with a customer's name (because they were labeled when you read them in with the `read.csv()` function), so you can also pull assignments by name using the `row.names()` function combined with the `which()` function:

```
> winedata.clusters$cluster[
which(row.names(winedata.transposed)=="Wright")
]
[1] 4
```

Cool! Furthermore, you can write out all these cluster assignments using the `write.csv()` function if you cared to. Use `?` to learn how to use it. Spoiler: It's like `read.csv()`.

Now, the main way you understood the clusters in Excel was by understanding the patterns in the descriptors of the deals that defined them. You counted up the total deals taken in each cluster and sorted. How do you do something similar in R?

To perform the counts, you just use the `aggregate()` function where in the "by" field you specify the cluster assignments—meaning "aggregate purchases *by* assignment." And you also need to specify that the type of aggregation you want is a sum as opposed to a mean, min, max, median, and so on:

```
aggregate(winedata.transposed,by=list(winedata.clusters$cluster),sum)
```

You'll use transpose to store these counts back as five columns (just as they were in Excel) and you'll lop off the first row of the aggregation, which just gives back the cluster assignment names. Then, store all this back as a variable called `winedata.clustercounts`:

```
> winedata.clustercounts <-t(aggregate(winedata.transposed,by=list
        (winedata.clusters$cluster),sum)[,2:33])
> winedata.clustercounts
```

	[,1]	[,2]	[,3]	[,4]	[,5]
V1	2	5	0	3	0
V2	7	3	0	0	0
V3	0	2	3	0	1
V4	0	5	1	6	0
V5	0	0	0	4	0
V6	0	8	1	3	0
V7	0	3	1	0	15
V8	0	1	15	0	4
V9	0	2	0	8	0
V10	1	4	1	0	1
V11	0	7	1	4	1
V12	1	3	0	0	1
V13	0	0	2	0	4
V14	0	3	0	6	0
V15	0	3	0	3	0
V16	1	1	0	3	0
V17	7	0	0	0	0
V18	0	1	4	0	9
V19	0	4	1	0	0
V20	0	2	0	4	0
V21	0	1	1	1	1
V22	0	17	2	2	0
V23	1	1	0	3	0
V24	12	0	0	0	0
V25	0	3	0	3	0
V26	12	0	0	3	0
V27	1	4	1	3	0
V28	0	5	0	0	1
V29	0	1	4	0	12
V30	0	4	4	1	13
V31	0	16	1	0	0
V32	0	2	0	2	0

All right, so there are your counts of deals by cluster. Let's slap those seven columns of descriptive data back on to the deals using the column bind function `cbind()`:

```
> winedata.desc.plus.counts <-
cbind(winedata[,1:7],winedata.clustercounts)
> winedata.desc.plus.counts
```

	Offer	Mth	Varietal	MinQty	Disc	Origin	PastPeak	1	2	3	4	5
V1	1	Jan	Malbec	72	56	France	FALSE	2	5	0	3	0
V2	2	Jan	Pinot Noir	72	17	France	FALSE	7	3	0	0	0
V3	3	Feb	Espumante	144	32	Oregon	TRUE	0	2	3	0	1

	Offer	Mth	Varietal	MinQty	Disc	Origin	PastPeak	1	2	3	4	5
V4	4	Feb	Champagne	72	48	France	TRUE	0	5	1	6	0
V5	5	Feb	Cab. Sauv.	144	44	NZ	TRUE	0	0	0	4	0
V6	6	Mar	Prosecco	144	86	Chile	FALSE	0	8	1	3	0
V7	7	Mar	Prosecco	6	40	Australia	TRUE	0	3	1	0	15
V8	8	Mar	Espumante	6	45	S. Africa	FALSE	0	1	15	0	4
V9	9	Apr	Chardonnay	144	57	Chile	FALSE	0	2	0	8	0
V10	10	Apr	Prosecco	72	52	CA	FALSE	1	4	1	0	1
V11	11	May	Champagne	72	85	France	FALSE	0	7	1	4	1
V12	12	May	Prosecco	72	83	Australia	FALSE	1	3	0	0	1
V13	13	May	Merlot	6	43	Chile	FALSE	0	0	2	0	4
V14	14	Jun	Merlot	72	64	Chile	FALSE	0	3	0	6	0
V15	15	Jun	Cab. Sauv.	144	19	Italy	FALSE	0	3	0	3	0
V16	16	Jun	Merlot	72	88	CA	FALSE	1	1	0	3	0
V17	17	Jul	Pinot Noir	12	47	Germany	FALSE	7	0	0	0	0
V18	18	Jul	Espumante	6	50	Oregon	FALSE	0	1	4	0	9
V19	19	Jul	Champagne	12	66	Germany	FALSE	0	4	1	0	0
V20	20	Aug	Cab. Sauv.	72	82	Italy	FALSE	0	2	0	4	0
V21	21	Aug	Champagne	12	50	CA	FALSE	0	1	1	1	1
V22	22	Aug	Champagne	72	63	France	FALSE	0	17	2	2	0
V23	23	Sept	Chardonnay	144	39	S. Africa	FALSE	1	1	0	3	0
V24	24	Sept	Pinot Noir	6	34	Italy	FALSE	12	0	0	0	0
V25	25	Oct	Cab. Sauv.	72	59	Oregon	TRUE	0	3	0	3	0
V26	26	Oct	Pinot Noir	144	83	Australia	FALSE	12	0	0	3	0
V27	27	Oct	Champagne	72	88	NZ	FALSE	1	4	1	3	0
V28	28	Nov	Cab. Sauv.	12	56	France	TRUE	0	5	0	0	1
V29	29	Nov	P. Grigio	6	87	France	FALSE	0	1	4	0	12
V30	30	Dec	Malbec	6	54	France	FALSE	0	4	4	1	13
V31	31	Dec	Champagne	72	89	France	FALSE	0	16	1	0	0
V32	32	Dec	Cab. Sauv.	72	45	Germany	TRUE	0	2	0	2	0

And you can sort using the `order()` function inside the brackets of the dataframe. Here's a sort to discover the most popular deals for cluster 1 (note that I put a minus sign in front of the data to sort descending. Alternatively, you can set the `decreasing=TRUE` flag in the `order()` function.):

```
> winedata.desc.plus.counts[order(-winedata.desc.plus.counts[,8]),]
```

	Offer	Mth	Varietal	MinQty	Disc	Origin	PastPeak	1	2	3	4	5
V24	24	Sept	Pinot Noir	6	34	Italy	FALSE	12	0	0	0	0
V26	26	Oct	Pinot Noir	144	83	Australia	FALSE	12	0	0	3	0
V2	2	Jan	Pinot Noir	72	17	France	FALSE	7	3	0	0	0
V17	17	Jul	Pinot Noir	12	47	Germany	FALSE	7	0	0	0	0
V1	1	Jan	Malbec	72	56	France	FALSE	2	5	0	3	0
V10	10	Apr	Prosecco	72	52	CA	FALSE	1	4	1	0	1
V12	12	May	Prosecco	72	83	Australia	FALSE	1	3	0	0	1
V16	16	Jun	Merlot	72	88	CA	FALSE	1	1	0	3	0
V23	23	Sept	Chardonnay	144	39	S. Africa	FALSE	1	1	0	3	0

V27	27	Oct	Champagne	72	88	NZ	FALSE	1	4	1	3	0
V3	3	Feb	Espumante	144	32	Oregon	TRUE	0	2	3	0	1
V4	4	Feb	Champagne	72	48	France	TRUE	0	5	1	6	0
V5	5	Feb	Cab. Sauv.	144	44	NZ	TRUE	0	0	0	4	0
V6	6	Mar	Prosecco	144	86	Chile	FALSE	0	8	1	3	0
V7	7	Mar	Prosecco	6	40	Australia	TRUE	0	3	1	0	15
V8	8	Mar	Espumante	6	45	S. Africa	FALSE	0	1	15	0	4
V9	9	Apr	Chardonnay	144	57	Chile	FALSE	0	2	0	8	0
V11	11	May	Champagne	72	85	France	FALSE	0	7	1	4	1
V13	13	May	Merlot	6	43	Chile	FALSE	0	0	2	0	4
V14	14	Jun	Merlot	72	64	Chile	FALSE	0	3	0	6	0
V15	15	Jun	Cab. Sauv.	144	19	Italy	FALSE	0	3	0	3	0
V18	18	Jul	Espumante	6	50	Oregon	FALSE	0	1	4	0	9
V19	19	Jul	Champagne	12	66	Germany	FALSE	0	4	1	0	0
V20	20	Aug	Cab. Sauv.	72	82	Italy	FALSE	0	2	0	4	0
V21	21	Aug	Champagne	12	50	CA	FALSE	0	1	1	1	1
V22	22	Aug	Champagne	72	63	France	FALSE	0	17	2	2	0
V25	25	Oct	Cab. Sauv.	72	59	Oregon	TRUE	0	3	0	3	0
V28	28	Nov	Cab. Sauv.	12	56	France	TRUE	0	5	0	0	1
V29	29	Nov	P. Grigio	6	87	France	FALSE	0	1	4	0	12
V30	30	Dec	Malbec	6	54	France	FALSE	0	4	4	1	13
V31	31	Dec	Champagne	72	89	France	FALSE	0	16	1	0	0
V32	32	Dec	Cab. Sauv.	72	45	Germany	TRUE	0	2	0	2	0

Looking at the top deals, it becomes clear that cluster 1 is the Pinot Noir cluster. (Your mileage may vary. The genetic algorithm doesn't give the same answer each time.)

So just to reiterate then, if you strip away all my pontification, the following R code replicates much of Chapter 2 of this book:

```
> setwd("/Users/johnforeman/datasmartfiles")
> winedata <- read.csv("WineKMC.csv")
> winedata[is.na(winedata)] <- 0
> install.packages("skmeans",dependencies = TRUE)
> library(skmeans)
> winedata.transposed <- t(winedata[,8:107])
> winedata.clusters <- skmeans(winedata.transposed, 5, method="genetic")
> winedata.clustercounts <-
t(aggregate(winedata.transposed,
by=list(winedata.clusters$cluster),sum)[,2:33])

> winedata.desc.plus.counts <-
cbind(winedata[,1:7],winedata.clustercounts)
> winedata.desc.plus.counts[order(-winedata.desc.plus.counts[,8]),]
```

That's it—from reading in the data all the way to analyzing the clusters. Pretty nuts! And that's because the call to skmeans() pretty much isolates all the complexity of this method away from you. Terrible for learning, but awesome for working.

Building AI Models on the Pregnancy Data

In this section, you're going to replicate some of the pregnancy prediction models you built in Chapters 6 and 7 of this book. Specifically, you're going to build two classifiers using the `glm()` function (general linear model) with a logistic link function and using the `randomForest()` function (`randomForest()` bags trees, which may be anywhere from simple stumps to full decision trees).

The training and test data are separated into two CSV files, called Pregnancy.csv and Pregnancy_Test.csv. Go ahead and save them into your working directory and then load them into a couple of dataframes:

```
> PregnancyData <- read.csv("Pregnancy.csv")
> PregnancyData.Test <- read.csv("Pregnancy_Test.csv")
```

You can then run `summary()` and `str()` on the data to get a feel for it. It's immediately apparent that the gender and address type data have been loaded as categorical data, but as you can see in the `str()` output, the response variable (1 for pregnant, 0 for not pregnant) has been treated as numeric instead of as two distinct classes:

```
> str(PregnancyData)
'data.frame': 1000 obs. of  18 variables:
 $ Implied.Gender        : Factor w/ 3 levels "F","M","U": 2 2 2 3 1...
 $ Home.Apt..PO.Box      : Factor w/ 3 levels "A","H","P": 1 2 2 2 1...
 $ Pregnancy.Test        : int  1 1 1 0 0 0 0 0 0 0 ...
 $ Birth.Control         : int  0 0 0 0 0 0 1 0 0 0 ...
 $ Feminine.Hygiene      : int  0 0 0 0 0 0 0 0 0 0 ...
 $ Folic.Acid            : int  0 0 0 0 0 0 1 0 0 0 ...
 $ Prenatal.Vitamins     : int  1 1 0 0 0 1 1 0 0 1 ...
 $ Prenatal.Yoga         : int  0 0 0 0 1 0 0 0 0 0 ...
 $ Body.Pillow           : int  0 0 0 0 0 0 0 0 0 0 ...
 $ Ginger.Ale            : int  0 0 0 1 0 0 0 0 1 0 ...
 $ Sea.Bands             : int  0 0 1 0 0 0 0 0 0 0 ...
 $ Stopped.buying.ciggies: int  0 0 0 0 0 1 0 0 0 0 ...
 $ Cigarettes            : int  0 0 0 0 0 0 0 0 0 0 ...
 $ Smoking.Cessation     : int  0 0 0 0 0 0 0 0 0 0 ...
 $ Stopped.buying.wine   : int  0 0 0 1 0 0 0 0 0 0 ...
 $ Wine                  : int  0 0 0 0 0 0 0 0 0 0 ...
 $ Maternity.Clothes     : int  0 0 0 0 0 0 0 1 0 1 ...
 $ PREGNANT              : int  1 1 1 1 1 1 1 1 1 1 ...
```

It's best for `randomForest()` that you actually factorize this response variable into two classes (a 0 class and a 1 class) instead of treating the data as an integer. So you can factorize the data like so:

```
PregnancyData$PREGNANT <- factor(PregnancyData$PREGNANT)
PregnancyData.Test$PREGNANT <- factor(PregnancyData.Test$PREGNANT)
```

Now if you summarize the PREGNANT column, you merely get back class counts as if 0 and 1 were categories:

```
> summary(PregnancyData$PREGNANT)
  0   1
500 500
```

To build a logistic regression, you need the `glm()` function, which is in the built-in stats package for R. But for the `randomForest()` function, you'll need the `randomForest` package. Also, it'd be nice to build the ROC curves that you saw in Chapters 6 and 7. There's a package specifically built to give you those graphs, called ROCR. Go ahead and install and load up those two real quick:

```
> install.packages("randomForest",dependencies=TRUE)
> install.packages("ROCR",dependencies=TRUE)
> library(randomForest)
> library(ROCR)
```

You now have the data in and the packages loaded. It's time to get model building! Start with a logistic regression:

```
> Pregnancy.lm <- glm(PREGNANT ~ .,
data=PregnancyData,family=binomial("logit"))
```

The `glm()` function builds the linear model that you've specified as a logistic regression using the `family=binomial("logit")` option. You supply data to the function using the `data=PregnancyData` field. Now, you're probably wondering what PREGNANT ~ . means. This is a *formula* in R. It means "train my model to predict the PREGNANT column using all the other columns." The ~ means "using" and the period means "all the other columns." You can specify a subset of columns as well by typing their column names:

```
> Pregnancy.lm <- glm(PREGNANT ~
Implied.Gender +
Home.Apt..PO.Box +
Pregnancy.Test +
Birth.Control,
data=PregnancyData,family=binomial("logit"))
```

But you're using the PREGNANT~. notation because you want to use all of the columns to train the model.

Once the linear model is built, you can view the coefficients and analyze which variables are statistically significant (similar to the t tests you conducted in Chapter 6) by summarizing the model:

```
> summary(Pregnancy.lm)

Call:
glm(formula = PREGNANT ~ ., family = binomial("logit"),
data = PregnancyData)

Deviance Residuals:
    Min      1Q   Median      3Q      Max
-3.2012  -0.5566  -0.0246   0.5127   2.8658

Coefficients:
                        Estimate Std. Error z value Pr(>|z|)
(Intercept)            -0.343597   0.180755  -1.901 0.057315 .
Implied.GenderM        -0.453880   0.197566  -2.297 0.021599 *
Implied.GenderU         0.141939   0.307588   0.461 0.644469
Home.Apt..PO.BoxH      -0.172927   0.194591  -0.889 0.374180
Home.Apt..PO.BoxP      -0.002813   0.336432  -0.008 0.993329
Pregnancy.Test          2.370554   0.521781   4.543 5.54e-06 ***
Birth.Control          -2.300272   0.365270  -6.297 3.03e-10 ***
Feminine.Hygiene       -2.028558   0.342398  -5.925 3.13e-09 ***
Folic.Acid              4.077666   0.761888   5.352 8.70e-08 ***
Prenatal.Vitamins       2.479469   0.369063   6.718 1.84e-11 ***
Prenatal.Yoga           2.922974   1.146990   2.548 0.010822 *
Body.Pillow             1.261037   0.860617   1.465 0.142847
Ginger.Ale              1.938502   0.426733   4.543 5.55e-06 ***
Sea.Bands               1.107530   0.673435   1.645 0.100053
Stopped.buying.cig      1.302222   0.342347   3.804 0.000142 ***
Cigarettes             -1.443022   0.370120  -3.899 9.67e-05 ***
Smoking.Cessation       1.790779   0.512610   3.493 0.000477 ***
Stopped.buying.win      1.383888   0.305883   4.524 6.06e-06 ***
Wine                   -1.565539   0.348910  -4.487 7.23e-06 ***
Maternity.Clothes       2.078202   0.329432   6.308 2.82e-10 ***
---
Signif. codes: 0 '***' 0.001 '**' 0.01 '*' 0.05 '.' 0.1 ' ' 1
```

Those coefficients without at least one * next to them are of dubious worth. Similarly, you can train a random forest model using the `randomForest()` function:

```
> Pregnancy.rf <-
randomForest(PREGNANT~.,data=PregnancyData,importance=TRUE)
```

This is the same basic syntax as the `glm()` call (execute `?randomForest` to learn more about tree count and depth). Note the `importance=TRUE` in the call. This allows you to graph variable importance using another function, `varImpPlot()`, which will allow you to understand which variables are important and which are weak.

The `randomForest` package allows you to look at how much each variable contributes to decreasing node impurity on average. The more a variable contributes, the more useful it is. You can use this to select and pare down the variables you might want to feed into another model. To look at this data, use the `varImpPlot()` function with `type=2` to pull rankings based on the node impurity calculation introduced in Chapter 7 (feel free to use the `?` command to read up on the difference between `type=1` and `type=2`):

```
> varImpPlot(Pregnancy.rf, type=2)
```

This yields the ranking shown in Figure 10-4. Folic acid ranks first with prenatal vitamins and birth control trailing.

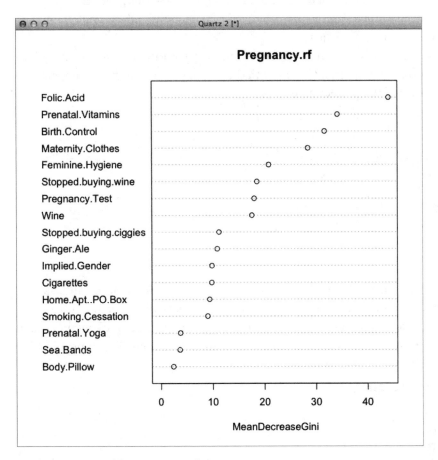

Figure 10-4: A variable importance plot in R

Now that you've built the models, you can predict with them using the `predict()` function in R. Call the function and save the results to two different variables, so you can compare models. The way the `predict()` function generally works is that it accepts a model, a dataset to predict on, and any model-specific options:

```
> PregnancyData.Test.lm.Preds <-
predict(Pregnancy.lm,PregnancyData.Test,type="response")
> PregnancyData.Test.rf.Preds <-
predict(Pregnancy.rf,PregnancyData.Test,type="prob")
```

You can see in the two `predict` calls, that each is provided with a different model, the test data, and the `type` parameters that those models need. In the case of a linear model, `type="response"` sets the values returned from the prediction to be between 0 and 1 just like the original PREGNANT values. In the case of the random forest, the `type="prob"` ensures that you get back class probabilities—two columns of data, one probability of pregnancy and one probability of no pregnancy.

These outputs are slightly different, but then again, they use different algorithms, different models, and so on. It's important to play with these things and read the documentation. Here's a summary of the prediction output:

```
> summary(PregnancyData.Test.lm.Preds)
    Min.   1st Qu.   Median     Mean  3rd Qu.     Max.
0.001179 0.066190 0.239500 0.283100 0.414300 0.999200
> summary(PregnancyData.Test.rf.Preds)
       0                      1
 Min.   :0.0000    Min.   :0.0000
 1st Qu.:0.7500    1st Qu.:0.0080
 Median :0.9500    Median :0.0500
 Mean   :0.8078    Mean   :0.1922
 3rd Qu.:0.9920    3rd Qu.:0.2500
 Max.   :1.0000    Max.   :1.0000
```

The second column from the random forest predictions then is the probability associated with pregnancy (as opposed to a non-pregnancy), so that's the column that's akin to the logistic regression predictions. Using the bracket notation, you can pull out individual records or sets of records and look at their input data and predictions (I've transposed the row to make it print prettier):

```
> t(PregnancyData.Test[1,])
                        1
Implied.Gender         "U"
Home.Apt..PO.Box       "A"
Pregnancy.Test         "0"
Birth.Control          "0"
Feminine.Hygiene       "0"
Folic.Acid             "0"
Prenatal.Vitamins      "0"
```

```
Prenatal.Yoga              "0"
Body.Pillow                "0"
Ginger.Ale                 "0"
Sea.Bands                  "1"
Stopped.buying.ciggies     "0"
Cigarettes                 "0"
Smoking.Cessation          "0"
Stopped.buying.wine        "1"
Wine                       "1"
Maternity.Clothes          "0"
PREGNANT                   "1"
> t(PregnancyData.Test.lm.Preds[1])
            1
[1,] 0.6735358
> PregnancyData.Test.rf.Preds[1,2]
[1] 0.504
```

Note that in printing the input row, I leave the column index blank in the square brackets [1,] so that all columns' data is printed. This particular customer has an unknown gender, lives in an apartment, and has bought sea bands and wine, but then stopped buying wine. The logistic regression gives them a score of 0.67 while the random forest is right around 0.5. The truth is that she is pregnant—chalk one up for the logistic regression!

Now that you have the two vectors of class probabilities, one for each mode, you can compare the models in terms of true positive rate and false positive rate just as you did earlier in the book. Luckily for you, though, in R the ROCR package can compute and plot the ROC curves so you don't have to. Since you've already loaded the ROCR package, the first thing you need to do is create two ROCR prediction objects (using the ROCR prediction() function), which simply count up the positive and negative class predictions at various cutoff levels in the class probabilities:

```
> pred.lm <-
prediction(PregnancyData.Test.lm.Preds,
PregnancyData.Test$PREGNANT)
> pred.rf <-
prediction(PregnancyData.Test.rf.Preds[,2],
PregnancyData.Test$PREGNANT)
```

Note in the second call that you hit the second column of class probabilities from the random forest object just as discussed earlier. You can then turn these prediction objects into ROCR performance objects by running them through the performance() function. A performance object takes the classifications given by the model on the test set for various cutoff values and uses them to assemble a curve of your choosing (in this case a ROC curve):

```
> perf.lm <- performance(pred.lm,"tpr","fpr")
> perf.rf <- performance(pred.rf,"tpr","fpr")
```

> NOTE
>
> If you're curious, `performance()` provides other options besides the `tpr` and `fpr` values, such as `prec` for precision and `rec` for recall. Read the ROCR package documentation for more detail.

You can then plot these curves using R's `plot()` function. First, the linear model curve (the `xlim` and `ylim` flags are used to set the upper and lower bounds on the x and y axes in the graph):

```
> plot(perf.lm,xlim=c(0,1),ylim=c(0,1))
```

You can add the random forest curve in using the `add=TRUE` flag to overlay it and the `lty=2` flag (`lty` stands for "line type"; check out `?plot` to learn more) to make this line dashed:

```
> plot(perf.rf,xlim=c(0,1),ylim=c(0,1),lty=2,add=TRUE)
```

This overlays the two curves with the random forest performance as a dashed line, as shown in Figure 10-5. For the most part, the logistic regression is superior with the random forest pulling ahead briefly on the far right of the graph.

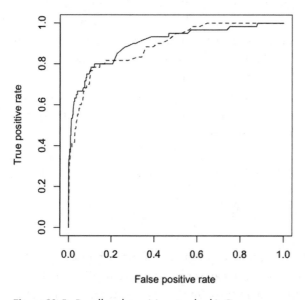

Figure 10-5: Recall and precision graphed in R

All right, so to recap here, you trained two different predictive models, used them on a test set, and compared their precision versus recall using the following code:

```
> PregnancyData <- read.csv("Pregnancy.csv")
> PregnancyData.Test <- read.csv("Pregnancy_Test.csv")
```

```
> PregnancyData$PREGNANT <- factor(PregnancyData$PREGNANT)
> PregnancyData.Test$PREGNANT <- factor(PregnancyData.Test$PREGNANT)
> install.packages("randomForest",dependencies=TRUE)
> install.packages("ROCR",dependencies=TRUE)
> library(randomForest)
> library(ROCR)
> Pregnancy.lm <- glm(PREGNANT ~ .,
data=PregnancyData,family=binomial("logit"))
> summary(Pregnancy.lm)
> Pregnancy.rf <-
randomForest(PREGNANT~.,data=PregnancyData,importance=TRUE)
> PregnancyData.Test.rf.Preds <-
predict(Pregnancy.rf,PregnancyData.Test,type="prob")
> varImpPlot(Pregnancy.rf, type=2)
> PregnancyData.Test.lm.Preds <-
predict(Pregnancy.lm,PregnancyData.Test,type="response")
> PregnancyData.Test.rf.Preds <-
predict(Pregnancy.rf,PregnancyData.Test,type="prob")
> pred.lm <-
prediction(PregnancyData.Test.lm.Preds,
PregnancyData.Test$PREGNANT)
> pred.rf <-
prediction(PregnancyData.Test.rf.Preds[,2],
PregnancyData.Test$PREGNANT)
> perf.lm <- performance(pred.lm,"tpr","fpr")
> perf.rf <- performance(pred.rf,"tpr","fpr")
> plot(perf.lm,xlim=c(0,1),ylim=c(0,1))
> plot(perf.rf,xlim=c(0,1),ylim=c(0,1),lty=2,add=TRUE)
```

Pretty straightforward, really. Compared to Excel, look at how easy it was to compare two different models. That's quite nice.

Forecasting in R

> **NOTE**
>
> The CSV file used in this section, "SwordDemand.csv," is available for download at the book's website, www.wiley.com/go/datasmart.

This next section is nuts. Why? Because you're going to regenerate the exponential smoothing forecast from Chapter 8 so fast it's going to make your head spin.

First, load in the sword demand data from SwordDemand.csv and print it to the console:

```
> sword <- read.csv("SwordDemand.csv")
> sword
SwordDemand
1          165
2          171
```

3	147
4	143
5	164
6	160
7	152
8	150
9	159
10	169
11	173
12	203
13	169
14	166
15	162
16	147
17	188
18	161
19	162
20	169
21	185
22	188
23	200
24	229
25	189
26	218
27	185
28	199
29	210
30	193
31	211
32	208
33	216
34	218
35	264
36	304

All right, so you have 36 months of demand loaded up, nice and simple. The first thing you need to do is tell R that this is time series data. There's a function called ts() that is used for this purpose:

```
sword.ts <- ts(sword,frequency=12,start=c(2010,1))
```

In this call, you provide the ts() function with the data, a frequency value (the number of observations per unit of time, which in this case is 12 per year), and a starting point (this example uses January 2010).

When you print sword.ts by typing it in the terminal, R now knows to print it in a table by month:

```
> sword.ts
    Jan Feb Mar Apr May Jun Jul Aug Sep Oct Nov Dec
```

```
2010 165 171 147 143 164 160 152 150 159 169 173 203
2011 169 166 162 147 188 161 162 169 185 188 200 229
2012 189 218 185 199 210 193 211 208 216 218 264 304
```

Nice!

You can plot the data too:

```
> plot(sword.ts)
```

This gives the graph shown in Figure 10-6.

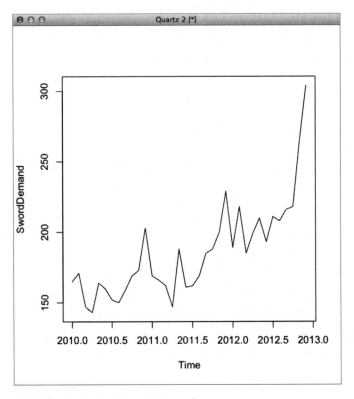

Figure 10-6: Graph of sword demand

At this point, you're ready to forecast, which you can do using the excellent `forecast` package. Feel free to look it up on CRAN (`http://cran.r-project.org/package=forecast`) or watch the author talk about it in this YouTube video: `http://www.youtube.com/watch?v=1Lh1H1BUf8k`.

To forecast using the `forecast` package, you just feed a time series object into the `forecast()` function. The `forecast()` call has been set up to detect the appropriate technique to use. Remember how you ran through a few techniques earlier in the book? The `forecast()` function is gonna do all that stuff for you:

```
> install.packages("forecast",dependencies=TRUE)
> library(forecast)
> sword.forecast <- forecast(sword.ts)
```

And that's it. Your forecast is saved in the `sword.forecast` object. Now you can print it:

```
> sword.forecast
         Point Forecast    Lo 80    Hi 80    Lo 95    Hi 95
Jan 2013       242.9921 230.7142 255.2699 224.2147 261.7695
Feb 2013       259.4216 246.0032 272.8400 238.8999 279.9433
Mar 2013       235.8763 223.0885 248.6640 216.3191 255.4334
Apr 2013       234.3295 220.6882 247.9709 213.4669 255.1922
May 2013       274.1674 256.6893 291.6456 247.4369 300.8980
Jun 2013       252.5456 234.6894 270.4019 225.2368 279.8544
Jul 2013       257.0555 236.7740 277.3370 226.0376 288.0734
Aug 2013       262.0715 238.9718 285.1711 226.7436 297.3993
Sep 2013       279.4771 252.0149 306.9392 237.4774 321.4768
Oct 2013       289.7890 258.1684 321.4097 241.4294 338.1487
Nov 2013       320.5914 281.9322 359.2506 261.4673 379.7155
Dec 2013       370.3057 321.2097 419.4018 295.2198 445.3917
Jan 2014       308.3243 263.6074 353.0413 239.9357 376.7130
Feb 2014       327.6427 275.9179 379.3675 248.5364 406.7490
Mar 2014       296.5754 245.8459 347.3049 218.9913 374.1594
Apr 2014       293.3646 239.2280 347.5013 210.5698 376.1595
May 2014       341.8187 274.0374 409.5999 238.1562 445.4812
Jun 2014       313.6061 247.0271 380.1851 211.7823 415.4299
Jul 2014       317.9789 245.9468 390.0109 207.8153 428.1424
Aug 2014       322.9807 245.1532 400.8081 203.9538 442.0075
Sep 2014       343.1975 255.4790 430.9160 209.0436 477.3513
Oct 2014       354.6286 258.7390 450.5181 207.9782 501.2790
Nov 2014       391.0099 279.4304 502.5893 220.3638 561.6559
Dec 2014       450.1820 314.9086 585.4554 243.2992 657.0648
```

You get a forecast with prediction intervals built-in! And you can print the actual forecasting technique used by printing the method value in the `sword.forecast` object:

```
> sword.forecast$method
[1] "ETS(M,A,M)"
```

The MAM stands for multiplicative error, additive trend, multiplicative seasonality. The `forecast()` function has actually chosen to run Holt-Winters exponential smoothing! And you didn't even have to do anything. When you plot it, as shown in Figure 10-7, you automatically get a fan chart:

```
> plot(sword.forecast)
```

To recap, here's the code that replicated Chapter 8:

```
> sword <- read.csv("SwordDemand.csv")
> sword.ts <- ts(sword,frequency=12,start=c(2010,1))
> install.packages("forecast",dependencies=TRUE)
> library(forecast)
```

```
> sword.forecast <- forecast(sword.ts)
> plot(sword.forecast)
```

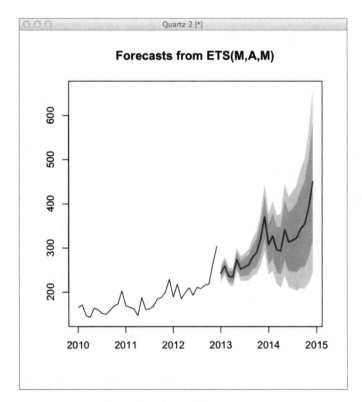

Figure 10-7: Fan chart of the demand forecast

Crazy. But that's the beauty of using packages other folks have written specially to do this stuff.

Looking at Outlier Detection

NOTE

The CSV files used in this section, "PregnancyDuration.csv" and "CallCenter.csv," are available for download at the book's website, www.wiley.com/go/datasmart.

In this section, you'll do one more of the chapters from this book in R, just to drive home the ease of this stuff. To start, read in the pregnancy duration data in PregnancyDuration .csv available from the book's website:

```
> PregnancyDuration <- read.csv("PregnancyDuration.csv")
```

In Chapter 9, you calculated the median, first quartile, third quartile, and inner and outer Tukey fences. You can get the quartiles just from summarizing the data:

```
> summary(PregnancyDuration)
 GestationDays
 Min.   :240.0
 1st Qu.:260.0
 Median :267.0
 Mean   :266.6
 3rd Qu.:272.0
 Max.   :349.0
```

That makes the interquartile range equal to 272 minus 260 (alternatively, you can call the built-in IQR() function on the GestationDays column):

```
> PregnancyDuration.IQR <- 272 - 260
> PregnancyDuration.IQR <- IQR(PregnancyDuration$GestationDays)
> PregnancyDuration.IQR
[1] 12
```

You can then calculate the lower and upper Tukey fences:

```
> LowerInnerFence <- 260 - 1.5*PregnancyDuration.IQR
> UpperInnerFence <- 272 + 1.5*PregnancyDuration.IQR
> LowerInnerFence
[1] 242
> UpperInnerFence
[1] 290
```

Using R's which() function, it's easy to determine the points and their indices that violate the fences. For example:

```
> which(PregnancyDuration$GestationDays > UpperInnerFence)
[1]    1 249 252 338 345 378 478 913
> PregnancyDuration$GestationDays[
which(PregnancyDuration$GestationDays > UpperInnerFence)
]
[1] 349 292 295 291 297 303 293 296
```

Of course, one of the best ways to do this analysis is to use R's boxplot() function. The boxplot() function will graph the median, first and third quartiles, Tukey fences, and any outliers. To use it, you simply toss the GestationDays column inside the function:

```
> boxplot(PregnancyDuration$GestationDays)
```

This yields the visualization shown in Figure 10-8.

The Tukey fences can be modified to be "outer" fences by changing the range flag in the boxplot call (it defaults to 1.5 times the IQR). If you set range=3, then the Tukey fences are drawn at the last point inside three times the IQR instead:

```
> boxplot(PregnancyDuration$GestationDays, range=3)
```

As shown in Figure 10-9, note now that you have only one outlier, which is Mrs. Hadlum's pregnancy duration of 349 days.

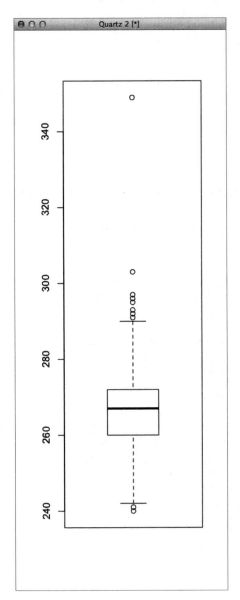

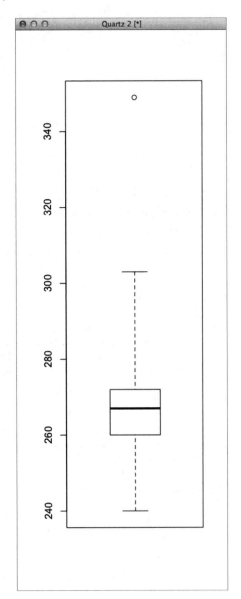

Figure 10-8: A boxplot of the pregnancy duration data

Figure 10-9: A boxplot with Tukey fences using three times the IQR

You can also pull this data out of the boxplot in the console rather than plot it. Printing the stats list, you get the fences and quartiles:

```
> boxplot(PregnancyDuration$GestationDays,range=3)$stats
      [,1]
[1,]   240
[2,]   260
[3,]   267
[4,]   272
[5,]   303
```

Printing the out list, you get a list of outlier values:

```
> boxplot(PregnancyDuration$GestationDays,range=3)$out
[1] 349
```

Okay, so that's a bit on the pregnancy duration problem. Let's move on to the harder problem of finding outliers in the call center employee performance data. It's in the CallCenter.csv sheet on the book's website. Loading it up and summarizing, you get:

```
> CallCenter <- read.csv("CallCenter.csv")
> summary(CallCenter)
      ID              AvgTix           Rating          Tardies
 Min.   :130564   Min.   :143.1   Min.   :2.070   Min.   :0.000
 1st Qu.:134402   1st Qu.:153.1   1st Qu.:3.210   1st Qu.:1.000
 Median :137906   Median :156.1   Median :3.505   Median :1.000
 Mean   :137946   Mean   :156.1   Mean   :3.495   Mean   :1.465
 3rd Qu.:141771   3rd Qu.:159.1   3rd Qu.:3.810   3rd Qu.:2.000
 Max.   :145176   Max.   :168.7   Max.   :4.810   Max.   :4.000
   Graveyards        Weekends         SickDays       PercSickOnFri
 Min.   :0.000   Min.   :0.0000   Min.   :0.000   Min.   :0.0000
 1st Qu.:1.000   1st Qu.:1.0000   1st Qu.:0.000   1st Qu.:0.0000
 Median :2.000   Median :1.0000   Median :2.000   Median :0.2500
 Mean   :1.985   Mean   :0.9525   Mean   :1.875   Mean   :0.3522
 3rd Qu.:2.000   3rd Qu.:1.0000   3rd Qu.:3.000   3rd Qu.:0.6700
 Max.   :4.000   Max.   :2.0000   Max.   :7.000   Max.   :1.0000
 EmployeeDevHrs  ShiftSwapsReq   ShiftSwapsOffered
 Min.   : 0.00   Min.   :0.000   Min.   :0.00
 1st Qu.: 6.00   1st Qu.:1.000   1st Qu.:0.00
 Median :12.00   Median :1.000   Median :1.00
 Mean   :11.97   Mean   :1.448   Mean   :1.76
 3rd Qu.:17.00   3rd Qu.:2.000   3rd Qu.:3.00
 Max.   :34.00   Max.   :5.000   Max.   :9.00
```

Just as in Chapter 9, you need to scale and center the data. To do so, you need only use the scale() function:

```
> CallCenter.scale <- scale(CallCenter[2:11])
> summary(CallCenter.scale)
     AvgTix            Rating           Tardies          Graveyards
 Min.   :-2.940189   Min.   :-3.08810   Min.   :-1.5061   Min.   :-2.4981
```

```
1st Qu.:-0.681684    1st Qu.:-0.61788    1st Qu.:-0.4781    1st Qu.:-1.2396
Median :-0.008094    Median : 0.02134    Median :-0.4781    Median : 0.0188
Mean   : 0.000000    Mean   : 0.00000    Mean   : 0.0000    Mean   : 0.0000
3rd Qu.: 0.682476    3rd Qu.: 0.68224    3rd Qu.: 0.5500    3rd Qu.: 0.0188
Max.   : 2.856075    Max.   : 2.84909    Max.   : 2.6062    Max.   : 2.5359
     Weekends            SickDays          PercSickOnFri     EmployeeDevHrs
Min.   :-1.73614    Min.   :-1.12025    Min.   :-0.8963    Min.   :-1.60222
1st Qu.: 0.08658    1st Qu.:-1.12025    1st Qu.:-0.8963    1st Qu.:-0.79910
Median : 0.08658    Median : 0.07468    Median :-0.2601    Median : 0.00401
Mean   : 0.00000    Mean   : 0.00000    Mean   : 0.0000    Mean   : 0.00000
3rd Qu.: 0.08658    3rd Qu.: 0.67215    3rd Qu.: 0.8088    3rd Qu.: 0.67328
Max.   : 1.90930    Max.   : 3.06202    Max.   : 1.6486    Max.   : 2.94879
   ShiftSwapsReq       ShiftSwapsOffered
Min.   :-1.4477    Min.   :-0.9710
1st Qu.:-0.4476    1st Qu.:-0.9710
Median :-0.4476    Median :-0.4193
Mean   : 0.0000    Mean   : 0.0000
3rd Qu.: 0.5526    3rd Qu.: 0.6841
Max.   : 3.5530    Max.   : 3.9942
```

Now that the data is prepped, you can send it through the `lofactor()` function that's part of the DMwR package:

```
> install.packages("DMwR",dependencies=TRUE)
> library(DMwR)
```

To call the `lofactor()` function, you supply it the data and a `k` value (this example uses 5, just like in Chapter 9), and the function spits out LOFs:

```
> CallCenter.lof <- lofactor(CallCenter.scale,5)
```

Data with the highest factors (LOFs usually hover around 1) are the oddest points. For instance, you can highlight the data associated with those employees whose LOF is greater than 1.5:

```
> which(CallCenter.lof > 1.5)
[1] 299 374
> CallCenter[which(CallCenter.lof > 1.5),]
        ID AvgTix Rating Tardies Graveyards Weekends SickDays
299 137155  165.3   4.49       1          3        2        1
374 143406  145.0   2.33       3          1        0        6
    PercSickOnFri EmployeeDevHrs ShiftSwapsReq ShiftSwapsOffered
299          0.00             30             1                 7
374          0.83             30             4                 0
```

These are the same two outlying employees discussed in Chapter 9. But what a huge difference in the number of lines of code it took to get this:

```
> CallCenter <- read.csv("CallCenter.csv")
> install.packages("DMwR",dependencies=TRUE)
> library(DMwR)
```

```
> CallCenter.scale <- scale(CallCenter[2:11])
> CallCenter.lof <- lofactor(CallCenter.scale,5)
```

That's all it took!

Wrapping Up

Okay, this was a fast and furious run-through of some of what you can do in R merely by understanding three things:

- Loading and working with data in R
- Finding and installing relevant packages
- Calling functions from those packages on your dataset

Is this all you need to know how to do in R? Nope. I didn't cover writing your own functions, a whole lot of plotting, connecting to databases, the slew of `apply()` functions available, and so on. But I hope this has given you a taste to learn more. If it has, there are scads of R books out there worth reading as a follow-up to this chapter. Here are a few:

- *Beginning R: The Statistical Programming Language* by Mark Gardener (John Wiley & Sons, 2012)
- *R in a Nutshell, 2nd Edition* by Joseph Adler (O'Reilly, 2012)
- *Data Mining with R: Learning with Case Studies* by Luis Torgo (Chapman and Hall, 2010)
- *Machine Learning for Hackers* by Drew Conway and John Myles White (O'Reilly, 2012)

Go forth and tinker in R!

Conclusion

Where Am I? What Just Happened?

You may have started this book with a rather ordinary set of skills in math and spreadsheet modeling, but if you're here, having made it through alive (and having not just skipped the first 10 chapters), then I imagine you're now a spreadsheet modeling connoisseur with a good grasp of a variety of data science techniques.

This book has covered topics ranging from classic operations research fodder (optimization, Monte Carlo, and forecasting) to unsupervised learning (outlier detection, clustering, and graphs) to supervised AI (regression, decision stumps, and naïve Bayes). You should feel confident working with spreadsheet data at this higher level.

I also hope that Chapter 10 showed you that now that you understand data science techniques and algorithms, it's quite easy to use those techniques from within a programming language such as R.

And if there's a particular topic that really grabbed you in this book, dive deeper! Want more R, more optimization, more machine learning? Grab one of the sources I recommend in each relevant chapter's conclusion and read on. There's so much to learn. I've only scraped the surface of analytics practice in this book.

But wait...

Before You Go-Go

I want to use this conclusion to offer up some thoughts about what it means to practice data science in the real world, because merely knowing the math isn't enough.

Anyone who knows me well knows that I'm not the sharpest knife in the drawer. My quantitative skills are middling, but I've seen folks much smarter than I fail mightily at working as analytics professionals. The problem is that while they're brilliant, they don't know the little things that can cause technical endeavors to fail within the business environment. So let's cover these softer items that can mean the success or failure of your analytics project or career.

Get to Know the Problem

My favorite movie of all time is the 1992 film *Sneakers*. The movie centers on a band of penetration testers led by Robert Redford that steals a "black box" capable of cracking RSA encryption. Hijinks ensue. (If you haven't watched it, I envy you, because you have an opportunity to see it for the first time!)

There's a scene where Robert Redford encounters an electronic keypad on a locked office door at a think tank, and he needs to break through.

He reaches out to his team via his headset. They're waiting in a van outside the building.

"Anybody ever had to defeat an electronic keypad?" he asks.

"Those things are impossible," Sydney Poitier exclaims. But Dan Aykroyd, also waiting in the van, comes up with an idea. They explain its complexities to Redford over the comms.

Robert Redford nods his head and says, "Okay, I'll give it a shot."

He ignores the keypad and kicks in the door.

You see, the problem wasn't "defeating an electronic keypad" at all. The problem was getting inside the room. Dan Aykroyd understood this.

This is the fundamental challenge of analytics: understanding what actually must be solved. You must learn the situation, the processes, the data, and the circumstances. You need to characterize everything around the problem as best you can in order to understand exactly what an ideal solution is.

In data science, you'll often encounter the "poorly posed problem":

1. Someone else in the business encounters a problem.
2. They use their past experience and (lack of?) analytics knowledge to frame the problem.
3. They hand their conception of the problem to the analyst as if it were set in stone and well posed.
4. The analytics person accepts and solves the problem as-is.

This can work. But it's not ideal, because the problem you're asked to solve is often not the problem that needs solving. If *this problem* is really about *that problem* then analytics professionals cannot be passive.

You cannot accept problems as handed to you in the business environment. Never allow yourself to be the analyst to whom problems are "thrown over the fence." Engage with the people whose challenges you're tackling to make sure you're solving the right problem. Learn the business's processes and the data that's generated and saved. Learn how folks are handling the problem now, and what metrics they use (or ignore) to gauge success.

Solve the correct, yet often misrepresented, problem. This is something no mathematical model will ever say to you. No mathematical model can ever say, "Hey, good job formulating this optimization model, but I think you should take a step back and change your business a little instead." And that leads me to my next point: Learn how to communicate.

We Need More Translators

If you've finished this book, it's safe to say you now know a thing or two about analytics. You're familiar with the tools that are available to you. You've prototyped in them. And that allows you to identify analytics opportunities better than most, because you *know what's possible*. You needn't wait for someone to bring an opportunity to you. You can potentially go out into the business and find them.

But without the ability to communicate, it becomes difficult to understand others' challenges, articulate what's possible, and explain the work you're doing.

In today's business environment, it is often unacceptable to be skilled at only one thing. Data scientists are expected to be polyglots who understand math, code, and the plain-speak (or sports analogy-ridden speak ...ugh) of business. And the only way to get good at speaking to other folks, just like the only way to get good at math, is through practice.

Take any opportunity you can to speak with others about analytics, formally and informally. Find ways to discuss with others in your workplace what they do, what you do, and ways you might collaborate. Speak with others at local meet-ups about what you do. Find ways to articulate analytics concepts within your particular business context.

Push your management to involve you in planning and business development discussions. Too often the analytics professional is approached with a project only after that project has been scoped, but your knowledge of the techniques and data available makes you indispensable in early planning.

Push to be viewed as a person worth talking to and not as an extension of some number-crunching machine that problems are thrown at from a distance. The more embedded and communicative an analyst is within an organization, the more effective he or she is.

For too long analysts have been treated like Victorian women—separated from the finer points of business, because they couldn't possibly understand it all. Oh, please. Let people feel the weight of your well-rounded skill set—just because they can't crunch numbers doesn't mean you can't discuss a PowerPoint slide. Get in there, get your hands dirty, and talk to folks.

Beware the Three-Headed Geek-Monster: Tools, Performance, and Mathematical Perfection

There are many things that can sabotage the use of analytics within the workplace. Politics and infighting perhaps; a bad experience from a previous "enterprise, business intelligence, cloud dashboard" project; or peers who don't want their "dark art" optimized or automated for fear that their jobs will become redundant.

Not all hurdles are within your control as an analytics professional. But some are. There are three primary ways I see analytics folks sabotage their own work: overly-complex modeling, tool obsession, and fixation on performance.

Complexity

Many moons ago, I worked on a supply chain optimization model for a Fortune 500 company. This model was pretty badass if I do say so myself. We gathered all kinds of business rules from the client and modeled their entire shipping process as a mixed-integer program. We even modeled normally distributed future demand into the model in a novel way that ended up getting published.

But the model was a failure. It was dead out of the gate. By dead, I don't mean that it was wrong, but rather that it wasn't used. Frankly, once the academics left, there was no one left in that part of the company who could keep the cumulative forecast error means and standard deviations up to date. The boots on the ground just didn't understand it, regardless of the amount of training we gave.

This is a difference between academia and industry. In academia, success is not gauged by usefulness. A novel optimization model is valuable in its own right, even if it is too complex for a supply chain analyst to keep running.

But in the industry, analytics is a results-driven pursuit, and models are judged by their practical value as much as by their novelty.

In this case, I spent too much time using complex math to optimize the company's supply chain but never realistically addressed the fact that no one would be able to keep the model up to date.

The mark of a true analytics professional, much like the mark of a true artist, is in knowing when to edit. When do you leave some of the complexity of a solution on the cutting room floor? To get all cliché on you, remember that in analytics great is the enemy of good. The best model is one that strikes the right balance between functionality and maintainability. If an analytics model is never used, it's worthless.

Tools

Right now in the world of analytics (whether you want to call that "data science," "big data," "business intelligence," "blah blah blah cloud," and so on), people have become focused on tools and architecture.

Tools are important. They enable you to deploy your analytics and data-driven products. But when people talk about "the best tool for the job," they're too often focused on the tool and not on the job.

Software and services companies are in the business of selling you solutions to problems you may not even have yet. And to make matters worse, many of us have bosses who read stuff like the *Harvard Business Review* and then look at us and say, "We need to be doing this big data thing. Go buy something, and let's get Hadoop-ing."

This all leads to a dangerous climate in business today where management looks to tools as proof that analytics are being done, and providers just want to sell us the tools that enable the analytics, but there's little accountability that actual analytics is getting done.

So here's a simple rule: *Identify the analytics opportunities you want to tackle in as much detail as possible before acquiring tools.*

Do you need Hadoop? Well, does your problem require a divide-and-conquer aggregation of a lot of unstructured data? No? Then the answer may be no. Don't put the cart before the horse and buy the tools (or the consultants who are needed to use the open source tools) only to then say, "Okay, now what do we do with this?"

Performance

If I had a nickel every time someone raised their eyebrows when I tell them MailChimp uses R in production for our abuse-prevention models, I could buy a Mountain Dew. People think the language isn't appropriate for production settings. If I were doing high-performance stock trading, it probably wouldn't be. I'd likely code everything up in C. But I'm not, and I won't.

For MailChimp, most of our time isn't spent in R. It's spent moving data to send through the AI model. It's not spent running the AI model, and it's certainly not spent training the AI model.

I've met folks who are very concerned with the speed at which their software can train their artificial intelligence model. Can the model be trained in parallel, in a low-level language, in a live environment?

They never stop to ask themselves if any of this is necessary and instead end up spending a lot of time gold-plating the wrong part of their analytics project.

At MailChimp, we retrain our models offline once a quarter, test them, and then promote them into production. In R, it takes me a few hours to train the model. And even though we as a company have terabytes of data, the model's training set, once prepped, is only 10 gigabytes, so I can even train the model on my laptop. Crazy.

Given that that's the case, I don't waste my time on R's training speed. I focus on more important things, like model accuracy.

I'm not saying that you shouldn't care about performance. But keep your head on straight, and in situations where it doesn't matter, feel free to let it go.

You Are Not the Most Important Function of Your Organization

Okay, so there are three things to watch out for. But more generally, keep in mind that most companies are not in the business of doing analytics. They make their money through other means, and analytics is meant to serve those processes.

You may have heard elsewhere that *data scientist* is the "sexiest job of the century!" That's because of how data science serves an industry. *Serves* being the key word.

Consider the airline industry. They've been doing big data analytics for decades to squeeze that last nickel out of you for that seat you can barely fit in. That's all done through revenue optimization models. It's a huge win for mathematics.

But you know what? The most important part of their business is flying. The products and services an organization sells matter more than the models that tack on pennies to those dollars. Your goals should be things like using data to facilitate better targeting, forecasting, pricing, decision-making, reporting, compliance, and so on. In other words, work with the rest of your organization to do *better business*, not to do data science for its own sake.

Get Creative and Keep in Touch!

That's enough sage wisdom. If you've labored through the preceding chapters then you have a good base to begin dreaming up, prototyping, and implementing solutions to the analytics opportunities posed by your business. Talk with your coworkers and get creative. Maybe there's an analytical solution for something that's been patched over with gut feelings and manual processes. Attack it.

And as you go through the process of implementing these and other techniques in your work-a-day life, keep in touch. I'm on Twitter at @John4man. Reach out and tell me your tale. Or to give me hell about this book. I'll take any feedback.

Happy data wrangling!

Index